Patriot Paths of Pennsylvania
... The Colonial Years
Or
The Memoirs of a Marine

By

SG Moyer USMC (RET)

Patriot Paths of Pennsylvania

The colonial years.

"A nation reveals itself not only by the men it produces but also by the men it honors, the men it remembers."

~President John F. Kennedy, Navy Lieutenant and the only American President to receive a Purple Heart and the Navy and Marine Corps Medal.

My initial vision for Patriot Paths of Pennsylvania was to develop a script for a YouTube series in which my daughters and I, as proud residents of West Chester, explore all the well-known and little-known Revolutionary War battle and skirmish sites in and around our hometown. We also explored mills, houses, taverns, and forges—people and places that contributed to Washington's desperate fight for independence. We even took a few steps off the beaten path to investigate local legends and lore that took place in 18th-century Pennsylvania. This book is a testament to our shared love for history and our community.

Our journey, which began as a celebration of our hometown's rich colonial history, quickly expanded to include the Philadelphia Campaign...Pennsylvania's piece of the American Revolutionary War pie. We picked up the historical trailhead in Buck's County in 1776 when Washington formulated a desperate plan to attack a Hessian garrison in Trenton, New Jersey, risking the destruction of his Army to show the world that he and the few skull-crusher patriots he had remaining were not yet beaten into submission as the British aristocracy supposed after sustaining several brutal defeats in New York. The trail took us to Trenton, Princeton, and Morristown, New Jersey, then on to Elkton, Maryland, Newark, Delaware, and eventually back to Pennsylvania. The trail eventually ended for us in the town where I grew up, in Selinsgrove, Pennsylvania. Although no Revolutionary battle or skirmish was fought in Selinsgrove, you will have to read the book and embark on your own journey along the

Patriot Paths of Pennsylvania to find out how it ties into the narrative. Get ready for a thrilling adventure through history!

As I began the research for the project, mapped out relevant historical sites to visit, and discovered sites I did not initially research but invariably stumbled upon, I realized that the project could also serve as a platform to tell my own martial stories spanning over twenty years of active duty service with the United States Marine Corps; a stage to tell my stories and to pass on my military experiences to my beloved daughters who will likely never hear daddy tell one of his war stories but will have them written in a book they can read and pass along to their children someday.

Written in the original manuscript as Marine Corps Tie-Ins, they are modeled loosely on Warrior Tie-Ins used when teaching martial arts to Marines. Although the 18th-century historical content in these chapters is ordered as the history unfolds, the Tie-Ins illustrating my active-duty service are not necessarily placed in chronological order. Instead, they are placed with chapters whenever they, either symbolically or by circumstance, connect.

~This work is dedicated to the strength and perseverance of military moms like my lovely and faithful wife; without your willingness to selflessly step in and up whenever duty deployed me to foreign shores and far away lands thousands of lonely miles away from home and family for long months at a time, I would have little inspiration or reasons (two of them) to write this book.

With special thanks to all the United States Marines I served with in Iraq and in other 'climes and places' who helped me fill in some of the gaps in my memory so I could write the Tie-Ins as authentically as possible. To the family members, friends, and mom-mom's red pen who read the rough draft manuscript or portions of it and gave me the confidence to publish. To my work colleagues local to the greater Philadelphia area who pointed me toward obscure historical sites that are little documented and easy to miss. And a very special thanks to my five-year-old sidekick, who has visited nearly all the historical sites mentioned in this book with her daddy. She enthusiastically asks to explore just about every house with stones on it she sees or to go on just one more adventure; she sometimes even talks her big sister and mom into coming along.

Last but certainly not least, I want to give a heavenly thanks to my father-in-law, William Hugh "Pop-Pop" Dutton, and to my Marine Corps brother, Staff Sergeant William M. Harrell. Pop-pop, thank you for reading as much of this manuscript as you could and for the valuable feedback you gave me before your Lord and Savior called you home. Billy, thank you for inspiring me to be a good Marine and an even better man and thank you for the ultimate sacrifice you made in that foreign land so my little ladies can sleep safely and peacefully every night. If the Army or the Navy were to look on Heaven's scene, they would surely find the streets are guarded by one of the finest Marines I had the honor of serving with...Semper Fidelis!

Table of Contents

Book One: A Prelude to War and an Unfortunate Retreat

Washington's Crossing, Pennsylvania 1

Trenton, New Jersey 18

Princeton, New Jersey 40

Elkton, Maryland 51

Newark, Delaware 64

Wilmington, Newport and New Castle, Delaware 77

Lewes, Delaware 92

Kennett Square, Pennsylvania 103

The Marshallton Historic District 116

Thornbury, Pennsylvania 120

Chadds Ford, Pennsylvania 126

Dilworthtown Historic District 145

Book Two: The Battle of the Clouds and a Massacre at Paoli

Glen Mills, Pennsylvania 153

West Chester, Pennsylvania 161

Downingtown, Pennsylvania 170

Aston, Pennsylvania 181

Edgemont, Pennsylvania 194

Goshen Township, Pennsylvania 199

Frazer, Pennsylvania 214

Uwchlan Township, Pennsylvania 219

The Great Valley 231

Chester Springs, Pennsylvania 239

East Vincent, East Coventry Township and the Charleston Village Historic District 250

French Creek, Pennsylvania 259

The Great Iron Furnaces of Chester, Delaware and Berks County, Pennsylvania 272

Bethlehem, Pennsylvania 282

Malvern, Pennsylvania 290

Parkesburg, Pennsylvania 310

Phoenixville, Pennsylvania 317

Book Three: Winter Hostilities Around Philadelphia, a Spring Withdrawal and the End of the War in the North

Philadelphia, Pennsylvania 336

Germantown, Pennsylvania 363

Schwenksville, Pennsylvania 380

Whitemarsh Township, Pennsylvania 386

Gloucester, New Jersey 395

Conshohocken, Pennsylvania 401

King of Prussia, Pennsylvania 409

Trappe, Pennsylvania 416

Wissahickon State Park, Pennsylvania 428

Tredyffrin, Pennsylvania 436

Newtown Square, Pennsylvania 452

Eastown Township, Pennsylvania 465

Lafayette Hill, Pennsylvania 478

Warminster, Pennsylvania.. *484*

Coastal Counties of New Jersey *494*

Marcus Hook, Pennsylvania.. *505*

Book Four: An American Revolution in the Pennsylvania Back-Country

York County, Pennsylvania... *512*

Lancaster, Pennsylvania.. *525*

Carlisle, Pennsylvania *535*

Berks County, Pennsylvania... *544*

Luzerne County, Pennsylvania *564*

Lycoming County, Pennsylvania 571

Danville, Pennsylvania 581

Northumberland County, Pennsylvania 593

Bedford, Pennsylvania.. 604

Selinsgrove, Pennsylvania... 613

About The Author 641

Bibliography 643

Book One: A Prelude to War and an Unfortunate Retreat

Washington's Crossing, Pennsylvania

"I'll take care of my men first. Frozen troops can't fight. If we run out of ammunition, we'll go to the bayonet!"

~Colonel Lewis B. Puller, the most decorated Marine in the Corps.

In July 1776, the British Army and Navy unexpectedly paid New York a visit when they landed at Staten Island. By late August, over 200 British warships, tenders, and transports had disembarked 23,000 British Army regulars and seventy-two artillery pieces on the American shoreline. This expeditionary force represented two-thirds of the British Army's might, and it was augmented by 10,000 Hessian soldiers. The expeditionary force sailed down the coast from Canada to snuff out Washington's amateur Army and put to bed any aspiration of American independence. Lord Richard Howe, Admiral of the Fleet, kept seventy-two warships in American waters to support his brother, General Sir William Howe, and his seasoned, professional British Army. In 1776, this was the largest projection of seaborne power ever attempted by any European nation.

Between 1755 and 1775, Howe's army fought on five continents and defeated every advisory that stood against it. Howe's fifteen generals averaged forty-eight years old with at least thirty years of military experience. On the other hand, Washington relied on twenty-one general officers, averaging forty-three years old with less than two years of military experience. General Howe's troops averaged nine years of military experience, while Washington's citizen soldiers averaged a scant few months of military experience and those few months were not good ones for the patriots.

By the end of November 1776, General Howe believed that most of the fighting was at an end in America after having broken Washington's Army to pieces in New York and eastern New Jersey. One fragment of the American Army had retreated across the Delaware River, another fled into northwestern Jersey, a third was driven into the Hudson Valley, and yet another third returned to New England. By late autumn, Howe ordered his Hessian mercenaries into the Jersey countryside to protect the Loyalist population and maintain civil order.

Surprisingly, General Washington also believed that the war was a lost cause. When his Army camped at the Thompson-Neely farm in Bucks County that winter, ninety percent of the Continental soldiers were either killed, captured, or deserted. Additionally, with their terms of enlistment expired, most of Colonel Bull's Flying Camp reserves had returned to their homes in Pennsylvania's backcountry. Washington's supplies were also dangerously depleted and to make matters worse; General Cornwallis threatened to bear down on his position with 8,000 British and 2,000 Hessian infantrymen, which outnumbered Washington's forces 3 to 1. The revolution was hanging on by a single fiber of the very last thread for an American bid for independence. On December 18th Washington wrote to his brother Lawrence, "I think the game is pretty near up...You can form no idea of the perplexity of my situation. No man, I believe, ever had a greater choice of difficulties and less means to extricate himself from them. However, under a full persuasion of the justice of our Cause I cannot but think the prospect will brighten, although for a wise purpose it is, at present hid under a cloud".

On December 22nd Washington called his officers together in a council of war. Bolstered by reinforcements who had recently returned from New England, Washington put a desperate plan proposed by Colonel Reed on the table for his general officers to debate. The audacious plan proposed crossing the Delaware to attack an enemy outpost or two in New Jersey before winter set in. The operation would be referred to as the citizen American Army's 10 Crucial Days, and the success or the failure of its desperate thrust at the Hessians in New Jersey would help shape world history. Washington's cabinet of officers enthusiastically agreed on the prudence of an attack, accepted the risks associated with the venture, and spent the better part of the next day working out the details of their battle plan.

Late in the evening of the 24th Washington reconvened his council of war in the Merrick House and developed his battle plan in detail. Although he had no idea, a British spy was in his midst at his headquarters who, within a day, reported the meeting to the Hessian high command in Brunswick. Other warnings of an impending American attack made their way to the Hessian Colonel Johann Rall, commander at the Hessian garrison at Trenton, Washington's intended target. A Hessian post near the town intercepted two American deserters after they crossed the river, who divulged the American Army's battle preparations. Also, a doctor and a gentleman named Mr. Wahl warned Rall of an imminent attack. Upon receiving the warning, the Hessian commander of the Trenton garrison arrogantly retorted, "Let them come."

Meanwhile, Washington ordered small patrols to cross the Delaware River to engage in preemptive skirmishes with Hessian outposts. They were instructed to hit quick, hit hard, and then return. Washington's intent was to harass the Hessians, wear them down, and keep them alert and exhausted. On a cold Christmas night, while a brutal winter storm commenced, Colonel Rall passed the time playing cards by a warm fire with a couple of his officers. One of his subordinates, Major von Dechow, proposed they send out their baggage as a precaution in case the Americans attacked their garrison. To this suggestion, Colonel Rall replied, "Fiddlesticks! These clodhoppers will not attack us, and should they do, we will simply fall on them and rout them". That night, after three days and nights of constant alarms, the duty officers, confident no major attack would occur during the storm, eased off security and allowed their men some respite. Major Dechow even canceled the next morning's patrol because of his confidence that no one would attack the garrison during the severe winter storm.

By late Christmas afternoon, the American Army began to move from their camps and assemble for their main attack on the Hessian garrison across the river. The plan called for Washington's subordinate commanders to lead their men across the river in four different locations simultaneously. Washington planned to cross the river with 2,400 men at McConkey's Ferry and Johnson's Ferry at present-day Washington's Crossing Historical Park, about ten miles upstream from Trenton, and attack the Hessian post from the north and west. 800 Pennsylvania militiamen, led by General James Ewing, were ordered to cross at Trenton Ferry, nearest the Hessian post, and seize the Assunpink Creek Bridge to deny the Hessians a route out of Trenton to the southeast. The fourth American force comprised of 1,200 Philadelphia Associators led by Colonel Cadwalader. They were tasked to embark on boats in Bristol, cross the river, and land at Burlington, twelve miles below Trenton. Cadwalader's mission was to conduct a feint to draw off Colonel Dunlop and Colonel Stirling's troops should they move to reinforce Trenton and keep them occupied during the American assault.

Time for this mission had priority. To initiate a sunrise attack, Washington needed his troops in their assembly areas by sunset so darkness would mask their crossing into New Jersey and give them enough time to march to their objective unobserved. For the Army to stick to the timeline, all the troop movements to the Jersey side of the river needed to be completed by midnight. Unfortunately, Washington's timeline was skewed before his Army even began to make its crossing. Every one of Washington's combat elements reached their assembly area late. One regiment didn't even leave their camp, five miles from the ford, until after sunset. The regiment didn't get to their assembly area until after 6 PM, yet they were among the first to reach it. This pushed Washington's timetable to H-plus two hours, or two hours after the attack was planned to commence, which would likely result in Washington losing the element and shock of surprise, potentially jeopardizing the entire mission.

As if the fuming Washington didn't already have enough to worry about, a courier from Philadelphia rode into his camp with a dispatch from General Gates addressed to the Commander in Chief. Just before Christmas, Washington asked Gates to command an assault element for the Trenton operation. Gates turned it down because of an undisclosed illness but instead asked for permission to return to Philadelphia. Washington reluctantly agreed and asked Gates to stop by Bristol on his way to Philadelphia to deal with a developing command problem. Again, Gates refused, claiming he was too ill to stop by Bristol. Ironically, sick as Gates claimed to be, he wasn't too ill to ride to Baltimore and seek an audience with the president of Congress to persuade him to overrule Washington's plan for operations in New Jersey and likely had even loftier ambitions to replace Washington as chief.

In the dispatch to Washington, Gates wrote that while Washington was engaged with the Hessians in Trenton, he believed the British would sneak across the river and take possession of Philadelphia. The courier dutifully informed Washington that he had overheard Gates suggest, "Washington ought to retire south of the Susquehanna River to reform the army." He also said, "It was his intention to propose the measure at Baltimore." It turns out that Gates wasn't really as concerned with the British backdooring Washington and moving into Philadelphia as much as he was looking for an opportunity to backdoor Washington to unseat him as

Commander and Chief of the American Army. He would more famously attempt this again during the failed Conway Cabal about a year later. Washington had every reason to give into feelings of betrayal and rage after reading the seditious dispatch, but, as he was known to do in the face of adversity, he composed himself and focused on the critical task at hand.

As it seems too often to be the case during Revolutionary War battles and skirmishes in the northeast, weather had a hand in the disposition and conduct of Washington's scheme of maneuver. John Greenwood, who had enlisted as a fifer, was with the Army at the crossing that night and wrote in his memoir, "A little after sunset it began to drizzle or grow wet." By the time they reached the river, the drizzle had become a cold, driving rain that developed into a winter nor'easter within a few hours. "It rained, hailed, snowed, and froze." John survived the crossing, the collective battles of the 10-Days Crucible, and a second enlistment before leaving the Army. After the war, he served George Washington again, but this time as his personal dentist. Greenwood made Washington four sets of wooden dentures that he used throughout his presidency and until the end of his life. He is also credited with the 1790 invention of the first foot-powered drill, which he called the dental foot engine.

As if the delays and weather were not enough, the river threatened to completely derail Washington's battle plan before it even began. The Delaware River is tidal below the falls at Trenton. When the tide came in, it caused the ice floating downstream toward the falls to reverse course and move upstream. This winter phenomenon caused a massive ice buildup, which, trapped between the falls and the tide, became a frozen, chaotic obstacle. With conditions as severe as they were that night, it took less than four hours for the ice to pile five feet high and cover a span of the river over half a mile, making passage impossible. Ewing's forces had no chance of crossing that night under those conditions.

Further south, Cadwalader's forces faced dangerous river conditions of a different sort. Near their crossing point at Neshaminy Ferry, the nor'easter had caused a quarter-mile expanse of the ice-clogged river to become extremely turbulent, and the current was nearly impossible to navigate. Cadwalader eventually called off the attempt and marched his forces six miles south to attempt the crossing at Dunk's Ferry. As Cadwalader's forces began crossing downriver, they encountered more problems. The river below Dunk's Ferry had a distinctive s curve that trapped ice between the eastern shore and the incoming tide, creating another massive ice jam, albeit a little less severe than the one at the falls. Cadwalader had to disembark his men and attempt to cross the ice jam on foot. Only half his forces made it across when Cadwalader again called off the attempt and returned to the Pennsylvania shore. After about three hours, Cadwalader gave up any more attempts to cross the river and, abandoning the mission, recalled the men who had managed to make the crossing. A debate on the Jersey side of the river between those men took place, arguing whether they should continue onto Trenton with only half of their men. They eventually decided not to make the march and returned to Pennsylvania; by the time they made it back, it was almost daybreak.

With just two of Washington's assault elements attempting the crossing, the entire operation was already on the verge of collapse. Fortunately for Washington, conditions where he intended to cross were improved, and the Army was better prepared to make the crossing. At the Thompson-Neeley Farm, a large flotilla of boats and barges stood ready to transport Washington's forces across the river. Many boats used were Durham Boats, large, sturdy bulk cargo boats typically used to ferry iron ore across the river. The boats were more than adequate for their vital task that night. Most of the men made the crossing standing up in the boats since the vessels had few seats to sit on, and they were constantly taking on the icy water. If you visit

Washington's Crossing Historical Park, you can see several replicas of these boats. Although the river conditions were better where Washington made his crossing, the storm had made visibility nearly impossible. Fortunately, General Knox, who was placed in charge of the crossing, was able to keep the boats together with his loud, booming voice. Several commanders who made the crossing believed the endeavor would have failed if not for the 'great lungs of Knox.'

Most people in the eighteenth century could not swim, which made the crossing even more treacherous. It was said that some soldiers had even joked that they "did not fear to drown, for they were born to hang." During the crossing operation, some men fell overboard into the frigid waters. One of these soldiers was Colonel John Haslet of Delaware. He was eventually fished out of the river but suffered severely from exposure. Amazingly, Haslet marched ten miles on swollen legs and even fought in the Trenton battle without complaint; incredibly, Washington did not lose a single man to the river that night.

To ensure the assault had a chance to succeed, Washington believed secrecy was the paramount concern. At the landing site on the night of the crossing, he sent an advanced force of sentries to secure it and allow no one in or out of the area of operations. Washington devised a challenge and password, a system still in use by modern Marines. After writing the challenge and passwords down on several slips of paper, Washington passed them out to his commanders before the river crossing. Dr. Benjamin Rush, who was with the Commander in Chief the night before the crossing, wrote, "While I was talking to him, I observed him to play with his pen and ink upon several pieces of paper. One of them by accident fell upon the floor near my feet. I was struck with the inscription upon it. It was *Victory or Death*".

The one-half of Washington's Army that had made the crossing was at least three hours behind the timetable, seemingly forcing him to forfeit the element of surprise. Later, Washington wrote, "As I was certain there was no making a retreat without being discovered and harassed on re-crossing the river, I determined to push on at all events." The assembly of Washington's Army on the Jersey riverbank was slow but was without any further major issues.

Marine Corps Tie In...You are Now Aboard Marine Corps Recruit Depot Parris Island, South Carolina.

I was a couple of years out of high school when I realized I needed to accomplish a dream I had for years: that of becoming a United States Marine. I already had a great job with a very generous employer who had offered to send me to his Alma Mater in Doylestown, Pennsylvania, to become a landscape architect. As gracious as the offer was, I instinctively knew I was not nearly mature enough for college, and I would seriously risk wasting the gratuitous opportunity if I accepted his offer. I decided the best course of action was to enlist in the Marines, and on 10 October 1995, I was on an airplane for the first time in my life. The destination was Savannah, Georgia, and a short bus ride to Marine Corps Recruit Depot Parris Island, South Carolina.

After a few days in a forming platoon, my first Friday as a recruit arrived, commonly dubbed 'Black Friday' at both recruit depots. Black Friday was the day we did the sea bag drag from the forming barracks to a squad bay in a training company, where we met our team of Drill Instructors and settled into our new home for the next three months. The group of recruits who formed to become Platoon 3050, Lima Company, 3rd Battalion, was quickly ushered into the squad bay and instructed to sit on the floor, cross-legged and in rows of ten. The series commander, a young first lieutenant, walked to the center of the squad bay and, after delivering a short welcome aboard brief, said, "I am going to introduce you to the Drill Instructors responsible for your training by administering the Drill Instructor's Creed. " The Lieutenant smartly faced about as four intimidating Drill Instructors marched briskly in front of and crisply faced the series commander. In perfect synchronicity, the Senior Drill Instructor and his team raised their right hands and loudly boomed the following indelible words:

"These recruits are entrusted to my care. I will train them to the best of my ability. I will develop them into smartly disciplined, physically fit, basically trained Marines, thoroughly indoctrinated in love of the Corps and country. I will demand of them and demonstrate by my own example the highest standards of personal conduct, morality, and professional skill."

On that black Friday, the thought had never crossed my mind that I was destined to raise my hand in the same way and affirm the same creed to eight training platoons as a Marine Drill Instructor in less than ten years. After the team of Drill Instructors recited the creed, the Senior Drill Instructor introduced his team and then addressed platoon 3050, delivering a gravitating speech.

After the Senior Drill Instructor's speech, he swiftly turned to his team of Drill Instructors and said, "Take charge of this platoon and train them to become United States Marines!" After exchanging sharp salutes, the Senior marched into the duty hut, the green belt Drill Instructors took over the deck, and hell rained down on the hapless recruits of 3050 well into the twilight hours. Known as the 'Heavy Hat' at Parris Island and the 'J-Hat' at San Diego, the Heavy was the Drill Instructor primarily responsible for teaching in-house procedures and close order drill; our Heavy was easily the most intimidating human being I had ever been around. His face was always a mask of hate and discontent; he shaved his head, leaving a small tuft of hair that looked a bit like a groundhog tail hanging above his sinister brow. Later in his career, this imposing Drill Instructor was appointed the 19th Sergeant Major of the Marine Corps.

The first training day was a complete and exhaustive blur of perpetual motion. First names and personal pronouns such as I, my, me and mine were expressly forbidden on the depot and were the first words to be forcefully removed from our vocabulary and replaced with 'this recruit' or 'recruit (insert last name).' The platoon members learned that any other proper nouns or pronouns would not be tolerated during our stay on the island. Through the day's chaos, the platoon somehow learned the gist of in-house procedures, including morning and evening basic daily routine (BDR).

The most humiliating event of the night was hygiene hour. We quickly learned this routine was to be strictly controlled and supervised by junior Drill Instructors, who were about as approachable as rabid dogs. When it was time for hygiene, the platoon stripped to shower shoes and a towel. A hygiene bag lay across the right forearm of each recruit, parallel to the deck, elbow tucked tightly into each rib cage. Half the platoon shaved and brushed 'fangs' by the numbers, led by one of the rabid dog DIs. His loud, rapid-fire commands confused recruits; some were shaving with toothpaste while others were frantically brushing their teeth with shaving cream. The other half of the platoon was led into the 'rain room' by the other rabid dog DI, where they shuffled around 'rain trees' and soaped on command, rinsed on command, then dried off on command...all in less than 30 seconds. Because everyone had their seabags dumped and kicked around the squad bay multiple times during inventory earlier in the day, few recruits even had their own hygiene gear. The chances were better than average that we had brushed our teeth with someone else's toothbrush, shaved with someone else's razor, and washed with someone else's bar of soap that night.

The Drill Instructors led this insane routine until the recruits had it perfected, and the Drill Instructor team was allowed 'off lights', which meant that the DI team was required to be with the platoon

24/7. This continued until the team sufficiently trained the platoon to a certain standard. After the series Chief Drill Instructor observed the team, evaluated the platoon's morning and evening BDR, and determined the process to be sufficiently mastered, the team was allowed to begin an overnight duty rotation. The process, depending on the aptitude of the platoon and the diligence of the DIs, lasted anywhere from a week to several.

After a week of acclimatizing to the rigors of recruit training, Platoon 3050 was assembled on the quarterdeck for a 'period of instruction,' which turned out to be an Incentive Training (IT) demonstration. Platoon 3050 was about to discover that IT was a Drill Instructor's favorite method of instilling good order and discipline, and the method was about to become a recruit's living nightmare. Five recruits from a senior training platoon appeared seemingly out of nowhere. They were very intensely 'smoked' for three minutes, left in a leaning rest position while the Drill Instructor made a few points, then smoked the group of recruits for another three minutes before sending them away. After the demonstration, the 'smoking lamp' was lit, and our Drill Instructors wasted no time dishing out an abundance of practical application and remediation for the next three months.

My first personal smoke session by a Drill Instructor occurred on one unfortunate day during grass week at the rifle range. Our Heavy was engaged in a heated argument with another series Drill Instructor over who had provided the best instruction to their platoon on rifle handling and safety rules. I was quickly called into the midst of the argument to give a winning example of my Heavy's outstanding instruction. My marksmanship skills were honed; I was confident I could easily recite the four safety rules or demonstrate any weapon handling technique. As I was put through intense questioning, I inadvertently called the Heavy a Drill Sergeant (a strictly Army term) instead of Drill Instructor (an inherently Marine term). I paid dearly for my display of temporary insanity and especially for embarrassing my Heavy. As the Heavy went to work on me in a barely veiled attempt to remove the soul from my nasty recruit body, I was determined that I would at least suffer my humiliation with intrepidity. I shouted as loudly as possible while trying to perform exercises the Heavy rapidly demanded. I was even ordered to scream the Army recruiting jingle, "Be all I can be in the Army" while I was being mercilessly smoked, to my abject embarrassment and mortification. In the Heavy's slightly disguised attempt to stop my heart, I must have somehow impressed him with my tenacity, if nothing else, because he fired a squad leader that evening and promoted me into the position. Unfortunately, yet somewhat paradoxically, I was relieved of the appointment before graduation because, try as I might, I could not get a particular close-order drill movement (column of files) mastered in time for the platoon's final drill evaluation.

I have many other unique memories of my time at Parris Island during recruit training. I remember a recruit dubbed the 'Gerber Baby' because he looked just like the Gerber Baby. Every morning, the recruit would line up opposite my rack, wearing just his skivvy drawers like all the rest of us, to count off for accountability and begin morning BDR. This was a spectacle the Gerber Baby recruit obviously could not handle tactfully, as he fought vainly every morning to maintain his military bearing. Subsequently, every morning would begin for him with a trip to the quarter deck for an attitude adjustment. In his professional genius, one of the junior Drill Instructors even implemented a plan to add extra incentive by ordering Gerber to choose nine of his 'girlfriends' to join him on the quarter deck for his morning smoke sessions. This failed to fix the Gerber Baby's bearing problem but did succeed in angering the many 'girlfriends' he had inadvertently acquired in the platoon.

There was a recruit in the platoon who evidently had a weak bladder, based on the absurd number of times in a day he requested permission to 'make a head call.' On one of these occasions, one of our green belt Drill Instructors was reviewing Marine Corps History with the platoon as we labored methodically over rifle maintenance. Like clockwork, the recruit interrupted the Drill Instructor's review to obtain permission to use a toilet. This particular recruit must also have had an undisclosed learning disability; after two and a half months, he never learned how to ask for permission to the standard the platoon was taught: "Good afternoon Sir, Recruit (insert name) respectfully requests permission to make a head call Sir!" The recruit was instructed to sit down every time he recited the line incorrectly. Finally, the recruit stood up again, this time holding himself while shouting for permission to use a toilet, adding that it was an emergency and, yet again, completely got the jargon wrong. That the recruit declared the request an emergency either amused or enraged the Drill Instructor, or possibly a little of both; the recruit was promptly instructed to run around the squad bay while making a siren noise. After a few laps, the recruit suddenly stopped, declaring he no longer had an emergency but needed to change his sodden trousers.

The recruit and his weak bladder failed to graduate with Platoon 3050. The platoon was a couple of days away from graduation and was being marched to the parade deck for practice. The Drill Instructor had halted the platoon to talk with someone when the recruit with the weak bladder started to do the pee-pee dance in the middle of the formation, along a high-traffic area. Evidently tired of waiting on the Drill Instructor to finish his conversation and march the platoon to the parade deck, he urinated in the street at the position of attention. The last we heard, the hapless recruit and his below-average bladder were dropped to a first-phase platoon for another three months of 'remediation.'

It has been nearly 28 years since I first stood on one of the iconic sets of yellow footprints one damp, misty mid-October night in Parris

Island, twenty of which I served my watch on active duty. During my career, I met and served with many Marines through good times and hard times. As age begins to fade my memory, I have trouble remembering all the fine men and women I had the honor of serving with. The names of the four Drill Instructors who molded me into a Marine, though they will remain somewhat anonymous in this work, have withstood the test of time and will always be remembered as I am sure it is with all who have gone to Parris Island or San Diego and earned the title Marine.

Historical places to visit in and near Washington's Crossing, Pennsylvania.

There are numerous points of historical interest within Washington's Crossing Historical Park. The park features 18th-century homes that would have existed in 1776, including the boathouse that contains restored Durham boats. A museum on site offers exhibits of several artifacts from the Revolutionary War period and showcases an ornately embossed cannon donated by General Lafayette. There is plenty of accessible parking in and around the park, and a bridge spanning the Delaware River provides a bird's eye view of the crossing site and leads to a restored historical building and a replica of a barge that would have been used to transport cannon and horses across the river. Informational signs within the park are plentiful and provide visitors with a good background of the history. On most days, plenty of knowledgeable park rangers provide guided tours of the crossing. If you plan your visit in December, you might even see Washington, Knox, and Cadwalader leading their men across the frigid expanse of river in the Durham boats.

Many more historical sites related to the Revolutionary War are well worth visiting within a thirty-mile radius. Bowman's Hill Tower is a short and easy drive through Bucks County. Although the tower was built well after Washington's famous crossing, the hill it stands on was used as a lookout post by Washington's Army. Visitors can climb the few hundred stone steps to the balcony of this tall tower and see miles of countryside, including the Thompson-Neely House. At this restored 18th-century farmstead, a Revolutionary War burial site is maintained.

Thompson-Neely House is located at 1628 River Road New Hope, Pennsylvania.

Washington's Crossing Historical Park is located at 1112 River Road Washington's Crossing, Pennsylvania.

Bowman's Hill Tower is located at the corner of Route 32 River Road and Lurgan Road, Washington Crossing, Pennsylvania.

Bogart's Tavern is located at 4705 York Road Buckingham, Pennsylvania.

Neshaminy State Park is located at Tidal Marsh Natural Area Andalusia, Pennsylvania.

Gabriela Barrantes Photography (Headquarters) is located at 1 Orchard Lane Doylestown, Pennsylvania.

Revolutionary Burial Ground (Langhorne Hospitals) is located at Bellevue and Flowers Avenue Langhorne, Pennsylvania.

Old Revolutionary Fort is located at 70 York Road New Hope, Pennsylvania.

Unknown Soldiers of the Continental Army Marker (Burial Site) is located along Taylorsville Road Washington's Crossing, Pennsylvania.

Justices House (Headquarters) is located at 111 South State Street Newtown, Pennsylvania.

Loyalist Raid of 1778 Marker is located at 100-114 S State Street Newtown, Pennsylvania.

<u>Newtown Presbyterian Church Marker (Burial Site)</u> is located at 76 North Sycamore Street Newtown, Pennsylvania.

<u>The Cross Roads Marker (Encampment)</u> is located at 1075 W Bristol Road Warminster, Pennsylvania

Trenton, New Jersey

We've got the Old Fox safe now. We will go over and bag him in the morning!

~ General Charles Cornwallis, The First Marquess Cornwallis

The crossing over the Delaware River was miraculously completed without loss of life or equipment, and Washington's Army slowly assembled for a march on Trenton. General Washington was still marginally hopeful for the two factors he considered vital for a successful assault on the Hessian forces garrisoned in the town: secrecy and surprise. The slow, treacherous river crossing, a difficult, cumbersome march over dangerous roads, and the misplaced ambition of an antagonistic subordinate threatened to compromise Washington's strategy.

Washington's Army wasn't assembled and ready to march until around four in the morning, putting it a conservative four hours behind Washington's timetable or H plus four in modern military language. The road conditions, icy and treacherous, made footing for men and horses exceedingly difficult. The attacking Army nearly lost its commanding general before it was well into the march when Washington's horse lost its footing and threatened to plummet down a steep embankment with its rider. As soon as he felt the horse slip, Washington, well known for his superb horsemanship, instinctively grabbed the floundering horse's mane and heaved its head up enough for the horse to regain its footing.

Dragging the heavy field pieces along the route took a physical toll on both man and beast, particularly while traversing ice-covered hills. Soldiers had to help the horses pull the heavy cannon up the hills, every step putting them at risk. Should the horses slip or the traces break, the guns could roll back down the hill, crushing anyone in its path. Going down the icy hills with the cumbersome guns was no less treacherous. Again, soldiers were required to assist the horses with the descent by manning draglines. This time, the risk shifted to the horses pulling the guns, should they break away.

By the time the Army reached the halfway point, the hour was already nearing six in the morning. At the Birmingham crossroads, the tired soldiers halted and began to check their weapons; to their dismay, many discovered the pieces wet, thus not in firing condition. The dismal news soon made its way up the chain of command to the general officers. General Sullivan reportedly asked, "What is to be done?" General St. Clair replied, "You have nothing for it but push and charge." Washington concurred and ordered his generals to "advance and charge." Before the Army moved on, Washington ordered his subordinate commanders to take out their timepieces and synchronize them to his pocket watch, one of the first documented instances of this action during an American military operation. Finally, after these final preparations were made, the Army divided and moved toward Trenton in two different directions in accordance with Washington's battle plan.

General Greene was tasked with leading his Army contingent uphill to Upper Ferry Road, into Trenton via Pennington Road, and attacking north to south. General Sullivan's Army division continued to River Road, entering Trenton on Water Street and attacking east to west. Since Sullivan had the shortest and easiest route, he was required to halt briefly to allow Greene to get into his attack position.

Unbeknownst to Washington, he still held the element of surprise, but it was almost forfeited less than three miles from the objective. Washington was riding along Greene's column, encouraging the soldiers to pick up the pace, when a group of fifty men were spotted marching from Trenton. Washington rode ahead to find that the men were his own, but they were not assigned to any of the advance parties in the Army's vanguard... they had a strange story to tell their commander-in-chief. A few days before the

American Army crossed the Delaware, Hessian Jaegers had killed one of General Adam Stephen's men of the Virginia Fourth Regiment, and the general immediately sent a raiding party across the Delaware to avenge the death of his soldier, contrary to Washington's general order for the raiding parties to stand down. On Christmas day, Captain Wallis took a raiding party across the river, not knowing that Washington had planned a large-scale attack on Trenton. Wallis attacked a Hessian outpost near the outskirts of the town, which alarmed the enemy garrison. Led by Colonel Rall, the Hessians attempted to hunt down the raiding party. They gave chase, but Wallis' party was able to evade the Hessians. After an exhaustive search, Colonel Rall returned to the garrison empty-handed. Instead of attempting to return to friendly lines across the river, Wallis hunkered down with his men on the outskirts of town and was fortunate to run into Washington's Army.

The more Washington heard the captain's story, the more convinced he was that the element of surprise had been compromised. He had ordered the harassing attacks to end by Christmas Eve, hoping to lull the garrison into complacency through a false sense of security. Washington immediately sent for his insubordinate general to verify the captain's story. In a rare show of anger, Washington, upon hearing his general admit he had sent the unauthorized raiding party, raged, "You, Sir! You, Sir, may have ruined all my plans by having put them on their guard". To understand Washington's unusually harsh reaction toward General Stephen, it helps to have some backstory between the two generals. Stephen was Washington's second in command during the French and Indian War but had gained a reputation for insubordination and intoxication while on duty, for which he was severely reprimanded. After the war, Stephen campaigned against Washington for an important political post in Virginia but lost. Neither wanted to serve together in the Revolution, but circumstance did not give them a choice. Based on this criterion, it is reasonable to surmise that Stephen was either willingly or carelessly insubordinate once again, this time at Washington's Crossing.

Quickly regaining his composure, Washington re-mastered his emotions during a moment in time when he really needed to remain calm and collected. He turned his back on his disputant general, thanked the captain for his services, and invited the captain's men to join his column. Whether Stephen was held accountable for his actions on this day is unclear. However, later, during the Battle of Germantown, his antics finally caught up to him, and he was found guilty via court martial of intoxication while in command of an active combat unit. The general was stripped of his rank and discharged from the Army.

By half past seven, Washington's Army was grossly behind its timetable and was still two miles from their assault position. Weather again became a factor, but this time to Washington's benefit when the ferocious nor'easter provided thick clouds and heavy snow, effectively masking Washington's attack on Trenton. Miraculously, both American assault positions attacked nearly simultaneously, and with the element of surprise, Washington had his coveted advantage.

A popular but inaccurate interpretation of historical accounts of the first battle of Trenton suggests that Washington achieved the element of surprise because the Hessian garrison suffered the ill effects of a long night of celebratory drinking that Christmas night, but there is no evidence to support this popular theory. Instead, the disdain the Hessian commander had for his American opponent, the effects of the severe winter weather on the Hessians, and days and nights of the garrison conducting long patrols and maintaining a constant, high level of alert might have caused them to be drunk with fatigue and ignorance, but not alcohol.

The Hessians had made General Dickinson's home their main outpost on River Road and defended it with a company of Jaegers. Colonel Stark, a patriot from New Hampshire known for his ferocity in battle, had trained and drilled his men to use the bayonet. Out of a raging, snowy torrent charged Stark's soldiers, howling with fixed bayonets toward the unbelieving Hessian defenders. The Hessians hastily retreated toward town as American batteries, massed on the Pennsylvania side of the river, began to suppress enemy positions. The bewildered Hessians suddenly found themselves under attack from three different directions. The three surprised Hessian regiments occupying the town regained their professional poise despite the shock of the sudden attack and were quick to respond to the unmistakable sounds of combat. Having slept in their uniforms, they formed ranks near their quarters much faster than one would expect from a camp of drunken revelers.

Colonel Rall was rudely woken by his adjutant, shouting, "The Enemy...Turn out!" Colonel Rall, still in his bedclothes, was informed that the Americans had completely surrounded the town. Had Colonel Rall been given an accurate depiction of the battle as it was unfolding, he would have discovered that the town was not completely surrounded as he had been told. The Hessians still controlled a small stone bridge that spanned the Assunpink Creek and led to an excellent defensive position on some high ground. Had Rall ordered his garrison into a fighting retreat across the bridge, the outcome of the Battle of Trenton might have been different. Based on the information Colonel Rall was given, he made a fatal decision to counterattack Washington in the town.

Although fatal, Rall's decision was not all that unremarkable; he had a shallow opinion of Washington's 'rebel rabble' and very high confidence in his professional Hessian regulars. In accordance with the German tactical doctrine of the time, Rall consolidated his forces to attack the strongest point of Washington's Army. General Knox began to unlimber his guns on the town heights while General Washington carefully watched the American attack develop in the town. Knox's guns began to bark, sending ball and grapeshot into the Hessians concentrated on King Street. As quickly as Hessian gunners manned their cannon, American shot cut them down, killing horses and men indiscriminately, forcing the surviving Hessian gunners to abandon their field pieces and run to safety.

American patriots soon gained a foothold in houses, and their muskets and rifles, sheltered from the weather, poured devastating small arms fire into the exposed Hessian soldiers, causing them to eventually break and retreat under the pressure of the massed fires. Colonel Rall was ultimately able to consolidate two of his regiments behind the English church in the center of town and oriented them north to attack the American guns on the heights. Observing Rall assemble his troops, Washington immediately ordered Colonel Hand and Colonel Haussegger's regiments to shift to high ground beyond the Hessian regiments. The move effectively disrupted Rall's plan, and his counterattack was aborted.

Colonel Rall received news that his artillery had been either captured or destroyed. Two of the abandoned guns belonged to Rall's own regiment, and their loss under those circumstances would have caused considerable embarrassment for the proud Hessian. In an attempt to rescue the guns and salvage his honor, Rall ordered the two regiments into the middle of the American infernal, where a cone of patriot fire instantly enveloped them from three directions. Rall recklessly ran the lead-laced gauntlet and recovered his guns but paid a heavy price for them in Hessian blood. The American marksmen, targeting officers, managed to drop four of Rall's captains during the attempt. Usually in the thick of any battle, Colonel Rall received two American balls for his effort, both of which were mortal, proof indeed that 'pride comes before the fall.' Beaten, leaderless, and completely overwhelmed, the surviving Hessians sounded the retreat and headed east and out of town, closely pursued by the victorious American Army.

The routed Hessians had lost their venerated commander and a total of 918 men, including twenty-two killed, eighty-three seriously wounded, and 813 taken prisoner. They also left behind valuable arms, equipment, and supplies. After the cessation of hostilities, Washington called a hasty war council and debated whether to push their luck and attack other garrisons in New Jersey or return to the relative safety of camp on the Pennsylvania side of the river. Prudence persevered, and the decision was made to return with the captured arms, equipment, and supplies. The prisoners were marched off to captivity in prisoner camps located at Lancaster, Reading, and Carlisle.

The Second Battle of Trenton or The Battle of Assunpink Creek

Back on the Pennsylvania side of the river, the American Army had scarcely settled into camp after their victory over the Hessian regiments in Trenton when Washington received an urgent message from General Cadwalader. Cadwalader eventually made it across the river to New Jersey but missed making the march to Trenton with the Army a few days earlier. Instead of returning to Pennsylvania, Cadwalader's men voted to remain in Jersey to reconnoiter. Cadwalader sent a message to Washington to advise his commander that while reconnoitering in the vicinity of Burlington, he had witnessed the British evacuate the town, some marching back to eastern Jersey. Cadwalader lobbied for another attack in the Jerseys, writing, "If we can drive them from west Jersey, the success will raise an army by next spring and establish the credit of the Continental money."

Washington called his subordinate leaders to a council of war late on the night of December 27th to discuss the plausibility of one more winter assault on British forces in the Jerseys. The question was soon answered as the officers debated among themselves; they decided that the Army should seize upon the opportunity for one more attack on British forces, and orders were quickly issued for the Army to re-cross the Delaware River. Washington's officers had decided on a December 29th crossing of the river, this time at eight different crossing points; Washington intended to have his entire Army intact for this last assault, and he wasn't taking any chances. At Bristol, General Mifflin assembled twenty-seven Pennsylvania regiments, including a detachment of American Marines, led them across the river to Burlington, and formed them into a brigade that marched with the main Army toward Trenton.

As the American Army began to settle into temporary camps around Trenton, Washington received valuable intelligence that around 6,000 British troops remained in the Jerseys, and another 4,000 were mobilizing in support. The intelligence suggested a strong British attack was imminent. Washington called his generals into a war council once more to discuss strategy. The council decided the obvious and best course of action was to receive the pending threat on ground of their choosing. Since they already knew Trenton well, they chose to defend it. Washington wasn't about to make the same mistake his late adversary made; he was going to fortify and defend the open hill to the south of Assunpink Creek instead of bottling himself up in the town as Rall had done.

The defensive position was a good one. Aside from commanding the high ground, it had natural barriers capable of stopping or slowing an assault on the hill; the Delaware River protected the western flank, and the Assunpink Creek protected the front. A virtually impregnable swamp protected the eastern flank, leaving the Assunpink Creek Bridge as the only likely avenue of approach. Preparations for a defensive battle were almost immediately set into motion by the American Army. The artillery was placed on high ground covering bridges and fords, reinforced pickets were sent onto every road leading into Trenton, and the infantrymen were set into three defensive positions on the hill.

General Cornwallis, who was preparing to return to England on leave, was aboard a ship and about to get underway when a British courier gave the general the dismal news of the Hessian disaster in Trenton. A very disgruntled Cornwallis had to disembark his baggage and get orders out to one of his most reliable lieutenants to "find the rebel army and destroy it." After issuing his order, Cornwallis began a fifty-mile ride from New York to Princeton on weather-beaten roads. By the time the general reached Princeton, a British Army of around 10,000 soldiers had been assembled for deployment against the American Army in Trenton.

Among Cornwallis' commanders was Hessian Colonel von Donop, a violent, ambitious professional soldier bent on avenging the Hessian embarrassment suffered during the battle a few days earlier. The Colonel issued a directive to his soldiers that they were to take no prisoners in the anticipated battle, at the risk of severe corporal punishment in the form of fifty 'stripes' to anyone found insubordinate to the Colonel's order.

Cornwallis set his Army in motion toward Trenton, but he soon found that the march would not be easy. The weather created a hazardous condition called freeze/thaw, which typically occurs in the spring but had unseasonably occurred during Cornwallis' January march. During the day, the roads would thaw, creating almost impassable, knee-deep, muddy conditions unfit for travel; Cornwallis' movement took too much time and sapped the strength of his struggling soldiers.

Colonel Hand, who had recently engaged Hessians at Princeton, wisely fell back toward Trenton instead of attempting a direct assault on the British column. At a large crossing at Shabbakunk Creek, Hand decided to take advantage of the terrain and set his men into a position on both sides of the crossing to ambush the approaching British column. When the British flanks and advanced guards came within close range, Hand ordered his riflemen to open fire. The ambush was so sudden and effective that it turned the British advance guard into the oncoming column. During the ensuing confusion, American guns continued to fire on the British column, effectively fixing it on the road. Hand's men, outnumbered six to one, bravely held their ground for a couple of hours, effectively stalling the British attack on Trenton, then slowly withdrew through the woods toward friendly lines.

Americans streamed towards Washington's lines and safety as the British column closed on Trenton. Not all made it in time; some, like an American chaplain, were destined to suffer Donop's wrath. Sitting in a tavern on the outskirts of town, the hapless chaplain heard the battle rattle and decided to get on his horse and ride to safety. When he got outside the building, he discovered his horse was gone, so he tried to run, but not in time to prevent his capture. The unfortunate chaplain soon became a victim of a deadly Hessian game. He was promptly stripped of his clothes, and the Hessians stabbed the naked chaplain with bayonets as he pleaded and prayed for mercy. His body was allegedly found later, naked except for thirteen bayonet wounds to his body and numerous saber slashes to the head.

Another critical moment for the American cause occurred on the little stone bridge spanning Assunpink Creek that helped shape world history. With Cornwallis finally in his attack position at Trenton, the appearance of his ten-thousand-man Army had to have been disheartening for the American defenders. But to attack Washington, Cornwallis was forced to funnel his forces over the Assunpink Creek Bridge. Three times, the British forces attempted to force their way over the bridge, and three times, the American defenders repelled the attack. Had the American troops failed in their endeavor to prevent the British from crossing the bridge, vastly outnumbered, they would have been quickly overwhelmed. The likely result was that Washington and his Army would have become trapped in their natural fortification and annihilated.

Sergeant White, an American soldier, wrote, "The enemy came on solid columns; we let them come on some ways. Then, by a signal given, we all fired together. The enemy retreated off the bridge and formed again, and we were ready for them. Our whole artillery was again discharged at them". Even after Washington's long lines of infantry poured concentrated fires on the British column, they watched in amazement as the enemy continued their attempt to cross the bridge until they were eventually compelled to withdraw. Cornwallis consolidated his forces and attempted to cross the bridge a second time. This time, withering American fires prevented the British from even getting halfway across the bridge before the troops broke and retreated. To the amazement of the American defenders, Cornwallis attempted a third crossing. Sergeant White wrote, "They came a third time. We loaded with canister shot and let them come nearer. We fired all together again, and such destruction it made, you cannot conceive. The bridge looked red as blood, with their killed and wounded and red coats". The British forces were forced to retreat a third time, and American troops moved forward and closer to the bridge.

Nevertheless, Cornwallis relentlessly continued to probe Washington's defense for any surface or gap he could exploit. The British tried three more attacks before darkness set in, this time at a couple of minor fording sites, but the American defenses were too strong, and each attack was repelled. Losses on the American side were minimal, estimated at around fifty killed and wounded; the British estimates were much higher, with 500 killed, wounded, or captured.

Darkness put an end to hostilities for the day, but each commander had some planning to do for the following day. In one headquarters, Cornwallis was busy planning a surprise attack at dawn the next day. He planned to use his Hessians to distract the Americans by conducting a diversionary attack and then attack Washington's vulnerable flank with his regulars. Under the cover of darkness, Cornwallis maneuvered his forces accordingly but decided against the advice of his senior officers for an immediate night attack, believing, "We've got the Old Fox safe now. We will go over and bag him in the morning."

Busily planning in his headquarters, Washington knew precisely what Cornwallis was up to via intelligence gathered by reconnaissance patrols and had no intention of allowing his Army to be outflanked. He presented the situation to his senior leaders as a problem that required a solution. Washington told his leaders that to remain in place assured a battle the next day they likely could not win, but a retreat on the only route known was conceivably as dangerous as a battle. Washington said, "The loss of the corps he commanded might be fatal to the country; under those circumstances, he asked advice." As the senior officers worked on the problem, a solution soon began to form...neither a general engagement at Trenton nor a retreat out of Trenton on a dangerously exposed road, but a stealthy escape and an attack on the enemy's rear in Princeton.

General St. Clair, recalling traces of paths he had discovered while patrolling in the area, suggested if the Army could somehow make it to the little-used paths undetected, it could march north six miles to Princeton before the British even noticed they were gone. The previous morning's road conditions had helped slow Cornwallis' movement toward Trenton, buying Washington valuable time to shore up his defenses. At such a perilous time for the Americans, road conditions were destined to help Washington rapidly move his Army out of Cornwallis' carefully laid trap. Although the roads during the day were a soggy mess, the temperature in the early evening dropped so suddenly that the muddy roads froze over within a couple of hours. Taking full advantage of this fortuitous phenomenon, Washington devised a diversion, ordering his men to build numerous fires as a ruse to cover their immediate withdrawal and stole a march on Princeton; the 'Old Fox' had escaped the hunter's trap.

Marine Corps Tie-In...Cold on the Mountain.

I have firsthand experience of what it is like to participate in sustained operations in cold weather conditions. During my career as a Marine, I had the opportunity to attend the Advanced Winter Mountain Leaders Course in Bridgeport, California. The course was a challenging, five-week school that taught students how to survive and operate in mountainous terrain in frigid weather. I fondly remember those five cold weeks in the High Sierras.

I started my cold weather experience by running a Physical Fitness Test at altitude. I was stationed at sea level but base camp at the Marine Corps Mountain Warfare Training Center (MCMWTC) is 6,800 feet above sea level. I never had an issue with a PFT and consistently scored perfect or near perfect. Although I scored yet another high PFT score, the combination of cold and altitude made the three-mile run through Pickle Meadows gut-wrenchingly challenging. After the PFT, we received mountain equipment and cold weather gear for our training and immediately set out on a timed, mostly uphill, individual hike with more gear than I had ever hiked with. I easily made the cut, but unfortunately, over 20 other students failed, were dropped from the course, and sent back to their units.

After the first cut, the class jumped right into the training. We needed to quickly acclimatize and become proficient in downhill/cross-country skiing, skijoring, mountain operations, establishing tactical bivouac sites (including constructing and sleeping in emergency snow shelters), mountain medicine, and mountain survival. Students were required to pass all tests and events with 100% proficiency, and failure to remediate resulted in being dropped from the course. Getting dropped from a formal school almost always had an adverse effect on a Marine's career.

I performed well in the school until the downhill skiing evaluation. Before I arrived at MCMWTC, I had never been on a pair of skis, so the learning curve was steep for me; I was not the only one. We all participated in a cross-country ski race on our first day at a ski resort in Nevada. Very few students were proficient on skis, so the 5k course resembled a demolition derby that I somehow won; I can only really credit my success to the attrition of the other students and sheer dumb luck. As I was nearing the finish, I noticed an instructor trying to overtake me. Determined to maintain my advantage, I skied hard and managed to finish just ahead of him. This little race became my saving grace later in the course when I failed to remediate a skills test on skis. I was eventually brought before all the instructors who notified me of my failure to pass or remediate with 100% proficiency. I was told I was being dropped from the course when the instructor I finished ahead of in the 5k advocated for me. After some discussion among the instructors, they agreed to allow me to continue the course. Unfortunately, others were not as fortunate and did not make the cut. During downhill training, a recon lieutenant and fellow student who enjoyed saying ridiculous things to civilians on the slopes while riding the lift didn't make it off the chair one afternoon when his tongue froze to it after licking the steel frame. We left him in the chair for a little while to reflect on his inappropriate behavior. Later in the course, he drank melted snow that was contaminated with stove fuel and ended up a medical drop.

After our ski trials at the resort, we returned to the snow-packed mountains of MCMWTC for a long week of survival techniques. We established a base camp in a secluded meadow and were told to build one-man shelters for the night. Those who dug snow caves, as we were taught, slept warm during the bitterly cold night, while others who were not so diligent spent the night in freezing misery. The following evening, the class started out on a night march; since we didn't carry packs, we expected a brief foray around the camp. We were about an hour into the hike when our instructor turned and informed us that we would spend the rest of the night where we were and gave us ten minutes to dig a trench large enough for all of us to sleep in. Our snowshoes became field expedient shovels as the class dug a trench as deep as we could make it in ten minutes. Relying on body heat to survive the night, the Marines were quite literally human rotisseries as we rotated around each other, from side to side and high to low. It was indeed a miserable but survivable night.

That week, we learned valuable survival techniques, such as primitive fire building, trapping with snares, and field medicine. During one class, we were being entertained by a captivating tale of a local legend called the High Sierra Mountain Bush Monster when an instructor brought out a soft, fluffy bunny and asked for a volunteer to assist with a demonstration. A Marine quickly volunteered and was told to find a short but sturdy stick. When he returned to the class with his stick, the instructor thrust the rabbit at him and said, "Dinner." I am not sure which looked more terrified, the rabbit or the Marine, as he clumsily tried to bludgeon it to death. The instructor eventually took the flailing, screaming rabbit from the Marine and briskly snapped its neck, ending its misery. During the spectacle, one of the rabbit's eyes popped out of its head. The instructor told the Marine to eat it, explaining to the class that an eyeball was a valuable source of electrolytes. Aided by a lot of peer pressure, the Marine very hesitantly gave in to the instructor's persistence. The Marine pulled the eyeball out of the rabbit's battered head with his teeth and, biting down, instantly began to spit and gag. The grinning instructor told the Marine he might have forgotten to recommend not chewing the eyeball but swallowing it whole instead. Perhaps this tale of the rabbit's demise was poor, but the soup it supplemented that day over a primitive fire was very rich.

The last day of our survival week was spent skijoring to the top of MCMWTC's highest peak, 9,494 feet above sea level. The day should have been easy; after all, we were towed up the mountain. We rendezvoused with a tracked vehicle, a static line was tied to the hitch by a hitch knot, and the class was instructed to tie into either side of the running ends of the rope. We all stood behind the vehicle in our skis with a large mountain pack on our backs and our ski poles attached to the rope with an overhand turn. The tracked vehicle suddenly lurched forward, spilling everyone in the snow, a precursor to how the rest of the day would be spent. The problem the class had with the skijoring exercise was multifaceted. For the course, we were given two types of boots: leather ski boots that fit well in ski bindings but would get soaked throughout the day and freeze solid at night or Mickey Mouse boots that kept our feet warm and dry but were cumbersome and did not fit well in ski bindings.

Since most had opted to wear Mickey Mouse boots, most of us would eventually lose a ski, and when one lost a ski, they suddenly found themselves being dragged behind the vehicle. The reason we were instructed to tie the ski poles into the running end of the line with an overhand turn was twofold. One, it was far easier to hold onto the ski poles like a handlebar than maintain a grip on the rope wearing heavy gloves. The second reason is that the overhand turn could be released with a quick twist of the poles. The Marines had at least a chance of avoiding tangled bodies when someone lost a ski, which was very often. During the event, the mountain was undergoing freeze-thaw conditions; by the time we reached the top, we were all completely soaked from frequent spills in wet snow and exhausted. We were told that base camp was already set up down the mountain, and the faster we skied to it, the faster we got into warm, dry clothes. The problem I now faced was the trail down was completely frozen, and as I mentioned, I am not a good skier. Although we had skins on our skis that worked great in snow, they slowed our descent very little on ice. I had nothing else to do but point my ski tips down the hill, and off I went. About the time I began to wonder how I would stop my ever-increasing momentum down the hill, a half-buried metal road marker suddenly solved the riddle. I hit the post, and Wilde E. Coyote like, kind of hung there for a few minutes until I slid from it and sprawled onto the snow. After gathering my breath and scattered gear, I decided walking was the fastest way to get to the base camp.

The five-week course ended with a field exercise combining all the hard and soft skills we obtained during the course. We collaboratively finished the field exercise two days ahead of schedule, reaching our raid objective in less than three days. We were told we could enjoy a few days of free time in the Tahoe area before class graduation. Little did we know there was to be more friction added to the course after our after-action brief on the objective. After the brief, we all crammed into a few tracked vehicles for the ride down to base camp and a warm shower; most of us were too tired to hold a conversation, much less speculate why the raid objective resembled a supply depot packed with cases of Meals Ready to Eat (MREs), water and fuel...we were just too tired to care, and we left it all behind.

About fifteen minutes into the ride, a few of us noticed that we were gaining elevation instead of losing it. In an instant, the vehicle lurched to a stop, and we were 'highly encouraged' to get out of the vehicles amidst a din of simulated machine gun fire, arty simulators, and smoke. One of our classmates was designated a battle casualty, and we had to treat and evacuate the Marine. The instructors threw a few random packs, several sets of mismatched skis, some mismatched snowshoes, and a sled into the waist-deep snow and gave us minutes to get out of the ambush site. We quickly treated the 'injured' Marine and strapping him to the sled, moved out of the notional ambush site. We embarked on a cold, grueling all-night movement down the mountain, broke a trail through waist-deep snow, and established a tactical patrol base before daylight. We spent the next three days attempting to survive, evade our instructors, and get off the mountain.

When the instructors dropped those random packs in the snow, there was very little food left in them; whatever was in the packs disappeared on the first day. Unfortunately, we left crates of unopened MREs on the objective site, and foolishly, we left them where they lay, thinking the course was completed. Some of us attempted to hunt, fish, or set snares, but to no avail since it was extremely cold, and we were utilizing primitive hunting, fishing, and trapping methods. Every now and an instructor monitoring our activities would place a bit of food in a snare set, and one time, a Marine attempting his luck at fishing was rewarded with an MRE floating down the stream. Everyone was tired, hungry, and very ill-tempered at this point of the training exercise. When I returned to the base camp from an unsuccessful hunting foray, an instructor was busily dumping snow on several fires the students had lit. Discovered by the 'enemy,' our base camp was compromised, and we had to move on, dragging another casualty on the sled.

Finally, on the third day, hunkered down in another primitive patrol base, we could smell stew cooking, and most of us were almost literally starving. We eventually decided to recon the source of the scent of cooking food and found staff members portrayed as partisan civilians making stew. They forced our leader to eat the hot strew and promised full stomachs and a ride to base camp for all of us...but a steep price was demanded. In trade, we were to give up all our warming layers and the few sleeping bags we had, and we would not leave the mountain until the next day. This resulted in outright mutiny from most of the students, and finally, cracking under fatigue, hunger, and the cold; most threw in the towel and refused to continue the training. An administrative timeout was called by the officer in charge of MCMWTC, and he sat us down as a class and held a very humiliating, one-way conversation with us. The result of the administrative timeout was that we would finish what we had started. We were going back to MCMWTC proper the next day, but we were going to hike back, dragging a new casualty along a rugged, circuitous route, and it would take another whole night to accomplish. When we finally got to MCMWTC proper the following morning, we thought the course was finished.

Little did we realize that the worst was yet to come. We were at MCMWTC proper for just enough time to unload our gear and turn in rifles and serialized gear when an instructor told us to strip down to poly-pro and sneakers and get back into the tracked vehicles. Back up another mountain we all went. When we reached our destination, we gathered around a large warming tent, AED, and a large hole cut into an ice-covered lake. We formed a line while an instructor soaked a mountain pack in the ice-cold lake. The officer in charge tied a bowline around his waist, threw the soaked pack over a shoulder, and stood in a pair of skis with the poles in one hand. With a tug of the rope, the OIC was plunged into the freezing lake. After a few seconds, the OIC, struggling to bring his shocked body and brain back to a functional state, was eventually able to get all the gear out of the lake and pull himself out with the poles. It all seemed like an easy but uncomfortable exercise to negotiate. A Marine is pulled into the lake, swims to the surface, throws the heavy pack onto the ice, sings a verse of the Marine Hymn, and pulls himself from the icy hole in the lake. Simple enough, except when I hit the freezing water, my body and brain temporarily shut down, much like hitting a light switch. Unfortunately, I had tinnitus in my left elbow from the downhill ski mishap I had earlier, which caused me to struggle with the pack. By the time I wrestled the pack out of the water and sang the hymn, my body had acclimatized enough for me to enjoy a cold, recreational swim.

Historical places to visit in and around Trenton, New Jersey.

Trenton, the capital city of New Jersey, has preserved many of its 18th-century structures and they help paint a historical picture of the two touchstone Revolutionary War battles that were fought there in 1776. Although a visitor will need to navigate urban sprawl to take in the historical points of interest, it is well worth the trip. Start your Trenton tour at the Watson House and then make a short drive to the waterfront park. Plaques and statues commemorating the battle are located just outside the baseball stadium. Although a historical trail exists, the area is currently under construction and is inaccessible. Visit the William Trent House and Museum next. The site offers plenty of free parking in a secure area and is within walking distance of the Old Barracks Museum and historical plaques at the site of the 13 Stars Tavern.

The next stop should be St. Mary's Church, where there is accessible parking near Fitch's Gun shop and a plaque marking the headquarters of Colonel Rall. Head over to is Mill Hill Park, where the second battle of Trenton occurred at Assunpink Creek. One can view several commemorative plaques and visit the Douglas House and Washington's statue. Parking is a bit sketchy and limited at the park, and I recommend a weekday morning visit.

The next stop in Trenton should be at the Trenton Battle Monument. There is much to take in at this majestic monument honoring the battle and the American patriots who fought it. Street parking can be accessed, but it is limited.

The last stop I recommend is Cadwalader Park, just a few miles outside Trenton. The site has little historical value, contributing to the Revolutionary War since the Washington Statue was moved to Mill

Hill Park. Still, a Civil War monument and a large cannon from that era are on display. The Trenton Museum is also located in this extensive, well-maintained park. The park is a great place to wind down and perhaps enjoy an afternoon picnic or boat ride down a restored portion of a 19th-century canal system that flows through the park. The park offers plenty of free parking and a large playground for children to expend excess energy before the ride home.

John A. Roebling Park is located at 30 Wedge Drive Trenton, New Jersey.

(The Watson House is located in the park)

Waterfront Park is Located at 300 Riverview Plaza Trenton, New Jersey.

(Several Revolutionary War Memorials are located in the park).

The William Trent House is Located at 15 Market Street Trenton, New Jersey.

Mill Hill Park is Located at East Front Street and South Broad Street in Trenton, New Jersey.

Historical sites at this location include: The Patriot's Plaque, 2nd Battle of Trenton Plaque, Washington's Arch Plaque, the Douglas house and Washington's Statue.

The Old Barracks Museum is located at 101 Barrack Street Trenton, New Jersey.

A block to the northeast of this location is the 13 Stars Tavern, Revolutionary War Meeting Place Plaque, and across the street to the North is the Abraham Hunt House.

First Presbyterian Church Burial Ground is located at Warren Street Plaza, N Warren St, Trenton, New Jersey.

1739 Friends Meetinghouse is located at 132 East Hanover Street Trenton, New Jersey.

St. Mary's Church is located at 151 North Warren Street Trenton, New Jersey. Fitches' Gun Shop and the Headquarters of Johann Rall plaque are nearby.

Trenton Battle Monument is located at 354 North Warren Street Trenton, New Jersey.

The Black Soldiers and Patriots Plaque is located in the vicinity of the monument.

Trenton Battle Monument is located at intersection of North Warren Street (U.S. 206) and West Hanover Street Trenton, New Jersey.

Cadwalader Park is located at Cadwalader Heights, Trenton, New Jersey.

Princeton, New Jersey

"It is a fine fox chase, my boys!"

~General George Washington, Commander in Chief of the American Army.

As the American Army approached Princeton, Washington split his forces, much like he had done for the first Battle of Trenton; General Greene led the left wing and General Sullivan led the right wing, which was the main effort of the attack. One part of Greene's force was tasked with dismantling a bridge at a road crossing near Worth's Mill and setting up a blocking position to stop traffic in both directions to contain the British garrison in the town and prevent it from being reinforced. The second part of Greene's force was tasked to attack the garrison on Nassau Street via Post Road. Sullivan's 5,000-man main effort wheeled right at their release point and, orienting east, moved toward Princeton via Sawmill Road. The road eventually led Sullivan's column to their attack point behind Princeton College.

Colonel Mawhood, the British commander of a relief force ordered to Trenton to support Cornwallis, saw the American Army maneuvering toward the town and was left with two choices: continue his march to Trenton to reinforce Cornwallis or return to Princeton and defend the town against the attacking Americans. Colonel Mawhood decided to defend Princeton, leaving his artillery in a support-by-fire position on Mercer Hill. He moved his infantry to close with Washington at the American center of gravity, which was typical British Army doctrine in those times. Remarkably, Mawhood marched on a converging line with Greene's column, each unaware of the other's proximity. Washington, who had a clear view of the converging columns, quickly sent a horseman to Greene warning him of the maneuvering British column, along with an order to prevent Mawhood from reinforcing the garrison.

Greene ordered General Mercer to move his men out of the ravine and attack Mawhood's column, but underestimating the size of the enemy force, Mercer only committed a part of his brigade to the attack. Both armies, now fully aware of one another, began to close within firing distance on the William Clark farm, where roads intersected at a fenced-in orchard. The British forces gained the orchard first and, with it, the tactical advantage. As Mercer's forces entered the orchard, Mawhood's dismounted dragoons fired on them but fired high and had little effect. Mercer's fire was more accurate, forcing the dragoons to fall back to the main column. The battle swung in favor of Mercer's smaller force but only temporarily, as Mawhood swiftly adjusted and committed more men to the fray. Mawhood's men had the advantage of firing the first volley again, and once more, the volley was high and ineffective. Mercer's men fired more accurately again, and the British troops suffered dearly for it. Eventually, the British found their range and gained the advantage with their superior numbers. Mercer's horse fell under the onslaught of British bullets, and as he fell, the brave and resolute patriot shouted a general retreat to his men.

Eventually, Mawhood ordered the hopelessly surrounded American General to surrender, but Mercer defiantly refused to give ground. Exquisitely uniformed, he received a debilitating butt stroke to the head that, in itself, was a fatal wound. Mercer miraculously regained his feet and feebly swung his saber at the offending British soldiers, but to no effect; they mercilessly bayoneted him numerous times, leaving him to die on the battlefield. After Mercer fell, Mawhood ordered a bayonet charge against Mercer's men, who, leaderless and having no bayonets, were forced to run. A small fenced area currently preserves the spot where Mercer was said to have died under the shade of an ancient oak tree. Although the original tree no longer exists, another oak from the seed of the original tree now graces the hallowed area.

As Mercer's men fell back, Cadwalader's men stepped into the gap. They held the line as American Artillery began to pour grape and canister shot into the British ranks, ultimately stopping their charge. Although Mawhood brought two cannon to bear on the Americans, the patriots continued to run gallantly toward the sound of the gun. Washington himself led some of his Army into the fight, eventually outflanking and overwhelming Mawhood's forces. The British line broke, but the veteran regulars fell back in good order and covered their retreat while Washington reputedly shouted, "It is a fine fox chase, my boys!"

The bulk of Mawhood's forces retreated to the west, but the colonel took a few files of soldiers and moved toward town. The irony of the moment came when the flamboyant commander rode toward Princeton with his two hunting spaniels prancing around his horse, making himself an easy target for American marksmen who were too amused by the spectacle to end it.

In town, the remnants of the British garrison prepared to repel the impending American attack and chose to meet its onslaught by advancing forward and establishing a defense in depth. The British soldiers stopped in a ravine, which gave it some protection, and sent a reinforced platoon to attempt to flank the Americans, but Sullivan's overwhelming numbers prevented the effort. The British were forced to retreat again, the disciplined regulars falling back to a secondary defensive position consisting of another prepared breastwork where they attempted to make a stand. Sullivan's artillery unlimbered their guns, fired on the British flank, and caught them in a double envelopment. The second British position now unattainable, they fell back to a tertiary defensive position at a final breastwork and faced to meet the American onslaught, who had now advanced to within fifty or sixty feet of the defenders. The British eventually surrendered to the relentless American surge, clearing the way for them to advance on holdouts defending the college. The American artillery, commanded by Alexander Hamilton, obliged the British challenge and directed devastating fires on Nassau Hall.

The attacks at Clark Farm, Frog Hollow, the redoubts around Princeton, and Nassau Hall, though considered American victories, were empty ones. Although the casualty rates were unusually high for the British defenders, the skirmishes were merely a series of delaying actions that allowed the remainder of Mawhood's garrison and most of their supplies and guns just enough time to escape the town and the victorious Americans. The British Seventeenth Regiment of Foot suffered a casualty rate of 45%, The Grenadier Company sustained a casualty rate of 53%, and Mawhood lost a little over 50% of his forces, numbering a total of approximately 450 killed, wounded, captured, or missing.

Washington pulled off his third unlikely victory in a row, but his ultimate goal was to seize the largest British garrison in the Jerseys. Located in Brunswick, the stores and magazines of munitions and supplies would go a long way to sustain the American Army through the long winter, and a chest reputedly containing seventy thousand pounds of sterling would help fund a larger Army, but it was not in the cards for Washington. The fight for Princeton drained the remaining energy and resources of the American Army, forcing it into winter camp at Morristown. At the same time, a frustrated Cornwallis, guessing Washington planned to attack Brunswick, moved his Army southeast and away from Washington, who was headed northwest and into winter camp.

The approximately 130 Marines attached to Cadwalader's forces fought in a land battle for the first time in their illustrious history during the Battle of Princeton. The Marines were in the thick of the fighting at a critical stage of the battle, participating in Washington's decisive counterattack against Mawhood's forces. When Cadwalader galvanized his inexperienced men into action, the Marine detachment held the right flank, near the fence between William and

Thomas Clarke's farms. This is close to the modern boundary between the Institute for Advanced Study and the Princeton Battlefield State Park. The only known Marine casualty was a Pennsylvanian Marine, Captain William Shippin. The Pennsylvania Marines normally served on the brig *Hancock*, which was a Pennsylvania privateer.

Marine Corps Tie-In...Riding with the Posse.

During Drill Instructor duty while on quota at the Weapons and Field Training Battalion in Camp Pendleton, California, I was fortunate enough to have time to volunteer more extensively with the Riverside County Sheriff's Department as a member of the Lake Elsinore Mounted Sheriff's Posse. I was not a sworn officer with the power to arrest, nor was I authorized to carry a sidearm, but there were a few reserve deputies in our ranks who were sworn. I had a couple of horses: an Arabian Saddlebred, which was hotheaded and not broken for riding, and an American Quarter Horse, thoroughly broken and trained for police work, searches, and rescue.

The horses and riders had to pass a yearly qualification course to represent the sheriff department in public as uniformed posse members. The qualification course was a mix of sensory evaluations for the horses and handling skills for the riders. The qualification began with an obstacle course that the horse and rider were required to navigate in a prescribed amount of time. To complete the course, the horse and rider were required to demonstrate mastery in backing, sidestepping, and maneuvering in tight places.

Next, a rider was given a balloon and instructed to ride around a corral at a canter. When told to do so, the rider was required to pop the balloon against the saddle to stimulate gunfire while maintaining control of the horse. Police units were driven into the training area with the light bars on; the horse and rider were required to ride in a tight circle around the unit. After several closed circuits, a deputy hit the siren and blew a horn at intervals. A helicopter was even flown into the training area, and posse members were required to control their mounts, keeping them standing in place on the perimeter of the landing zone until the helicopter flew away.

The final part of the qualification was formation riding, where a team of posse members had to demonstrate proficiency in various offensive and defensive formations. Once the posse unit passed the qualification course, horses and riders were authorized to participate in policing events such as DUI Checkpoints, fatality callouts, patrols, crowd and riot control, and search and rescue; only qualified riders on a qualified horse were cleared to participate in public events representing the Sheriff department.

As a posse member, horse and rider were offered unique opportunities to participate in para-police training and other qualification events. I was fortunate to participate in SAR City search and rescue training, a three-day training exercise in Barstow, California. SAR City is organized and run by the Barstow Desert Rescue Squad, San Bernardino County Sheriff, the Office of Emergency Services (OES), and Barstow Community College. Before the SAR City event, my mount injured himself in the trailer on the ride to the desert, and I was on foot for the long weekend.

While attending the event, one of my favorite courses was a man-tracking course offered by a world-renowned professional tracker. This man shared account after account of difficult tracking details that led to rescuing survivors or recovering victims. Most of his tracking missions resulted in rescue instead of recovery of remains. The man was so good at his craft, whether mounted or ground tracking, that he could literally follow a set of tracks where no recognizable tracks were presented. He even demonstrated this by having someone in the class lay a set of tracks to fool him, including walking on a blacktop road for a distance. The instructor picked up the student's trail in no time; as he worked out the trail, he explained his process in minute detail.

During my service with the posse, I responded to two fatality callouts. The first one involved seven people in a single-vehicle accident. The driver had accelerated at a high rate along Lake Elsinore, lost control, and sheared off several roadside phone poles. The vehicle, an SUV, was almost unrecognizable, and the victims were all violently ejected and deceased. The callout took nearly all night to clear because of the wreckage that needed to be recovered and the various body parts that needed to be picked up; there was not one body that was recovered intact.

I participated in one other fatality callout that involved a person struck by a vehicle. A very intoxicated man was attempting to cross a busy road when a speeding car struck him, taking a leg off around the knee. The vehicle failed to stop and was soon involved in a high-speed chase, while the victim bled out before EMS arrived at the scene. When the high-speed chase ended somewhere near Paris, California, then considered the Meth capital of the world, the sheriff deputies had a fugitive drug dealer in custody.

DUI checkpoints were set up almost every weekend in the county, but the posse was not required to support every one of them. During my first checkpoint, I helped monitor entry control points while the deputies looked for vehicle violations and suspicious activity. People under the influence of drugs and alcohol were taken off the roads regularly, people were cited for vehicle violations, and the deputies even took people into custody with outstanding warrants. I was asked to help search a vehicle that was pulled over because the occupants were smoking pot. We were about to clear the car when I reached under the seat and found a large sandwich bag full of weed. The deputy I was searching the vehicle with seemed a bit miffed because it turned out that quite a bit of hallucinogenic mushrooms was mixed with the weed, which meant the deputy had a lot more work to do before he ended his shift.

Another DUI checkpoint was interesting right from the start. The road the deputies chose to set up on was busy, particularly at night, and we soon had a longer backup than usual for us to deal with. I was asked to walk toward the end of the growing line and start pre-screening vehicles. I did this by quickly scanning the car for violations and making verbal contact with the drivers to explain why everyone was stopped. While speaking with the drivers, I was able to scan the inside of the cars for drug paraphernalia and open containers of alcohol. If I found anything, I walked away and called it to the checkpoint deputies.

As I was working my way down toward the checkpoint, I came upon a car whose driver was acting very strange; he was moving around behind the wheel in a manner average drivers do not. When I got to the driver's side window, the man quickly closed it. I was concerned about my safety, so I ordered the driver to place his hands on the steering wheel. When I took a glance inside the vehicle, I immediately noticed the man's pants were down and around his ankles.

I called it in, and when the man pulled up to the deputies screening the checkpoint, he was directed to pull his car into a designated search area and required to perform a field sobriety test...he failed the test, but at least his pants were pulled back up.

The Sheriff's Department thanked me for well over 500 hours of volunteer service to Riverside County by presenting a certificate of appreciation, and the Marine Corps recognized my dedication to service by awarding me the Military Outstanding Volunteer Service Medal. The award was created under Executive Order 12830 by George H. W. Bush in 1993, the year I graduated high school. It is awarded to military personnel who perform substantial volunteer service in the local community that is considered above and beyond the duties required as a member of the United States Armed Forces.

Historical places to visit in and near Princeton, New Jersey.

The historic sites that tie Princeton to the Revolutionary War are expansive, and an overnight stay and multiple visits are recommended to take in all the rich history. Start at Princeton Battlefield State Park, where there is plenty of parking and a lot to see, including the Mercer Oak, where the beloved American General it is named for fell in battle, and the Thomas Clarke House, which is a restored 18th century home where Mercer was said to have died of his wounds. Also on the battlefield is the Colonnade and Revolutionary War burial ground and numerous plaques, cannon and monuments commemorating the battle.

The tour's next stop takes you into the city and the Richard Stockton House. Stockton, a signer of the Declaration of Independence and former Governor of New Jersey built the mansion, which has been converted into a museum that exhibits furnishings and relics that once belonged to the first family of New Jersey and also showcases five permanent galleries that take visitors on a historic tour from the struggle for Independence to the Governor's era. The property also includes a small gift shop and a well-manicured 18th-century garden. Near the Stockton House is the Princeton Battle Monument and several other Revolutionary War monuments.

The next stop on this historical adventure should take visitors to the Ford Mansion and Washington's Headquarters Museum. The home has been beautifully preserved in its 18th-century splendor, and the museum, with its interactive exhibits, is well worth the entrance fee. Across the street from the Ford Mansion is a beautiful life-sized equestrian statue featuring Washington. Just down the road, well within walking distance, is a turnabout featuring a monument and period cannon. A quick visit to Nassau Hall at Princeton University, dinner, and hand-made ice cream are excellent ways to round out the day before checking into a hotel or Airbnb for the night.

The next day, head out to Morristown National Park and swing into the Rockingham Historical Site, featuring a replica of an 18th-century fort and stockade along the way. Morristown National Park is where Washington encamped his Army during the winter of 1776-77, just after its improbable victory at Princeton. The park is comparable to Valley Forge National Historic Park and features miles of historic trails, restored cabins, a working 18th-century farmstead, monuments, and a visitor's center.

After your visit, I recommend a quick drive to Fort Nonsense. Although the fort no longer exists, a pair of cannon and the vague remnants of earthworks can be viewed at the site along with several informative historical signs and plaques; the view alone is well worth the drive. Close your trip with a visit to Hacklebarney Park, which offers miles of scenic trails, rock-hopping beside beautiful waterfalls, and plenty of places to enjoy a quiet picnic. On your way out, visit Hacklebarney Farms and Cider Mill, especially if you visit in the fall, and enjoy homemade eats, a hayride, and plenty of fresh pressed cider.

Princeton Battle Monument is located at Stockton Street and Bayard Street Princeton, New Jersey.

Marines in the Revolution Marker is located at Stockton Street and Bayard Street Princeton, New Jersey.

Nassau Hall is located at Nassau Hall, Princeton University, New Jersey.

Richard Stockton House is located at 55 Stockton Street Princeton, New Jersey

Thomas Clarke House is located on the battlefield.

Battle of Princeton Monument is located at Henry Hall, Princeton, New Jersey.

Princeton Battlefield State Park is located at 500 Mercer Road, Princeton, New Jersey.

Colonnade and Gravesite is located across the street from the battlefield.

Fort Nonsense is located along Fort Nonsense Access Road Morristown, New Jersey.

Morristown National Historic Park is located at 30 Washington Place Morristown, New Jersey.

Ford Mansion & Washington's Headquarters Museum is located at 30 Washington Place, Morristown, New Jersey.

Washington Equestrian Statue is located across the street from the Ford Mansion.

Hacklebarney State Park is located at 119 Hacklebarney Road, Long Valley, New Jersey.

Hacklebarney Farms Cider Mill is located along 104 State Park Road, Chester Township, New Jersey.

Rockingham Historic Site is located at 84 Laurel Avenue Kingston, New Jersey.

Elkton, Maryland

"I can hear you, the rest of the world can hear you and the people who knocked these buildings down will hear all of us soon."

~George W. Bush, 43rd President of the United States.

The British ground phase of the Philadelphia Campaign began at the mouth of the Elk River and the northern shore of Chesapeake Bay. Turkey Point, an easy mile-and-a-half walk on a good trail from a small and very busy parking lot, overlooks the bay just south of the Head of the Elk. In the autumn of 1775, General Sir William Howe was appointed Commander in Chief of His Britannic Majesty King George III's Army operating on the American continent. By 1777 Howe, believing he had the beleaguered American Army on the ropes, wanted to bring the conflict to a quick end. The problem he faced was that Washington and his Army were camped in the highlands of New Jersey, which was easy to defend and difficult to attack. Fresh off three improbable victories at Trenton and Princeton during the Ten Days Crucible, Washington's Army was not in the beleaguered condition Howe believed it to be.

Occupying a defensive position on high ground, Washington was also not about to be drawn out onto the plains and into open combat against Howe's vastly superior and well-equipped Army. After ten days and a halfhearted effort to draw Washington's forces out of the hills, during the Battles of Short Hills and Bound Brook, Howe withdrew his forces to Sandy Hook, New Jersey, crossed the Hudson into New York, and rendezvoused with his brother's fleet.

The Howe brothers formulated a plan to embark 15,000 troops on 211 ships and move the Army up the Delaware River to take the American capital at Philadelphia. This plan was designed to exploit an asset Washington did not have available: a dependable navy with speed and mobility on the seas and major waterways. The plan, which somehow remained secret, was to take their task force down the coast to the mouth of the Delaware, work the fleet up the river, and disembark the troops at Chester or Marcus Hook just outside the city for a short, overland march to Philadelphia.

When the fleet reached the mouth of the Delaware, however, the Howe brothers received intelligence from Loyalists that the river was blockaded with three sets of river obstacles called Cheval de frise, which consisted of long poles with iron spikes placed in wooden boxes at 45-degree angles. The boxes were filled with rocks to sink the spikes under the water line at low tide. Any of the valuable ships running into one of these obstacles risked tearing the bottom out of the deeper drafting vessels. The intelligence reports also indicated that the river just west of Philadelphia was defended by three forts: Fort Mifflin on the Pennsylvania side and Forts Mercer and Billingsport on the Jersey side. Had Howe known that Fort Mifflin was defended by a militia force of a mere 60 untrained militia, of whom none were even familiar with employing the fort's cannon, or that Fort Mercer wasn't even garrisoned and Fort Billingsport wasn't really a fort at all, he may have risked the Cheval de frise.

Based on the information provided to the Howe brothers, they decided to move up the Chesapeake Bay and disembark at the Head of the Elk landing. This was a controversial decision in parliamentary circles for a few reasons. First, Howe could have disembarked near the mouth of the Delaware and then marched a much shorter distance overland toward Philadelphia. It is reasonable to assume that the landing would have likely been uncontested, sparing valuable time and resources. Secondly, since the original plan was designed to be a short coastal voyage to the mouth of the Delaware and a comparably quick transit upriver to Philadelphia, the fleet was only provisioned for a 6 to 10-day cruise. The horses embarked for the cavalry, ammo and supply trains were birthed in very tight stalls lined with sheep skin to save space and protect the horses from friction. During the sweltering month of August, it was typical for the eastern coast to experience winds from the southwest, which slowed down the sailing ships headed in that direction. In addition, sailing through the Chesapeake meant that the armada would have to sail all the way down the coast to Norfolk, Virginia, just to access the Chesapeake Bay, which added weeks to the voyage. It took the fleet over a month to reach the Head of the Elk, by the time the ships reached their destination, 27 died men due to hunger and sickness. The horses faired far worse for the experience; over half of the horses embarked on the stifling ships died during the long transit.

At historical Elk's Landing, Maryland, just two days before the British ground forces landed, General Washington, whose network of spies alerted him to the British movement at the mouth of the Delaware River, traveled through the state of Delaware in a driving rainstorm on horseback to reconnoiter and plan a counter to Howe's ensuing invasion. Washington overnighted in the Jaccob Hollinsworth house, which, in the 18th century, doubled as an inn, against the advice and protests of his general staff. Just two days later, his antagonist, General Howe, stayed in the same inn, the same room room and was waited on by the same servant!

By August 25th Howe's Army was disembarked from the ships, and had set up a hasty encampment at the Head of the Elk because it was in no shape to move. Provisions were critically low, all the gunpowder was wet from a three-day torrential downpour, and they had serious issues with the horses that had survived the voyage. Of the horses that were healthy enough to disembark, half of that number died when, in their deprived condition, they broke into a field of green corn and literally ate themselves to death. Howe was bogged down in Elkton for some time, which allowed Washington the time he needed to position his Army on terrain that offered his forces the best tactical advantage.

Although this brief interlude in Howe's plan worked out great for Washington and the Continental Army, it turned out to be a terrible set of circumstances for the Marylanders who inhabited Elkton and the surrounding area. The British soldiers, already infamous for depravations committed on American civilians, had plenty of time and, frankly, motivation to commit more atrocities. Although Howe strictly forbade any of his forces from pillaging, the hungry troops did it anyway. One example of the brutality of some of the deprivations committed is a local story of a woman's fingers being cut off for the rings she wore on them. After this and many other alleged brutal acts committed by crown forces, the people of Elkton apparently had enough and took matters into their own hands. Two soldiers of the 71st Regiment of Foot were reportedly found along a road with packs full of plunder, and their throats slit. Two other British soldiers were found hanging from a tree with packs full of plunder still on their backs. Howe pulled his subordinate commanders into a meeting and issued an order that any soldier caught with plunder or who was caught straggling was to be immediately executed. This standing order helped stem but did not stop the plundering.

While Howe's Army was busy requisitioning horses and provisions, an amusing coincidence occurred when Washington and his staff were on Iron Hill, approximately nine miles away in Delaware, reconnoitering Howe's encampment via spyglass. At the same time, Howe and his general staff were keeping an eye on Washington and his party via their spy glasses on Grey's Hill overlooking Elkton, Maryland.

The weather was a constant factor during the Philadelphia Campaign as each General attempted to maneuver the other into decisive engagements; if there was no dry powder, there was no way to fire muskets and cannon at opposing armies. Even if there was an opportunity to conduct close combat with the sword and bayonet, Washington would certainly avoid such an encounter whenever possible; the British were well-trained and equipped for such engagements, while Washington's soldiers were notoriously ill-equipped and poorly trained in 1777. The stalemate at the Elk's Head ended a few days later on September 3rd when, with a break in the weather, Howe finally moved his forces east along Old Wilmington Pike toward Philadelphia.

The landing at Head of the Elk held tactical significance on at least two more occasions during the Revolutionary War and at least once after the Revolutionary War when the British landed at the site to invade America during the War of 1812. In March 1781, Continental Major General Marque De Lafayette returned to the landing with 1,200 American troops to embark on ships from a small French fleet, set sail to Yorktown, Virginia and began a campaign to capture the traitorous Benedict Arnold. Unfortunately, the Marque could not complete his mission because the small French fleet that Lafayette's troops were to embark on sailed into the teeth of the larger British fleet. This resulted in the French Fleet disengaging and returning to Rhode Island, giving the British control of the Chesapeake. The action stranded the bulk of Lafayette's landing force in Annapolis, forcing him to make an overland journey from the Head of the Elk to link up with the rest of his men and march them south.

In September 1781, the combined forces of Washington and the French General Rochambeau embarked on ships of the French Fleet, which recently returned to the Chesapeake from Rhode Island and joined with Lafayette's troops already in Virginia. Within six months, the Americans secured a free and independent nation with the victory at Yorktown and the surrender of Cornwallis, but Lafayette's contribution to the American cause, his martial exploits, and the Battle of Yorktown are stories for another day.

Michael Rudolph, a son of Elkton, was a Revolutionary War officer and served as a cavalry lieutenant in Henry Lighthorse Lee's Legion. In 1776, Rudolph was meritoriously breveted the rank of Captain for his actions during the Battle of Paulus Hook, where he forded a canal in the dead of night to lead an attack on a British stronghold. As a result of his extraordinary bravery, Rudolph was thanked by Congress, Lord Sterling, and George Washington. Rudolph remained with the Continental Army for the duration of the war and then returned briefly to civilian life. In 1793, Rudolph accepted an appointment as Adjutant and Inspector General of the Army. Unfortunately for Rudolph, this appointment only lasted five months. During the Indian wars in the Ohio Valley, Rudolph was in command of Fort Hamilton but was infamous for the harsh treatment of his subordinates. The desertion rate was excessive, and because of this, Rudolph was known to order severe punishments, including running the gauntlet and death. When General Anthony Wayne became Commander in Chief of the American Army, he found out that Rudolph had put to death three soldiers who were waiting on their appeals process. Wayne demanded Rudolph's resignation. Rudolph decided to sail to France and join the revolution that had begun there, but he never made it; the ship was lost at sea, and Rudolph disappeared with it.

Partridge Hill was the home of Colonel Henry Hollingsworth. He was the deputy quartermaster for the Continental Army when he warned the Continental Congress that Howe's landing force was approaching Elk's Landing. He was also responsible for moving a large supply of provisions for the Continental Army to prevent them from falling into British hands. Hollingsworth made multiple attempts to get much-needed supplies to the encampment at Valley Forge in 1778, but unfortunately, the British had all the feasible routes blocked. A historical marker on Partridge Hill at the local American Legion marks the location as the revolutionary home of Henry Hollingsworth.

Another historical marker is located at the former home of Robert Alexander, a Baltimore lawyer who was a member of the Sons of

Liberty and appointed a deputy congressman for Maryland in 1776. Just one year later in September, Alexander hosted General Washington at his residence, which in those days was known as the Friendship Tract. Three days later, Alexander hosted and subsequently offered his allegiance to General Howe, left his wife, and headed back to Philadelphia, this time with the British Army. He never returned to his home in Elkton, and in 1778, after Howe evacuated the city, Philadelphia became a place where he was suddenly not welcomed. He booked passage to London, where he died alone in 1805. Maryland tried him for treason in absentia. A guilty verdict resulted in the confiscation of all his holdings, which became the property of the city of Elkton. His wife, who remained a staunch patriot, was allowed to stay in the home, which eventually became known as the Hermitage.

The Mitchell House, located at 131 East Main Street, is the site of a former 18th-century hospital. Built by Dr. Abraham Mitchell between 1769 and 1781, the celebrated doctor grew up in Lancaster County, Pennsylvania, but settled at Head of Elk, as Elkton was originally called, in 1767. A Mitchell family tradition suggests that Mitchell completed his medical education and was rewarded with a horse, saddle, saddle bags, and $500 cash from his father, which allowed him to seek a place to set up his medical practice and home. The money didn't last because he used most of the funds as security for a friend, but he still managed to lease a lot in Elkton by 1769. He eventually built the historic Mitchell House on the leased lot. Throughout the years, he purchased large tracts of land throughout the surrounding countryside, having always maintained a strong interest in agricultural pursuits. Mitchell was also a dedicated patriot, loyal to the cause of freedom and independence. During the Revolutionary War, he used his large Georgian house in Elkton as a hospital to treat wounded soldiers of the Continental Army.

Betty Murphy, a former resident of the Mitchell House, said that ghosts of those who came before her time at the Mitchell House never left it. She told her story to historian, author, and tour guide Mindie Burgoyne, who included the tale in her book "Haunted Eastern Shore: Ghostly Tales from East of the Chesapeake." The story Burgoyne recorded tells of dogs reacting to some unseen entity in the home; items are mysteriously hidden, and a cackling laugh is sometimes heard from an unknown source. She mentioned a story of the apparition of a man sometimes seen in the house. Perhaps she was just hearing an old house groan in the wind or maybe the doctor is still working his craft at the Mitchell House.

Marine Corps Tie in...the Calm Before the Shamal.

On September 11th 2001, I was a young sergeant assigned to Bravo Company, 1st Battalion 5th Marines, conducting routine inspections of my Marines in Camp Pendleton, California, when one of my subordinates ran from his room shouting that the World Trade Center had been 'bombed.' Any other tasks or training we had planned for the day quickly fell by the wayside as every set of eyeballs in the barracks was glued to TV screens. We watched in abject horror as the second tower was struck by a plane and subsequently collapsed. We all probably had the feeling that this attack would inevitably draw a strong American response very soon. It didn't take long for us to find out just how strong that response would be. In the autumn of 2002, I attended Sergeant's Course at Camp Pulgas. I had completed about two-thirds of the course when the class was informed it was graduating weeks early because some units were receiving warning orders to prepare for combat operations in the Middle East.

By January 2003, we were on our way to Living Support Area Five (Camp Coyote) on the Kuwaiti side of the Iraqi border. I was the leader of a well-trained squad of Marines and was extremely confident in their fighting ability. As we waited in the Kuwaiti desert for the order from President Bush to begin combat operations in Iraq, we prepared ourselves mentally and physically in anticipation of the prelude to war. When we arrived at LSA Camp Coyote, no 'living support' existed. Nothing was there except a vast expanse of desert surrounded by triple-strand Concertina wire protecting rows of two-man tents. Within a few weeks, port-a-pots and hodji tents arrived on site, followed by a few shower trailers and, several weeks later, a chow hall. During our occupation of the relatively spartan Kuwaiti camp, we had very little access to any media sources or modern modes of communication back home; there was no internet and very limited access to sat-phones. Hence, as the weeks passed, uncertainty began to set in, and boredom became more challenging to stave off. Bored Marines are nothing to trifle with. During our stay in Camp Coyote, we had an 'accidental' stabbing in one of our battalion's hodji tents, one of our sister battalions had a negligent discharge of a rifle into a clearing barrel, and another battalion even had a male corpsman accused of hitting on male Marines.

Marines played around with the Atropine and 2 PAM Chloride Injectors that we each were issued to counter chemical and biological attacks despite being explicitly ordered not to. The threat of accidental injection was very real, and a Marine working at a distant Ammo Supply Point almost died when she injected herself during a chemical attack drill.

Each combat unit was provided a live chicken and a cage while we prepared for combat in the LSA. Someone had decided since canaries were often used in 19th Century mines to detect dangerous gasses, chickens could be used in the same way to detect chemicals or biological hazards during combat operations. Unfortunately, the cages were mounted on the hoods of Humvees, which with the added engine heat, simply amplified the already scorching temperatures and baked the NBC chickens alive. The irony for the chicken was that each Marine already had detection strips attached to our uniforms, which would have been much more reliable than trying to figure out why a caged bird was suddenly doing the 'funky chicken'.

Before OIF, I was chosen by the Sergeant Major to represent the battalion as its Color Sergeant. I had the custodial duties of the unit colors to add to my responsibilities in Kuwait and Iraq. My collateral duty required me to be around the crusty, stogy-smoking battalion Sergeant Major more than I wanted, but despite frequent visits to the command tent to tend to the battalion colors, I learned no more than I would have in my platoon's assigned hodji tent.

I fondly remember the extreme excitement when, after about a month of eating MREs, it was announced hot chow would be served for breakfast. The excitement quickly faded to a profound letdown when it was discovered that the hot chow consisted of powdered eggs and sausages that smelled suspiciously like goat was being served. Marines were quick to give the 10-inch sausage links a unique moniker that had something to do with camel parts. Constant long lines at the enlisted shower trailers eventually resulted in Marines sneaking into the officer's trailer for showers. One evening, all the NCOs in the battalion were ordered to clean them after the officer's trailer was mysteriously broken into and trashed.

I also fondly remember an amusing moment during our first experience of a Middle Eastern shamal, which is an intense sandstorm. The winds were so strong that they sometimes pulled the retaining pins out of tents, causing havoc throughout the camp. The swirling sand reduced visibility to near zero conditions and even penetrated the heavy canvas tents when they were not pulled from their anchors. A row of port-a-pots was placed across a dirt road from our tent. To get to one during a shamal without getting lost required Marines to run guidelines from the tents to the port-a-pots. Also located near the row of the johns were large trash bins for cardboard and recyclables. Although a smoking pit was in a designated area well away from any infrastructures or flammable material, Marines would sometimes smoke near the trash bins because, well, why would you walk 100 feet to smoke if you only had to walk ten?

One day during a particularly fierce shamal, our Jamaican Marine was taking a number two in one of the port-a-pots when an errant cigarette butt was flicked into one of the trash bins, which, fanned by the strong winds, rapidly erupted in flames that spread to the johns. We heard a choked scream and ran out in time to see a port-a-pot melting around a rifle. The Jamaican Marine stumbled out of the flames, a magazine in one hand with white eyes wider than saucers through his thick portholes...true to the priorities of typical young Marines, he managed to save the magazine but left his rifle behind in the melted Port-a-pot.

Toward March, we began to get conflicting news regarding the political tensions between Washington, D.C., and Baghdad. One night, we were told that Saddam was going to cooperate with UN inspectors and there would be no invasion, and the next night, we were told we were going to attack; it was always a toss-up day to day whether we were getting ready to go home or invade Iraq. One day, the battalion participated in an athletic field day and was treated to hamburgers and ice cream, followed by a talent show put on by our peers. The rare opportunity to indulge in burgers and ice cream should have been an obvious indicator of what was about to follow. In the middle of that night, we were rudely woken and ordered to pack all our gear and strap it to our designated Amphibious Assault Vehicles (AAV) as the Company Gunnery Sergeants began issuing live ammunition to Platoon Sergeants; we were finally headed across the border and into Iraq.

Historical Sites to visit in and around Elkton, Maryland

For this historical excursion, I recommend beginning a tour within city limits where the Mitchell and Rudolf houses can be visited along with the Hermitage and the plaque marking the place where the Bicentennial tree once stood. Travel down the road a bit to the Jacob Hollinsworth House but be aware of your surroundings. A prison stands within sight of the Hollinsworth House, and a run-down neighborhood is adjacent to the historic property. End your visit at the Elk Neck State Park, which provides visitors with ample hiking trails along the scenic Chesapeake Bay. Some trails lead to the Turkey Point Lighthouse, which stands on a beautiful vista, providing an unobstructed view of the Bay. On your way home from your adventure, stop by Hart's Methodist Church and read the historical marker beside the church's entrance. For an extended experience, drive a few miles west to historic Havre De Grace and walk the Lafayette trail, visit a life-sized bronze statue of the Marque, and visit another landmark lighthouse overlooking the Bay at the mouth of the Susquehanna River.

Hart's Methodist Church (Historical Marker) is located 3203 Turkey Point Rd Elkton, Maryland.

Turkey Point Lighthouse Trailhead is located along Turkey Point Road, Elkton, Maryland.

The Jacob Hollinsworth House is located at Landing Lane Elkton, Maryland.

The Bicentennial Tree plaque is located at 157 East Pulaski Highway Elkton, Maryland.

The Michal Rudolph Marker is located at 129 East Main Street Elkton, Maryland.

The Mitchell House is located at 131 East Main Street Elkton, Maryland.

Partridge Hill is located at 129 West Main Street Elkton, Maryland.

The Hermitage is located at 330 Hermitage Drive Elkton, Maryland.

Historic Lafayette Trail is located at 811 North Adams Street Havre De Grace, Maryland.

Newark, Delaware

"The raising of that flag on Suribachi means a Marine Corps for the next 500 years."

~James Vincent Forrestal, US Secretary of the Navy and the first United States Secretary of Defense.

The skirmish at Cooch's Bridge near Newark, Delaware is historically significant for a few reasons; it was the first combat test for Washington's newly formed Light Infantry Unit, it was the only land-based Revolutionary War battle in the state, and purportedly the very first American engagement that the Betsy Rose flag was flown.

After the now famous reconnoitering of the opposing Chiefs of Staff on opposite hilltops, one in Delaware and the other in Maryland, the British Army was finally ready to maneuver. Washington had the preemptive opportunity to choose the ground to defend, which could have been anywhere between Elkton and Philadelphia, but also had the burden of predicting the route the British would likely take. There were options to consider other than marching directly to Philadelphia for General Howe to decide on. Another of his campaign objectives was to cut Washington off from the supply depots feeding and arming Washington's Army, primarily located in Pennsylvania's backcountry. Washington knew he had to protect his gunpowder, ammunition, and provisions stored in Lancaster, Downingtown, and Reading, Pennsylvania. Washington also knew he had to remain flexible enough to counter Howe's next move whenever and wherever it came.

Howe could force a fight with Washington and risk losing more men and equipment than he could replace in a reasonable amount of time; Howe had expected much more Loyalist soldiers to augment his Army and replace his combat losses, but he didn't get them. Most

Loyalists were eager to support the Crown behind the scenes but were much more reluctant to take on an active role against their neighbors. Howe could take an easier avenue of approach to Philadelphia by re-embarking ships waiting in the mouth of the Delaware and bypass Washington's Army altogether. But for Howe to do so meant accepting the risk of leaving a well-provisioned American Army nipping at his heels and he still had Washington's backcountry stores to consider. Howe's most probable course of action remained an assault on the American capital at Philadelphia by marching overland on the Old Baltimore Pike toward Philadelphia to force Washington into a critical tactical mistake or at least keep him off-balanced by threatening the Continental Army's supply lifeline, either of Howe's choices played into Washington's strategy as long as he could manage to keep his Army one step ahead of Howe's Army.

Another consideration to factor in was that Howe was fighting a decidedly 'European war' on American soil, which generally meant that taking the capital city of an opposing force by rank and file inevitably resulted in victory over that adversary. However, the British aristocracy would learn throughout the conflict that in America, the game was played a bit differently than they would expect in 'civilized' Europe. There was no American King to depose in Philadelphia and the Continental Congress could and literally did pick up and move to a more secure location more than once because they had the flexibility and the need to do so. Washington was once a British Officer schooled in a gentleman's approach to prosecuting wars, but as a veteran of wilderness warfare, that hypocrisy was only going to go so far; he understood economy of forces; with the fledging Army he led, this was important. He also knew he didn't need to beat Howe on a battlefield to win; he just needed to keep his Army intact and fight a protracted war. Philadelphia was merely a pawn that could be sacrificed by the patriots for the greater good.

Washington's game plan was to choose the most adventitious ground, fortify it, and with a tactical advantage, wait for Howe's forces to attack. Initially, Washington moved his Army out of Wilmington and set it in a defensive line oriented southwest along White Clay Creek, Delaware. Washington quickly relocated the Army east in favor of better ground across Red Clay Creek, Delaware, where it was more protected by better terrain features oriented southwest from Newport to Stanton, Delaware. The stronger position could block Howe's most likely avenue of approach to Philadelphia along the Old Baltimore Pike. While the Army was busy with its priorities of work in the defense, Washington ordered General William Maxwell of New Jersey to conduct delaying ambushes against the British column that was slowly moving along the pike, with his newly established Corps of Light Infantry. This unit comprised 100 elite soldiers from each of Washington's nine divisions formed to engage and disengage with enemy formations quickly. Most of the soldiers selected for the new unit were experienced woodsmen who could live off the land, were experienced in guerrilla warfare, and were expert riflemen.

Maxwell's Light Infantry was expected to continuously harass Howe's forces and delay his march toward Philadelphia. By September 3rd Maxwell had his Corps set in multiple positions along the Old Baltimore Pike, where he hoped to engage the Jaeger column marching in Howe's vanguard with hit-and-run assaults. Maxwell eventually moved into ambush positions below Iron Mountain after a two-mile running fight with the Jaegers between Atkin's Tavern in Glasgow, Delaware, and Cooch's Bridge.

Maxwell's Corps initiated an ambush and engaged the German Jaegers, about 400 in number, commanded by Lieutenant Colonel Ludwig von Wurmb. The Jaegers (the term means hunter) were light infantry troops armed with rifles and short hunter's swords in lieu of the longer and more cumbersome musket and bayonet issued to regular troops. Ambushed by Maxwell's Corps on both sides of the pike just west of the bridge, the Jaegers formed a battleline and supported by close combat against Maxwell's center of gravity, attempted to outflank the Americans. The battle reputedly lasted most of the day until Maxwell's forces eventually ran out of ammunition and had to resort to hand-to-hand combat. After about seven hours of continuous fighting, Maxwell withdrew from his position and retreated across Cooch's Bridge.

During this running fight and ensuing ambush, Captain Johann Ewald, a Hessian Jaeger, reported that "he was leading a mounted patrol of six Jaeger Dragoons when they were fired on from ambush. At the sound of the gun, his horse reared up and took several musket balls. He was the only member of the party that wasn't either killed or wounded, his horse taking shots surely intended for him". Ironically, he may not have even been mounted at all if not for an injury he received earlier in a skirmish near Bound Brook, which forced him to temporarily perform his duty on horseback.

Howe ordered reinforcements to the bridge and eventually secured it for the British, while Maxell moved his Corps east to rejoin the American Army at Red Clay. For an entire day of fighting, casualties were remarkably light, even given the notoriously inaccurate reporting from both sides. Around twenty Jaegers and forty of Maxwell's men were killed and buried in a common grave somewhere in the vicinity of the bridge. Although Maxwell's Corps was eventually forced to relinquish Cooch's Bridge to the British forces, they were successful in delaying the British Army. For a brand-new military unit, they acquitted themselves professionally and with honor.

After the battle, Howe and his column encamped between Aiken's Tavern and Iron Hill. They remained there for the next five days, setting up their headquarters in the tavern and establishing a temporary field hospital at Pencader Church. While Howe occupied

Aiken's Tavern, General Cornwallis commandeered the Cooch House as his headquarters for five days. Cornwallis even stabled his horses in the dining room (which appears to have been a common practice of British commanders) until his Army burned the family's mill and moved toward Kennett Square on September 8th.

In 1746 the Cooch family sailed for America. Thomas purchased a grist mill and an adjoining 200-acre parcel of land from John Dayett in what is now the State of Delaware. In 1760, Thomas Cooch built a stone house on a small hill facing the Christiana River. Cooch was commissioned a Captain by Lieutenant Governor John Penn and fought in the French and Indian War. After the war, he was appointed a New Castle County, Delaware judge. On March 20th 1775, he became the Colonel of the Regiment for the Lower Division of New Castle County. On November 16th 1788, Thomas Cooch died at the age of 88. He is buried in Old Welsh Tract Baptist Cemetery in Newark, Delaware.

Two urban legends suggest that Cooch's Bridge and the nearby Walsh Tract Church are haunted by Revolutionary War-era apparitions engaged in an eternal search for their heads. Legend says a hessian scout wearing a steel breastplate, dressed as a specter, and riding a pale horse probed Maxwell's line, drawing fire to locate the Patriot positions. Bullets striking his chest apparently did little to slow him down and convinced American soldiers that he was indeed a ghost until one flying a bit higher cleared the breastplate and took him in the head. Ironically, the scout dressed as a specter may have become one himself and perhaps looks for his missing appendage in the vicinity of Cooch's Bridge on misty, moonless nights.

Another legend epitomizes Delaware's very own headless horseman. On the day of the battle, a Patriot by the name of Charlie Miller was galloping his horse past the Welsh Tract Church when an enemy cannonball struck the unfortunate rider and sent his head with the cannonball through the church's brick wall. If you drive along I-95 near Newark, you might find Charlie looking for his head or what's left of it. If you visit the church, you might even see where bricks were patched in to repair the damage. There are two problems with this story. First, early architectural drawings of the building show a window that was cut into the wall to allow light to shine on the pulpit. When the pulpit was relocated, the hole was bricked in. Second, no other damage was reportedly repaired, yet the cannonball had to exit the building somewhere. Finally, Charlie has yet to be found on any revolutionary muster roster, so you will probably be disappointed if you visit these historical sites looking for these particular spirits.

Many interesting debates have arisen over the question, did the Star-Spangled Banner really make its debut at the Battle of Cooch's Bridge, as a local legend suggests? My hypothesis is probably not for several reasons. First, several Revolutionary War sites have claimed that the Betsy Ross flag was first flown over their location, including the Moland House and the Middlebrook encampment, but this can only be true for one or none of the sites. Second, there is still some disagreement in historian circles about when the first authentically American flag was initially carried into battle; most historians believe the Betsy Ross flag design didn't even appear until 1792, well after the Revolutionary War, and that was in a painting.

Although in May of 1777, the new congress addressed the topic of an official national flag, it only specified that the official design of the American flag was to have 13 stars and 13 stripes, with no specific design for the layout of the stars given and the resolution was likely addressing the design of official Navy standards since ships sailing the seas in the 18th Century were identified by their nation's colors. The Betsy Ross flag appeared again in two more paintings in the late 19th Century; one was a portrait of Ross sewing her controversial flag, and the other was the 1851 painting called *Washington Crossing the*

Delaware, but it likely did not exist as a physical flag on an American battlefield during the war.

There are also problems with the popular tradition that Betsy Ross created the first American flag after Washington personally gave her the design in 1776, as her grandson claimed a century later. If Washington had given her written instructions, we could have expected an event as significant as this to have been well documented; primary source documents or receipts have either not surfaced, not been preserved, or never even existed in the first place. However, there is documentation that Washington had once ordered bed drapes from Ross, which could have been a catalyst for the Ross tradition. Another problem with the tradition is when it surfaced, which wasn't until after the American Civil War when her grandson made a claim to Betsy's fame in 1870.

Betsy Ross Flag or no Betsy Ross Flag, it is improbable that any flag or standard was present during the battle of Cooch's Bridge because General Maxwell's Light Infantry Corps was pulled together literally days before the engagement at Cooch's Bridge occurred and would not have had time to make or acquire a national flag. Carrying a standard into ambushes would not have been a priority, nor would it have been tactically sound; Maxwell would not have been inclined to wave around a large banner when he was trying to be stealthy.

If a flag representing Maxwell's Corps had been flown in the battle, it would have been an earlier design featuring 13 stars in three horizontal rows and the more familiar 13 stripes on a scarlet background. Captain Wilson's company of the 7th Pennsylvania Regiment carried such a banner, which may have been one of the first to display the stars and stripes, and the flag was with Maxwell's Light Infantry Corps at Cooch's Bridge.

This flag, known in modern times as the Brandywine battle flag, was verified to have been uncased during the Battle of Brandywine and may have been present at the Paoli Massacre and Battle of Germantown as well since Wilson's company was present at both engagements; the Betsy Ross flag was verified not present at either of these engagements. Perhaps Wilson survived the Battle of Cooch's Bridge because he had the good sense to keep his standard cased.

Marine Corps Tie-In...Ghost Stories at the Oldest Post of the Corps.

Many ghost stories are associated with old buildings or places of tragedy. My first duty assignment as a young Marine was ceremonial duty, National Capital Region security, and presidential support at Marine Barracks 8th and Eye in Washington, D.C. The location for the barracks and the home of the Commandant of the Marine Corps were chosen by President Thomas Jefferson and Colonel William Ward Burrows, the second Commandant of the Marine Corps, in 1801.

When the British attacked and burned most of Washington D.C. in the War of 1812, the Commandant's home was spared. Commodore Joshua Barney led a joint contingent of 360 sailors from the Washington Navy Yard and 120 Marines from Marine Barracks 8th and Eye eight miles north to a small town called Bladensburg, Maryland, to augment the army and militia who were attempting to defend the National Capital against a British landing party. As the battle raged, the militia bolted and fled with the American Army retreating at their heels. But the small Navy and Marine unit remained in place and held their ground. The gallant men refused to give up an inch of American soil, firing cannon loaded with grape and canister into the attacking British Light Infantry, commanded by General William Thornton. Although the Marines were badly outnumbered and eventually forced to withdraw, they refused to panic and conducted a fighting retrograde to the city. The Commodore received a British ball during the battle that lodged so deeply in his thigh that it could not be removed. The wound would eventually result in the Commodore's death in 1818; he is buried in the Allegheny Cemetery in Pittsburgh, Pennsylvania.

Because of the Marine's relentless effort in the face of insurmountable odds, it is traditionally held that the British, who generally had a pretty contemptuous view of most American fighters, made a point to leave the Marine barracks strictly alone and intact as a sign these warriors were the only Americans who had earned their respect. The Commandant's House is the only original building left in the complex; the barracks and officer's quarters were rebuilt in 1900 and 1907.

While stationed at the barracks, I heard of a few run-ins Marines had claimed to have with unusual entities. The first, while probably not a ghost, is still worthy of mention. The name of this anomaly was called the Station Wagon Lady. Rumor had it that the Station Wagon Lady (who purportedly wasn't a lady at all) parked her station wagon across the street from the barracks every Friday night and would pick up unsuspecting or intoxicated Marines after the Evening Parade for a 'night out' in the town. Although I had never seen the infamous Station Wagon Lady or even personally knew of a Marine who had, she or it is undoubtedly a legendary if not completely fabricated, facet of barracks life.

The second ghost story has a more somber spin to it. As this story goes, a child was playing with her ball in the barracks parking garage one evening when a derelict motorist ran her over, killing her instantly. Some Marines have claimed to have heard the sound of a bouncing ball during the late hours of the night, and some have even claimed to have seen an old red ball roll down the parking garage ramp and disappear through a concrete wall. As a young resident of the barracks and a parking permit holder, I routinely parked my car in the garage and occasionally did so in the middle of the night. The lower garage was used during inclement weather to practice close-order drill, and it was an eerie place to train because it was tight, dark, damp, and smelled of gas fumes. The garage was particularly unnerving because the World-Famous Marine Corps Body Bearers prepared for funerals in the lower garage and even stored a couple of coffins there to practice full honor funeral routines. I cannot claim to have ever seen or heard anything paranormal, and the research I have conducted, although not exhaustive, did not turn up any news articles of a child being killed in the garage. The only deaths at the barracks my research did verify was a death ruled as murder due to the negligent discharge of a Marine sentry's sidearm in 2019, and the death of a Marine ruled a suicide in 2021.

Another ghost story that floated around the barracks while I was stationed there had something to do with an account of wall lockers moving on their own. As the story relates, one late night after a Friday Evening Parade, a young lieutenant assigned duty as the Officer of the Day heard loud noises coming from a large, multi-purpose room called the Brown Baggers Locker Room. The room was large and consisted of multiple rows of wall lockers assigned to Marines who lived out in town and needed a place to store uniforms and parade gear. The young officer allegedly entered the Brown Bagger Locker Room after unlocking the door to find the wall lockers sliding around the room by some inexplicable, invisible force. Scared beyond reason, the lieutenant drew his service pistol, emptied the magazine into the lockers, and fled the area. The following morning, the lieutenant was said to have turned his rank into the commanding officer. The lieutenant was not named, and to my knowledge, the event is not documented and likely never happened, but it makes an exciting bedtime tale nonetheless.

The last Ghost story told while I was assigned to the barracks claimed that legless apparitions sometimes appeared and disappeared on the parapet over the band hall directly opposite the Commandant's home. Again, I have never seen a ghastly apparition in the barracks quad or knew of a Marine who had, but I thought I heard one on a late night during a Fourth of July Friday Evening Parade. At a point during the parade sequence, the lights are all turned out except for a spotlight fixed on a lone bugler who stands on the parapet opposite the crowd and plays Taps. On this summer night, as Taps was played, a Vietnam veteran in the crowd let out a loud, blood-curdling scream when the only other sound that could be heard was the bugle. I imagine the veteran carried ghosts of his own; memories brought back from that horrible war in a faraway place.

Historical Places to visit in and around Newark, Delaware.

Aikin's Tavern Historic District consists of a few 18th-century buildings, two of which have not been preserved as historical attractions. One of these buildings is an 18th-century home, which is now a private residence; another, which used to be the tavern, is either being demolished or renovated; and the other is Pencader Church and cemetery with a bronze historical plaque along its parking lot. The Daniel Nichols House no longer exists, but a historical sign marks the approximate site it once occupied.

A visitor will want to spend more time at Cooch's Bridge. Although the original bridge has long since been replaced, it is the location of the battle site and subsequent mass grave of both British and American soldiers who died on the hallowed ground. There is a small parking area facing a field and a creek where the men fought and several historical signs commemorating the event. Just across the bridge is the Cooch House which has been preserved and is open to tourists. Along the road is a beautiful stone and bronze memorial featuring four cannon.

Drive a few miles north to the Welsh Tract Church and burial grounds, where visitors can easily see where the brick had been patched (perhaps after a cannonball tore through the church). The burial ground is where you will find Thomas Cooch's gravesite.

Your last stop on the Newark, Delaware, historical path should be Iron Hill State Park. This park is well-maintained and has a small, interactive nature center great for children, miles of well-maintained hiking trails, and a historical plaque marking where Washington had observed British activity at the Head of the Elk landing.

Marine Barracks 8th and Eye in Washington, D.C., is an active-duty post, and visitors are admitted by invitation only. A Friday Evening Parade offers the best opportunity for a visit and can be arranged by contacting the protocol office at the barracks.

Bladensburg's Historic Balloon Park marks the location of the 1812 battle of Bladensburg and showcases a magnificent marble structure called The Undaunted Monument. This monument features beautifully wrought bronze reliefs of the American heroes who fought and died defending their nation's capital. If you look closely at the relief of Commodore Joshua Barney, you can see the wound he received on his thigh during the battle.

Newark History Museum is located at 429 South College Avenue Newark, Delaware.

Iron Hill State Park is located at 1500 Iron Hill Road Newark, Delaware.

Welsh Tract Church is located at 1 Welsh Tract Road Newark, Delaware.

Cooch's Bridge is located at 961 Old Baltimore Pike Newark, Delaware.

Thomas Cooch House is located at Old Baltimore Pike Newark, Delaware.

Pencader Museum is located at 2029 Sunset Lake Road Newark, Delaware.

<u>Aikin's Tavern Historic District</u> is Located at Route 40 and Glasgow Avenue Glasgow, Delaware.

<u>Marine Barracks 8th and Eye</u> is located at the intersection of 8th and I Street Washington, D.C.

<u>Bladensburg's Historic Balloon Park</u> is located at 4401 Upshur Street Bladensburg, Maryland.

Wilmington, Newport and New Castle, Delaware

"By their victory, the 3rd, 4th, and 5th Marine Divisions and other units of the Fifth Amphibious Corps have made an accounting to their country which only history will be able to value fully. Among the Americans who served on Iwo Island, uncommon valor was a common virtue."

~Fleet Admiral Chester W. Nimitz, the last surviving US officer who was appointed the rank of fleet admiral.

Although only one land battle was fought in the state of Delaware during the Revolutionary War, several touchstone naval battles were fought when the British Navy attempted to blockade and control the Delaware River. These battles are near and dear to me because some involve the world's finest: the United States Marines!

Before we delve into Delaware's river battles, let's talk about how my Marine Corps came alive! The United States Marine Corps was modeled after the British Royal Marines. After the Peace of Utrecht in 1713, the British Marines were, for all intent and purposes, disbanded with only four invalid companies remaining in service. With the outbreak of hostilities with Spain in 1739, King George II re-established the Royal Marines. On November 15th in his address to the House of Commons, George II stated that "the prosecution of the war would require a number of soldiers to serve on board the fleet" and the King "judged it proper, that a body of Marines should be raised." The following month, an Order decreed the formation of six regiments of Marines, each with an authorized strength of 1,100 men. Additional regiments were formed soon after the original six, including three regiments organized in the colonies and placed under the command of Colonel Alexander Spotswood of Virginia. Men willing to enlist for a war against France in the New World were scarce in England, and the Crown seized upon the idea of using men from the colonies. The King also believed that the Americans, being acclimated, were better suited for the service they were destined for than Europeans.

By the end of the Seven Years' War (French and Indian War) in 1763, during which Americans served as Marines in the British fleet, historical sources suggest that numerous colonists possessed the training and experience that made them the best sort of raw material for an efficient American Marine force to be created. But in 1775, before the advent of the Revolutionary War, Americans lacked a true naval tradition or rigorous military discipline. Combined with the poverty of the colonies, these circumstances created limitations, which, considering the overwhelming force of the British troops, seriously threatened the enterprise. Despite all the adversity it faced, an American Marine Corps was eventually established; the American Revolution and the cause for independence were greatly aided by the activities of American Marines fighting on land and at sea.

On November 10th 1775 at 10 AM, President Hancock struck a gavel on his table, and the delegates to the Second Continental Congress who were gathered in the Assembly Room of the State House in Philadelphia were brought to order. Among several topics discussed that morning was the creation of two battalions of Marines from the forces under the command of General Washington. The First and Second Battalions of American Marines would consist of one colonel, two lieutenant colonels, and two majors, with the remaining commissioned and non-commissioned officer corps structured along the lines of a Continental Army regiment. Excluding officers, each battalion would have 500 men assigned to it.

Washington believed that raising two battalions of Marines from his ranks was impractical, and he balked at the notion. On November 28th Congress commissioned its first Marine officer, Captain Samuel Nicholas, who was a young Philadelphian Quaker. On November 30th

Congress relieved Washington of the responsibility to raise the two battalions from his ranks and ordered they be created independently of the army.

By late December, the five companies of Marines had been recruited, and each man paid a month's advance. With Samuel Nicholas' appointment, the recruiting of men and the selection of their officers began. Among the first officers picked were Joseph Shoemaker and Isaac Craig. Recruitment of men was carried out by the three captains (Nicholas, Shoemaker, and Welsh) and the two ranking lieutenants (Craig and Wilson). Several rendezvous were held early in December, probably in several Philadelphia public houses such as Tun Tavern, traditionally recognized as the official birthplace of the Corps. In addition, drummers with highly decorated drums paraded the streets to attract recruits. On one such drum was painted a coiled rattlesnake about to strike and bore the motto "Don't Tread on Me."

I have read many documents and primary source material while conducting research for this manuscript. Occasionally, I have encountered contradictions that challenge historical traditions I was previously taught in classrooms and during my time in the Marine Corps. For example, the Betsy Ross flag tradition was one of these, and unfortunately, I may have to add the Tun Tavern tradition to my growing list, but we will see how the history unfolds. Though Marine Corps history and tradition acknowledge Tun Tavern as the first recruiting post and the birthplace of the Marines, historian General Edwin Simmons deduced from his research that it was more likely a tavern owned by the Nicholas family called the Conestoga Waggon, where the Marine Corps was born. I believe General Simmons is partly correct. The tavern was built on the Post Road east of Tun Tavern in the early 1700s by John Jenkins, a prominent businessman. It served as a way station along the main north-south route through the colonies. Samuel Nicholas became the tavern's proprietor in the early 1770s. In 1766, Nicholas formed the Gloucester Fox Hunting Club at the Conestoga Wagon and later transformed it into The Light Horse of the City of Philadelphia, considered a "gentlemen's militia," which Nicholas also led. Nicholas focused on officer procurement from his own tavern, and many of them, including Joseph Shoemaker, were pulled from Nicholas' Light Horse Company for officer accession. Recruitment did take place at the Tun Tavern, but almost exclusively for enlisted men. The recruits needed to be "good seamen, or so acquainted with maritime affairs," and Tun Tavern, because of its location in the rough and tumble Philadelphia waterfront district, was ideal for recruiting scrappy soldiers of the sea.

During the Revolutionary War, one of the most formidable backcountry militia units was a Pennsylvania Rifleman regiment known for the black hunting shirts they wore into battle. Colonel Edward Hand of Lancaster County was elected the regiment's commander. Colonel Hand's militia often carried tomahawks and scalping knives into combat; some wore hunting shirts with the words' Liberty or Death' sewn in white letters across the front instead of black hunting shirts. An additional piece of equipment they likely carried in battle to maintain their savage image was their battle flag. The flag was embossed with the image of a coiled rattlesnake ready to strike with the words 'Don't Tread on Me.' Many other backcountry units also adopted the flag and carried it into battle.

The flag, known as the Gadson flag, was named for Christopher Gadsden, a South Carolina delegate to the Continental Congress and a Brigadier General in the Continental Army. Gadsden designed the flag in 1775 and gifted it to Commodore Esek Hopkins, who had it unfurled on the main mast of his flagship, USS Alfred, on December 20th 1775. Two days later, Congress made Hopkins commander-in-chief of the Continental Navy. Hopkins adopted the Gadsden banner as his personal flag, flying it "from the mainmast of his flagship" whenever he was aboard. The Continental Marines also flew the flag during the early part of the war.

The Marine Corps flag has changed many times since the 18th century. The Gadson Flag was carried into battle by early Marines but the present-day official flag of the Marine Corps, called the Battle Colors, was adopted on January 18th 1939. The flag features the Marine Corps emblem in gray and gold with a scarlet background and gold fringe. The emblem traces its roots in the designs and ornaments of the early Continental Marines and British Royal Marines. The globe on the U.S. Marine emblem signifies the Corps' readiness to service in any part of the world. The eagle represents the United States. The anchor, which dates to the founding of the Corps in 1775, acknowledges the naval tradition of the Marines and their continual service within the Department of the Navy. The official Battle Colors of the United States Marine Corps is adorned with 56 streamers and silver bands to commemorate all the military campaigns in which Marines have participated. They span the entire history of our nation, from the American Revolution to the present. Every Marine Corps unit possesses its own Battle Colors, representing its combat legacy.

In the spring of 1776, Marines became heavily engaged in defending the Delaware River from the invading British Navy. On May 5th a dispatch was sent to Philadelphia with news that British warships were sighted entering the mouth of the Delaware River. By midnight, another dispatch, this time from Port Penn, about 20 miles south of Wilmington, was received: "Two Ships of War, a Top Sail Schooner & three small Vessels, supposed to be tenders, were sighted."

This British expedition up the Delaware River was not ordered to bombard or capture the city of Philadelphia but to clear the river of obstructions and open it to navigation for deep-draft vessels. Soon after the two frigates entered the Delaware, they sighted the American schooner Wasp and gave chase. By late afternoon on the

7th the British frigates were off the mouth of Christiana Creek, having forced the *Wasp* to seek refuge up the shallower creek. The frigates anchored at the mouth of the creek for the night, preventing the *Wasp's* escape and allowing crews to refill the water casks and make minor repairs to the damaged ship.

Also, on May 7th after Commodore Thomas Read received orders from the Committee of Safety to move his fleet of thirteen armed boats downriver to intercept the British warships, he immediately called a conference of his captains. The following morning, Wickes, Captain of the *Reprisal*, dispatched a party of men to the boats. First Lieutenant Robert Harris and ten seamen were assigned to the pilot boats while Captain Miles Pennington, two sergeants, and twenty-four Marines, "equip'd with Small arms, all in great Spirits" were assigned to the fire boats. The thirteen row-galleys of the Pennsylvania Navy rendezvoused at Hog Island in the early morning of May 8th and proceeded to make their way through the chevaux-de-frise and down the Delaware. However, the American frigates *Reprisal* and *Montgomery* could not pass the obstructions and remained above the barrier. Around 2 PM, a report was received that HMS Roebuck, armed with forty guns, and the *Liverpool*, armed with twenty-eight guns, along with their tenders, were in the vicinity of New Castle, Delaware.

Also, on the river during a foggy late morning were the two British frigates still at anchor off Christiana Creek. As the fog cleared around 1 PM, a fleet of fifteen vessels was sighted coming down the river composed of the row-galleys, each carrying a single heavy gun (either an 18, 24, or 32-pounder), a floating battery armed with ten 18-pounders, and a sloop "fitted as a fire ship." The 15 ships appeared neither formidable nor impressive to the crews of the larger, well-equipped British warships. However sluggish and incompetent the American fleet might have appeared, the two British frigates immediately cleared their decks and opened their gunports for action. The American galleys opened fire with no more than a mile separating the two forces but failed to inflict any damage on the British ships. Under sail, the frigates moved closer, brought their broadsides to bear, and began a thunderous counterfire. The river combatants exchanged shots for two hours until the *Roebuck* somehow managed to go aground, but the American galleys retired, failing to capitalize on their advantage. Although numerous attempts were made to refloat the *Roebuck*, it was not until 4 AM the following day that the British could free the ship. Meanwhile, the Americans returned upriver to their anchorage in Chester.

On the morning of May 9th the galleys left their anchorage at Chester and slowly approached the two British frigates moored downriver. The *Roebuck* and *Liverpool* headed downstream, hoping to draw the galleys into deeper water where they "could run near them and have a better chance of destroying them." The galleys immediately followed, keeping "up a smart fire," but cautiously remained at their usual distance. By sunset, the galleys had pursued the frigates as far as New Castle when the cannonade ceased, it being too difficult to sight the guns. The two British frigates, however, continued to drop down the river, and the galleys finally broke off their pursuit and anchored for the night at New Castle.

The damage done to the *Roebuck* and *Liverpool* during the second day's engagement was extensive. Several balls had penetrated the *Roebuck's* hull just above the water line on both her sides and stern. Likewise, an 18-pound ball had entered an upper port, destroyed a 9-pounder, killed one man, and wounded two others. The rigging, sails, and spars of the 44-gun frigate also suffered extensive damage. The *Liverpool* had "several Shot through our Sails, some few in our Hull, and one in our bowsprit." The American galleys, however, suffered minimal damage. The British fleet spent the next few days moored at Reedy Island while the American fleet anchored at Newport, awaiting a resupply of munitions.

On May 15th the *Roebuck* and *Liverpool* pulled in their anchors and, abandoning their effort to clear the Delaware, moved downriver toward the Delaware Capes. Noting that little could be done "without more Ships, a Bomb brig, and a body of Troops to act with them," Captain Hammond went out to sea the next morning, the *Liverpool* with orders to cruise off the Delaware Capes, and the *Roebuck* to proceed southward.

Marine Corps Tie In...Sea Stories.

Every active-duty Marine infantry battalion begins a deployment cycle by replacing the Marines at the end of their enlisted contracts or Marines who rotate to other duty stations. Officers and Staff Non-Commissioned Officers (SNCOs) will transfer from a Special Duty Assignment to a victor unit (infantry battalion) at or near the beginning of its deployment cycle. Junior Marines below the rank of corporal are usually assigned to a battalion from schools, primarily the School of Infantry, where new Marines learn basic infantry combat skills before transitioning to fleet units. Training for deployment begins at the fireteam level and progresses to battalion-level training. Typically, a battalion work-up for a deployment consists of a Combined Arms Exercise held at 29 Palms, California, a summer or winter mountaineering package at MCMWTC in Bridgeport, California, and a Blue/Green work-up which is an amphibious familiarization exercise, working with the Navy on ships. The training, which takes over a year to complete, culminates in a ten-day tactical exercise called the Marine Corps Combat Readiness Evaluation (MCRE). After successfully completing the MCRE, the battalion receives the designators Battalion Landing Team (BLT) and Special Operations Capable (SOC). The battalion is then temporarily assigned to one of seven Marine Expeditionary Units (MEU), which, in turn, is assigned to an Amphibious Readiness Group (ARG) for a six-month deployment.

The MEUs are assigned to various Naval fleets worldwide and are considered America's front-line Force in Readiness, first to fight as the President of the United States directs. For example, a battalion participating in the Unit Deployment Program (UDP) will fly to Okinawa, Japan, and join the 31st MEU, the only MEU permanently stationed overseas. The MEU will usually link up with the America ARG, which operates with the US Seventh Fleet and participates in unilateral training with host nations in the Pacific theater. If a battalion is assigned to the 26th MEU, the battalion will link up with the Bataan ARG, assigned to the Sixth US Fleet stationed at the Naval base in Norfolk, VA. The three ships the battalion is embarked on will become its floating base for the deployment and will work with host nations in the Mediterranean Sea and the Persian Gulf area.

I spent time at sea on several naval vessels and was fortunate enough to have experienced both types of MEUs. I deployed with the 31st MEU twice as a member of BLT (SOC) 1/5 and BLT (SOC) 2/4. During those deployments, I cruised to Australia, Iwo Jima, South Korea, and Mainland Japan. As a member of BLT (SOC) 2/6, I cruised to Israel, Spain, Sicily, Qatar, Bahrain, United Arab Emirates, and Kuwait and transited the Suez Canal twice.

My first MEU experience was with Bravo Company BLT 1/5 on board the USS Juneau (LPD-10). The *Juneau* was an Austin-class amphibious transport dock that transported the MEU's Amphibious Assault Vehicle (AAV) assets in her well deck. The Juneau, or 'Jolly J' as her navy handlers called it, was one the smaller of the three ships BLT 1/5 was assigned to. She was older and had seen better days, but it beat doggy-paddling to Australia. A few memorable events happened on the ship during our transit: Sewage pipes burst and left about four inches of poop water sloshing around in our assigned birthing area, we became Golden Shellbacks, conducted a rare amphibious landing on Iwo Jima and were entertained by a 'gong show gone wrong' in the 'Upper V' of the ship.

Bravo Company embarked on the *Juneau* out of Red Beach, Okinawa. It began a long transit south of the Equator to Australia, participating in Exercise Crocodile 99 and making port calls in MacKay and Brisbane. During the port call in MacKay, I volunteered for a Community Relations project (COMREL) and helped repair a public picnic area. During our port call in Brisbane, I volunteered for a COMREL and helped restore a playground at an orphanage. Although most Marines use their port call to 'explore' the local scene, I found the COMREL projects the best way to take in the scenery and they provided a unique opportunity to interact cross-culturally with people. Somewhere between the two port calls, while operating in the Australian bush, our company commander drew down on a startled wombat that jumped up in front of him in the thick brush. Fortunately for the wombat, the captain did not have live ammunition in his sidearm at the time.

When the 31st MEU crossed the Equator at the International Date Line, several unusual events occurred. First, we lost an entire calendar day, and second, that time-lapse was filled with a naval rite of passage called the Golden Shellback Ceremony. Before the process of becoming a shellback begins, a sailor or Marine is called a Pollywog. The eve of the equatorial crossing is called Wog Day, a reversal of the next day. Wogs are allowed to capture and interrogate any Shellbacks they can find but are made aware that the ceremony will be much harder on them if they do.

After crossing the dateline, Pollywogs on the 'Jolly J' received subpoenas to appear before King Neptune and his court. The court consisted of his first assistant, Davy Jones, her Highness Amphitrite, and other dignitaries (all represented by the highest-ranking sailors who were Shellbacks). The court officiated the ceremony, which was preceded by a beauty contest of sailors dressing up as women, and each department of the ship introduced one contestant in swimsuit drag. Afterward, some pollywogs were "interrogated" by King

Neptune and his entourage, and a concoction of hot sauce, aftershave, and whole uncooked eggs was sometimes used as a 'truth serum.' During the ceremony, the Pollywogs underwent several humiliating ordeals such as wearing clothing inside out and backward, crawling on hands and knees on rough, nonskid-coated decks, being 'locked in stocks' and pelted with rotten fruit, being 'locked in a water coffin' of salt-water and bright green sea dye (fluorescent sodium salt), crawling through lanes of rotting garbage and finally kissing King Neptune's hairy belly which belonged to a very fat Navy Chief, was coated with lard and hair clippings. The Officers and Staff NCOs received the harshest treatment, while the NCOs and non-NCOs, who vastly outnumbered the officers and staff, got through the ordeal relatively unscathed.

In the 18th century and earlier, the line-crossing ceremony was a much more brutal event, often involved beating pollywogs with boards and wet ropes and sometimes throwing the victims over the side of the ship, dragging the pollywog through the surf from the stern. In more than one instance, sailors were reported to have been killed while participating in an 18th-century line-crossing ceremony.

As late as World War II, the line-crossing ceremony was still rather rough and involved activities such as the "Devil's Tongue," which was an electrified piece of metal poked into the sides of those deemed pollywogs. Beatings were still common, usually with wet firehoses, and several World War II Navy deck logs contained reports of sailors visiting sickbays after crossing the dateline.

Baptism on the line, also called equatorial baptism, is an alternative initiation ritual sometimes performed as a ship crosses the Equator, involving water baptism of passengers or crew who have never crossed the Equator before. The ceremony is sometimes explained as an initiation into King Neptune's court. This was certainly not an option on the day we made our crossing.

On our return trip from Australia, we had a rare opportunity to visit Iwo Jima, which is generally considered hallowed ground for Marines. With the 'Jolly J' within view of the famous volcanic island, the Marines of Bravo Company climbed into AAVs and participated in an even rarer event, one of just a few beach landings conducted by a Marine Combat unit since World War II. Since I was the first squad leader in third platoon, I sat under the troop commander (TC) hatch adjacent to the vehicle commander. After the AAV resurfaced from its splash off the ship's fantail, I got an unforgettable view of the island and the towering Mount Suribachi. When the AAV reached the beach, we all had an inimitable opportunity to walk the black sands, see Japanese WW II bunkers, and hike Mount Suribachi. Our platoon hiked the volcanic mountain together, took in the fantastic view at the top, and honored the fallen at an ID tag-covered memorial.

The battle of Iwo Jima began on February 19th 1945, and ended on March 26th. It was a major battle of the Pacific Campaign during World War II and was the first U.S. ground attack on the Japanese home islands. The Japanese army positions were heavily fortified with vast bunkers, hidden artillery, and over eleven miles of tunnels. After landing on the beachhead, one of the first objectives was the taking of Mount Suribachi. At the second raising of a flag on the peak, Joe Rosenthal famously photographed six Marines raising the United States flag on the fourth day of the battle. The 36-day assault resulted in more than 26,000 American casualties, including 6,800 dead. Of the 21,000 Japanese defenders present at the beginning of the battle, over 19,000 were killed or committed ritual suicide, and only 1,083 were taken prisoner.

On one of our last days embarked on the 'Jolly J,' some Bravo Company Marines starred in a gong show. We had some pretty interesting Marines in Bravo Company during our deployment, including a very belligerent 3rd award Lance Corporal and a Company Gunny who was lovingly known by his callsign W.A.R.D.O.G.G "don't hate me cause you ain't me" The Gunny made himself famous with the Marines with his saying: "it doesn't matter if I am dog-faced ugly; All I need is my tattoos, a bottle of Aqua Velva and a set of dog tags to pick up ladies." As the Marines of Bravo Company were gathered in the Upper V' of the 'Jolly J' enjoying the gong show, another act approached center stage, which was the company's 3rd award Lance Corporal, dressed as a wizard, fake beard and all. The 'wizard' promptly stated that he could predict someone's future simply by sniffing their footwear. The owner of the first shoe the wizard sniffed predicted he would live a long, happy life, and the owner of a black, spit-shined boot would have a successful military career. For the last prediction, the esteemed wizard requested the footwear of the company Gunny, but the W.A.R.D.O.G.G wasn't having it. Unfortunately for the W.A.R.D.O.G.G, the company commander 'highly encouraged' him to play along with the skit. The wizard sniffed the Gunny's boot and, wrinkling his nose in mock disgust, sniffed it again to the same effect. After taking a third sniff, the wizard said, "I predict you are about to take a long journey," and threw Gunny's boot deep into the Lower' V' of the ship, which, quite predictively, ended the gong show with scattering Marines and an audacious uproar. If the gunny had been able to catch the Lance Corporal, he probably would have thrown him overboard. The USS Juneau was decommissioned in 2008 and is part of the National Defense Reserve Fleet; she is currently berthed in Oahu, Hawaii, waiting for a one-way cruise to a scrapyard.

Historical Places to visit in and near Wilmington, New Castle, and Newport, Delaware.

Most of these historical places of interest are located among urban sprawl in Wilmington and New Castle but are easily accessible. Start your tour by visiting Fort Delaware State Park. Plan your visit in the summer when the ferry boats are transporting visitors to the island fort. Although the fort did not exist during Delaware's river battles, one can look out on the waters and imagine ships maneuvering in position to fire a decisive broadside. The Civil War fort, which is kept in a well-preserved state, functioned as a prison for Confederate prisoners of war, privateer officers, political prisoners, and federal convicts.

Next, take a short drive to New Castle and visit historical sites in the town including the First State National Historical Park. Here, you can tour the 1730s courthouse museum where Delaware's colonists voted for independence from England and Pennsylvania in 1776. While gazing at a full-sized sculpture of William Penn inside the park, one might wonder why it is in Delaware. The Penn statue is in Delaware for a couple of reasons. It commemorates Penn's first landing site in the Americas and the lower counties of Delaware were once leased from the Duke of York so Penn's colony would have more access to the coast. Tour the sheriff's House while you are here, walk a short distance to the river, and visit Battery Park. If you don't want to walk, there is plenty of parking, accessing a beautiful trail along the river. Take time to visit several museums at the eastern end of the trail.

End your day visiting several historical sites in the city of Wilmington; make sure to visit Fort Christina Park and a tall memorial marking the site of the Dutch fort. Park at the Kalmar-Nichol Museum, view the 17th Century Dutch artifacts on exhibit, or take advantage of a lazy summer day, and book passage on a replica of the ship the museum is named for a short cruise of the Delaware River.

Grand Opera House is located at 818 North Market Street Wilmington, Delaware.

Brandywine Village is located at 915 Hutton Street Wilmington, Delaware.

Pulaski Park is located at 5 Broom Street Wilmington, Delaware.

<u>Fort Delaware State Park</u> is located at 45 Clinton Street Delaware City, Delaware.

<u>Fort Christina</u> is located at 1110 East 7th Street Wilmington, Delaware.

<u>The Joseph Tatnall House</u> is Located at 1803 N Market Street Wilmington, Delaware.

<u>Kalmar Nyckel Museum</u> is Located at 1124 East Seventh Street Wilmington, Delaware.

<u>Sign of the Ship Tavern Marker</u> is located at 3rd Street and North Market Street Wilmington, Delaware.

<u>Old Swedes Church Walking Tour</u> is located at 612 North Church Street Wilmington, Delaware.

<u>Kosciuszko Park</u> is located at South Broom Street and Sycamore Street Wilmington, Delaware.

<u>Battery Park</u> is located along Battery Park Trail in New Castle, Delaware.

<u>Dutch House Museum</u> is Located at 32 East 3rd Street New Castle, Delaware.

<u>Hale-Byrnes House</u> is Located at 606 Stanton Christiana Road Newark, Delaware.

<u>First State National Historic Park</u> is Located at 211 Delaware Street New Castle, Delaware.

Lewes, Delaware

"A ship without Marines is like a garment without buttons."

~Admiral David D. Porter, the second U.S. Navy officer ever to attain the rank of admiral.

Following three days of battle on board the provincial galleys, Captain Miles Pennington and his Marine company returned to Philadelphia to find the *Reprisal* ready for service. The Marine detachment of the *Lexington* also returned to Philadelphia but found their ship in the same condition as when they departed...still under repair. The excess time, however, was not wasted. Marine recruiting parties scoured the city and had little trouble enlisting men for the next cruise. Among those enrolled was John Barry (no relation to Captain John Berry), who appears on the brigantine's muster roll as "John Barry, Serjant."

On May 17th the *Lexington*, far better armed and manned than she had been in March, joined the *Reprisal* and *Hornet*, both anchored at Chester. Under orders from the Marine Committee, the two brigs and sloop were ordered to convoy merchantmen vessels idled by the recent battle, down the river and into the open sea. Soon after obtaining pilots, the three Continental vessels moved down the river and anchored near Cape May on the 25th. There, they found both friend and foe. In mid-channel stood the HMS *Liverpool*, while in the upper reaches of the bay lay the *Wasp*. The following day, the British frigate unexpectedly put to sea, only to reappear on the 27th give the four vessels chase, and then retire beyond the Capes. The two American brigs, sloop and schooner, played cat and mouse with the *Liverpool* for several weeks. After *Liverpool* returned to New York, the American ships resumed the game with her replacements, the frigate *Orpheus* and sloop *Kingfisher*.

On June 8th Kingfisher spotted the American privateer *Nancy* sailing toward Cape May loaded with supplies from the Caribbean Islands and began to chase her, followed by the Orpheus. Finding the capes effectively blocked by the two British warships, the *Nancy* attempted to navigate through shallower waters into Turtle Gut Inlet off the Jersey side of the river where the deep draft ships couldn't follow. In the darkness and fog, she managed to run aground and became hopelessly trapped. Captain John Berry aware that the *Nancy* was being pursued by the Kingfisher and Orpheus, devised a plan to assist, but with darkness and fog upon them, they could not locate her.

The following morning the British warships, locating the *Nancy* first, began to fire on her as they sailed toward the stranded ship. Captain Berry quickly devised a plan for his ships to fire on the *Kingfisher* and the *Orpheus* to prevent them from boarding the *Nancy* while he and Captain Wickes' brother Richard, who served together on the *Reprisal*, gathered a party of seamen and Marines, and set out to unload the brig's valuable cargo. All but 100 barrels of powder had been removed before the *Orpheus* and the *Kingfisher* finally anchored close to the Nancy and opened fire. The Americans quickly ignited the remaining powder and retired. Several boats from the *Kingfisher* were dispatched to take over the brig, but the powder ignited five minutes after they boarded. The battle to save the *Nancy's* cargo left Captain Wickes' brother dead but allowed the *Reprisal* and the merchantmen safe passage through the capes. On July 3rd after the British frigates had withdrawn up the coast, the *Reprisal* and her convoy set out to sea, leaving the *Lexington*, *Hornet*, and *Wasp* behind to secure the bay.

Twenty-three-year-old Lieutenant Joshua Barney of the Continental Navy commanded the privateer sloop *Hyder Ally* during the river battles. She was owned by Pennsylvania businessman John Willcocks and was issued a letter of marque. The sloop-of-war was armed with 16 six-pounders and had a crew of about 110 men, officers, and Marines, and was named after Hyder Ali, the ruler of the Kingdom of Mysore on the Indian subcontinent and a British enemy. With Lieutenant Barney were two privateer sloops: 10-gun *Charming Sally* and 12-gun *General Greene*.

Barney's first task was to escort an American fleet of five merchantmen to Delaware Bay. Three British ships were sighted during this cruise, and a battle ensued. British forces included the 32-gun frigate HMS Quebec under Captain Christopher Mason, the 24-gun sloop-of-war HMS General Monk commanded by Captain Josias Rogers, and a New York privateer brig named *Fair American* crewed by American loyalists. *Fair American* was the former American privateer *General Washington*, commanded by Silas Talbot before she was captured.

At nightfall on April 7th 1782, the American convoy anchored within Cape May for shelter until after the wind had abated from a storm. Later that night, the British on the *Quebec* and the *General Monk* sighted the American fleet, anchored off the cape, and prepared to attack *Hyder Ally* because she was considered the most formidable ship of the American fleet. Unaware of the British vessels nearby, the Americans spent the night believing they were safe. The following morning, three British privateers were spotted, and Captain Mason signaled them to join him, but only *Fair American* responded. At 10 AM, the Americans sighted the British vessels approaching. Lieutenant Barney ordered the merchantmen to flee up Delaware Bay under the protection of *General Greene* and *Charming Sally*, while *Hyder Ally* remained behind to engage the British.

The fleet was directed to sail as close to the shoreline as possible to prevent pursuit. The larger British vessels would have difficulty following in the shallow water. *General Greene* disobeyed Barney's orders and prepared for battle. *Charming Sally* grounded on a shoal and was abandoned by her crew. At about 11 AM, the Americans identified the three British vessels. The *Quebec* stood off nearby Cape Henlopen to prevent the Americans from escaping Cape May and into the Atlantic. However, this was unnecessary as the Americans were headed into the bay rather than into the open sea. *Fair American* led the advance, with *General Monk* following in trace. Sometime after noon, the British came within range of the two American privateers. Lieutenant Barney turned his ship about as if attempting to flee to lure *General Monk* closer. *Fair American* opened fire with a broadside, followed by another; the shots were accurate but caused minor damage.

Still, in a mock retreat, *Hyder Ally's* gun ports remained closed, and the Continentals had yet to fire a shot. *General Greene* did the same as *Hyder Ally* and turned around, but she grounded just outside British gun range. The tactic had worked: *Fair American* broke off the effort to attack *General Greene* as *General Monk* proceeded forward to attack *Hyder Ally*. Fortunately for Continental forces, *Fair American* grounded in shallow water and was put out of the action permanently because of damage to her hull. Heading forward, Captain Rodgers decided to slow down and launch a boat to take the abandoned *Charming Sally*, after which he continued until he caught up with *Hyder Ally*. When within range of pistols, Rodgers ordered her to surrender. Barney answered with a broadside of grape, canister, and round shot that raked the deck of the British sloop, killing some sailors and Marines. *General Monk* replied with her bow guns, which were the only weapons bearing down on the Americans at the time.

Barney ordered his ship to port and unleashed another broadside whose shots passed through the sails and rigging of *General Monk* and damaged her main and top-gallant masts. Before the battle, the British bored their six-pounders on *General Monk* to fire nine-pound balls. This proved fatal when the British came within a few yards off *Hyder Ally's* beam for a full broadside of their own.

When they fired the modified guns, *General Monk's* cannon exploded, ripping them from the deck and flipping them over. Several sailors burned themselves as they tried to right the cannons.

A few minutes later, the two sloops had drifted close enough to each other that the British and Americans could hear each other shouting commands. Barney took the opportunity to reload his cannon, but he waited to give his gunners the order to open fire. Instead, the lieutenant shouted, "Hard a-port, do you want him to run abroad of us?" which was another deception. Hearing this, Captain Rodgers ordered his ship to port as Lieutenant Barney ordered his vessel to starboard.

As a result, the two vessels collided and became entangled in each other's rigging. The American sailors fastened *General Monk* to their ship to prevent her from breaking loose and fired their broadside. The shots knocked out some of the British guns and sent the crew into confusion. The American Marines sat high in the rigging of *Hyder Ally* and poured musket fire into the British. Barney's men boarded while he remained on the compass box to direct the attack. About this time, the box was shot out from under the lieutenant, but he suffered only a slight injury. Barney also ordered that his port-side guns be turned around to the starboard so they could assist in the battle. After only 26 minutes of close-quarters combat, Captain Rodgers was wounded, and all of his officers were killed except a midshipman who struck the colors.

A total of 20 British sailors died and 33 were wounded. *General Monk* was captured, and *Fair American* was aground and stranded, so Captain Mason in *Quebec* fled without even engaging in the fight. American forces suffered the loss of four killed and 11 wounded. *Charming Sally* was captured without a fight, *Hyder Ally* was damaged considerably, and *General Greene* was grounded but re-floated after *Quebec* began her retreat.

The Battle of the Delaware Capes, also known as the 3rd Battle of Delaware Bay, was a naval battle fought off the Delaware River towards the end of the American Revolutionary War. The battle occurred on 20th and 21st December 1782, three weeks after the signing of the preliminary articles of peace between Britain and her former American colonies. The battle on the bay pitted three British Royal Navy frigates, the HMS *Diomede*, *Quebec*, and *Astraea*, against five American ships: South Carolina Navy's 40-gun frigate *South Carolina*, the brigs *Hope* and *Constance* along with the schooner *Seagrove*.

The pursuers skillfully took up a position to limit South Carolina's options in getting away, and the British windward ship attempted to mask South Carolina's wind. For eighteen hours, the British chased *South Carolina*. When she came in range, she fired her stern chasers at *Diomede*, which returned fire from her bow-guns. By around 3 PM, the British ships were close enough to exchange shots and could each swerve, fire a broadside, and return to the chase while preventing *South Carolina* from doing the same. The first of the British broadsides did significant damage to *South Carolina,* leading Joyner to call his officers together to discuss whether to fight or to continue the flight. The decision was to continue to flee. By 5 PM, *Quebec* and *Diomede* came up alongside *South Carolina*, with *Astraea* behind in support, along with *Hope* and *Constance*. The British were soon in a position to fire six broadsides, five from the *Diomede* and the other from the *Quebec*, all aimed at *South Carolina's* masts, sails, and rigging, which within two hours were in tatters. Joyner, now seeing the hopelessness of *South Carolina's* situation, decided to fire her guns one last time, not wishing to surrender with his cannon loaded. He then struck his colors, ending the battle. The British took possession of *South Carolina* and transferred their prisoners to the British ships.

The British had suffered no casualties, and damage to their three frigates was light, most damage being to masts and rigging. *South Carolina* had a crew of about 466 men when captured, of whom she had lost six killed and eight wounded. *Hope* had 42 crew members. *Constance*, with another 30 men, brought the total number of American prisoners to nearly 530. Fifty German and eight British prisoners that the Americans had recruited out of captivity in Philadelphia were released, as they had once served as soldiers in General John Burgoyne's army. Because of the number of men involved, the British treated their American prisoners harshly, locking them under hatches and not allowing more than two to come up on deck at the same time.

Prize crews then took *South Carolina*, *Hope*, and *Constance* to New York, where all three vessels were tried and condemned. The Royal Navy did not purchase *South Carolina*; the war was ending, and with it, the need for a large navy. *South Carolina's* design also had flaws the British didn't want to repair. Instead, she was sold for service as a merchantman. Prize money for the captured vessels was awarded in 1784.

Marine Corps Tie In...More Sea Stories.

I met my wife the same year I deployed with the 26th MEU. The Marines of BLT 2/6 out of Camp Lejeune, North Carolina, took a short ride up the coast to the Naval base in Norfolk, Virginia, and embarked on our ships. I was the weapons Platoon Sergeant for Fox Company and was assigned to the USS Iwo Jima (LHD-7). The *Iwo Jima* is a Landing Helicopter Deck and the largest of the three ships the battalion was assigned to. Shipboard life on the *Iwo Jima* was much more bearable than on the *Juneau*, and on the flight deck of the *Iwo Jima* somewhere in the Mediterranean Sea, I was promoted to the rank of Gunnery Sergeant. What I appreciated the most about the *Iwo Jima* was the chow; as a Gunny, I ate my meals in the Chief's Mess. The ship's captain made sure steak and crab legs, two of my favorite food groups, were on the menu weekly. The Chief's Mess was seldom crowded, and one could eat as much as they wished.

After a port call in Haifa, the USS Iwo Jima made a two-week transit of the Suez Canal. Since flight operations were highly restricted during the transit, I spent most of my free time on the flight deck, taking in the sights of the Egyptian coast. After transiting the Red Sea, we had a few more weeks before entering the Persian Gulf and participating in unilateral training with Qatar military units. In Qatar, I led a small team of Marines that trained Qatari soldiers in marksmanship techniques. After the marksmanship training, my platoon provided security for Operation Native Fury for a few weeks, during which one of my Staff NCOs decided to sell his serialized SAPI plates to a Qatari soldier, resulting in a grueling series of gear inspections for the company back on board the Iwo Jima and for the staff sergeant, an eventual Bad Conduct Discharge.

We spent Christmas and New Year's with the *Iwo Jima* docked in Bahrain and enjoyed a low-key, unadventurous lull in the deployment tempo. I had the incredible opportunity to golf on a PGA Sawgrass course outside of Dubai and I visited the Dubai Mall, which features an indoor ski slope and a parking garage full of expensive abandoned sports cars. When Fox Company embarked on the *Iwo Jima* to continue the deployment, it was with a new ship's captain. We later found out that the former captain was relieved of his duties after his alleged promiscuous behavior involving a female junior sailor was reported. Unfortunately for the ship and its crew, the *Iwo Jima* was dubbed the USS Love Boat, and unfortunately for me, the new captain was not a fan of crab legs.

The ARG received orders to chase Djibouti pirates after Christmas, and since most of the battalion was not needed, the Navy dropped us off in Kuwait. From the Kuwaiti docks, Fox Company bussed to Camp Buehring, a staging point to Iraq in the northern part of the country, for a few weeks. Camp Buehring is also known as the

Udairi Range Complex and is largely uninhabited except for a few nomadic Bedouin tribes herding camels, goats, and sheep. During trips to live fire ranges, it was common to see the primitive Bedouin camps with vast herds of animals surrounding them.

At the camp itself, communication back home was more accessible, but the near opposite time zones made it more challenging to call home because it could only be made from a phone trailer with limited phones and restricted times to use them. Communication through email was possible but slow, so waking up in the middle of the night in Kuwait to call home was still the better option. The camp featured a Burger King, Subway, and Dairy Queen, but the foodstuff tasted different, it was expensive and cash only. The caveat to spending cash at these vendors was that the change received was in tokens that could only be used in the camp instead of currency.

During our stay in Kuwait, the battalion tragically suffered a casualty when a young sergeant overdosed on bodybuilding supplements and succumbed to heart failure. The sergeant is survived by his wife and children. The tragedy produced a trickle-down effect resulting in a ban on supplements; every Marine's personal effects had to be searched, and any supplements destroyed. When we met our ships at the pier for our voyage home, only officers and staff were allowed to board to inspect all the Marine birthing areas for contraband. During a search of a storage area, a heavy coffin rack shifted off its support and crashed down on my head, nearly rendering me unconscious.

The transit home was remarkably uneventful except for a quick, two-day stop in Sicily and an unscheduled stop at the Naval base in Rota, Spain, to wait out a severe Mediterranean storm that created swells large enough to rock the big-decked Iwo Jima violently. In Sicily, I took a couple of trips inland and toured the city of Syracuse on one day and the Syracuse Archaeological Site in Siracusa on another. The Roman amphitheater is located in the suburb of Neapolis. It features a row of Gladiator sarcophagi in what is now an archaeological park near the Greek theatre and the Altar of Hieron. I walked the city for an entire day, taking in sites like the massive and highly ornate Cattedrale Metropolitana della Nativita di Maria Santissima, the statue of Diana, the Temple of Apollo, and other ancient Greek and Roman ruins.

While in Spain, I volunteered for a COMREL project at a monastery in Seville. The Monastery of Santa María de las Cuevas, also known as the Monastery of the Cartuja, is located on the Isla de La Cartuja in southern Spain. Christopher Columbus stayed here to plan his second voyage, and his remains were interred at the Monastery of the Cartuja by the will of his son Diego. In 1542, the remains were transferred to Colonial Santo Domingo.

During the Napoleonic invasion of Spain, the monks were expelled, and monastery buildings were used as barracks by Napolean's troops, who unfortunately damaged the buildings while they occupied them. The troops left in 1812, and the monks moved back in until the closing and confiscation of many religious properties was ordered in the 1830s.

The COMREL project involved basic landscape maintenance and cleanup. During the visit, we had the opportunity to tour the monastery, its grounds, and a museum. Some memories that stand out during my visit are the stables traditionally believed to have housed Napoleon's horses, a statue of the Apostle Peter minus a nose, and a traffic circle with a large statue of a bull featured in its center.

Historical places to visit in and near Lewes, Delaware.

Begin your tour in the Lewes Historic District, where you will find several 18th-century houses to explore. Be sure to visit Henlopen State Park, explore the many World War II-era military displays, and check out the Cape Henlopen Lighthouse. Finish your day relaxing on a lightly used beach that provides an excellent view of the bay. For the more adventuresome types, drive your 4x4 out on the beach and spend the night fishing in the surf...just be mindful of high tide.

Cape Henlopen State Park is located in Lewes, Delaware.

Cannonball House is located at 1812 Park on Front Street Lewes, Delaware.

David Hall House is located at 101 East Third Street Lewes, Delaware.

Fort Miles Historic District is located in Cape Henlopen State Park Lewes, Delaware.

Major Henry Fisher Home is located at 618 Pilottown Road Lewes. Delaware.

Cape Henlopen Lighthouse is located in Cape Henlopen State Park, Lewes, Delaware.

Lewes Historic District is located in Lewes, Delaware.

Kennett Square, Pennsylvania

Demonstrate to the world there is "No Better Friend, No Worse Enemy" than a U.S. Marine.

~General James Mattis, 26th US secretary of defense

Kennett Square is the Mushroom capital of the world and where about 50% of America's mushrooms are grown. The Lenape Indians originally inhabited Kennett Square, but when European settlers colonized the land, the town was named Kennett Square, a throwback to Kennett, Cambridgeshire in England. 'Square' referred to the original land grant from William Penn, which included one square mile. On September 10th 1777, Howe led his troops into Kennett Square and camped for the night. The next day the village served as the British Army's release point to exploit unguarded fords north of Washington's defensive position and flank Washington's Army.

Before daylight on September 8th Howe, leaving some of his forces to feint an attack and fix the American Army in their defensive position along Red Clay Creek, displaced the rest of his Army and moved. Instead of moving east toward the entrenched American center of gravity as Washington predicted, Howe ordered his forces north and around the waiting Washington, taking a route through Newark and Hockessin into Pennsylvania. Cornwallis led the match, followed by General Grant and Knyphausen; Ewald took on his customary role of scouting the road ahead of the Army.

If Howe's goal was capturing Philadelphia, why would he move his Army north toward Kennett Square when the more direct route to Philadelphia would have been due east through Wilmington via the Old Baltimore Pike? Why wouldn't Howe choose a route close to the Delaware River where he wouldn't be far from his brother's fleet and provisions?

Howe had already acquired a reputation for outmaneuvering and outflanking Washington and his rag-tag Army with his better-armed, provisioned, and disciplined professional Army. If Howe could maneuver north and around Washington's Army along Red Clay Creek, he could trap it between his Army and his brother's Navy, which commanded the Delaware River. This would give Howe unlimited access to Washington's supplies in the Pennsylvania backcountry and put Washington in an unattainable position should Howe choose to engage him or give the British Army an uncontested route to Philadelphia.

Howe wanted to destroy Washington's Army quickly, but he also wanted to avoid any needless loss of his men and equipment by facing a full-frontal assault on the ground of his enemy's choosing. It was difficult for him to replace his men and equipment and took several months for either to transit the Atlantic Ocean on sailing ships. By moving north on Lancaster Road, Howe hoped to gain a tactical advantage or at least keep Washington off balanced and guessing what the British Army's next move would be.

While Ewald rode through White Clay Creek country, scouting in advance of the Crown Forces north of Newark, he could hardly believe Washington had given up such an advantageous piece of ground to defend. As he rode through rocky heights, forming a defilade that took him about 30 minutes to ride through "where 100 riflemen could have held up the army a whole day and kill many men…hair stood on end as we crammed into the defile and I imagined nothing more certain than an unexpected attack at the moment when we would have barely stuck our nose out of the defile".

I learned that history tends to fold on itself, repeating events at various times just as it often did in this conflict on American soil. Just three days after Ewald rode through a defile at White Clay Creek that was ideally situated for an enemy ambush unopposed, he rode through another, this time in Pennsylvania on Birmingham Road and unbelievingly unopposed again. Had Washington known the lay of the land or had more advanced notice of Howe's flanking movement, he could have used the undulating terrain at White Clay Creek and shaped the battlefield to his advantage.

Unfortunately, stuck in his defensive position along Red Clay Creek, Washington did not have access to good intelligence if he had it at all. The lack of viable intelligence resulted in another proverbial fold in history when Washington found himself neatly boxed into another trap sprung by Howe, who, once again, gained Washington's flank using his favorite maneuver. Although Howe held a distinct tactical advantage in Delaware and could have easily attacked Washington's right flank, containing the Continental Army below Wilmington, Delaware, he chose not to attack his vulnerable enemy. Historical sources agree that Washington, waiting for the British to approach from the east, had no idea Howe had outflanked him again.

After Howe's column cleared the defile near Washington's previous defensive position at White Clay Creek, they continued to march north through Mill Creek Hundred, ransacking farms and taking livestock and supplies. When the British Army marched into Hockessin, Howe set up headquarters in the Daniel Nichols House, which stood approximately 100 yards east of a historical marker commemorating this historical event. The house served as Howe's headquarters during his Army's encampment along Limestone Road, which extended almost five miles between Milltown to New Garden on September 8th and 9th 1777.

Although minor skirmishes occurred near Hockessin, Howe's jaegers and light infantry had little trouble brushing them aside. One of these skirmishes is known in historical circles as General Weedon's foray in Spring Grove. Washington's Army remained in the defense along Red Clay Creek for the entire day of September 8th fixed by Hessian feints, but one of his units was not. General Weedon's brigade was mobile and operating near Mill Creek, while Howe marched his Army up a hillside west of Mill Creek. At some point during the day, Weedon located and closed with the Hessian Jager Corps across a steep valley on Mill Creek, near modern-day Delcastle Technical High School. Captain Friedrich von Muenchhausen, an aide to General Howe, wrote:

"We saw two regiments coming from Newport on two different roads... I was ordered by the General...to lead the Hessian Jaegers diagonally through the woods to cut off these troops... but the rebels... retreated quickly. Notwithstanding this, the jaegers got close enough to send a few amusette balls at them." A four-year-old boy found one of these amusette balls in a creek near Delcastle in 1992.

There are no records of bloodshed on either side of the brief skirmish. However, Weedon's position was the closest eyes and ears that General Washington had on the British movements that afternoon and evening. There are unconfirmed stories that Washington visited Milltown on the evening of September 8th perhaps to meet with Weedon or his aides and assess the situation for himself.

The knowledge that the British units were encamped along Limestone Road was critical for the American Army, which was bogged down in defensive positions, waiting for an attack that was not going to happen at that place or time. Around 2 AM on September 9th, Washington led his Army on a desperate moonlit march to head the British off at John Chads' ford.

From a historical standpoint, Weedon's foray was a significant military event that happened in Delaware during the Revolutionary War because of its strategic importance; acting on the intelligence obtained by Weedon, Washington was able to prevent his Army from becoming completely enveloped, trapped, and destroyed by the British Army and Navy. Unfortunately for the American Army, Howe's unexpected march north allowed him to avoid fording a creek and attacking a strong defensive position on high ground where his Army was sure to sustain a high casualty rate at the hands of the entrenched American Army. More important, Howe had successfully placed his Army in an advantageous position where it could effectively deny Washington from accessing his vital backcountry supply depots.

The next defensible piece of ground between Howe and Philadelphia were the fords of the Brandywine River. The logical crossing for Washington to defend was Chads' ford because the Great Post Road (modern route 1) crossed the Brandywine at the site. As tempting as it is to start a rumor that the Brandywine Creek was named so because the early settlers poured all their brandy wine into the stream to keep it out of British hands, that probably did not happen; the stream was most likely named for Andren Brainwinde, an early settler of the region. The creek is about 60 miles long with relatively narrow, steep banks averaging depths of 5 to 6 feet when it isn't swollen by storm surge. It branches a few miles north of the Great Post Road. Over the creek's 60-mile course through the countryside, only three major roads crossed it: the Great Post Road, The King's Highway (present-day Route 13 in Delaware), and the Lancaster Road (present-day Route 30), which was too far north for Howe to consider as a route toward Philadelphia. Although these roads are paved highways today, in the 18th century, they were not much wider than a cart path and were usually challenging to travel.

By the end of the day, on September 9th Washington had moved his Army twelve miles north from Newport on a course roughly parallel with Howe's and crossed the Brandywine at Pyle's ford about a mile south of Chad's ford. The Army began establishing new defensive battlelines near Chad's ford just east of the creek, re-gaining the defensive advantage it forfeited to Howe the day before.

By mid-day on the 9th Howe and Cornwallis crossed the state line and moved into New Garden, Pennsylvania, while General

Knyphausen and the baggage train reached Kennett Square, six miles west of Washington's position, by late night. Howe did not intend for Knyphausen to move into position so close to Washington but expected to catch up with him and the slower-moving baggage train at New Garden. Knyphausen ordered a cold camp with Washington's picket posts located dangerously close to his camp at the Anvil Tavern just east of Kennett Square; 'amazingly' Knyphausen's column nor the baggage train were discovered by the American pickets.

On the morning of September 10th Howe moved his second column, led by Cornwallis, up to Kennett Square and once again consolidated his Army. Howe spent the rest of the day scouting routes and terrain and gathered as much information as possible from cooperating Loyalists living in the area to formulate a battle plan. Three of these Loyalists, Joseph Galloway, Curtis Lewis, and John Jackson had been guiding Howe's Army since its landing at the Elks.

On the morning of the Battle of Brandywine, Howe decided on a strategy to fix Washington's forces along the Brandywine in the vicinity of Chad's ford, using Knyphausen's forces as a feint while maneuvering the rest of his forces north to reach Washington's exposed right flank. If he could pull this off seamlessly, chances were good that he would achieve all three of his strategic goals, end the revolution, and be back home in England in time for Christmas goose.

During the Revolutionary War, the Quakers adopted an official attitude of neutrality. Ironically, it was likely that on September 11, 1777, the first shots of the Battle of the Brandywine were fired from the cemetery adjoining the Old Kennett Meetinghouse. Knyphausen's forces received a rude surprise from their American antagonists as they marched east from Kennett that morning.

As they passed by a long stone wall in front of the meeting house, they were suddenly ambushed by riflemen. The initiative gained by the small American force led by General Maxwell was soon forfeited as they were quickly driven back to the hills north of Chad's ford by overwhelming numbers. During Maxwell's fighting retrograde with Knyphausen's column along the Great Post Road, his men acquitted themselves well, buying precious time for the Continental lines to fortify their defensive positions and inflicting enemy casualties; the Queen's Rangers reported 14 KIA and 57 wounded while Ferguson reported 2 KIA and eight wounded. The soldiers killed in the battle that afternoon are buried in the Old Kennett Cemetery, the grave marked with a simple stone marker and Betsy Ross Flag.

The Kennett Monthly Meetinghouse, known as Old Kennett, was first constructed in 1710 on land owned by Ezekiel Harlan, which was deeded from William Penn. In the 18th century, Kennett and Marlboro Townships were being colonized by farming Quaker families who joined with members of New Castle Meeting House, Hockessin Meeting House, and Centre Meeting House (near Centerville, Delaware) every four to six weeks for business meetings at Newark Meeting House. The meetinghouse can be visited and exists in a preserved state, much like in 1777. There is also an information board and the original stone wall Maxwell's forces used to fire from covered positions, and the cemetery is still intact east of the building.

While Knyphausen was doing his best to convince Washington he was facing the entire 15,000-man British Army in mass, Howe and Cornwallis, led by Ewald and their Loyalist guides, departed from the Marlborough Meetinghouse and marched up the Great Valley Road toward Red Lion Inn. The route took the column to the first of two fords they had to cross, Trimble's ford on the west branch of the Brandywine. At around 1030, Cornwallis began to ford the Brandywine at Trimble's ford; local legend has it that two well-known patriots, Squire Cheyney and Colonel Hannum, witnessed Howe and Cornwallis cross the Brandywine that morning.

Trimbleville, Pennsylvania, also known as Trimble's Ford and the Trimbleville Historic District, is a community of about six homes.

Trimble's ford is located in southern Chester County Pennsylvania, about two miles south of Marshallton. James Trimble first bought land in the area on the banks of the west branch of the Brandywine River in 1744, with his descendants living in the community until 1948. Several buildings from the eighteenth century survive, including Trimble's farmhouse, a mill, blacksmith and wheelwright shops, and a boarding school. Aside from the historic homes and horse farms in the area, there are two landmark markers for Trimble's ford. While the ford is surrounded by private property, the marker that denotes the general location where the Crown Forces crossed can be viewed along the public road.

After marching ten miles from Kennett Square, Jeffries's ford was the second unguarded ford the British column needed to cross to outflank General Washington's defense at Chads' ford. From this point, they continued their march up the "Great Defile" of Birmingham Road to Osborne Hill, where they rested near Strode's Mill before launching a mile-wide flanking attack on Washington's Troops on Birmingham Hill. The ford was near present-day Jeffries Bridge, and several historical markers along the road intersection north of the bridge mark the crossing. There are walking paths near the ford and plenty of parking with trail access at Stroud's Preserve.

Marine Corps Tie In...the 2003 March to Baghdad.

In the early morning hours of March 19th we pulled out of LSA 5 (Camp Coyote) but not to the Kuwaiti airport and back home. We crossed the line of departure and into Iraq as the first ground force (The tip of the spear) to cross the border and engage Saddam Hussain's forces. During the first day of the invasion, we breached a giant berm and defensive obstacles placed by the Iraqis. That night, we hunkered down in hasty fighting positions and experienced the first of several danger-close encounters with scud missiles that caused us to seal ourselves in all our Mission Oriented Protective Posture (MOPP) gear and gas masks for days. We were in the MOPP suits and rubber booties for so long that our leather combat boots began to fall apart around our feet. The only time we unsealed the suits was to pee, and even that was taking a chance. Bravo Company received orders to secure one of four Gas and Oil Separation Plants (GOSP) in the Rumaylah Oil Fields before the Iraqi Army had an opportunity to destroy them as they had during Operation Desert Storm.

We were on the way to our company objective at GOSP 3 when an attachment of M1 Abrams from the 2nd Tank Division operating in our vanguard started to fire on unseen targets in the distance. As the tanks charged toward the Rumaylah Oil Fields, the desert and the sky were lit with crisscrossing flashes and tracers. One of my Marines, a wide-eyed SAW gunner, asked where the incoming tracers were coming from. I looked at him and said, I assume from the bad guys. For the young Marine, who often boasted about the body count he would rack up if given a chance in combat, the war suddenly became very real.

Years later, I had the honor of training the son of the 2nd Tanks Commander at Villanova University's NROTC Unit. The son, an artillery officer, honorably served as a Marine Officer, like his father before him. I believe he would have been a tank officer like his father had the Marine Corps not removed the asset from its organization after OIF. That night, 2nd Tanks destroyed around 18 enemy tanks, three trucks, a motorcycle, and piles of RPGs, Small arms, and 120 mm mortars. They also captured around 240 EPWs who surrendered to the American iron beasts.

When the ramp of our AAV dropped inside GOSP-3, my squad of Marines disembarked into shaddowy chaos. The Iraqis had preemptively dug a ditch around the GOSP, flooded it with oil, and then ignited into a wall of fire as we were charging toward them. As the Marines of Bravo Company worked to clear the fighting positions just inside the flaming moat, I fondly remember a fellow squad leader of the third platoon tossing hand grenades into fighting positions of resisting bad guys like he was tossing candy to children in a parade. Years later, I was reminiscing with this re-tread sheriff's deputy, who had nobly reenlisted to take the fight away from the American home front and to the streets of Iraq. He laughed when I suggested he reminded me of Donkey Kong throwing barrels at Mario in the famous 1990s Nintendo game as he threw grenades into the enemy fighting positions that night.

After a long night of demonstrating to the Iraqis that fighting Marines was not in their best interest, we gathered hundreds together who had wisely surrendered, into a hastily established security area. We treated the wounded and searched as many of the EPWs as we could for weapons or intelligence. We found out later that the defenders were mostly conscripted farmers who were pressed into defending the GOSPs and had little desire to die for their soon-to-be-deposed dictator. As we searched the area in the morning light, we found crates of unopened ammunition, firearms still in packing grease, and dumpster bins full of stale bread, indicators that we didn't face Iraqi regulars that night. Later, a contingent of British soldiers took over the responsibility of safeguarding the Enemy Prisoners of War (EPWs), and Bravo Company got back on the road to Baghdad.

Historical sites to visit in and near Kennett Square, Pennsylvania.

If road-tripping is one of your passions, then this segment of the Patriot's Path is for you. These historical sites trace the paths of both Armies as they maneuvered north into Pennsylvania and an eventual showdown along the banks of Brandywine Creek. Visiting these sites can be done in a day of crisscrossing the countryside or by following the routes each Army took into Chester County in 1777. Pick up the trail where Washington held his Army in defensive positions along Red Clay Creek. Look toward the creek beyond the historical marker where a portion of the American Army's breastworks are still distinguishable. Jump back into your vehicle for a short ride to Spring Grove, where you will find General Weedon's Foray historical marker. Finally, head toward Greenville and visit the site of the Crooked Billet Tavern, where Washington and his generals talked about strategies two days before the Battle of Brandywine.

To follow the British Army's movement to Chester County, begin at the historical Marker where the Daniel Nichols House once stood. General Howe used the house as a temporary headquarters while marching north toward Kennett. Along the path, swing by New Garden Friends and Marlborough Friends Meetinghouses before driving to the Crown Forces Encampment Historical Marker and the 1768 Historic Farmstead markers in Kennett.

From here, drive east on the Baltimore Pike to the Old Kennett Meetinghouse. Swing in, stretch your legs, and walk around the well-maintained meetinghouse. In front of the building, you will find a large panel detailing its rich historical heritage involving the Revolutionary War and its role as a stopping place along the Underground Railroad. Along the meetinghouse's western front is an original stone wall where Maxwell and his Light Infantry fired on German columns marching toward Chadds Ford. On the eastern side of the building, you will find a large cemetery and the mass grave of Revolutionary War soldiers who died for liberty.

Continue your drive east on the Baltimore Pike, stopping at historical markers where Knyphausen conducted his feint. Then, end your foray at the historic Barnes-Brinton House. Although the ford sites are listed in this chapter, I recommend including them in a Battle of Brandywine tour to better understand the British troop movement as they attempted to flank the entrenched American Army.

<u>Washington's Earthworks Historical Marker</u> is Located at 1417 Newport Road Wilmington, Delaware.

<u>General Weedon's Foray at Spring Grove Historical Marker</u> is Located at 3200 Stoney Batter Road Wilmington, Delaware.

<u>Crooked Billet Historical Marker</u> is Located at the Intersection of Kennett Pike and Brindley Way Greenville, Delaware.

<u>The Daniel Nichols House</u> is located at Limestone Road and Sheringham Hockessin, Delaware.

<u>New Garden Friends Meetinghouse</u> is Located at 875 Newark Road Avondale, Pennsylvania.

<u>Traversing the Red Clay Valley Historical Marker</u> is located at 541 Chandler Mill Road Kennett Square, Pennsylvania.

<u>Crown Forces Encampment Historical Marker</u> is located at 120 North Union Street Kennett Square, Pennsylvania.

<u>1768 Historic Homestead</u> is located at the intersection of South Union Street and James Walter Way Kennett Square, Pennsylvania.

<u>Marlborough Friends Meetinghouse</u> is Located at 361 Marlborough Road Kennett Square, Pennsylvania.

<u>Brandywine Valley Tourism and Information Center</u> is Located at 300 Greenwood Road Kennett Square, Pennsylvania.

<u>Old Kennett Meetinghouse</u> is Located at 1113 East Baltimore Pike Kennett Square, Pennsylvania.

<u>Battle of Brandywine Historical Marker</u> is located along Independence Way Chadds Ford, Pennsylvania.

<u>American Light Infantry Historical Marker</u> is located at 423 Baltimore Pike Chadds Ford Pennsylvania.

<u>Barnes-Brinton House</u> is located at 632 Baltimore Pike Chadds Ford, Pennsylvania.

<u>Trimble Ford Historic District</u> is located at 301 Northbrook Road West Chester, Pennsylvania.

<u>Stroud's Preserve</u> is Located at 454 North Creek Road West Chester, Pennsylvania.

(Jeffrie's ford is located at the southern boundary of the preserve)

The Marshallton Historic District

"The most important six inches on the battlefield is between your ears."

~General James Mattis, 26th Secretary of Defense

Martin's Tavern, located in the Martin's Tavern/Humphry Marshall Historical Park, is where local patriots Colonel Hannum and Square Cheyney overnighted before making a morning trip to Trimble Ford and unexpecatantly observed thousands of scarlet troops fording the Brandywine. Cheyney was undoubtedly a frequent visitor to Marshallton since he was married to one of Marshallton's esteemed daughters, Mary Bennett. In marrying Mary, Thornbury-bred Squire Cheyney had joined one of Marshallton's most prolific families, the Woodwards, and could call at least five of his wife's uncles or aunts in the immediate Marshallton area his relatives. Cheyney's wife was the first cousin of Abigail Woodward Clayton, whose initials and marriage date of 1750 were found during renovation on the roof gable of the original dwelling, which later became the Tavern.

Although the building has collapsed, the tavern ruins have been painstakingly preserved and reinforced to preserve the original footprint of the historic inn. Its surviving walls, window frames and fireplaces give a visitor an idea of what it might have looked like in the 18th Century. The ruins are now surrounded by manicured lawns and award-winning landscaping. Period documents and maps are displayed within the ruins, describing the tavern's role as a local watering hole, traveler's stopover, and local militia meeting place. The Marshallton Historic District encompasses 65 contributing buildings and three contributing sites. It includes the separately listed Humphry Marshall House, Marshallton Inn, and Bradford Friends Meetinghouse.

The Blacksmith Shop was built in 1750 on the Woodward family property and was operated continuously through the 1950s. The names of the individuals who ran the shop and a wagon repair business on the second story of the building are listed on the wall inside the shop. When the last working blacksmith left the building in the 1950's most of the tools were left behind and are still displayed today. Relics of the second-floor wagon repair shop have also been preserved.

After the 1950s, the building deteriorated until Duke and Mary Cann Evans made the structural repairs and upgrades necessary to safely permit its use as a shop. They opened the shop in 1965 and operated it for 35 years. Substantial efforts were made to return the structure to its original condition and appearance; the building is much the same as it existed in the 1700s.

The life of famous American botanist and author Humphry Marshall is also celebrated in the historic district. Humphry Marshall was born near the village and educated in a Quaker family. Encouraged in his botanical interests by his cousin John Bartram, who is generally considered the first British colonial botanist in the Thirteen Colonies, Marshall established a garden at the family homestead. Marshall published his first book, *A Few Observations Concerning Christ, Or the Eternal Word,* in 1755. However, Marshall is best known for his 1788 publication *Arbustrum Americanum,* the first formal scientific description of trees and shrubs native to North America. Also skilled as a mason, Marshall may have built his impressive stone house himself.

Marine Corps Tie-In...Knowledge is Power.

Along Iraqi Highway 1 in the vicinity of a stretch of the highway that US forces converted into an improvised runway, Bravo company had stopped at dusk and dug hasty defensive positions. During the night, a Marine artillery unit across the highway from us received a fire mission, and they began to discharge their thunderous guns. The noise and concussions were so intense most of us thought we were taking incoming fire and ducked for cover. I learned a rude lesson about why it is not a good idea to doze off under the iron hull of an AAV. Aside from nearly knocking myself out after I jumped up from my slumber and smashed my head against the AAV, it is also the last place you want to be if the vehicle suddenly needs to move; fortunately for me, the AAV remained in place that night.

The next day, our officers and NCOs were called to a brief by our Company Commander to let us know that coalition forces had previously dropped thousands of small anti-personnel bomblets in our area of operation, and unit leaders needed to be able to identify them and mitigate the risk; in other words, make sure our Marines knew what to look for and to avoid the battery like bomblets. The bomblets were M864 DPICMs and were employed to cover the battle space with thousands of anti-personnel bomblets. The DPICMs are designed to detonate upon ground contact but have a high failure rate, which is why so many of them were left unexploded on the battlefield.

Before the Captain even finished his brief, we heard an explosion. It turned out that a few Bravo Company Marines found the bomblets and, not knowing what they were, had decided to have batting practice with them. A Marine made solid contact with a bomblet, which exploded on impact, tearing the Marine's E-Tool apart and spraying a few onlookers with shrapnel, but fortunately, no one was seriously hurt.

Historical places to visit in and near Marshallton.

The historical points of interest in Marshalltown are within walking distance of this small historic village. Parking is limited and can be challenging, so a morning or evening trip is recommended. Martin's Tavern ruins have been stabilized and well preserved with informational plaques throughout the structure, giving readers an excellent background into the history of its small role in the fight for independence. Take a short walk down a narrow sidewalk and visit the Blacksmith shop, which now serves as a gift shop. The Humphrey Marshall House stands across the road from the tavern site and blacksmith shop and is open seasonally for tours. If you are into meetinghouses, stroll along an old lane to the Bradford Meetinghouse and burial ground where American Patriots like Colonel Hannum, whose grave is unmarked, are interred.

Marshalltown Historic District is located along West Strasburg Road, West Chester, Pennsylvania.

Martin's Tavern Ruins is located at 1400 West Strasburg Road West Chester, Pennsylvania.

The Blacksmith Shop is located in the Marshalltown Historic District, West Chester, Pennsylvania.

Bradford Meetinghouse is located at 521 Northbrook Road, West Chester, Pennsylvania.

Humphrey Marshall House is located at 1371 West Strasburg Road West Chester, Pennsylvania.

Thornbury, Pennsylvania

"Because I am hard, you will not like me. But the more you hate me, the more you will learn. I am hard but I am fair."

~R. Lee Ermey, Actor and US Marine Drill Instructor

Squire Cheyney, one of four brothers was born on the Cheyney farm in 1730, but not in the existing farmhouse within sight of the Cheyney Preserve. The land that Cheyney University of Pennsylvania is built on was from the original 500-acre Cheyney farm but was not part of Thomas Cheyney's 150 acres where his home stands today. When the Revolutionary War started, Thomas Cheyney was in the prime of his life. He was in his mid-40s, married, and father of nine children with a 150-acre farm that provided plenty of income. His neighbors regarded his character so highly that they later gave him the honorary title of Squire.

Having decided to support the American cause, Cheyney quickly immersed himself in war-related appointments. Within a month, he helped organize and equip the county's militia. A week later, he was appointed a commissioner to seize Loyalists' property. He also took subscriptions to finance the Continental Army because the Continental Congress, America's government until 1781, could beg, borrow, and steal money, but it could not levy taxes. He was dismissed from membership in the Religious Society of Friends for his active involvement in the American Revolution.

On the morning of September 11th 1777, Squire Cheyney and Colonel Hannum famously rode to Trimble Ford and witnessed the bulk of the British Army crossing the Brandywine in an attempt to flank Washington's Army. The Hannum family history relates the event as follows:

"At the time the British army invaded Chester County, on its way from the Head of Elk to Philadelphia, Colonel Hannum resided at the

"Centre House" (now in the village of Marshallton), between the two main branches of the river Brandywine, and the night of September 10th 1777, was passed by Thomas Cheyney, Esq, a relative of Hannum, at the house of the latter. (At that perilous crisis, it was not deemed prudent for Squire Cheyney to lodge at his own home.) On the morning of September 11th the two set out together to visit the American army, known to be in the vicinity of Chad's Ford. As they descended towards the west branch of the stream, near Trimble's mill and Ford, they discovered coming down from the hills opposite a very numerous bodies of soldiers, evidently British. This very much surprised Hannum and Cheyney, and they moved round the adjacent hills, in order to observe the direction taken by the enemy. Finding them going toward Jefferies' Ford, on the east branch, and believing them to constitute the chief portion of the English army, the two decided to immediately, and at some personal risk, to proceed with the intelligence to Gen. Washington. Squire Cheyney, being mounted on a fleet hackney, pushed down the stream from Jefferies' Ford until he found the American commander-in-chief."

The road they chose that morning was called the Great Valley Road, which continued past Trimble's Ford. The Great Valley Road followed an ancient and well-used trail called the Warrior's Path, where a century earlier, marauding Iroquois used the trail to travel from their ancestral homes in the northeast to attack distant Indian villages as far south as the Carolinas and Georgia. This path was featured in a Sackett novel by Louis Lamour titled *The Warrior's Path*. The historical fiction tells the story of the Seneca tribe sending their young men to North Carolina to test themselves against the strength of Barnabas Sackett, a Welsh settler, and his sons.

According to the Hannum family legend, Cheyney reached Washington, who was busy conferring with his Generals at the Ring House. Cheney pushed through some guards to inform the commander-in-chief of the imposing British force he had just discovered Trimble's ford. When Cheyney perceived that Washington was not taking him seriously, Cheyney told Washington that Colonel Frazer and General Wayne would readily endorse his credibility, after which Washington purportedly considered Cheyney's report. This is a great local legend, and although entirely plausible, it has its problems with historians because of the lack of primary source collaboration, which should have existed in letters and documents for such an important event to have occurred.

At the end of the war, Cheyney continued to serve locally for many years as a Justice of Peace and as a Judge of the Court of Common Pleas. In 1787, he capped his political career by voting at Pennsylvania's Ratifying Convention to have the Keystone State adopt the U.S. Constitution, the second state to do so.

Major John Harper, a close friend of Cheyney, received a wartime commission as Quartermaster of the Fourth Battalion of Pennsylvania. Below is his commissioning appointment, not unlike modern promotion warrants used in our Armed Forces; the order reads as follows:

"We reposing especial Truth and Confidence in your Patriotism, Valour, Conduct, and Fidelity, Do these presents, constitute and appoint you to be Quarter Master of the Fourth Battalion of Pennsylvania Troops in the Army of the United Colonies raised for the defence [sic] of American Liberty and for repelling every hostile invasion thereof. You are therefore carefully and diligently to discharge the Duty of Quarter Master by doing and performing all Manner of Things thereunto belonging. And we do strictly charge and require all Officers and Soldiers under your command to be obedient to your Orders as Quarter Master, And you are to observe and follow such orders and Directions from time to time as you shall receive from this or a future Congress of the United Colonies, or Committed of Congress for that purpose appointed, or Commander in Chief for the Time being of the Army of the United Colonies, or any other your superior Officer, according to the Rules and Discipline of War, in pursuance of the Truth reposed in you. This commission to continue in Force until revoked by this or a Future Congress. Philadelphia February 9th 1776."

By order of the Congress,

President John Hancock

Major John Harper was a committed patriot and a brave soldier. After his appointment to Quartermaster of the Fourth Pennsylvania Battalion, under Colonel Anthony Wayne, he was commissioned an ensign in Captain Taylor's company of the same Battalion on October 12th 1776. By January 1st 1777, he was appointed first lieutenant of the Fifth Pennsylvania Line and was brigade major of Second Brigade at the battle of Brandywine. A few days after the battle, Major Harper, accompanied by Colonel Persifor Frazer, was on a reconnaissance patrol when the whole party was captured by British dragoons at the Blue Ball Tavern and taken to Philadelphia. Colonel Frazer successfully escaped, but Harper, after the British evacuation of the city, was sent to a prison hulk anchored off New York, where he remained a prisoner for over three years. He survived his terrible ordeal and was exchanged on November 4th 1780.

Towards the end of the Revolution, Major Harper acquired the tavern now known as the City Hotel and became host of the inn. He likely purchased the tavern property, knowing that the Suspension Act of 1785 which formed Delaware County, would be passed. After the county seat was subsequently moved from Chester to West Chester, Harper, believing there was little to gain by remaining in Chester, emigrated to the new county seat and became the landlord of the Turk's Head Inn. He died at Dilworthtown shortly after the beginning of the 19th century and was buried in the Cheyney family graveyard across the road from the university.

Marine Corps Tie-in...a Bridge Over the Saddam Canal.

After successfully conducting a relief in place (RIP) with British forces at GOSP-3, RCT-5 received orders to move up Route 27 to seize a key bridge over the Saddam Canal just outside Al-Nasiriyah. The U.S. Army had met significant resistance in the city before RCT-5 arrived at the location. Al-Nasiriyah was also the scene of a well-publicized event when Iraqi forces captured a female soldier and six others after their convoy took a wrong turn, were held as prisoners, and brutally treated.

First Battalion Fifth Marines led the attack as the RCT's main effort, followed in trace by 3rd Battalion. An enemy company-sized element put up strong resistance from defensive positions north and south of the canal. Iraqi fighters were notorious for ambushing American conveys moving north on highways leading toward Baghdad, from pre-excavated trenches that stretched for miles along either side of Iraq's main highways. After taking a few small arms potshots or occasional RPG shots at the convoys, the Iraqi soldiers would 'ditch' their weapons, uniforms, and military equipment and mill around with other civilian noncombatants along the route, making it impossible to identify them as enemy combatants. This tactic employed by the Iraqi army caused considerable confusion in the battle space and really irritated the Marines of Bravo Company.

When Bravo Company reached the city's outskirts, the enemy engaged us with mortars and heavy machine guns from positions on both canal banks. While crossing the bridge, I glanced at an Iraqi prostrate beside the road, fallen against a small concrete encasement with a hole through his midsection that a basketball could have easily passed through, an obvious recipient of an American 50. Caliber round that impacted its intended target center mass.

The Iraqi mortar fire was so inaccurate it seldom came close enough to threaten our convoy. However, we were close enough to see a few rounds impact among herds of sheep and goats grazing along our route, resulting in a grotesquely colorful spray of wool, pink mist, and sheep parts. The enemy mortar positions, including a couple of anti-air batteries, were eventually spotted and destroyed after a 50. Cal gunner from a Counter Mech Platoon (CMP) Gun truck engaged the positions. A couple of Cobra gunships were quickly walked onto the enemy gun placements to mop it up.

Once Bravo had secured the far side of the bridge and gained a foothold, Charlie Company continued the attack, pursuing the enemy along with elements of Bravo Company. My squad had an opportunity to engage the bad guys when several Iraqi fighters, uniformed in black, tried to maneuver through some wadis to attack the company's flank. They were fixed by fire from my squad while another squad, led by Donkey Kong, the grenade enthusiast, enveloped and aggressively assaulted through the enemy force.

Historical places to visit in Thornbury, Pennsylvania.

This stop along the Patriot Path will not take a visitor long to take in the few historical sites it offers. The farm park is on a small preserve that features an improved path along a circuitous route. Along your walk, visit Cheyney, his compatriot Major Harper, and other American Patriots buried in the family burial ground. There are also historical plaques along the path to read, and toward the end of your walk, the trail offers a great place to look at the Squire Cheyney Farm. Unfortunately, the farm is privately owned and is not open for tours. For history enthusiasts who are just passing through, consider combining this visit with a visit to Marshalltown.

<u>Squire Cheyney Farm Park</u> Located at 1740 Towne Drive West Chester, Pennsylvania.

<u>Cheyney Family Burial Grounds</u> Located just off the trail located at 1740 Towne Drive West Chester, Pennsylvania.

Chadds Ford, Pennsylvania

"Men do not fight for flag or country, for the Marine Corps or glory or any other abstraction. They fight for one another. And if you came through this ordeal, you would age with dignity".

~William Manchester, Historian and recipient of the National Humanities Medal and the Abraham Lincoln Literary Award.

John Chads operated a ferry service at the ford near his home along Brandywine Creek from 1729 until his death in 1760. In 1737, Chads operated a ferry across Brandywine Creek. The location became commonly known as Chadds Ford. On September 11th 1777, just before the Battle of Brandywine, Chads' wife Elizabeth refused to evacuate their home and hid her silver spoons in her pockets. An artillery exchange occurred near the house, resulting in British cannonballs damaging the springhouse. After the battle, Elizabeth lived in the home until her death in 1790.

Washington was on the other side of the Brandywine River just east of Chads' ford, committed to his defensive strategy had his army busily fortifying their positions. Washington established his headquarters at the Benjamin Ring House, just east of Chads' ford. Although he attempted to make a general reconnaissance of the surrounding area, Washington was a lot less successful than Howe, who had enlisted the help of several local Loyalists. When the day had ended, conflicting reports, a failed effort to gain reliable intel from locals and Washington's distrust of local militia left him ignorant of the other fords, key terrain, and roads in the vicinity of his defensive position.

Greene's division established a defensive position just south of the Great Post Road to guard a ferry crossing but was close enough to support the defense of Chads' ford. On Greene's right, in an elevated position, was General Wayne's division, whose primary duty was to defend the ford. Proctor's artillery occupied a position 600 yards northeast of Chads' ford on a hill to the right of and behind Chadds House. General Sullivan's division was occupying a defensive position to the right of Wayne's division, about a mile and a half to the north at Brinton's Mill, and the Army's right flank was guarded by Colonel Hazen's Canadian Regiment, which included three fords to the north of Chads' ford.

While Knyphausen maneuvered closer to Chads' ford, two of his field pieces were unlimbered on a hill near present-day Chads' Ford Elementary School, opposite Proctor's artillery park, and began firing on the American batteries. The long-range barrage had a negligible effect on Proctor's position, but the primary purpose of the cannonade was meant to signal to Cornwallis that Knyphausen had reached the American center of gravity and was beginning his diversionary assault to fix Washington's Army in place while Howe and Cornwallis conducted yet another flanking maneuver. Parties of Knyphausen men and American patriots started skirmishing on both sides of the Brandywine. During one of these skirmishes, Captain Ferguson, who commanded an experimental rifle corps armed with breech-loading flintlocks he developed, claimed to have gotten a party of American officers in his gun sights about 100 yards distant. He ordered three sharpshooters to fire on them, but the idea of shooting a man in the back from ambush disgusted Ferguson, and he rescinded the order, admiring the boldness in which one of the American officers was carrying out his duties. Ironically, not long after the incident, a ball struck and shattered Ferguson's right elbow, and the wound took over a year to fully heal. The day after the battle, while Ferguson was convalescing, a day a doctor informed him that Washington was in the area when he had the American officer in his gunsights. Ferguson later wrote, "Even if the officer were the General, he did not regret his decision."

His Ferguson Rifle did not remain in service much past the Battle of Brandywine. It took six months to produce 100 at a price four times the cost of a standard musket, so the experimental corps was disbanded; Ferguson's soldiers were rearmed with standard muskets and returned to Light Infantry units.

Howe had not quite reached Trimble's ford before Washington (around 8 AM) began to receive contradicting reports that a possible flanking movement by Howe was being conducted to the north of the entrenched Americans. Washington sent some of his dragoons to investigate. The Dragoons returned to report that they found no British troops in the vicinity of Trimble's ford, probably because Howe's column had not yet reached it. Around 10 AM, Colonel Hazen sighted the British column at Buffington's ford and reported to Sullivan, who, in turn, sent an aide riding back to Washington's headquarters to report the flanking movement.

The next ford the British crossed was Jeffries ford on the east fork of the Brandywine; Washington's only presence above Buffington's ford consisted of a few light dragoon patrols. Although Washington had confirmation that a flanking attempt by Howe was indeed in progress on his right flank, he hesitated because he received the information from his militia, and Washington was notorious for distrusting his militia. Washington waited on further confirmation from his dragoons operating in the area before making a tactical adjustment. When Washington finally acted to protect his right flank, he ordered Lord Sterling and General Steven's reserves to shift north. Once they had reached Birmingham Hill, about a mile and a half from Chads' ford, the reserve troops halted and began forming a battle line.

Around noon, Washington had another close call on his life. He rode up to Proctor's position on the hill above the Chads House and was reconnoitering west of the Brandywine when Knyphausen's cannons began dropping balls near Proctor's guns. A local named

Amos House and a few others, likely encouraged by curiosity, were near Washington when composed as he usually was in battle, said to Amos and the other spectators, "Gentlemen, you perceive that we are attracting the notice of the enemy. I think you had better retire." This was confirmed by James Parker of the Queen's Rangers, who stated, "About noon I saw Washington come out of a farmhouse...I had in short enough to get a canon fired at the group...my prayers went out to the ball that it might finish Washington and the rebellion together".

Washington, sure he was only facing a part of Howe's forces at his front, decided to launch the first offensive made by the Continental Army against a significant portion of the Crown Forces in the war for independence when he ordered Sullivan to attack. Maxwell pushed across the Brandywine and engaged Knyphausen's pickets while Colonel Ramsey pushed across Brinton's ford and skirmished with the 4th Regiment of Foot and Ferguson's Riflemen. The skirmishes quickly escalated into a large-scale battle when Washington, after ordering the bulk of his Army across the Brandywine, quickly rescinded his order because of yet another contradictory report he received. Now believing Howe's flanking maneuver was a feint, Washington ordered his Army back to their defensive posture, anticipating Howe to attack through Knyphausen's frontage. Sullivan, however, was convinced that a British attack on the American flank was imminent, and he was right.

By 1 PM, Cornwallis had reached Jefferies ford and was crossing it, moving his column briskly along Birmingham Road and ever closer to Washington's right flank. While leading the column in the vanguard, Ewald must have had a bout of de ja vu as he moved through another steep defile, which would have been a perfect ambush site for Washington's Army, had his intelligence reports been consistent and trustworthy. As it was, Ewald, leading Cornwallis' column, safely transited the defile and waited until the rest of the

British column caught up near Sconneltown near a grist mill that still stands. After a brief rest, the British moved onto Osborne's hill about two miles north of Washington's exposed flank, where they began to form for battle. On Osborne Hill, Cornwallis reorganized the British Army into three separate columns. The center column, consisting of the Jaegers and light infantry, remained on Birmingham Road. The second column, consisting of the elite British Guards and the 16th Light Dragoons, formed about 400 yards west of the road, and the third column, consisting of the 4th Brigade, formed about 400 yards east of the road. Once assembled, the battle line was approximately a mile long.

At about 1:15 PM, Sullivan again received intelligence that Cornwallis had crossed the Brandywine, this time at Jefferies ford. By 2 PM, an aide was once again sent to deliver the intelligence to Washington. While Cornwallis was finishing his Pre-Combat Checks (PCCs) and Pre-Combat Inspections (PCIs), Washington decided that Stirling and Stevens would need support defending the right flank at Birmingham Hill adjacent to the Birmingham Meetinghouse, which would be converted into a field hospital for both armies after the battle. Now assuming that Knyphausen was the smaller of the two British forces, Washington shifted Sullivan's division and some artillery north to support Stirling and Stevens.

On Birmingham Hill, Stirling set in a defensive line oriented northwest, beginning at the intersection of Wylie Road and Birmingham Road and extending for about 800 yards. His Aide de Camp and future President of the United States, James Monroe, sat his horse beside Stirling's. Stevens established his line near Stirling's right flank along Birmingham Road and extended it through the woods to Sandy Hollow. Sullivan, whose division was about a mile from Birmingham Road at Brinton's Ford, had finally begun to move into place on Birmingham Hill about a mile and a half from Stirling's left flank. Sullivan's division arguably had two of the worst commanders in the American Army: French General Preudhomme de Borre and Maryland's General Smallwood. Sullivan was the ranking officer on Birmingham Road, which left him in command of the American forces gathered there.

Consequently, de Borre assumed command of Sullivan's division in his absence. By the time both armies had maneuvered their formations, about 5,300 Americans faced roughly 9,000 British regulars. Sullivan and Stirling were located in the vicinity of a stone house, which is still standing at the intersection of Birmingham and Wylie Roads. Five limbered field pieces were positioned between Sullivan and Stirling near a civil war era cannon placed to mark the location of the field pieces during the battle.

Around 3 PM, Ewald was ordered with the advanced guard to attack the American infantry and dragoons spotted ahead of their battle formation in the vicinity of the meetinghouse. A skirmish soon broke out between Ewald and the Americans, which turned out to be Maxwell's light infantry, who pushed Ewald's advanced guard back to a fence line along Street Road. Once Cornwallis became aware of the American disposition, he ordered his columns into battlelines and prepared to begin his attack.

Around 4 PM, Cornwallis moved the British columns down Osborne Hill while Howe remained on top of the hill in the best position for him to observe the battle unfold. The position was also centralized, providing Howe with good ground for command and control. When the columns reached the bottom of the slope on Street Road, they quickly formed a line of battle, unlimbering a pair of cannon to oppose the American guns and cover troop movements. Cornwallis planned to attack the American forces with three battlelines: his elite troops holding the center of the formation, the Jaegers and light infantry on the left flank, and two battalions of grenadiers and General Mathew's Brigade of Guards on the right flank; the rest of his forces were held in reserve.

Cornwallis' left wing of 3,000 troops advanced south and engaged Steven's line of 2,100 Americans, while his right wing of 3,700 troops engaged the divisions of Sullivan and Stirling lines of 3,200 Americans. Before the British lines were ordered forward to close with the Americans, the grenadiers took off their foraging caps, pulled their tall bearskin caps from their packs, and brushed them out before putting them on for battle, adding a good foot of height to their already physically imposing posture. With the British drummers and fifers playing patriotic tunes, the Crown Forces paraded into the largest land battle of the Revolutionary War.

Around 4:30 PM, as Cornwallis was crossing Street Road, American guns began to lay down exploding shells in the beaten zone; Ewald renewed his attack on Marshall's 3rd Virginians located around the Jones home, forcing them into a supplemental defensive position behind the north-facing wall of the meetinghouse.

The American guns were causing a lot of British casualties but not enough to really slow down their momentum. When Cornwallis' lines were within 500 yards of the guns, the American gunners switched to grapeshot and canister rounds. Soon cannon from both armies combined with thousands of small arms fires, creating a thick fog that limited the vision of combatants and concealed battle formations. As soon as the British could move their guns up from Street Road, they began to fire rounds of grape and canister into the American ranks of Stevens and Stirling, exacting mass casualties of their own.

While these engagements took place, Sullivan's division found themselves out of position west of the battlefield near Street Road and had to loop south to get into an effective line of battle. Sullivan quickly realized the danger of Cornwallis getting around his right flank and shifted Stevens and Stirling to counter the threat. Howe, able to see the American shift from Osbourne Hill, ordered the 4th Brigade out of its reserve position and continued to extend his battle line to the east.

Although the American shift of Stevens and Stirling was pulled off with few issues, the same cannot be said of Sullivan's division, which the incompetent French General De Borre was temporarily commanding. After Sullivan finished shifting the two divisions of Stevens and Stirling, he rode out to check on his division and found them moving south but still too far away from the battle to form an effective line. Soon after finally getting his division onto Birmingham, Sullivan realized a large gap had opened between his division and Stirling's left flank and yet again rode off to Stevens and Stirling to make the adjustment, leaving De Borre to shift the division right and online with the rest of the American forces. De Borre was way too slow to move the division to the right; instead of simply shifting the division laterally, he attempted a complex European maneuver that, under the circumstances, would have been difficult for a well-trained European division to accomplish. He marched the division down the hill's south slope, turned east for some distance, then attempted to wheel it in precise position on Stirling's left flank. While De Borre was attempting his maneuver, the British Guards on Cornwallis's right flank were able to move uncontested within closing distance of Sullivan's floundering division and fired a single devastating volley, killing twenty-six men, including an American commander, before the battleline was even formed. This completely demoralized Sullivan's division and collapsed his lines, the men retreating in all directions. De Borre was observed galloping his horse away from the din of battle as fast as it could carry him.

As Sullivan's lines were scattering toward the southeast, Colonel Smith organized about 1,000 men into a rough battleline in Sandy Hollow. When De Borre rode up to Smith's newly formed line, Smith offered command to the senior French general, who immediately declined the responsibility. Smith later wrote that De Borre showed him scratches on his cheek the French general claimed were caused by the British firing fishhooks from their cannon but Smith guessed that the scratches were more likely caused by briars as De Borre shamefully fled the battle on Birmingham hill. After the battle, De Borre attempted to acquit himself of his cowardly actions in a letter addressed to Congress. He claimed he could not hold the division together because the Americans would not stand up and fight. He also added that he was grazed on the cheek by a British ball. Multiple eyewitness accounts directly contradicted De Borre's poor assessment of the American patriots and testified during a hearing that De Borre made no effort to re-form the division but instead, fled the battle. De Borre resigned from the Army three days later and returned to France.

One element of Sullivan's division, led by Colonel Hazen, did not flee the battlefield but remained resolutely defending the American guns. Consequently, his regiment, grossly outnumbered, was badly beaten by the British. Hazen's regiment sustained four officers and seventy-three enlisted casualties in the battle within a few short minutes.

While Sullivan's division was being routed by the British Guards, the British Grenadiers closed with Stirling's division. When the grenadiers were within 40 paces of Stirling's line, the Americans fired devastating volleys into the British ranks. The grenadiers fired one volley at the Americans and dropped to the ground. When they came back up, they did so with fixed bayonets, charged the American line with their usual ferocity, and forced Stirling's division from Birmingham Hill.

During this stage of the battle, the Marques de Lafayette entered the war as a combatant on American soil for the first time. Likely because of the young Marque's close ties with the French monarch, Lafayette was always near Washington, who was still located in the vicinity of Chads' ford. As he witnessed the intense fighting on Birmingham Hill, Lafayette appealed to Washington and was granted permission to immediately join Sullivan. When Lafayette reached

Conway's Brigade at the western edge of Sandy Hill, he dismounted and frantically tried to get the panicked Americans to form a battleline, fix bayonets, and charge at the surging British. As Lafayette was hopelessly attempting to get the routed Americans to take a stand, a British musket ball took him in the leg. Because Conway's forces, in full flight towards Dilworthtown, were closely pursued by the British, Lafayette's French Aide could barely get Lafayette onto a horse and off the field.

When Stirling's line finally gave way to the British assault around 6 PM, the American gunners finally abandoned their cannon to the British and fled the field. The last Americans to quit the battle was Steven's division, which was holding a battle line on the north crest of Sandy Hollow. Stevens was arguably defending the best ground in the battle space with two field pieces attached in support, but realistically, he could only hope to delay the surging British charge enough to cover Stirling's retreat. When Steven's division was finally forced to withdraw in a fighting retrograde through Sandy Hollow, they had to abandon the field pieces because the horses needed for moving them had all been killed by British bullets.

When Knyphausen heard the thunder of cannon to the north, he assumed (rightly) that Cornwallis had completed his flanking march and was in the attack. This was his cue to attack Greene on the other side of Chads' ford. Unfortunately for Knyphausen, he had his forces spread out too far up and down the western side of the Brandywine, and it took a considerable amount of time to consolidate and re-form battle lines. At around 5 PM, Washington ordered Greene to displace and move north to support the collapsing American lines. The only remaining Americans for Knyphausen to attack when his forces were finally ready was General Wayne's division which was augmented by the bulk of Maxwell's light infantry.

Marine Corps Tie In...H-Hour, Into Baghdad.

During Operation Iraqi Freedom, the intonation had always been, "Baghdad is the enemy's center of gravity. The campaign's purpose was to remove the regime, and the means to that end was capturing Baghdad. It was where Saddam's power resided, both symbolically and logistically. US Central Command (CENTCOM) and its subordinate leadership were consistent in their assumption that Saddam would attempt to defend the capital. While he had stationed relatively weak regular army divisions in the south, Saddam had kept his best forces, the Republican Guard and the Special Republican Guard, close to Baghdad. Coalition commanders believed the Iraqis would set up concentric rings of defense around Baghdad in response to an eventual coalition attack on the capitol.

As Bravo Company, 1st Battalion 5th Marines fought closer to Baghdad, we encountered a more determined enemy. During a particularly intense night as US artillery fired barrages on targets in the city prior to Bravo Company entering Baghdad's suburbs, I remember watching the streaking artillery rounds mingle with hundreds of Tomahawk missiles through the lenses of my night vision goggles. It was difficult for me to imagine that any infrastructure in the city could withstand such devastation, and I fully expected to roll into Baghdad unopposed to find nothing left but a pile of smoking rubble resembling Sodam and Gomorrah, those defiant ancient cities destroyed by God in a rain of fire.

As we drifted closer to Baghdad, my platoon was tasked with setting up a cordon outside the suburban town of Saddam City. We soon found ourselves entirely engulfed by refugees. These Iraqi refugees had been evacuated from the town so it could be cleared of suspected insurgents by coalition forces. The disoriented people were gathered in huge, surging crowds across the river from their homes. We were ordered to contain the crowd and prevent people from re-entering the town, but the effort was hopeless. We witnessed some people attempting to swim the river to return to the town while others constantly appealed to us in their language to return to their homes. The problem we had was that we had no interpreter, and our Arabic wasn't very good.

We eventually found an Iraqi doctor who had studied in the States and had a good command of English. He volunteered to help translate, but we soon realized that it would have been easier for us if the language barrier had persisted. When they learned they could effectively communicate with us, we were quickly inundated with a horde of frantic people who had one hundred and one problems we couldn't help them with. One of the many appeals from people in the crowd that stood out to me was from a woman who insisted she accidentally left her infant behind in her home. She passionately pleaded to be allowed to go back and get her baby. I dutifully forwarded her request to my platoon commander, even knowing it was a hopeless waste of time. Even if her story was true, we were ordered to allow no one into the city for any reason. I hope to this day that her request was simply a ruse in an attempt to gain access to the town.

At the end of that long and stressful day, we were relieved by another coalition unit, and we moved to our next objective. The movement was slow because the roads were literally choked with refugees pushing overloaded wheel barrels or dragging carts piled with household goods and loot. Each of our AVVs had a small surplus of humanitarian rations that we were 'highly encouraged' to pass out to people in crowds, and we tried our best to toss them to children as we passed through the crowded streets in the AAV, but adults would quickly descend on the children, beat them and take the rations from them. This demonstration of greed and abuse really pissed the Marines off, who were trying to get the foodstuff to the starving children. One Marine devised an amusing remedy to deter the greedy adults from descending on the children. He removed the food contents from a few MRE sleeves and taped a brick into each.

He scattered the foodstuff to the children as we rode by and waved the 'MRE bomb' at the unsuspecting adults to get their attention. When they were well within the Marine's range, he would violently throw the improvised missile at them, often striking them with breathtaking results.

An amusing phenomenon occurred during our operations around Saddam City where Marines suddenly 'acquired' a massive resupply of cigarettes. By the time our company moved into the Baghdad suburbs, Marines had run out of whatever tobacco products they brought to the theater. To describe some Marines as tobacco fiends might be too modest. Marines were selling re-dip to each other, often demanding unbelievable prices for their well-used ware. Inside city limits, Marines discovered a cigarette factory run by one of Saddam Hussein's cousins until US forces took over the compound. Camp Marlboro, as US forces later named it, turned out to be the source of the blue packaged contraband cigarettes Marines were suddenly in possession of copious amounts. Called hodji cigarettes by Marines, Bravo Company had a temporary fix for their habit, and nonsmokers had some valuable bartering items.

1st Battalion 5th Marines eventually received orders to seize Azimiyah Palace, one of Saddam's presidential palaces located in northeastern Baghdad. As we moved through the suburbs of Baghdad on the night of April 9th I vividly remember how eerie the experience was. The streets were empty, and the buildings were void of light or sound. Through night vision goggles, I could see hundreds of Infrared Target Pointer/Illuminator/Aiming Light (AN/PEQ-2) lasers dancing on the seemingly vacant buildings and overpasses as Marines continuously scanned for potential threats. Suddenly, along the road in the direction I was facing as our AAV rumbled down the road, an intense explosion of light and energy surged toward our vehicle after an Iraqi fuel tanker was detonated by a Rocket Propelled Grenade (RPG). My Marines were unscathed, if not a bit shaken by the encounter, but other Marines in our company convoy were not as fortunate. Two fellow NCOs, one of whom was a close friend of mine, sustained egregious injuries as RPGs slammed into the side of their vehicle. They were safely evacuated by helicopter after our company secured the palace complex the next morning. They both thankfully survived their injuries but will carry their battle scars for the rest of their lives.

In the early dawn light of April 10th with Alpha company in the lead, the battalion was suddenly engulfed in intense RPG, heavy machine gun, and small arms fire from every direction. The battalion's lead company somehow got turned in the wrong direction. As they turned around and fought their way back on course, Bravo company seized the initiative and took point, pushing toward the battalion objective. Supported by the battalion's 81 mm mortar platoon, Bravo reached the palace and quickly secured the eleven buildings within the walled compound.

The effort to secure the buildings in the palace compound can be described as barely controlled chaos at best. After securing the sector my squad was tasked to clear, and after confirming there was no other way to support the company effort inside the compound, I took the initiative and moved my squad outside the compound walls where our AAVs were parked, to provide overwatch security and augment their up-gun systems. I immediately noticed that we were in a courtyard lined with several layers of fighting positions orienting away from the compound. My squad quickly cleared and occupied the first few rows of fighting positions, setting in a hasty defensive line to support the AAVs.

As my team leaders were establishing sectors of fire, two RPGs, undoubtedly aimed at the AAVs, impacted the compound wall just above the tracked vehicles. Almost simultaneously, my squad came under small arms fire from buildings outside the courtyard. My Marines quickly returned suppressive fires as rounds were snapping and kicking up dirt around our defensive positions. A Mk 153 Shoulder-Launched Multipurpose Assault Weapon (SMAW) team attached to my squad found a covered position on a low rooftop and fired a high explosive round into a building where we located concentrated enemy fires. As suddenly as the attack began, the courtyard went quiet.

During the combat action at Azimiyah Palace, 1st Battalion 5th Marine sustained 1 KIA and 60 wounded. The battalion defeated the enemy forces in zone and killed several hundred Special Republican Guard soldiers and Saddam Fedayeen Fighters. After the attack, the city eventually settled into an end-of-hostilities phase, and thousands of grateful Iraqi citizens took to the streets to thank the American Marines and Sailors around the palace for liberating them from Saddam's tyrannical reign.

Bravo Company spent the rest of our stay in Baghdad running post-war operations from the palace we had secured. Remarkably, most of the palace was left standing, although tomahawk missiles surgically gutted a portion of it. The prevailing rumor was that the gutted section of the palace was specifically targeted based on the intelligence that high-value targets were occupying the damaged portion on the night of the strike and that the high-value targets were Saddam's sons or maybe even Saddam himself. Regardless, the space must have been lavishly decorated, as evidenced by bits and pieces of gilded debris found throughout the complex and in a destroyed swimming pool outside the targeted area. I even found a tattered lion skin rug as I sifted through the debris for intelligence.

Historical places to visit in or near Chadds Ford, Pennsylvania.

For this significant stop along the Patriot Path, you will want to take a day to visit the many historical points of interest that encompass the Battle of Brandywine. Unlike other historical battles, where one can visit a preserved battlefield, only small pockets of the

Brandywine battlefield have been preserved. A great place to start is the Brandywine Battlefield Park. Although this location does not offer a lot of the actual battlefield to tour, there is a small museum and gift shop that offers many great resources to get you started on your tour. The gift shop also provides guided tours of the Benjamin Ring House, where Washington was headquartered, and Gilpin Homestead, where Lafayette stayed. Roads lead to each location so I recommend driving to each site unless you want to stretch your legs. While visiting the Gilpin Homestead, check out the giant ancient Sycamore Tree in the yard that existed when the Battle of Brandywine occurred. Also near the homestead is a monument dedicated to all the men and women who fought for our great nation since the Revolutionary War.

After your battlefield park visit, drive west a few miles to Chadds Ford Elementary School. Although there are no historical signs or monuments commemorating the site's role during the Battle of Brandywine, this is where the British unlimbered their cannon and fired on Chads' House just across the creek. Jump back onto the road and visit John Chads' House, fording site, and contributing buildings. If you plan your visit for mid-September, you will likely run into a Revolutionary War encampment and reenactors representing both sides of the American conflict. Although Brinton Mill is listed as a place to visit, it is private property. I recommend asking permission before visiting this beautifully maintained historical farm that Sullivan's division occupied briefly before the battle. You can either continue your drive on Creek Road to Osbourne Hill or retrace Howe and Cornwallis' flanking movement to the hill.

To retrace the British flanking movement, drive to Longwood Gardens and jump onto East Doe Run Road. Turn onto Northbrook Road to Wawaset Road and turn left. In about a quarter of a mile, turn right and back onto Northbrook Road. Continue on Northbrook, where you will eventually cross the Brandywine Creek. The one-way bridge is narrow, so use caution and judgment when crossing. You are now in the Trimbleville Historic District. Continue along Northbrook to Broad Run Road on the left; a historical Marker is along this Road. Continue on Northbrook until you reach Camp Linden Road. Turn right, and about a quarter of a mile on the right side of the road beside a driveway is the Trimble Ford Historic Plaque. Continue on Camp Linden Road to North Wawaset Road and turn right. Continue on Wawaset Road to Allerton Road and follow it to Jefferies ford on the other side of the bridge, where you will find several historical plaques.

Finish tracing the British flanking movement by traveling on Allerton Road to Birmingham Road. Turn right onto Birmingham Road and enter the natural defilade that bothered Ewald so much as he rode through it on September 11th 1777. Look carefully for the Sconneltown plaque on the right before you reach Strodes Mill. The mill site is now an artist's studio, but visitors can park, walk across the road, and take pictures of the old buildings. Continue to the Osborne Hill Marker on the left side of the road intersection. There is no parking lot, so I recommend parking along Country Club Road to visit the marker and take in the incredible view the vista offers; congratulations, at this point, you have successfully flanked Washington's Army.

Follow Birmingham Road to the Birmingham Meetinghouse and Lafayette Cemetery on the left side of the road. There is a lot to see here as you walk around the old meetinghouse used as a field hospital by both Armies after the battle. The sight of a mass grave containing the remains of American and British soldiers is marked with a boulder and plaque. A stone wall separating the meetinghouse and Lafayette Cemetery is the same one Maxwell's troops used as they engaged Ewald's advanced force. In the cemetery, you will find a large battle monument and a few smaller ones honoring the Patriots of the battle. Across the road, you will find Birmingham Hill, where the bulk of the battle occurred. There are historical plaques detailing the battle and two Civil War-era cannon placed where the American guns were unlimbered during the battle.

After visiting these historical sites, drive down the road to Thornbury Road and turn left. The General Stevens Last Stand Historical Marker is across the road from a farm market. Continue along the road to South New Street. Turn right and proceed to Sandy Hollow, where there is a parking lot on the right. Sandy Hollow features an improved trail that wraps around this small section of the battlefield. It is where Lafayette fought on American soil for the first time and received a wound for his effort to turn American soldiers from their full-fledged retreat. On the outskirts of Sandy Hollow along Birmingham Road are two more cannon, sisters to the ones mentioned before. They are pointed toward Sandy Hollow, marking the spot where Lafayette was wounded. A Lafayette monument is just down the road from the gun placement, but it is on private property.

To finish your Brandywine Battlefield tour, drive to the second Lafayette monument, which is located along a private driveway, then continue east on Birmingham Road to a few historical plaques containing information about the closing moments of the battle. The plaques are in a field with mowed paths, but parking is limited to only a few vehicles.

Brandywine Battlefield Park is located at 1491 Baltimore Pike Chad's Ford, Pennsylvania.

Gilpin Homestead is located at 198 Harvey Road Chads' Ford, Pennsylvania.

Benjamin Ring House is located at 1491 Baltimore Pike Chad's Ford, Pennsylvania.

John Chad's House is located at 1719 North Creek Road Chad's Ford, Pennsylvania.

Brinton Mill is located at 1400 South Creek Road (Private Property) Chads' Ford, Pennsylvania.

Sconneltown Marker is located at 204 south Birmingham Road Chad's Ford, Pennsylvania.

Strodes Mill is located at 1000 Lenape Road West Chester, Pennsylvania.

Osborne Hill Marker is located at 901 Birmingham Rd Chads' Ford, Pennsylvania.

General Howe Command Post is located at 901 Birmingham Road Chads' Ford, Pennsylvania.

Birmingham Meetinghouse and Lafayette Cemetery is located at 1245 South Birmingham Road Chads' Ford, Pennsylvania.

Birmingham Hill is located at 1270 South Birmingham Road Chad's Ford, Pennsylvania.

General Steven's Stand Historical Marker is located at 1241 Thornbury Road Chads' Ford, Pennsylvania.

Sandy Hollow is located at South New Street Parking lot Chad's Ford, Pennsylvania.

Lafayette Marker #1 is located at 1311 South Birmingham Road (Private Property) Chads' Ford, Pennsylvania.

Lafayette Marker #2 is located at 1340 Fieldpoint Drive (Private Property) Chads' Ford, Pennsylvania.

Brandywine Battlefield Historical Markers is located at 370 South Birmingham Road (limited parking) Chads' Ford, Pennsylvania.

Dilworthtown Historic District

"People sleep peaceably in their beds at night only because rough men stand ready to do violence on their behalf."

~Richard Grenier, Newspaper Columnist

During the waning hours of the Battle of Brandywine, Washington stood on or near William Brinton's yard as Sullivan's division fled the battlefield, and Greene maneuvered his division to the south of the house to cover the routed Continentals. It was almost dark when the last shots near Dilworthtown were fired. Greene's final battle line of 2,000 Continentals was positioned on both sides of Wilmington Road in an L-shaped formation, essentially creating a giant ambush zone for the pursuing British.

Generals Weeden and Muhlenberg, supported by General Knox's guns, stood up to the surging British Army one final time before retreating toward Chester, Pennsylvania, behind the rest of the Continental Army. The two brigades displaced from their position near Chads' ford and moved east on the Old Post Road. They continued their march north onto Harvey Road toward Dilworthtown and arrived at the Wilmington and Oakland Road intersection.

While Greene's division was establishing their final protective line, the 4th British Brigade, led by General Agnew, continued to advance toward Dilworthtown on a line parallel to Brinton's Bridge Road. His skirmisher line was established east of Wilmington Road and was arranged left to right: 37th, 64th, 46th, and 33rd Regiments of Foot.

As Agnew's brigade cleared Dilworthtown, it came within range of Knox's guns. The American batteries fired canister and grapeshot from their cannon, filling the beaten zone with hot metal fragments, causing momentary havoc and disorder in the British ranks. Within a few minutes, the British got their 12-pound cannon placed and unlimbered, oriented their fires toward Knox's position and forced Knox to displace his two guns. Knox moved his guns into a secondary defensive position and began to fire into the British ranks again.

Meanwhile, the left flank of the British assault, consisting of the 2nd Grenadier Battalion and the 42nd Royal Highland Regiment, was maneuvering within closing distance of the American line beyond the William Brinton House. Greene held the superior position and established interlocking fires, but the British were well aware of the danger. Weedon, in position on the right flank, waited until the British were almost directly in front of him in an open field before he ordered his men to fire on them. The Americans delivered concentrated, devastating fires into Agnew's line. According to written testimony, the skirmish lasted for the better part of an hour. According to Ewald, nearly all the officers of the 46th and 64th were killed during the American fires, and General Agnew himself almost lost his life when an American cannonball nearly struck him. As fate would have it, General Agnew would lose his life on American soil to a sniper's bullet a few weeks later as the battle of Germantown was winding down. The fighting at Dilworthtown continued until British guns began to shell the American line again, eventually forcing Greene into an orderly retreat that finally ended the battle of Brandywine. Although the retreat was not as disorganized as in past defeats, the only American units that withdrew with their unit relatively intact were Wayne, Greene, Maxwell, and Nash's units.

As dusk quickly settled in, the British consolidated their forces on their hard-fought but otherwise worthless ground and chose not to pursue the fleeing Americans by foot, which invariably became Washington's saving grace. Although the British had driven the American Army off another battlefield, they failed to destroy it again.

Factors that contributed to the cessation of hostilities and Howe's decision not to pursue Washington's retreating Army came down to a flawed estimate of the strength of the American line during the final skirmish, the onset of darkness, rough terrain, and fatigue. Howe later conceded that the American Army fought so well that day he was convinced Sullivan defended Birmingham Hill with 10,000 troops.

Major John Andre, then Aide de Camp to General Grey, wrote, "Night and the fatigue the soldiers had undergone prevented any pursuit." Major Andre also survived the battle but forfeited his life on American soil a few years after his service at Brandywine. After being implicated in Benedict Arnold's treason, he was executed near West Point, New York, as a convicted spy.

After the battle with Greene's forces, the exhausted British soldiers camped on the forward edge of the battle area and consolidated in or near Dilworthtown the next day while Howe established his headquarters at the George Gilpin House. Howe's forces remained in the Dilworth area, burying their dead where they lay, treating or evacuating the wounded to the British fleet now anchored in Wilmington and patrolling the countryside for fleeing American officers and food.

The Dilworthtown Inn was set up as a field hospital, and casualties from both sides of the battle were treated at a make-shift hospital set up in the Birmingham Meetinghouse. American and British soldiers who succumbed to their wounds in the Meetinghouse are buried in a common grave just outside its walls, which is marked with a memorial stone.

There were so many American wounded left on the battlefield that Howe requested help from Washington's surgeons, including Dr. Benjamin Rush, who was almost captured on the battlefield while treating the wounded. As an original signer of the Declaration of Independence, he was surely near the top of Howe's most-wanted list. Ironically, the day after the battle, Howe personally received Rush at his headquarters in the George Gilpin House and was even introduced to several of his officers. Four days later, Dr. Rush was given leave to accompany some of the American wounded to a schoolhouse converted into a hospital at the intersection of Gay and High Streets in West Chester. Some of those soldiers eventually succumbed to their injuries and were interred in the school yard.

The battle went down as an American defeat in the history books, but the inexperienced, novice Continental Army had acquitted itself well against the vastly superior British professional Army. The Battle was one of the war's bloodiest, with estimated KIA's from the American Army hovering around 300 with an additional 600 recorded as wounded; the Americans also lost 11 valuable, hard-to-replace field pieces which were either spiked or abandoned. Howe's reported battle damage assessment (BDA) was around 90 KIAs and an additional 490 wounded; however, several other witnesses accounted for many more injured or killed on the British side.

During the Battle of Germantown, American officers came into possession of an official British memorandum on the Battle of Brandywine that reported 1,032 killed or wounded during Cornwallis' flanking attack. During Knyphausen's feint, 944 were reported killed or wounded. The total number of British forces killed or wounded was reported at 1,926, but the British were notorious for underestimating battlefield casualties, so the number may have been even higher.

The outcome of the Philadelphia Campaign and perhaps the entire war may have had a significantly different outcome favoring the British cause had Howe pursued and destroyed Washington's Army or immediately crossed the upper fords of the Schuylkill River. Taking Washington's backcountry supplies or destroying the American Army were stated goals of Howe during the planning phase of the Philadelphia campaign. Howe could have pursued and mopped up Washington's scattered Army around Chester or at least positioned his Army to deny Washington access to his valuable supply depots in Reading as he tried to reorganize his Army. But Howe chose to rest his troops in Dilworthtown for five days, giving up the initiative and failing to bring the war to a close.

The British officers might have won the battle at the Brandywine. but they could not ignore the fact that a badly outmaneuvered and beaten amateur American Army had gathered itself together enough to hastily defend a strong position and delay the British advance, buying valuable time for Washington's soldiers to evacuate the battlefield. Washington limped away from another defeat but once he pulled his Army back together again, the patriots would live to fight another day.

Marine Corps Tie-In...Through the Heart of Baghdad.

After the smoke cleared and the Al-Azimiyah Presidential Palace was secured by Bravo Company, it soon became apparent that it would become our base of operations while the rest of Baghdad was falling under the control of US and coalition forces. Baghdad was declared secured on April 14th (my birthday). The following day, President Bush formally declared victory, and for the next several weeks, Bravo Company participated in the post-hostility mop-up of the streets of Baghdad.

We made our temporary home inside the walled compound, using a courtyard and a couple of outside buildings as a temporary bivouac. Our days were spent guarding the compound, patrolling the streets, and, on occasion, a special task would be assigned to the company from the battalion. While the security of the compound was routine and mundane, the patrols in the ravaged streets of Baghdad were anything but that.

The patrols usually ranged from platoon-sized to squad-sized, were typically conducted on foot and in the vicinity of our assigned zone. Most of the time, the Marines were operating in a heightened state of alert because it seemed like every Iraqi citizen was carrying an AK-47, including children. Although most Iraqis we met were friendly, one never knew which one was not. Unfortunately, in one of our sister battalions, a tragedy of this very nature occurred when word circulated that a Saddam Loyalist had infiltrated a Marine patrol and shot its leader in the back of the head execution style. The Marines in the patrol shot the Iraqi infiltrator to rags, but the Corps lost another one of its very best SNCOs that day.

During a squad-sized patrol somewhere in the city, my Marines encountered and nearly engaged a group of Iraqi police officers dressed in distinctive Iraqi army uniforms and armed with AK-47s. Fortunately, we were able to quickly confirm via radio that the group of Iraqis were friendly and narrowly avoided an international incident. We carefully kept a close eye on the Iraqi police force, and since they displayed no hostile intent, we all safely went about our business. The Iraqi police force eventually transitioned from Iraqi army uniforms and wore more easily recognizable civilian police uniforms.

One of the most impressive displays of American might I witnessed during OIF-I happened on a darkening evening while patrolling the streets of Baghdad. The platoon was already a little edgy after encountering children who engaged our patrol with toy guns earlier in the evening. We were working our way down a street when we suddenly took fire from a mosque. Pinned down inside an abandoned building, it was decided that the best course of action was to request close air support. Expecting a Marine Cobra Gunship, what came on station instead, was an Air Force A-10 Warthog.

A complicated nine-line was abruptly interrupted by the pilot, who wanted to keep communication simple and brief. The pilot only wanted to know where the bad guy was, where we were, and a good egress route for his aircraft after his gun run. Within seconds of the transmission, the jet screamed overhead, made a lazy pass of the mosque, and suddenly, diving from behind us, unleashed a devastating stream of hot death from its cannon. After a loud, brief burp of the jet's big gun, we could hear the heavy brass casings from the cannon's massive rounds rattle off cars as the mosque was surgically reduced to dust. We safely resumed our patrol and there was no reason to recon the sight for a Battle Damage Assessment; there was nothing left to assess.

Historical Sites to visit in and near the Dilworthtown Historic District.

The Dilworthtown Historic District marks the end of your Brandywine tour. Begin your tour at the William Brinton House, where Washington stood watching the end of the Brandywine battle. The William Brinton 1704 House was built on a 450-acre land grant from William Penn and has been restored to its original state by descendants of the Brinton family. The house is furnished with period furniture, lead casement windows, an indoor bake oven, and a colonial herb garden in the backyard. The Brinton Association of America maintains the house and the caretaker is a sixth-generation Brinton. Famous Brinton descendants include Civil War General George B. McClellan and President Richard M. Nixon. The home is now a museum and can be visited by appointment or during regular hours between March and October. Across the road is a small walking preserve with limited parking and an informational bulletin board.

Across the street is a small preserve featuring mowed paths where some of the last fighting occurred. Just down the road is the George Gilpin House that Howe used as his headquarters and entertained the good doctor and signer of the Declaration of Independence, Benjamin Rush. Unfortunately, this house is not well preserved or available to tour, but it sits along the road and offers an unobstructed view for pictures.

Finish your tour back at the Dilworthtown Inn, which is beautifully restored and still in operation as a restaurant. Just be sure to call ahead for a reservation before you drop by. Across the road is another period building that functions as a store, and a plaque commemorating Dilworthtown's role in the Revolutionary War can be found in front of the Inn.

William Brinton House is located at 21 Oakland Road West Chester, Pennsylvania.

Dilworthtown Inn and Historical Marker is located at 1390 Old Wilmington Road West Chester, Pennsylvania.

George Gilpin House is located at 2-88 Harvey Road West Chester, Pennsylvania.

Book Two: The Battle of the Clouds and a Massacre at Paoli

Glen Mills, Pennsylvania

"The future success of the Marine Corps depends on two factors: first, an efficient performance of all duties to which its officers and men may be assigned; second, promptly bringing this efficiency to the attention of the proper officials of the government, and the American people."

General John A. Lejeune, 13th Commandant of the Marine Corps.

Colonel Persifor Frazer, the son of John and Mary Smith Frazer, was born in Newtown Square, Pennsylvania, just west of Philadelphia. He married Mary "Polly" Taylor on October 2nd 1766, and managed a prosperous farm in the woods north of the former Glen Mills School. Frazer became a leading regional political figure and resisted the growing British tyranny in the colonies before the Revolutionary War. In early 1776, Persifor was chosen as commanding officer of Company A, Fourth Pennsylvania Battalion, and later received a promotion to lieutenant colonel of the Fifth Pennsylvania Line, commanded by General Wayne.

For Persifor to have been made a British prisoner during the war must have been his destiny. On the night of the 11th just after the closing shots of the Battle of Brandywine were exchanged, Persifor returned to his home in nearby Glen Mills for some rest before traveling toward Chester to rendezvous with Washington's retreating Army. A group of American riflemen warned the Frazers that some local Loyalists had informed the British of suspected ammunition and baggage Persifor had hidden on his farm and that a patrol was en route to the farm to confiscate the supplies and take Persifor into custody. Although Persifor downplayed the danger to his wife, he did take the precaution of hiding the ammunition and baggage before departing for the Continental Army near Philadelphia.

On Sept 13th Persifor left home to link up with the Army, just ahead of a detail of over 250 British troops who paid his wife Polly an unwelcomed visit at their homestead, situated just behind the back nine of the famous Glen Mills golf course. Polly, alerted by the sound of several wagons moving toward her home, quickly hid her children, servants, and a wounded American soldier in the woods and returned to the house. On her porch and alone, she was met with British soldiers who, intent on plunder, burst through the home's front door demanding the whereabouts of stores of ammunition, baggage, and "those damned rebels." Without hesitation, Poly denied anyone else's presence or knowledge of any ammunition or stores hidden on the property. This reply didn't sit well with the officer questioning her, sending him into a rage of profanity and destruction. The British plunderers soon found Persifor's liquor stash and promptly began to get drunk. Captain DeWest (not the interrogating officer) stopped a drunken soldier about to strike Polly and cleared the home of the soldiers. He then explained to Polly that the British rewarded American soldiers who turned to the British effort. Laughing the suggestion aside, Polly said, "You don't know Colonel Frazer, or you wouldn't suggest such a thing, nor would he listen to me if I proposed it." She added with a flair, "If Persifor chose to side with the British, I would never consent to have anything more to do with him." Her courage that day must have made an impression on Captain DeWest, who, having orders to fire the house and barn, chose instead to spare them. The home ironically burned down years later when a fire broke out while Italians were baking bread for quarry workers, but this was long after the Frazers left the farmstead.

Polly did not end her heroics with the farmstead event; she eventually traveled to the Walnut Street prison in Philadelphia to visit her incarcerated husband after his capture at the Blue Ball Inn. At that time, the jail at Walnut Street was notorious for the harsh treatment of American prisoners by the British jailers; hundreds of prisoners were reportedly abused. Some prisoners even died under prison commandant Captain William Cunningham's supervision and were dragged off to the potter's field and unceremoniously tossed in a ditch. Washington Park now occupies the site of the infamous burial ground, and a monument featuring a life-sized bronze statue of Washington facing an eternal flame that commemorates the sacrifices of hundreds of unknown Patriots interred within its boundaries.

Cunningham and his jailers took precautions to ensure word of conditions in the prison never reached higher authorities outside its walls. But Polly Frazer and Jane Gibbons were going to do something about that and arranged to smuggle out a letter the prisoners wrote. During one of her visits, Polly smuggled spoiled and moldy food the British jailers were feeding American prisoners along with a letter describing the horrid treatment out of the jail in some folds of her petticoat. She was able to make her way unmolested through the pickets to Washington's encampment and got the evidence into the hands of the commander-in-chief. Washington, horrified with the alleged poor treatment of prisoners under the rules of war, petitioned Howe for better treatment of the prisoners. Treatment of the prisoners suddenly became a bit better; in a few short months, after Howe evacuated Philadelphia, the tables turned on some of the British jailers who themselves became prisoners. Frazer wrote an affidavit describing prison conditions:

An undated affidavit from Presifor, which Chester County, Pennsylvania, has validated, reads: "I Persifor Frazer late Lieutenant Colonel of the fifth Pensylva Regt do declare, that I was prisoner of War with the British Forces from the 16th of Septemr 1777.' till the 17th March 1778. that Colonel Hannums was taken & put into confinement at the State House in Philada about the 9th or 10th

October 1777. About the 4th day of January We were remov'd to the New Goal, where I remain'd till about the 20th, when I obtain'd a parole to go to Sick quarters in the City; I remain'd in this situation till about the last of Feby following, when I was orderd by a deputy of Mr Ferguson the British Commissary of Prisoners, to repair to the Sign of the Golden Swan in Third Street. Colonel Marbury who also was out on parole and myself went together the same afternoon, & were put into confinement, no Paroles being demanded of either of Us— Here we found Colonel Hannums & a Number of other American Officers who had been remov'd from the New Goal to this place— about this time the greatest part of the Officers who were on parole at Sick quarters in the City were order'd in & confin'd here also—upon enquiry I understood that those Gentlemen who had been remov'd from the New Goal, had been persuaded to Sign Paroles upon promises made to them of many Liberty's & priviledges w[hi]ch I found in almost every instance violated; As they as well as myself were under as much restraint here as We had been either at the State House or New Goal—Two Centries were plac'd at the front & two others at the back part of the House, who frequently prevented any of our acquaintance from holding any conversation with Us threatning to run their Bayonets into those who attempted it—Our provision & Cloathing was frequently search'd by the guard to prevent as I understood any intelligence being convey'd to or from Us, And the persons who brought those necessarys for our Use were often prevented from coming to Us—during our confinement at this place Mr Ferguson came into the Room where Colonel Hannum myself & sundry other Officers were in confinement when Colonel Hannum complaind in a very spirited manner, that, the priviledges promis'd by the said Mr Ferguson to him and others, at the time of their removal to that place, had not been complied with, and mention'd many of the hardships We at that time suffer'd contrary to the agreement—upon the relating of which Mr Ferguson express'd surprize, & said, the guards had misunderstood their Orders, but that he would rectify the matter & for the future We should have more Liberty—For a few hours after this conversation, We were suff[ered] to speak to some friends who came to Visit Us—but the same Evening the Serjeant or Corporal of the guard inform'd some of Us, that they had receiv'd fresh orders not to suffer Us any more to enjoy those indulgencies—and without any cause that We could learn, we were afterwards under very Severe restrictions—Two Prisoners were as I was informed walking in the Stable Yard under the eye of the guard, the Town Major coming by at this time, reprimanded the guard for allow[in]g 'those fellows' (as he call'd Us) so much Liberty, I remain'd in this siutation 'till the evening of the 17th of March when I made my escape & the same evening as I understood Colonel Hannum & Major Williams likewise escap'd—When we got clear of Philadelphia We made all possible haste to Camp & went to Head Quarters, and upon a just & particular Account given to his Excellency General Washington by Colo. Hannum of the circumstances of his confinement and escape (as far as I was acquainted with the matter) His Excellency, express'd himself satisfy'd with his conduct During the whole time of Colonel Hannum & myself being Prisoners (except some small time when We were at Sick quarters in the City) We constantly mess'd together and Lodg'd in the same Room, by which means I became acquainted with some of the facts here Stated".

After the war, Persifor became an iron manufacturer and merchant; he owned and operated Sarum Forge in Thornbury Township, where Glen Mills Train Station now stands. He and his wife, Polly, are buried at the Presbyterian Church in Middletown, Pennsylvania.

Sarum Forge, owned by John Taylor and later by Persifor Frazer, was built in 1739; the forge contributed to the history of the Revolutionary War before the conflict began. It was the first to create and use a rolling mill, which allowed the forge to mass produce iron bars, nails, and other goods better and cheaper. Sarum discovered that by passing steel sheets through large rollers, he could make the iron much denser, producing finished products of a much higher quality. Sarum's process allowed him to mass produce his iron products better and cheaper than any other manufacturer worldwide and evolved into modern-day steel-making processes.

Sarum's pioneering process in the American iron industry, along with the efforts of other American iron masters, led to Great Britain passing the Iron Act of 1750. The Act was contrived to try to reduce the production of iron goods in the colonies because England did not want the colonists to become technologically independent, and they had the foresight to assume that Sarum's process could also mass-produce weapons and munitions. The Act decreed that colonists were no longer authorized to manufacture their products from raw material; everything was to have a 'made in England' stamp fixed to the product. The Act was generally disregarded by Sarum and other colonial iron masters who continued to produce high-quality iron products.

In 1836, Sarum Forge became Glen Mills and was converted into a paper mill. Among other paper products, the mill produced currency and became internationally famous for its anti-counterfeiting measures. In 1878, the mill closed, and a few years later, the buildings were torn down to make way for the present-day Glen Mills Station, built where it stands today.

Marine Corps Tie-In...a Children's Prison in Iraq.

When I shared my manuscript idea with the Sergeant Major of Marines who was my platoon sergeant during OIF-I, he reminded me of an important event our platoon participated in that definitely has its place in this story. On April 8th 2003, the French news service AFP reported that U.S. Marines had liberated a children's prison in Northeast Baghdad. The report said that 100 to 150 children poured out of the unlocked prison gates and swarmed around their Marine liberators. A Marine officer told an AFP embedded reporter that the children looked undernourished and were wearing threadbare clothing. My platoon sergeant during OIF I reminded me that the Marines featured in the report were the warriors of Bravo Company.

Ironically, the children we liberated may have been the lucky ones. During the nineties, international organizations had repeatedly reported on the imprisonment, torture, and execution of children by the Saddam Hussein regime. Children were among the nearly 300,000 people who have "disappeared" in Iraq since the late 1970s. Children had been routinely and repeatedly arrested to force their parents to confess to crimes against the regime. For example, a March Boston Globe story detailed the interrogation of a former Iraqi secret policeman who happened to specialize in torture. The police officer admitted to torturing children as young as five or six to "get their mothers talking." He claimed that Iraqi torturers never killed the children, just "beat them with steel cables." But he was contradicted by a BBC story in which another former regime torturer said, "It was common to kill children if their parents wouldn't talk." The BBC had it right based on what we saw and heard on that forlorn day in Iraq.

Historical places to visit in and near Glen Mills, Pennsylvania.

Pull on your hiking boots because you will need them for this stretch of the Patriot's Path. Begin your adventure at Bonner Park; although parking is limited, it is seldom packed. Start on well-used but rugged paths that take you through the woods and along the creek for about a two-and-a-half-mile loop. Along the way, you will encounter an abandoned bridge, glimpse a view of an old mill that has been converted to a private residence, and see numerous ruins, remnants of the Dyer Quarry that once occupied the wooded land. About halfway into your hike, you will walk into a clearing where you will find the Frazer Farmstead site. Fortifications have been started to preserve the remains of the house, but they still need to be completed, so use caution when exploring the site. Also at the site are ruins of Persifor's barn and a few historical plaques explaining the site and the Frazers' role during the Revolutionary War. When you return to the parking lot, it is enticing to follow the train tracks to your vehicle instead of beating brush but be warned: the tracks are still used for seasonal train excursions.

On your way to Newlin Grist Mill, swing by the Glen Mills Train Station, which used to be the site of Sarum Forge. A historical marker is just around a bend in the road, and the station is occasionally open to visitors. You will find ample parking, restrooms, and a small gift shop at Newlin Forge. Although there is no documentation that Newlin Grist Mill played a role during the Revolutionary War, it existed in the 1770s. Explore the 18th-century mill, houses, and buildings. You can also explore miles of manicured trails that meander along a stream, through fields, and lightly wooded areas. Enjoy a picnic lunch at one of several tables near the parking lot to close out your stroll through history.

Frazer Farmstead and Dyer Quarry (Ruins) are located in Bonner Park. Trailhead is along Lockley Road Glen Mills, Pennsylvania.

Sarum Forge (Glen Mills Train Station) is located at 128 Glen Mills Road Glen Mills, Pennsylvania.

Newlin Grist Mill and Park is located at 219 South Cheyney Road Glen Mills, Pennsylvania.

West Chester, Pennsylvania

"The Marines I have seen around the world have the cleanest bodies, the filthiest minds, the highest morale, and the lowest morals of any group of animals I have ever seen. Thank God for the United States Marine Corps!"

~ Eleanor Roosevelt, the longest-serving first lady of the United States

West Chester was originally known as Turk's Head and was named after the tavern that once bore the same name. During the Revolutionary War, Loyalist Jacob James was the proprietor of the Turk's Head Tavern. He joined the British Army after the Battle of Brandywine and served as a scout and recruited spies from his tavern. James also participated in kidnapping operations and was commissioned a captain of the Goshen Troop of Light Horse which was a local Loyalist unit.

A schoolhouse was located at what is now High and Gay Streets in West Chester, Pennsylvania and served as a hospital for recovering American soldiers after the Battle of Brandywine. Although the building no longer exists, a plaque and historical marker commemorate the school and its small role in achieving American independence. On September 16th 1777, as British columns were marching along present-day High Street in West Chester, Knyphausen's advanced guard was fired on by American scouts, resulting in one British killed and several wounded. Captain Mathews pursued the scouting party up Pottstown Pike (Route 100), and Knyphausen continued marching toward the Goshen Meetinghouse via Old Wilmington Pike. Matthews, failing to locate and engage with the American scouts, ended his pursuit in the vicinity of Indian King Tavern, which once stood at the intersection of Pottstown Pike and Boot Road.

Colonel John Hannum was a militia officer of the 1st Battalion of Chester County Militia during the Revolution. He was a native of Concord township, but when he purchased a large farm in East Bradford, he became a Removalist or an outspoken advocate of splitting Chester County.

During the Revolutionary War, he was one of the Committee of Seventy, appointed at a county meeting held at Chester on December 20th 1774. Colonel Hannum was present with General Wayne during the Battle of Brandywine. That winter, he was captured by British troops one night while asleep in his bed. The troops were led to his house by a Loyalist neighbor.

He was taken into custody and held prisoner in Philadelphia. Hannum also wrote a letter to General Washington describing his rough treatment and had it smuggled out of the prison. Hannum escaped his confinement, but his accomplishment became a subject of discussion from a Board of General Officers who, in 1779, determined Hannum had broken parole.

To George Washington from a Board of General Officers, 28 June 1779

From a Board of General Officers

New Windsor 28th June 1779.

"The Board of General Officers ordered to sit the 25th to decide respecting a number of persons prisoners With the Enemy, who of them have broke their Parole, and who of them are Military Prisoners. Beg leave to Report the following state of their Cases and their Opinion upon them.

Colonel John Hannom was a Militia Colonel in Chester County Pennsylvania; was in actual service and made prisoner by the Enemy on their way from Brandiwine to Philadelphia. He was afterward admitted to a limited parole at the Golden swan in the City: That from an indulgence of walking the street, granted him by Serjeant Serrit without authority, he took the opportunity of a dark night of making his escape. The Board are of opinion that he broke his parole."

Colonel Frazer, also a prisoner in Philadelphia, wrote a letter to Washington detailing prisoner treatment and specifically named the Golden Swan".

On March 22nd 1784 the Pennsylvania General Assembly authorized Colonel John Hannum, Isaac Taylor, and John Jacobs to build a new courthouse and prison for Chester County and sell the old courthouse in Chester. Work began on a new courthouse in Turk's Head during the summer of 1784. Cheyney's friend, Major John Harper, who became a Chester tavern keeper after the war, was unhappy with the splitting of Delaware County from Chester County, so he led a militia force with the intent of destroying the unfinished courthouse at West Chester in 1785.

Harper and the non-removalists spent the night at the General Greene Tavern, appeared near the Turk's Head early in the morning and took up an assault position about two hundred yards southeast of the present Quaker meetinghouse. They placed a cannon near the meetinghouse and prepared for the attack. Although they were formed and ready, they appeared reluctant to proceed. After having remained several hours in the assault position, a truce was negotiated between the parties by the intervention of some pacifist locals, who used their influence to prevent the attack. The non-removalists were offered an opportunity to inspect the defenses that had been prepared by the Removalists, on condition that they would not attack them. The Non-Removalists then agreed to abandon their plan and to return peaceably to their homes.

The cannon, which had initially been aimed at the unfinished walls, was turned in another direction, and fired in celebration of the truce. Colonel Hannum ordered his men to leave the courthouse, stack their firearms and wait until the non-removalists finished their visit.   .

During the visit, rashness nearly caused a renewal of hostilities when one of Harper's men entered the fort and pulled down a Removalist flag displayed on a wall. Enraged at this treatment of their standard, the removalists rushed to their weapons and were, with difficulty, prevented from firing upon the major and his cohorts. Efforts on the part of the leaders on both sides of the conflict calmed the infuriated men, and the parties eventually separated quietly without loss of life or limb.

Hannum changed the name of the town of Turk's Head to West Chester and began selling lots along Gay Street. By 1795, he had mapped out the original streets, which are Church, High, Gay, Market, Chestnut, and Walnut. On March 28th 1799, West Chester was incorporated as a borough from Goshen Township by an act of state legislature. Colonel John Hannum's home still stands along the Downingtown Pike at 898 Frank Road as a private residence. Hannum died in 1779 and was buried at the Bradford Friends Burying Ground in Marshallton, Pennsylvania.

Colonel Thomas Taylor was a commander of a battalion of Chester County militia and trained them on his Westtown farm. He and some of his men were disowned by the Quakers for fighting against the British, primarily during the Battle of Brandywine. Since Taylor was disowned by the Quakers, he was not allowed to be buried at the meetinghouse with his loved ones. Taylor established his own family burial ground on his farm, and it is rumored that hundreds of soldiers who died at Brandywine are interred at the site, although only Taylor and four others are named in historical documents.

A memorial marker was placed in a small roadside meadow in 2023 to honor the five soldiers named and the unnamed hundreds of other patriots, but it does not mark the exact location of the burial site. A memorial erected earlier in 2001 by the Taylor family is likely closer to the burial ground; it is located on the fringe of a housing development, and easily accessible. The burial ground was once surrounded by a stone wall and gate, but it fell to ruin by the late 19th century. By 1905, only a few stones were visible. According to a late local resident of over 70 years, the markers from the graveyard were removed during the 1920s or 1930s and used as steps for an old house built nearby. That house was demolished after 1980; only one of those headstones was saved by a West Chester University professor who studied the site.

Another American patriot who lived near West Chester was General William Harris. Harris enlisted in Colonel Bull's Flying Camp at the age of 18, about the time the Revolutionary War broke out. He worked his way through the ranks and was commissioned a lieutenant by 1777. His militia regiment eventually became the Thirteenth Regiment of the Pennsylvania Line, which saw combat action in the battles of Brandywine, The Clouds, and Germantown. He also fought at Paoli and several other minor skirmishes that took place after the Battle of Germantown. He remained with the Continental Army, although where he fought if he continued to fight after the war moved south, is ambiguous. He must have stayed in the area or returned to Pennsylvania toward the end of the war because he aided in the capture of the Loyalist Joseph Doane, a highwayman who robbed a treasury in Bucks County with his sons.

Harris continued to serve in the local militia after the war and participated as a captain in the Whiskey Rebellion. In 1811, he received a commission as a Brigadier General. When the War of 1812 broke out, Governor Snyder called his unit into service, but he died before the unit saw action.

His son, Colonel John Harris, served in the United States Marine Corps for 45 years before being appointed the 6th Commandant of the Marine Corps, his service spanning the War of 1812, the Indian

Wars, and the American Civil War. At the age of 66, Harris is the oldest officer to be appointed Commandant of the Marine Corps. Just before the beginning of the Civil War, half of the officers in the Marine Corps had resigned their commissions to fight for the Confederacy, including Lieutenant Israel Greene, who led a contingent of Leathernecks from Marine Barracks Eighth and Eye to put down John Brown's rebellion at Harper's Ferry in 1859. Harris was one of three consecutive Commandants of the Marine Corps hailing from Pennsylvania and was followed in office by 7th CMC, General Zeilin, who approved the EGA insignia, and 8th CMC, General McCawley, who approved Semper Fidelis as the official Motto of the Marine Corps.

I want to thank a friend and WCASD Campus Safety Officer colleague who has been filling in local historical gaps such as the Taylor monuments, for me ever since I shared my vision for this manuscript with him; he is much esteemed in the community and his many and continued years of service to the citizens of West Chester is indelibly valued and much appreciated.

Marine Corps Tie-In…Riding the Rocket.

The days of sudden peace after weeks of sustained combat operations were a little challenging to adapt to after the smoke cleared around the Al-Azimiyah Palace in northeast Baghdad. Our days became longer as we waited on mail, care packages, chow, frag-o's or conducted rather routine mop-up patrols in our sector. During one of 1/5's mop-up patrols, a tractor-trailer loaded with frog-7 missiles and a mobile missile launcher were found in the city.

The FROG-7 missile has a range of 70 kilometers and is typically equipped with a 550-kilogram warhead, giving it a casualty radius of approximately 2.8 km by 1.8 km, although the missile is capable of delivering conventional, nuclear, or chemical warheads. A Marine was able to hot wire and drive the tractor-trailer to our palace compound within our battalion's assigned sector. The trailer with the rockets was parked in the immediate vicinity of Bravo Company's bivouac area.

Marines are sometimes at their stupidest when they try to be funny especially when boredom sets in. When I think of a typical young modern Marine, I tend to compare most of them to Roman legionaries of old. They proudly march under scarlet and gold standards, with the sign of the eagle ever-present. They are notorious for crude drawings on anything that presents itself as a canvas for their art. It was common to come across perversely defaced portraits of Saddam or palace walls decorated with course graffiti after Marines grew tired of exploring the palace compound in search of spoils of war. One of the more common methods of defacement was to relieve oneself in the palace, usually on the ornate but tacky furniture, statues, or portraits of Saddam. After the Frogg-7's were secured inside the palace they received the same treatment by the Marines.

Along with the strange practice of defecating on artwork and weapons of mass destruction was the bizarre practice of posing with the rockets in odd positions. As Marines were messing around with the rockets, I was keenly reminded of a scene in the movie Armageddon when Steve Buscemi's deranged character is literally straddling a nuclear delivery system on an asteroid in the face of his assumed demise, riding it like a bronc-breaker when another movie character very tersely orders him to "get off the nuclear warhead."

One afternoon, a Nuclear, Biological, and Chemical (NBC) team showed up at our bivouac area, sealed in large, high-speed contamination suits, to examine the content of the warheads with Geiger counters and other detection equipment. For years, I regretted peeing on those rockets, not knowing if I inadvertently contaminated myself with some unknown nuclear, chemical, or biological agent. It wasn't until I recently read an account of the rockets 20 years after the event that I learned the delivery tanks on the rockets were empty.

Historical Sites to visit in and near West Chester, Pennsylvania.

Take a morning trip into West Chester before the town wakes and park along Gay Street just past High Street. Along the sidewalk, you will find a historical marker and brass plaque marking the site of the old schoolhouse that was used as a hospital after the Brandywine battle. Walk around the corner and along High Street to the Courthouse, where you will find more historical signs and plaques, including the 10 Commandments. The Old Glory Memorial stands just outside the Courthouse, and an 18th Century equestrian watering fountain sits along the street. Cross High Street, look left on the building that used to be The Turks Head Tavern and read the two bronze plaques that tells its story. Visit the Chester County Historical Society and see the original Turks Head Tavern sign and other local historical exhibits. If you are into Lafayette, a historical marker commemorating his visit to the town years after the Revolutionary War stands just outside a local park. A small white marble slab marks the spot where Lafayette stood to view a parade in his honor, but it is obscure and easy to miss.

Just outside town, along Pottstown Pike, is the Oakland Cemetery, where you will find the graves of several Pennsylvania Patriots, including Marine Corps General Smedley Butler, recipient of two Congressional Medals of Honor. Round out your trip driving by Colonel John Hannum's House, now a private residence called Tulip Hill Farms.

If you are into 18th Century homes and buildings, consider visiting the Taylor-Cope Historic District in West Whiteland Township, it comprises of 15 well-preserved contributing buildings constructed between 1724 and 1906. You can also take a driving tour of the Paradise Valley Historic District in East Bradford Township with its 25 contributing 18th Century homes and buildings. Some of these stone structures include a stone bridge, two mill races, and a small family graveyard. Some of the historic properties include the William Mercer Farm, Samuel Starr Farm, Enoch Pearson Farm, George Jefferis Farm, Thomas Price Farm, Spackman's Mill, and Hannum Mill.

Period Schoolhouse used as a Field Hospital was located at Gay and High Streets West Chester, Pennsylvania.

Chester County Courthouse is located at 2 North High Street at Market Street West Chester, Pennsylvania.

Old Glory Memorial is located at West Market Street and North High Street West Chester, Pennsylvania.

The Sign of the Turk Tavern Marker is located along East Market Street West Chester, Pennsylvania.

Lafayette's Parade #1 is located at East Lafayette Street and Clover Alley West Chester, Pennsylvania.

Lafayette's Parade #2 is located along Matlack Street West Chester, Pennsylvania.

Camp Wayne is located at West Rosedale Avenue west of South Church Street West Chester, Pennsylvania.

Oakland Friends Burial Grounds is located at 1041 Pottstown Pike East Bradford, Pennsylvania.

Colonel John Hannum House is located at House 898 Frank Road East Bradford, Pennsylvania.

The Taylor Burial Ground Monument is located at 1147 South Concord Road West Chester, Pennsylvania.

The Taylor Burial Ground Marker is located in the vicinity of 1135 Cockburn Drive West Chester, Pennsylvania.

Downingtown, Pennsylvania

"I want to go where the guns are"!

General Lewis Chesty Puller, The Most Decorated Marine in the Corps.

The village of Downingtown was first called Milltown because of the mills that were built on the edge of the unsettled western frontier in the 18th Century. Thomas Moore built a water corn mill in 1716, and Roger Hunt established a gristmill in 1739. In 1761, John Downing opened a tavern on the east side of Brandywine Creek called the Downing Mill Inn; his father Thomas, developed an industrial complex of mills on Lancaster Road in Milltown.

Milltown was changed to Downingtown around the beginning of the Revolutionary War to honor one of its leading citizens and a prominent businessmen, Mr. Thomas Downing. In the 1970s, the town celebrated its Revolutionary War roots with a day of re-enactments and festivities. At least one local historian refused to participate because he contended that there was no actual fighting in or around Downingtown. The disgruntled historian was correct; there is no evidence that British troops were ever in Downingtown. As to Downingtown and its ties to the war, however, there are several. The mills in and around the town produced goods the Army relied on for sustainment, and magazines located in the town were used to store these provisions. The town even saw its share of soldiers when the Pennsylvania Militia was ordered to muster in Downingtown before the Battle of Brandywine.

The morning after the Paoli massacre, Maryland's General Smallwood was busy in the vicinity of Downingtown trying to gather the remnants of his roughly 1000-man army that had deserted. His troops had bolted from Paoli and scattered across the Pennsylvania backcountry as fast as they could run without even encountering the enemy the night prior. General Smallwood wrote, "The Field Officers in general behaved firm and well and many of the captains and lieutenants; but there are others of the latter two classes who have not been heard of since and who I believe set the first example of flying."

General Wayne sent Captain Thomas Buchanan of the First Pennsylvania Regiment to the Whitehorse Tavern to try to find Smallwood on the night of the massacre. He wrote of the spectacle that unfolded before him that night, "I was sent forward by Wayne to Smallwood, that lay at the Whitehorse to get him to cover our retreat and fix a place of rendezvous. He sent me forward to try to stop as many of his broken troops that had taken the road to Downingtown. On coming near to there, I found where some of his artillery had thrown a field piece into a limekiln and had broken the carriage. I went on to Downingtown and fixed a guard on the road to stop the runaways; got a wheeler and blacksmith to mend the carriage and went down and put the cannon on the carriage."

The name and location of the lime kiln where Captain Buchanan recovered the cannon has not surfaced in primary sources to my knowledge, but given the rough location provided by Buchanan, I believe it was probably ditched then later recovered from a limekiln established just east of Downingtown in the vicinity of the Wee Grimmet House. In the early 1800s, the house served as a tenant house for people who worked in the limestone quarry about a quarter mile south of the house along the 30 bypasses. The remnants of a small lime kiln lay in the woods just south of the Lancaster Pike.

The original Sign of the Ship Inn was located a mile west of Downingtown and was operated by Thomas Park, another British Loyalist. Just after the Battle of Brandywine, several patriot soldiers came by the inn for a drink, but Park refused to serve them. Angered, the soldiers fired thirteen shots into the signboard of the inn, cursing the inn as they left. The story soon made its way around the countryside, and Park's patronage soon fell off, and he was forced to close his business.

After the massacre at Paoli, American casualties were taken to the Sign of the Ship tavern to have their wounds treated. One of these wounded soldiers was 21-year-old Private James Reed of the 10th Pennsylvania. He joined Colonel Bull's flying Camp in 1776 and served five months before being taken prisoner at Fort Washington, New York, and held in a prison hulk for 13 weeks until he was paroled. In violation of his parole, he enlisted in the Continental Army at the risk of death if he were captured and recognized. He, like many others at Paoli, was put to the bayonet, suffered numerous wounds, and was left on the field for dead. He never fully recovered from his wounds and so was unable to rejoin the army. The wounded were eventually evacuated to Lancaster hospitals, one of which was located at the Ephrata Cloister, and those who did not recover from their wounds were buried in the cloister cemetery.

In 1796, John Bowen bought the signboard and hung it at his new tavern in Exton, where his wife Susie helped him establish the new Sign of the Ship Inn. Many years later in 2021, The Ship Inn at Exton was featured on a July episode of the Food Network's *Restaurant: Impossible*, and the historical inn was treated to multifaceted overhaul by celebrity chef Robert Irvine, who now sponsors First Battalion Fifth Marines' annual OIF reunion in Camp Pendleton.. Unfortunately, the intervention failed, and the inn fell under new management a couple of years later with a different name and new sign (VK Brewing) for the first time since its revolutionary days. I contacted the new owners and asked if I could look at the old sign; unfortunately, the sign went with the previous owner.

Another important Downingtown inn was built in 1761 along Lancaster Avenue. The General Washington Inn was known as the "King of Arms" or "King George" before the Revolutionary War. The inn was a Stage Stand in the 18th Century and was considered a first-class establishment. It provided bedrooms, washrooms, and the best dining facilities along the road. A Stage Stand was often named for a prominent hero and sometimes indicated the feelings of the people at the time. During the Revolutionary War, the 'King George' in Downingtown became the 'George Washington' simply by painting the red coat blue and converting the 'Crown' into an 'Eagle.'

Known in some historical circles as the original fighting Quaker, Richard Thomas of Downingtown was elected a colonel of the 5th Battalion of Associators on April 19th 1776. Consequently, he was disowned from Uwchlan's Friends Meeting for accepting the commission. Whenever a Quaker disowned one of its congregants, it was similar to the present-day Amish tradition of excommunication. The church disowned the abolished member, who could have no further affiliation with its congregants. This form of banishment included burial in the church cemetery along with their loved ones. Thomas, who survived the war and became a US senator, died in 1832, was denied interment in Uwchlan's Friends burial grounds, and was consequently buried in a Philadelphia cemetery. Ironically, the meetinghouse was eventually used as a hospital, and several soldiers who died from wounds or disease are buried somewhere within its cemetery walls.

My favorite local Downingtown story is about Richard's wife, Thomazine, who was also Thomas Downing's daughter. An unforeseen consequence of Thomazine's marriage to an American officer would be an unwelcome visit by British troops because her husband was one of the American officers sought by the British after the Battle of Brandywine.

Sometime in mid-September, British troops visited Thomas's home looking for the Colonel but, not finding him, began to plunder the farm. They then turned to Thomazine to try to squeeze the Colonel's whereabouts from her. Thomazine was not talking, so the troops decided the thing to do would be to hang Thomazine by the neck from wooden pegs driven into the kitchen wall until she 'spilled the beans'. Thomazine was described as a somewhat portly lady and, at the time of the incident, very pregnant, which must have made the British game harder to play. Fortunately for Thomazine and her unborn child, none of the pegs would hold their combined weight. The frustrated troops departed the residence, either tired out from the effort or concerned they might soon be discovered. Had they been more persistent, they would have found the next peg was made of iron and firmly anchored in the stone wall, which would have probably resulted in the demise of Thomazine and her child.

A small stone building banked into a slope near Valley Creek and known locally as the Woodcutter's Cottage is all that remains from the so-called Thomas mansion tract. The homestead was acquired in 1843 by a grandson, Richard Ashbridge, who built a large colonial mansion with the same floorplan as the old farmhouse that stood for a long time on the property; the new house, however, was much more extravagant. This house is still known today as the Richard Ashbridge House. It has recently been restored as a community building for the Ashbridge Preserve apartment complex located just across the street from the Exton Walmart. Whitford Lodge, Whitford Hall, and the Ivy Cottage are all local historical homes also attributed to Richard's building efforts after the war.

Yet another story centers around the Thomas family's mill located at 130 West Lincoln Highway, where, according to family tradition, the Colonel's brother George, although a pacifist, supported the American cause in his unique way. George, much like his neighbors, was also an object of British plundering during 1777. While managing the family grist mill in the absence of Richard, George produced a special blend of flour intended only for enemy use. This flour may have 'accidentally' contained ground glass. During and after the Revolutionary War, George's focus centered almost exclusively on his Oaklands farm; his innovations in agriculture earned him a high degree of respect within the region. In addition to managing one of the largest farms in the Great Valley, George pioneered the introduction of lime as a soil supplement in 1787.

Although mills in Downingtown were common in the 18th Century, the Roger Hunt Mill is the only one I know that survives within city limits. The Roger Hunt mill was built in 1759 and was one of the first mills established in the area. The building is a two-story stone structure with a gambrel roof and a one-story frame addition. The main house, built in 1740, now a row of condos, stood just across the street from the mill complex. The house was a two-story, five-bay stone structure with Georgian design details. In 1865, the grist mill became a plaster mill and then a feed mill in 1900 until it closed for good around 1930. Sometime after the 1930's, the roof collapsed, causing the walls to fall in, but stabilization efforts have slowed down further determination of the structure.

Dowling Forge was operated from 1785 to 1881 and was once a thriving part of Chester County's iron industry. A successful iron forge needed iron ore, limestone to use in the purification process, wood to make charcoal, and a water source to provide power. The Dowlin Forge site had all four. The creek was dammed to provide power, and the large logs that formed the dam's base are still visible in the creek. The process began when impure iron from local furnaces was hauled to Dowlin Forge. The metal was heated with lime flux, called a bloom, and reworked into bars of iron with two giant hammers driven by a water wheel. The pounding hammers beat out impurities in the iron; the resulting iron was then sold to rolling mills.

At one point, the forge was leased to Lukens Steel of Coatesville, Pennsylvania. Iron was prepared at the forge, then packed in sand to keep warm and hauled on carts in eight-mule teams to Lukens Steel. Metal plate on the USS Monitor, a famous Civil War ironclad battleship, was built from iron prepared at the forge. Chunks of pig iron, another name for the crude iron and the slag, or the forge's waste product, are abundant at the ruins. A walk along the Struble Trail will take you past the ruins and signs describing the site.

Marine Corps Tie-In…recovering a 50 cal. Barrel.

After shifting to post-war operations in our assigned sector of Baghdad, we received a fragmentation order (frag-o) to patrol near the Abu Hanifa Mosque. During Alpha Company's push toward the Al-Azimiyah Palace on that intensely embattled night, Alpha Company lost an AAV to a mobility kill, and the Marine Corps lost a real American hero: a very professional, dedicated, and much-loved company gunnery sergeant who was killed while courageously directing fire at enemy positions. In 2016, during NASCAR's Salute to Heroes-themed Coca-Cola 600 race, the gunny's name was featured on the race-winning cup car. That driver went on to win the NASCAR championship the following year.

My squad was tasked with locating the disabled AAV and recovering any crew-served weapon components, radios, and other sensitive equipment that might not have been destroyed. Specifically, we were looking for a spare 50. Caliber barrel that, for some reason, was missing.

We patrolled a little over half a mile northeast to the mosque and came upon a truly war-torn scene. The ancient mosque and the buildings around it had sustained quite a bit of collateral damage. On a narrow side street in the vicinity of the mosque, we found the disabled AAV, a burned-out hull wedged between a couple of buildings. A hasty search of the AAV netted us nothing; no crew-served weapon components or sensitive equipment remained except the remains of a radio suite the vehicle commander destroyed with a thermite grenade before quickly abandoning the vehicle in the midst of the firefight.

We conducted a hasty search of the buildings within a block or so of the AAV. We were about to return to the palace empty-handed when one of my Marines, a salty 2nd or 3rd award yet proficient and dependable private first class, happened to look up into the rafters of a building to discover a 50. Caliber barrel wedged between the steel sheeting and wooden frame.

Although we returned to the palace having accomplished our mission, we were starkly reminded of the high cost and sacrifice of our success in Iraq. The gunny was one of two Marines from our battalion killed in action during OIF I.

Years later, at the Philadelphia Union League, I had the rare opportunity and honor of personally meeting the general who had commanded the First Marine Division during OIF I. Remarkably, as we briefly reminisced our time together in Iraq, the general, whose call sign was 'Chaos', recalled the exact number of 1st Battalion Fifth Marine warriors who were killed and wounded during the 'Push to Baghdad'.

Before departing for Kuwait, 'Chaos' famously issued his Blue Diamond letter to the NCOs of 1/5 at the Fifth Marines Grinder in Camp San Mateo. I placed my letter between my front Sappi plate and flak and only removed it when I returned to the States. Years later, I was tasked to escort some of my Villanova Marine option midshipmen to the Union League to hear the general speak; I pulled my Blue Diamond letter out of its frame and brought it along. After exchanging war stories with the general for a minute or so, I gave a Villanova NROTC Unit coin to the general. While I expected a coin in return from the general, then commander of the United States Central Command (CENTCOM), the exchange didn't happen because his aide had no coins on hand. The general smiled when I asked him if he would autograph my Blue Diamond letter. He was probably a little amazed I even kept it. The letter is one of my most prized military keepsakes and reads in the general's hand, "Gunny, thank you for your combat leadership."

Historical places to visit in or near Downingtown, Pennsylvania.

For this portion of the Patriot's Path, I like to bookend the historical sites between Bondsville Mill Park and the Dowlin Forge ruins which are located along the Struble trail in Downingtown. Bondsville Mill Park is an ongoing restoration project to preserve the historical significance of the mill. A grist mill was originally established at the site in the early 1700s and transitioned into a wool mill in the early 1800s. The wool mill produced jeans and during the Civil War, uniforms for the Union Army. The wool mill also produced fabric for Air Force jackets during World War II but eventually closed sometime after the war. There are paths that meander around the old buildings, mill races and a water tower. There are also butterfly gardens to explore and a soldier's monument to check out. The buildings are currently not accessible, but you can get a glimpse of some of the old machinery through windows and holes in the walls.

Drive toward Downingtown and swing by the Roger Hunt Mill ruins. Although the buildings are in a state of ruin, the site can be visited, and by walking its grounds, one can see the mill ruins, a large industrial scale, the mill traces, and much of the equipment used in various milling processes through the years. Next, visit the many historical homes that are situated on either side of Lancaster Avenue from the George Washington Inn to the Sign of the Ship Inn (now VK Brewery). To my knowledge, the George Washington Inn, Wee Gimmet House, Whitford Lodge, Ivy Cottage and Whitford Hall are now private property.

The Ashbridge House and Historical Society can be visited. I recommend grabbing a Chick-fil-a meal while you are taking in the building's rich heritage. The Ashbridge House in Exton has been restored but has become a recreation building for the residents of the apartment community. You can walk around the house and the outbuildings that used to belong to the Ashbridge estate but like the house, businesses now occupy the 18th Century structures.

The last leg of your historical experience should be a casual stroll along the Struble and Uwchlan Trails. Along the Struble Trail, look for the old Dowlin Forge and the Dowlin mill ruins, dam, and mill traces as you cross a footbridge onto the Uwchlan Trail.

Bondsville Mill Park is located at 1647 Bondsville Road Downingtown, Pennsylvania.

Roger Hunt Mill is located at 101 Race Street Downingtown, Pennsylvania.

Downingtown Log Cabin is located at One Park Lane Downingtown, Pennsylvania.

The George Washington Inn is located at West Uwchlan Avenue and East Lancaster Avenue Downingtown, Pennsylvania.

The Ashbridge House and Downingtown Historical Society is located at 849 East Lancaster Avenue Downingtown, Pennsylvania.

Wee Gimmet House is located at 628 West Lancaster Avenue Downingtown, Pennsylvania.

Whitford Lodge is located at 229 West Lancaster Avenue Downingtown, Pennsylvania.

Ivy Cottage is located at 225 West Lancaster Avenue Downingtown, Pennsylvania.

Thomas Mill and Mill House is located at 200 West Lancaster Avenue Downingtown, Pennsylvania.

Whitford Hall is located at 145 West Lancaster Avenue Downingtown, Pennsylvania.

Ashbridge House is located at 210 Main Street Exton, Pennsylvania.

The Zook House is located at 100 Exton Square Exton, Pennsylvania.

Sign of the Ship Inn is located at Ship Road and route East Lancaster Avenue Exton, Pennsylvania.

Dowlin Forge Ruins is located at Dowling Forge Road and Struble Trail intersection Downingtown, Pennsylvania.

Aston, Pennsylvania

"How lucky I am to have something that makes saying goodbye so hard."

~A.A. Milne, World War I & II Veteran and author of Winnie-the-Pooh.

Aston Township, originally called Northley, was one of the first townships in Pennsylvania and was first settled in 1682. Edward Carter, an early township constable, changed the name from Northley to Aston in honor of his old home of Aston in Oxfordshire, England.

The first time I heard of Aston Township, Pennsylvania, I was a young Staff NCO stationed at Camp Lejeune, NC. I came across a profile called UNCBlue on a Christian dating site. After a few visits to Aston Township, where UNCBlue was from, I married her. She is the mother of our two beautiful daughters. Her father bears the Dutton name, a name as popular in the township now as it was in ancient England.

My wife grew up in a home at the intersection of PA-452 and Meetinghouse Road. The house and property now belong to a Royal Farms convenience store, which is fitting since the property was originally part of the family farm my father-in-law grew up on before it was subdivided. Just down the road from where my wife grew up is the Chichester Meetinghouse, the namesake for the road it still sits along.

The meetinghouse, built in 1688 and rebuilt after a fire in 1769, is a great surviving example of early Quaker heritage. Interestingly, building Quaker meetinghouses in England was illegal until the Act of Toleration of 1689. Because meetinghouses were built in this area of Pennsylvania at an earlier date, and because the 1769 meetinghouse is believed to reflect the style of the earlier meetinghouse, the Chichester Meetinghouse is believed to be an example of early

"English" Quaker architecture. A caretaker's house was built in 1703, and in 1783, a two-story barn with a six-bay shed was added. Both buildings are still in use.

History diverges a bit as to why musket balls scar the doors of the Chichester meetinghouse. One prevailing story is that the doors, which still have visible bullet scars, were from minor skirmishes when locals attempted to defend their property from being plundered by Cornwallis' men who were camped nearby. Another story speculates that British Soldiers shot into the door for target practice.

Unfortunately, a few historical intricacies challenge both theories. Ammunition was valuable during the Revolutionary War; wasting it on target practice with notoriously inaccurate muskets wasn't encouraged by either Army. A minor skirmish between locals and British soldiers on pillaging expeditions is more plausible, but the theory still has challenges. Although British soldiers had permission to forage for items it needed for sustenance, they were expressly forbidden to pillage or rob noncombatants. Although pillaging still happened to noncombatants, the prohibition against it reduced the number of times it occurred. Most of the township's inhabitants were Quakers, which meant they tried to remain neutral in the conflict; the British did not want to alienate the population by mistreating them or, worse, encourage them to become patriotic and support the American cause by making them angry and vengeful.

With his land grant in 1681, William Penn became the 'sole' proprietor of the lands he called Sylvania (wooded land). Penn's Woods eventually became Pennsylvania when the King added the Penn prefix to honor Sir William Penn, the proprietor's father. Penn Jr. had helped establish the colony of New Jersey, but his focus was on setting up his 'Holy Experiment' in religious and political freedom, exactly as he saw fit, in Pennsylvania. He advertised for settlers, many of whom were being persecuted for their religious beliefs in Europe, pitching the idea that Pennsylvania would be democratic, tolerant of all religions, and a place where people from all walks of life would be welcome. His sales pitch worked, and in 1682, twenty-three ships sailed up the Delaware, carrying about 2000 settlers on them. They came from all over Britain, particularly Wales, Yorkshire and the Midlands. Many German Mennonites came, too, thanks to Penn's visit to the Rhineland in 1677. A wave of Irish Quaker settlers arrived in the following years, thanks to William Edmundson's missionary work in that country.

The second generation of Quakers was invariably different from the pioneers who had fled persecution. Quakerism was the dominant religion, and they were comfortable in their peaceful, pacifist lives and Quaker routines. Some eventually mixed with non-Quakers and adopted some of their ways. Because of this, several left or were forced to leave the church when they married non-Quakers. By the mid-18th century, members of the Religious Society of Friends lived throughout the thirteen British colonies in North America, but the largest numbers were concentrated in Pennsylvania.

The American Revolution created an awkward situation for many of these Friends, informally known as "Quakers," as their nonviolent religious tenets often conflicted with the emerging political and nationalistic ideals of their new homeland. Early in the conflict's history, Quakers participated in the revolutionary movement through nonviolent actions such as embargoes and other economic protests. However, the outbreak of war created an ideological divide among the group. Most Quakers remained true to their pacifist beliefs. They refused to support any military actions, but a sizable number of Quakers actively participated in the conflict in some form and dealt with the repercussions of doing so.

On the night of September 11th after the Battle of Brandywine, Washington retreated to the town of Chester to gather his Army and regroup. The next day, Washington, still endeavoring to defend Philadelphia, marched his Army east of the Schuylkill River, the last natural barrier between Howe's forces and Philadelphia, instead of occupying the city. The Continental Army marched from Chester through Darby and crossed a floating bridge at the middle ferry, which was located in the vicinity of present-day Market Street Bridge; no permanent bridge spanned the Schuylkill in 1777. The bridge was called the floating bridge because it was precisely that. Imagine crossing the Schuylkill River over rickety planks on unstable, floating pontoons. It reminds me of some of the bridges some Marines used to cross over Iraqi canals in OIF. I was happy, on those occasions, to be crammed into over-packed Amphibious Assault Vehicles due to breakdowns and bump plans because those vehicles could forego chancing unstable bridges and ford water obstacles instead. After the army crossed the Schuylkill, they moved toward East Falls and camped about five miles from Germantown while Washington established a hasty headquarters in the home of Henry Hill on the outskirts of the village.

On September 13th Cornwallis was sent to pursue the remnants of Washington's Army. At 4 PM, he and his staff reached Village Green, where they drew rein before the side porch of 'The Stars'. James Fennell, the landlord, despite his Patriotic bias, hid his disappointment with a smile and watched the unusual scene unfold at his doorstep. Cornwallis naturally was the center of attention. He sat his horse with precise military bearing; his uniform, impeccable and rich, consisted of a voluptuous scarlet coat loaded with gold lace and decorations, his white sheepskin britches, high black boots, and his superior horsemanship all combined to give anyone who saw him a memorable example of the regality of a professional British soldier. Cornwallis established an encampment between Mount Hope and Village Green in Aston Township and used the Seven Stars Tavern as his headquarters.

For the next several days, Cornwallis remained at the Stars while his army searched for remnants of the American Army, rested, foraged, and prepared for the next fight. On September 15th Howe received intelligence that Washington had re-crossed the Schuylkill River and was moving west along the Old Lancaster Road. He rode to the Stars to meet with his subordinate General officers and plan the next phase of his campaign based on the intelligence report.

On Sept 16th Cornwallis broke camp and moved his column north on Chester Road towards a rendezvous with Howe and his Crown forces at the Goshen Meeting House, located at the intersection of Paoli Pike and Chester Road. But before the march, some unpleasant business had to be conducted.

Remember when, after the British landing at the Elk, Howe had problems controlling the looting, pillaging, rape, or worse atrocities that some British and particularly the Hessians were likely committing against noncombatants? Howe, in response, issued a standing order that such activity would result in prompt prosecution and subsequent execution of the accused if found guilty.

Unfortunately, there are no accounts of British officers actually carrying out the capital punishment Howe had ordered for convicted offenders of his order until a pillaging incident was reported in Aston.

According to eyewitness accounts and corroborating evidence, three soldiers who had been members of a party of foragers strayed away from the main body and, crossing Chester Creek above Dutton's mill, entered Jonathan Martin's home and plundered the family of valuables. Among the items were some personal trinkets belonging to his daughter, Mary Martin. Mary, who was 18 years old at the time, boldly chastised the men for their dishonest and cowardly acts. One of the soldiers became enraged at the girl and struck her with his bayonet, inflicting a slight wound on her hand when she attempted to ward off the blow.

The same evening, the three soldiers went to the residence of Mr. Cox, about a mile distant, where they committed similar acts of pillage, including the theft of a distinctive silver watch. Miss Cox was about the same age as Miss Martin, and early next morning, the two girls visited the British headquarters, where they had an interview with General Howe, who had just arrived that morning from his camp at Dilworthtown.

It also chanced that the troops encamped at Village Green were mustered for inspection that morning. Howe told the young women that if they could recognize the men guilty of the theft, they should be punished as prescribed in his general order. The British commander-in-chief, with the girls at his side, walked in front of the entire length of each line of soldiers, and the women pointed out three men they identified as the culprits. To ensure the girls made no mistake in identity, the officers were instructed to march the troops by a given point, and again, the girls selected the same men. A third trial resulted in their recognition of the three culprits out of the three or four thousand soldiers assembled, and Howe ordered the men searched. After some of the stolen articles were found in their possessions, they were immediately tried by court-martial. As the evidence was direct and uncontradicted, they were found guilty and sentenced to death.

Only two of the three were hanged; the third was required to act as executioner for his companions. The one selected to do service as 'Jack Ketch,' an old English term generally used for executioner, was determined by drawing straws. That evening after General Howe and his escort of dragoons returned to Dillsworthtown, the sentence of the courts-martial was carried out. An apple tree near the roadside was used for the gallows, and the men were executed in full sight of the officers who stood on the porch of the tavern watching the ghastly sight.

Interestingly, several historical accounts identified the soldiers as Hessian, which would make the most sense since the German troops would have had the most motivation for looting. However, written testimony by British officers witnessing the event and an entry recorded in an Orderly Book that Captain Thomas Armstrong of the 64th Regiment's Light Infantry maintained, correctly identified the guilty members. According to the Orderly Book, "Willim Mirret, a Grenadier assigned to the First Grenadiers and William Harrison of the First Battalion of Light Infantry are this day to be executed a 11 o clock in front of the Grenadiers encampment for plundering in disobedience to General Howe's orders."

An excerpt from the diary of Captain-Lieutenant John Peebles of the Royal Highland Regiment's Grenadier Company also correctly identified the culprits. "A light infantryman of the 5th regiment and grenadier from the 28th regiment were executed at 11 o clock...for marauding, the first examples made though often threatened, and many deserved."

Thomas Dutton, a local who was over a hundred years old and sometimes called Thomas the Centurion, once told the story that on the evening of September 13th British troops under Cornwallis made camp at Village Green in Aston Township. Thomas, then a child, was afraid the soldiers would kill his mother's cows, which were in a pasture close to the bivouac area for the British troops. Thomas, not ten years of age at the time, marched resolutely to the camp and drove the cows home. An officer noticed the boy's action and, probably thinking that where those cows were going, a good time could be had, ordered four soldiers to follow while he walked with young Dutton to his home. The child answered every question the officer asked him, and when the two reached the Dutton home, the soldiers waited outside to guard against the capture of their commander, who had entered the house with the boy.

The widow Dutton was considerably agitated, but the officer assured her that the soldiers did not come to rob the people, but advised her that as long as the troops were in the neighborhood, to bolt and bar every door and window, "in case camp-followers, under the ruse of lighting a pipe, getting a drink of water, or other calculated distraction, would attempt to get into the house and plunder it ." The British officer, a gentleman who had lost one of his hands during a battle at Flanders' Fields, paid for his meals then quietly returned to camp. The timely warning, in all probability, saved the widow from losing some of her property.

Marine Corps Tie In...a Blessed Wedding.

In the spring of 2008, while assigned to a Marine unit in North Carolina, I was managing my account on an online dating service called Christian Mingle when I came across a possible match that immediately caught my eye. The girl's username was UNCblue, and she lived in Aston Township, Pennsylvania. After a few online chats, I discovered that UNCblue had many admirable and very attractive traits; she was a physical education teacher who loved Jesus, otters, and the FBI. She is descended from a long line of English gentry, and she is absolutely beautiful.

Online chats led to an eventual 3- or 4-hour phone call with the girl; she had my undivided attention from the beginning of that mesmerizing night. I grew up in the backcountry of central Pennsylvania, where it is common to see the Amish and their traditional and old-fashioned way of life. I discovered that the girl's hometown of Chichester was a bright and bustling Philadelphia suburb, completely opposite of my quiet hometown in the mountains. Plans were eventually made to meet in person over Memorial Day weekend, and it was tough for me to curb my excitement. She arranged for me to stay in a lovely suite close to Valley Forge National Historical Park. Our first meeting, the night I arrived, was a brief but unforgettable one as we made plans for the following day. When she arrived the next morning, I thought I would impress her by showing off my 2001 Corvette, but to my chagrin and true to her personality, she was unimpressed with it.

She took me to the Knox headquarters farm inside the historical park, where we enjoyed a leisurely walk over a covered bridge and along picturesque Valley Creek. We stopped for a brief rest and sat together on a rustic bench along the trail. I love that old weathered bench, and I try to get out to it around Memorial Day every year to relive the memory. I felt as nervous as I did when I first tried to hold a girl's hand as a young boy, and I was probably as clumsy when I reached out for hers. Her touch was as electric as our first kiss, and as I held her close by that whispering stream, I knew intuitively, we would always be together. That night, she took me to a worship night in a church she served at, and we ended the evening at a local restaurant with two of her closest friends who interrogated me mercilessly.

The next day was Memorial Day, a truly sacred time when I reflect on brother Marines, who had made the ultimate sacrifice while defending the freedom we should all cherish as Americans. The day has an even more profound significance for me because I passed a very important test on that day. The girl invited me to her parent's home for a Memorial Day picnic, where I met and fellowshipped with her family and the rest of her friends. Unbeknown to me, her father was quietly and carefully evaluating me. Later, I learned the girl's father had told her if he had discerned anything negative about my character, I would not be invited back to his home. Aside from an incident where I lost my grip on a whiffle ball bat and sent it careening into traffic during the picnic, I passed his test.

After the Memorial Day visit, we realized many more visits would follow. On one of my last weekend visits before going on deployment with the 26th MEU, I went with her father to a Christian book store. On our way back to the house I very nervously asked him for his daughter's hand in marriage. He looked over at me and asked, "Why do you want to marry my daughter?" Before I even thought of the best reply, I blurted out "Because I love her to death." He was as unimpressed with my answer as my wife was of my corvette. He let me stew in my words for a bit, then talked to me about why he did not like the statement I had just made. From my perspective, what I had said, I had heard a lot of people say and I thought it was a perfectly acceptable explanation. But for her dad, 'perfectly acceptable' or the 'norm' was never going to be good enough for his beloved daughter, and his standards were going to be much higher for whoever was going to become his son-in-law. I sat there miserable, feeling like I blew my opportunity, but he happily gave his blessing, and I never used the phrase again. Eventually, I embarked on a Naval ship that took me on a six-month deployment halfway around the world, but the girl and I communicated as often and as best we could. In Israel, I bought the diamond she wears on her ring finger but narrowly avoided disaster with it. After I returned from the deployment, I made plans to propose marriage to her when she and her friend visited my North Carolina beach rental. I had planned an elaborate scavenger hunt to engage her 'spy' skills which would eventually lead to her discovery of the engagement ring. The plan was flawed and fell through before it was even set in motion.

I lived in a rented condo right on the beach in North Topsail Island, and I planned to bury a locked box containing the ring that only a sequence of codes and puzzles could unlock, in a sand dune right below the stairway that led out onto the beach. I didn't plan on her flight being extremely delayed or on the impending high tide that night. I had rented a limousine to pick the girl and her friend up from the airport but had to cancel the limo and drive a rental an hour and a half to the airport instead. My timeline was thrown off considerably, so I put my backup plan into motion, which was to have a confederate of mine set the stage at the condo while I was on the way to the airport. The box and the ring were hidden in a roof rafter outside the apartment, and the words 'Will you Marry Me' in colored construction paper were stapled to the condo wall. For theatrics, my accomplice intentionally left a trail of sandy footprints on the floor, and with the front door ajar, he watched the apartment from the parking lot until I arrived with the girl.

When we walked up to the entrance, door ajar and a sandy trail leading into the condo, I acted surprised and tried to convince her to go in first because I wanted her to be the first to see the construction paper proposal. She wanted no part of my stupid idea and had no intention of going into the apartment alone, but somehow it all worked out. Thankfully, the flawed plan A was shelved because, by the time we arrived from the airport, the tide had risen over the stairway where I had planned to bury the ring. In the end, she said yes to my crazy proposal after she located the box, unlocked the coded lock with her amazing spy skills, and saved the ring from becoming lost at sea.

Although the hour was late, we decided to go out for dinner. I drove the two ladies to a 'luxurious' five-star restaurant that served a fine selection of seafood cuisine. When we pulled into the parking lot, the girl took one glance at the dilapidated old building and refused to get out of the car, trusting her intuition over my poor judgement. As I drove the two hungry ladies around, looking for a better place to eat, I almost ran the car out of gas; in my excitement, I didn't even notice the gas light was on. I got gas in the car before we it left us stranded and eventually stumbled onto a sports bar; although a little loud, the food and atmosphere were great.

We married that July at her family church. The ceremony was a very special event and one I will have the fondest memories of forever. The building was packed with family and friends from at least four different states. Marines from Camp Lejeune made the long trip north to stand beside me as groomsmen and to welcome my bride into the Marine Corps family as only Marines do. As we walked from the church after the ceremony, the four Marines, swords drawn in an arch, waited for us to pass through. At the end of the arch, a sword was dropped in our path and my wife was formally brought under the protective umbrella of all Marines, before being ceremoniously dismissed with a tap on her bustle by a sword-wielding Marine Officer.

We had a small reception at an American Legion Hall and ended the long day with a visit to her grandmother, who could not attend the wedding. We celebrated our honeymoon night at the historic Warren Inn and enjoyed a Fourth of July picnic with family and friends the next day before flying to Maui for our honeymoon. We are going on fifteen years of marriage and celebrate our anniversary each year, along with four very special birthdays: ours in April, our oldest daughter in June, and our youngest daughter in May.

Historical places to visit in and around Aston, Pennsylvania.

This portion of the Patriot Path will take you to Aston Township, Pennsylvania, for a few stops at historical points of interest. Chichester Meetinghouse and Aston Township Memorial Garden will highlight this short trip into the Philadelphia suburbs. Pull into the meetinghouse, walk up to the caretaker's house, and knock on the door. Chances are she will be available and happy to open up the meetinghouse and let you look around. Drive to the memorial garden and check out the beautiful monument erected to honor those who served and sacrificed in uniform. Walk across the street and grab a burger at Zac's on the ground the Seven Stars once stood on. Gallows Hill and the 1724 Courthouse are in a rougher part of the Chester neighborhood, so I recommend limiting a visit to a drive-through, if at all. Unfortunately, the Clam Digger has long since closed its illustrious doors, and I only list it as an inside joke for my lovely wife.

1724 Chester Courthouse is located at Avenue of the States Street Aston, Pennsylvania.

Gallows Hill is located at Edgemont and Providence Avenue Aston, Pennsylvania.

<u>Chichester Meetinghouse</u> is located at 611 Meetinghouse Road Upper Chichester, Pennsylvania.

<u>Historic Neighborhood of Logstown</u> is located at Valleybrook Road and Logstown Road Aston, Pennsylvania.

<u>Aston Township Memorial Garden</u> is located at Concord Road and South Pennell Road Aston, Pennsylvania.

<u>The Clam Digger</u> was located at NC 210 Snead's Ferry, North Carolina.

Edgemont, Pennsylvania

"They say you can lead a horse to water, but you can't make him drink. In the Marine Corps, you can make that horse wish to hell he had."

~Fred Larson, Lawyer and producer of the films, Star of Bethlehem and the Christ Quake.

Along the Edgemont Road traveled an American scouting party consisting of Colonel Persifor Frazer, Major John Harper, and Jacob Vernon. Their reconnaissance of Chester complete and with Cornwallis settling into an encampment in the vicinity of Seven Stars Tavern in Aston Township, the scouting party prudently took a more circuitous route back to the Continental Army, and the three stopped at the Blue Ball Tavern for refreshments.

While enjoying their meal, Major Harper happened to glance out of a window and saw a group of horsemen approaching the tavern. Mistaking the riders for members of the Virginia Light Horse who typically conducted scouting missions dressed in captured British uniforms, the Major was not concerned by their approach. Unfortunately for the three American patriots, the riders were British dragoons. Once the three realized their mistake, Vernon escaped by jumping through a window. The two officers were not so fortunate. Attempting to follow Vernon out the window, they were fired on and subsequently forced to surrender once they found themselves surrounded. They would both eventually find themselves reluctant guests of the Walnut Street prison along with Colonel Hannum, who was captured from his home earlier. With the exception of Hannum, who broke his parole and left the city, the friends would remain incarcerated in Philadelphia until the city fell back into American hands in the Spring of 1778 after Howe abandoned it. The Blue Ball tavern was re-visited by the British within a few short days of this little episode in history when, after the Battle of the Clouds, Cornwallis passed by and established camp a couple of miles east of the tavern, where they stayed for a few days to support the infamous Paoli Massacre.

The tavern survived the Revolutionary War but still had more noteworthy stories worth telling. Prissy Robinson, who was a granddaughter of one of the tavern's early proprietors, was rumored to have bludgeoned to death hapless visitors who happened to flash their money in her presence. According to legend, Prissy would get the party started by serving copious amounts of hot rum to her unsuspecting victims at dinner. After they retired to their rooms, they would find kegs of whiskey conveniently stored there. Prissy would lurk around until they fell into a drunken stupor, enter the room, administer a quick, sharp blow to the skull, and drag the limp body into the cellar where she would bury her crime. Another similar account regarding a female patron was added to Prissy's legend. The female patron flashed her money during dinner and was found hanging from the boxed stairway (which still exists) the following day, apparently by suicide. As folks became aware of Prissy's little side gig, the tavern business started to fall away. After Prissy passed away in 1860, these accounts were generally chalked up to Prissy's generally disagreeable disposition instead of actual murders taking place.

Years later, new owners of the tavern discovered six skeletons with cleft skulls and other broken bones buried in the cellar during renovations, and theories about Prissy's morbid activities were recalled. A search of a nearby orchard yielded yet another skeleton, further bringing the urban legend to life.

Today, the tavern, now a private home, retains much of its colonial originality; along with the boxed staircase, it is easy to discern the tavern layout with its massive walk-in fireplace and its original flooring hewn from Long Leaf Pine. The Long Leaf Pine is an endangered species and no longer exist north of Virginia.

Marine Corps Tie-In...Things Buried.

After the firefight outside of the walled compound of the Al-Azimiyah, where my squad had suppressed the RPG and small arms attack from the Iraqis, I quickly checked my squad and our attachments for injuries, and we spread-loaded our ammunition. A few hours of observing the cityscape in front of our position for enemy activity netted nothing, so I decided to clear the remainder of the fighting positions that were dug in the small, vacant lot outside the wall. We discovered a mixture of uniform items and equipment, ammunition scattered around, and some scant food items, but strangely, no weapons. I found Iraqi Dinars featuring Saddam's portrait in the pocket of one uniform and a folding knife ornately decorated but cheaply made in another fighting hole. Iraqi helmets were found in nearly every fighting hole. When I picked up one of these helmets, it reminded me of a child's costume piece; I doubt if it could have stopped an air rifle pellet from penetrating it.

Suddenly, I heard a Marine cuss loudly near the compound wall; I immediately went over to investigate the cause of the Marine's outburst, only to see half of him protruding from a hole. We helped him out of the hole and discovered he had fallen through a thinly disguised weapons and ammo cache. After tearing off a few thin boards, we found a vast assortment of small arms, including various types of Soviet-made handguns, submachine guns, rifles, carbines, light and medium machine guns, and RPG launchers. Along with the weaponry, we found crates and belts of ammunition, including RPGs and hand grenades.

We reported our discovery to higher and were advised to secure the cache and cordon off the area until the contents could be safely removed and destroyed. It was very tempting to take one of the weapons as a war trophy and try to smuggle it back home, but we avoided the risk of prison or worse by leaving the stuff as it lay. Sometime before an EOD team came onsite to remove the weapons and ammunition, a team of Special Forces arrived and began to sort through the enemy stockpile, throwing various weapons into their vehicle. The vehicle looked like a Range Rover we were used to seeing military personnel roll around in Kuwait. The Special Forces guys sported full beards and were dressed like they were auditioning for a Chuck Norris movie. They sported utility blouses with sleeves ripped off, wore shemaghs around their necks, baseball caps on their heads, and Oakley sunglasses protected their eyes. We were preparing to defend our cache from getting plundered when higher informed us they could take whatever they wanted from the stockpile. Oddly, they avoided the Iraqi grenades, which were known to be unreliable at best and dangerous to handle.

One cringe-worthy story made its way through the ranks as our baggage was being searched for contraband for our return trip back to California and served as a great deterrent for would be smugglers. According to the story, a service member sent a live Iraqi hand grenade he intended to keep as a souvenir back to the States. While holding their child, his wife unknowingly opened the package after it arrived. As she handled the unstable grenade, it detonated, killing both. I have not been able to find content to support this story, so for now and hopefully forever, we can attribute it to an urban legend told to encourage young Marines to give up unauthorized war trophies during the amnesty period.

Another popular smuggling story that made its way around camp was that of an SNCO who modified the floor of a Conex box (shipping Container) to hide several Iraqi firearms he intended to smuggle back to the States. The weapons made it to the States, but diligent customs inspectors found the cache, and the Marine was subsequently court-martialed.

The Blue Ball Inn (private property) can be viewed from across the road at 1250 Old Lancaster Road Berwyn, Pennsylvania.

Goshen Township, Pennsylvania

"We've backed off in good faith to try and give you a chance to straighten this problem out. But I am going to beg with you for a minute. I'm going to plead with you, do not cross us. Because if you do, the survivors will write about what we do here for 10,000 years".

~James Mattis, 26th Secretary of Defense

East Goshen was originally part of the Welsh Tract granted to Welsh immigrants, mostly Quakers. Because of its beauty, it was named for the biblical land of Goshen. Robert Williams is generally considered the first settler of Goshen and lived in a cave somewhere south of East Boot Road. In 1702, Friends of Haverford donated 19 English pounds so Williams could build a proper house. The homestead was established in the vicinity of a clocktower, which is located just south of East Boot Road.

The battle of the Clouds, consisting of three minor skirmishes fought in and around West Chester and East Goshen, took place almost literally in my backyard. If I had lived at the same location in the 18th century, I would have undoubtedly witnessed the long German and British columns marching along Boot Road toward the Sign of the Boot Tavern, and I would have certainly heard the subsequent battle rattle of skirmishing soldiers.

On September 14th Washington, deciding it was more important to protect his supply depots than wait for Howe to move toward Philadelphia, broke camp, marched his Army down Ridge Road (Route 23), and crossed the Schuylkill at Levering's ford near Manayunk. From the ford, the Continental Army moved along the Old Lancaster or Conestoga Road toward Downingtown to protect Washington's backcountry iron, gunpowder, and supply depots by blocking the main routes. Downingtown, Chester County's largest backcountry town, was also an essential depot for flour and other supplies the Continental Army relied on. When the day's march ended, the 10,000-man American Army was strung along the road from Radnor Meetinghouse to Merion Meetinghouse; Washington established his headquarters at Buck's Tavern.

Around 4 PM, Howe received intelligence that Washington was moving west into the Great Valley; acting on the information, Howe moved to position his Army at the White Horse Tavern, built along the junction of five vital roads leading into Pennsylvania's backcountry, to deny Washington access. On the evening of the 15th Howe met with his officers and issued orders to move into the valley. The following morning, Howe's forces, still bivouacked at Dillsworth, broke camp and marched toward White Horse Tavern to intercept Washington. General Knyphausen and Captain Matthews broke camp before the main British column and moved in advance toward the Goshen Meetinghouse. Orders were also dispatched to Cornwallis to move his column north from Aston to Goshen Meetinghouse via Chester Road and he moved his columns north beyond the Seven Stars Tavern.

On September 15th Washington breakfasted with a local silversmith, sent a detachment toward Aston to observe Cornwallis' activities, and moved his Army twelve miles west on the Lancaster Road (present-day route 30) and camped in the vicinity of Malvern and Frazer. Colonel Potter and Maxwell's troops remained camped near Colonel Richard Thomas' home in Exton. Washington headquartered at Randel Malin's home at the (intersection of Lancaster and Swedesford), General Wayne was at Whitehorse Tavern, and General Greene was encamped at the Paoli Tavern.

On the morning of September 16th Colonel Maxwell was re-positioned near Colonel Richard Thomas's Mill on Pottstown Pike. Colonel Potter's militia was lined up on the ridge behind Boot Tavern. Potter's line extended between the Thompson House and the John

Bull House. Around 3 PM Hessians led by Colonel Carl von Donop detached from Howe's main force at Goshen Meetinghouse and moved west on Boot Road past where Knyphausen's Hessians were holding. The Hessian column's vanguard ran into Potter's battleline near the Sign of the Boot Tavern.

The run-in at the Boot Tavern almost had dire consequences for the over-ambitious Colonel Donop. The Colonel had come to the war in the Americas with lofty plans to expand the war to include Mexico and Peru and become wealthy from the venture. Donop probably had some revenge in mind because of the presumed humiliation he suffered earlier at the hands of the Americans at Trenton. He also had some negative stigma to overcome when he was caught with his pants down (possibly literally) while spending Christmas 1776 with a beautiful young widow, rumored to be a well-known seamstress from Philadelphia. Donop, then the senior Crown Forces officer in southern Jersey, was too far away from Trenton to support Colonel Rall, whom he had little respect for in the first place in the first place, when he received word of the American attack. If Donop had been willing and able to support Rall, there likely would have been no American Army to skirmish with at the Boot Tavern on September 16th.

Donop spurred his horse toward Potter's forces near the Sign of the Boot and outdistancing his vanguard, soon found himself way ahead of and cut off from his detachment. Had he been dismounted, his rashness probably would have ended in his capture or demise. As it turned out, a rainstorm began during the brief skirmish, and gunpowder soon became worthless. When Donop's men caught up to him, retreat for Potter and Maxwell soon became their best course of action. The Hessian Jaegers were great fighters with their hunting swords and were more than willing to use them, while most American soldiers didn't even have bayonets, much less swords. It likely would have been a lop-sided afair at best, and Donlop would have won back some of his lost prestige.

As it turned out, he lost five jaegers killed, seven wounded, and very narrowly avoided capture, while Potter and Maxwell lost 8-11 killed, several wounded, and some taken prisoner. Boot Tavern became a temporary headquarters for General Howe after the skirmish. American dead from the Boot Tavern skirmish were said to have been buried near the George Meredith house along 1421 South Ship Road, which was used as a field hospital. The house was demolished in 2007, and a new one was built on the site. Other American wounded from the Boot Tavern skirmish were taken to the home of Daniel Thomas. The house is located east of south 1454 Ship Road and remains a private residence.

Around 3 PM at Goshen Meetinghouse, Cornwallis ordered the 1st Light Infantry, commanded by General Abercromby, to move north on Chester Road. Along the road, approximately a mile from the meetinghouse, the 1st Light Infantry closed with the Pennsylvania Militia, which had been ordered, along with Wayne's regular brigades, to establish a skirmish line in the vicinity of the Rees farm (present-day Alcott Circle and North Chester Road) to block the northern approach to the valley and protect the Continental Army's left flank. Considered a minor skirmish, Wayne's regulars didn't even have an opportunity to engage the 1st Light Infantry before the militia (as General Pickering stated) "shamefully fled the first fire." When a steady rainfall caused multiple misfires of their carbines, the jaegers, attached to the 1st Light Infantry, pulled out their hunting swords, forcing Wayne to withdraw north toward King Road. The skirmish resulted in 12-14 Pennsylvania militiamen killed, while the 1st Light Infantry reported no casualties. Immaculata University has a monument commemorating the engagement just outside one of its main buildings. There is also an unsubstantiated claim that there is a gravesite on its campus that is traditionally believed to contain soldiers killed in the battle.

While Colonel Donop attempted to maneuver around Potter at Boot Tavern, Wayne's brigades desperately tried to get back in position with the rest of Washington's Army, which was still forming near Immaculata College (most likely just north of Kings Road). During the chaotic attempt to quickly form an American battle line, the rainstorm morphed into a nor'easter, forcing Washington to make a quick decision; stay on the high ground and face Cornwallis' forces with wet gunpowder while Donop attempted to gain his right flank or retreat before the roads were rendered impassible because of the torrential downpour that had developed.

Washington's generals conferred, and Pickering's advice was succinct, "The order of the battle is not completed. If we are to fight the enemy on this ground, the troops ought to be immediately arranged. If we are to take the high grounds on the other side of the valley, we ought to march immediately, or the enemy may fall upon us in the midst of our movement." Washington's decision must have been relatively simple if not frustratingly ironic; once again, he had the tactical advantage with the high ground, but this time, with the rain making gunpowder useless and his lines not formed, he could not rationally commit to close combat against a much better trained and equipped professional British Army, armed with bayonets and swords. "Let us move," was Washington's response, and the Army turned back toward the White Horse Tavern and marched down into the valley.

Cornwallis and a large part of the British Army remained encamped on George Hoopes' farm a short distance north of the meetinghouse, while Howe and the remainder of his Army camped near the Sign of the Boot Tavern. With Cornwallis were several hundred soldiers who had been injured at the Battle of the Brandywine, numbers of whom died of their wounds, both British and Hessian. According to local tradition, many of the British and Hessian dead are buried in an unmarked mass grave in Section A (east side) of the Goshen Burial Ground and on high ground somewhere on the old Hoopes farm.

The William Everhart House is a historic home built at the junction of Boot and Ship Roads. It was built about 1810 and is a two-story, five-bay, brick Federal-style dwelling with a gable roof. It was the home of Congressman William Everhart who also built the William Everhart Buildings in West Chester. Before he made a substantial fortune developing West Chester and getting elected to Congress, William Everhart lived at the Boot Inn between the 1810s and 1820s. While operating a general store he built his home at the intersecting "V" of Ship and Boot Roads. The house still stands at the intersection of Boot and Ship Road in Goshen. Some historical accounts place this as the lot where the Sign of the Boot tavern once stood.

I'm afraid I must disagree with proponents of this theory since the Sign of the Boot would have still been standing years after William Everhart's house was built...two buildings cannot occupy the same space at the same time. From 1772 through 1776, Samuel Oliver registered a tavern at the intersection of present-day Boot Road and Phoenixville Pike under the name "The Sign of the Boot." The popular crossroads kept the tavern in business until 1865, when Edwin Oakley registered it as The Boot Tavern.

Before I close the chapter on Goshen, I would be remiss if I failed to include a little-known local legend. Goshen Township narrowly avoided a Salem-like witch trial in the mid-1700s. Around the 1770s, a seven-year-old Goshen Township girl named Rebecca Ashbridge began acting very strangely. The young girl appeared demented; the only words she would say were the repetition of the barely intelligible phrase "molotley, molotley, molotley." For the residents of Goshen

Township in the 18th century, this was clear evidence that a local widow named Mary Moll Otley bewitched the innocent child.

According to the legend, the local constable, James Gibbons, went to arrest the widow, Mary Otley, on charges of performing witchcraft. While Gibbons made the arrest, other residents stayed behind to draw Mary's image on a board. They then fired at it with pieces of silver because they believed lead would not hurt a witch. While in the presence of the accused witch, Gibbons monitored her behavior and appearance. If she expressed pain or was visibly uncomfortable, then the constable would have strong evidence of witchcraft.

A period book about the history of West Chester made equally ridiculous claims, such as the idea that Gibbons made Mary walk across salt. This version also alleged that residents escorted her to a nearby mill where they weighed her against the Bible. "For it was held," according to the book, "that a Holy Bible would always outweigh a witch." After passing this archaic test, they proposed throwing Mary in the mill dam, believing that if she were a witch, she would swim out quickly but, if innocent, sink to its depths. Fortunately, cooler heads prevailed and Mary was not thrown into the mill dam to either sink or swim.

This is an interesting local story, but is there enough source evidence to suggest it happened? To determine the authenticity of a historical account, scholars rely on eyewitness testimony in the absence of empirical evidence such as primary source documentation, which this witch trial legend certainly lacks. Many histories produced during the 18th century and earlier relied on word of mouth and local tradition, especially since most people of the period were illiterate. Until the twentieth century, methodological, evidence-backed history was uncommon, especially for local history. In contrast, historians today have a responsibility to defend every assertion with evidence.

Although no record has surfaced to definitively prove Mary Moll Otley practiced witchcraft, there are records at the Chester County Archives that can provide circumstantial evidence against the story. Historian Douglas Harper contextualized the Otley witch story using the records at the Chester County Archives. Harper used the local tax assessments and pauper records to delegitimize the story, and he also pointed out that "belief in witchcraft generally subsided as the eighteenth century progressed...It is extremely unlikely that such hysteria could have broken out in Goshen as late as 1780. Although less secular compared to today's standards, people in the late eighteenth century would have avoided mass hysteria over witchcraft".

There is another angle to this evidence-based problem, loosely based on the adage that there is always a little truth behind every rumor. Sometimes legends are told simply for the entertainment they provide, but making allegations as serious as witchcraft in the 18th century transcends simple storytelling, and one could even suggest there was an ulterior motive for propagating a story such as Mary Otey's. The Ashbridges, for example, would have had such a motive. Nearly every account of the legend begins with Mary Otley bewitching Rebecca, the seven-year-old daughter of Joshua Ashbridge, who happened to be George Ashbridge's son. The best evidence lies in the relationship between the Otleys and Ashbridges. The Otleys were a poor family that regularly required assistance from neighbors. The Ashbridges, on the other hand, were well-respected and wealthy.

George Ashbridge was a prominent figure in the township and surrounding community. He was the fourth generation 'George' in the family. He owned and operated several mills including Dutton Mills, which provided flour to Washington's Army encamped at Valley Forge in 1777-78. His uncle was Richard Ashbridge, who owned the farmland in Exton, Pennsylvania, which has since been developed into a Walmart and apartment buildings.

Before 1799, Chester County did not have a poorhouse to aid struggling families. Instead, each township assigned an Overseer of the Poor to ensure the needy received necessary help. In 1753, Goshen Township's Overseer of the Poor reimbursed George Ashbridge for aiding Jonas Otley, a relative of Mary's who was also a poor blind man.

The two families clearly knew each other, but the relationship might have become strained in 1765, when George Ashbridge, along with two others, "...did beat, wound and evilly treat other Harms to the said Mary Otley...." Although the specifics of the case remain unknown, the fact that George Ashbridge injured Mary Otley indicates animosity between the two families. Not only did Ashbridge allegedly malevolently injure Otley, but he was also publicly humiliated as he was tried in front of the Chester County Court of Quarter Sessions in 1765. The court ruled 'Ignoramus Returned' or not enough evidence to justify prosecution, which was a ruling in favor of Ashbridge. For George to have suffered embarrassment due to the trial would have been detrimental to his community status, which was very important to the Ashbridges. Ashbridge would have certainly gained some of his precious prestige back with his neighbors and business associates if Mary was seen as a victimizing witch instead of a poor, bullied, and abused woman.

It would have been relatively easy for the Ashbridges to propagate such a scandal as witchcraft in the 1700s and conveniently label Mary Otley the antagonist. Mary Otley's lifelong poverty and the trial against Ashbridge harmed her reputation within the community. There is also a historical account that could have provided a catalyst for the witchcraft legend. Interestingly, records at the Chester County Archives connect Otley to a more evidential event than witchcraft, which leads us to the 'little truths' part of the narrative I alluded to earlier.

In May 1744, the County Commissioners paid William Jones twenty shillings for "the examination of Ann and Mary Otley concerning the murder of Ann Otley's child." Based on the wording of the entry, it is not known whether Mary Otley was charged directly with murdering Ann's child or just assisted and or concealed the murder. Because she was not hanged, we can reasonably conclude she was either acquitted of her crime or at least pardoned. There is no record of this case being reviewed by the Chester County Court of Common Sessions. However, Mary does appear on record as having provided testimony against George Ashbridge in 1765.

So, has the US government been using hyped-up hysteria regarding alien invasions as a cover for secret weapons projects at Groom Lake, or is the government secretly using alien technology to develop advanced weapons? Conversely, was Mary Otley held on trial by her peers for the commission of witchcraft in a small Pennsylvania township, or was she a victim of her impoverished circumstances that fed into a story that grew into a legend that was weaved to regain lost prestige and preserve a prominent family's affluence in the same small community? Until this author sees a person riding a broomstick or being abducted by a flying saucer, I am persuaded to believe that humans will continue to do things that make them uniquely...human.

Marine Corps Tie-In...Winning the Hearts of the Iraqi People One Child at a Time.

During my first combat deployment in Iraq, I saw firsthand how a disruption in or a lack of medical infrastructure can adversely affect populations, particularly in third-world countries. When President Bush declared a cessation of hostilities in Iraq, I was a young squad leader for third platoon, Bravo Company 1/5, operating out of a Presidential palace in Northeast Baghdad. One afternoon on a routine patrol in the vicinity of the palace, a distressed Iraqi man approached the patrol with his young daughter, seeking medical aid for her.

I stopped the patrol to have the corpsman try to diagnose and hopefully treat the girl's ailment. The corpsman informed me that the child had an infection in her eye and likely needed the kind of antibiotics that only a medical doctor could prescribe and provide. Our battalion medical officer back at the palace complex was the only doctor available to us. Unfortunately for the child, Operational Security (OPSEC) protocol prohibited Iraqi nationals from entering our Battalion Forward Operating Base (FOB). At a loss for a solution, I turned to my Company Commander, who had accompanied the patrol. The captain was a hard-nosed Marine Officer from Louisiana who stressed to his subordinate leaders, "When in charge, be in charge." When I turned to him for guidance, he shrugged his shoulders, reminded me I was the Marine in charge of the patrol, and told me to "make a decision."

We escorted the child and her father to our FOB where the Medical Officer was able to examine her. The decision was a lifesaving one because it turned out that the little girl had a Chlamydia infection in her eye. If she had not received medical attention when we intervened, she at a minimum, would have lost sight in the infected eye but likely would have eventually succumbed to the infection. Before we departed Baghdad, the little girl and father returned to the palace; the father was very grateful that his child was restored to good health. The little girl gave me a small red silk flower, and we had our picture taken together, but the flower and picture have been misplaced over the course of time and multiple moves.

Historical places to visit in and near Goshen, Pennsylvania.

Welcome to beautiful Goshen Township and my backyard! Begin your historical tour of Goshen Township at the Grove Methodist

Church, where you will find a Revolutionary War Patriot's grave, then check out the ten contributing 18th-century houses and buildings that comprise the Grove Historic District. Drive east on Boot Road, look left and find a development named for the Indian King Tavern. The tavern no longer exists and would have stood a mile east of the development at the eastern corner of Boot Road and Pottstown Pike. Continue on Boot Road to Ship Road; look left where the roads fork, and you will see the William Everhart House, now a dentist's office. Continue south on Ship Road and see the small hill Colonel Potter's troops marched down on their way to the Sign of the Boot Tavern and their skirmish with Colonel Donop. The next stop is at the Daniel Thomas House, which is also a private residence, but one can easily discern the home's historic bones, and an old stone wall is exposed along the road. Drive to the Rite Aide on the Corner of Phoenixville Pike and Boot Road. Opposite the road is a private residence and commercial building separated by the remnants of a stone barn bridge. I believe it is all that remains of the old Sign of the Boot Tavern based on a study of an existing period picture of the tavern and old maps. Here is where Potter temporarily halted Donop's flanking march and nearly captured the ambitious Hessian commander. Continue your tour on East Boot Road, the same road the Hessians marched to attempt to flank Washington's Army, which was massing on King Road near Immaculata University. Turn left on Paoli Pike and drive down to East Goshen Park, where you will find ample parking and picnic areas to enjoy a quick lunch.

The Goshen Historic District is at the park's southern border, and its paths will lead you there. The old blacksmith shop and the Tory Inn are just across the road. If you visit on a Wednesday or Saturday morning, chances are good you will hear the ringing of a heavy hammer against steel and get a whiff of woodsmoke. Look inside and find a friendly blacksmith willing to take you back to when the shop produced plow shears, nails, and tools for 18th-century farmers. Also a wheelwright, the gentleman will share his extensive knowledge of his trade and show you his well-preserved Conestoga Wagon. The Tory Inn was once a Bed and Breakfast but is now a private residence. Walk east on Boot Road up a slight hill to the Bell Tower.

Although the tower is on private land, it's still worth looking at and puts you near where Goshen's first settler lived in a cave. After visiting the clock tower, head north along Chester Road to the Goshen Friends Meetinghouse, where Howe consolidated his Army and planned his next move in what would be known as the Battle of the Clouds. An unmarked mass grave of Hessian soldiers is said to be somewhere in the meetinghouse's eastern section of the burial ground. Walk through the cemetery toward an old stone entrance beside Paoli Pike, and you will find a bronze historical sign. Look across the road and see the old George Hoops farmhouse, now a private residence faced with Serpentine Stone from a local quarry. Drive along North Chester Road to Alcott Circle. There is nothing to see here but urban sprawl, but this is the general location where historians agree the second skirmish of the battle took place. Continue to Greenhill Road and turn left. Drive to Hershey Mill's Road, turn right, and into a small parking lot.

Here, you can walk around a small historical preservation established on the old mill site. Hershey Mills Road will take you to Immaculata University, built on the ridge where Washington once massed his Army for a decisive engagement with the British Army. A historical marker is displayed in a small garden outside a large building, and another historical marker is located at an entrance to a development along King Road.

Finish this portion on the Patriot's Path with a walk through the Ashbridge Preserve. Bring hiking boots and insect repellent if you are visiting in the summer and avoid this hike if it has rained because these trails can get muddy. Your walk will take you through beautiful woods, glades, and meadows along the tranquil Ridley Creek. The trail crosses this creek a few times, but there are no footbridges, just concrete pilings to sort of hop across. In places, the woods take on an eerily countenance as if a certain 'witch' might have gathered her ingredients there a long time ago.

George Meredith house is located at 1421 South Ship Road West Chester, Pennsylvania.

William Everhart House is located at 1300 Ship Road West Chester, Pennsylvania.

Daniel Thomas House is located at 1454 South Ship Road West Chester, Pennsylvania.

Grove United Methodist Church is located at 490 West Boot Road West Chester, Pennsylvania.

Blacksmith shop is located at 1600 East Boot Road West Chester, Pennsylvania.

Goshen Meetinghouse is located at 807 North Chester Road West Chester, Pennsylvania.

The Clocktower is located at 1680 East Boot Road West Chester, Pennsylvania.

The Joseph Garrett House is located at 1610 Paoli Pike West Chester, Pennsylvania.

William Sharpless House (and in 1800 the Tory Inn) is located at 734 North Chester Road West Chester, Pennsylvania.

Hershey Mills Park is located at 1034 Hershey Mill Road West Chester, Pennsylvania.

Immaculata University is located at 1145 West King Road Immaculata, Pennsylvania.

<u>Ashbridge Preserve</u> is located at Wast Strasburg Road Malvern, Pennsylvania.

Frazer, Pennsylvania

"I'm not scared of very much. I've been hit by lightning and been in the Marine Corps for four years".

~Lee Trevino, a Marine Machine Gunner and regarded as one of the greatest players in golf history.

During the Revolutionary War, the White Horse Tavern was operated by John Kerlin, who was a staunch patriot. On July 5th 1776, the Declaration of Independence was read for the first time at two sites in Chester County, and the "White Horse" was one of those sites. The tavern also served briefly as General Washington's headquarters while he attempted to maneuver his Army to engage the British Army during the Battle of the Clouds.

The tavern was located at the junction of six important roads and, from a tactical perspective, one of the most crucial intersections in northern Chester County. Downingtown, where a supply magazine for the American Army was located, was seven miles west of the tavern along the Old Lancaster Road, and Lancaster was another 33 miles away. To the east, the Old Lancaster Road led to Philadelphia, which was 26 miles away. Swede's ford, the best crossing on the Schuylkill River, was 12 miles northeast. North Chester Road ran southeast to Goshen, Edgemont, and Chester. To the southwest was a road leading to the Sign of the Boot tavern, Turks Head, and eventually Wilmington. These last two roads were strategically crucial as blocking positions for the American Army because Howe's Army was camped along these roads, just a few miles south of the Whitehorse, and Washington still wanted to deny Howe access to the fords and Philadelphia. To the northwest ran a road toward Yellow Springs and the iron region of French Creek and beyond. In addition, the back-country furnaces of Warrick, Redding, and Hopewell could be accessed using this road. The last road, running northeast, led to Judge Moore's Phoenixville home and Valley Forge. From

Phoenixville, roads led to Reading, yet another essential American supply depot.

On September 16th 1777 around 5 PM, Washington was retreating from his high ground near present-day Immaculata University; the rain ruined gunpowder for both armies, and the roads quickly dissolved into soupy quagmires, forcing Howe to stop his pursuit of Washington. Cornwallis sent his contingent into camp on the George Hoopes farm and Howe, his British soldiers, and the Hessians camped along East Boot Road between present-day Paoli Pike and Route 202. Washington moved his Army beyond the Whitehorse Tavern and probably camped near what is now the Philadelphia Memorial Park just north of the tavern. The next day, Washington's main Army moved toward Yellow Springs.

Maxwell and Potter moved east toward Valley Forge to secure the Army's baggage and supplies because Valley Forge was being used by Washington as a supply depot. A plausible primary route for Washington into Yellow Springs would have been the Paxton Road, the main road to Harris's ferry (Harrisburg). The route roughly followed Valley Road west through Exton Park to Ship Road, avoiding the steep climb up Conestoga Road (Route 401) and north to Lionville, which in the 18th Century was the location of the Red Lion Tavern. From there, Kimberton Road (Route 113) led directly to Yellow Springs, but there is currently no primary source document verifying that Washington used this as his primary route. Some historians think it is more likely that the Army, already out of marching order, would have taken any passible route to Yellow Springs. Regardless of which roads were used, when the rain-soaked, exhausted Army reached Yellow Springs, they made a hasty camp in a meadow behind the tavern and creek while Washington set up his headquarters in a tavern located in the village.

When the weather broke a few days later, Howe mobilized his Army and marched them toward the Schuylkill River. Along the way,

Howe stopped at the Whitehorse and set up temporary headquarters. During the short time the British occupied the property, Kerlin suffered heavy financial losses.

While the Continental Army was encamped at Valley Forge in the winter of 1777-78, the tavern continued to be of importance to the American cause for independence because it was the first stopping place and served as a relay station for express riders going between the Army's headquarters and the temporary capital in York. The tavern also served as a patriot stronghold throughout the war after the brief British occupation.

Marine Corps Tie-In...A Pair of Gifts in a Baghdad University.

Our platoon received a frag-o on my birthday to search an Iraqi university located in our battalion's sector for suspected munitions. Word on the street was Saddam converted some of Iraq's universities into sweatshops to mass produce weaponry; we were looking for mortars. We all quickly geared up and moved out into the streets of Baghdad in search of our objective.

When we reached the university building, it was deserted and pockmarked with battle scars. Once inside, our squads worked independently to search for weapons and munitions. This would turn out to be no wild goose chase as we began to find thousands of components for mortar projectiles. We found an abundance of stabilizer fins, mortar bodies, and fuses but not the high-explosive filler that makes mortars go boom.

As my squad searched our assigned sector, we found ourselves in a suite of science or chemistry laboratories. Desks were overturned, broken beakers and tumblers crunched beneath our feet, and strewn chemicals stained the walls and furniture. None of this alarmed us much... until one of my Marines discovered a biohazard decal on a broken glass pane.

We eventually found an access ladder to the building's roof and made our way up for a bird' s-eye view of the city. The one' war trophy' I wanted to bring home was an Iraqi flag; on my birthday, I finally found one within my reach, fluttering away on the university's roof. One of my team leaders secured the flag for me, and we moved off the roof and worked our way to a platoon rally point in the school's auditorium.

While waiting for the platoon to consolidate, we explored the area and discovered a large chalkboard near the front of the room. On the board was written "For our American Friends" in English, followed by a long paragraph in Arabic that none of us could read. Below the paragraph was a chalk arrow pointing to a box, 'gift wrapped' in silver paper, complete with a bow. In a cynical mindset, I imagined the writing on the chalkboard served as a warning for anyone who could read Arabic that leaving the package for the Americans to open would be in the reader's best interest. Before one of my Marines got the notion to open the 'gift', we took the precaution to move out of the building as quickly as possible. Once we were at a safe distance, higher was called to request an Explosive Ordinance Disposal (EOD) team to inspect and dispose of the package.

Places to visit in or near Frazer, Pennsylvania.

The two 18th-century buildings on this historical tour of Frazer are private residences but are within easy view of the roadside. The third stop on this small segment of the Patriot's Path should be the Battle of the Clouds Park. Here, you will find a couple of historical signboards that provide information on the Battle of the Clouds and the White Horse Tavern.

White Horse Tavern is located at 606 Swedesford Road Frazer, Pennsylvania.

The Malin House is located at 74 Malin Road Malvern, Pennsylvania.

Battle of the Clouds Marker Chester Valley Trail is located at 133 Phoenixville, Pennsylvania.

Uwchlan Township, Pennsylvania

"In the last analysis, what the Marine Corps becomes is what we make of it during our respective watches. And that watch of each Marine is not confined to the time he spends on active duty. It lasts as long as he is "proud to bear the title of United States Marine."

~General Louis H. Wilson Jr. 26th Commandant of the Marine Corps and recipient of the Congressional Medal of Honor.

As travelers began using the roads in Chester County, many inns were built along them. They served food and drink but were much more important than a simple watering hole. During the eighteenth century, there were few newspapers and even fewer people who could even read them. Pennsylvania's inns and taverns were publishing houses of information for locals and travelers. One of these was the Red Lyon Inn, identifiable by its colorful sign of a lion for the many people who could not read. The inn began as a log cabin, and in 1725, it was rebuilt of red brick and offered respite to drovers until 1888. While men slept in the house, cattle were corralled in lots beside it. Red Lyon was the village's name until 1826, when the post office opened. However, since several 'Red Lyons' existed in Pennsylvania, the village was renamed Lionville.

The Lionville is a national historic district in Uwchlan Township, Chester County, Pennsylvania. The district consists of 39 contributing buildings in the crossroads community of Lionville. These 18th and 19th-century buildings include a variety of residential, commercial, and institutional buildings. Notable historic buildings include the Cadwalader House, Vaughan House, Red Lion Tavern, Uwchlan Meeting House, and Wagonseller House.

The original Uwchlan Meetinghouse was built in 1715 after Joseph Cadwalader bought a large piece of land from David Lloyd and donated a small lot to the Society of Friends for their meeting house and burial ground. This first meetinghouse was a log cabin, which some historians think burned down. A new building was constructed, another log cabin, but upgraded with glass windows. This meetinghouse was eventually replaced with the current meeting house, using field stone.

During the winter of 1777-78, the meetinghouse was used as a hospital by the Continental Army, who then camped at Valley Forge. It was staffed by Dr. Bodo Otto. Many soldiers who died there were buried behind the meetinghouse. The minutes of the Uwchlan Meeting recorded on Jan 8th 1778, reads, "A few days ago, the key for the Meeting House was demanded by some of the physicians of the Continental Army to convert the same into a hospital for their sick soldiers. The caretaker of the meetinghouse refused to deliver the key, so some soldiers forced their way into the house and stables." Although the Friends were not in favor of this action, they made no further protest and met in member's homes until the Army was done using it.

General Washington stayed across the street at the Red Lion Inn when he visited the sick soldiers at the meetinghouse. Dr. John Latimer resided at the inn while he oversaw the meetinghouse hospital. Dr. James Craik, another army surgeon, mentioned Uwchlan in a letter he wrote in 1778. "On my way to Manheim I visited Yellow springs and Red Lyon hospitals, which I found in excellent order and they have but few sick at present. However, as the army is becoming more sickly, we may expect they will soon be full."

Some Uwchlan residents who were not Quakers enlisted in the Continental Army. The mustering lists did not list names by residence, so it would be impossible to locate all those who fought. As of 1777, Uwchlan residents who served in the Pennsylvania Regiment were listed under the 7th Battalion of the Chester County Militia.

The Uwchlan Township Administration Building in Baird Park was constructed around an 18th-century home built in the early 1700s by wheelwright Hugh Pugh. An original room called the Hugh Pugh Room has been preserved and can be visited during regular business hours. An 18th-century stone barn at the site has also been refurbished to preserve the exterior. Visitors to Baird Park can walk the property, which includes three ponds that feed into one another, a monument dedicated to the veterans of the Armed Forces of America, and a statue of a Revolutionary War Soldier. The bronze statue, which memorializes the Flying Camp Militia, faces the very road that General Washington, Wayne, and other celebrated patriots have ridden or marched on as they traveled to and from Warwick Furnace, Coventry Forge, Yellow Springs, and Valley Forge during the war.

Also in Baird Park is a tiny log cabin with some fascinating history attached to it. A local man named Joe Hoffecker donated his 21-acre property to the township and lived in the original house until his death. His donation became the Foster Field Township Park, located along Route 113. When the park was expanded, the township was surprised with what they found while demolishing Hoffecker's home. Hidden within the modern-day home were the wood logs for the walls on three sides of a 1780's era house. Demolition was temporarily halted, and restoration efforts began. The logs were recovered, transported across the township to the administration complex, and reassembled into a cabin on a small hill just north of the Uwchlan police station. What is hard for modern visitors to grasp is the cabin's small size. Typical period homes were initially built small and usually expanded as the family grew. There was very little privacy in a typical 18th Century home. The entire family usually lived in the same room, close to a fireplace, with children sometimes sleeping in a loft area. Doorways were built low, and window frames were made small to preserve heat. While most of the joints are pegged, an original beam with dozens of nail holes remains intact on the ceiling. Visitors can even hold an original nail should they choose to.

For me, the more intriguing story in this chapter is a synopsis of the life and fate of the first owner of Baird Park. Hugh Pugh has the dubious distinction of being the subject of the first homicide trial in the original Chester County Courthouse located in present-day Delaware County. The first homicide in Chester County was, in the consequences that followed the execution, the most historic in the annuals of Pennsylvania after Hugh Pugh and Lazarus Thomas were hanged in Chester on May 9th 1718, for the murder of Jonathan Hayes, a resident of Marple Township and one of the judges of the county court.

The case agitated the public to such an extent that in October of 1715, the Court instructed three men to find a place "more Convenient than the Court House for holding the Supreme Court for ye Tryail of these persons ye are holden in ye Jail of ye County on Suspition of murder." The minutes of the Provincial County indicate that the accused parties had been allowed to post bail for some reason "and through the indolence of a former administration." The minutes also indicate that the men were not brought to trial until April 17th 1718, when Chief Justice Lloyd and the four associate justices of the Supreme Court were present, as was Governor Sir William Keith.

Pugh and Thomas were likely the leaders of a "Lawless Gang of Loose fellows, Common Distrurbers of the public peace," and "were so hardened and became so audacious as still to continue in their publick Rioting, Caballing and fighting." The men were known to brag openly that it was not within the power of the colonial government to try any capital case, according to the common and statute laws of England, which the prisoners claimed as a right since they were English subjects.

On May 8th the day previous to the time set for their hanging, Pugh and Thomas petitioned Sir William Keith for a stay of execution until the desire of the King could be ascertained and, at the same time, formerly lodged with the governor and council, their appeal to King George I, in which they gave three reasons why their conviction was illegal: Seventeen members of the Grand Jury and eight of the Petit Jury were Quakers, who had not been sworn. That the Act of Assembly permitting affirmations by governors and witnesses was enacted in violation of the Act of Parliament, passed in the first year of King George's reign. And because the Act of Assembly permitting affirmation to be made in all legal proceedings was not enacted until after said murder was supposed to be committed, therefore was *expost facto* and not applicable to their case because the Act of Assembly was objectionable to reason and in conflict with the laws and statutes of England, and thus void.

The governor and council refused to pardon the prisoners, and Sheriff Nicholas Fairlamb was instructed to execute the two men according to the death warrant imposed, which, signed by Chief Justice Lloyd and the Associate Justices of the Supreme Court, had already been placed in his hands. The men were executed on Gallows Hill, and public excitement dissipated.

After the execution, the authorities began to second-guess the legality of it since the appeal to the King had not been forwarded, although it accompanied the petition for a stay of execution or at least a reprieve. At that time, the King and his ministry did not approve of the mild criminal code framed by William Penn, which was recognized in the Pennsylvania providence and had repeatedly urged the colony to adopt the criminal policies of England. In Penn's Woods, capital punishment was awarded only for homicide and treason convictions while in England, conviction of any of 220 capital offenses could result in execution.

Only a few days had passed when the legal reasons which the executed men urged to set aside their conviction alarmed the leading class in the providence as to the legality of the trial and subsequent execution of the sentence. Twenty-two days after the execution, the Assembly passed an act that substituted Penn's criminal code with a modification of the more aggressive criminal code of England. The act included over seventy offenses punishable by death. The Assembly felt confident that the little matter of illegally executing two "bad men" would not weigh heavily with the King if it accomplished his policy of substituting a rigorous system of punishment for crimes in Pennsylvania.

The King approved and confirmed the Act of the Assembly early in 1719. The legal points raised by the accused in their petition were never made the subject of judicial consideration and decision, but the effect of their petition radically changed the criminal code of Pennsylvania, and today, the consequences of the Pugh trial are the forebearers of our modern penal laws.

Marine Corps Tie-In...Battlefield Miracles.

Efforts to eliminate any reference to God in schools and our American history have resulted in ignorance of certain facts involved in the birth of the United States, specifically, the role miracles played in the American Revolution. Some historians (I am one of them) advocate that our nation was literally won through divine influences.

During the French and Indian War, George Washington was second in command of 1,400 British troops led by General Braddock. The expedition was organized to capture Fort Duquesne, near present-day Pittsburgh. On their way to the fort, they were attacked by a party of French soldiers and their Indian allies. During the battle, Braddock and every officer on horseback were shot, except Washington. Braddock died of his wounds during the British retreat and was buried in the middle of a path. Washington wrote to his brother Lawrence, "But by the All-Powerful, I had four bullets through my coat, and two horses shot under me, yet escaped unhurt, although death was leveling my companions on every side of me." A warrior allied to the French, who fought in the battle, later stated, "Washington was never born to be killed by a bullet! I had seventeen fair fires at him with my rifle and after all could not bring him to the ground". This was just the first of several instances where historians advocating divine influences would draw evidence to support their theory.

Inexplicable, sudden changes in weather patterns were a predominant theme throughout the Revolutionary War. Instead of executing an amphibious assault on Washington's forces in Boston, Howe had to abort the plan due to what he called "a hurrycane or terrible storm... a southeaster of gale proportions" and evacuated the city.

In the Brooklyn Heights, Howe maneuvered his force of 15,000 men behind Washington's lines, effectively pinning his tiny Army against the East River. But before Howe could destroy Washington's forces, inclement weather again influenced the outcome of Howe's plan when a torrential rainstorm stalled his attack and an ebbing tide prevented Howe from maneuvering ships to cut off an escape route for the beleaguered Patriots.

Washington, always one to seize an advantage, ordered a nighttime evacuation of the Heights. Miraculously, the wind abated, and a thick fog settled in, masking the American evacuation.

Following an improbable American crossing of a frozen Delaware River with his Army barely intact, an even more unlikely American victory was won the following morning when, in the thick of a driving snowstorm, Washington surprised and defeated a Hessian garrison of over a thousand professional Hessians in less than an hour with only a part of his already depleted Army.

The Second Battle of Trenton was another weather-related miracle worthy of mentioning. If you will recall, in the second chapter of this book, January freeze-thaw conditions slowed General Cornwallis' march to Trenton, giving Washington's Army more time to prepare for an attack. Marching on the muddy roads, sometimes knee deep, due to rain and thaw, fatigued Cornwallis' troops, sapping valuable energy they would need for battle. Then, later that night, after being denied victory at a little bridge three times, Cornwallis, convinced he had trapped the American Army, decided to wait until the next day to "bag the fox." However, the temperature dropped, froze the ground, and allowed Washington to quietly withdraw and quickly march to Princeton.

Most people believe Washington's failure to defend Philadelphia was his undoing. However, Washington's actions in 1777 helped turn the tide of the war despite the British occupation of the city by keeping his Army intact and American hope for independence alive. Howe had planned for a speedy annihilation of Washington's Army and the eventual capture of the American capital. Once Washington's Army was destroyed and the capitol secured, Howe could move the bulk of his Army north to Albany, New York, and link up with Burgoyne's northern Army to close with and destroy the remnants of the American Army.

Although Howe had defeated Washington's forces at Brandywine, Paoli, and Germantown, he failed to reduce Washington's forces enough for them not to be a regional threat. Washington's Army went into winter camp a day's march from Philadelphia, effectively bottling up Howe's forces. Burgoyne was left to face an American Army more than twice the size of his roughly 7,000 troops, resulting in an astonishing American victory over one of Britain's most gifted generals. The defeat, at the hands of an inexperienced colonial Army, shocked people in London, but it was viewed as a miracle in Paris. This was the defining moment that finally drew France into the conflict on the side of the Americans and completely changed the course and outcome of the war.

In Yorktown, Virginia, Cornwallis unexpectedly found himself surrounded by a combined force of American and French troops. Cornwallis attempted to escape under the cover of darkness by moving his troops across the York River on boats. The first wave made it safely across the river, but a sudden and severe rain squall blew the second wave of soldiers downriver. This left Cornwallis without the strength of his Army and any realistic chance of breaking the American siege. This miraculous "adverse turn of the weather completely disrupted the attempted breakout." A British colonel summed it up best when he said, "Thus expired the last hope of the British army."

George Washington wrote, "It will not be believed that such a force as Great Britain has employed for eight years in this country could be baffled in their plan of subjugating it... The singular interpositions of Providence in our feeble condition were such as could scarcely escape the attention of the most unobserving, while the perseverance of the Armies of the United States, through almost every possible suffering and discouragement for the space of eight long years, was little short of a standing miracle".

During the hostilities in Iraq during OIF, it was evident that God also had a hand in shaping the battlefield and protecting the Marines of RCT-5 through its own series of miraculous events. Events such as near misses from scud missiles, Frog-2 rockets with empty payload compartments, bullets impacting all around my squad's position at Al-Azimiyah Palace with zero effect, RPGs slamming into packs mounted on the outside of AAVs but not detonating, and even a case of an RPG striking a Marine in the helmet but failing to explode I believe, were all genuine battlefield miracles.

First Battalion Fifth Marine's Chaplain Cash, nephew of the late, great Johnny Cash, did an outstanding job preparing his Marines spiritually before they crossed the line of departure and sustained them spiritually during the long march to Baghdad. The chaplain also did a superb job recording battlefield miracles that helped protect and sustain the Marines of RCT-5 in a book he wrote titled *A Table in the Presence*. After OIF, Chaplain Cash was featured in a video titled *Military Miracles*. The video chronicled four well-known extraordinary events I can only attribute to divine providence.

The first miraculous event he recorded took place amid an enemy mortar barrage. The platoon sergeant for a platoon of gun trucks and one of the unit's embedded reporters were well within a mortar's casualty radius when it impacted and exploded. Both men were thrown violently to the ground, several feet from where they were standing; each miraculously survived without sustaining so much as a scratch. The same gun truck and platoon sergeant were the subject of yet another set of unexplainable circumstances weeks later when they came under an RPG attack that sent a rocket through the truck, packed with four Marines and their gear. Witnesses of the event were so sure there could be no survivors they began preparations to send the deceased home. The RPG pierced the gun truck on the driver's side, passed through, and exited on the other side, and nobody was seriously injured. An impact of that magnitude surely should have resulted in all four Marines killed or severely injured. Yet, every one of them seemed to be under a supernatural hedge of protection.

A platoon sergeant in another RCT-5 company was sitting in the troop commander seat of the AAV he was traveling in when something struck him violently in the head. The dazed Marine picked up the helmet he was wearing to find the entry and exit holes of an enemy 7.62 mm round. The round entered on one side, traveled around the inside of the helmet, and exited on the other side without so much as touching the Marine's head. The heavy caliber of the round and the high velocity at which it traveled should have given it plenty of energy to prevent the round from deflecting off its course. It could be explained in no other way but that it was a miracle that the Marine survived the encounter unscathed.

The fourth miraculous event the video chronicled is perhaps the most profound of them all. A platoon of phantom AAVs suddenly appeared on an overpass that did not exist, to prevent 1st Battalion 5th Marine's beleaguered command AAV from being overwhelmed and destroyed by the enemy.

Eyewitnesses say the vehicles on the overpass looked clean and brand new when they should have been covered with weeks of desert grime. Although officers in the command AAV were utilizing a Blue Force Tracker and were well-versed in where friendly and enemy forces were located in the battle space, they had no idea where the platoon of AAVs came from or where they went. Days later, the Executive Officer of First Battalion Fifth Marines traveled on the exact route the event took place and found no evidence an overpass even existed at the location.

Chaplain Cash commented on the assault on Al-Aziriyah: "When I talked with some of the Marines, I had felt like I stumbled upon a group of men who just walked through the Red Sea, and I was just as much a witness as them. I was witnessing men whose lives had been changed by things they could not explain from the night before... the way I see it, we can choose to believe that we are at the mercy of a chaotic universe that occasionally hiccups and defies its own laws, or we can believe in the prospect that there is a loving God who, from time to time decides to break through to our lives, to punctuate our existence with the reminder that I am here, that I love you and that I want you to know Me".

The battalion commander of First Battalion Fifth Marines, already a seasoned combat veteran before OIF, said of the assault on the Baghdad palace, "There was absolutely no doubt that someone was watching over us that night; we should not have survived that fight like we did."

Places to visit in Uwchlan Township, Pennsylvania.

A walk along the Uwchlan Trail will take you to remnants of the region's iron heritage. One can view ruins of the forges and mills that once operated in the area, including an old springhouse, a dam from the late 1700s, a forge, and a mill. Descriptive plaques at these sites will help one learn more about the region's history. The trail intersects with the 2.6-mile Struble Trail at Dowlin Forge Road and ends at Pennypacker and Milford Roads. Visit historic Lionville and its 18th-century houses and buildings, including the Uwchlan Meetinghouse. Finish this piece of the Patriot's Path with a stroll around Baird Park. Take a look at the tiny cabin along Ship Road, walk along several ponds, visit the life-sized Revolutionary War Patriot statue, go inside the township building, and ask to see the historic Hugh Pugh Room.

Uwchlan Meetinghouse is located at 5 North Village Avenue Exton, Pennsylvania.

Red Lyon Inn is located at South Village Drive and Whitford Road Exton, Pennsylvania.

Uwchlan Trailhead is located at Shelmire and Dowlin Forge Roads Downingtown, Pennsylvania.

Baird Park is located at 715 North Ship Road Exton, Pennsylvania.

Hugh Pugh Room is located in the township building at 715 North Ship Road Exton, Pennsylvania.

The Great Valley

"Emphasis in the Marine Corps isn't on talking about your feelings".

~Adam Driver, AKA Kylo Ren and Marine Corps Mortarman

September 17th found the wet weather in southeast Pennsylvania still not abating. Washington's Army was strung along the road through Yellow Springs, and Washington made his headquarters at the Yellow Springs Tavern. Sometime in the afternoon, Washington issued orders for cannon, firearms, and supplies to be sent to Warwick furnace via present-day route 23, which was to be the Army's next destination.

By September 18th it finally quit raining, and Washington found his Army in desperate need of gunpowder and ammunition. With Howe and his Army only a few miles away and danger close, Washington mobilized his men and headed west toward Warwick Furnace. His plan was for the Army to go into camp, repair arms, re-provision, and be in a better location to protect his back-country resources. The only primary account of the movement to Warrick Furnace is from Captain Robert Kirkwood of the Delaware Regiment, who reports that he "crossed French Creek Bridge," a route that would have taken the Army through East Pikeland past the Black Bear Tavern and the Continental Powder Works near Rapp's Dam. They made camp that night "about three miles further," which placed the Army along modern-day Route 23 in East Vincent Township. Although there is no documented evidence of the location of Washington's headquarters that night, local tradition is that he stayed at Brownback Tavern.

While the bulk of the American Army headed deeper into the backcountry, Wayne remained in the Great Valley with his division of 2,000 men to guard the routes to the furnace. The absence of an official record does not definitively locate the area where Wayne camped; however, Colonel Thomas Hartley gives us some indication of the camp location. He stated, "They made camp three miles from the Red Lion." Some historians believe the likely location was the home of Christian Hench along Pickering Creek.

While Washington was moving west toward Warwick Furnace, Howe moved east toward the upper fords of the Schuylkill River and camped three miles from Valley Forge. Howe's forces divided into two columns took slightly different routes through the Great Valley and reunited at Howel's Tavern in Tredyffrin Township, where they went into camp. On the 21st Howe marched his column to the mouths of French and Pickering Creeks at present-day Phoenixville and camped there until the 23rd.

Phoenixville, as we know it today, did not exist as a town in the 18th century, and the land around Howe's encampment would have comprised local farms, mills, and a tavern. A main road near the encampment and Howe's likely goal was Nutt Road, which connected Reading and Philadelphia. The road was named for Samuel Nutt, an Iron Master who used it to ship pig iron to forges and blacksmiths in the area.

Valley Forge was named for iron works owned by William Dewees, a Colonel in the Pennsylvania militia. He was not particularly happy about the Continental Congress's decision to establish a military depot in the vicinity of his iron works, sawmill, and grist mill for fear that the Crown Forces would confiscate the Continental arms, munitions, and supplies and destroy the mills; he was also worried that his mills would be the target of loyalist sabotage. On September 18th his fears were realized.

As the Crown Forces slowly trickled toward the Schuylkill River, Congress began evacuating to Lancaster. The vulnerable supply stores at Valley Forge needed to be moved to the backcountry, out of reach of the Crown Forces. Unfortunately, no one was available to remove the supplies because of confusion over military jurisdiction; locals were already mustered into the militias, and because of the general panic the proximity of the British Army was causing.

Captain Henry Light Horse Lee, with a small contingent of eight dragoons, along with Washington's aide de camp Alexander Hamilton, with a small detachment of only eight militiamen, were given the overwhelming task of removing the stores at Valley Forge or destroying them in place to prevent them from falling into British hands. Two mounted troops from the 16th Dragoons led by the infamous Colonel Tarleton, a detail of 200 dismounted dragoons, and three companies of Light Infantry commanded by Major Craig were ordered to Valley Forge to confiscate the supplies. Tarleton was about to have the second of at least three separate engagements with his American Dragoon counterpart, Captain Lee.

During the afternoon of Sept 18th Lee and Hamilton arrived at the forge, located along the mouth of Valley Creek and the Schuylkill River, and established two vedettes (mounted sentries) on the crest of Mount Joy, overlooking the mills and magazine. Although they had orders to try to remove the stores, it quickly became apparent they would have to destroy them. When the British advanced on the summit of the hill named Mount Misery, they discovered that some of the intelligence from the loyalist spy was inaccurate; instead of finding an unguarded magazine left abandoned by the militia guards, they found Lee and Hamilton's detail attempting to destroy the supplies in the magazine. Lee and Hamilton were warned by the vedettes who, sighting the British column, fired on it, alerting the men working in the magazine of the impending danger.

After the vedettes fired on the column, the British Dragoons ran their horses down the hill to engage the vastly inferior American detail before they could flee. Lee immediately embarked his dragoons on a flat-bottomed barge large enough to hold 50 men along with Hamilton, who earlier acquired the boats for just the purpose. When Lee realized the two vedettes were barely ahead of the British dragoons and in danger of being overtaken, he and two of his dragoons got off the boat to support the vedettes rather than detain the boat from moving across the river and out of range of British small arms. Hamilton's barge, taken by the swollen river, was quickly swept downstream and out of control while Lee and his dragoons relied on the speed of their horses, which, despite close fires, escaped westward with the vedettes.

Lee's distraction and escape bought Hamilton a little time but not enough to avoid drawing fire from the British forces. The strong current held the barge in place, making Hamilton and his men sitting ducks as the British lined the riverbank and fired on the exposed vessel. Hamilton was only able to escape by diving into the water. A strong swimmer, he was able to swim underwater for extended intervals to avoid the volleys; he stayed underwater so long that his soldiers thought he had drowned. He was eventually able to swim to the other side of the river and to safety.

He would later report to Congress that he lost his horse when the barge was fired on. In addition, one man was killed and another wounded; on the British side, only Major Craig's horse was killed. As for the forge and mills, Sarah Stevens, an eyewitness, reported that "the place being left to the mercy of the enemy, they set fire to the buildings which the stores were deposited, the forge and all of the buildings appertaining to it, all of which with their contents destroyed." Before the buildings were set on fire, the British were able to remove vast amounts of supplies stored in the magazine.

Marine Corps Tie-In...The Combat "V"

for:

"Heroic performance while serving as squad leader, third platoon, Company B First Battalion Fifth Marines, First Marine Division in support of Operation Iraqi Freedom, from 20 March to 20 April 2003. He led the collection and search of 38 enemy prisoners of war and ensured the proper security for 341 prisoners at the Rumaylah Oil fields. On 10 April, during the battalion's movement into Baghdad, Sergeant Moyer subjected himself to constant Rocket Propelled Grenade and small arms fire to direct fire against enemy positions along the route. At the compound, he dismounted his squad to provide security for the breaching element and then cleared through the compound. He then led his squad outside the palace walls on the eastern side to provide security for elements coming into the palace. He directed withering fire on enemy positions, and that enemy fire ceased after his squad returned fire. Sgt Moyer's initiative, perseverance, and total dedication to duty reflect credit upon himself and were in keeping with the highest traditions of the Marine Corps and the United States Naval service".

Historical places to visit in or near the Great Valley, Pennsylvania.

This segment of the Patriot Path will guide you to the Great Valley's 18th-century churches, field hospitals, graveyards, and headquarters that played a part in the Revolutionary War. Begin your tour of the Great Valley at The Baptist Church in the Great Valley, where you will find the graves of several American patriots. One of these graves is marked with a beautiful obelisk and plaque commemorating the resting place of Captain Benjamin Bartholomew. In 1776, Bartholomew raised a company of militia and served under Colonel Persifor Frazer. He was wounded in the leg at Brandywine but continued to serve throughout the war. Another famous patriot buried in this graveyard is Reverend David Jones. Jones pastored the Baptist Church of the Great Valley briefly until the start of the Revolutionary War. An ardent patriot, well-known for his love for liberty, Jones volunteered his services to the Continental Army and served as Wayne's chaplain throughout the war. He was known to carry a pair of derringers on his person and once held a suspected British spy under them until an arrest could be made. He was so persuasive in convincing his countrymen to fight for the American cause that Howe put a bounty on his head.

Next, take a drive over to the Valley Friends Meetinghouse, which served as a field hospital during Washington's winter encampment at Valley Forge. Across the road from the meetinghouse, you will find a well-maintained graveyard. A lone stone with an inscription, "The memorial is dedicated to those buried here who lost their lives in the cause of American Independence during the Valley Forge Encampment." Historical documents estimate over three hundred Revolutionary War Patriots are buried in the graveyard in unmarked graves. Next, drive over to the Church of Saint Peter in the Great Valley. This church was founded by The Church of England missionaries in 1704. The surviving church building was constructed in 1744 and used as a field hospital by both the Continental Army and the British forces. After the Paoli massacre, Captain Wolfe, who commanded the Light Company of the British 40th Regiment of Foot, and at least two other unidentified British soldiers who died of wounds sustained during the engagement at Paoli, were buried together with five unidentified American Patriots who died of wounds received during the massacre. It was rare for the British to have documented burials during the Revolutionary War. It is believed the reason this particular burial was documented was because of the church's affiliation with the Church of England. Today, if you visit this church and graveyard, you will find these graves marked with American and British flags waving in the breeze in unison. You will also find several other graves of patriots, and if you look hard enough, you will find the grave of an ancestor of a patriot who fought in the War for Independence.

Head back over to the southern side of the valley and visit two historic 18th Century homes that served as headquarters for a French officer and chief engineer who designed the defenses for the Valley Forge winter encampment, along with a mansion that served as Howe's headquarters while his Army was encamped on the once sprawling estate. The 1740 John Harvard House served as the headquarters of General Louis Duportail during the winter of 1777-78. Duportail also designed the siege works during the Battle of Yorktown. After the war, Duportail returned to France and participated in its Revolution. He was forced to flee his home country and returning to America, he bought a farm near Valley Forge. Unfortunately, he was lost at sea while attempting to return to France. The grounds are open to the public every Sunday from 1 PM to 3 PM. The Teegarden Park in Berwyn, Pennsylvania was established on a plantation that once belonged to Samuel Jones. In mid-September, after waiting for the nor'easter to blow through Goshen, Howe marched his Army to the Jones plantation and established another camp because the Schuylkill was swollen with storm surge and rendered impassable. Howe stayed in the Jones mansion which still stands adjacent to the park along Contention Lane as a private residence. The log barn, believed to be among a very few surviving of its kind, was saved from demolition and carefully dismantled. It has been reassembled on a new foundation at the nearby Duportail house where it is now open to the public. The mansion is in easy view of the road along with another barn and various outbuildings.

Finally, finish your visit to the Great Valley at the Gunkle Spring Mill. Although the mill wasn't in operation until after the Revolutionary War, it is still a great example of a well-preserved 18th-century grist mill. A new water wheel was recently constructed, and the mill is open to visitors during the summer months along with the miller's house and other contributing buildings.

The Baptist Church of the Great Valley is located at 945 North Valley Forge Road Devon, Pennsylvania.

<u>The Church of Saint Peter in the Great Valley</u> is located at 2475 Saint Peters Road, Malvern, Pennsylvania.

<u>Valley Friends Meetinghouse</u> is located at 1121 Old Eagle School Road Wayne, Pennsylvania.

<u>The Duportail House and Federal Barn</u> is located at 297 Adams Drive Chesterbrook, Pennsylvania.

<u>Teegarden Park</u> is located at 440 Old State Road, Berwyn, Pennsylvania.

<u>Gunkle Spring Mill</u> is located at 210 Conestoga Road Located at 44 Moore Road Malvern, Pennsylvania.

Chester Springs, Pennsylvania

"I want to walk into a room, be it a hospital for the dying or a hospital for the sick children and feel that I am needed. I want to do, not just to be".

~Princess Diana

The Lenape people gave Yellow Springs its name long before any European settlements were established in the area. As the people in Philadelphia got word of the yellow-tinted waters' healing properties, many visited Yellow Springs to drink and bathe in the mineral-rich water.

The Revolutionary War was fought with weapons that caused devastating injuries; heavy lead musket balls, cannons, swords, and bayonets killed, maimed and wounded an estimated 1,000 Continental soldiers each year of the War. Unbelievably, disease and exposure killed nine times that number. As the men from the colonies gathered from the thirteen colonies to fight, their germs mingled, spreading typhus, tuberculosis, smallpox, and influenza. Unsanitary conditions bred typhoid and dysentery. Food shortages caused scurvy and malnutrition.

Before the American Army marched out of the Valley Forge encampment in June of 1778, between 1,800 and 2,000 men died of illness, more men than were killed at any single battle of the War because 18th-century medicine was unable to cure most ailments, infections, or diseases. Sometimes, the patient's condition would even worsen due to primitive medical procedures. Bloodletting was such a procedure, thought to be beneficial to patients. Doctors used lancets and sometimes leeches to remove large amounts of blood from the sick. A common medical theory during the 18th Century was that the immune system could only deal with one illness at a time. If a second illness occurred, the first would leave. This inspired doctors to irritate the skin to cause blistering, using all manner of noxious materials to achieve this. Another method doctors used to treat an illness was to induce a patient to vomit or purge the bowels.

During the encampment at Valley Forge, General Washington requested that the Continental Congress build a hospital to serve the soldiers of his Army. Dr. Kennedy loaned a portion of his Chester Springs land to Congress for a hospital site. On January 3rd 1778, with disease rates in the American Army rising, the Continental Congress ordered that the construction of a new military hospital begin at Yellow Springs. Yellow Springs Hospital became the Continental Army's first permanent military hospital. 1,300 soldiers were treated at Yellow Springs throughout the Army's six-month encampment at Valley Forge.

The hospital, called Washington Hall, was built by Zachariah Rice. When the hospital was completed, it measured one hundred and six feet by thirty-six feet. The first floor consisted of a kitchen, dining room, and utility rooms. Two hospital wards were built on the second floor, and private rooms took up the third floor.

Zachariah Rice's wife, Abigail Hartman, is regarded as the hospital's first nurse. In the summer of 1750, she immigrated to Pennsylvania with her parents, Johannes and Margaret Hartman. In 1757, when she was sixteen, Abigail married Zachariah in a ceremony performed by the Reverend Muhlenberg. She probably met Zachariah, who was a Pennsylvania militiaman, before her adolescence. Two years later, Abigail gave birth to their first child; according to the Rice family bible, Abigail gave birth to a baby thirteen times in the next fourteen years.

The hospital at Yellow Springs was about a mile from the Rice family farm along Pickering Creek, and although it is unclear why Abigail first visited Yellow Springs, a logical assumption would be to visit her husband since he was building the hospital. Period documentation suggests that Abigail began to travel to the hospital at Yellow Springs regularly to support convalescing soldiers and to help with their morale. One of Abigail's descendants wrote, "Abigail came on her errands of mercy, carrying foods and delicacies to the sick and wounded soldiers."

Unfortunately, Abigail paid the ultimate price for her selfless service at Washington Hall. Sometime during her work at the hospital, she contracted typhoid fever from one of the patients. She had several complications from the illness and failed to recover. She was buried at St. Peter's Church near Yellow Springs. On her first tombstone was inscribed: "Some have children, some have none, here lies the mother of twenty-one."

Few doctors in colonial times had formal education in medicine. Surgical and medical techniques were learned by apprenticeships, and the title "Doctor" was taken by those who wanted to practice medicine. One of these was Dr. Jacob Erhenzeller, who was certified to practice medicine by Dr. William Shippen Jr. although he did not receive a medical degree. Erhenzeller became an assistant surgeon for the Continental Army, serving with distinction during the Battle of Monmouth. After the war, he returned to his home in West Goshen and opened his own practice; he is buried at Grove Methodist Church near West Chester, Pennsylvania. During the 18th Century, there was a shortage of medical practitioners, particularly in rural areas. The Army's medical department had struggled from its inception due to a shortage of trained personnel. Dr. Bodo Otto was an exception to the norm. He was born in 1711 in Hanover, Germany. His father was Christopher Otto, controller of the district of Schartzfels, and his mother was Maria Magdalena Nienecken. He was named for his baptismal sponsor, Privy Councilor Baron Bodo von Oberg. Bodo Otto received an excellent education and planned to practice medicine. He served an apprenticeship with physicians and surgeons in Harzburg, Hildesheim, and Hamburg. He was also an intern at the Lazaretto in

Hamburg. Bodo Otto began his career as a surgeon with the Duke of Celle's Dragoons. After settling in Luneburg, he was accepted as a member of the College of Surgeons and became a surgeon to the prisoners and invalids in the fortress of Kalkberg. In 1749, he was appointed chief surgeon for the district of Schartzfels. He held this position until he emigrated to America with his family on the *Neptune*. He opened an office in Philadelphia late in 1755, but in 1760, he moved to New Jersey, where his practice is said to have covered Gloucester, Salem, and Cumberland counties.

Otto was a staunch Lutheran and, through the influence of the Reverend Henry Muhlenberg, moved to Reading, Pennsylvania, in 1773. Later, in 1776, he was appointed senior surgeon of the Middle Division of the Continental Hospitals and treated the wounded from the battle of Long Island. On February 17th 1777, Congress ordered him to Trenton to establish a military hospital for the treatment of smallpox. In 1777, he was assigned to a hospital in Bethlehem, Pennsylvania. In the spring of 1778, he was placed in charge of the hospital at Yellow Springs.

At Yellow Springs, Bodo Otto described how some nurses "refuse to serve any longer, as they have received no pay." Nurses in the 1700s were typically marginalized by society and often considered the physical property of their husbands. Nurses at Yellow Springs demanded the money they had been promised; Washington and Congress heard their protests and quickly resolved the problem. By the end of the War, some nurses earned better pay than enlisted men.

After Congress reorganized the medical and hospital departments in 1780, Otto was one of the fifteen physicians selected for the hospital department. He was among the last to leave the service on February 1st 1782. At the time of his retirement from the Army, Dr. John Cochran, the director-general, wrote a testimonial commenting on Otto's humanity and the success of his medical practice. After the

War, he reopened his Philadelphia office but soon returned to Reading.

Otto's sons were also Army physicians, assisting him as Junior Surgeons and Surgeon Mates. Otto died in 1787 and was buried at the Trinity Lutheran Church Cemetery in Reading, Pennsylvania. Many of his surgical instruments as well as a portrait of him and his wife, are in the collection of the Historical Society of Berks County in Reading.

The Vincent Baptist Church and Graveyard were so close to the Revolutionary War Hospital that it was natural that deceased soldiers were buried in its cemetery. In addition to the Revolutionary War, there are also stone markers for soldiers who served in the French and Indian War and from more recent conflicts. In 1894, it was discovered that there were approximately 200 unmarked graves in the cemetery. White marble stones, which were said to be of the earliest members of the congregation and of unknown Revolutionary War soldiers from the Yellow Springs Continental Hospital, were purchased to be placed on these gravesites. The "unlettered stones" were mentioned again in September 1902 as follows:

"In Vincent burial ground are many grave markers that bear no inscriptions, just small square white marble stones. When the Yellow Springs was used as a hospital during the Revolution, the dead were buried in this enclosure, and rough stones marked their graves. The church people, in their recent renovation, placed these new stones, for which they deserve the thanks of the nation."

At least two Revolutionary War Soldiers buried in the cemetery lay in marked graves. John and Mary Philips came from Wales in 1755. Their sons, John and Josiah, both served in the Revolutionary War. John was a captain, and Josiah was a lieutenant in the Continental Army. Both are buried in the Cemetery.

Not only has the church served as a burial place for soldiers of the American Revolution, but it has also welcomed the children who were orphaned during the American Civil War. The children attended services at the church after the Chester Springs Civil War Orphans School opened in 1869. They decorated the graves of the veterans each year on what became known as Decoration Day, now more commonly referred to as Memorial Day.

On Decoration Day 1907, "At 8:30 a.m., the boys' battalion, headed by the school band, followed by the line of girls, marching in true soldierly precision to the cemetery where a most beautiful service was rendered. A dirge was played by the band, a prayer offered by the Rev. C. H. Wilson, the graves of all the pupils and "old soldiers" who lie buried there were strewn with the beautiful flowers of springtime, a salute to the dead was fired by the battalion, after which Rev. E. C. Sult delivered a most beautiful address... "America" was sung, benediction pronounced, and "Taps" sounded by the buglers."

The church provided a burial plot for the children who died while attending the school. An inscribed granite obelisk marks the resting place of 21 children in addition to the two straight lines of white marble stones downhill from the monument.

Have you ever watched the 2017 movie *The Greatest Showman,* which was based on the life and showmanship of P.T. Barnum? In 1850, Barnum brought European opera singer Jenny Lind, known as the Swedish Nightingale, to America and put her on tour. Barnum paid Lind an astounding $1000.00 per appearance during her two-year tour. From 1850-52, she performed in 93 concerts and appeared five times in Philadelphia. Cinematically, the two had an affair of sorts that went wrong, prompting her abrupt return to Europe. Historically, nothing of the sort happened. She and Barnum did not enjoy an intimate relationship, and looking for a break from Barnum's overbearing personality, Lind traveled to Yellow Springs to rest and relax. In May of 1852, just before she returned to Europe, she held a concert at Yellow Springs, as evidenced by an article mentioning an 1852 concert ticket at Yellow Springs that had been discovered. A spring and guesthouse are named in Lind's honor at modern Yellow Springs.

Marine Corps Tie-In...Naval Hospitals.

On an autumn day in 29 Palms, California, my platoon played a game of tackle football in one of the few grass fields on base. Concerned that our aggressive nature would cause injuries, our company commander mandated that Marines wear flak jackets to minimize injury when playing tackle football. The flacks issued in those days were post-Vietnam War era and old, even to Marine standards. One of our platoon members was lightning-fast on his feet and was always challenging to tackle. During one game, the Marine ran a quick slant and caught the ball right in front of me. I instinctively went for the tackle which somehow, I successfully made, but only after he dragged me down the field a bit. Everyone on my team was stoked that I was able to tackle the speedster, and I was pretty excited, too.

When I attempted to high-five a teammate, I felt what I thought was a piece of athletic tape flopping against the back of my hand. When I looked down at my hand, I found that my right middle finger was the object I felt against my hand. It hung limp and opposite its usual posture. The injury wasn't pleasant to look at but wasn't very painful, so I had another Marine yank on it to turn it around; I balled up my hand and continued to play. After the game, it was apparent, given the massive swelling, that I probably broke the finger. A corpsman who examined it quickly referred me to the Emergency Room at the base hospital.

I rarely had an occasion, if any, before that day to visit a hospital emergency room and had never been the subject of a medical operation. The hand was x-rayed, and the injury was determined to be severe enough to prompt immediate surgery. I was soon prepped for the procedure, which required an IV placement, to administer regional anesthesia for the nerve block procedure they decided to go with.

A navy nurse prepped me for the IV and went for a vein... repeatedly. I already did not have a fondness for needles, so every time she missed a vein and went for another, I was becoming more inclined to stick myself with the IV. Frustrated and probably humiliated, she burst into tears and ran out of the room. Another nurse thankfully came in and hit a vein with his first attempt.

In a few minutes, I started to feel the effects of the anesthesia, and I was wheeled into an operating room. The surgeon told me they were not going to put me completely under for the operation and they would let me know what was going on procedurally. The doctor performed the nerve block and started flopping and chopping; he even positioned a mirror so I could watch his team do their work. I probably asked too many questions as the drugs loosened my usually reluctant tongue when, after an incision was made to access the twisted and shattered bone, a mask was abruptly placed over my face. I asked no more questions until I woke from the procedure with my hand in a soft cast and pins protruding from my finger to hold it in traction.

The next time I visited a Navy hospital, it was to repair a double hernia I acquired from being an 'intense' new Drill Instructor. I had a pretty good idea what my injury was before I was examined, so the doctor's diagnosis did not surprise me. What surprised me was the doctor's request after he had examined the herniated area. Apparently, the hernia was so severe he wanted a few of his resident practitioners to study the phenomenon. When I reluctantly agreed, I didn't anticipate five or six resident students to file into the room to physically examine the hernia, and the affair left me as embarrassed as I had probably ever felt before. I am thankful I took the precaution of changing my drawers prior to the visit.

The procedure was supposed to be an outpatient operation, and I was informed by a nurse prior to the surgery that I could go home once I recovered from the anesthesia and demonstrated I was stable enough to leave the hospital by walking around the nurse's station on my own. As soon as I woke up, I kicked my legs over the side of the bed and stood to take my walk. As quickly as my feet touched the floor, the rest of my body followed.

Unfortunately, my adventures with hernias did not end at the Naval Hospital in San Diego, as the repair failed several years later. I was working at Villanova University this time, and since I was nowhere near a naval hospital, the repair was conducted at a local surgical group. This time, I thought I would avoid humiliation by preparing better than I had before the last repair. I thought I had prepared the area of the operation thoroughly, but to my astonishment, the attending nurse came to my bedside with a razor and a pair of clippers. When she was done prepping the surgical area, I realized I had been fleeced, and I told her so in the presence of my wife and father-in-law. This time, I was probably a little less embarrassed due to the drugs that had been administered to prepare me for surgery, but that didn't spare my wife from the embarrassment my outburst had caused, although my father-in-law apparently got a good laugh out of it.

Historic places to visit in and near Chester Springs, Pennsylvania.

Begin your tour of historic Chester Springs at Yellow Springs Historic District, where Washington's Army stopped to weather the storm that ended the Battle of the Clouds before it could begin. Take a look at the old inn that Washington used as his headquarters, tour the ruins of the first American military hospital, and take in the sites of the mineral springs for which the district was named.

Drive down the road for a short distance to Vincent Baptist Church and Graveyard, where you will find the final resting place of several Revolutionary War Patriots who died at the hospital in Yellow Springs. Next, head over to St. Peters Lutheran Church and visit the grave site of Abigail Rice and her husband Zachariah, American Patriot and builder of the Hospital at Yellow Springs. The church was used as a hospital while the American Army camped at Valley Forge; at least a dozen Revolutionary War Patriots are buried alongside Zachariah and Abigail. Between these two stops, make sure to pull off the road and walk a short distance through a roadside meadow to the Old Root Cellar, which existed before the Revolutionary War.

Finish your trip on this portion of the Patriot's Path with a visit to the Mill at Anselma. Long before a mill was built at this location, the Lenape occupied the land. The grist mill was constructed in 1747 by Samuel Lightfoot and grinding flour when Washington's Army was operating in the area, so it is possible that the mill helped sustain American Patriots. Walk around the beautiful twenty-two-acre property and visit the well-preserved mill, house, and contributing 18th-century buildings. Book a tour and see the exhibits in the house, then walk through the only mill in America that has an intact colonial-era power transmission system. Plan your visit in October and enjoy some freshly pressed apple cider as you enjoy this rich cultural site.

Yellow Springs Historic District is located at 1685 Art School Rd Yellow Springs, Pennsylvania.

Yellow Springs Historical Marker is located at Yellow Springs Road and route 113 Yellow Springs, Pennsylvania.

Washington's Headquarters is located at 1701 Art School Road Yellow Springs, Pennsylvania.

Vincent Baptist Church and Graveyard is located at 2109 Art School Road Yellow Springs, Pennsylvania.

The Old Root Cellar is located at 1811 Horse-Shoe trail Chester Springs, Pennsylvania.

St. Peter's Lutheran Church is located at 1239 Clover Mill Road Chester Springs, Pennsylvania.

The Mill at Anselma is located at 1730 Conestoga Road Chester Springs, Pennsylvania.

East Vincent, East Coventry Township and the Charleston Village Historic District

"Freedom is not free, but the U.S. Marine Corps will pay most of your share".

~Ned Dolan, Captain of Marines and CIA Officer.

In 1777, the land where Ellis Woods Cemetery is located on Route 23 and Hill Church Road in East Vincent township was owned by John Hiester, a member of a prominent family of early settlers, and his barn was likely used as a hospital. John Hiester served as a captain in the Chester County Militia. He also had two brothers: Daniel Hiester Jr, a colonel in the Philadelphia County Militia, and Joseph, a lieutenant colonel in the Berks County Militia. It would be a convenient coincidence if one of the Hiester brothers was traveling with the Continental Army on September 19th and was involved with arranging for the care of the sick and wounded on John's property.

The small Revolutionary War cemetery contains the mass grave of 22 Revolutionary War Soldiers from the Battle of Brandywine and the encampment of Valley Forge. These unknown soldiers died in the adjacent German Reformed Church in 1778, which is located a short distance up the hill from the cemetery and was used as a hospital. The Church is not far off the route Washington's Army could have taken on their march to Warrick Furnace.

Inscriptions on the Obelisk are as follows:

On the Northeast Side *"Sacred to the memory of Twenty-two Revolutionary Soldiers, who in the fall of 1777, when the American Army had encamped at the Valley Forge, were lodged in the German Reformed Church, (in sight) then occupied as an hospital; who there, distant from their homes, uncomforted by friends and kind relations, deceased in the spring of 1778, of a fever then prevailing in the camp; who were interred in this ground and where they slumbered in their peaceful but neglected tomb (except that Mr. Henry Hipple Sr, preserved the ground) until the Union Battalion of Volunteers of Chester County, aided by the generous and patriotic people of this vicinity, resolved to have them enclosed and a monument placed over them; the foundation of which accordingly was laid on the l9th of November, 1831, upon which occasion regular military ceremonies were observed, and a funeral oration delivered, to perpetuate the profound regard due the individuals who paid the forfeit of their precious lives for our sacred rights, and for privileges which they were never permitted to enjoy, and to contribute to generations unborn, the memory of the precious price of the Liberty and Independence of our happy Union. They raised this monument on the 25th of October 1833, and they also dedicate to the memory of several other Revolutionary Soldiers who, the same time and same manner, deceased in the Lutheran Church (then used as a hospital and are buried near it and in other places of this vicinity)."*

On the Southeast Side, *"Within these walls surrounding them, they Can yet be thought to claim a tear; Oh, smite thy gentle breast, and say, 'The friends of freedom slumber here.' "We hear their humble graves adorn, We, too, may fall and ask a tear, 'Tis not the beauty of the morn That proves the evening shall be clear.*

On the Northwest Side, "Their names, though lost in earth below and hence are not recorded here, are known where lasting pleasures flow, Beyond the reach of death and fear" "Their feet have trod misfortune's sands, their lives by hardships worn down; They're gone, we trust, to better lands, To brighter sunshine of their own."

On the Southwest Side is the inscription *"Virtue, Liberty, and Independence."*

Near East Vincent Church stands the Zion Lutheran Church. Both congregations shared the East Vincent church until 1762, and the first building on this site was erected in 1775. The present building was built in 1861 and is still in use today. Like East Vincent Church, Zion was used as a hospital during the Valley Forge encampment, and soldiers are known to have died there as well. However, their grave sites are unmarked and unknown. They were likely buried in the original cemetery or somewhere nearby.

It is a little-known fact that East Coventry Township is home to another old cemetery at 580 Ellis Woods Road where several more Revolutionary War soldiers are buried. The little hill in East Coventry Township serves as the final resting place for some of Washington's soldiers who succumbed to injuries and disease during the winter encampment of the American Army at Valley Forge. Seventeen graves are marked; but according to local tradition, upwards of around 150 soldiers were likely buried in the woods surrounding the cemetery based on body parts and buttons unearthed over the years from road widening projects and other improvements. Since none of the remains were ever identified, government-issued marble markers were not provided. Today, the remains rest together, their graves marked with a simple period flag and a shared memorial.

Revolutionary War soldiers are buried in the Charlestown Presbyterian Cemetery located on the Phoenixville-Charlestown Road just north of the historic village of Charlestown. The cemetery is part of the Charlestown Historic Village, along with 21 contributing buildings. The cemetery is associated with the Charlestown Presbyterian Church, founded in 1743 on a portion of land given by Job Harvey. The Church once stood in the Northwest portion of the present graveyard. Around 200 or 250 graves are marked by a rough stone with no inscription at all. The graveyard is likely the final resting place of many more American patriots than there are crumbling grave markers and tombstones. The Old Charleston Cemetery was halfway between the winter encampment and the Yellow Springs Hospital. Injured and diseased men were transported back and forth between the encampment and the hospital. Unfortunately, many men did not survive and were left at local cemeteries, which were overwhelmed with disease-ridden bodies. The soldiers were often hastily buried in large, unmarked graves to avoid the spread of disease, with only a funeral shroud or blanket to cover their bodies due to the lack of proper caskets. The unmarked graves of the fallen were thought to be lost forever until a hand-drawn map of the cemetery turned up in a wall at the Chester Springs Hospital during the early 1800s.

The present graveyard was situated on one of the earliest laid-out roads in the township. One of the first persons buried in this graveyard was Lewis Evans of Vincent Township, who died May 19th 1762. Also buried here was Dr. Samuel Kennedy, who died on January 19th 1776; he was a Surgeon for the 4th Battalion of Pennsylvania Troops. A prominent marble obelisk in the cemetery was erected by the people of Phoenixville, dedicated to the memory of Dennis Dempsey, who was enlisted with Captain J. Siddan's Company, a Delaware regiment under Colonel John Haslett. During the Battle of Germantown, a soldier named McQuade was pierced through the leg by the sword wielded by a British soldier. Dempsey freed him from the sword and carried him to safety.

Marine Corps Tie-In...a Sacred Duty.

While assigned to Marine Barracks 8th and Eye, located in the National Capitol Region, our primary duty was presidential support. We also had a few collateral ceremonial duties we were regularly assigned. One of the more sacred duties was providing ceremonial support for funerals at Arlington Cemetery. Funeral duties included providing full honor escorts, firing parties, and casket bearers.

The casket bearers, dubbed the World-Famous Body Bearers, were assigned to Bravo Company and consisted of hand-picked, very buff Marines. They practiced their routine over and over with weighted caskets until their routine was perfect. They operated large field pieces during Friday evening parades and spent the rest of their time eating and bodybuilding. The barracks gym would close for general use during specific times of the day to give the Body Bearers exclusive use of the facility.

During a funeral, usually in Arlington National Cemetery, the Body Bearers gently lifts a flag-draped casket from a hearse or caisson. They march it solemnly to the graveside while the band plays The Marines Hymn in slow time. At the graveside, the team lifts the casket high three times before lowering it gently to rest on putlogs placed over the grave. The team, with great precision and ceremonial pose, folds the flag and hands it to the presiding officer, who, in turn, presents it to the family before the funeral is concluded.

The team performed their solemn duty in every clime and place except for particularly adverse weather conditions if the funeral can be postponed. On one snowy winter morning in Arlington Cemetery, while my platoon was providing a ceremonial escort for a funeral, we almost witnessed a mishap that would have been unfortunate, if not catastrophic, if the worst had occurred. As the team was slowly maneuvering the casket to the gravesite, they had to negotiate a slippery slope to reach their destination. The team almost reached the gravesite when two of the lead bearers lost their footing and lurched violently forward. The forward momentum caused by the sudden slip forced the lead bearers nearly to their knees as the rest struggled to maintain their grip on the casket. One could almost envision the casket sliding down the hill, casket open, the dead guy sitting up 'Weekend at Bernie's' style, resembling an Olympic luge, as the casket leveled headstones in its path. The World-Famous United States Marine Body Bearer's motto... 'The last to let you down'.

Assignment to a seven-man firing party was considered a prestigious duty and went to the most seasoned Marines in the ceremonial platoons. During the routine, the firing party performs a three-volley salute by aiming their M1 Grand rifles in a precise direction over the casket and firing blank cartridges into the air three times in perfect unison. Taps are played directly following the three-volley salute. After the flag is folded and presented to the family of the deceased Marine, spent rounds are typically gathered and carefully placed within its folds.

The custom of the gun salute at funerals originates from the European dynastic wars. When battles ceased and after the dead and wounded were removed from the battlefield, three shots were fired into the air to signal that the battle could resume. Interestingly, because each of the seven-member firing party fires three volleys, I was under the impression that the three-volley salute we performed was called a 21-gun salute. To my admonishment, a 21-gun salute is reserved only for the President of the United States, former presidents, presidents-elect, chiefs of state, heads of government, and reigning monarchs to announce their arrival. Of these dignitaries, only a POTUS receives a 21-gun salute during their funeral.

My assignment to a Marine firing party resulted in hours of extra practice, dry-firing M1s as a team, and then finally working with blanks until the team performed flawlessly and consistently. At my first firing party detail, the seven of us stood at ceremonial parade rest in the cemetery adjacent to the burial site with our rifles, each loaded with three blank rounds. At the prescribed time, the detail commander, an NCO from our platoon, snapped to attention, performed a crisp about-face, and commanded us to the position of attention, half right face and port arms. The NCO in charge then smartly marched himself to a position just right of the detail and issued the following commands: "The first count is the dead count (meaning we were in the ready position) standby...ready, aim fire!

Ready, aim, fire! Ready, aim, fire! Safeties, ready two! Present, Arms"! After the detail had presented arms, the NCO returned to his position centered and six paces from the detail, manipulating his sword in a sweeping motion, and rendered a salute as Taps was played for the fallen. The long hours of training paid off and the team performed flawlessly.

The platoons of ceremonial marchers at Marine Barracks 8th and Eye often received taskers to support funerals at Arlington National Cemetery. Whenever we received an assignment, we carefully dressed in white trousers, black undershirts, and unblemished, high-gloss Corfam shoes. We drew our rifles from the armory and boarded buses for the short trip to the cemetery. Every Marine on the bus remained standing on the bus ride to ensure our trousers didn't get wrinkled by sitting on them, and we all carried our blouses on hangers and pulled them on at the cemetery for the same reason.

The full honors escort detail typically started just outside of Fort Myer's Old Post Chapel, located on the fringe of the cemetery. The escort, including an army caisson team from the Army Old Guard, maintained a ceremonial posture until the service inside the chapel concluded and the Body Bearers secured the casket on the caisson. An escort was usually led by a company commander or the senior presiding officer, and the unit's guidon bearer. These two Marines were followed immediately by the band. Marching in the file directly behind the band were two or more ceremonial marching platoons separated by the color guard. Behind the platoons marched a chaplain followed by the caisson team and the eight Body Bearers who were the last to handle the casket.

The gloss-black caissons were initially built for a 75mm cannon in 1918, then equipped with ammunition chests, spare wheels, and tools used for the cannon. For funeral caissons, the gun and equipment box are removed and replaced with the flat deck on which the casket rests. Directly to the right of an exquisitely mounted Army caisson commander, six matched horses pull the flag-draped casket on the caisson, the horses adorned with meticulously maintained ceremonial tack and harness unique to their solemn duty at Arlington National Cemetery. Although all six horses are saddled, only those on the left have mounted riders. This tradition began in early 19th-century artillery units when one horse from each team was mounted while the other carried supplies and horse feed. Traditionally, a rider-less, caparisoned horse follows the casket of any Army or Marine Corps commissioned officer holding the rank of Colonel or above. As Commander in Chief, U.S. presidents are accorded the same honor. The horse is led behind the caisson equipped with an empty saddle, and the rider's boots are reversed in the stirrups, indicating the warrior will never ride again.

On one hot and muggy August afternoon we were scheduled for back-to-back funeral escorts and were required to bring an extra uniform to change between details. We arrived at the chapel dressed, were inspected then marched into a position where we assumed a ceremonial at-ease posture until the chapel service ended. Around 30 minutes had passed when our platoon sergeant, centered six paces from the platoon, began to frantically shift his weight from one foot to another. He eventually placed his gloved hand in the center of his back and began to tap vigorously, signaling that he needed a supernumerary to assume his position. Once another Marine took his position, the platoon sergeant hastily sought a place to relieve himself. By the time he returned to the platoon, the caisson team had arrived and was in position between the escort platoons and the chapel. We stood for another fifteen minutes when one of the team horses let loose a gusher. Suddenly the platoon sergeant started to do his pee-pee dance again and promptly started frantically signaling for the supernumerary to relieve him. Unfortunately, at about that time, the chapel doors swung open, and the Body Bearer team appeared with the flag-draped casket... the platoon sergeant had to remain in place.

We could clearly hear him quietly cussing as he struggled to maintain his bearing, which, in turn, made it difficult for us to keep straight faces. Resistance became futile, however, when out of the chapel walked a little old white-haired lady leaning precariously on a cane. As she slowly descended the marble steps, she walked directly behind the caparisoned horse, whose handler had difficulty controlling the animal. In an almost predictable, surreal moment, the horse's tail came up and a massive explosion of corrupted air was emitted from deep within its bowels. It fairly moved the old woman's hairdo and prompted her to shake the cane angrily at the horse's offending orifice. I quickly attempted to at least bite my cheek and maintain my composure although I could plainly hear my platoonmates snort and gasp as they lost their bearing.

Somehow, during the commotion, the platoon sergeant must have lost his personal struggle with his weak bladder and managed to sneak off unnoticed because, by the time we were on the march, the platoon commander was in his place in front of the platoon, but the supernumerary was marching in the platoon sergeant's position at the rear of the platoon.

Locations of the cemeteries mentioned above.

<u>The Revolutionary War Soldiers' Cemetery</u> is located at Route 23 and Hill Church Road in East Spring City, Pennsylvania.

<u>Ellis Woods Revolutionary War Cemetery</u> is located at 580 Ellis Woods Road, Pottstown, Pennsylvania.

<u>Old Charlestown Cemetery</u> is located at 2470 Charlestown Road, Phoenixville, Pennsylvania.

<u>Arlington National Cemetery</u> is located at One Memorial Avenue Arlington, Virginia.

French Creek, Pennsylvania

"Marines I see as two breeds, Rottweilers or Dobermans, because Marines come in two varieties, big and mean, or skinny and mean. They're aggressive on the attack and tenacious on defense. They've got really short hair and they always go for the throat".

~Rear Admiral Jay R. Stark

Gunpowder is a mixture of sulfur, charcoal, and potassium nitrate that must be combined in specific ratios to produce a dependable product. While this sounds simple enough, in 1775, chemistry was a rudimentary process at best. Potassium nitrate is a compound of nitrogen and potassium, and neither element had even been identified in the 1770s. What early chemists did know was that an ingredient they called nitre was needed. Some nitre-producing recipes involved soaking soil in urine from animals and humans than allowing it to dry. The dried urine-infused soil was then boiled to produce saltpeter. Recipes for nitre varied in method, which added to the problems of making gunpowder in volume. The Process required half a year or more to produce nitre-bearing soil, significantly reducing gunpowder production in America.

In 1774, the Frankford Mill was the only gunpowder mill operating in the colonies but it produced a minuscule amount of the black powdered propellant compared to what Washington would need to wage a successful war. To make matters worse, the mill was not producing the high-quality powder needed for American artillery pieces. It remained in operation until the British seized it after they occupied Philadelphia in 1777. A year later, the owner of the mill was accused of underhanded dealings with the British and was convicted of treason by the Supreme Executive Council of the Commonwealth of Pennsylvania, resulting in the confiscation all his property, including the mill.

Another Pennsylvania Powder mill operation was built in 1775 and was located on Crum Creek, about three miles from Chester and was managed by Dr. Robert Harris, who was a relative of John Harris, namesake of Pennsylvania's capital. The mill, consisting of a 30'x20' mill house and a 20'15' drying house, was built to produce a ton of powder a month. Harris received a ton of saltpeter and 500,000 pounds of Sulphur from the Continental Congress to mix into gunpowder, but that mill was not producing nearly enough either.

In early 1776, the Continental Congress commissioned the construction of a powder mill and gun factory on French Creek, intended to supply the Continental Army during the war, and it was the only powder mill and gun factory commissioned by the Continental Congress. A 1776 report described the powder works complex as "buildings consisting of a powder mill (or stamping mill), a graining mill, a saltpeter house, and four drying houses." By early winter that same year, the powder mill and a gun factory, complete with its own boring and grinding mill to manufacture gun barrels, were built along French Creek because the stamping mill and the graining mill depended on waterpower. Since raids by the British forces were a real threat, barracks were built to house a company of militia tasked with protecting the works.

The French Creek Works operated successfully until March 10th 1777, when an unexplained explosion destroyed the stamping mill. Because sabotage was suspected, Congress demanded an inquiry into the incident. However, an official investigation concluded that an unfortunate accident contributed to the explosion of the stamping mill and not sabotage. No historical records indicate that the stamping mill was rebuilt, but the gun factory continued operations during the spring, summer, and early fall of 1777.

On August 29th all remaining weapons from the French Creek complex were ordered to be sent to Washington's Army. By September 10th intelligence of a probable British raid on the complex compelled Colonel DeHaven to request additional soldiers to guard the powder works as wagons began moving powder and guns out of the reach of the British forces.

The threat to the complex was very real. Captain Johann Ewald of the Hessian Field Jager Corps commanded a detachment of approximately 140 men and officers, including mounted and dismounted Jagers, Light Infantry, and grenadiers, and was operating in the French Creek area that autumn. On the morning of September 22nd Ewald's patrol marched Pikeland Township "...near to the rear of the army, where an enemy party was believed to be stationed" and stumbled upon a deserted powder works complex. "I passed the village, which consisted of perhaps forty to fifty buildings but had been completely deserted by the inhabitants. I deployed on the other side behind the hedges or walls and searched through the village, where I found a blown-up powder magazine and a rifle factory, in which several thousand pieces of fabricated and unfinished rifles and sabers of all kinds were stored". After Ewald's patrol secured the area, they began to destroy the complex. "I ordered everything smashed to pieces, set fire to the factory, and marched back."

Washington soon realized if he was going to have any chance of victory, the colonies needed to import their powder from overseas. To import gunpowder from other countries, the colonists had to trade through Britain since imports with the American colonies from other European countries were controlled by Britain through the parliament's Navigation Acts. Industrial production was discouraged in the colonies by various laws. One of the results was that the colonists allowed American powder mills to close as it was far more convenient and cost-effective to import gunpowder from Britain. Because of these factors, the colonies perilously needed powder supplies at the beginning of the war since they could expect no further shipments from Britain. Had it not been for the French stepping in and supplying the Americans with arms, supplies, and gunpowder from 1776 through the war's end, American forces would not have been able to sustain an effective Army to fight and win the battles they did.

The Seven Stars Inn began as the homestead of Gerhard Brumbach, who settled in Vincent Township in 1718. The land was then new and uncultivated, with a small village of Lenape Indians located below the homestead. Gerhard made friends with them and even engaged them to work for him, paying them in provisions for their labor. The Lenape honored Gerhard with the name "Minquon," meaning "never violent or wrong in dealings."

Around 1720, Samuel Nutt, a local Iron Master, opened the first road in Vincent Township, Chester County, at his own expense. The road, called Ridge or Nutt Road, extended past Gerhard's homestead. Traffic was heavy along the road due to the growing iron industry in the region, along with a steady addition of new settlers on Ridge Road. Gerhard found he was frequently sheltering drovers and travelers. On May 25th 1736, he petitioned Pennsylvania to run a "Publick House on the ground that he frequently oppresses by travelers whom he was obligated to entertain, and that there were no publick houses within twenty miles below, not thirty miles above his place on the Great Road which leads to Philadelphia to the Iron Works, and from thence to Conestoga."

Gerhard's inn prospered, and he was able to improve his land and build a grist mill, the first to be constructed in the French Creek region. In 1741, he gave a plot of ground to Brownback's German Reformed Church "for a burial place for his family, his descendants, and his neighbors." The church still in use today is known as Brownback's United Church of Christ and stands just below Ridge

Road. Gerhard died in 1751, but the inn remained with the family for two more generations.

His son Benjamin, who was commissioned a first lieutenant and assigned to the 2nd Battalion of the Chester County Militia, inherited the inn, and ran it during the Revolutionary War. The inn became a frequent meeting location because of his role and popularity in the militia. In 1776, Colonel John Beaton taught locals how to make gunpowder in an old log building that stood in a vineyard on the property, and on August 30th 1776, Colonel Grubb submitted a receipt to Congress "for 55 Breakfasts of Captain Adam's Company at Benjamin Brownback's." Historical documents show that Washington and his army marched on Ridge Road to protect the military supplies at the Reading Furnace. Tradition has it that Washington departed the inn on September 18th 1777, to cross the Schuylkill River at Parker's ford with his Army.

Benjamin's inn thrived for nearly thirty years and did well enough to build a large house, now called Hiestands Corner, at the junction of Lancaster and Ridge Roads. Sometime after Benjamin died in 1786, his 85-year-old widow, Rachel Parker, was murdered, and the murderer was never brought to justice. The inn, then known simply as the "Tavern," was left to Benjamin's son Henry, who ran it until his death in 1804. After Henry's death, the inn finally left the Brumbach family when it was sold to John Baker. Baker is the man credited for naming the inn "Seven Stars." Under Baker's management, the Inn became the region's center of gravity. During the peak of the Conestoga Wagon days, it was a natural gathering place for town meetings, elections, and celebrations.

In 1848, John Yeager, an avid Fox Hunter, bought the inn, and it became well known throughout Chester County as a hunter's retreat. During the Prohibition years, the inn turned to other means of financial stability in the absence of alcohol sales. The inn would change ownership eleven more times until the Canterino Family acquired it. The family operates a tavern and restaurant, continuing the inn's rich legacy.

The reason Baker named the inn "Seven Stars" remains ambiguous. Some say it used to be called Seven Crossroads or Seven Daughters. Others say it is named for the seven stars in the Big Dipper constellation or to honor the seven years of America's War for Independence.

Marine Corps Tie-In…Welcome to the Stumps.

After three years of Presidential support at Marine Barracks 8th and Eye in Washington, DC, I received orders for 3rd Battalion 7th Marines, based at the Marine Corps Air Ground Combat Center (MCAGCC) located just outside of Twenty-Nine Palms, California. The new barracks Sergeant Major at 8th and Eye had just been reassigned from MCAGCC, and word on the street was he was going to make sure all the 8th and Eye Marines scheduled to rotate to the fleet that year would receive orders to his old stomping grounds.

I had wanted to serve in California anyway and even requested the West Coast as an enlistment incentive before boot camp, but I had sun and surf in mind, not cactus, roadrunners, coyotes, and desert rats. When my plane landed in Palm Springs, California, I stepped onto the tarmac and smelled the desert for the first time; the creosote, desert sage, and desert lavender combined to produce an unexpectantly pleasant aroma that will linger with me forever. In time, I learned to love these desert scents, especially after a rare storm when rain intensified the desert fragrance.

But when I arrived in Palm Springs on a late winter evening and rode on a military shuttle van that took me through Yucca Valley, Joshua Tree, Twenty-Nine Palms, and into the heart of the Mohave where my new duty station was situated, I had anything but love for the desert. The scene during that long, moon-lit December ride was like no other I had ever experienced. Endless desert on either side of

California Route 62 was dotted here and there with a few small shacks and Joshua trees that strangely silhouetted the pale, silver desert floor. Yucca Valley, Joshua Tree, and 29 Palms were the only three small towns between Palm Springs and the base; since the base supplied everything a young Marine could want, I spent little time outside its gates.

Marine grunts assigned to 29 Palms are a breed apart from other Marines. They are typically wilder and grungier than a Marine stationed elsewhere in the fleet. The trouble they get into, although relatively confined to base proper, ranged at times from typical to lunacy. There was little to do with any free time the Marines had; there were no iPhones or personal computers in those days, and few Marines had a vehicle to get off base. It was, however, a great place to conduct combat training because every training event was live fire; there were no fire hazards in the desert to limit training to blank fire, or no fire, such as conditions tend to be from Spring through Fall on Camp Pendleton, California. The base was a very poor place for physical conditioning because the environment was nearly always hot and dusty, and a bite from the desert wildlife (rattlesnakes, scorpions, and black widows) had the potential to kill you or make you wish you were dead.

The base had great terrain features like Sugar Cookie Hill, a sand dune Marines attempted to run down and named for the condition they find themselves in when they inevitably fall and tumble to the hill's base, covered in sweat and sand. The base also featured Lake Bandini, a series of sewage sanitation holding ponds, and a road around its perimeter serving as the route for the three-mile run portion of the Physical Fitness Test every Marine had to record semi-annually. There were few places where grass grew, and the few grassy areas on base were the carefully irrigated athletic fields, golf course, and the Base General's lawn. If a Marine was caught even walking on the General's grass, the base Sergeant Major would have his foot up the offending Marine's backside. The dare in those times was to attempt to pee on the General's grass without getting caught, and it was visually evident that several Marines had taken up the dare successfully.

The Base General ruled his Marines with an iron fist and even had the ability to reach into the local domain and shut down car dealers who preyed on unsuspecting junior Marines by selling them used cars at 35 percent interest. Local establishments like an infamous were club were also within reach of the General's long arm of justice. One year, the club brazenly advertised "Dollar a wife night...last night for 2nd Battalion 7th Marine wives" on their marquee sign, referring to the spouses of Marines scheduled to return home the following week from a long deployment in Okinawa. The club mysteriously closed down the following week.

One night, a Marine standing duty at the rifle range was sent to the brig for firing a round into a television set in the duty hut. According to the story, the Marine was practicing his quick drawl with a service pistol he was required to carry as the OOD when he 'accidentally' discharged it. In the Marine Corps, unintentionally discharging a firearm isn't considered accidental; it is considered negligent. Attempting to outdraw Clint Eastwood on a television screen with a service pistol that is only supposed to be placed in condition 1 (round in chamber) for a critical threat was negligent at best.

During a routine field day (room cleaning) inspection, a platoon member's room was being inspected when a mysterious noise from a locked wall locker overhead compartment caught the inspecting NCO's attention. The Marine (our platoon barber) was immediately ordered to unlock the overhead compartment, which the Marine refused to do. When the lock was finally cut, and the door opened, a very small female nearly rolled out and fell to the floor. As she was assisted out of the small compartment, belts of live ammunition fell out with her. A quick search found a virtual ammunition supply point in the Marine's locker. He had smuggled everything from belted ammunition to smoke grenades and pyro flares. He even had a few M203 high explosive grenade projectiles stashed away in the overhead.

On the day he was supposed to be administratively discharged from the Corps for his 'ammo and human trafficking,' the Marine decided to light up a victory reefer on the catwalk outside his room. Instead of being escorted off base with a very generous administrative discharge, he spent a little bit of time in the brig while waiting on his court martial and subsequent dishonorable discharge.

Two of the oddest events I witnessed while at 29 Palms didn't even happen while I was stationed at the base. The first occurred during Combined Arms Exercise (CAX) while assigned to 1st Battalion 5th Marine and the other during a site survey while assigned to 2nd Battalion 4th Marines as the battalion Logistics Chief. During the CAX, I was a young squad leader for 1st Battalion 5th Marines, and our platoon commander was a very arrogant Naval Academy grad. Our platoon was in a support-by-fire position, firing live rounds into targets on our company objective. The plan was to shift our fires on signal and to cease on another just before a sister platoon enveloped and assaulted through the objective. The signal to shift and a cease-fire was controlled by 'Coyotes,' senior infantry Marines assigned to 29 Palms to work with units conducting a CAX, so the chances of a fatal training accident were greatly minimized.

Our platoon commander had a different plan in mind and ordered elements of our platoon to continue firing, determining there was plenty of standoff between the beaten zone and the maneuvering platoon. He argued that training should be more realistic and that tactically, the signal plan to cease fire was unrealistic and initiated too early. The Marines knew better and calmly refused his order to continue to fire. The frustrated young lieutenant was on the verge of losing his mind when up the hill came our company gunnery sergeant, ol' WAR DOGG.

The WAR DOGG promptly got knee-deep in the lieutenant's business. Their argument quickly escalated to the point where an enraged, red-faced gunny took command of the situation and ordered the platoon off the hill. We were promptly displaced from our support-by-fire position, followed by a sobbing lieutenant repeatedly crying, "I am confident in my tactical skills," while big tears rolled down his cheeks.

I had my own unfortunate run-in with the young lieutenant several weeks after we returned from CAX. A week before the unit was scheduled to deploy to Bridgeport for a summer package, a duplex in base housing opened so I reserved a moving truck and asked my fireteam leaders to help move before I lost the house to someone else on the waiting list. The lieutenant found out my team leaders were going to help me move and called me into his office. He informed me I could not ask my team leaders to help me move because that would be abusing the chain of command. An argument quickly escalated into a shouting match that was abruptly interrupted by the WARRDOGG. The WARDOGG ordered me out of the platoon commander's office and asked me what the argument was about. When I finished telling my brief account, he ordered me to stand by and angrily marched into the office to confront the lieutenant. After a fair amount of screaming, a red-faced WARDOGG emerged and slammed the door. He pointed at me to go to his office and told me very tersely that the team leaders could help with the move if they wanted, but if he ever found out I talked to an officer like I did to the lieutenant again, he was going to make me wish I had not. My team leaders and I managed the move in less than a day and they were well compensated for their help.

The lieutenant, unfortunately, would not escape his propensity for making bad decisions. After a routine and uneventful deployment to Okinawa, the lieutenant, after returning to Camp Pendleton, was reassigned as the weapons platoon commander and, while on a static mortar range, commanded mortarmen to drop rounds on coordinates way outside the lateral limits of the range. I knew his coordinates were wrong, and the other NCOs on the hill practicing call for fire knew it, and the mortarmen, who fired live rounds on the range regularly, especially knew it. The Marines refused to drop rounds in the tubes, so the enraged lieutenant dropped a round into the tube himself and splashed a high explosive mortar round danger-close to a tent full of School of Infantry Marines.

The second event occurred near the end of my career when I went to MCAGCC to conduct a site survey of Camp Wilson for unit training. The camp is located along the base's airstrip, which accommodates helicopters, F-18s, F-35, and C-130s. When I was stationed at MCAGCC, Camp Wilson historically billeted visiting units training on the base, was not modernized and widely considered the base boondocks if there can even be such a thing in the Mojave Desert. It only consisted of a control tower, tarmac, and several rows of hot, metal Quonset huts built to house visiting units. Years after my assignment with the 7th Marines had ended, the transient camp had been modernized. The Quonset huts were replaced by cooler K-Span buildings. A mini-mart, enlisted club, laundromat, and gym have also been built at Camp Wilson.

My site survey team, which included a sergeant and a few company gunnery sergeants, were busily inspecting the K-Spans and marking them for company assignments. I had just returned from mainside, where I had arranged for the use of air conditioner units for the K-Spans that were set aside for heat-sensitive electronics when the sergeant came to me with an unusual request. While I was at mainside, a British Marine, a member of a visiting unit training at the facility, had noticed our small team milling around the K-Spans. The British Marine found our young sergeant and invited him to a K-

Span they were billeted in for alcoholic indulgences. When I glanced in that direction, I couldn't help noticing several British Marines running around their K-Span with cans of beverages, bodies girdled with MRE sleeves, and wearing nothing else but smiles. When I astutely pointed the scene out to the young sergeant, he suddenly had no desire to join the festivities of the Royal Marine Unit. When I related this story to my current boss, who had served in the French Foreign Legion and retired as a British Marine Commando, he smiled cynically, a silent verification of British Marines' love for their 'Nakey Time.'

Ironically, many years later, and after I retired from the Marines, I became a teammate with the Marine who served as base Sergeant Major while I was assigned to 29 Palms. We served as TAC officers at a military boarding school in Pennsylvania. We had many fond memories in common of that desert oasis, including PFTs around the breathtaking (literally) Lake Bandini, keeping Marines out of trouble at a local watering hole called the Mouse Trap, the joy of frequently navigating the rigors of range 400, and the mysterious powers of the Base Commanding General.

Historical places to visit in or near French Creek, Pennsylvania.

The Continental Powder Works historic sites can be accessed via several preserved trails. Convenient parking can be found at a parking lot near Rapp's Covered Bridge. A trail out of the parking lot will take you to where the powder stamping mill once stood. If you cross the road, an existing but earlier mill building can be explored, and trail systems will take you past the mill races, dam, and the newly opened Powder Works trail, where one can imagine wagons frantically moving valuable gunpowder away from the reach of the British Army. If you want to get out and enjoy a longer hike along the beautiful countryside on a relatively flat, improved trail, park at the French Creek Trailhead along Hare's Hill Road. There is usually plenty of parking and an informational sign at the trailhead will show hikers the system's various routes. I would like to recommend a dinner reservation to experience the Seven Stars inn or include it when you visit Pennsylvania's great iron furnaces which you will read about in the next chapter of Patriot's Path.

<u>Seven Stars Inn</u> is located at 262 Hoffecker Road Phoenixville, Pennsylvania.

<u>French Creek Heritage Park</u> is located at 1145 Rapp's Dam, Phoenixville, Pennsylvania.

The Great Iron Furnaces of Chester, Delaware and Berks County, Pennsylvania

"Casualties many; Percentage of dead not known; Combat efficiency; we are winning".

~General David M. Shoup, 22nd Commandant of the Marine Corps and recipient of the Congressional Medal of Honor.

Around the time the Revolutionary War began, the Committee for Safety for Pennsylvania commissioned the Warwick, Reading, and Hopewell Furnaces to begin casting cannon to support the American war effort. This was the same committee that commissioned the Continental Powder works to be established along French Creek.

Warwick Furnace was founded by a woman named Anna Nutt in 1737, who was prompted by the death of her husband, Samuel Nutt to continue his iron empire. Samuel Nutt had made plans for the establishment of a furnace on a tract of land included in his holdings, and he had the prudence of mentioning his desires in a will naming his wife, Anna Nutt, a nephew, Samuel Nutt, Jr. and Samuel Savage as his successors in this initiative. As an indication of the scope of the operation, records indicate that wood from 240 acres of woodland was required just to keep the furnace in production every year. The large bellows that were operated by a giant water wheel cost 200 English pounds which is roughly equivalent to 29,000 dollars today. The weekly output of the plant amounted to twenty-five tons of iron, comprised of pig iron and castings for pots, stoves, kettles, andirons, smoothing irons, clock weights, and similar household devices. In 1750, Warwick Furnace was managed by John Potts Sr. Samuel Potts, in the meantime, having bought out the other heirs, owned it in partnership with Thomas Rutter until his death in 1790 when it reverted to the heirs of Samuel Potts. The furnace remained in the Potts family until it was abandoned in 1867.

One historian has recorded the story of a large bell made at Warwick Furnace by Rutter and Potts. The bell was rumored to have been used to call furnace workers to work from 1757 until 1874. During the revolution, when the Hessians were passing through the town, the bell was rung to summon the citizens to assist in burying the cannons cast at the furnace awaiting delivery to the Continental Army. With Howe's forces near the Ironworks, the Iron masters began to bury cannon on and near the Ironworks to prevent the British from confiscating them. The effort to conceal the cannon was wasted because the British didn't bother the Ironworks. The buried cannon were never dug up and laid there for almost 100 years, unmentioned but not completely forgotten. Seven were dug up in 1875, and five more were found in 1895. On May 17th 2022, four more cannon were discovered after Ray Bentley commissioned geophysical surveys that detected large iron objects in the ground. The four cannon are nearly identical, measure seven feet long, and weigh over 4,500 pounds each. The guns were cast to fire 18-pound balls, and two of the cannon were discovered with an 18-pound ball lodged in the barrels. During the restoration process of the guns, one ball remained lodged and the other rolled out when the guns were cleaned. Six cannon that were produced at Warrick, although Civil War-era pieces, are displayed at the Paoli and Brandywine Battlefields. In addition, steel from the Iron Clad Civil War ship USS Monitor was produced at Warrick Furnace.

On September 18th Washington and his Army arrived at Warrick Furnace, and the commander-in-chief set up his headquarters at Reading Furnace Mansion, the home of Colonel Thomas Bull. Unfortunately, the Colonel was indisposed at the time and temporarily shared a prison barge with American Patriot Ethan Allen. However, the Colonel's wife hosted Washington and his staff, doing her part to support the revolution. Colonel Thomas Bull was a patriot and Revolutionary War hero who commanded the Chester County

'Flying Camp' Militia Regiment during the American effort to repel the British occupation of New York City. He was captured after the surrender of Fort Washington and sent to one of the infamous British prison ships in Brooklyn Harbor along with Ethan Allen. The Colonel was eventually paroled and returned to manage nearby Warwick Furnace. Later in life, he served as a Member of the Conventions, which drafted the Federal and State Constitutions from 1787 to 1790. He became a Presidential Elector in 1792 and represented Chester and Delaware Counties in the State Assembly from 1793 to 1801. Colonel Bull was instrumental in establishing the Conestoga Turnpike, building St. Mary's Church in Warwick Township, and his own 'Mount Pleasant' mansion (across the road) in 1784. The barn, Sawmill, Grist Mills, Blacksmith shop, and other buildings along French Creek near the intersection of Routes 345 and 401 were collaboratively known as Bulltown.

Hopewell Furnace was founded in 1771 by Mark Bird, son of William Bird, a prominent Pennsylvania ironmaster. In 1761, Mark Bird took over the family business after his father's death. This included two forges and a furnace on 3000 acres. Bird expanded the business to 8000 acres by 1763 and added the Hopewell and Jones Good Luck mines. In 1770, he purchased several tracts of land in Berks and Chester Counties where he planned to build a furnace on French Creek near his father's forge and the Hopewell mine. By 1771, the Hopewell Furnace was in operation, and an early stove plate was imprinted with a 'Mark Bird-Hopewell Furnace-1772' stamp. By 1775, Bird was a member of the Pennsylvania Committee of Correspondence and the Pennsylvania Provincial Conference.

During the Revolutionary War, Bird served as a colonel of the Second Battalion of Berks County militia, was elected to the Pennsylvania General Assembly, and served as a judge for Berks County. As Deputy Quartermaster General of Pennsylvania, his furnace conveniently provided cannon and shot to the Continental

Army and Continental Navy. However, payments from Congress were not enough to cover his over-expanded business, and Bird was forced to close his Berks County ironworks in 1784 following a national economic downturn. Bird wrote, "...I was Ruined, by the Warr, it was not Drunkeness, Idleness or want of Industry." Following floods and fire, Bird was forced to mortgage his Hopewell and Birdsboro properties in 1786. In 1788, the Hopewell plantation was auctioned off to James Old and Cadwallader Morris, and Bird moved to North Carolina, which was an 18th-century debtor's refuge. Bird died there in 1816. In 1938, the property was designated Hopewell Village National Historic Site under the authority of the Historic Sites Act. It became one of the earliest cultural sites of the National Park System. Hopewell Furnace consists of 14 restored structures on 848 mostly wooded acres. Hopewell Furnace National Historic Site is well protected, bordered by French Creek State Park on three sides and State Game Lands on the south side, preserving the lands the furnace utilized for its natural resources.

Marine Corps Tie-in...Recruiting Duty.

After completing my first four years in the Marine Corps, I left active service and returned to central Pennsylvania. Within a few weeks, I was hired by an organization that facilitated a placement camp for court-ordered, at-risk adolescent boys; the camp was structured around a military model. I completed a two-week training course and then went to work at the barracks to which I was assigned. The barracks consisted of low-security buildings where a couple of staff members monitored the kids at night. There was a high-security Juvenile facility on site, which was the immediate destination of those who stepped out of line. My job was mundane at best, primarily consisting of troop handling and low-level security. A day would begin with a quick march to the chow hall for a light breakfast. After breakfast, the platoon of 'lost boys' would be led in a physical exercise. There was a schoolhouse at the facility, and the instructors would monitor the classrooms until noon meal. After school, the kids were allowed to play pick-up sports until evening chow. On weekends, activities were scheduled to keep the kids occupied throughout the day.

It did not take me long to realize that the camp wasn't being run according to the rules and some of the staff were not what they represented themselves to be. Few of the instructors were professional, and fewer even had prior military experience. One instructor even ran the squad bay by imitating Full Metal Jacket's Gunnery Sergeant Hartman, sometimes mimicking some of the movie scripts word for word. Part of the mandatory training required to work with youth was a course called Handle with Care, and it was made very clear the kids could only be physically handled using the prescribed techniques. I saw very few incidents where kids were 'handled with care' and many more where it couldn't be called anything but abuse. If a kid's behavior became unacceptable, he could be ordered to perform pushups or side straddle hops for a prescribed amount of time. If a kid's behavior puts himself or others at risk, Handle with Care methods were authorized to prevent injury from occurring. I was monitoring a 7-year-old whom I had ordered to do pushups for using profane language and disrespect. He refused when I ordered the kid to transition to side straddle hops. Suddenly, doors behind the kid burst open, and two tall instructors grabbed the kid by his arms and, heaving his feet off the floor, carried him outside the building and violently faceplanted him in a bed of mulch.

I spoke with the instructors, and not getting the response I was hoping for, I reported the incident to our senior supervisor, a reserve Navy officer. The following morning, I was pulled aside and told to go home and return for the night shift. Within a couple of weeks, I quit the job and began working with a Landscaper I had been employed before enlisting in the Corps. Years later I learned that the camp had been permanently closed after an instructor broke protocol and took his platoon of boys into a nearby quarry for physical training by himself. The boys bludgeoned the instructor to death and several escaped.

As grateful as I was for the landscaping job, I knew I didn't want to settle into the vocation for the rest of my life, so during the winter layoff, I decided to reenlist. I went to the local Marine Corps recruiting office and told the recruiter I wanted to reenlist. He wasn't sure of the procedure since I had only recently come off terminal leave. As it was, he told me he was pretty sure I would not retain my current rank of sergeant even if I could reenlist. I then talked with a Navy recruiter who was ready to sign me up and send me to the next SEAL/BUDs course that was available but told me I had to enlist as a yeoman. I also spoke with an Army recruiter who wanted to sell me every infantry-oriented job it had to offer but who was clearly reluctant to talk about any other opportunity in the Army. I decided to trust my instincts and keep moving.

I eventually got a call from the Marine recruiter, who, realizing I was an easy 'bone,' informed me I could reenlist and retain my rank after all. I signed the paperwork, but I had to be medically screened again, which necessitated a trip to Harrisburg, where I was unpleasantly subjected to an old-school prostrate check and multiple hearing tests until, guessing right, I was able to pass it. I cleared the Military Entrance Processing Station (MEPS) process, reenlisted, and assigned PTAD (Recruiter Assistance) at my local Recruiter substation. I assisted a gunny and his staff sergeant until my orders came through. I spent long hours canvassing, conducting phone contracts, and home visits. The few months of supporting the recruiting efforts were long enough to convince me to avoid recruiting duty at all costs in the future.

During my career as a Marine, I have heard numerous stories of the shenanigans that commonly happen during recruiter duty. One example is sleeping with an applicant, called dipping in the Pool, and if caught, a recruiter will be relieved. Applicants waiting on a ship date enter the Delayed Entry Program (DEP); those individuals are referred to as a Poolee. Infidelity on recruiter duty was also a frequent occurrence, and promiscuous behavior with an applicant's mother or sisters was expressly forbidden. I once had a friend who, already struggling in his marriage, was assigned recruiter duty and was sent to a recruiting station near his hometown. He made it a year before he was relieved for cause for committing adultery.

I was pretty sure it was happening at the station where I worked as a recruiter's assistant. There were several late nights when an attractive young woman, who had rather mysteriously dropped from the DEP, would arrive at the office late in the evening. Whenever she arrived, I was told to canvas the mall for a couple of hours or call it a day and go home, which was fine by me; I wanted no part of their late-night forays.

If the recruiters were getting contracts and making mission life was good. When the recruiters were not making their bones, the duty could be unbearable. While I was assigned to the RSS, there was a recruiter under the supervision of the gunny who had been struggling to make mission. An artilleryman by trade, he was likely volun-told to report to Recruiter School and was less than enthusiastic to begin with. The gunny met with the three other recruiters in his charge and conducted a role-play session to help the struggling recruiter.

The role play did not have its desired effect, and the gunny decided to evaluate the struggling recruiter a final time before writing an unfavorable performance review or what career Marines call a double-signer. When an adverse fitness report is written, the Marine is counseled on the deficiency, and the report is permanently filed in the Marine's Service Record Book. In most instances, a double-signer is career-ending. On the day the staff sergeant was being evaluated, I was tasked by the gunny to assist the recruiter by helping him set up and run a recruiting booth at one of his schools. A young high school senior from the school was already working through the enlisted process with the gunny and had verbally committed to enlisting after high school. The gunny decided to throw his recruiter a bone by sending the 'ringer' to the booth we had set up, and all the recruiter had to do was close the deal. I was aware because the gunny wanted an insider report on how the recruiter interacted with the students. The problem was the recruiter wasn't interacting with anything in the school but the cafeteria. I was left to manage the booth as best I could and even managed to score a few referrals. When the ringer arrived at the booth to speak with the recruiter about enlisting, he was nowhere to be found. When I finally did locate the recruiter sitting in the cafeteria, he nonchalantly told me to get the kid's contact information because he did not have time to talk to him. A few weeks later, the recruiter was in the emergency room for a stress-related illness, an occurrence that was apparently a reoccurring condition the recruiter was suffering from. He eventually received the double-signer, was relieved for cause, and sent back to the fleet.

Sometimes, to make mission, a recruit would have to ship to boot camp whether they were ready or not. One afternoon, I was ordered to drive an overweight kid down to a hotel near the MEPS, an hour away from the substation, and put him on a treadmill until he was under his ship weight, then walk him into the station the next day. I had the kid on a treadmill until midnight, then put him in bed and drove him to the MEPS the following day. Once I checked him in at the MEPS, I jumped in the car and drove back home. I was almost home when the recruiter called asking when I was going to leave the MEPS. When I told him I was nearly home, he was livid because he apparently implied that he wanted me to stay with the applicant until he had a plane ticket in hand, but I failed to pick up on the implication. It turned out well in the end when the kid shipped to Parris Island on a weight waiver.

Places to Visit in Pennsylvania's Iron Furnace District.

To explore these historic sites more fluidly, I recommend three separate trips. For the first trip, I begin at Warwick Furnace Farm. Here, you can walk along rustic country trails, explore the fortified remains of the furnace site, cross a historic bridge, and see the beautifully preserved 18th-century farmhouse and its contributing buildings. After exploring Warwick Furnace Farms, jump back in your car and drive a short distance to Reading Furnace Historic District. Although this site is privately owned, everything is within view from the roadside. Next, head to Bulltown, the final leg of this tour. On your way, look for a historical sign at the intersection. Bulltown consists of the Colonel Bull House, which is a private residence, a cluster of period buildings on the opposite side of the road, and a historical sign providing information on Colonel Bull and the Pennsylvania Flying Camps.

Hopewell Furnace Historic District is a great place to spend an entire day. Stop at the visitor shop, pick up a park map, buy a souvenir, or link up with a park ranger for a guided tour. Explore the furnace site and see a restored water wheel in motion; look around at all outside exhibits, including the furnace ruins, Conestoga Wagons, and iron products. Take a look inside the old company store and visit several period tenant houses. French Creek State Park is within easy walking distance and can be accessed via several trails. Enjoy beautifully maintained picnic areas or hike the miles of well-marked trails, including one that links to the Horseshoe Trail System.

The Cornwall Furnace is another 18th Century Furnace beautifully preserved and open to the public for tours. There are several buildings to explore on the property and a small gift shop is on site where you can pick up refreshments or a souvenir. Consider visiting nearby Fort Zeller which was built to protect settlers during the French and Indian War. The fort, considered the oldest of its kind, is actually a fortified blockhouse featuring a natural spring in its cellar and has an interesting legend tied to its historical roots. One of the fort's early inhabitants known as 'the young countess' claimed to have single-handedly killed several raiding Indians who had attacked the fort. According to the legend, she ran to the fort and hid in the cellar where she decapitated an Indian who foolishly exposed his head through a rather prominent opening to the spring. Then, disguising her voice, she fooled several more Indians into the fort and and treated them to a similar fate. The number of Indians slain differs from one to several depending on who is telling the story. Regardless, the fort can be visited by appointment where you will find the well-preserved fort with its spring in the cellar also features a carving of the Zeller family coat of arms. A beautiful stone monument stands in front of the fort with a bronze plaque inscribed with the deed to the property.

Warwick Furnace Farm Located at 810 Warwick Furnace Road, Glenmoore, Pennsylvania.

Hopewell Furnace National Park Located at 2 Mark Bird Lane Elverson, Pennsylvania.

Reading Furnace Historic District Located at 123 Mansion Road Elverson, Pennsylvania.

Bulltown Located at 106 Orchard Hill Lane, Elverson, Pennsylvania.

Cornwall Furnace Located at 94 Rexmont Road, Cornwall, Pennsylvania.

<u>Fort Zeller</u> is located at 10 North Zeller Road Newmanstown, Pennsylvania.

Bethlehem, Pennsylvania

"You cannot exaggerate about the Marines. They are convinced to the point of arrogance, that they are the most ferocious fighters on earth- and the amusing thing about it is that they are."

~ Father Kevin Keaney, a chaplain who served with Marines in Korea

From December 1776 to May 1777, Dr. William Shippen, a relative of Peggy Shippen, Benedict Arnold's second wife, operated an Army hospital in the Brethren's House building. General Gates and Arnold stopped in Bethlehem when they brought their troops down from New York to Pennsylvania to join forces with Washington. Arnold had a reputation for combining his training as an apothecary with his concern for the well-being of his troops and was known to have worked in the hospital to help care for his soldiers.

The house was used as a hospital again from September 1777 to May 1778, when Washington's medical officers commandeered it as a military hospital. At the time, the multi-level stone building housed clergy, who lived in a dormitory-like setting. It is generally believed that at least 500 soldiers who died during treatment were buried in the vicinity of the house.

A more famous Revolutionary War soldier was also treated in the Moravian settlement. In September 1777, the Marquis de Lafayette was wounded at the Battle of the Brandywine and was initially treated by Washington's personal physician after he was evacuated from the battlefield. When he was stabilized, Lafayette was taken to Philadelphia, then across the river to Bristol. From Bristol, he was transported to the Sun Inn at Bethlehem in Congressman Lauren's personal coach to recuperate from his wound. During the two-day trip, Lafayette and Laurens developed a close relationship that, in turn, helped Washington navigate the Conway Cabul in York,

Pennsylvania, when Laurens, the new President of Congress, advocated for the embattled Washington at Lafayette's request.

Lafayette returned the favor years later after Laurens was captured by the British while on his way to Europe and imprisoned in the Tower of London. Lafayette's wife, Adrienne, appealed to the British to grant Laurens all possible consideration, making his imprisonment a bit easier and perhaps shorter than it may have been without her intervention. After one day in the overcrowded Sun Inn, Lafayette moved to George Frederick's house and was nursed back to health by George's wife, Barbara Beckel, and their daughter, Liesel.

While Lafayette was convalescing, he wrote several letters to his wife and continued to appeal to Washington for a command. Even more vital to the American cause, Lafayette wrote letters to his countrymen hoping to influence French intervention by inflaming their patriotic passion for American Independence. The house, located on present-day Main Street in Bethlehem, is no longer standing but is memorialized with a historical marker.

A small monument was designed and placed to commemorate American Revolution soldiers who died in the hospital at the Brethren's House. During the monument's construction, one soldier was reburied in the tomb around 1931. Several more soldiers were reburied at the site on Memorial Day in 1996 after remains were discovered during an urban construction project. The city typically hosts a ceremony on Memorial Day, and other small historical events are occasionally held at the site.

Facing an inevitable British occupation of Philadelphia in 1777, Pennsylvania ordered that several important bells in Philadelphia be whisked from the city to prevent the British from melting them down to make cannon balls. This included the Pennsylvania State House bell, better known as the Liberty Bell. The Liberty Bell was hidden on a hay wagon and taken away from Philadelphia to present-day

Allentown under heavy guard. It was brought to Zion Reformed Church, where it was hidden, along with several other bells, in the church's basement. The bell remained hidden at Zion Reformed Church until June 1778, when it was returned to the State House after the British evacuated Philadelphia. The replica of the Liberty Bell was on display in a small museum in the basement of the historic church, which provided safekeeping to the famous icon of American Independence many years ago. Unfortunately, the church was sold in 2023, and the museum failed to secure a lease for the basement space it occupied, from the new owners. Many exhibits have been moved to the Lehigh Valley Heritage Museum, where they will be on public display.

Marine Corps Tie-In...A Port Call in Israel.

Our first opportunity to get off the ship during BLT (SOC) 2/6's 2008 deployment came with a two-week port call in Haifa, Israel. During the port call, I participated in a COMREL project at a monastery called Stella Maris on the slopes of Mount Carmel, which encompasses Elisha's ancient cave. The COMREL project entailed pulling weeds, outside cleanup, and picking olives from ancient trees on site.

I also took advantage of a rare opportunity to visit Biblical sites at Jerusalem, Jericho, the Jordan River, the Dead Sea, and Masada. I knew little of Masada's history before my visit to Israel. I learned that between 37 and 31 BC, Herod the Great built two fortified palaces on a mountain overlooking the Dead Sea. In 66 AD, an extremist Jewish splinter group called the Sicarii overran the Roman garrison of Masada. After the Second Temple was destroyed in 70 AD, more members of the Sicarii fled Jerusalem and hid on the mountaintop fortress.

In 73 AD, Lucius Flavius Silva, the Roman governor of Judaea, laid siege to Masada with the Roman legion X Fretensis (The tenth legion of the Strait), several auxiliary units, and Jewish prisoners of war. The Roman task force of over 15,000 men surrounded Masada, built a circumvallation wall, and then constructed a large earthen siege ramp against the mountain's western face. A giant tower with a battering ram was constructed and moved up the completed ramp with incredible difficulty. When Roman troops eventually entered the fortress, they discovered that its defenders had set all the buildings but the food storerooms on fire and either committed mass suicide or killed each other, totaling 960 men, women, and children.

During our visit, the siege ramp and the ruins of Roman defensive works below the mountain were easily distinguishable. Adventurous tourists could choose to hike the ramp to the top of the mountain as a cheaper alternative to the tram service that was offered. To access the mountain stronghold, we rode the tram from the visitor center to the top of the mountain, where we found the fortresses and other well-preserved building ruins. The ground was still littered with tiny pottery shards. At various sections of the defensive fortifications, large round stones were stacked where ancient defenders had staged them to use as missiles against the invading Roman Legion.

Just to the south of Masada is the famous Dead Sea where we spent the rest of the day resting and relaxing. Some of the ship's Navy pilots indulged in a mud bath at a nearby spa, but most of us just made a beeline to the water. Salt was heavy in the air and crystals crunched under our feet. When we got to the water we noticed several pipes jutting out into the sea. We soon discovered these provided fresh water so swimmers could flush the salt out of their eyes. The salt content is so high in the Dead Sea that it is nearly impossible for swimmers to sink in its depths, but you do not want to drink the water or get any in your eyes.

Also, during the port call, I took the opportunity to spend the day as a tourist in Jerusalem. That epic day was filled with sights and experiences I hope to experience again someday. The tour began when the tour buses stopped along a vista on the Mount of Olives overlooking the Garden of Gethsemane. After taking in the panoramic view and posing for a picture with a camel, I made my way into the garden. The experience was profound, and the feeling was surreal to walk amongst ancient olive trees that once hosted Jesus and his disciples during his ministry. The garden was where Jesus was betrayed by one of His own. It is also the place of His passionate prayer, where all four gospels collaborate to indicate He sweated blood. The Church of All Nations is beside the garden, nearly covered inside and out with religious frescos. The church is believed to contain the very rock Jesus prayed over on the night of His betrayal. The Church of Mary Magdalene is also located on the garden's outskirts. It is easily the most prominent, easily recognizable building on the Mount of Olives, but it was one I did not have the opportunity to visit.

The tour made its way through one of Jerusalem's ancient and massive gates and into the narrow alley systems streaming through what is referred to as the Old City. Beyond numerous tables of merchants and purveyors of religious souvenirs are temples and churches, Holy places built over significant Christian sites. I visited the Church of the Holy Sepulchre, which houses the Anointing Stone. This predominantly Catholic tradition claims the stone slab is placed at the spot where Jesus' body was prepared for burial by Joseph of Arimathea. Here, I stopped to pray. Until the writing of this manuscript, the prayer remained a secret, but one that I will reveal in this manuscript. While others crowded around me, placing souvenirs and other objects on the stone to 'anoint' them, I knelt, put my left hand on the marble slab, and prayed for my wife and our future marriage.

Scholars believe the Church of the Holy Sepulchre was built on Golgotha, the hill where Jesus was crucified. Evidence is good that the site is also Mount Moriah, the place where God instructed

Abraham to take his son Isaac and sacrifice him as a burnt offering. Ironically, according to Scripture, Isaac asked his father where the lamb was for the sacrifice, and Abraham answered that the Lord would provide the lamb...and He did. The Lord provided a young ram in place of Isaac that day, foreshadowing the day when God, 18 centuries later, provided another lamb for the sacrificial atonement of man's sin. This time, the lamb was in the form and nature of His Son, a blood atonement of sin for all who will believe in His perfect sacrifice.

The Church of the Holy Sepulchre is also believed to be the location of Jesus's empty tomb, where he was buried and resurrected. After the Roman Emperor Constantine the Great began to favor Christianity, he signed the Edict of Milan legalizing the religion and sent his mother to Jerusalem to look for Jesus' tomb. With the help of Bishop Eusebius and Macarius, three crosses were found near a tomb. One of the crosses purportedly reversed the effects of death and was presumed to be the true cross Jesus was crucified on, leading Constantine to believe that he had found the tomb. In 326 AD, Constantine ordered that the temple to Jupiter and Venus, which was initially built over the site, be replaced by a church. In an area of the church believed to have been the site where the Romans crucified Jesus and the two Thieves is a worn hole in bedrock that is believed to have stabilized Jesus' cross. People (including me) stood in a lengthy line for the opportunity to kneel and place their hands inside a hole that Jesus' blood may have poured into as He hung from the cross.

I also visited the Wailing Wall and a small anti-chamber in an ancient home designated as the room of Jesus' last supper with His disciples. There are many more important and revered places within Jerusalem's massive stone walls I didn't get an opportunity to explore; there are far too many to take in during a day-long tour.

Historical places to visit in or near Bethlehem, Pennsylvania.

All the historical points of interest in this chapter are located in urban sprawl, so begin your trip to Bethlehem by visiting the Brethren's House. Once you have seen the Brethren's House, take a stroll along this charming small town and visit the rest of the Revolutionary War-era signs and monuments. Take a leisurely drive north to Allentown and see a replica of the Liberty Bell. Although the bell and its exhibit are no longer located at the Zion Reformed Church, a brass historical plaque is mounted by the church entrance, and the bell can now be visited at the Lehigh Valley Heritage Museum.

Historical Marker of the Beckel House is located at 534 Main Street Bethlehem, Pennsylvania.

The Sun Inn Marker is located at 564 Main Street Bethlehem, Pennsylvania.

Pulaski's Banner Marker is located at the Moravian Cemetery Bethlehem, Pennsylvania.

The Old Chapel Marker is located at Single Sisters' House 44 West Church Street Bethlehem, Pennsylvania.

Continental Army Honored Dead Marker is located at 85 West Church Street Bethlehem, Pennsylvania.

Brethren's House and Marker is located at 85 West Church Street Bethlehem, Pennsylvania.

Tomb of the Unknown Soldier is located at 427 1st Avenue Bethlehem, Pennsylvania.

Moravian Historical Society Museum is located at 214 East Center Street Nazareth, Pennsylvania.

<u>Zion's Reformed United Church of Christ</u> is located at 622 West Hamilton Street, Allentown, Pennsylvania.

<u>Lehigh Valley Heritage Museum</u> is located at 432 West Walnut Street Allentown, Pennsylvania.

Malvern, Pennsylvania

"I'm going to fight my way out; I'm going to take all my equipment and all my wounded and as many dead as I can. If we can't get out this way, this Division will never fight as a unit again".

~General Oliver P. Smith, World War II and Korean War Veteran.

The Battle of Paoli has been given several different monikers by people who described the action that night through their own lens, the most common among them being the "Paoli Massacre." The first recorded name for the battle was "Last Night's Affair," which is how Wayne described the battle in his letter to General Washington. Congressman Laurens called the battle "General Wayne's False Step, while Major Andre called it "Surprise of a Rebel Corps in the Great Valley." Other names given were "The Action at the Warren," "The Attack made by General Grey against the Rebels near White Horse Tavern," and "The Payola Battle or Sticking Night."

On September 18th with Wayne's division camped near Yellow Springs, about three miles from the Red Lion Inn, Washington developed a strategy to keep Howe away from Philadelphia. The wet weather and resulting high water had made most roads impassable, and the fords were considered inaccessible, which slowed Howe's movements to a grinding halt. At the White Horse tavern, Howe split his forces. Howe's column, consisting of General Grey and Knyphausen's troops, moved along Swedesford Road and established headquarters at the Sign of George III and the house of Samuel Jones near the Great Valley Baptist Church in Tredyffrin. Cornwallis headed east along the Lancaster Road toward the General Warren tavern, then camped further east past the Paoli tavern, two miles north of the Blue Ball tavern, on a bluff overlooking Howe's encampment.

Washington ordered Wayne and Maxwell's forces to begin a harassing campaign on the flanks and rear of Howe's 15,000-man force while he prepared to move the bulk of his Army sixteen miles to Parker's ford. In addition, Washington hoped to confuse Howe's intelligence-gathering efforts by giving the impression of a more significant American force by screening the regular Army with militia. Smallwood was supposed to link up with Washington's main Army, but because Smallwood was bogged down in Oxford, Pennsylvania, dealing with his rebellious Maryland militia, he was re-routed toward Yellow Springs with his 2000-man force to reinforce Wayne's effort. He got as far as Cochran's Tavern in West Fallowfield Township by the 18th.

Anthony Wayne grew up near Paoli on his family's homestead prior to the Revolutionary War. At 32 years of age, Wayne had no military experience but received a commission as brigadier general in February 1777 along with a Frenchman named De Haas. Wayne was given command of the 1st Pennsylvania brigade and De Haas the 2nd brigade. De Haas never took command of his brigade and resigned his commission. The division commander, General Lincoln, was sent to northern New York with General Gates, leaving Wayne in charge of the entire Pennsylvania Line.

The two-year-old American Army already had a history of leadership issues. Officers were typically chosen and promoted for political reasons over merit or experience, and to complicate things even more, European officers were often promised high ranks to fight for the American cause. It got so bad that a frustrated John Adams wrote, "I am wearied to death with the wrangles between military officers high and low. They quarrel like cats and dogs. They worry one another like mastiffs scrambling for rank and pay. There is as much pulling and hauling about rank and pay as if we had been accustomed to a military establishment here 150 years."

Unfortunately, this would also prove to be an issue for Wayne and his junior officers at Paoli. Colonel Richard Humpton, a British Army veteran 12 years Wayne's senior, was one of Wayne's subordinate commanders. Humpton was a native of Yorkshire, England, where Wayne's grandfather also hailed from. His other subordinate commander and third in command was Colonel Thomas Hartley, a prominent resident of York, Pennsylvania.

The Pennsylvania line consisted of nine regiments and, at full strength, should have numbered around 6,000 men. However, because of the short enlistments and difficulty with desertions, Wayne's command only numbered around 2,000 men. Despite its size, the Pennsylvania Line had a reputation for being a stubborn, well-disciplined fighting unit.

Although Wayne thought his movement toward Paoli and the British rear had gone unnoticed, Howe was well aware of Wayne's proximity to his encampments from intelligence gathered by reconnaissance patrols, deserters, and captured American dragoons carrying dispatches between Wayne and Washington. On the night of September 18th Wayne's Pennsylvanians made their way through the Great Valley under a bright, full harvest moon. They moved east on the Lancaster Road and past the General Warren Tavern through Warren Pass, following the same route Cornwallis took with his troops earlier that day. Wayne's forces reached the Paoli Tavern just a couple of miles from Cornwallis' camp, close enough to hear the British drummers' and fifers' sound reveille. Wayne still believed his forces had not been detected by the British, but he could not have been more mistaken, nor the danger to his men more real. Although Washington's march to Parker's ford had completely outflanked Howe's forces, it left Wayne alone and in a dangerously exposed position.

The first indication to Wayne that the British might have known of his position at the Paoli Tavern occurred shortly after he wrote his second dispatch to Washington on Sept 19th when he ordered his Pennsylvanians to retire to a piece of high ground a mile and a half to the west of the Paoli Tavern to avoid a perceived British attack.

Captain von Munchhausen, attached to Cornwallis, wrote, "...the Second battalion of light infantry and English riflemen were dispatched to break camp quietly and attempt to surprise Wayne. They found Wayne 2 and a half miles behind us, and they almost surrounded him when fate intervened. Two drunken Englishmen fired at a picket, which touched off an alarm and permitted their escape though in great confusion."

The Americans located high ground in the fields of Ezekiel Brown and Cromwell Pierce, a major in the militia. Wayne had his right flank facing east and his left flank facing west near Sugartown Road. To the front of his position were corn fields and woods instead of the present-day urban sprawl. Behind the camp were woods owned by Levi Bowen. Wayne used a house on the Pierce property as his headquarters.

The camp was intended to be temporary until Smallwood's militia joined him. Unfortunately, Smallwood's militia was nowhere near Malvern and had just begun to march toward Downingtown from James McClellan's Tavern in Parkesburg, about twenty-five miles to the west. For some unexplained reason, Wayne displaced his troops and moved his columns north on Sugartown Road and then west on King Road to North Chester Road, where he halted. Around seven in the evening, Wayne ordered his troops back to the ground they had just left and reestablished a hasty camp.

While Wayne was maneuvering around Paoli, Washington, on the east side of the Schuylkill, had completely outflanked Howe. His Army occupied a blocking position that extended eight miles from Valley Forge to Norristown, putting Howe in a precarious position between the main American Army and Wayne's troops.

By September 20th Smallwood, with 2,100 men and three cannon, had reached Downingtown, a scant eleven miles away from Paoli. Wayne had sent Colonel Chambers to Downingtown to guide

Smallwood to the camp at Pierce's fields, and Wayne expected the augmentation of his forces by 2 PM that afternoon. Anticipating Smallwood's arrival, Wayne ordered his troops to prepare for a march, and the division was subsequently formed, but because rain once again threatened, Wayne ordered booths built to stack and keep his muskets and powder dry and for the troops to rest.

Although Wayne did not expect an attack to occur that night, he was warned there would be one. Mr. Jones, a local sympathetic to the American cause, rode into camp around 10 PM while Wayne was reconnoitering a road on the British right flank. Jones came to inform Wayne that while at the Paoli Tavern, a man who had been in the British camp was told by a soldier that there would be an attack on Wayne that night, and it would have happened the night prior had Wayne not moved his division to North Chester Road. When Wayne returned to camp, he had a crucial decision to make: either remain in place and wait for the overdue Smallwood he expected at any minute and risk attack or move his division to avoid one.

Meanwhile, Howe needed to decide how he was going to break out of the American encirclement he found himself in. Howe decided to march toward the Schuylkill River the following day but not toward Sweedes' ford, where Washington expected him. Howe planned to march north toward Phoenixville along the Nutt Road in a maneuver designed as a series of feints to pull Washington out of his blocking position. As for Wayne's division, Howe was determined to attack and destroy it with General Grey as the main effort and with Musgrave in a blocking position at the Paoli Tavern where he was close enough to quickly reinforce Grey or attack Wayne's forces should Grey successfully turn them into Musgrave's troops.

Howe entrusted the effort of the attack to General Gray, who would lead some of Howe's most elite troops in the attack on Wayne's troops. Major John Andre described the force that would attack Wayne. It consisted of the 40th and 55th regiments, numbering

500 troops led by Colonel Musgrave. In comparison, General Grey would lead a force of 1,500 soldiers comprised of the 42nd and 44th regiments and the second battalion of light infantry with an escort of the Queen's Own Light Dragoons; Grey's columns marched at 10 PM with a vanguard of 500 Light Infantry led by Major John Maitland of the Royal Marines; Musgrave marched toward Paoli an hour later. The assault forces were highly trained and well-disciplined, specifically trained and experienced in light infantry or ranger tactics. They were well versed in carrying out specialized missions requiring speed and stealth and usually found themselves posted at danger points or covering the front and flanks of British columns.

That night, General Grey famously ordered his troops to remove the flints from their muskets before the assault so no one could inadvertently fire a musket and give away the attack. For this order, he received the moniker 'No Flint Grey.' Major Andre wrote that "no firelock was to even be loaded the plan being total surprise than a shock attack using only bayonets. It was represented to the men that firing discovered us to the enemy, hid them from u, killed our friends and produced a confusion favorable to the escape of the rebels and perhaps productive of disgrace to ourselves. On the other hand, by not firing we knew the foe to be wherever fire appeared and a charge of bayonets ensured his destruction; that amongst the enemy those in the rear would direct their fire against whoever fired in front, and they would destroy each other".

Grey did not rely on his troops to lead them to where Wayne was hunkered down. Local Loyalist guides are verified to have been recommended to Howe by the treacherous Joseph Galloway. Curtis Lewis, a blacksmith from East Caln township, was one of these Loyalist guides who, sometime after the Paoli Massacre, found himself detained for high treason for guiding the British assault force to General Wayne's encampment. The other guide was thought to have been a deserter from Wayne's division, Private John Farndon, "of whom it is said deserted from our army to the enemy, and piloted some of the bloody highlanders in the night to General Wayne's brigade". Farndon, captured by American forces that night or soon after, was hanged on a gallows built for the purpose. His body was left hanging from noon to sunset to serve as a deterrence to others who might have thought of betraying their comrade in arms.

As Grey's forces marched west on Swedesford Road toward Wayne's position, they took every inhabitant with them as they passed along to prevent any warnings from reaching Wayne. According to an anonymous account, a corporal's guard entered the home of Captain Bartholomew along the Swedesford Road and took his elderly uncle out in the cold, damp night dressed in only his nightshirt. He died shortly after from exposure and rough treatment at the hands of the British.

Just before midnight, two of Wayne's vignettes spotted horsemen approaching the crossroads of Swedesford and Long's ford (Route 401). They challenged them three times without receiving a reply before firing on the horseman and then galloped down Long's ford toward the General Warren and Wayne's camp beyond the inn. When the vignettes rode into camp and warned Wayne, he had the division up and under arms.

When Grey's assault force reached the General Warren, they knew Wayne was in the vicinity but did not know precisely where the encampment was located or its disposition. A local tradition is that Peter Mather, a Loyalist and tavern keeper for the General Warren, was the man who led Grey to Wayne's position, but the tradition lacks evidence to support Mather's cooperation with Grey. Years later, his daughter, who was eight years old on the night of the massacre, stated that although Grey's forces stopped at the tavern and urged her father to guide them, he adamantly refused and never left the tavern that night. The British account by Major Andre did not mention Mather one way or another. He explained that Grey's "column approached the General Warren where having forced intelligence from a blacksmith, they came upon the out sentries, piquet and camp of the rebels." The blacksmith's intelligence provided to the British actually aided Wayne instead. Had the blacksmith guided Grey's column down Sugartown road, they would have assaulted Wayne's troops from west to east and driven them into Musgrave's waiting column at the Paoli, enveloping them in a pincer movement that could have resulted in the complete destruction of an entire American division. But the blacksmith, coerced into cooperation, either intentionally or not, pointed Grey's column eastward on the Lancaster Road toward the Warren Pass on a more direct route, placing the attacking British column between Wayne and Musgrave.

Around midnight, General Wayne rode through the encampment, encouraging the division to form battle lines. Within about five minutes, the division was armed and formed into platoons. Wayne's division was arranged as follows: on the right flank along present-day Channing Avenue, Hartley's brigade formed with the artillery company with four cannon to his right, and on the left near Sugartown Road, Humpton's brigade was formed oriented north toward the Lancaster Road. As the Americans formed for battle, a light rain began to fall, so Wayne commanded the division to take off their coats and cover the ammunition with them. Once the ammunition was covered, Wayne ordered an evacuation of the camp by wheeling to the right in sub-platoons, taking them from their battleline formation into a column facing to the east of camp. The next command, 'to the left face,' had them facing north again, but this time in columns of two that could quickly march off in any direction in a column of files.

The first Americans to die that night were the four to eight-man piquets positioned around Wayne's encampment. These men were quickly overwhelmed and mercilessly bayonetted to death. The

British Light Infantry moved along Longford Avenue and halted adjacent to the American camp. They faced right, fixed bayonets, and let out a thunderous Huzza! Before rushing the American right flank.

As the piquet was being attacked on the American right flank, Wayne ordered the artillery and baggage to immediately displace and move west on King Road toward the White Horse tavern, with the rest of the division following in trace. Wayne ordered the 1st Pennsylvania regiment to the right flank to cover his retreat and form a battleline to delay the British attacking force in the woods along Long Ford Road (Longford Ave). The 1st Pennsylvania regiment was quickly overrun by Grey's forces and driven in confusion toward Wayne's camp. The British, relying on the bayonet, had not fired a shot and took few casualties from the Americans firing into the darkness. Major Andre's prediction that the Americans would inadvertently fire on one another at this stage in the fight came to fruition. As the Americans fired at the attacking British, other Americans, mistaking the muzzle flashes for the British, began to fire on each other. In defense of the 1st Pennsylvania regiment, they were improperly provisioned for a night attack and were already at a distinct disadvantage. Though more accurate than smooth-bore muskets, they were armed with rifles that were much slower to reload and lacked a stud to attach a bayonet. During a bayonet attack, whether day or night, a soldier armed with a rifle rarely had a chance to win the engagement, much less come away from it alive.

As all this took place, Wayne, realizing that the column had still not moved out of camp, rode to the left flank to issue his order a third time with all his light horse accompanying him. As the British Light Infantry entered Wayne's camp representing the first wave of the British attack, the British took their first recorded casualties of the assault. Captain Wolfe was killed, and Lieutenant Hunter took a ball to the hand. The Americans, unfortunately, fared much worse. The 7th Pennsylvania, which was the rear unit, bore the brunt of the Light

Infantry attack, which, upon entering the camp, struck the 7th and surrounded it, inflicting heavy casualties. Behind the first British wave, the second wave of the assault was forming along Long Ford Avenue, consisting of the Queen's Own Light Dragoons and 350 members of the 44th Regiment of Foot.

The British tactic for the attack on Wayne's division was designed to psychologically impact Wayne's men. Taking advantage of darkness and surprise to instill panic and confusion among the men of Wayne's Pennsylvania Division, the British attack worked to perfection. As the second wave of the British attack hit Wayne's confused regiment, a dozen of the Queens Own Light Dragoons charged the ground with swinging sabers, and the 44th regiment of foot swarmed the Pennsylvania 1st brigade with fixed bayonets, causing even more panic among the Americans.

Meanwhile, on Sugartown Road, one of the cannon carriages lost its rear wheels and broke down in the middle of the road. This caused the baggage wagons to stop, obstructing the road and bringing the fleeing division to a grinding halt. It took several crucial minutes to drag the cannon off to the side of the road. Damaged too much to prevent the reassembly of its carriage, a rope was fastened around the gun, and it was dragged off with the others.

Back in the camp, the assault intensified, with Grey's men moving through it, chasing down Americans and indiscriminately putting them to the bayonet. A few of the attackers were killed or wounded by American fires, but steady rain and confusion wrought by the charging British made any semblance of an organized counterattack impossible; as the attack progressed, any organized resistance turned futile.

On Long Ford Avenue, the third and largest wave of the British attack was preparing to storm the camp. This consisted of two battalions of the Royal Highland Regiment, also known as the

Blackwatch. Six hundred fighting Scotsmen fixed bayonets and charged the camp; the disciplined battalions maintained their rank and formation, thoroughly sweeping up whatever resistance that remained of Wayne's men. The Blackwatch battalions killed and wounded no less than three hundred Americans while Wayne was somewhere around Sugartown Road trying to stand up a rear guard to cover the rest of his division's retreat.

With orders to find Smallwood, Major North rode westward along King's Road, finding some units of the Pennsylvania division moving in good order while encountering others who, in a panicked state, fired at or fled from anything that moved along the roads. Just prior to the British assault, Smallwood had reached the summit of the hill on North Chester Road and had turned east on King's Road. They were about a mile away from Wayne's camp when pandemonium struck. According to Smallwood, the enemy ambushed his column; in reality, he was fired on by panicking Pennsylvania soldiers fleeing the British. This occurred somewhere within the boundary of North Chester Road, King Road, Hickory Road, and Forrest Road in East Goshen Township. Smallwood ended up chasing his fleeing militia through Downingtown and beyond, losing an estimated 50 percent of his militia to desertion along the way. The other half of his forces consolidated with Wayne at the Red Lion, many of them no longer with arms. Wayne retreated with his division west on Swedesford to Ship Road, then north on Pottstown Pike to the Red Lion Tavern across the road from the Uwchlan Meetinghouse. Like so many others in the area, the Meetinghouse was used as a hospital to treat Wayne's wounded men. Tradition has it that so much blood lay on the floor after treating Paoli's wounded that the stains were visible for years after the massacre.

The affair at Paoli was not called a massacre because the battle produced a large number of killed or wounded. After all, Wayne was able to escape with his division relatively intact. But why was this affair considered a massacre instead of just another battle or skirmish during the Philadelphia Campaign, especially given the small size scale of the event? It is regarded as a massacre because of the atrocities committed that September night by the British forces. Although no documentation has ever surfaced proving that Grey or his officers ordered their troops to give no quarter or to commit the depravations they were accused of at Paoli, there is ample evidence that the acts committed by British soldiers went well beyond acceptable military standards of the period nor was it limited to a few isolated incidents on the battlefield. A British historian, James Murray, wrote, "General Grey conducted this enterprise with equal ability and success though perhaps not with the humanity which is so conspicuous in his character...A severe and horrible execution ensued...the British troops as well as the officer that commanded them gained but little honor by this midnight slaughter -it showed desperate cruelty than real valor".

Colonel Hubley of the 10th Pennsylvania Regiment later testified that he heard British troops calling 'no quarters' as his regiment rallied on the field. "The greatest cruelty was shewn on the side of the enemy. I, with my own eyes see them, cut and hack some of our poor men to pieces after they had fallen in their hands and scarcely shrew the least mercy to any, they got very dew prisoners from us."

Hubley, himself, had a narrow escape from the carnage. "In the affair I was remarkably lucky. About the middle of the engagement I unfortunately fell into the hands of some of the British troops viz one light horseman and four infantrymen. When they took me I damned them for a parcel of scoundrels and asked them what the meant by taking one of their own officers upon which they begged my pardon and I desired him to follow on. The four infantrymen filed off to the right in the man time. He came on with me until I got him amongst a party of our men."

About an hour after Wayne's retreat, the British consolidated on the campsite. Major Andre wrote, "About 200 killed or wounded remained on the field. We brought away nearly 80 prisoners and of those who escaped a great number were stabbed with bayonets or cut with broad swords, as great a number at least never stopped till they got to their own homes, in short, this harassing corps is almost annihilated by the loss of that night and by the subsequent desertions. On our part we only had 7 or 8 killed and wounded. We returned to camp before day break with 8 or 10 wagons and 30 or 40 horses 'borrowed' from Mr. Wayne".

At the time of the attack, the American regiment was the largest in the Continental Army, numbering 325 men. Of that number, fifty-six were killed, wounded, or missing during the massacre. In the camp, blood stained the ground around the bodies of the dead Americans. The hideous condition of some of the remains showed evidence of unspeakable horrors. Trails of blood crisscrossed the field, along with scattered muskets, clothing, and equipment. 52 Americans who lay dead in Pierce's fields were buried together with their arms and equipment in a common grave near the center of Wayne's encampment. The soldiers were placed in two rows of 26, oriented east to west in a 12 by 60-foot common grave. On the 40th anniversary of the massacre, veterans of that night gathered to mark and dedicate the hallowed ground where their comrades lay, with a marble monument similar to the one General Wayne is buried under at St. David's Church.

General Wayne continued to serve his country with distinction after Paoli, demanded his own court-martial to defend his decisions during the battle at Paoli, and fought in other critical battles of the Revolution. After the Revolution, he was appointed Commander in Chief of the American Army and traveled west to fight the Indian Wars in the Northwest Territory. During the most famous of these Indian battles, the Battle of Fallen Timbers, Wayne's soldiers engaged and defeated a coalition of British forces and a confederation of Indian tribes. The Indians were led by the Shawnee Chief Tecumseh (Panther Eye in the Sky) and his one-eyed brother, known as the prophet, in the Northwest Territory during the Battle of Fallen Timbers.

Although Wayne fought and won many battles in his illustrious lifetime, he would lose his battle with gout before he was able to return to his beloved Waynesborough Estate in Chester County, giving him the unusual distinction of being buried in two separate places. Upon his death in 1796, Wayne was buried at Fort Presque in Erie, Pennsylvania, at the foot of the post's flagpole, as he had requested. Twelve years later, his son Isaac traveled to Erie to bring his father's remains home. Expecting mere bones when the body was disinterred, Isaac was dismayed to find that the uniform had nearly rotted away from his father's corpse, but the body was in a remarkable state of preservation. Because of the long travel distance, it was not practical for Isaac to take Wayne's body hundreds of miles to the family cemetery at St. David's on a small, rickety cart. Dr Wallace, a local surgeon, devised a plan to boil the flesh off Wayne's bones so the son could carry them home. After the procedure, the doctor was so disgusted by the procedure that he buried his surgical tools with Wayne's flesh when it was re-interred at the foot of the flagpole. The grave in Erie is marked with a monument, and the cauldron in which his remains were boiled is on display at a local museum.

Of course, two burial sites and a boiled body provide a perfect median for a good ghost story, and Wayne is probably the second most popular ghost on the East Coast, second only to Abraham Lincoln's. This may be hard to believe, but Pennsylvania roads were even worse in the early 1800s than they are now. In those days, the roads were merely cart trails, muddy paths full of rocks, ruts, and tree stumps. When Isaac finally arrived at the gravesite at St. David's, he attempted to reassemble his father's skeleton, only to discover, to his horror, that several of the bones were missing. Some of the bones likely had tumbled out of the wagon while making the arduous trip across Pennsylvania along present-day route 322. Isaac was devastated by this turn of events and regretted his decision to relocate his father's bones for the rest of his life.

After Isacc's discovery was made known, stories began to surface that every New Year's morning, on Wayne's birthday, his ghost supposedly appears to make the long journey from St. David's to Erie and back on a fleshless horse in search of his missing bones. People have insisted that they witnessed a man dressed in a Revolutionary War uniform riding a horse and stopping occasionally to look for something. Wayne's ghost has been allegedly seen throughout Pennsylvania, including along Route 1 in Chadds Ford, near the site of the Battle of Brandywine. Wayne's ghost allegedly appears in full army dress riding a galloping white stallion with red eyes and flaming hoofs, which abruptly vanishes, reminiscent of the Hessian's steed in the Legend of Sleepy Hollow. His ghost also allegedly haunts Valley Forge National Park and battle sites in New Jersey, New York, Virginia, and Canada, all locations he fought during the Revolutionary War. Some people say Wayne's ghost looks menacing yet determined, whether alone or on horseback, as though he is still fighting against the British and Hessians.

The Admiral Vernon Inn, later named the Warren Inn in East Whiteland Township, was one of the earliest inns west of the courthouse in Philadelphia. George Aston built the inn on the Provincial (Lancaster) road in the Great Valley in 1744 and was granted a license to open a public house the following year. Aston must have felt that his inn was destined for fame when he gave it such a distinguished name since Admiral Vernon was the idol of England at this time. (Mount Vernon was also named after the admiral.) However, he was soon replaced in the minds of the people by another naval hero, Admiral Warren, so in 1748, the old Vernon sign was replaced, proclaiming the inn the 'Admiral Warren.'

Aston was also a prominent and popular man in the area. He was one of the vestrymen at St. Peter's Church and one of the first men in the county to form a company for defense when the French and Indian War broke out. The inn became the center for the military in the area, and it is mentioned several times as a landmark or stopping place in General Braddock's reports. In 1763, Captain Aston sold the inn to Lynford Lardner, a brother-in-law of Richard Penn and the agent for the Penn family in America. Lardner had several tenant innkeepers. Caleb Parry was an innkeeper from 1767 until the Revolution. At that time, he was commissioned a lieutenant colonel in Colonel Atlee's first regiment of Pennsylvania Musketry. He never returned to the inn, as he was killed in the Battle of Long Island.

In 1774, Lardner died, willing the inn to the Honorable John Penn of Philadelphia. Peter Mather became Penn's innkeeper, and the inn soon became a meeting place for Tories and British officers in the vicinity; notable among them was Major John Andre, a paroled prisoner of war at the time. Local belief was extraordinarily strong that Mather played a part in the Paoli Massacre; he denied it, and it could not be proved, but suspicion remained attached to him for the rest of his life. In any event, patronage at the inn dwindled, with only the chance traveler stopping by.

After the Revolution, when there was renewed discussion about moving the county seat from Chester to a more central location, the three suggested places were "Downing's," the "Turk's Head," and the "Admiral Warren." When the "Turk's Head" was selected, Penn was anxious to sell his property, which was sold in 1786 to Casper Fahnstock from Ephrata.

Marine Corps Tie-In...My First Trip to the Gulf.

My first of several trips to the Persian Gulf occurred in 1998 when Lima Company, 3rd Battalion 7th Marines, was tasked to fly to Kuwait and provide force protection in support of Operation Native Fury. I was a young, recently promoted corporal with very little operational experience, having recently been assigned to the unit from Washington, DC.

The company bussed to a reserve Air Force base in southern California and boarded a civilian plane for our flight to Kuwait. On the way to the Middle East, our plane unexpectedly diverted to Sigonella, Sicily, due to an engine fire. Although the company was stranded on the Mediterranean island while the engine was being repaired, there was little opportunity to take in much of the local sites. I did experience life living in the shadow of a giant active stratovolcano named Mount Etna, which lay dangerously close to the navy barracks where we temporarily lodged for a few days.

The plane engine was eventually repaired, and the company was soon airborne on the last leg of our journey. Lima 3/7 was stationed in the Mojave Desert, so we were relatively used to the hot, arid conditions, but as we soon found out, the Middle East is a different kind of desert environment, and most of us were ill-prepared for it.

Our company was tasked to secure the Kuwaiti Naval Base for the duration of Operation Native Fury, and we took the opportunity to hone our force protection skills, from squad-sized security operations to company-level security operations. We were housed in a rustic barracks-style building featuring wall-to-wall tile, which helped keep the hot temperature tolerable during the day. The small base provided slips for the few small Kuwaiti military craft based at the facility. Several floating docks in the artificial harbor were protected by a long seawall that jutted out into the Persian Gulf. Near the end of the seawall, a missile-gutted Kuwaiti naval vessel, a relic from Desert Storm, barely floated where it was moored.

Early morning and evening were the best times to train or stand sentry duty in Kuwait because a gulf breeze would kick up and cool things down during these intervals. The breezy conditions did not last long and gave way to scorching temperatures day and night. I volunteered to stand sentry at an M2 50. Caliber heavy machine gun (Maw Deuce) placement at the end of the pier as much as possible because I wanted to learn the weapon system, and it was much more peaceful at the end of the pier. The day was divided into three shifts, and each squad rotated through the shifts. The shifts were set up to give each squad eight hours on sentry duty, eight hours on react, and eight hours off. The squad on react had to stay in a designated location and on standby in case sentry posts needed support. Most of the eight-hour shift was spent waiting in a semi-alert posture, with an occasional drill called in for training purposes during the interval. The training scenarios varied from support by force, EPW search procedures, crowd control, and responding to suspicious packages. During the eight hours of free time, a Marine could sleep, PT, or wander the confines of the base.

Interaction with Kuwaiti nationals was limited, although a contingent of Kuwaiti navy personnel did invite our platoon to their compound for tea one morning. Tea is an important drink in Arab culture and is usually served with breakfast, lunch, and dinner. For Arabs, tea symbolizes hospitality and is typically served to guests. Called jaei and pronounced Shey, it is one of the most important aspects of hospitality and business etiquette in Arab culture. It is important not to reject tea when offered because it may be considered rude. Tea in Arab countries is usually a robust and dark drink, similar to breakfast tea served in other parts of the world. Jaei is often brewed with sugar and served in long glasses.

I have always been a coffee drinker since earning the title Marine, and I always drink coffee hot, black, and strong; I never add foo-foo to my coffee, and I consider it offensive to do so. I like to pride myself on the idea that the pots of coffee I make are strong enough to float a horseshoe, but the jaei our Kuwaiti hosts served us was in a league of its own. I cannot recall a cup of coffee more potent than the tiny glass of jaei I drank that morning in Kuwait.

Just before the end of our mission in Kuwait, we received devastating news from 29 Palms. Four of our young NCOs had remained in CONUS to attend a professional development course. After a night of drinking in San Diego, a series of bad choices led to tragic consequences. Somewhere on one of the four northbound lanes of Highway 5 near Camp Pendleton, one of the inebriated NCOs lost control of the vehicle he was driving and crashed into a guardrail, which ejected an NCO who was 'sleeping it off' in the back seat. The officer who called our company commander with the news reported that the young NCO, a squad leader who was well-liked by everyone, never had a chance and was instantly killed after his body impacted guardrail posts at a high rate of speed.

Historical places to visit in and near Paoli, Pennsylvania.

All these historical locations in this segment of the Patriot's Path can be visited in one day in Malvern, Pennsylvania. Begin your historical tour at the Paoli Battlefield, where you will find the common grave of the brave soldiers who fell to the British bayonets on the night of the massacre. Walk around the well-maintained park, where you will discover a walking trail, monuments, historical signs, and even a replica of a cannon on a broken carriage. Plan your visit in September when the battlefield comes alive yearly with reenactors and vendor booths. Make the short drive to historic Sugartown and its rich heritage of 18th-century homes and buildings. Visit the period country store for light refreshments before driving to the Warren Inn. The Inn is still in operation and is a great place to dine or stay for the night. My wife and I spent our wedding night in one of the Inn's historically preserved rooms and it was a fantastic experience. There is a historic plaque just outside the main entrance, and around the corner is the 18th-century blacksmith shop mentioned in this chapter of the Patriot's Path.

Paoli Battlefield is located at West 1st Avenue and Wayne Avenue Malvern, Pennsylvania.

Historic Sugartown is located at 273 Boot Road Malvern, Pennsylvania.

General Warren Inn is located at 9 Old Lancaster Road, Malvern, Pennsylvania.

Parkesburg, Pennsylvania

"Any officer can get by on his sergeants. To be a sergeant you have to know your stuff. I'd rather be an outstanding sergeant than just another officer."

~Sergeant Major Dan Daly, one of only two Marines to be awarded the Congressional Medal of Honor for two separate campaigns.

Among the early local settlers of Parkesburg was Arthur Parke, the first of the family after which the town is named. The Parkes owned much of the land on which Parkesburg was built, and Parvin Smith owned most of the west and south areas. Descendants of the Parkes and Smiths still reside in the borough.

The Fountain Inn, the original name for Parkesburg, was a tavern along Strasburg Road that served as a stop-over for those traveling between Philadelphia and Lancaster, which was the country's largest inland town in that era. James McClellan held a petition for the tavern built in 1734, and it still stands at 133 Main Street as a private residence. One of the original stone steps of the inn is on exhibit in the Upper Octorara Church Museum.

By 1720, local settlers built the Octorara Church where several Indian trails intersected. First known as Sadsbury, it was changed to Octorara, the name of the "mother church" of seventeen Presbyterian daughters and granddaughters in Chester and Lancaster Counties. Upper Octorara United Presbyterian Church is on Route 10, one mile north of Parkesburg. The church cemetery across the street from the church is the final resting place of several Revolutionary War patriots.

There is no recorded British pillaging of local property in or around Parkesburg. However, neighborhood Quaker families assisted in the care and transportation of some of those wounded at the Battle of Brandywine. American soldiers were familiar sights at the

Fountain Inn and along area roads. General Hand's company often patrolled the area to prevent British foraging efforts in the backcountry.

General Smallwood and his Maryland militiamen stopped in Parkesburg on their way to augment General Wayne at Paoli, and the tavern was used as a hospital after the battle at Paoli. A few days after the massacre, a Quaker brought an American soldier he had found by the roadside to the Fountain Inn. He had found the soldier lying in the woods with his coat, shirt, and trousers so stiff with gore they would have stood up by themselves when removed from the man. The wounded man later recounted his experience of the massacre. He told the patrons at the tavern that more than a dozen British soldiers had fixed bayonets and formed a circle around him. He said that every one of them took turns stabbing him in various parts of his body and limbs until, with a last desperate effort, he got out of their circle and fled, but not before receiving a vicious bayonet slash that opened his scalp. As a doctor cleaned and treated the man's wounds, he counted 46 different bayonet wounds deep enough to kill had they been thrust into the man's vitals. The man was later identified as James Martin, a Virginian serving with the 13th Virginia Regiment.

Local tradition has it that when Lafayette visited the US in 1824, he stayed at the Fountain Inn. The owner of the Fountain, a comrade-in-arms of Lafayette during the Revolution, personally escorted the General around the area.

The 'Hand's Pass' trail is located in Valley Township just west of Coatesville, Pennsylvania. At the Pass, General Edward Hand, one of Washington's staff officers and a hero of the Battle of Princeton, was scouting with a small company of soldiers when he stumbled upon a group of Hessians from a British camp. The Hessians immediately retreated without an exchange of gunfire. The Pass was later named for General Hand because of the bravery he and his men showed during the encounter with the Hessians. The Pass was eventually widened to accommodate the Lincoln Highway (Route 30), which is an east-to-west route through Hayti and divides the township.

Marine Corps Tie-In...Marine Corps Martial Arts Instructor Course.

The current Marine Corps close combat training model is the Marine Corps Martial Arts Program (MCMAP), which replaced the Linear Involuntary Neural-override Engagement (LINE) training, which was the Marine Corps's close-quarters combat system, in 2002.

MCMAP is considered a highbred model, combining hand-to-hand and close-quarters combat techniques with morale, team-building activities, and instruction in the warrior ethos. The program trains Marines in unarmed combat, edged weapons, weapons of opportunity, and rifle and bayonet techniques. It also stresses mental and character development, including the responsible use of force, leadership, and teamwork.

The techniques used by MCMAP vary in degrees of lethality, allowing a Marine to choose the most appropriate (usually the least) amount of force. The program is developed from several martial arts disciplines, including Brazilian jiu-jitsu, Wrestling, Judo, Capoeira, Sambo, Bujinkan Budo Taijutsu, boxing, Savate, kickboxing, Isshin-ryū Karate, Muay Thai, Taekwondo, Kung Fu, Aikido, Hapkido, Eskrima, Sayoc Kali, Jujutsu, Krav Maga, Iaido, Kendo, and Kobudo.

MCMAP is a synergy of mental, character, and physical disciplines with application across the full spectrum of violence. The disciplines are the foundation of the MCMAP system because they serve a dual purpose. The physical discipline comprises of about a third of the program and includes training Marines in fighting techniques, strength, and endurance. MCMAP also supports the sustainment of skills and techniques already taught to improve skills and develop weak-side proficiency. Ground fighting, grappling, pugil bouts, bayonet dummies, and other techniques are used to familiarize

Marines with the techniques used. In addition, physical strength and endurance are tested and improved with various techniques that often require teamwork or competition, such as calisthenics, running with full gear, log carries, and boxing matches. Techniques can also be practiced in water or low-light conditions to simulate combat stress.

I went through the MCMAP Instructor course as a young sergeant at Camp Pendleton when it was a new program. The course was extremely challenging, consisting of five weeks of constant mental and physical beatdowns. I remember an occasion where, while on a particularly grueling run, an NCO from my company had verbalized wanting to receive an injury so he could get out of the course without quitting because by quitting, he might receive an adverse fitness report from the school. Some Marines did quit, and several were dropped for injuries, but the NCO graduated.

During one training block, the class was led to a field that featured a long, wide, sandbag-reinforced trench. In and around the trench, several weapons of opportunity, such as pugil sticks, padded batons, and rubber knives, were scattered about. The rules for the training block were simple...survive. It reminded me of a spin-off of a recruit training event called Pugil Sticks 3, where recruits armed with pugil sticks would charge into a large, sandbagged bunker to confront whatever threat was present physically. The scenario changed from bout to bout; a recruit could charge into an empty bunker and wait a few seconds to jump 1-3 attackers running through an adjacent entrance or charge into a 1-1 scenario. The concept in the MCMAP training block was the same, but the bouts were longer, the weapons unpredictable, and many students were engaging at once, so it was every man for himself.

Another training block I fondly remember in the course was dubbed the 'Unit Cohesion' Room, where the school's dojo was converted into a WWE Hell in a Cell-styled venue. Again, the rules were pretty simple...survive. Although surviving the room took a lot of intestinal fortitude, some teamwork was encouraged, though the method was unorthodox. Several stations were set up in the converted dojo, enough for one Marine to rotate to and be painfully engaged for four-minute intervals. Ground fighting on the mats and hand-to-hand fighting in the ring were the featured events, and everyone in the class rotated through each. A timekeeper was centrally located in the room whose duty was to catch anyone not performing an exercise during a four-minute interval and tally the occasion on a whiteboard. After a certain number of room infractions, the four-minute interval would start over. Here is where the unconventional teamwork took place; since the timekeeper couldn't possibly see everyone in the room simultaneously, it became everyone's unspoken duty to sufficiently distract the timekeeper enough to avoid infractions to help each other successfully get through the interval and rotate.

The grappling mat was dominated by a huge 2nd-degree black belt Marine who specialized in ground fighting techniques. If anyone grappling with him somehow managed to make him tap out, the interval would immediately end, and everyone would get a brief respite before rotating, except that never happened. To simply survive four minutes was to succeed; no one even got close to tapping out the black belt.

In the sparing ring, our opponent was a female Marine brown belt instructor, working on logging sustainment hours towards her blackbelt. She was having her way with every inexperienced Marine who stepped into the ring, and we all kind of accepted the reality that when it was our turn, we would get a beatdown from a girl. When it was finally my turn to rotate to the ring, I was already through half of the stations, had been smothered and painfully manipulated for over four minutes on the grappling mat, and was already completely smoked. I was quickly dressed in a head and groin protector, shrugged into a flak jacket, and had gloves pulled over my hands. Each fighter was escorted to the center of the ring and reminded that strikes of any kind to the head, neck, or groin were strictly prohibited. After the safety brief, we touched gloves and waited for the whistle to start the bout.

At the whistle blast, the female Marine punched me full in the face and quickly backed off. I was stunned, surprised, and expected to win via disqualification, but the bout was not even paused. She circled rapidly, closed, and punched me full in the face a second time, and I lost it. Head down; I started pounding her with everything I had, with all the technique and finesse of a berserk madman, until I had her against the ropes, then into a corner where I began to work her over with knees and elbows. I did not hear the whistle blasts and barely felt another instructor pulling me off the offending Marine until he had me incapacitated with some technique that was new to me.

After I had composed myself, the instructor released his hold, and the class got to rotate to another station a little early after a brief respite. As I removed the protective gear, I saw another instructor dressing for the ring to replace the one I had just pummeled. To this day, the female Marine, the 'thing in the ring', was the only girl I ever hit with intent to injure.

Historical Sites to visit in or near Parkesburg, Pennsylvania.

There are only a few historical sites to visit on this leg of the Patriot's Path. The Fountain Inn is now a private residence in the heart of Parkesburg and not easily accessible although there is a historical plaque mounted on the front of the house. The Octorara Museum is more visitor friendly and there is plenty to see at this historic church. Go inside and ask for a tour of the museum exhibits then go across the street to a plethora of Revolutionary War Patriot graves in the cemetery. If you visit in the fall make sure to drive down the road to a small country booth that sells homemade apple cider doughnuts.

The Fountain Inn is located at 131 Main Street Parkesburg, Pennsylvania.

Octorara Church Museum is located at 1121 Octorara Trail Parkesburg, Pennsylvania.

Hand's Pass is located in the vicinity of 1145 West Lincoln Highway, Downingtown, Pennsylvania.

Phoenixville, Pennsylvania

"There are only two kinds of people that understand Marines: Marines and the enemy. Everyone else has a second-hand opinion."

~General William Thornson, U.S. Army

Phoenixville began as a 1600s-era village with a population of about four hundred settlers. One of the first Europeans in the area was a lawyer named Charles Pickering. Pickering immigrated from England with fellow Quaker William Penn, seeking wealth and treasure. Finding what he believed were traces of silver along a Schuylkill River feeder stream, he bought a land grant consisting of just over 5,300 acres of land from Penn, established the village of Charlestown along the banks of the creek that now bears his name, and began mining operations.

Unfortunately for Pickering, the ore he dug from his Pickering and Mining tracts was not the valuable silver he had expected to extract and proved to be worthless, so he resorted to counterfeiting Spanish silver bits. His skill as a lawyer must have been as poor as his minting skills because he was convicted of that crime in 1685. Pickering was fined forty English pounds to help fund the construction of a courthouse and ordered to pay full restitution to anyone who had bought into his scam. Around 1700, Pickering was conveniently lost at sea during a voyage to England, and his lands were split among 16 of his friends.

Around 1730, Moses Coates and James Starr arrived in the area. They purchased 1,000 acres of land along the French Creek near Phoenixville from David Lloyd, a Chester County political figure who originally called the area the Manavon Tract after his home in England. Starr built a grist mill, and the town of Phoenixville rapidly developed in the vicinity. Around 1734, Starr built what is regarded to be the oldest house still standing in Phoenixville.

In the 18ᵗʰ Century, most of the residents of Phoenixville were either Quakers or Mennonites. Regarded as pacifists, their religious principles prevented them from bearing arms. Most of the town's population did not approve of an armed conflict against England, but around thirty men from the Phoenixville area bravely served in the Revolutionary Army. Some of the town's early residents believed they could hear the noise of the cannon during the Battle of Brandywine over twenty miles distant. Sometime after that battle, wounded American and British soldiers trickled into local churches, meetinghouses, and taverns for treatment.

Phoenixville is also believed to be the furthest point in the Pennsylvania backcountry that the British Army occupied during the war. While Washington held the fords between Valley Forge and Norristown to deny Howe from crossing the Schuylkill and occupying Philadelphia, Wayne began his march from Chester Springs to rejoin the Continental Army. They moved fourteen miles northeast to Jones's Tavern on Ridge Road (Route 23), 20 miles west of the British Army's camp. The tavern was named for the father of Colonel Jonathon Jones of the 2ⁿᵈ Pennsylvania Regiment. Jones served with Benedict Arnold in Canada in 1775, and with General Wayne at Three Rivers and Fort Ticonderoga in 1776 where wounded, he lay for almost a day buried in snow. In 1777, he resigned his commission, having never fully recovered from the ordeal.

Meanwhile, while camped near Valley Forge, General Howe decided on a series of feints to determine Washington's reaction. Washington's response would shape Howe's decision to either cross the Schuylkill River at one of the lower fords and march south to Philadelphia or maneuver north toward Washington's backcountry supplies. On September 22ⁿᵈ Howe sent a strong reconnaissance patrol up Route 23 toward Reading and Pottsgrove. Intelligence of Howe's patrol forced Washington to make a tough decision; pull out of his well-established blocking position and protect his valuable stores or remain in place to deny Howe the fords and Philadelphia. Washington decided that while it would be unpopular to leave Philadelphia defenseless, the result of the British occupation would be primarily psychological since the Continental Congress had already evacuated to York, Pennsylvania. On the other hand, failing to protect his backcountry stores could prove catastrophic to the American cause of freedom. Washington pulled his Army away from the fords, moving them north and into the backcountry near Pottsgrove, allowing Howe uncontested access to the lower fords.

By September 25th Wayne's Pennsylvania division had reached Trappe, Pennsylvania, six miles south of the Continental Army, and no longer threatened Howe's Army. With Washington's Army out of the way, Howe could use the lower fords to cross his Army over the last remaining natural barrier separating him from his goal of occupying Philadelphia, and he did it without a fight.

During the three days that they were in the Phoenixville area, the British allegedly ransacked every home and business in the town. A monument in town was placed in front of Pat's Pizza to mark the forward edge of Howe's occupational force, but it is likely misplaced by a few miles since Howe had advanced his Army as far as French Creek which is west of town. Pat's Pizza was established in the same historic inn Howe headquartered during his brief occupation of Phoenixville and it was known as the Fountain Inn in those days.

Phoenixville was also the home of an interesting local Judge named William Moore. Moore was born in Philadelphia on May 6th 1699. Moore was sent to England for his formal education and graduated from the University of Oxford in 1719. Moore returned to Pennsylvania and moved onto 240 acres of the original Pickering tract in 1729. He built a simple frame house, later upgraded to a stone mansion overlooking the river. The mansion is still standing, and although it is now a private residence, it has always been called

Moore Hall. Moore also built a sawmill and the Bull Tavern, a popular watering hole in the area during colonial times.

Moore was Colonel of one of the Chester County militia regiments during the French and Indian War. As was the custom of gentlemen of wealth and standing in those days, he immersed himself in political affairs. In 1733, he was sent to the Pennsylvania Assembly and was re-elected each succeeding fall until 1740.

Moore was a patriot but not one who supported war as a means of gaining independence from England. An anonymous author wrote the following satire describing Moore, "I once made myself believe I could act the Patriot and accordingly made Interest to be chosen for a Representative, then I opposed loudly all Proprietary Innovations and was warm for the Liberty of my Country but getting nothing but the Honour of serving my Country I found that a Post of Profit might with my skill be more advantageous."

In 1741, the governor of Pennsylvania appointed Moore a justice of the peace and judge of Chester County Court. He acted in the capacity of these duties for forty years but was known for certain biases he had toward influential friends and Pennsylvania elitists. Moore also actively participated in disputes between the governor and the Pennsylvania Assembly. In November 1755, he wrote to 'warn' the Assembly that a group of two thousand men was going to travel to Philadelphia from Chester County to force them to pass a militia law, which the Quaker majority, with their pacifist views, would have been naturally opposed to.

During the next two years, several petitions were presented to the Assembly, charging Moore with tyranny, injustice, and extortion while adjudicating certain cases as a judge, and they wanted him to be removed from Office. The petitions were thought to have been generated by Moore's political opponents, including Issac Wayne, who was Anthony Wayne's grandfather. The names signed to these petitions are numerous and were garnered from a population of mostly illiterate people who were easily manipulated. In a rant Moore published in a local newspaper, he explained the circumstances of each of the charges in detail. He suggested that the petitions were gathered by Isaac Wayne, with whom he had had a personal quarrel, writing that they were obtained "through spite and rancor, by "riding night and day among ignorant and weak Persons using many Persuasions and Promises." After a hearing of the petitioners, the Assembly found Moore, "guilty of extortion, and many other fraudulent, wicked, and corrupt practices" and recommended he be removed from office as the county's judge.

Moore did not attend the hearings because he believed the Assembly had no authority to investigate the charges on the petitions. Immediately after the meeting of a new Assembly, composed primarily of the same people from the last, an arrest warrant was issued to the sheriff to have Moore incarcerated. He was arrested at Moore Hall by two armed men on a January Friday evening in 1758 and taken to Philadelphia, where he was confined in jail, where he steadfastly refused to defend his actions. The Assembly ordered that he be confined in jail until he recanted statements the Assembly considered loyal to the Crown. He was released in about three months after he finally recanted his statements. In August, the governor, after a series of disagreements with the Assembly regarding its ruling on Moore's case, questioned several witnesses, went through the form of a trial, and declared that "Moore had purged himself of every one of the original charges, and that he had never known a fuller and clearer defense."

The Crown eventually had the final say in the matter when it intervened on February 13th 1760, after Dr. William Smith traveled to England to appeal for his friend. The appeal resulted in the Crown notifying the Assembly of "His Majesty's high displeasure at assuming power that did not belong to them and invading the royal prerogative and the liberties of the people."

By the time the Revolutionary War broke out, Moore was a seventy-six-year-old man suffering from gout. He was, however, keenly aware of the importance of the struggle between the Crown and Patriots, and his sympathies, like most wealthy men of the country, were still entirely aligned with the Crown. Moore's disdain for the rebels was obvious, and he regarded them as a "rude rabble." Jacob Smith, known as a political eavesdropper, made an affidavit that he heard Moore say in his own home on May 7th 1775, that "the people of Boston were a vile set of rebels" and that "he was determined to commit every man to prison who would associate or muster."

The accusation caused a bit of excitement in Chester County, and patriots who were just coming into power during the Revolutionary War tended to go about the countryside and force people they suspected of having Tory views to recant. On June 6th the Chester County Committee, whose chairman was Issacs's grandson, Anthony Wayne, visited Moore Hall to force Moore to recant...again. This time, Moore was too old and ill to put up much of a fight and consequently signed a recantation. However, the spirit with which, twenty years earlier, Moore had defied the Assembly and went to jail was still determined. The paper he signed containing his recantation said, "I also further declare that I have of late encouraged and will continue to encourage learning the military art, apprehending the time is not far distant when there may be occasion for it." The veiled sarcasm was overlooked entirely, and the committee unanimously accepted Moore's recantation.

Sometime after Wayne visited with his grandfather's antagonist, a party from the Continental Army, including a member of Congress from the district, was sent to the Phoenixville area to confiscate the firearms from suspected Tories. They went to Moore Hall, where they found him restricted to his easy chair. During their search for firearms, they discovered a beautifully made sword with a handle inlaid with gold and silver, which had likely been a family heirloom. They were about to confiscate it when Moore asked permission to see it one last time. As soon as it was handed over to Moore, he stepped on the sword, snapping the blade from the handle. Then, gripping the hilt tightly, he threw the useless blade at them and, with a gesture of contempt, shouted, "There! Take that if you are anxious to fight, but you have no business to steal my plate."

Judge Moore spent the remainder of his long, eventful, if not controversial, life in Phoenixville until his death on May 30th 1783. Ironically, he and his old antagonists, the Waynes, rest together in the graveyard at St. David's Episcopal Church in Wayne, Pennsylvania. Moore is buried directly in front of the church door, and everyone who visits or attends the church walks over the venerable old judge as they enter the church. Although Judge Moore's home is historically preserved, it is a private residence.

While the Continental Army was encamped at Valley Forge, Colonel Clement Biddle and the Army's quartermasters were accommodated at Moore Hall, and Washington was Headquartered at the Issac Potts House. During the winter of 1778, representatives sent by Congress called the Continental Camp Committee traveled to Moore Hall to formally reprimand Washington for his perceived failures during the Philadelphia campaign. When the five-man committee arrived, Washington greeted them with his usual courtesy and gave them comfortable rooms in Moore Hall. Nothing in Washington's noble character resembled the whining, complaining, indecisive general that his Congressional critics used to describe him. Instead, they met a man whose bearing emanated serene authority. Congressman James Lovell, who was roommates with committee leader Francis Dana when they attended Harvard, was not a fan of Washington. Lovell wrote a letter to Sam Adams informing him that the committee's purpose was to "rap a demi-god over the knuckles." Unfortunately for Lovell, the visit did not turn out how he envisioned.

A bit of backstory will form a picture of what was happening behind the scenes.

The ominous realities of the condition of the Continental Army at Valley Forge in the opening weeks of 1778 were mirrored in York, Pennsylvania, where a depleted Congress and its statesmen tried to govern a new nation. Reduced to a mere eighteen members, the Continental Congress met in the small backcountry town after their perilous flight to escape capture, a sure conviction of treason, and death by hanging by the British Army that was in control of Philadelphia. Henry Laurens of South Carolina sat in the president's chair. Just before the meeting, a late arrival had nondescriptly handed the president a sealed letter he had 'found' on the stairs, entitled "*Thoughts of a Freeman*." The manuscript, penned by an anonymous author, listed a series of propositions, all denouncing Washington. Laurens looked up and realized that the congressmen in attendance were all staring at him, anticipating him to present the manuscript. They expected Laurens to submit the document to them, as the president was required to do with any mail he received, because of Congress's paranoia regarding executive power. Once Laurens submitted the letter, they planned to debate it for several days and would have likely approved some of the more insulting proposals regarding Washington. Could anyone, including a 'demi-god,' continue to serve the Continental Army as Commander in Chief in the face of such adversity and contempt from his own Congress?

Fortunately for the besieged Washington, Laurens had other loyalties besides obeying the wishes and whims of his congressional contemporaries, namely his son, Colonel John Laurens, who was one of Washington's trusted aides. Through this back channel, Washington was in constant communication with the president and had long since won his support and admiration. Instead of submitting the letter to the congressmen, Laurens quietly stashed it away. At the same time, he gave an offhanded remark that "the fireplace was the best way to dispose of such an anonymous production." But the letter was on its way to Washington at Valley Forge by courier within hours.

"Sir,

While I was sitting in Congress yesterday, a Member came in and delivered me the enclosed paper just in its present state except the broken Seals, the Gentleman's declaration as he was putting the thing into my hand, that he had picked it up on the Stairs, was a sufficient alarm—I passed my Eye cursorily over the pages, put them into my pocket and intimated to the House, that it was an anonymous production containing stuff which I must be content with, as perquisites of Office—that the hearth was the proper depository for such Records. I have shewn it to no body and have long hesitated upon the propriety of troubling Your Excellency with the knowledge of an attempt for which I want a proper stigma."

The congressman and their political counterparts, every one of them ignorant of military affairs, had turned on the man who had saved the struggling Revolution with improbable victories at Trenton and Princeton in the closing days of 1776, with a mere shell of an Army. The same man also skillfully avoided destruction at the hands of the world's premier military power during the Philadelphia Campaign. They used praise previously showered on Washington after those victories by the public to declare him an "idol with feet of clay." The congressmen's new hero became the devious and ambitious Horatio Gates, who defeated the British at the Battle of Saratoga. This emboldened congressmen and their political allies, including promotion-hungry Continental Army officers like Thomas Conway, to openly scorn Washington in letters and conversations in taverns all over Pennsylvania.

Back at Moore Hall, the Continental Camp Committee was surprised to receive a written report Washington calmly handed them, describing the desperate condition of the Army. It was approximately 16,000 words long and in letter form, making it evident that it illustrated Washington's personal opinions and recommendations to improve the state of the Army. The ghostwriter was Washington's aide, Colonel Alexander Hamilton, who had been helping Washington craft the letter for two weeks. Although they didn't realize it then, the five-man committee held America's first great state paper in their hands. With it, they also experienced Washington's political agility, which they did not even know existed.

The report's central theme was emphasized in its opening sentences, "Something must be done-important alterations must be made... The alternative was the dissolution of the Army at worst, or its continued existence as a feeble, languid, ineffectual force, a second best that would only delay the inevitable for a year or two." Along with reading this formidable document, which called, among other things, for providing officers a postwar pension to stay in the Army, the committee was subjected to another shock; the committee witnessed firsthand that the Continental Army was rapidly deteriorating. On February 2nd New York congressman Gouverneur Morris told his friend John Jay that "he had seen the skeleton of an army...in a naked starving condition, out of health, out of spirits."

The content of Washington's letter created the dismal atmosphere in which he invited Committee Chairman Francis Dana to dinner at his headquarters at the Issac Potts House. For several hours, they discussed the condition of the Army and what needed to be done to improve it. Washington specifically emphasized his plan to provide pensions for the officers in an effort to retain their service, an idea he felt would push Sam Adams and his followers over the edge. These men believed that "true revolutionists should be motivated by pure virtue, with no necessity for other rewards."

Washington told Dana that "over fifty officers had resigned already from a single division, bringing the total departures to over three hundred American officers."

Washington and Dana spoke until the combination of fatigue and a dying fire brought the conversation to a close. The hour was too late and the roads too hazardous for Dana to travel to his quarters in Moore Hall. Washington invited him to spend the night at his headquarters, and Dana accepted Washington's hospitality. While Dana was preparing for bed, he felt a sudden urge for fresh air. He stepped outside the house and began pacing up and down in the brisk January night. A few feet away from Dana was a large man doing the same thing. After a moment's hesitation, Dana spoke to Washington. Out of the cold darkness came words Dana would never forget. "Mr. Dana- if Congress does not trust me... I cannot go on thus."

In a moment that must have been surreal, the stunned Dana was speechless. When he gained his faculties, he hastily spoke the words that leaped involuntarily into his mind. He told Washington that "most of Congress still trusted him, and that included Delegate Francis Dana." Several years later, Dana told his son that "this was the proudest moment of his life."

To the immense chagrin of James Lovell, Sam Adams, and the other uncompromising and dogmatic statesmen, Francis Dana and the other committee members became ardent supporters of Washington that winter. Ironically, Congress voted for all the reforms Washington had called for in his report, and a much-improved system of supplying and equipping the Army was initiated. The reforms allowed the commander-in-chief to appoint the Quartermaster General and Commissary General of the Army, something Congress had previously insisted was their prerogative, although their efforts inevitably proved to be catastrophic.

On the most critical issue, half-pay pensions for the officers, resistance from the stubborn politicians was fierce. They refused to approve half-pay for life. Gouverneur Morris, who supported Washington, suggested a compromise: half pay for seven postwar years. Still, the antagonists of the idea pushed back. A vote resulted in a 5-5 deadlock, with Pennsylvania's two delegates on opposite sides of the debate. A third delegate, merchant Robert Morris, who was no relation to Gouverneur Morris, was usually extremely busy and seldom attended Congressional meetings. Gouverneur Morris quickly sent him a blunt message: "Think one moment and come here to York the next." On May 15th Robert Morris arrived just in time to put Pennsylvania and Congress in the pro-pension column, six states to five.

By another single fiber of the very last thread, Washington finally had the tools to build an Army with the stability and manpower to win a protracted war for independence at Yorktown, Virginia, three years later. One can read a copy of the letter "*Thoughts of a Freedman*" from the Henry Laurens Collection and Washington's letter to the Continental Camp Committee from the Washington Papers Collection.

Marine Corps Tie-In...No Better Neighbor Than a US Marine.

Billy was a Marine's Marine. He was well-liked, hardworking, relentlessly devoted to his wife and son, would give the shirt off his back for anyone in need, and at times, he was a terrible pain in the rear end.

We spent a lot of evenings beside a firepit, and he had a habit of tossing empty bottles on a slope behind the duplex we shared in our Camp Pendleton base housing neighborhood. I knew intuitively that someday, a base housing representative would make us clean up the bottles, fine us, or both. When the day of that inevitable visit finally came, I was the one at the house, so I received the warning and was awarded the task of cleaning up the slope. As I crawled through the scrub brush picking up bottles, Billy rolled up in his truck and, with a huge grin, said, "They finally caught you, didn't they"? Before I could reply, he emptied a bottle of pop and sent it arching through the air, landing danger-close to where I was working.

Billy cut me a break and stopped sending more bottles onto the slope after I had it cleaned up, but true to form, he moved on to the next thing, which was to send bottlecaps spinning into well-manicured landscaping I had meticulously maintained. That was Billy, though, always looking for a thread to pull, but the thing with Billy was, if he didn't like you, he wouldn't bother with you at all.

His son was cut from the same cloth as the father, always looking for adventure or chasing their family dog, a boxer the family called Pebbles. I spent a lot of time with his son and watched him whenever Billy and his wife needed a sitter. His favorite movies were "*The Emperor's New Groove*" and "*Blackhawk Down*," and like his dad, his favorite college football team was the Washington Huskies. To this day, I have not been able to watch Blackhawk Down because of the bitter memories it brings, but I have a little girl who likes Kuzco and llamas, and I like college football, so I watch the Disney movie with my daughters and I enjoy a Huskies game whenever I can.

For a cautious introvert who didn't make friends very easily, I instantly warmed up to Billy and considered him one of the very few whom I considered a close friend...in fact, I regarded him more as a brother. Billy was a Texas boy who grew up on the Huntington Beach, California, surf and could ride a shortboard better than most Texans could ride a tame horse. I on the other hand, grew up amongst the Amish in Central Pennsylvania and only saw an ocean once before my career in the Marine Corps, so I was not inclined to spend a lot of time in the ocean and could care less about surfing.

An enduring attribute of Billy's was his persistent nature. As I got to know him and spent time with his family, it became harder to resist his insistence that I learn to surf. Finally, I decided that the best way to appease Billy and get him to stop bothering me about surfing was to get out there and try it a couple of times. I surmised that Billy, invariably conceding defeat, would stop trying to get me out on the surf after seeing me flounder in the ocean a few times. I finally bought an old, worn funboard made by a company called Midget Smith, from a Marine who was leaving the Corps. The idea had its challenges—the fatal flaw was underestimating the level of Billy's persistence. Day after day, I would go out into the cold autumn surf to prove to Billy that I would never develop the skills or passion to ride a frigid ocean wave. Day after day, he would show up outside my bedroom window early in the morning, standing in his boardshorts and Uggs, holding a cup of coffee in one hand while tossing pebbles at my window with the other until I was awake and grudgingly agreeing to hit the surf again. He often told me, after a day of watching him carve up wave after wave while I tried literally to just keep my head above water, that the first wave I rode would have me hooked. The more I failed, the more I doubted his intuition until I finally dropped into a perfect, glassy-smooth wave and rode it to the beach. The experience was peaceful, exhilarating, and addictive all at the same time, and he was right: I was hooked on surfing. Although I never developed even a fraction of his skill on the waves, I developed a love for it.

Once, after a Thanksgiving weekend, a significant swell rolled into San Onofre, our local beach, following an autumn storm surge, and he wanted to drop in on a big wave before work. I harbored serious doubts that I even had the skill to survive the drop on a wave of the magnitude that was breaking that morning and the remarks of bystanders on the beach saying, "Dude, don't do it, man, you're gonna die" didn't boost my confidence level much. Billy looked back at me and said, "You do not have to do it; if you want to wuss out, go ahead, but I am not going to miss this." His lightly veiled insult replaced my healthy fear of getting crushed by a massive wave and I adopted his reckless abandon.

By the time we paddled through the powerful, crashing sets, we discovered that the riptide pulled us about a mile south of the beach, and as tired as we already were, we had to paddle back toward the beach to catch a wave where they were breaking. I had never been so far from shore on a surfboard, and I had serious doubts that Billy had either, although he was putting on a great show that for him it was merely a level or so above mundane. As we floated just outside the breaks, Billy said, "I am not paddling another two miles to catch a wave, so it's one and done." He was not finished talking when a set started to roll in, and seizing my opportunity, I nosed my board into the second wave in the set, paddled a couple of times, stood up, and looked down into the steepest drop I ever experienced. My life seemingly flashed before my eyes as I felt the board buckle violently beneath my feet, but I somehow made the bottom turn and carved the thick-railed Midget Smith back into the wave. I settled into the most magnificent ride I would ever experience or ever try to experience on a surfboard as the wave smoothed itself out. As I glided down the length of the wave; all I could feel was the wind and ocean spray hitting my face. I could not see anything but a great wall of water behind me, but I had a long view of the rapidly approaching beach. Eventually, the ride ended as my board swept smoothly onto the sandy beach, and I was saddened by the sudden thought that I would probably never have another ride like that again on a surfboard.

I looked around in time to see Billy carving up a huge wave, taking every bit of energy he could from it as he hit lip tricks and tail whips and rode back into the power of the wave to ride through its curl. On that epic morning, he was every bit as good as any professional surfer I had ever seen. When Billy hit the beach, he had a smile on his face that stayed with him for a long time, and judging by the radiance of the smile, what he had just experienced was anything but mundane. As we walked our boards back to the truck, people congratulated us with well-wishes and sporadic clapping as if we were conquering heroes. Once in the truck, he looked at me, shook his head, and said, "Dude, did you hear what I was trying to tell you before you took off on that wave?" I said, "No, what did you say?" Billy gave me a crooked smile and said, "I was trying to tell you to wait for the last couple of waves because if you bit it on the bottom turn of the first couple of waves...you know, one of the waves you just dropped into, you would probably not make it out of the Pacific alive". I tried to laugh it off, but he came back and said, "seriously, that was freaken awesome, but I was a little worried brother, I didn't think you were gonna stick the bottom turn on that old board."

Though we didn't know it then, we never had another opportunity to surf a big wave together again. After I returned from Iraq, I traded the Midget Smith to him for the beat-up Carter he rode the big wave on. That summer, he had planned to teach his son to surf on the Midget Smith, and he was going to teach me the fine art of shortboard surfing on the Carter. Sometimes, life throws its proverbial curveball. After OIF, the Marine Corps lifted the stop-loss stop-move order that froze all pending transfer orders for Marines. When Billy found out that stop-loss was going to keep him out of Iraq during OIF I, he was utterly devastated. He was a young Staff Sergeant assigned to instructor duty at the School of Infantry, and although he was very good at what he did, he didn't want to miss out on a combat deployment. He sucked it up as great Marines tend to do when faced with adversity and promised to take good care of things for me while I was gone. Shortly after our return from OIF, Marines could finally transfer or get out of the Corps. Billy soon found himself in receipt of a set of orders to Hawaii and the big surf opportunities the assignment would give him during his free time.

The Marine Corps prioritizes organizational needs ahead of the individual needs of a Marine. Although Billy had his coveted orders, the Corps only gave him a couple of weeks to execute them. Billy wasn't about to go to Hawaii and leave such a massive move to his young family to deal with on their own, so he very agonizingly had to turn his orders down, and he was promptly given orders to my old unit, which was on a short turn-around to deploy to Okinawa and the 31st MEU.

Billy was the kind of guy who could see the silver lining in everything. Although he wasn't going to get to drop in on a monster wave in Hawaii any time soon, he still had Onofre, had his family beside him, a career he loved, and he didn't even have to move his family out of the duplex for the next several years. Besides, he anticipated having plenty of time left in his career to get another coveted duty assignment to Hawaii.

Historical sites to visit in and near Phoenixville, Pennsylvania.

Swing into Pat's Pizza in Phoenixville, Pennsylvania, grab a bite to eat, and check out the historic building that once served as Howe's Headquarters during the Revolutionary War. Inside the restaurant, you will find vintage pictures and a brief history of the former 18th-century Tavern. Outside the building along the Road is a memorial marking the site of the British occupation of the town. Drive by Moore Hall and the Starr House, which is believed to be the oldest building in Phoenixville, now private residences. Visit the Phoenixville Ironworks and the Phoenixville Foundry, which houses exhibits from the Ironworking days of the town.

Go to Reeves Park, visit the war memorial, and check out one of the 1,400 Griffin Cannon that was forged at the Phoenixville Ironworks for the Union Army during the American Civil War. Then check out a full-sized bronze statue of David Reeves, the president of Phoenixville Ironworks in the early 1800s.

Finish your visit of this segment of the Patriot's Path at Morris Cemetery. Although the cemetery is not full of Revolutionary War patriots, it does have a large monument commemorating the Civil War veterans who are interned around it. Interestingly, Morris Cemetery is also the final resting place of the parents of a Wild West icon. Henry Longabaugh, alias the Sundance Kid, grew up on the outskirts of Phoenixville before heading west, where he partnered with Robert Parker, alias Butch Cassady. These two have the dubious distinction of being the most prolific train robbers of their time. They took their crime spree all the way to Argentina, where their luck finally ended, and they supposedly died in a shootout with law enforcement officers. Years later, the bodies were exhumed, and DNA tests were done on the remains, which confirmed the bodies were not those of the famous outlaws. Either Butch Cassady and the Sundance Kid were not killed in Argentina, or those looking for their graves looked in the wrong spot. Henry was known to make the long journey home on several occasions to visit his family in Phoenixville. Years later, researchers, acting on a rumor that Henry died during one of the trips he made to Phoenixville and was buried in the family plot, discovered an unmarked grave with Ground Penetrating Radar. Plans have been made to exhume the body and conduct DNA testing, but this work has not yet begun.

The Revolutionary War Monument is located at the intersection of routes 23 and 113 Phoenixville, Pennsylvania.

Moore Hall (private property) is located at 1001 Valley Forge Road Phoenixville, Pennsylvania.

<u>**Morris Cemetery**</u> is located at 428 Nutt Road Phoenixville, Pennsylvania.

<u>**Phoenixville Foundry**</u> is located at Two North Main Street Phoenixville Pennsylvania.

Reeves Park is located at 148 Third Avenue Phoenixville, Pennsylvania.

Mattias Pennypacker Farm is located at 55 Mill Road Phoenixville, Pennsylvania.

The Starr House is located at Ten Main Street Phoenixville, Pennsylvania.

Phoenixville Ironworks is located at 2 North Main Street Phoenixville, Pennsylvania.

The Fountain Inn is located at 498 Nutt Road Phoenixville, Pennsylvania.

Book Three: Winter Hostilities Around Philadelphia, a Spring Withdrawal and the End of the War in the North

Philadelphia, Pennsylvania

With their survival as an institution and as individual human beings at stake, the Marines have had to ruthlessly and endlessly examine, discard, define, refine, and redefine their approaches to achieve the ultimate in rapid, effective response to dynamic challenges.

~David A. Freedman

At 5 PM on September 26th with Washington out of the way, the British Army crossed the Schuylkill River at Gordon's ford and Fatland's ford and occupied Philadelphia, but not before burning the mill complex and anything else they could not carry away from Valley Forge. While Howe was moving into Philadelphia, Washington was breaking camp at Pottsgrove and moving his Army to Pennypacker Mills, ten miles closer to Philadelphia but still 20 miles away, ending a grueling march of 140 miles in just eleven days. General Howe gave Cornwallis the honor of formally occupying Philadelphia, the fourth largest city in the British Empire in the 18th century. Cornwallis selected around 3,000 troops and marched them into the city from Germantown. Ahead of Cornwallis' column rode several well-known Torys, including Joseph Galloway and the Allen Brothers.

As Galloway rode in front of Cornwallis' column, they passed Christ Church, where he had married his wife. Coincidently, Patriot General Anthony Wayne was married in the same church. The column eventually halted in front of the State House where Galloway once served as Speaker of the Pennsylvania Assembly. The State House was converted into the Captain's Main Guardhouse during the

British occupation of Philadelphia. Joseph Galloway was a Philadelphian renowned for his career in law and politics and was an ardent Loyalist or a Royalist, as my esteemed boss would put it. I met my boss at Valley Forge Military Academy and College, a military academy we both worked for. He was a member of the French Foreign Legion and retired from military service as a British Royal Marine Commando. On a 1777 battlefield, we would have been the fiercest of enemies, but when my boss married a 'Yank,' he also married his bride's country and has since become a citizen of the United States of America. We regularly rib each other about which Marine Corps is better, debate Royalist versus Rebel idiosyncrasies, etcetera. But it's all in good fun and keeping with the venerated Espirit de Corps our respective Marine Corps communities endear. Galloway was speaker of the Pennsylvania Assembly for 14 years prior to the Revolutionary War, and his closest friend is said to have been the venerable Benjamin Franklin. Galloway advocated reconciliation with Great Britain at the First Continental Congress by proposing a moderate Plan of Union.

Franklin, one of the more ardent advocates for Independence, tried to persuade him to become a patriot, but his efforts came to no avail, and their friendship eventually soured. Galloway refused to attend the second Continental Congress, resulting in outward animosity and even threats from his countrymen. He retired to his estate in Bucks County instead of remaining in the city and suffered from the patriotic fervor around him, but his exile to Bucks County was short-lived. In November 1776, the American Army was retreating from defeats in New York and crossed New Jersey near Galloway's estate. This prompted him to flee from his estate and place himself under the protection of General Howe. During Howe's Philadelphia Campaign, Joseph served as Howe's chief guide and spymaster and personally recruited upwards of 80 spies in support of the British cause. After the British abandoned Philadelphia in June

1778, Galloway exiled himself to England. Not very long after, he was tried and convicted of high treason in absentia by the Assembly, and his estates were confiscated. Galloway never returned to America, nor would he ever see his wife again, whom he had left behind hoping to recover his seized properties through her.

William Allen and his four sons advocated for American Independence in the days leading up to the American Revolution. William, a member of the Pennsylvania Assembly, led the Proprietary faction, which supported the Penns as rightful proprietors of Pennsylvania during the 1740s and 1750s. William championed American rights and lobbied against the infamous Stamp Act. In 1750, he built a country estate outside Philadelphia called Mount Airy, which eventually became part of Philadelphia. In 1762, he founded Allentown, Pennsylvania, and maintained a hunting lodge there. The Allen family continued to support the cause for Independence and even offered to donate munitions from their iron works for the Continental Army to defend Philadelphia should British forces attack the city. But as a radical populist political party in Pennsylvania rose in fervor, the family was forced to cling to their British ties and withdrew their support from the American cause in the Revolutionary War.

William Allen believed that the colonies should resolve their differences with England through constitutional means and did not support Independence through revolution. In 1774, Allen traveled to England, where he published *The American Crisis: A Letter, Addressed by Permission of Earl Gower, Lord President of the Council, on the present alarming Disturbances in the Colonies*, which proposed a plan for restoring the American colonies to Crown rule. He remained in England throughout most of the American Revolution and did not return to Philadelphia until 1779. Allen died at Mount Airy in 1781 before the end of the war.

William's eldest son, John, was elected to the Provincial Congress of New Jersey in 1776, but like his father, he left over his opposition to the war. He married Mary Johnston, a daughter of merchant David Johnston, in 1775; he died in Philadelphia in 1778.

Andrew became Pennsylvania's Attorney General in 1769. He served in several other public offices, including Philadelphia Recorder, and as a member of the City Council. Allen was also co-founder of the First City Troop. In 1776, Allen became a delegate to the Continental Congress but resigned shortly after his appointment because he opposed Independence. He traveled to New York, where he was supposed to advise the Committee of Safety on the city's defense. When the British drove Washington's Army out of New York and began their long occupation of the city, Allen sought British protection because he feared for his safety. Safely under British skirts, Allen took the required oaths of allegiance to the king and fled to England. Allen was tried in absentia and convicted of treason by the Assembly and his estate was confiscated. He died in London in 1825.

William's third son, James, was a notable lawyer and also a member of the Assembly. In 1775, he became an officer of the Pennsylvania Associators and joined the Continental Army the following year. In September 1776, James traveled to New York and was a distinguished guest of Washington and his staff. He was in the city to witness the battle of Harlem Heights on September 16th. The next day, he was escorted to his New Jersey estate where he became a Loyalist. On December 19th 1776, James was served with an arrest warrant from the Council of Safety. He was escorted to Philadelphia and put on trial and admitted to not supporting the cause of liberty. He rationalized his confession by stating "that while he did not support the cause of liberty, he never publicly interfered with it." Although James tried to remain neutral, he and his family were continuously harassed by New Jersey militiamen for their Tory sympathies. James died in Philadelphia in September 1778.

The youngest brother, Billy, also initially supported the American cause for Independence and received a commission as a captain in William Thompson's rifle battalion, which is considered the first unit raised by the American Army. The following year, Billy was promoted to lieutenant colonel of the 2nd Pennsylvania Battalion and distinguished himself on the fields of battle during the American defeat in Canada in a rear guard action that helped save the retreating American force from destruction at the hands of British forces. Anthony Wayne reported, "Allen and myself were now left on the field with only twenty men and five Officers, the Enemy still Continuing their whole fire from Great and small guns upon us . . . the Enemy who were Strong in Number had Detatched in two or three bodies about 1500 men to cut off our Retreat . . .I believe it will be Universally Allowed that Col. Allen and myself have saved the Army in Canada." Not long after Billy's heroic actions in Canada, the Declaration of Independence was penned, which, along with the rest of his family, he believed was too radical. Although the Continental Army wanted to promote him, Billy turned it down and resigned his commission. Billy then began to actively side with the British, and he raised a regiment of provincial troops called the Pennsylvania Loyalists to fight alongside the British regulars. Billy's lands and estate were also confiscated, and he fled to England, never returning to America.

For General Howe, occupying the city was going to present a few significant problems. After his lengthy campaign, he had many battle casualties that needed to be convalesced or replaced, and his Army had to be provisioned. The provisioning was a significant problem; with Washington's Army intact and hovering around the city, foraging parties would be limited and vulnerable to attacks. While Howe's brother had plenty of provisions on the more than two hundred ships under his command, river obstacles and two American forts still defending the Delaware River below Philadelphia's harbors prevented the British admiral from accessing city docks. Adding complexity to Howe's problem was a small but annoying Pennsylvania Navy patrolling the Delaware almost uncontested.

One of these annoying river raiders was John Hazelwood, who was commissioned a commodore in both the Pennsylvania and Continental Navies during the Philadelphia campaign. Hazelwood commanded Fort Mifflin and all American naval vessels operating on the Delaware River during the British invasion. He kept the British Navy at bay for weeks and contributed significantly to developing riverine warfare doctrine for colonial navies. Hazelwood was chosen by Washington and his counsel to lead an operation to move a large fleet of American ships and riverboats upriver and out of British hands before their inevitable occupation of the city. Congress even awarded him a ceremonial military sword for his bravery and distinguished service.

In late September 1777, Hazelwood assembled a defensive flotilla near Fort Mifflin to deny Admiral Howe's Royal Navy access to Philadelphia. His flotilla consisted of the 24-gun frigate *Delaware*, 32-gun frigate *Montgomery*, 8-gun sloop *Fly*, and numerous fire barges.

On Sept 27th when Commodore Hazelwood's combined armada rounded Gloucester Point, just south of Philadelphia, British drummers alerted the garrison, and artillerymen quickly manned their guns while the 1st Battalion of British Grenadiers hastily formed for battle. A six-gun battery commanded by Captain-Lieutenant Downman was placed on the City's southern waterfront behind unfinished earthworks. British Chief of Artillery General Cleaveland arrived on the scene after the alert was sounded and ordered Downman not to fire his guns unless the Americans fired on the battery. Downman ordered Lieutenant John Wilson to find a good spot to place one of the exposed guns. Wilson, who acquitted himself well at Brandywine, moved the gun to the end of a wharf in the shipyard and aimed it at the approaching American armada.

Downman failed to pass Cleaveland's engagement order to Wilson. When the frigate *Delaware* came within range, Wilson fired on her, managing two ineffective shots before Downman could order him to cease fire. The *Delaware* returned fire, unleashing her 12-pound guns loaded with grapeshot, at the gun placement. This exchange of fire prompted a second exchange from the battery and Hazelwood's ships, which fired a mixture of grape, 12, 18, 24, and 32-pound shot at the British defenders. Wilson, whose gun had run out of ammunition, ran to the other gun placements for more, leaving the gun and its crew to fend for itself. When he returned, the gun and its crew had somehow disappeared.

Unfortunately for Captain Alexander, who was commanding the *Delaware*, he accidentally grounded the ship while engaging the battery, and it became the prime target of the British guns. A British ball struck the ship's galley, and flaming ambers started small fires on the ship's deck, which were not easily extinguished. Alexander attempted to turn the *Delaware* about, but the sailors mismanaged the sails in the confusion. As the flaming ship floundered, a British ball penetrated the foredeck near the bow and set the hull on fire. The vessel became hopelessly grounded on the lower end of Windmill Island, only 250 yards from the British battery. Captain Alexander had to strike his colors, and the British immediately sent a boat with 10 Grenadiers to the ship to take possession and put out the fires. Marine Lieutenant Neilson and a group of men were able to lower some boats over the side of the Delaware and get away before the detachment of British Marine grenadiers boarded and took control of the frigate. The American sailors (152 men), including Alexander who remained on the *Delaware*, were placed into boats and taken to shore near Old Swedes Church and marched to prison at the State House.

While all this took place on the *Delaware*, the British trained their guns on the remaining American ships, which were busy tacking sails for a withdrawal. The *Fly* was also a casualty of the relentless British guns. After taking repeated shots that hulled her and shot the foremast away, killing four and wounding six, the *Fly* eventually ran aground on the Jersey side of the Delaware River. While the *Montgomery*, out of range of the British battery, returned safely to her station by Fort Mifflin, the schooner *Mosquito*, which also tried to withdraw downriver, was forced aground on the Jersey side of the Delaware River. Unbelievably, a fixed, six-gun battery in an unfinished, defensive earthwork with guns capable of only firing 12-pound shot had soundly defeated Hazelwood's armada of two frigates and five galleys. The *Delaware* was eventually repaired, floated off the sandbar, refitted, and pressed into British service behind the forts and obstacles guarding the Delaware River. Incredibly, the *Delaware* was manned by 53 British sailors from the HMS Roebuck located in the vicinity of Chester (below the American forts and obstacles) and former crewmen of the *Delaware* who decided to switch sides instead of remaining British prisoners in the city.

The one-hour river engagement was just the beginning of the fighting between American and British forces to control the Delaware River and its valuable navigational channel, and it would take the next two months to decide who would emerge victorious. Although the British now possessed the most powerful ship in the American Navy, it was hopelessly trapped behind three lines of river obstacles and three American forts (Mercer, Mifflin, and Billingsport), which still guarded the deep Delaware River channel below Philadelphia. Howe decided to attack Fort Billingsport, two miles below Fort Mifflin on the Jersey side of the Delaware, first since it was the furthest from the city than work his way upriver. Fort Billingsport, built to protect the first line of river obstacles, sat on ninety-six acres of land on the Jersey side of the Delaware. It was the first land purchase ever made by the United States. Although the fort was augmented by two floating barges each armed with nine and ten 18-pound guns anchored near it, Billingsport was the least defendable of the three river forts. It was unfinished, poorly designed, undermanned, inadequately armed with only five guns, and it could not be defended from a land attack.

On September 28th General Howe ordered the 10th and 42nd Regiments, consisting of about 1,000 troops, commanded by Colonel Thomas Stirling (no relation to Lord Stirling), to attack and destroy Fort Billingsport. Colonel Stirling's forces left Germantown and, on the morning of the 29th linked up with two battalions of the 71st Highlanders in Chester. He planned to move his augmented force across the river, turn north, destroy Fort Billingsport, and remove the first line of obstacles blocking the river. Sterling's forces were ferried across the Delaware and landed at Paul's Point on Raccoon Creek just south of the present-day Commodore Barry Bridge; the force then moved east on Center Square Road and north on King's Highway.

On September 27th Washington ordered Colonel William Bradford of the Pennsylvania militia to assume command of the few militiamen garrisoning Fort Billingsport. Bradford had enlisted in one of Pennsylvania's Flying Camps as a private and was promoted to major within the year. On September 29th Washington changed his mind and ordered the Pennsylvania militia garrisoning the fort to remove any stores, burn the fort and reinforce Fort Mifflin. Washington had decided to abandon and destroy Fort Billingsport, but a lack of manpower combined with the American Navy's fear of losing the fort delayed the fulfillment of the executive order.

So, when Colonel William Bradford arrived at the fort on the 29th he discovered that General Silas Newcomb of the New Jersey militia, the fort's commander, was conspicuously absent from his post. Newcomb had apparently taken one of the fort's guns and 300 New Jersey defenders with him, leaving behind the remaining guns, 12 artillerymen, and around 100 Pennsylvania militiamen to defend the fort. Newcomb was described by his contemporaries as "a man who was never where he should be and extremely indecisive...although a very sincere and well-meaning man, he should never have been entrusted with a command." Sometime after Bradford arrived, 100 Jersey militiamen returned to the fort, and on the 30th 50 more were sent by Newcomb, who stayed away from the fort.

On October 4th Newcomb wrote an account, from his perspective, of what had happened and sent it to New Jersey Governor Livingston. "On Sept 29th I made my headquarters at Woodbury 7 miles northeast of the fort. I posted a guard of 50 men at Big Timber Creek Bridge to prevent boats from crossing the river to the British and sent 150 men to the Bradford at Billingsport to augment the defenders. On October 1st I was informed of an enemy party of about 400 landed on the shore opposite of Marcus Hook and decided it was better to engage the British as far from the fort as it could and did so".

Colonel Sterling's forces were advancing inland when he spotted Newcomb's militia maneuvering opposite his position. Newcomb wrote, "About 9 in the morning...the enemy advanced within a few hundred yards of where we were drawn up, with 2 or 3 field pieces, when a pretty brisk fire from both sides issue. We now know their numbers to be superior to what they had been represented." Stirling's forces engaged with and drove Newcomb past the intersection of Salam Road and a road leading west toward Billingsport, more than 3 miles from the fort. Newcomb's forces crossed Mantua Creek and turned to make a stand. The British troops followed and again engaged the New Jersey militia. Newcomb withdrew to Woodbury, and Sterling, leaving 3 or 4 dead behind, turned his forces toward Fort Billingsport again.

Hearing the skirmishes unfolding around him, Bradford knew he could not adequately defend the fort from a strong land attack; he ordered the fort fired and cannon spiked that they could not extract from the fort. He put the guns he could take and the defenders into boats and sent them across the river to Fort Mifflin. Bradford remained on a brig near the fort to ascertain the strength of the attacking force. When the British broke through the corn fields surrounding the fort, they discovered the brig just offshore and fired on it. Guard boats commanded by Marine Lieutenants Dennis Leary and William Barney of the Continental brig *Andrew Doria* worked feverishly until all the ammunition and men were transferred from the fort to safety. The brig returned fire before safely moving out of range and upriver. Stirling's men moved to occupy the fort while American row galleys were still shelling it. British ships in Royal Navy anchorage near Marcus Hook moved upriver and eventually drove the row galleys away.

Although the fort was in British hands, it would take them more than three weeks to remove the first line of chevaux-de-frise and level the obsolete fort. Colonel Sterling, wishing to maintain the initiative, requested permission to attack Fort Mercer, but his request was subsequently denied. Unfortunately for Howe, at the time of the attack on Fort Billingsport, Fort Mercer, although equipped with artillery, was only defended by a few non-combatants. If Sterling had been given his leave, he would have been able to occupy Fort Mercer without a fight and be in a position to force the immediate evacuation of Fort Mifflin.

In 1778, a Revolutionary War skirmish occurred near the ruins of Fort Billingsport when about three hundred Loyalist and British troops marched from Fort Billings to Swedesboro, hoping to capture local militiamen. Finding the Patriots gone, the English pillaged homes and burned the log schoolhouse that had recently been used as a jail for Tories. Patriot Militia soon returned, taking a position on a wooded hill overlooking the town, and began shooting. The British returned fire, and bullets flew in all directions, endangering soldiers and citizens alike before the sides retired.

As for Colonel Bradford, he continued to serve in the Revolutionary War with distinction until poor health forced him to resign in 1779. A year later, William Bradford became Pennsylvania's Attorney General and Register of the High Court of Appeals at the age of 25. Bradford continued to serve as Attorney General until he was appointed a Justice of the Pennsylvania Supreme Court in 1791. Three years later, he served on President George Washington's Cabinet as United States Attorney General until his death in 1795. Bradford County, Pennsylvania, was named in William's honor.

Fort Mercer was the strongest of the three Delaware River forts and was located two miles upriver on the Jersey side of the Delaware. It was built to provide the final layer of protection for the Philadelphia riverfront and to defend the last line of river obstacles. The fort was armed with fourteen guns and designed for a garrison of 1,500 defenders, although it was never manned with anything close to that number of men. The fort was built in a position to overlook and help protect Fort Mifflin.

The ever-ambitious Colonel Carl von Donop, commander of the Hessian Grenadiers, would not survive his next attempt to cover himself in vain glory. Donop appealed to General Howe to attack and seize Fort Mercer under the auspice that it was under-defended. In a hurry for the Delaware River to fall under British control, Howe granted him the honor. On October 22nd Donop crossed the Delaware River to the Jersey side with 2,000 Hessians and, surrounding the fort, demanded its surrender. Called the Battle of Red Bank, a chagrinned Donop soon found out that the fort, no longer undefended, was occupied by Colonel Christopher Greene and his 1st Rhode Island Regiment and Colonel Israel Angell's 2nd Rhode Island Regiment, the combined American forces numbering around five hundred men. The two very capable colonels, sitting behind strong defenses with plenty of ammunition, had no intention of surrendering the fort without a fight. Donop made three attempts to attack and overwhelm the

Rhode Islanders, and three times, they were repelled, aided by American riverboats who began to hurl artillery rounds into Donop's ranks. After the Hessians retreated and the smoke cleared, around four hundred were either killed or wounded while the American defenders suffered fourteen dead and 27 wounded. Among the Hessian dead was Colonel Donop; his ambitions and luck in America finally played out. Donop, who lingered for three days before succumbing to his wounds, may have finally realized how fatal his ambition was. While speaking with one of his officers, he said, "It is finishing a noble career early, but I die a victim of my ambition, and of the avarice of my sovereign." Von Donop is buried at the Red Bank Battlefield Park near the old fort ruins.

The night before the battle for the fort, two of the British War ships, the 64-gun ship-of-the-line HMS Augusta and the sloop of war HMS Merlin, were positioned just below the hidden chevaux-de-frise so they could support Donop's attack the following day. Admiral Reynolds failed to account for the ebbing tide, which left both ships grounded on a sand bar. HMS Roebuck moved upriver overnight to help the grounded vessels, but attempts to free the ships were unsuccessful. Fort Mifflin artillery and the Pennsylvania Navy commanded by Hazelwood engaged the stranded ships the next morning with cannon and fire rafts. Within an hour of the tantum barrages, HMS *Augusta* caught fire. The fire eventually reached the magazine, and the ship exploded with such force that it was audible thirty miles away. The *Augusta* was the largest ship lost by the British in both the Revolutionary War and the War of 1812.

Accounts vary as to the cause of the fire. In one version, the loss of *Augusta* was attributed to the British's accidental ignition of the powder magazine. Navy historian and prolific author James Fenimore Cooper claimed that the sides of the hull of the *Augusta* were packed with hay to repel musket and cannon shot, and during the exchange, the hay caught fire, and the fire rapidly spread. Crew members gave their testimony, but none could be definitively verified. No one remembered having seen or heard the explosion of any powder on the decks. Only Midshipman Reid ventured to suppose that the fire originated from the cannon wads and Admiral Lord Howe had apparently accepted this explanation. Soon after, the crewmembers of *Merlin* were ordered to abandon their ship and set fire to it.

Ann Cooper Whitall lived in a brick home on the banks of the Delaware River near Fort Mercer with her husband, James, and their children. On October 22nd 1777, with British warships in the Delaware River, local residents of the towns along the river were urged to leave their homes to find a safe haven. Ann Cooper Whitall refused to leave her home, even at the insistence of her own family. A devout Quaker, Whitall placed her trust in God instead and remained in her home. She resolutely worked at her spinning wheel as the battle raged around her. When a cannonball suddenly burst into the room where she was sitting, Whitall reputedly picked up her spinning wheel and moved it to the basement, where she continued her work. Later that evening, after the Americans repelled the Hessian invasion force, Ann Cooper Whitall ministered to the wounded and dying Hessian soldiers, earning herself the nickname "the Heroine of Red Bank."

On November 11th 1777, American soldiers at Fort Mercer tested two cannon recovered from the *Augusta*, each weighing approximately 5,400 pounds, that were capable of firing 24-pound projectiles up to one-half mile. Both cannon exploded when tested, killing and injuring members of the gun crew. Archaeologists found a large fragment of one of the cannon using ground-penetrating radar and excavated it on September 11th 2015. The fragment of the original cannon weighs 848 pounds and lay undisturbed for over 230 years, only two feet below ground. The fragment is currently displayed a few feet from where archaeologists uncovered it.

Fort Mifflin was initially called Fort Island Battery or Mud Island Fort before it was renamed for Thomas Mifflin in 1795, who was the first post-independence governor of Pennsylvania. The fort was built on a mudflat previously owned by Joseph Galloway and exists today just off one of Philadelphia Airport's runways. It is surrounded by swamps on all sides except the front, which faces the riverfront. The fort was constructed of logs, ship spars, and old rafts set in the mud. Most of Mud Island was submerged at high tide, and the entire island, including the fort, could be flooded by cutting the dikes on the Pennsylvania shore. Ironically, the fort was built in 1771 under the direction of John Montresor, who, by 1777, was serving as General Howe's chief of engineers; he was ordered to attack and reduce the fort he had designed and built years earlier. The fort was positioned to defend the second line of chevaux-de-frise placed in the river's navigational channel.

Washington initially wanted Hazelwood to transfer 200-300 sailors from his ships to augment Fort Mifflin's garrison, his rationale being that sending sailors to operate the fort's cannon was the best option. However, Washington was unaware that many of Hazelwood's ships were sitting at anchor because they did not have enough sailors to put out to sea. Washington changed his mind and assigned command of the fort's defenses to the Continental Army, placing Colonel D'Arendt, a Prussian Baron described as having exceptional engineering skills, in command. Colonel Smith of the 4th Maryland Regiment was ordered to augment the garrison with regular Army soldiers. Unfortunately for Colonel Smith, D'Arendt was ill and could not report to the fort for several weeks.

On September 26th Colonel Smith arrived at Fort Mifflin to augment the sixty militiamen already defending the fort. Smith was not overly impressed with the poor disposition of the fort's defenses or the men who defended it; none could even load or fire the fort's cannon. Smith soon discovered that the sixty-man garrison, commanded by Colonel Lewis Nicola, were untrained invalids. The disabled soldiers were, believe it or not, assigned to the official

American Army unit established in 1776 to free up combat units by garrisoning forts and posts with troops that were unfit for combat duty. Given the tactical significance of Fort Mifflin, it is unfathomable that it was left without a single artillery officer, engineer, or artilleryman to defend the river and its obstacles. Smith and Hazelwood discussed the river's defense and, particularly, of Fort Mifflin. Hazelwood dismissed Smith's apprehensions regarding the poor disposition of the fort, saying, "a mosquito couldn't live there under the fire of my guns," ironically foreshadowing the demise of the schooner *Mosquito* at the hands of a British shore battery a day later. The disagreement between the American Army and Naval services would certainly not be the last in history.

On October 10th Captain Montresor and an escort of 20 Grenadiers crossed to Providence Island, located on the Delaware River adjacent to Fort Mifflin, to survey the high ground and flooded swamps surrounding the fort. A few locals, finding out about the British reconnaissance party, abandoned the island and the Pest House built on it in 1743. The evacuation of the island provided an option for the British to bombard the fort from the island and use it as a staging point for an assault or both. The Pest House, or the Old Lazaretto as locals also called it, was a quarantine hospital that treated people who contracted contagious diseases. A second hospital was built in 1799 on Tinicum Island, just southwest of where the Schuylkill and Delaware Rivers meet, along present-day Penrose Ferry Road. The hospital has the dubious distinction of being the oldest surviving quarantine station in the Western Hemisphere and one of the ten oldest in the world.

After Donop's failed attempt to seize Fort Mercer and the additional loss of two valuable warships, a frustrated General Howe focused his attention on Fort Mifflin. On November 10th Howe ordered a sustained bombardment of Fort Mifflin. The bombardment lasted for five days before the fort's defenders, low on munitions and rations and sustaining 250 killed and wounded, were finally forced to abandon the fort. After the Revolutionary War, the Army began rebuilding Fort Mifflin, maintained a garrison into the 19th century, and even housed prisoners of war during the American Civil War. In 1962, the U.S. Army finally decommissioned Fort Mifflin for active-duty infantry and artillery units. After the fort was decommissioned, the older portion of the fort was given back to the City of Philadelphia. However, a portion of the fort is still actively used by the U.S. Army Corps of Engineers, making it the oldest fort in use in the United States.

After the inevitable fall of Fort Mifflin, The Rhode Islanders at Fort Mercer were forced to abandon it to the British, finally giving Howe his coveted unrestricted control of the Delaware River and uncontested passage to Philadelphia for his brother's fleet. Although Howe finally gained the Delaware River, the four months it took him to complete the action gave Washington precious time to rest and resupply his Army.

The prevailing attitude regarding the British occupation of Philadelphia from those on the patriot side was interesting. In a letter to his wife, Lafayette wrote, "Philadelphia is taken, the capitol of America, the rampart of liberty! You must politely answer, "You are the great fools! Philadelphia is a poor, forlorn town, exposed on every side, whose harbor was already closed: though the members of Congress lent it, I know not why, some degree of celebrity. This is the famous city which, be it added, we will, sooner or later, make them yield back to us". Benjamin Franklin, on a 'diplomatic mission' in France more humorously wrote, "Instead of saying Sir William Howe had taken Philadelphia, it would be more proper to say, Philadelphia has taken Sir William Howe." General Pickering used the occasion to take a swing at the large Loyalist population in the city when he wrote, "I feel in some degree reconciled to Howe's entering Philadelphia, that the unworthy inhabitants (of which til' apparent a majority of the state is composed) may experience the calamities of war, which nothing but their own supineness and unfriendliness to the American cause would have brought them. Possibly Heaven permits it in vengeance for their defection, that their country should be the seat of war". General Hartley probably summed the situation in Philadelphia best when he wrote, "Our worthy Commander in Chief feels for his country. He is sorry to lose an inch of ground, but the loss of cities may sometimes be the salvation of states."

Howe achieved his goal of taking the American capital, but the victory turned out to be an empty one. The Continental Congress was nowhere near the city, and Washington, with his Army intact, remained a formidable regional threat, which effectively fixed Howe in Philadelphia to counter that threat. Howe realized the threat was very real when Washington unexpectantly attacked his Army garrisoned at Germantown within two weeks of the British occupation of Philadelphia. Although the British Army somehow managed to repel the attack, other skirmishes soon followed. On December 19th Washington moved his Army into winter camp, where Von Steuben would eventually mold it into a disciplined and professional Army.

The Revolution was still very much alive and Washington's valuable back-country supply depots in Downingtown, Reading, and Lancaster remained unmolested. Washington's Army fought valiantly across Chester County and although he failed to win a decisive victory against the British Army, General Howe, with his tested and proven professional Army, failed to destroy Washington's amateur Army and bring an end to the American bid for Independence.

The Continental Army had managed to survive against insurmountable odds and would soon gain a valuable ally in its bid for Independence. An improbable American victory at Saratoga, New York, combined with the Continental Army's demonstrated ability to stand toe to toe with the British, impressed the French enough to become more than a silent partner in the American venture for independence. France's formal entrance into the American Revolution expanded the regional conflict into a world war, and it was instrumental in turning the tide toward the American cause for freedom.

Marine Corps Tie-In...A Marine's Marine...Always Faithful.

I made it just beyond the first thirty days of Drill Instructor School when I received a phone call that radically and forever changed my life. I had just finished shaving my head and was trying to study a teach-back while meticulously preparing my uniforms for the following day's battery of inspections when my cell phone rang. The voice on the other end informed me that what I was about to hear was going to be difficult to accept. The voice on the phone told me that 'he' was gone. I remember saying, "ok, who's gone"? The voice said, "Billy... Billy's gone." Reflecting on the moment, I think I knew right away what the voice was saying to me, but my mind refused to accept the bitter news. The voice spoke again, "Did you hear me? Billy's gone."

My mind still refusing the reality and totality of the message, I replied, "I know he's gone... Billy deployed to Okinawa with First Battalion, Fifth Marines several months ago." The voice, a little less patient than before, said, "Billy is gone. He was killed today in Iraq, and a CACO team just notified his wife and son." I could form no words past the growing lump in my throat, and as I abruptly ended the call, the harshest of realities took hold of me and slowly strangled my heart. My neighbor, dear friend, and brother Marine was killed in Iraq. In a selfless act of heroism, he sacrificed his life to save the life of one of his Marines on the outskirts of a tiny, dirty, insurgent-infested town called Fallujah, Iraq.

For me, the irony couldn't be more stark. Billy was assigned the platoon sergeant of the very platoon I left behind after OIF-I to attend

Drill Instructor School. Bravo Company, third platoon rapidly re-deployed to augment the 31st MEU in Okinawa with 1st Battalion 5th Marines. They were not on the 'Rock' very long before the 31st MEU received marching orders to Iraq, where it was assigned to RCT-7. That morning, the platoon lost their platoon commander, a young lieutenant from California, to small arms fire. The officer's replacement was the staff sergeant who deployed with third platoon Bravo during OIF-1. Over the years, I have heard variations of the circumstances surrounding Billy's death. I did not get an opportunity to read Billy's Bronze Star citation, nor was I able to read the Summary of Action for his medal. A recent conversation with the Marine who led me and third platoon in 2003 summed up the events of that tragic day and helped me fill in some significant gaps in Billy's story. His account and verification of other versions of the events of 8 April 2004 was as follows:

Third platoon was ordered to clear two houses in the company's zone, and the two SNCOs leading the third platoon divided it in half to quickly clear them of insurgents. During the ensuing mission, Billy's half of the platoon took a significant amount of enemy fire. As Billy directed fire for his Marines, he and my old platoon sergeant briefly argued over the radio about the enemy's position. Billy began to lay down suppressive fire to cover his Marines while they moved into cover when two of them were cut down by the enemy fire. Billy unhesitantly left his covered position and, exposing himself, pulled the Marines to safety. As a corpsman was triaging one of the wounded Marines at the 'Cloverleaf,' the corpsman, noticing a large amount of blood on Billy's flak jacket, asked if he had been hit. Billy, indeed, had been hit by an enemy round, and the mortal wound was exposed after his flak jacket was removed. Several eyewitness accounts of the event consistently state that his last thoughts and words were exclusively of his beloved wife and son.

It took a long time for me to recover from the shock I had just experienced. I remember seeking out my squad advisor at Drill Instructor School to let him know what had happened. I knew I wanted to be as available as possible to help Billy's family in any way I could. Little did I know, the harshness of reality was about to take a full swing at my face. I requested the time off that I would need to escort Billy's body home from Dover. My request was almost immediately denied. The explanation was that I was attending one of the Corp's premiere formal schools and would fall too far behind my peers in the time it would take me to bring Billy home.

I almost dropped from the school on request, even knowing that to do so meant that I would undoubtedly be flushing my career down the drain. I wrestled with the decision for days. Finally, a close mutual friend and neighbor who lived in a duplex down the sidewalk with his young family talked me through it. More flexible at his unit than I was in a formal school, he took leave and caught a flight to Dover, Delaware, to fulfill the very sacred duty of bringing Billy home.

Our friend made sure Billy was carefully uniformed in his coveted dress blues, which were adorned with a Bronze Star and Purple Heart, pinned on his chest posthumously for the valorous manner in which he sacrificed his life, along with various other medals representing his storied and meritorious career. Over his left shoulder hung the prestigious French Fourragere, a unit award worn only by members of the Fifth and Sixth Marine Regiments. His flag-draped coffin was carefully loaded onto a commercial flight to California, where he was eventually laid to rest in his hometown.

His son, robbed of a life full of the lessons his father would have lovingly taught him, stood brave and tall beside his grieving mother, vulnerable in his youth yet protective of her throughout the funeral, a miniature image of his brave father. Contributing to Billy's obituary, the resolute 7-year-old son described his father as a great citizen and a great man. With insight remarkable for a young man of his age, he said, "He fought the war for a reason, and that reason was because he wanted our family to live in peace, and I miss him."

The composer of Billy's obituary went on to say, "He was that rare man who got it right, a true American hero ."A family member also wrote this final goodbye: "A hard body, a soft heart, a warrior, a gentle husband and father, a soldier dedicated to country, a devoted and loyal friend. A broad smile, a laugh now silent, a loving memory, a thought carried in our hearts forever. Dear Billy, you made the world a better place. We love you and miss you."

To this day, I am ashamed to say that I could have and should have supported Billy's family better. I could have and should have repaid him for the time he devoted to our friendship with something more substantial than an awkward farewell. Assuming I was doing what he would have wanted me to do, I focused on my career instead of selflessly setting it aside to be there for his family. I could have honored his legacy better than I did. I should have been there to support his son as he grew into the man and the Marine Officer he has become, molding himself into the man his father was, equipped with childhood memories I am sure he keeps close.

My guilt is my own, a result of the decisions only I am responsible for. I no longer grieve for Billy; he had an uncanny knack for having everything his way, and an honorable death on a battlefield defending his nation is the way I think he would have chosen instead of growing old in peace. The real tragedy is that I believe that he would not have chosen the time of his passing, not with so much to do with his wife and son still left on the table; he was not that kind of man. I struggle with the shameful idea that Billy kind of went to Iraq in my place. After all, I tried in vain to set aside orders in lieu of one more combat deployment with my Marines. Billy had orders to Hawaii, but ironically, circumstances handed him orders to my former unit and the very platoon I left behind to become a Drill Instructor.

The reality of it is, even if we had deployed to Iraq together, he still would likely have died a hero's death in Iraq, and I could not have supported his family in their hour of need anyway. I know if I could have altered the sands of time before I met my wife fifteen years ago, I would have set aside the narcissistic notion of becoming a Marine Drill Instructor to support Billy's family. I would have done that even if it meant that to do so would have ended my military career early; I have a nagging feeling that is what Billy would have done had our fortunes been reversed.

The enduring notion that gives me peace is that his sacrifice inspires me every day to be a loving and dedicated husband of an amazing woman and a patient and loving father of two beautiful young ladies; Billy would have wanted nothing less than that for me. He indeed has his place secure in heaven, and I know in my heart that he holds no grudge against me; I am confident he is as proud of my young ladies as I am every day, and someday, maybe... we will hit the surf together again.

Historical Places to Visit in Philadelphia, Pennsylvania.

If you really want to experience all that Philadelphia has to offer consider taking a few days to visit the battle sites, forts, museums, and historical points of interest in and around this history-rich city in Pennsylvania. Take a guided walking tour of the many city sites, where a knowledgeable tour guide will take you on a visit to several historical homes, statues, monuments, and other important places. Or park in a secure parking lot at Independence State Park, where you will be within minutes of Independence Hall, the Liberty Bell, and a bronze statue of George Washington and Commodore John Barry.

Walk across the street to Washington Park and visit the Tomb of the Unknown Soldier, which commemorates the hundreds of American Revolutionary War soldiers buried in the mass grave below the park. While you are visiting, look for a Sycamore Tree planted from a seed carried to the moon on Apollo fourteen by Astronaut Stuart Roosa in 1971.

Walk downtown and visit City Hall and Welcome Park, where you will find statues of William Penn. Also within walking distance of Independence Hall are the Ben Franklin National Memorial, Arch Street Meetinghouse, where Captain Samuel Nichols is buried, and Christ Church, where you can sit in the very pew reserved for Washington and his family when they attended services.

Stroll over to Penn's Landing and visit four beautiful parks along your way. Take Samson Walk toward the river, and the first of these parks, Welcome Park, is where you will find a beautifully crafted statue of Wiliam Penn. I-95 Park is further along Samson Walk but is currently under renovation. It is the location of the Scottish Immigrants Memorial and a stone marker indicating the spot where the Tun Tavern once stood. The third park to visit is about a block walk to Spruce Street and Foglietta Plaza, where you will discover the Philadelphia Korean War Veterans Memorial and the Beirut Memorial. The Philadelphia Vietnam Veterans Memorial is on the other side of Spruce Street.

Cross Christopher Columbus Boulevard and visit Penn's Landing and the Independence Seaport Museum. Take a tour on the U.S. Naval Submarine Becuna, then cross her deck to the U.S. Olympia, which served as Commodore Dewey's flagship in the Battle of Manila Bay. As you tour their historic vessels, the wonderful smell of culinary cuisine will probably propel your appetite at full steam ahead. The smells are likely coming from the four-masted steel barque, Mashulu. The Mashulu is the largest windjammer in existence, the largest surviving square-rigged ship still floating, and now serves as a floating restaurant.

After visiting Penn's Landing, head back to the city via Market Street, which will take you to City Hall. Buy a souvenir at its gift shop and take a look at a William Penn Statue, which gazes east toward a Penn statue in Wissahickon Park that looks west toward City Hall.

Give yourself the day to explore Philadelphia's Museum of the American Revolution. If you limit your visit to the Museum of the American Revolution to half a day, consider visiting the National Constitution Center along Arch Street. Consider spending another day exploring the Philadelphia Art Center, where you will discover several bronze statues of Revolutionary War heroes among its outside exhibits.

In front of the Art Center, you will find the Iconic Rocky statue and the Washington Memorial Fountain. Take a short drive west of the city to the Philadelphia Navy Yard, America's first U.S. Naval Yard, which began construction in 1776 along Front Street. The iron-clad ships of the Civil War made wooden ships obsolete, and in 1871, the Philadelphia Navy Yard was moved to League Island. In 1917, the Naval Aircraft Factory was built on the Navy yard, and some of the Navy's first aviators flew from a field just in front of the Marine Barracks built there in 1901. Today, the Navy Yard is being developed into a center for commerce. However, remnants of the Navy mothball fleet are still birthed there, including the aircraft carrier USS John F. Kennedy. "Big John," as she was called during her days in service, was the only ship of her class and the last conventionally powered carrier built for the Navy. If you want to visit this massive piece of American history, hurry because she is slated for a tug to Brownsville, Texas, where she will be scrapped.

Last, head over to Laurel Hill Cemetery where you can explore over 200 hundred acres of graves, monuments, and statues. Among the thousands of graves are Revolutionary War soldiers and Sailors, Colonel Hugh Mercer, General George Meade, commander of the Union forces at the Battle of Gettysburg, and Jacob Zeilin, 7th Commandant of the Marine Corps and first Marine to achieve the rank of general. If you look around just inside the main gatehouse you will even find the headstone of the fictional character Adrian Balboa featured in the Rocky movies.

Fort Mifflin is located at 6400 Hog Island Road Philadelphia, Pennsylvania.

Pest House (Lazaretto Quarantine Station) is located at Wanamaker Avenue and West 2nd Street Tinicum Township, Pennsylvania.

Fort Mercer is located at Red Bank Battlefield Park 100 Hessian Avenue National Park, New Jersey.

Independence Seaport Museum is located at 211 S Columbus Boulevard Philadelphia, Pennsylvania.

Fort Billingsport Park is located at Clonmell Road and North Delaware Street Paulsboro, New Jersey.

Tomb of the Unknown Soldier is located at Washington Square Philadelphia, Pennsylvania.

Tun Tavern is located at the intersection of South Front Street and Samson Street Philadelphia, Pennsylvania.

Penn's Landing is located at 601 North Columbus Boulevard, Philadelphia, Pennsylvania.

The Revolutionary War Center is located at 101 South 3rd Street Philadelphia, Pennsylvania.

National Constitution Center is located at 525 Arch Street Philadelphia, Pennsylvania.

Independence National Historic Park is located at 143 South 3rd Street, Philadelphia, Pennsylvania.

The Chapel of the Four Chaplains is located at 1201 Constitution Avenue Philadelphia, Pennsylvania.

Christ Church is located at 20 North American Street Philadelphia, Pennsylvania.

Old Swedes Church is located at 916 South Swanson Street, Philadelphia, Pennsylvania.

Ben Franklin National Memorial is located at 222 North 20th Street Philadelphia, Pennsylvania.

Pennsbury Manor is located at 400 Pennsbury Memorial Road, Morrisville, Pennsylvania.

Arch Street Meeting House is located at 320 Arch Street, Philadelphia, Pennsylvania.

Historic Strawberry Mansion is located at 2450 Strawberry Mansion Drive Philadelphia, Pennsylvania.

Declaration House is located at 701 Market Street Philadelphia, Pennsylvania.

Philadelphia Vietnam Veteran's Memorial is located at 10 Spruce Street Philadelphia, Pennsylvania.

Laurel Hill Cemetery is located at 3822 Ridge Avenue Philadelphia, Pennsylvania.

Tun Tavern Coming to Philadelphia in 2025 will be located at 19 South Second Street, Philadelphia, Pennsylvania.

Germantown, Pennsylvania

"This was the first time that the Marines of the two nations had fought side by side since the defense of the Peking Legations in 1900. Let it be said that the admiration of all ranks of 41 Commando for their brothers in arms was and is unbounded. They fought like tigers and their morale and esprit de corps is second to none."

~Lieutenant Colonel D.B. Drysdale, Commanding Officer, 41st Independent Commando, Royal Marines

General Washington had decided on one more attempt to draw Howe into a decisive engagement before the close of the campaign season, and the ground he chose was Germantown. On October 2nd Washington set his plan and his Army into motion, marching it to Methacton Hill, where he established his headquarters at the Peter Wentz Jr. homestead. The homestead served a dual purpose of giving him an excellent view toward Philadelphia while providing his Army with the defensive advantage of holding the high should the British attack unexpectantly. The homestead is now an active historical farm where reenactors take visitors on a tour of what colonial farming was like in the 18th century.

Three local brothers, Andrew, Jacob, and John Levering operated as spies for the American cause between Methacton and Philadelphia. Jacob used the disguise of a farmer peddling produce on the Schuylkill and gathered intelligence from neighbors sympathetic to the patriot cause. Whenever he returned home from one of his intelligence-gathering excursions, he would send one of his brothers to the American camp with the information. On September 30th British dragoons looking for Jacob arrested John instead. John had a pass from Washington that he managed to chew and swallow before he was apprehended. Thinking John was Jacob, the British took him to an oak tree in the vicinity of the middle ferry to execute him as a spy when neighbors intervened, testifying that the man the

British were about to hang was John, compelling the British to release him.

The Continental Army preparing to march into Germantown was different from the one that had almost folded a year earlier. This Army, about 14,000 strong, had its ranks filled with experienced, battle-hardened men hungry for a victory; the Army was also seeking revenge for losses suffered at Brandywine and atrocities committed at Paoli. It was organized into cohesive, fighting divisions, and Washington's generals had gained valuable experience in troop movement and tactical knowledge, emerging as competent combat leaders.

Washington had formed his battle plans on intelligence he received that indicated Howe had detached a significant number of defenders to attack and reduce the forts along the Delaware River to open up the shipping lane for his brother's flotilla. Taking advantage of the situation, Washington planned to divide his Continentals into four columns, move toward Germantown, and meet simultaneously at the northern and western edge of the town at 5 am and form for the attack. This plan required the columns to silently perform a 20-mile precision movement over poorly marked roads spanning difficult and rugged terrain in the pitch black of night.

Washington's right column consisted of Pennsylvania militia units, with John Armstrong's 1,500 Pennsylvania militiamen moving on the right flank. Colonel Potter marched up Ridge Road with 1,000 of these men, four cannon and an escort of Philadelphia Light Horse. His objective was to assault the Jaegers camped at Vanderin's Mill located along the Wissahickon Creek; they represented the British left flank. Armstrong planned to acquire guides at Levering's Tavern, cross Wissahickon Creek near Vanderin's Mill dam, and turn the British left flank. Armstrong's mission was to cross the Schuylkill toward Philadelphia with 500 militiamen and perform a series of feints. Washington hoped Armstrong could isolate the British defenders at Germantown by fixing the garrison in Philadelphia and prevent them from sending reinforcements.

The left column comprised of Smallwood's Maryland militia and New Jersey Militia, which formed on Washington's left flank with 1,600 men. Their objective was to hit the British right flank held by the Queen's Rangers to make way for the Continental Army's main effort. The two middle columns of Generals Greene and Sullivan's divisions represented the American main effort to attack the British main camp.

General Smallwood's route was the longest and most difficult, but if he could pull it off, it would put his forces behind Howe's right flank near the Stenton House and threaten the rear of the British defense at Germantown. The Stenton House was built after James Logan met and accompanied Pennsylvania founder William Penn to America in 1699; Logan named the house after his father's birthplace in Scotland. Logan was a renowned politician, merchant, justice, scientist, and scholar. Washington and Howe both headquartered at Stenton at different times before the Battle of Germantown.

Sullivan's column, augmented with Conway and Wayne's Pennsylvania troops, numbered about 3,500 men and represented the right half of Washington's main effort. On order, they were to march down Skippack Road to the Bethlehem Pike and onto the Germantown Pike near Chestnut Hill to attack the British left center, · a movement of about ten miles. Greene's column of 4,400 soldiers, the largest of the four columns, represented the left half of Washington's main effort. Their route followed Smallwood's troops to Whitemarsh, then onto route 73, entering Germantown on Limekiln Road to attack the British right center. Washington rode behind Sullivan's column with the reserve element of General Sterling's troops following. Having disbanded Maxwell's Light Infantry after the Battle of the Clouds, Washington had no vanguard to effectively screen his Army's movement.

Washington did not gain the element of surprise he had hoped for. Johann Ewald's diary contained an entry for the night of October 3rd that indicates he was warned of a potential American attack by a gentleman known as Professor Smith. Ewald wrote, "Toward evening, Professor Smith from Philadelphia came to me who owned a country seat close to the jaeger post, for which I had provided protection. He asked me to take a little walk with him, which I was quite willing to do since we had enjoyed several days' rest. Behind the camp and when he thought no one else would discover us, he addressed me with the following words: My friends, I confess to you that I am a friend of the states and no friend of the English government, but you have rendered me a friendly turn. You have shown me humanity, which each soldier should not lose sight of. You have protected my property. I will show you I am grateful. You stand in a corps which hourly is threatened by the danger of the first attack when the enemy approaches. Friend, God bless your person! The success of your arms I cannot wish. Friend! General Washington has marched up to Norristown today!" Ewald immediately alerted his chain of command. When word of the warning reached Howe, he scoffed at the idea saying, "That cannot be."

On October 4th around 3 am, British and Hessian patrols discovered Washington's approach, and Howe's camp was ordered to arms. The order, however, did not reach Royal Marine Major Maitland, whose position was farthest from the British main camp, and his troops were not under arms when the sun rose that morning around 6 am; the lounging 2nd Light Infantry was in for the shock of their lives. Just before sunrise, Sullivan's column was a scant mile from the Second Light Infantry's outpost at Mount Airy and three miles from the British main camp. Sullivan sent two regiments ahead to neutralize the British outposts and ordered his column into battle lines. As the sun came up, bullets began to fly. The weather would be a factor in determining the outcome of Washington's attack yet again when the morning brought a dense fog that rapidly descended over Germantown. When Washington's attack began, gunpowder from thousands of muskets produced a thick choking smoke over the battle space that thickened the already dense fog, creating mayhem and confusion for both sides of the embattled soldiers.

The British outposts were quickly overrun, but the firing alerted the rest of the 2nd Light Infantry, which were camped about three-quarters of a mile away at Mount Pleasant. Here, we need to remember that the 2nd Light Infantry were members of the British force that massacred Wayne and his men at Paoli, and Wayne, attached to Sullivan's column, was about to get his revenge for that terrible night. Lieutenant Hunter of the 52nd Regiment of Foot recalled that upon the commencement of Sullivan's attack, "So much had they in their recollection of Wayne's affair that many of them rushed out the back part of their huts."

Although Sullivan's attack completely routed the 2nd Light Infantry, Lieutenant Hunter thought it was very fortunate that they had moved from houses they previously occupied in Beggerstown onto the open field two days prior "for I am certain, had we been quartered in town when we were attacked, we should all have been bayonetted...indeed thoughts of Wayne's Affair hung over the light infantry like an ill-fitting shroud". As the fighting intensified, Lieutenant Hunter recalled hearing a loud cry of "Have at the Bloodhounds! Revenge Wayne's Affair!"

The 2nd Light Infantry charged the Americans twice, but the battalion suffered so many killed and wounded that the survivors had no choice but to retreat. Hunter went on to recount, "Indeed, had we not retreated at the time we did, we should all have been taken or killed, as the columns of the enemy had nearly got around our flanks." Hunter, struggling with what he was experiencing on the battlefield, wrote, "This is the first time we had ever retreated from the Americans, and it was with great difficulty that we could prevail on the men to obey orders."

Sullivan continued his assault, pushing the British defenders beyond the Cliveden House, about a mile from the British main camp. They were fired at from second-story windows, but the firing resulted in no American casualties. At this point of the attack, Washington, concerned that Sullivan's line was expending too much ammunition, dispatched his aide, General Pickering, to order Sullivan to conserve his combat resources. Adding to the battle friction was the thickening fog and smoke, which almost rendered it impossible for commanders to maintain command and control on the battlefield.

In a letter to his brother, Lieutenant Cliffe of the 46th Regiment of Foot recalled, "We who were a good distance on the right of the light infantry moved towards them and see them quite broke, flying like devils. We heard the word stop light infantry stop, which made us wait expecting we would rally, when a devil of a fire upon our front and right flank came ding dong around us. We had but 60 men could not cope, were abliged to fly. For the first time, I ever saw the 46th turn, but alas, it was not the last that day".

Wayne, in a letter to his wife, explained, "When we advanced on the enemy with fixed bayonets, they broke at first without waiting to receive us but soon formed again when a heavy fire took place on each side. The enemy again gave way. The Pennsylvanians, remembering Paoli, took ample vengeance for that night's work. Our officers exerted themselves to save many of the poor wretches who were crying for mercy but to little purpose; the rage and fury of the soldiers were not to be restrained for some time, at least not until a great number of the enemy fell by our bayonets." The proud Light Infantry unit that attacked Wayne at Paoli just over two weeks prior was routed from their Germantown camp by the survivors of that horrific night.

By 7 am, the American forces drove into the heart of Germantown, but the effort was taking its toll on the attackers. Enemy counter-fire, the depth of the advance, dwindling ammunition, limited visibility, fences, and other obstacles had hindered the Army's organization and eventually conspired against a decisive American victory at Germantown. In addition, the flanking effort Washington expected from Armstrong near the mouth of the Wissahickon was ineffective because the Hessians held their ground. Although the Hessians were occupied at the Wissahickon and unable to reinforce the British main camp, the effort failed to draw British troops from the path of Sullivan's main effort, which Washington depended on. To add to Washington's problems, General Irvine's 500 militiamen failed to create a diversion convincing enough to fix Cornwallis' troops in Philadelphia, which gave Cornwallis the flexibility to march to Germantown with his relief column.

Many contemporary historians claim the other flanking effort led by Smallwood never engaged the British at Germantown, but eyewitnesses disagreed. They got there, although a bit later than the rest of the Army, because of the time it took to negotiate their long and arduous route to the battle. They eventually pushed through British pickets and engaged the Queen's Rangers and Brigade of Guards, considered elite amongst their British peers. The experience of these elite troops, aided by a cannon firing grapeshot, unfortunately, proved to be a force too strong for Smallwood's militiamen to reckon with.

Meanwhile, much like Sullivan, Greene managed to surprise three Light Infantry companies on the left flank northeast of Cliveden. Greene's column pushed the British onto property owned by Isaac Woods. According to a historical account of the battle, Woods had inadvertently exposed himself to fire while observing the action from an open cellar door. Unfortunately for Woods, he was killed by an errant musket ball. Greene completely collapsed the three British companies and continued his thrust to the south. The retreating British forces fell back to Lukens' Mill, where they regrouped and attempted to defend their ground. Abercrombie's force of five hundred men was barely formed for battle before Greene's forces overwhelmed and routed them. Unfortunately, as Greene approached Germantown, the issues working against his American compatriots soon began adversely affecting his attack, resulting in an eventual loss of command and control.

General Stephen's drive toward the center of the Germantown defenses was the least organized and poorly led of the American attackers that morning and is generally attributed to his drunken condition during the assault. During his push, his negligence caused his troops to drift right into the rear of Wayne's line; incredulous as it sounds, they fired a volley into the backs of the Pennsylvanians, halting Wayne's forward movement.

While all this was taking place on the front lines, the turning point of the battle actually came from behind the battle lines at the Cliveden house. The American forces had the reeling British defenders on their heels when nearly surrounded; British Colonel Musgrave decided to fortify and defend the stone house with his regiment of a little over one hundred men instead of the more logical decision to retreat. As his men began to fire on Sullivan's men, Colonel Proctor unlimbered four cannon across the road in the yard of the Upsala House and started to lob balls at the house. The barrage had no effect on the defenders because the side of the house they were shelling was also the strongest, built with two-foot thick stone walls the cannon balls barely dented. Washington's staff began to debate what should be done about the defenders of the Cliveden House. Knox was strongly in favor of calling back Sullivan's infantry to attack the house because, in his words, "it would be unmilitary to leave a castle in our rear." Pickering, on the other hand, absolutely opposed attacking the fortified house. Pickering believed the Army "should maintain their momentum and continue the attack. Stopping to deal with a handful of the enemy was unnecessary and bordered on madness. The better policy to have pushed our advantage, leaving a party to watch the enemy in that house."

Although several of Washington's staff officers agreed with Pickering, Knox pressed his position, and being high in Washington's esteem, his opinion prevailed. Washington's deputy adjutant, Colonel Smith, volunteered to carry a truce flag to the house to convince the defenders to surrender. Pickering fully expected the British to shoot Smith dead, and he was almost right; Smith returned to Washington with a leg shattered by a defender's musket ball.

Major Benjamin Tallmadge wrote, "attempts to dislodge them were ineffectual, and although they would have been harmless in a few minutes if we had passed them by, yet the importunity of General Knox (which I distinctly hear) General Washington permitted him to bring his artillery to bear upon it, but without effect." After nearly a half hour of shelling with minimal effect, Washington called up Sterling's reserves. Although Washington had not intended for infantrymen to assault the house, they did so anyway, and the effort proved too difficult to gain entry or advantage. The assault was called back, and the house was left alone.

Although the house and grounds were torn up by cannon balls and left in bloody tatters, the home was restored to its colonial patina but with ample evidence of the siege preserved on the grounds and the house itself. Around the turn of the 20th century, roadwork unearthed a mass grave of Revolutionary War soldiers on the property. The remains were reburied together at the corner of Johnson and Morton Streets.

Stephen's men firing into the backs of Wayne's Pennsylvanians, combined with the sounds of intense fire at Cliveden behind the American line convinced Wayne and other commanders that the

British had somehow gotten behind them, so they began to reverse their forward attack. With the flanking attacks unsuccessful, Greene and Sullivan's men ran out of ammunition, and their attack stalled. The confusion and chaos of the action at Cliveden and the arrival of Cornwallis' reinforcements, led to a successful counterattack by the British and resulted in yet another American retreat. Part of the British counterattack included Knyphausen's regiments, augmented with a few field pieces, which the Hessians soon had unlimbered and fired into the retreating Americans.

Near the end of the battle, North Carolina lost a leading citizen and an accomplished general when an artillery round bounced down a road and tore through the side of Francis Nash's horse, taking his leg with it. The ball continued its momentum, smashing into the side of Major Witherspoon, who was an aide to General Maxwell. The wounded horse collapsed on Nash's severed leg. General Nash was pulled from the bloody horse and placed in a carriage, the severed leg placed beside him, and taken twenty miles back to camp at Pennypacker Mill. Nash lived for five days before succumbing to his injury; he is buried at the Towamencin Mennonite Church.

British General Agnew, who was wounded earlier at Brandywine, was pushing the British counterattack along the west side of Germantown Road and was riding into a village with his servant when a party of Americans opened fire on the pair from behind a house near a Mennonite meetinghouse. While wheeling his horse and calling out to his servant, Agnew took a volley of fire from the Americans, a ball entering the small of his back and exiting his chest. His servant got him into a house called the Grumblethorpe, where he was previously headquartered. A doctor was hastily summoned but arrived in time to see his would-be patient expire. Agnew's blood still stains the floor where he bled out; he is buried in the De Benneville Family Burial Grounds in Philadelphia, Pennsylvania.

Around 9 a.m., a frustrated Washington was on Germantown Pike, desperately trying to turn his retreating Army. He even ordered Major Tallmadge to block the road with his troop of horse. Still, the effort could not turn his panicked Army from its retreat. Fortunately for the American Army, the rough terrain prevented an effective British pursuit and allowed Washington to escape once again with most of his Army intact.

Whitemarsh church was located at three critical road intersections: Bethlehem Pike, Church Road, and Skippack Road, each about five miles from the Cliveden House. The intersection was critical because the bulk of Washington's retreating Army had to pass through it to reach safety. General Wayne remained at the church to keep the intersection open and collect stragglers. Cornwallis, with 2,000 men, soon approached the intersection in pursuit of the American Army but was forced to retire from the effort after Wayne, on the high ground, fired at the British with a few cannon and small arms. Washington reported his battle losses as 152 men killed, 521 wounded, and around 400 captured, including 54 officers. Sullivan lost two aides, White and Sherburne, who are buried near Pennypacker Mills. General Howe's forces suffered eighty killed, 426 wounded, and 14 missing, including the loss of General Agnew.

A real-life Mulan story emerged from one of the many improvised field hospitals set up to treat the wounded after the Battle of Germantown. Anna Maria Lane's husband had enlisted in the Continental Army in 1776. Anna apparently dressed as a man and served alongside her husband and was wounded at Germantown. Treatment of her injury undoubtedly revealed her true gender, but the discovery did not result in banishment from the Army. Lane's story can be told in two ways. If she enlisted in the Army, which is doubtful, her story should be told from a soldier's perspective. If she did not, her story illustrated the boldness and diversity of female camp followers such as she and Molly Pitcher.

Marine Corps Tie-In...Making the Cut- Selection to Drill Instructor School.

Shortly after returning home from Operation Iraqi Freedom, I was promoted to Staff Sergeant and told I needed to decide where I wanted to transfer; after four or five years with 1st Battalion, 5th Marines, it was time for me to rotate. I was between my second and third enlistment, which gave me career designation. To be competitive for promotion, a Marine must successfully complete a B billet. B billets can be one of the following special duty assignments: Drill Instructor, Recruiter, Marine Security Guard, or School of Infantry Instructor.

I fell in love with the Sierra Mountains while attending the Advanced Winter Mountain Leader's Course and, later, a unit training package. I had long decided I wanted to become an instructor at the MCMWTC in Bridgeport, California, but the move would have been a career killer. Although a successful tour would allow me to retire, I would likely do so as a Staff Sergeant because I wouldn't be competitive for promotion with Marines who completed a B billet.

I already knew through discussions with MCMWTC instructors that most of them either stayed on the mountain for the remainder of their careers or returned to the mountain after a brief stint with a fleet unit, and I was at peace with that. I requested orders for Bridgeport, and they were approved, but a couple of things caused me to change my mind. I found out that the 1st Battalion 5th Marines would likely return to Iraq sooner than later, and several Staff NCOs I looked up to convinced me I would be a good Drill instructor and become Sergeant Major someday; they were right about the first but wrong about the second.

When I heard the rumor that my unit might end up doing another tour in Iraq, I decided that I did not want my Marines to go into harm's way without me. Because I had the Bridgeport orders in the system and because of my overseas control date, I needed to request mast because my unit commanders did not have the authority to cancel my orders or allow me to extend with 1st Battalion 5th Marines. I painstakingly went through the long process, but it was an unsuccessful endeavor. The only option my career monitor gave me was to proceed to Bridgeport or cancel my Bridgeport orders in lieu of Drill Instructor Duty. I reluctantly agreed on career progression and rapidly found myself in possession of orders to Marine Corps Recruit Depot, San Diego, California. For thirteen weeks, I attended Drill Instructor School as a member of Class 2-4.

I was a combat veteran and was recently promoted to Staff NCO. I thought I was at the top of my game and thus prepared for Drill Instructor School. I received Permissive Temporary Additional Duty (PTAD) orders, which meant that my parent unit was still 1st Battalion, 5th Marines until I either graduated and received Permanent Change of Station (PCS) orders or failed the school and returned to 1st Battalion, 5th Marines with my derogatory, double-signed Fitness Report to serve out my enlistment; with a double-signer, I would not be approved for another re-enlistment. I checked into Drill Instructor School in Service Alphas and began the long administration process.

During the long wait at in-processing, an NCO walked by and told us all that we had better hydrate. None of us took the NCO seriously because we were all seasoned Marines and did not need a mere corporal to suggest we needed to hydrate. Everyone assigned to the Drill Instructor class was of a consensus that the school would be among the hardest we had ever attended. We would be challenged physically, mentally, and emotionally every day for 13 weeks, and it is well-advertised as such throughout the fleet. We were all about to discover an element of difficulty that was not well-advertised and one we were ill-prepared to deal with as the in-processing was completed and the class was herded into the Drill Instructor classroom for staff introductions.

At the time of my assignment at the school, I was a Marine for around nine years, and as I mentioned earlier, I was feeling pretty salty. The school's director and First Sergeant spoke to the class and introduced our instructors and squad advisers. If any of us had remembered our first introduction into the Corps when we met our own Drill Instructors on a dark Friday long ago, the introduction would have been eerily similar. What followed the introduction took us through the annuals of time and thrust us into our first day as a recruit once again when the First Sergeant snapped to attention and said, "Drill Instructors, take charge and carry out the plan of the day." The room figuratively and almost literally exploded in pandemonium as six or eight Gunnery Sergeants, intimidating in black duty belts and campaign covers, started to loudly scream orders at a cyclic rate. As seasoned and salty as I felt, nothing, including combat, could have prepared me to be treated like a recruit again.

The tone was quickly and brutally established- no one assigned to the class could move fast enough or scream loud enough to satisfy the instructors, and suddenly, no one could seemingly complete even the simplest tasks. I wish I had hydrated because a urinalysis by the numbers was a tone-setting friction point everyone had to work through as we all tried (some of us several times) to pee in a small bottle while three or four instructors were screaming instructions all at once. I typically had issues trying to fill the little bottle to the required level without someone screaming at me, even though it was a task I had performed in the Corps many, many times. The moment's intensity made it almost impossible for me to make my deposit in a timely manner so I could move on.

The days and nights continued throughout the first month the same as the first night: intense, demanding, and humiliating. After having my large slice of humble pie shoved violently in my face a few times, I finally learned some measure of humility as I trained to be a Drill Instructor. The first thing I had to learn was that a training schedule drives the day, and there is nothing routine about training days on the depot.

The second lesson I had to learn was that 'good enough' would never be good enough at the depot. The high standards the DI school instructors constantly demanded of us epitomize a Marine Drill Instructor. Personal appearance-uniform and hygiene had to be absolutely impeccable at all times; zero excuses were ever accepted for a less-than-perfect appearance. Uniform and hygiene inspections were conducted at least once a day. Haircuts were required about every other day and uniforms needed to be carefully prepared every day. Since there was almost no personal time to waste on going to a barber for a fresh haircut or to the cleaners for freshly cleaned and pressed uniforms, most students, including myself, shaved their heads bald every other day and laundered and pressed uniforms at the barracks.

My squad instructor was a gunny who looked like the actor who played the character 'Bear' in Armageddon. During one of his inspections, the usually morose instructor inspected uniforms and hygiene while simultaneously testing our knowledge. He tended to find a reason to fail every one of us for some minor infraction or another, and we were getting used to the inevitable. One morning during an inspection, 'Bear' stepped in front of one particularly immature and arrogant young sergeant and, without even looking at him, turned to the Marine with a clipboard and said, "Failed, breath is astronomically heinous!" That was as near as 'Bear' ever came to cracking a joke, and it was remarkably successful given the number of Marines who lost their bearing, albeit ever so slightly, with that remark.

Historical places to visit in and near Germantown, Pennsylvania.

I recommend planning an autumn tour around annual re-enactments held at the Cliveden House in Germantown. The grounds are open for the community to enjoy as a public park, weather permitting, from 9 am-5 pm. The property includes four buildings: the main house, kitchen dependency, wash house, and carriage house. Tours of Cliveden are available May through August, Thursday through Sunday, from 12–4 pm, September through November, Friday through Sunday, 12–4 pm. The Johnson House, Concord Schoolhouse and Upper Cemetery, Wyck House and Garden, the Grumblethorpe House, and St. Thomas Church are all located along Germantown Avenue, but only the Johnson House and Concord Schoolhouse are within a short walking distance of the Cliveden House.

You will probably want to drive to the remainder of the historical sites listed below. Be aware that the Lower Burial Ground is in a bad neighborhood with limited parking, so you may want to skip this stop. I like to visit the Towamencin Mennonite Church separately and spend a winter evening at the Peter Wentz Farm when the historic home is lit with candles; tours are provided by folks dressed in period garb, and hot cider is served. The farm provides a Spring through Autumn interactive 18th-century farming experience where reenactors give visitors a glimpse of living history on a working farmstead.

The Chiveden House Located at 6401 Germantown Avenue Philadelphia, Pennsylvania.

The Johnson House Located at 6306 Germantown Avenue, Philadelphia, Pennsylvania.

The Concord Schoolhouse and Upper Cemetery Located at 6309 Germantown Avenue, Philadelphia, Pennsylvania.

Wyck Historical House and Garden Located at 6026 Germantown Avenue Philadelphia, Pennsylvania.

The Grumblethorpe House Located at 5267 Germantown Avenue Philadelphia, Pennsylvania.

The Stenton House Located at 4601 North 18th Street Philadelphia, Pennsylvania.

Widow MacKinett's House Located at 262 East Girard Avenue Philadelphia, Pennsylvania.

St. Thomas Church Located at 3020 Germantown Avenue Philadelphia, Pennsylvania.

Lower Burial Ground Located at Germantown Avenue and Logan Street Philadelphia, Pennsylvania.

Grave Site Located at the corner of Johnson and Morton Streets Philadelphia, Pennsylvania.

De Benneville Family Burial Grounds Located at Green Lane and Broad Street Philadelphia, Pennsylvania.

Peter Wentz Farm Located at 2030 Shearer Road Lansdale, Pennsylvania.

Towamencin Mennonite Church Located at 1980 Sumneytown pike Kulpsville, Pennsylvania

Schwenksville, Pennsylvania

"Marines I see as two breeds, Rottweilers or Dobermans, because Marines come in two varieties, big and mean, or skinny and mean. They're aggressive on the attack and tenacious on defense. They've got really short hair and they always go for the throat".

~Rear Admiral Jay R. Stark, 47th President of the Naval War College.

On the evening of October 4th Washington's Army eventually made camp at Pennypacker Mills after a long night march, intense combat, and a bitter retreat from Germantown. Some men were wounded, and all were tired and hungry; they were so plumb tuckered out that they pretty much dropped where they halted with little semblance of organization. To put things in better perspective, the Army the night prior, averaged a 15-mile foot movement in the dark on rough roads, then attacked a veteran Army set up in the defense at dawn. They fought through dense fog and gun smoke for up to five hours, then retreated 20 miles in just over 24 hours.

While the Americans recuperated at Pennypacker Mills, another interesting story emerged. Remember Mel Gibson's movie 'The Patriot' where Mel Gibson's character kidnaped Cornwallis' prized Great Danes gifted to him by the king? There is no historical account that Cornwallis had hounds kidnapped from him in South Carolina or that he even had any dogs in America. It is a historical fact, however, that General Howe had a fox terrier named Lila with him while he occupied Philadelphia.

A French officer, Chevalier de Pontgibaud, attached to Washington's Army, recalled, "We were at table at headquarters-that is to say the mill, which was comfortable enough, when a fine sporting dog which was evidently lost, came to ask for some dinner. On its collar was General Howe. It was the commander's dog. It was sent back under a flag of truce, and General Howe replied with a warm letter of thanks to this act of courtesy on the part of his enemy our General." According to Washington's papers, the dog was returned to Howe with the following dispatch. "General Washington's compliments to General Howe. He does himself the pleasure to return him a dog, which accidentally fell into his hands, and by the inscription on the collar appears to belong to General Howe."

Marine Corps Tie-In...Making Smarty Disciplined Drill Instructors.

A difficult lesson I learned as a Drill Instructor School student was that I needed to demonstrate lessons taught by the DI School instructors at a mastery level if I was going to be trusted to make Marines and make them well. General knowledge was reiterated in the classroom, and since it was at a basic level, it was easy for me to memorize. What was extremely difficult to master was the many complex intricacies of close order drill. We were expected to learn and master every close-order drill movement in the Drill Manual, one of two living documents almost as important to Drill Instructors as the Bible is to pastors. From the Position of Attention to Column of Files, every single drill movement ever used to train and discipline recruits is recorded in detail in the Drill Manual. We learned to teach close-order drill by memorizing the step-by-step process of each movement, conducting teach-backs with a school instructor, and through practical application on the parade deck with classmates.

Conducting teach-backs was always an intimidating endeavor; it was hard to find the time to adequately study each movement, harder to schedule an appointment with a squad instructor to conduct the teach-back, and extremely difficult to pass a teach-back on the first attempt and have it signed off. The class soon discovered that the most accessible instructor to recite a teach-back to was my squad instructor because he seldom paid attention. Unfortunately, he was rarely available because everyone tried to book him. The worst instructor to conduct a teach-back with was the Chief Instructor, a hardnosed gunny who scrutinized every word and challenged every method. The instructor was so intimidating almost no one was successful in getting him to sign off on a teach-back. The teach-backs were a graduation requirement; every drill movement in the manual had to be mastered, so everyone needed to be completely signed off in order to graduate. Although students had most weekends off, weekend drill practice was 'highly encouraged' with instructor supervision, but the instructors adamantly refused to sign off-teach backs over the weekends.

One of the worst things that could happen in DI School was to get behind in teach-backs, and one Friday afternoon, I found myself in just that predicament. Most of that day was spent between hopelessly trying to pass a Drill Instructor School Field Day Inspection and working teach-backs on the parade deck. Conducting a teach-back on the parade deck was a daunting feat at best. The adage 'there is no pressure like peer pressure' takes on a whole new meaning as each student competes with one another while also contending with the constant noise reigning over the parade deck. A tactic that amused our instructor cadre was to have a student conduct a teach-back seven paces away on the parade deck and, at the first slip of the tongue, order the student to march off another seven paces and start over. The further a student got from an instructor, the louder a student had to be to overcome the ambient noise. The attempt was considered a failure if a student ran out of parade deck. The most significant contributor to the ambient noise came from the San Diego Airport, located beside the depot. Every time a jet took off from the busy tarmac, the roar of its engine would drown out every other sound on the depot. If a student was in the middle of a teach-back when a jet took off, the instructors assumed the instruction was incorrect since it was not audible, and seven paces of precious real estate had to be forfeited.

That Friday, I failed my teach-backs to the surprise of no one, and I had to get one or two signed off before I departed for the weekend. Unfortunately, my failures of the day combined with just enough procrastination to set me up with a teach-back date with the intimidating Chief Instructor. That afternoon, I found myself in the Chief Instructor's office with two Korean military exchange students who both spoke broken, rudimentary English at best. The Chief Instructor sat through a teach-back delivered by the Koreans first. He allowed them to teach a drill movement together because of their language barrier. I could not even discern what drill movement they were teaching, but to my astonishment, when the Koreans concluded, the Chief Instructor signed them both off.

I was instructed to begin my teach-back while the Koreans prepared for another. Despite my situation, I knew the drill movement I was teaching, was well-prepared, and felt good about my chances of having the teach-back signed off. After I completed teaching the movement, I made a move to retrieve my teach-back logbook from the chief, feeling confident that my endeavor was successful. Then, with a wave of his hand, he stopped me. To my astonishment, the chief verbally humiliated me for what felt like five minutes for my failure to communicate effectively in my native tongue while simultaneously extolling the Korean students' ability to teach in a language foreign to them effectively. After sitting through another Korean teach-back that I, for the life of me, couldn't figure out which drill movement was even being taught, I passed on my second attempt, delivering an almost identical teach-back to the one I had just failed.

The other important depot document was the Recruit Training Standard Operating Procedure (SOP). The SOP is a comprehensive rule book governing the conduct of Drill Instructors who were working with recruits. Although it did not necessarily need to be memorized while I was a DI, one needed to be extremely familiar with its content. Every cycle, a DI was required to take a SOP exam and pass it with a score of 100 percent before he or she is allowed to work with recruits. The requirements are the same for DIs working with officer canidates at Quantico, Virginia although the SOP differs from the recruit training SOP.

Historical Places to visit in or near Schwenksville, Pennsylvania.

Plan to visit Pennypacker Mills in late May to experience an annual reenactment event called the Patriots Along the Perkiomen. This event is a two-day Revolutionary War living history event where reenactors hold close-order drill exhibitions, demonstrate camp life in 1777, and even hold a recreation of one of several courts-martials held by Washington's staff during the Army's brief encampment along the Perkiomen. Tour the well-preserved 18th-century home built by Samuel Pennypacker, a former governor of Pennsylvania, and visit the gravesites of American Patriots who died of wounds sustained during the Battle of Germantown.

Take a short drive to the Idenhofen Farmstead, which served as a tavern in the 18th Century. These buildings have been preserved and are open to the public. Although there are no rumors or known Revolutionary connections, the tavern was in operation when Washington's Army was camped nearby, so it is conceivable that it once served thirsty Continental Army soldiers.

Head over to the Mill Grove Historic District, where a barn was once used as an improvised Army field hospital. You will also find a historic church building, the Timothy Matlack Historical Marker, and a small stone monument. If you are into art, visit the John James Audubon Center, which is in this historic district.

Pennypacker Mills is located at 5 Haldeman Road Schwenksville, Pennsylvania.

<u>Abington Presbyterian Church Graveyard</u> is located at 1090 Old York Road Abington, Pennsylvania.

<u>Timothy Matlack Marker</u> is located at 1233 Pawlings Road Norristown. Pennsylvania.

<u>Soldiers of Washington's Army Memorial</u> is located at 2779 Audubon Road Norristown, Pennsylvania.

<u>Mill Grove Historic District</u> is located at 1201 Pawlings Road Audubon, Pennsylvania.

<u>Idenhofen Farmstead</u> is located at 1285 Evansburg Road Harleysville, Pennsylvania.

Whitemarsh Township, Pennsylvania

"Hardness, I was learning, was the supreme virtue among recon Marines. The greatest compliment one could pay to another was to say he was hard. Hardness wasn't toughness, nor was it courage, although both were part of it. Hardness was the ability to face an overwhelming situation with aplomb, smile calmly at it, and then triumph through sheer professional pride."

~Nathaniel Fick, author and Recon Marine Captain

On October 8th Washington, having received intelligence that Howe had moved his troops from Germantown and consolidated them in Philadelphia, decided to move his Army closer to the city. Washington marched his Army east on Skippack Pike, then Forty-Foot Road to Sumneytown Pike, where they camped on Frederick Wampole's farm near Kulpsville. On October 16th Washington moved his Army to Methacton Hill in Worchester Township. On October 20th Washington moved his Army to Whitepain, 5 miles closer to Philadelphia. On November 2nd at the recommendation of his council of war, Washington marched his forces to Whitemarsh, approximately thirteen miles northwest of Philadelphia, where he established his headquarters at the Emlen House. At Whitemarsh, Washington's Army began to build redoubts and defensive works, including abatis, to protect their new encampment.

Washington did not know that Howe was leading his Army on the offensive in the vicinity of his new camp while his Army was was busily working on their defensive posture. Just after midnight on December 5th Cornwallis' vanguard, consisting of two British Light Infantry battalions, skirmished with Captain Allen McClain's mounted patrol near Three Mile Run and Skippack Road. McLane immediately sent a messenger to Washington, warning him that British troops were operating near the American encampment. While Cornwallis' troops marched through Germantown, Beggarstown, and Flourtown, cannon were fired to alert the American Army, who immediately manned their defensive positions. At 3 am, Cornwallis halted his column just south of the American defenses on Chestnut Hill and waited a few hours until daybreak. In an attempt to delay Cornwallis' attack by projecting a more significant force than he had, Washington ordered his troops to build multiple campfires, reminiscent of a tactic used to save the American Army one cold night in Trenton. Just as it did in Trenton, Washington's ruse worked. Hessian Major Carl von Bauermeister wrote, "...It looked as if fifty thousand men were encamped there. By day, we could see this was merely a trick..."

Expecting a delayed attack, Washington took the precaution of loading his tents and supplies on wagons before sunrise and sent the baggage north to Trappe. He then sent General James Irvine of the Pennsylvania militia and 600 soldiers on a reconnaissance patrol to determine the size and disposition of Cornwallis' column. Irvine marched his troops through the Wissahickon Valley toward Chestnut Hill. General Potter's brigade of about 1,000 Pennsylvania militia and Colonel Charles Webb's 2nd Connecticut Regiment of 200 men were ordered to screen Irvine's right flank. Around noon, Irvine's detachment closed with Cornwallis' men on the northern slope of Chestnut Hill. They got off the first volley but were immediately routed by the British. While attempting to turn his fleeing troops toward the skirmish, Irvine had three fingers shot off and was taken prisoner after he fell from his horse. Potter's brigade also fled despite orders to advance and engage the British Light Infantry. The 2nd Connecticut bravely made a brief stand, killing three and wounding eleven, including British Captain Sir James Murray-Pulteney.

Commanding the British Light Infantry, Colonel Abercromby continued to take the initiative after scattering Irvine's troops. He pushed north to the St. Thomas Episcopal Church, which is located on a prominent hill, and secured it. Howe arrived a short while later and, climbing to the top of the church's bell tower, studied the

American defensive positions. After deciding the American defenses were too strong for a successful attack, he ordered his field pieces to shell the American position, but his small guns did not have the range to hit Washington's defenses. Howe's troops camped on Chestnut Hill that night and planned a new attack for the following day.

The two armies spent December 6th watching each other across the Wissahickon Valley. Howe hoped that Washington would leave his strong position to attack the British, but Washington did not, preferring instead to stay in the defense and allow Howe to do the maneuvering. By day's end, Howe decided to flank the American left toward Jenkintown and Cheltenham Township while General Grey's forces created a feint on the American center. On December 7th around 1 AM, Howe marched his Army through Germantown to Jenkintown, where they remained until noon. Washington did not become aware of Howe's flanking attempt until 8 AM because the British moved below the military crest of a ridge on Chestnut Hill, effectively concealing their advance. Washington immediately moved Morgan's Rifle Corps and Colonel Gist's Maryland militia east to reinforce his left flank.

About a mile to the right of this detachment, recently promoted General Potter's brigade of Pennsylvania militia and Webb's 2nd Connecticut Regiment, commanded by Colonel Sherman, marched down Limekiln Road toward Edge Hill. The British rear guard, including the Jaegers and the Queen's Rangers, was slowed by their own Army burning the villages of Cresheim and Beggarstown at the front of the column. Howe's right was near the Abington Presbyterian Meeting; his main force moved to Edge Hill, which was a mile in front of the American lines and roughly parallel. Grey's column broke off from the main column and moved up Whitemarsh Church Road toward the American center.

General Grey had been instructed not to attack until he heard the sound of gunfire, indicating Howe's column was in position, but after several hours, he became impatient and decided to proceed on his own initiative. He formed his column in a skirmisher formation with the Queen's Rangers on the left, the Jaegers on each side of the road, and the Light Infantry on the right, oriented towards Tyson's Tavern along Limekiln Road. As Grey closed the distance to Washington's center, Morgan's Rifle Corps and Gist's Maryland militia occupying Edge Hill, fired on his troops. While Grey's troops returned fire, a small group of Americans moved down the hill to attack Colonel Twistleton's Light Infantry but were quickly repulsed. Lord Cantelupe, attached to the British Light Infantry, recorded in his journal that the 4th and 23rd regiments engaged the Americans, killing nine and wounding 19. Major John André reported that only one American was killed.

Regardless, the militia was routed, and fifteen were taken prisoner. General Cadwalader and General Reed, who were out reconnoitering near Twickenham, attempted to rally Potter's fleeing Pennsylvania militia, but the British quickly had the militia surrounded and outnumbered, and they again panicked and fled. The 2nd Connecticut made a stand, firing up to five rounds per man; Sherman waited to give the order to retreat until the Jaegers were within 15 or 20 yards from his battle line. During the skirmish, Cadwalader and Reed became separated from the militia after Reed's horse was shot out from under him. A detachment of Hessians charged at the two dismounted officers with bayonets, but Captain McLane rode up on the scene with a few dragoons in a charge that scattered the startled Hessians; the light patrol took the two American officers to safety. The Queen's Rangers and Jaegers gave chase to within yards of the American position, then fell back to Edge Hill, in a position between Grey's troops and Howe's column.

Meanwhile, Morgan's and Gist's militia engaged Howe's main column in dense woods, where they fought from cover and concealment, moving from tree to tree. British officers were used to encountering militia who would run away at the first sign of battle, but at Whitemarsh, they couldn't help admiring the grit and tenacity displayed by Morgan's and Gist's men. Cornwallis eventually ordered the 33rd Regiment of Foot into the fray, and the beleaguered militia was finally forced to retreat to the American lines.

On the morning of December 8th British generals and engineers once again looked for exploitable surfaces or gaps in Washington's defenses, but in a move that astonished British and American officers, Howe suddenly and inexplicably withdrew from the field and returned to Philadelphia. Although Howe was successful in two major skirmishes over the previous days, he could not maneuver around Washington's flank as he had hoped, and his Army was running out of provisions. The nights were getting chilly, and the troops had left their tents and cold-weather gear in Philadelphia.

At 2 PM, the British began their withdrawal; they lit numerous campfires, mimicking the tactic used by Washington three days prior, to conceal their withdrawal. Captain McLane observed a British column marching back down Old York Road into Philadelphia and sent the information back to Washington. Morgan's troops harassed the enemy's rear, especially Grey's column, which was bogged down by the weight of the artillery it was guarding. A contingent of Hessians formed to cover Grey's column with their fieldpieces, forcing Morgan's troops to retreat for the last time in this battle. The British arrived safely in Philadelphia later that day.

Marine Corps Tie-In...Physically Fit Drill Instructors.

I was a Marine grunt, a hard charger who trained extremely hard; I routinely achieved high physical fitness test scores and was no stranger to long hikes under heavy loadouts. Unit Physical Fitness rarely challenged me, but an NCO in my unit did challenge me one day. The NCO had recently joined our battalion and was assigned to my platoon. He wanted to take the Force Reconnaissance

Indoctrination and become a Recon Marine, so he focused almost exclusively on training and preparation. He looked like he could have done hard time in a California prison and his skin was tattooed in a manner to suggest he might have. He had a hard look in his eye and a rare but sinister smile that revealed rows of broken teeth, intuitively warning most people to stay well away from him. This young sergeant rarely listened to anything but hardcore metal music and was a fan of the rapper group Insane Clown Posse. He would tell violent stories reflecting on his days running the streets of Anaheim. Based on the stories he used to tell, it is hard to believe he wasn't criminally disqualified from enlisting in the Marines.

No one wanted to work out with this psycho-sergeant, and he couldn't find anyone who could maintain his blistering pace on long-distance runs. He came to me one Saturday morning and asked if I would go on a run with him. When I expressed doubt that I would even survive the experience, he shrugged and said he would wear a gas mask to slow his pace. He looked at me and continued, "I am not looking for a running buddy; I just need someone who can hang with me today because I am going to push myself until I pass out." I remember gaping at him, trying to determine whether he was serious, but that ended when he pulled on his gas mask and started to trot toward the infamous fire breaks of Camp Pendleton.

I followed after the NCO and maintained his pace for about five miles before I began to struggle; I was wearing no gas mask, but the pace was really beginning to hurt me. By the time we were out of the Talega Hills, where the movie Heartbreak Ridge was filmed, I had fallen behind until I eventually lost sight of him. When I finally caught up to the sergeant, he was negotiating the obstacle course along San Mateo Road. While I was trying to catch my breath, the guy wheeled around and ran through the course again. He beckoned me to follow when he finished and turned toward First Sergeant Hill. The hill is steep and challenging to climb, and ropes have even been installed at places to aid in the climb. The psycho-sergeant didn't touch the ropes once; by the time I was halfway up, he was halfway down. I turned to follow him...we ran for another half mile before he abruptly collapsed in a cloud of dust.

I pulled his mask off and got him to come around, and after a few minutes, we were trotting back to the barracks, his gas mask tucked under his arm. He tried to get me to go to the swim tank a few times, but I adamantly refused; I was not a good swimmer, and he would have ended up decorating the bottom of the tank had he passed out under my watch. I do not know what happened to the psycho-sergeant; I can only guess that he passed his coveted recon indoctrination and made it to a team or, failing, went out in a shootout with police as he often threatened.

Drill Instructor School humbled me yet again, and I realized through numbing daily Physical Fitness routines that I was far from the standard the depot set. Our Physical Fitness Instructor was recently named the most physically fit Marine of the Year, even though he likely didn't compete against the psycho-sergeant for the honor. Class 2-4 soon found out the hard way, why he was so aptly titled as we all hopelessly attempted to keep up with him during PT events. The physical fitness routines he taught were routines we would teach and lead recruits through over and over again once we graduated from school and earned our coveted duty belt and cover. The routines were not complicated and easy to master, but the physical level at which we were expected to perform them was not.

A week would not be complete without going through one of the PT Instructor's infamous beatdown sessions he led the class through every Thursday behind the schoolhouse. The incentive to perform was simple, obvious and a bit devious. Thursdays on the depot were visitor Thursdays for graduating recruits, and the schoolhouse is in a high-traffic area, which drew a lot of spectators. I can only describe the routine as something akin to the bitter memories I have when I was a recruit receiving Incentive Training (IT). The PT Instructor would lead us on a brisk three-mile run, the last half to three quarters, nearly an outright sprint. Before students could catch their breath, the PT Instructor quickly formed the class for Daily Sevens and had us attempting to play a twisted game of Keep-Up with the 'Most Fit Marine in the Corps.' The attempts hurt, I mean, it really hurt, and we soon found out that none of us were going to be able to keep up with the instructor as he cycled us through many, many push-ups, side straddle hops, mountain climbers, leg lifts or any other static exercise he could come up with. I gave it the good ol' collage try but succumbed to muscle cramps, dehydration, and eventual muscle failure along with the rest of the class on nearly every visitor Thursday.

It was very embarrassing and humbling to fail in the presence of anonymous civilian spectators. The beatdowns did serve as a reminder to each of us that there is an image and the reputation of a Marine Drill Instructor that, once earned, would have to be fiercely defended as we prepared to take our places in the training trenches; failure in the presence of a recruit would tarnish the image and reputation of the Marine Drill Instructor and not be tolerated by our peers.

Historical Places to visit in and near Whitemarsh, Pennsylvania.

This segment of the Patriot's Path will take you on a driving tour on the fringe of suburban Philadelphia. Begin your tour at Hope Lodge, a beautifully preserved 18th-century farmstead that is open to the public from Spring through Autumn. Explore the grounds and tour these historic buildings, then swing into the gift shop for a souvenir to take home. Drive around the rest of the historical points of interest listed below and consider ending your tour with a picnic, take in the amazing view of the countryside from an observation deck, and enjoy some hawk-watching at Fort Washington Park.

The Emlen House is located in the vicinity of Piszek Preserve Pennsylvania Avenue, Fort Washington, Pennsylvania.

St. Thomas' Church Whitemarsh is located at 7020 Camp Hill Road Fort Washington, Pennsylvania.

Fort Washington is located at State Park 500 South Bethlehem Pike Fort Washington, Pennsylvania.

Lawnveiw Memorial Park is located at 500 Huntingdon Pike Jenkintown, Pennsylvania.

Lafayette Marker is located at 2327 Barren Hill Road Fort Washington, Pennsylvania

Hope Lodge is located at 553 South Bethlehem Pike Fort Washington, Pennsylvania.

The Old Conestoga Road Memorial is located at 919 Conestoga Road Fort Washington, Pennsylvania.

Mather Mill is located at 575 Skippack Pike Fort Washington, Pennsylvania.

Gloucester, New Jersey

"There was always talk of espirit de corps, of being gung-ho, and that must have been a part of it. Better, tougher training, more marksmanship on the firing range, the instant obedience to orders seared into men in boot camp."

~James Brady, 17th White House Press Secretary under President Ronald Reagan. During the assassination attempt on President Reagan, Brady was permanently disabled when he was struck in the head by a bullet.

On November 20th Washington ordered General Greene to conduct a reconnaissance mission of Fort Mercer to gather intelligence on the British disposition there and along the Delaware River. Lafayette, who had been in the Whitemarsh camp less than a month and still favoring his injured leg, quickly volunteered to accompany Greene on the mission. Greene decided the safest way to conduct his reconnaissance was to cross the river and observe the fort and river from the Jersey side.

On November 24th in what would be known as the Battle of Gloucester, Greene ordered Lafayette to reconnoiter the British positions but to make sure his force of four hundred men avoided any unnecessary risks. Lafayette advanced within range of British pickets and, finding a force of Hessians about the size of his force, engaged it. Lafayette had the element of surprise, and when his forces fired on the Hessians, they fled the field. Lafayette's forces remained engaged in a running fight with the Hessians that lasted about an hour and inflicted an estimated sixty casualties on the Hessian patrol. Cornwallis promptly sent reinforcements to assist the beleaguered Hessians, and Lafayette astutely returned to friendly lines with a reported loss of one killed and five wounded. Upon completing the mission, Greene gave Washington a glowing review of Lafayette's heroism and leadership.

Lafayette described his actions against the enemy at Gloucester in his memoirs: "At Gloucester, I advanced to a strip of land called Sandy Point. For my imprudence, I would have paid dearly (as almost captured or killed). I found myself about two miles from the English camp of 400 Hessians and their cannon at 4 PM with only 350 men, mostly militia, I attacked the Hessians and drove them away. Cornwallis came to the field but was driven back to Gloucester. Greene arrived during the evening but wouldn't attack. The British retreated over the river, and Greene and I returned to Whitemarsh and Washington. The slight success at Gloucester gratified the army, especially the militia". Lafayette also wrote a letter to Washington hoping "his little expedition gave the general some pleasure."

Lafayette's leadership and initiative pleased Washington so much that he wrote a letter to his good friend President Laurens, requesting congressional approval for Lafayette to be awarded a vacated division command. On December 1st Lafayette was promoted to Major General and given his choice of several divisions, from which he chose a Virginia division.

The Benjamin Clark farm was built in Gloucester during the late 18th century. The east section has a stone marker engraved '1804'. Clark was a Revolutionary soldier and a consequence of Clark's well-known patriotism was that British troops and Loyalists raided his home several times. While delivering a load of grain to Valley Forge during the winter encampment, Clark had his four-horse team confiscated by the British. Late that night, Clark snuck into the British camp, cut his horses loose, and hid them on an island in Mantua Creek. When the British arrived at Clark's farm to take the horses back, they only found one old cow in the barn. Clark told the British they had taken everything else.

In 1772, Dr. Bodo Otto Jr. bought one hundred acres of land in New Jersey for four hundred ninety-seven pounds. The property formerly belonged to William Scull, who had purchased it in 1766 from Benjamin Lodge at Mickleton. Otto Jr. followed in his father's footsteps and served as a surgeon in Washington's Army at Valley Forge In 1777. When a Tory party raided his home, the house was partially burned; the original property dates to 1688.

Another prominent Gloucester home, the Hunter-Lawrence house, was built in 1765 by Judge John Sparks. The Reverend Andrew Hunter, one of the 'Tea Burners' of Greenwich and a chaplain in the Revolutionary Army, owned the home in 1792. Six years later, the house became the residence of John Lawrence. Lawrence's younger brother, James, also lived in the house. In 1813 James, who was in command of USS Chesapeake in the War of 1812, was fatally wounded during a battle with HMS Shannon. His dying words, "Don't give up the ship," have since become the motto of the U.S. Navy.

Marine Corps Tie-In... 8511...you made it!

For 13 weeks, Drill Instructor Class 2-4 embraced the suck. Throughout those long weeks, we worked through pain, fatigue, and humiliating moments. We had to be broken down so our instructors could build us back up and mold us into Marines capable of fulfilling the duties and rigors of a Drill Instructor. Those 13 weeks were packed full of moments that constantly tested the strength, fortitude, and bearing of the staunchest student in the class.

There was a time a student (the one with the astronomically heinous breath) almost dropped on request over a sandwich he thought someone had taken out of a shared fridge. He was temporarily filling the billet of class commander. Before calling the class to attention for another long and tedious afternoon class, he used his platform to conduct his 'sandwich inquisition.' He demanded that the Marine who was guilty of filching his sandwich step forward. So passionate was he to find the guilty party that, driven to tears, the sergeant promised that he would find the thief and make him pay.

Then there came a day when the class was introduced to the depot gas chamber, and a gunny on his second Drill Instructor tour temporarily lost his mind. Going to the Confidence Chamber, aka gas chamber, is an annual requirement for all Marines fleetwide. Every year, units pilgrimage to the gas chamber, protective masks tucked under an arm, for five or so minutes of testing the mask's seal. Marines also get the opportunity to practice in a contaminated environment, quickly dawning the mask and clearing it of residual gas...in this case CS gas. CS gas is a riot control agent the Marine Corps uses in capsule and smoke form. Exposure causes a burning sensation to the skin, tearing of the eyes to the extent that a Marine cannot keep their eyes open, and a burning irritation of the mucous membranes of the nose, mouth, and throat; the result is uncontrollable coughing, foot long snot-rockets, disorientation, and difficulty breathing.

We were all herded into the depot's gas chamber and quickly learned that we would not be subjected to a relatively quick, mild fleet chamber. A couple of junior Marines in the center of the chamber began to cook up the CS capsules, and the small room rapidly filled with thick gas. The class was instructed to break the seal with two fingers; everyone held this posture until the instructors thoroughly inspected each class member for compliance. Inevitably, some Marines could hold their breath no longer and quickly succumbed to the effects of the CS gas.

During the next iteration of the confidence chamber, the class was required to remove the mask altogether, slide it to the top of the head, and wait for each to be inspected. This process took longer than it should have because some Marines had already had a bad experience with the CS and were not eager for another.

The last iteration required Marines to remove the mask altogether and hold it out in front of their bodies. While the future DIs struggled to maintain their composure, a loud banging sound was coming from the vicinity of the gunny, who was donkey-kicking the metal panel behind him. Suddenly, the whole building shuddered with a crash when he burst through a door that was explosively unhinged. The gunny took a couple of instructors through the door with him; it was apparent to the class that the gunny had enough of the CS.

Our last week had finally arrived, and with the teach-backs, unit leader drill evaluations, and final PFTs in the books, Drill Instructor Class 2-4 had just two milestones to complete before graduation: bird-dogging for a week with a third phase recruit platoon and the battalion commander's inspection. I was assigned to a Kilo Company platoon in the Third Recruit Training Regiment (RTR) for the bird-dogging phase and very nearly forfeited my belt and cover before I even had a chance to put them on. We were still students and wore a duty belt and soft cover to distinguish us from the working hats. The distinction was unnecessary since the recruits already knew we were mere students. We were very limited with what we were allowed to do, and interaction with the recruits was almost forbidden.

One of the Drill Instructors showed me and another student how we were expected to make corrections and reminded us that was the only time we would ever touch a recruit. I was 'tightening elbows' exactly as I was instructed during a drill period when the RTR Sergeant Major came streaking from his office, snatched me up, and demanded I give him a good reason why I was 'manhandling' his recruits. I probably developed some streaks of my own in my drawers as I tried to utter some semblance of a reasonable answer. Fortunately, I made it through the course, received my belt and cover, and was assigned a Drill Instructor for Lima Company, Third Recruit Training Regiment, and the additional MOS of 8511. Coincidently, I was a recruit in platoon 3050, Lima Company, Third RTR on Parris Island, South Carolina.

Historical places to visit in or near Gloucester, New Jersey

Consider including the historical points of interest listed below with your visit to Red Banks Battlefield Park. The Hunter-Larence House now belongs to the Gloucester County Historical Society and serves as a museum that exhibits historical items from the county, some of which date to the Revolutionary War. Take a drive past the Colonel Bodo Otto House which is a private residence. Visit Wiggin's Waterfront Park and check out the Adventure Aquarium, then take a short walk across the promenade and tour the decks of the most decorated US battleship in American history, the Iowa Class USS New Jersey. At Proprietors Park you will find a few historical plaques that provide information on the Battle of Gloucester, the British landing of the British troops after they evacuated Philadelphia in 1778, and a beautiful monument marking the general location the HMS Agusta was towed to after it exploded during the Battle of Red Bank but the attraction here lay in the beauty and tranquility of the park nestled along the Delaware River.

Hunter-Lawrence House is located at 58 North Broad Street Woodbury, New Jersey.

Colonel Bodo Otto House is located at County Road 551 Mickleton, New Jersey.

Wiggin's Waterfront Park is located at 2 Riverside Drive Camden, New Jersey.

Proprietors Park is located at 100 Powell Street Gloucester City, New Jersey.

Conshohocken, Pennsylvania

"There's a mindset of flexibility and adaptability that comes with us. We don't mind hardship. We don't mind somebody saying – Go in and do this nasty job. Whatever the job is, we can do it. That's why the nation has a Marine Corps."

~General James F. Amos, 35th Commandant of the Marine Corps and first aviator to be appointed CMC.

On December 10th while camped in the vicinity of Broad Axe Village, Washington's war council decided on the prudence of moving into winter quarters and that the new camp should be established somewhere west of the Schuylkill River. On the morning of December 11th 1777, the Continental Army marched through Plymouth Meeting and crossed the river at Matson's ford. The route followed present-day Butler Pike across a temporary bridge of thirty-six wagons anchored in the river end to end with timber rails spanning the top. Washington ordered General Potter and his Pennsylvania militia to establish three advance pickets west of the river in preparation for the crossing to warn of British troop movements. The first picket was located at Middle ferry, near the modern Market Street bridge, the second at Black Horse Inn at City Line and Old Lancaster Road, and the third at the Harriton House along Old Gulph Road. The Harrington House was the home of Charles Thomson, secretary of the Continental Congress.

Unbeknownst to the Americans, General Cornwallis had led a sizeable British force out of the city on a foraging expedition early that morning. The force consisted of several battalions of Light Infantry and Grenadiers, regular infantry, two troops of dragoons, and a detachment of Jaegers. The force had six small cannon in direct support. Cornwallis had planned to forage in the country just south of Matson's ford and was unaware of the Continental Army operating in the vicinity. Cornwallis employed a resident named John Roberts to guide him, who, despite protests that he acted under duress, was later convicted of assisting Cornwallis and hanged by patriots in 1778.

Cornwallis and his foraging party crossed the Schuylkill at Middle Ferry, drawing a barrage of musket fire from the American picket before it withdrew. Cornwallis continued marching up the road toward Matson's ford. Soon after Cornwallis crossed the Schuylkill, the American picket positioned at the Black Horse Inn engaged the British troops. Outnumbered and flanked by the larger force, the militia began to fall back in confusion, taking casualties along the way. Battle reports were delivered to Potter, who was with the militia waiting at Harriton House. Potter concluded that "the British were advancing in force up Gulph Road and towards his location."

Potter had the bulk of his militia, consisting of five regiments, in skirmishers between the British forces and Harriton House. The militia was quickly overrun a second time, forcing a hasty retreat through Gulph Mills to Swede's Ford near present-day Norristown. This time, the retreat was reportedly "so chaotic that militiamen literally threw away their muskets and ammunition as they ran". This was an offense subject to corporal punishment for which some militiamen would later be fined or publicly whipped". After Cornwallis routed the Pennsylvania militia, he discontinued pursuit and established a strong position on the heights overlooking Matson's ford.

General Potter estimated his casualties at five killed, twenty wounded, and twenty taken prisoner. Potter estimated the British casualties to be higher than his. Captain Johann Ewald, who commanded the attachment of Jagers, recorded that "the British captured about 160 men in the battle after a stubborn resistance".

The following day, two Continental Army divisions, commanded by General Sullivan, started to cross the river at Matson's ford. The American divisions had almost completed the crossing when they realized the British held the tactical high ground on the heights. Sullivan quickly withdrew the two divisions back across the river and destroyed the makeshift bridge behind him.

The Continental Army spent December 11th and 12th on high ground above Swede's ford, and Washington sent out scouting parties to determine the disposition of the British force across the river. However, Cornwallis had already left the area, taking a roundabout route that brought him safely back to Philadelphia with wagons loaded with foraged provisions. On the evening of December 12th the Continental Army crossed the Schuylkill River at Swede's ford, again using makeshift wagon bridges. Washington then marched to King of Prussia, where they remained camped along the Gulph Road from December 13th until December 19th.

Marine Corps Tie-In...Surviving the Trenches as a New Hat.

After the DI graduation ceremony, the newly minted Drill Instructors were given a couple of weeks of leave to check out of their owning units, formally check into the depot, and move families onto the depot's base housing for those who required it. The two weeks came and went too swiftly, and I soon found myself walking into the squadbay of a platoon of Lima Company third-phase recruits. I did not have a foot across the threshold of the duty hut when the Senior Drill Instructor informed me that my appointed place of duty was with the recruits. He brusquely told me to place my ditty bag outside the duty hut hatch because neither the bag nor I had any business in the office. I was about as confused as I had ever been. There I was, standing in a squadbay full of recruits, donning the world-famous belt and cover of a Marine Drill Instructor, and I had no idea what I was supposed to do next.

A seasoned Greenbelt Drill Instructor soon popped his head out of the hut and screamed, "Do not try to teach them anything and don't answer any of their questions; in fact, don't talk to them at all.

The only things you will do with the platoon are make constant corrections, be demanding, and IT the crap out of the recruits. Unless the Senior or I tell you otherwise, keep the quarterdeck hot; we want you to continuously destroy recruits ten at a time."

I put down my ditty bag and went to work, looking for the smallest reasons to IT a recruit. A strict set of rules governs Incentive Training (IT), and they are carefully printed on a card that Drill Instructors must carry on their person at all times. Since there were very few occasions when a Drill Instructor was around recruits uncovered, most hats kept the card tucked in the headband of the campaign cover. I had never subjected a recruit to an IT session before stepping on deck that day, and it is something not practiced in DI School or while bird dogging because Drill Instructors are the only Marines in the fleet authorized to conduct IT.

Despite my gross lack of experience, I did not consider myself utterly inept. I gathered ten at a time to run them through the exercises authorized for IT...until an experienced Greenbelt from another platoon saw my quarterdeck action. He pushed me aside and said, "My first lesson is free motor scooter." He zeroed out the deck, called the platoon guide to the quarterdeck, and ordered him to gather nine of his 'girlfriends' to join him. When they were all hastily assembled in front of the hat, he promptly screamed at them to get on their faces and push.

As soon as the guide dropped down in a push-up position, the hat grabbed two pillows and, screaming an unintelligible tirade directed at the guide, viciously smacked the recruit with them. The hat looked like an animated, enraged toy monkey smashing two symbols together around the head of the hapless recruit. The hat had the dazed recruits in and out of various exercises faster than I could even think of the physical exercises authorized for IT. That afternoon, I learned a few lessons: a Drill Instructor doesn't need a good reason or even a reason at all to IT a recruit, the exercises themselves don't smoke a recruit, but the rapid transition of exercises will quickly destroy them and the more volume you demand of them and the fiercer you demand it, the quicker the recruits succumb to the grueling punishment.

Day in and day out, a pattern developed as I learned my role as 'Nick the New Hat.' I was expected to run everywhere I went, I would never sit down in the presence of a recruit, I would never eat in the presence of a recruit, I would scream louder and be more intense than any recruit, I would never show physical weakness in front of a recruit and etcetera- every day from lights to lights.

After a morning PT session a few weeks into my new role, my Senior DI told me to return to the duty hut, shower, dress, and eat something. He said he and the J-hat were going to march the platoon back to the squad bay instead of the customary cooldown jog to give me time to transition. I ran back, rinsed off, and dressed. I had a feeling the recruits would return before I had an opportunity to eat, so I slammed down my typical Drill Instructor's breakfast of a Slim Fast and Red Bull Chaser. I was about to open a granola bar when I heard the platoon...it had been less than seven minutes since I left them on the PT field.

Close-order drill periods for new hats are a terrible ordeal every single time the platoon is on the grinder (parade deck). A new hat is expected to continuously run up and down the long ranks of marching recruits, making constant corrections and blasting them at every opportunity. The only break from this was when a frustrated Senior or J-hat would run them back and forth or shift them right or left to wake the platoon, re-establish the recruits' undivided attention, and reinforce discipline. Although I was expected to chase the platoon like a rapid Pitbull, I considered it a break because it was a brief pause from the mundane.

I had heard stories about new hats being so exhausted they would doze on their feet if they stopped moving, and it happened to me once at a pivot point while the platoon was practicing columns one hot afternoon on the grinder. To tighten up columns, the J-hat put me at a pivot point where I was supposed to order one rank to pivot together while holding the oncoming rank back to maintain proper interval. With swinging arms, I spent what seemed like hours screaming, pivot, holdback. Pivot, holdback. Pivot, holdback. That afternoon I did this for about an hour when a recruit inadvertently marched into me; I had literally fallen asleep on my feet at the pivot point. Startled awake, I blasted the recruit as if he were at fault, but I knew the truth of it, and I think the disconcerted recruit did too.

I didn't get an opportunity to go home until my second full cycle, and only when the platoon had transitioned to the Weapons and Field Training Battalion at Camp Pendleton after their Initial Drill evaluation, 30 days into the cycle. On the morning of the second day of rifle qualification, my Senior told me to go home after I marched the platoon to the range and got the recruits staged. Unfortunately, most of the recruits who required corrective lenses left their 'portholes' locked in footlockers in the squad bay. Since the greenbelt Drill Instructors failed to inspect the recruits, I, having been one of the negligent greenbelts, had to return to the squad bay, unlock every locker of recruits requiring glasses, and deliver them to the range along with anything else the recruits had forgotten to take with them.

I lived about an hour from Camp Pendleton when traffic on the four lanes of CA-15 was moderate, and I didn't get to go home until late afternoon. I remember getting to the house and going directly to bed; I didn't even take the time to undress or take off my boots; I was that tired. Sometime in the middle of the night, I woke up, thinking a recruit was standing over me and I was in the duty hut. I jumped from the bed and began to scream...at a vacuum cleaner with clothing heaped over it, in my own bedroom. I had to be back on base by 0400 to wake the platoon anyway, so I jumped into my car and headed south. Arriving at the platoon barracks at Weapons and Field Training Battalion, I was rudely startled into alertness when I nearly drove my Dale Earnhardt Edition Monte Carlo SS Intimidator into a platoon of Marines standing in formation in a parking lot I wasn't even supposed to be in.

Historical places to visit in or near Conshohocken, Pennsylvania.

Begin your historical site survey of Conshohocken at the Broad Axe Tavern. The tavern began to serve its patrons around 1681, making it the oldest tavern in Pennsylvania. The tavern likely served Washington and his officers while briefly camped nearby. Rumor has it that General Grey visited the tavern and boasted that he would capture Lafayette. Fortunately for the boy general, Grey's plan was overheard by American general James Grant, and the plan was foiled. Another unsubstantiated account is that several Continental Soldiers are buried in unmarked graves along the road near the tavern.

Harriton House is another beautifully preserved 18th-century home. The 1704 house was owned by Charles Thompson, who was the first and only Secretary of the Continental Congress. Tour the outside of the home and explore the property, or schedule a tour of the interior of the house and period artifacts on exhibit. Tours are by appointment only; visitors must be 14 or older to be admitted, so plan accordingly.

Another place to visit is the Lower Merion Baptist Church. The Church was built on a parcel of land donated from the Harrington property in 1808. Reverend Horatio Gates Jones became its first pastor and served in that capacity for forty-six years. The church cemetery is where the history is at this stop along the Patriot's Path. Eighteen soldiers who served in the Continental Army, thirteen veterans of the War of 1812, thirty-six veterans of the Civil War, and sixteen descendants of William Penn are buried in the cemetery. You will find beautifully preserved headstones, well-maintained graves, and a stone monument in the northwest corner.

The best way to visit Matson's ford is to take a leisurely walk or run along the Schuylkill River Trail. With Access to the trail from Reading to Philadelphia, there are plenty of places to access the trail and enjoy the history and beauty of the Schuylkill River basin.

Broad Axe Tavern is located at 901 Butler Pike Blue Bell, Pennsylvania.

Matson's Ford is located off the Schuylkill River Trail in the vicinity of the Fayette Street overpass Conshohocken. Pennsylvania.

Harriton House is located at 500 Harriton Road Bryn Mawr, Pennsylvania.

Lower Merion Baptist Church is located at 911 New Gulph Road, Bryn Mawr, Pennsylvania.

King of Prussia, Pennsylvania

"They told (us) to open up the Embassy, or we'll blow you away. And then they looked up and saw the Marines on the roof with these really big guns, and they said in Somali, Igaralli ahow, which means Excuse me, I didn't mean it, my mistake".

Karen Aquilar, an American Journalist in Somalia.

Gulph Road, which runs through a deep valley between Rebel Hill and Widow's Hill, was one of the first highways opened west of the Schuylkill River, leading out of Philadelphia. Because of the physical surroundings, the name 'gulph' was given to the valley by local settlers. 'Gulph' is a Welsh word meaning, "an arm of the sea, a depression in the earth, a chasm or abyss". Rebel Hill, to the west of the road, traditionally received its name because, during the Revolutionary War, the locals supported the American cause so vigorously that Tories and Loyalists called the place Rebel Hill. Widow's Hill to the east of the road got its name after the Civil War because so many of the women were deserted by their husbands who enlisted to fight or some perhaps, who may have found the attraction of the Dixie Belles in the South too alluring to return home.

Gulph Mills was originally named Bird-in-Hand after the old tavern that used to stand at 977 Trinity Lane. The tavern was built about 1740 and originally consisted of a log building. A large stone structure was eventually built around it, but only the original well and springhouse remain. A grist mill was built at Gulph Mills in 1747 and supplied flour to the Continental Army during their stay at Valley Forge.

Washington's Army encamped in the area for about a week, then departed to Valley Forge, where they camped for the winter. Washington also used the Gulph Mill region as a nearby place to cache ammunition and powder during the autumn of 1777, skirmishing with the British nearby. The encampment is marked by a memorial erected by the Sons of the American Revolution in 1893.

A small toy mill was operated near the flour mill, and some of its foundations can still be seen opposite the Hanging Rock spring. A sawmill operated near the flour mill as well. Hanging Rock is a rock formation that existed along Gulph Road. Washington and the Continental Army would have passed by this natural formation on their march to Valley Forge. The rock was dedicated as a memorial to that march by the Valley Forge Historical Society in 1924. In 1917 and 1954, holes were drilled into Hanging Rock for dynamite to remove the rock and widen the road, however, the formation remains today.

Records do not detail where Washington's headquarters were located during the Army's encampment because some of his letters were dated "Headquarters Gulph Mill," others "near the Gulph," and one letter to the Board of War was dated "Headquarters Gulph Creek, 14th December 1777". Historians believe the headquarters was likely established in the Hugh House at the Walnut Grove Farm, now part of the Gulph Mills golf course.

On December 18th in a small, obscure camp near Gulph Mills, Washington's Army celebrated a day of "Thanksgiving and Praise." The day was set aside for fasting, prayer, and Thanksgiving at a time when American victories were sparse, to thank and praise God for the much-needed victory at Saratoga. Although many similar proclamations followed, this observance was the first national holiday recognized by all thirteen colonies. Later, after Washington became America's first president, he was inspired by its first Congress to issue an official Proclamation of Thanksgiving under the new Constitution and on behalf of the fledgling nation.

The origin of the proclamation is unique in that it was formally requested by a congressional vote from both chambers. On September 25th 1789, the House declared that Washington "could not think of letting the session pass over without offering an opportunity to all the citizens of the United States of joining with one voice, in returning to Almighty God their sincere thanks for the many blessings He had poured down upon them." Boudinot, a founding father, proposed "that a joint committee of both Houses be directed to wait upon the President of the United States, to request that he would recommend to the people of the United States a day of public thanksgiving and prayer to be observed by acknowledging, with grateful hearts, the many signal favors of Almighty God, especially by affording them an opportunity peaceably to establish a Constitution of government for their safety and happiness."

Washington's Thanksgiving Proclamation read, "May the children of the Stock of Abraham, who dwell in this land, continue to merit and enjoy the good will of the other Inhabitants; while everyone shall sit in safety under his own vine and fig tree, and there shall be none to make him afraid. May the father of all mercies scatter light and not darkness in our paths and make us all in our several vocations useful here, and in his own due time and way everlastingly happy."

Adopting a phrase from Seixas's letter, Washington wrote the deceptively simple sentence that, for all its brevity, resonates as one of the most definitive descriptions of the ideals of our nation. "Happily, the Government of the United States, which gives to bigotry no sanction, to persecution no assistance, requires only that they who live under its protection should deem themselves as good citizens in giving it on all occasions their effectual support."

On October 3rd 1863, President Lincoln followed with his own official proclamation on the 74th anniversary of Washington's proclamation. Lincoln's proclamation nationalized America's day of Thanksgiving and standardized its observance to be celebrated on the last Thursday of each November. In 1920, the nation's first Thanksgiving Parade took Place in Philadelphia. The parade, founded by the Gimbels Department store, featured fifteen ceremonial cars that paraded down the Benjamin Franklin Parkway. Over the years, the parade grew and has become an annual holiday event.

Marine Corps Tie-In…An American Homecoming.

After Bravo Company, First Battalion Fifth Marines conducted a Relief in Place (RIP) with an allied occupational force, we began our retrograde out of Baghdad and the Middle East. We linked up with our Amphibious Assault Vehicles and moved south to an old Iraqi Army base. During our brief stay, I explored some buildings, exercised my squad, and tried to avoid the burn pits as much as possible.

While exploring the base, I found military murals painted on the walls, discarded Iraqi uniforms, equipment, and French-made gas masks. I could have brought any of these items home as souvenirs, but I wanted to save my limited extra space for something much more valuable. While exploring the presidential palace in Baghdad, I found a beautiful bronze vase in a pile of rubble. The vase was about two feet tall, about a foot wide, and covered with ancient engravings. I cleaned it up, worked out a large dent, and decided to take it home and gift it to my mother.

But my platoon sergeant had found out about the vase and my plan. He took me aside and eventually convinced me that taking the vase home would be a bad idea. I was pissed with the staff sergeant because I really wanted the vase and didn't understand at the time, why I couldn't keep it since I literally pulled it out of a pile of palace rubble. The staff sergeant was definitely more perceptive than I was in the moment. Speculating the vase was likely an irreplaceable artifact, he told me it needed to remain in Iraq, and finally relenting, I found a safe place for it and left it behind.

Years later, I was glad I had. It turns out I wasn't the only American servicemember who had found museum-quality artifacts in Iraq. As recently as 2023, the Iraqi Ministry of Foreign Affairs, with the help of some of America's famous three-letter agencies, has recovered tens of thousands of ancient artifacts from the United States alone. Although most of the artifacts were removed from Iraq by smugglers and sold internationally while the country was in chaos in 2003, I am happy the staff sergeant prevented one of these agencies from possibly visiting me about an old vase I found in an Iraqi swimming pool.

After a few weeks at the Army base, the battalion loaded our gear on tractor-trailers, boarded buses, and headed south to the Kuwaiti International Airport. Our bags were randomly searched for contraband, and everyone was physically searched for munitions prior to boarding our flight.

When we arrived in Atlanta for a brief layover, we received a hero's welcome from appreciative American citizens. After we landed in California, our gear was quickly offloaded onto tractor-trailers again; we boarded buses and were escorted to the base by flag-waving bikers. Weapons and serialized gear were quickly secured in the armory, and our staff sergeant proudly marched the platoon to the Fifth Marine Grinder for our long-awaited reunification with family and friends. Post-deployment leave had been planned prior to the retrograde home, and Marines were dismissed from the grinder after they found their gear, to travel home to family and friends.

The next day, I packed up my dog and embarked on a three-day road trip to Pennsylvania. When I finally arrived in Flint Valley, I got out of the car with my dog and walked the final mile or so home. I was dressed in my dessert fatigues and wore my flak because I wanted to take the American flag I had carried throughout Iraq from behind the Sappi plate and hand it ceremoniously to my father. That done, it was finally time to sit back and enjoy being back home.

A pleasant surprise was in store for me when my brother inexplicably drove us to an old church grove I visited for summer festivals as a kid. When we arrived, the grove was full of cars, and the picnic pavilion was crowded with grateful people...my people. Every family member from both sides came together to welcome me home and honor my combat service; my Bakersfield brother was also there, along with childhood friends I had not seen in years. They had planned a homecoming for me, and they were all there, including my uncle, who had served in the Marines in the 1960s and had fought multiple combat tours in Vietnam. As I stood at attention while the National Anthem and Marines Hymn played for me, I couldn't control the proud tears rolling down my cheeks.

The occasion was emotional, and I stood proud, but I couldn't help feeling a twinge of guilt as I saw the grizzled Vietnam veteran stand and wave an American flag to honor my return because I knew that he didn't get a hero's welcome when he came home from Vietnam. Instead of honor escorts and flag-waving patriots, he came home to his countrymen spitting at him and treating him with scorn, pelted with insults from the very people he took a sacred oath to serve and protect, even if the cost was his own life. He suffered throughout his life from PTSD, although they didn't call it that in those times, and he carried deep, painful internal scars from witnessing fellow Marine brothers die horrifically in combat and return home in flag-draped boxes. Those comrades in arms who had made the ultimate, selfless sacrifice did not come home to a mournful but appreciative nation, police escorts, or full-honor funerals either; they came home uncelebrated...to lonely graves.

Historical places to visit in and near King of Prussia, Pennsylvania.

Most of these historical points are immersed in urban sprawl, but they are still well worth visiting. Begin your adventure with a drive-by visit to a gated private house that used to be the 18th-century Bird-in-Hand Tavern. Drive down to the Trinity Episcopal Church, where you can see a historical Marker commemorating Washington's first Thanksgiving.

Head over to 1271 Gulph Road, where you can park your vehicle, cross the road, and view a Revolutionary War memorial. Walk along a faint path beside South Gulph Road, and you will find a historical Marker for Gulph Mills Village. Gaze across the road and to the north, and you will see the locally famous Hanging Rock. The Hanging Rock is usually covered in vegetation in the summer, so it's best to plan for a winter visit. If you are into the wealth of meetinghouses southeastern Pennsylvania has to offer, check out the Radnor Meetinghouse down the road from Villanova University.

Finally, head towards the King of Prussia Mall, where you will find the King of Prussia Inn along the way. The historic Inn has been converted into a local business, but the old bones remain, including the original signboard for the Inn. You will also find a plaque with information on the building's history and a beautifully constructed Revolutionary War memorial.

Bird-in-Hand Tavern is located at 977 Trinity Lane King of Prussia, Pennsylvania.

Trinity Episcopal Church is located at 966 Trinity Lane King of Prussia, Pennsylvania.

Revolutionary War Memorial is located at 1271 Gulph Road Conshohocken, Pennsylvania.

King of Prussia Inn is located at 101 Bill Smith Boulevard King of Prussia, Pennsylvania.

Gulph Mills Historical Monument is located at 1030 Longview Road King of Prussia, Pennsylvania.

Radnor Meetinghouse is located at 610 Conestoga Road Villanova, Pennsylvania.

Trappe, Pennsylvania

"Some people wonder all their lives if they've made a difference. The Marines don't have that problem."

~Ronald Reagan, 40th President of the United States of America.

General John Peter Gabriel Muhlenberg was born October 1st 1746 in Trappe, Pennsylvania. His mother, Anna Maria Weiser, was the daughter of Pennsylvania Dutch pioneer and Indian diplomat, Conrad Weiser. John's father was Henry Muhlenberg, a German Lutheran pastor. He and his brothers, Frederick Augustus and Gotthilf Henry, were sent to Halle, Germany, in 1763 where they were educated in Latin at the Francke Foundation. John Peter left school in 1767 to work as a sales assistant in Lubeck but returned that same year to Pennsylvania.

John Muhlenberg served with the British 60th Regiment of Foot and briefly served in the German dragoons, where he was affectionately nicknamed "Teufel Piet" (Devil Pete). He received a classical education from the University of Pennsylvania, then called the Academy of Philadelphia. Muhlenberg was ordained in 1768 and pastored a Lutheran congregation in New Jersey. After a few years, he moved to Woodstock, Virginia, and pastored another Luthern church. Even though Muhlenberg was already an ordained minister, the Anglican Church was the state church of Virginia, and he was required to be ordained in the Anglican church to serve any congregation in that colony. In 1772, Muhlenberg sailed to England and was ordained into the priesthood of the Anglican Church.

Muhlenberg was also the chairman of Dunmore County's Committee of Safety and Correspondence, was elected to the House of Burgesses in 1774 and was a delegate to the First Virginia Convention. In 1775, the colony of Virginia authorized Muhlenberg to raise the 8th Virginia Regiment of the Continental Army and was commissioned a colonel. George Washington personally asked him to accept command of the regiment.

Muhlenberg's brother Fredrick, also a minister, did not support John taking an active role in the Revolutionary War, that is until the British burned down his church in front of him. After that, he was just as eager to join the American cause. Muhlenberg's great-nephew wrote his biography in the mid-19th century and stated the following:

"On January 21st 1776 Reverend Muhlenberg gave a sermon on the third chapter Ecclesiastes, which begins with "To everything there is a season...". After reading the eighth verse, "a time of war, and a time of peace," he declared, "And this is the time of war," and removed his clerical robe to reveal his Colonel's uniform. Outside the church door, drums began to roll as men turned to kiss their wives and then walked down the aisle to enlist; within half an hour, 162 men were enrolled into the Continental Army. The next day he led three hundred men from the county who formed the nucleus of the 8th Virginia Regiment".

The Muhlenberg Regiment's first assignment was to defend the coasts of South Carolina and Georgia. In the winter of 1777, Muhlenberg's Regiment was sent to Morristown, where it joined Washington's Army. Muhlenberg and the Virginia Line fought at Brandywine, Germantown, and Monmouth Courthouse. After the Battle of Monmouth, the fighting shifted to the South, and most of the Virginia Line was sent back to the war on their home front. General Muhlenberg was assigned to defend Virginia, but most of his command consisted of poorly trained and equipped militia units. In 1781, he commanded the first brigade in Lafayette's Light Division during the climactic Battle of Yorktown.

At the war's end, he received a brevet promotion to major general and settled in Montgomery County, Pennsylvania. Muhlenberg's post-war service includes election to the Supreme Executive Council of Pennsylvania and election to Vice-President of the Council, a position comparable to a modern Lieutenant Governor. In 1801, Muhlenberg received an executive appointment as supervisor of revenue for Pennsylvania and customs collector for Philadelphia in 1802 from President Jefferson. Muhlenberg was also an original member of the prestigious Pennsylvania Society of the Cincinnati. He died on his 61st birthday at Gray's Ferry, Pennsylvania, and is buried at the Augustus Lutheran Church in Trappe, Pennsylvania.

Marine Corps Tie-In...An Answer to an Important Question.

During my years at Villanova NROTC Unit, I served as its Assistant Marine Officer Instructor. Concurrent with the duty assignment, I took advantage of my nondeployment status and pursued a college degree. Concerned I would only have enough time to complete a two-year associate degree, I started an Associate's Degree in Psychology program through Liberty University. Halfway through my first semester, I got a call from an academic advisor who asked if I was interested in pursuing a bachelor's degree. When I told her of my concerns, she asked if I could send any college transcripts I had earned and my Navy SMART transcript to determine where I would matriculate in a traditional four-year bachelor program.

The advisor called a few days later to inform me that the school had reviewed the combined transcripts and would give me credit for two academic years and matriculate me into a bachelor's program as a junior. I enthusiastically accepted the proposition and began an undergraduate program in Religion. Ironically, I had felt the call to ministry but did not think I could realistically earn the degrees most churches require as a prerequisite for ordination. I took a huge leap of faith, and the Lord provided a way for me to earn an undergraduate degree and a Master of Divinity degree in just over three years of hard work and course overloads through distance learning programs.

While I was working on finishing my master's degree, I requested an extension at Villanova to complete a Navy Chaplain package and to obtain a conditional release and interservice transfer from the Marine Corps to the Navy. The process was long and tedious; I had to work through hours of medical screening, background checks, and chaplaincy-specific prerequisites. The Navy Chaplain recruiter I was working with either wasn't very experienced or not very dedicated to his job, and I had to walk much of the package through its various stages myself. I was glad I had three years of experience constructing officer commissioning packages at Villanova to fall on.

Ordination and a DOD Letter of Endorsement were the two main prerequisites for the package, the former driving the latter. While working on the package, I asked a pastor if I could be ordained through the church I was attending. I received counseling and advice and was asked to draft an Ecclesiastic dissertation. I was also required to ask six ordained ministers (three of whom were required from other churches) to agree to serve as members of the ordination board with whom I would defend the dissertation a couple of weeks after I sent each pastor the points paper. The board would then discuss the proceedings, pray, and vote on whether or not they felt I should be ordained. I needed a two-thirds majority vote among the pastors; if the vote was for ordination, their recommendation would be forwarded to and reviewed by the church elders, who had the final say.

I spent a few weeks drafting a lengthy dissertation and preparing for the ensuing ordination board. I studied my dissertation and was confident I could defend its points well. I was as nervous to walk into that board as I was during a Marine meritorious promotion board I once attended. When I walked into the room, I shook hands with each of the board members, and the church's lead pastor invited me to sit at the conference table. I was surprised that the board members asked me to explain only a few of my points in the dissertation; the conversation focused more on my candidacy and what ordination meant. They were all very supportive of my calling to become a chaplain and pledged their mutual support. Just before the pastors adjourned the board to discuss my candidacy, one of them, a Christian Counselor by vocation, asked me a profound question. He explained that sometimes a pastor's calling might not entail what one envisioned, and he asked me if I was prepared to accept the possibility that I might not become a Navy chaplain. He asked me if I could accept that possibility if it happened and be open to whatever ministry the Lord had set aside for me.

I was so fixated on being a chaplain that I didn't think not being a chaplain was a likelihood. Reflecting on my chaplaincy journey so far, it was plain to me that the Lord was executing His plan every step of the way. I confidently told the pastor that I was open to any plan the Lord had for me, even if, for some reason, it was not as a Navy Chaplain. The board chairman asked me to step outside the room while the pastors deliberated. After a few minutes, I was called back into the room and informed that the board had reached a unanimous decision to recommend to the Elder Board that I be ordained. I did not understand the depth of the pastor's question until the day realization hit me that I would not become a Navy Chaplain.

After I was ordained, I applied for the required DOD Ecclesiastic Endorsement from a Liberty University-affiliated endorsing agency. While vacationing with my family in Vermont, I got an unfavorable email from the endorser. The endorser informed me that due to a lack of pastoral experience, they would not endorse my candidacy for military chaplaincy. After several phone conversations with the endorser, he eventually agreed to accept two years of pastoral internship as pastoral experience and the last piece of the complex package fell into place.

After several long months of appointments, medical waivers, and interviews with DOD chaplains who provided strong recommendations, I finally completed my package, which was submitted to the Navy Chief of Chaplains. Unfortunately, that is where my aspiration to become a Navy Chaplain hit an insurmountable snag. I was informed that the Chief of Chaplains was absolutely opposed to allowing inter-service transfers into the Chaplaincy Corps and would not budge on her position. Two high-ranked chaplains, both captains in the Navy, advocated for my candidacy; each contacted the Chief and presented my case to her. One of the chaplains, whose son I had mentored at Villanova as a midshipman, even requested a congressional exception to policy but to no avail; the answer was no, and the door to the Navy chaplaincy was slammed shut.

It took a while for me to adjust to the realization that I would retire as a Marine instead of continuing my military service as a Navy Chaplain. I struggled to want to do any kind of ministry, but shortly after reporting to the 2nd Battalion 4th Marines, I began to work closely with the battalion chaplain and served as the battalion's protestant lay leader. I also offered marital, pre-marital, and family reunification classes for anyone who was interested before the battalion returned home from Okinawa, Japan. Prior to my assignment with the battalion, I became familiar with a recovery program called Celebrate Recovery (CR) during my pastoral internship. Shortly after arriving in Okinawa, the battalion experienced a sharp rise in alcohol-related incidents, which prompted the frustrated commander to ask his chaplain to set up an Alcoholics Anonymous program. The chaplain explained that while he could not set up an AA group and require Marines to attend, he knew of an alternative program that might work out and suggested to the Colonel that he have a talk with me.

I set up a PowerPoint brief and presented it to the battalion commander. He liked the CR program I showed him but wanted a few modifications. First, he wanted me to take out anything related to

Jesus. When I told the commander that Jesus was the program's foundation, he balked. His concern was that he would not be able to order the Marines to attend a religious program, and he asked if I could at least water down the religious annotations.

I assured the commander I would not use the CR model as a platform to apostatize and offered a few solutions to get Marines to attend the program. I proposed we hold a one- or two-hour meeting in the base chapel every Wednesday and work out a small budget for pizza and refreshments to provide to those in attendance. When asked why I would choose a day in the middle of a work week, I said, "It is all about waving a proverbial golden carrot under the noses of the Marines. Offer an incentive...while you cannot order Marines to attend a program with religious connotations, you could order your commanders to allow their Marines to attend the event if they choose and provide transportation to the chapel from field training events if necessary". Under the auspice that something is better than nothing, the battalion commander decided to allow me to implement a CR program.

I had worked with the CR model for a couple of years at my home church. I even had the opportunity to attend CR's annual three-day summit, which focuses on equipping CR leaders, so I had much of the material I needed to start the program. On the first Thursday afternoon, only a handful of Marines attended the program, but after two or three Thursdays, the room I was using was nearly filled with attendees as word got out that 'Gunny' was taking care of the Marines. At first, getting Marines to open up and work through the program's 12-step model was difficult, but as Marines began to share, trusting in the confidential safety nets in play, it encouraged others to share. I didn't always see the same faces every Thursday, but I did notice a corporal who had attended every meeting but seldom said a word. I made it a point to talk with him, and he eventually told me his story.

The Corporal told me that he was religious before enlisting in the Corps and attended church regularly. He also told me he raced stock cars, specifically Roush Fords, in a feeder system that would have eventually landed him an upper-tier ride in NASCAR. His parents supported the young man throughout his racing career, and he developed into a talented and successful young driver. He started to win, and with the wins came the celebrations and falling into addictive rabbit holes that sometimes come with the success of winning. The young man eventually lost his ride and, with it, his will to overcome the addictive adversity he was facing. His racing career was likely cut short, and he turned to the Corps, but it did not give him an antidote for his underlying problem.

Something about the CR model resonated with the young man, and week after week, he began to gather himself together. Eventually, he shared that he had destroyed the last bottle of alcohol he possessed, celebrating a symbolic break from his hurt, habit, and hang-up. The Corporal became more outspoken, endorsing the merits of the CR model as often as possible with others.

After a few months, the unit was preparing to embark on warships for a quick deployment to South Korea when the Corporal came to the weekly meeting a bit troubled, assuming we would have to suspend CR for a little while. I told him I had prepared for the upcoming deployment by pre-recording the teaching and testimonial weeks and would make them available for anyone who wanted them. He also asked if he could share the videos with others if they wished to, and I told him that would be great.

At the docks in Okinawa after the deployment, I ran into the young man, and it was like looking at a completely different person. It is evident that his life took a radically positive turn, and his heart was on fire for the Lord. He told me that so many Marines wanted to watch the videos that he started a group that met regularly on the ship he was on. Years after I retired, I ran into the young man on a social media platform where he informed me he was doing great, was out of the Corps and back in NASCAR, not as a driver but as a technical developer for the sport.

During the deployment, I spent a lot of time with a fellow SNCO, an awesome Marine and a man I respected tremendously but a man who also walked among shadows. I tried ministering to him throughout the deployment but could not break through the barrier he had built to insulate his hurt from others. One evening, his defensive barrier wavered just enough for him to share his story. He was burdened with a heavy tragedy, the worst heartbreak a loving father could ever endure...the loss of a child. He was one of the first responders to his child's fate, and the image was seared into his breaking heart. He spent years blaming himself for not being there before it happened or getting there in time to save his child. In a moment of vulnerability that night, the Marine opened up just enough to be receptive to what God was whispering to his trembling spirit. The window of opportunity for me to talk with him was narrow but just wide enough to remind him that although he had lost a child, he was still the father of another and that he had a Father in Heaven who would never leave or forsake him. I didn't know until years later that the tiny opening in his defenses was also a saving one.

I also did not know how vital that brief talk was that night or how important the flash drive I gave to him, containing a copy of the movies *God's Not Dead* and Billy Graham's *My Hope America*, until I received an odd text message from him a couple years after I retired. The text simply read 'God's Not Dead!' Indeed, God is not dead; at the time of the text, I was holding a perfect demonstration of this statement in the form of a tiny bundle of girl-child. My wife and I prayed and tried for years, even through medical intervention to conceive a second child, but with the passage of fruitless time, we eventually lost all hope that her older sister would have a sibling.

God is not dead. He is alive; His omnificence, omnipresence, and omnipotence remind me of His great love for us every day. He is the Alpha and the Omega, and through His mysterious ways, the pastor's profound question during my ordination board was answered; God's plan might not have been for me to become a chaplain, but had I not chosen to continue to serve in the ways He provided, lives would not have been so radically touched through His Word and the planting of a few simple seeds.

Historical places to visit in and near Trappe, Pennsylvania.

Trappe has several historic properties open for tours throughout the summer season. The Center for Pennsylvania German Studies, located in the Dewees Tavern, has five exhibition galleries filled with various antique furniture, textiles, and other historical objects. A research library and archives are also housed in the old tavern. The Henry Muhlenberg House is a fully furnished museum. The Speaker's House, which was the home of Frederick Muhlenberg, is undergoing a restoration. Built in 1763 for John and Silence Schrack, the beautiful stone house was owned by Frederick from 1781 to 1791. During this time, Frederick served as a member of the Continental Congress, Speaker of the Pennsylvania Assembly, the first president judge, recorder of deeds, and register of wills for Montgomery County, and the first Speaker of the U.S. House. From 1791 to 1803, the house was owned by Francis and Mary (Muhlenberg) Swaine; it later served as a Ursinus dormitory from 1924 to 1944, known as Highland Hall. Tours are available by appointment. The Trappe Historical Society also owns the Muhlenberg parsonage. Built in 1745, it is currently undergoing architectural investigations in preparation for restoration.

Originally known as the Fountain Inn, the Trappe Tavern building has served as a tavern since it was built in the late 1700s. A 'Big Spring' nearby provided water via underground wooden pipes to a distillery and the inn, which had three fountain pumps in the yard for watering thirsty horses. Traces of the spring remain by a pond located in Rambo Park. By 1823, the inn's barn sheds and stables could accommodate up to seventy-five wagons and 150 horses.

A drive through the countryside to the New Hanover Lutheran Church and Cemetery is well worth the effort. The stone church, built in 1700, was once pastored by Henry Muhlenberg and his son Fredrick and served briefly as a field hospital for Washington's wounded. If you stroll around the cemetery, you will find at least fifty marked graves of Revolutionary soldiers. At the intersection of Swamp Pike and Lutheran Road, you will also find a historical marker about Muhlenberg.

Just southeast of New Hanover Lutheran Church is another historically significant church. The Faulkner Swamp Reformed Church was built in 1790; its congregation holds the distinction of being the oldest Reformed or Evangelical church in continuous existence. After visiting these two historic churches, drive to the Colonel Antes House a short distance away, where the Faulkner Reformed Church congregation met before the church was built in 1790. Washington headquartered at the house upon invitation from Henry's son, Colonel Philip Frederick Antes, while the Continental Army camped nearby.

Interestingly, Fredrick held a British commission before the Revolutionary War. He became an outspoken patriot and supporter of American Independence, so he resigned his commission, accepted a commission in the 6th Philadelphia militia, and became a scout and guide for Washington. General Howe even offered a substantial bounty for Fredrick's head during the Revolutionary War. Henry's other son, John Henry, was a Colonel in the Pennsylvania militia, served under Colonel Potter, and built Fort Antes in Lycoming County. The 1736 Henry Antes House has been preserved in its 18th-century spender and serves as a living history museum. Just down the road, you will find a beautiful stone monument commemorating the three-day Continental Army camp in Pottstown, Pennsylvania.

The Henry Muhlenberg House is located at 209 West Main Street Trappe, Pennsylvania.

Dewees Tavern is located at 301 Trappe, Pennsylvania.

The Speaker's House is located at 151 West Main Street Trappe, Pennsylvania.

Muhlenberg Parsonage is located at 201 West Main Street Trappe, Pennsylvania.

Trappe Tavern is located at 418 West Main Street Trappe, Pennsylvania.

New Hanover Lutheran Church Cemetery is located at 2941 Lutheran Road Gilbertsville, Pennsylvania.

Revolutionary War Memorial is located at 275 Evansburg Road, Evansburg, Pennsylvania.

Camp Pottstown Memorial is located at Swamp Pike and Faust Road, Pottstown, Pennsylvania.

Colonel Henry Antes House is located at 318 Colonial Road, Perkiomen, Pennsylvania.

Saint James Perkiomen Church Cemetery is located at 3814 Germantown Pike Collegeville, Pennsylvania.

Wissahickon State Park, Pennsylvania

"My only answer as to why the Marines get the toughest jobs is because the average Leatherneck is a much better fighter. He has far more guts, courage, and better officers... These boys out here have a pride in the Marine Corps and will fight to the end no matter what the cost."

~2nd Lt. Richard C. Kennard, author and World War II Veteran.

Learning a valuable lesson from his defeat at Brandywine Creek, Washington had spies everywhere in and around the city of Philadelphia. He relied heavily on his spy network and had agents feeding him information from everywhere. Although a lack of intelligence hurt him in past defeats, historians agree that his much-improved spy network was instrumental in defeating the British forces later in the war. Molly Rinker was one of his network spies, and he relied on the information she and others gave him.

Molly, who was sympathetic to the patriot cause, was a tavern keeper for the Buck Tavern in Germantown when Washington was camped with his men a few miles away at Whitemarsh. Molly usually had a tavern full of drunken British soldiers and constantly overheard things...sometimes very useful things that could aid the patriot cause. The British soldiers who hung out in her bar and slept in her tavern were forced upon her. The British Army had occupied Germantown, and whenever British troops occupied a city, they were quartered in people's homes or somewhere on their property; the colonists had no choice in the matter.

Molly also knitted socks for the American Army. To openly knit socks or provide any other service to 'rebels' in a British-held city was tantamount to sedition, punishable by imprisonment or worse, but 'Mom Rinker' reputedly was not concerned about the possible consequences of her patriotic sympathies, which was pretty bold since the majority of her patrons were Torys or British soldiers.

Whenever Molly overheard helpful information to pass on to the Continental Army, she would take her knitting and sit on top of a huge rock that overlooked a narrow trail in Wissahickon Park. She wrote the things she overheard on bits of paper and hid them in small balls of yarn. When she determined the time was right, she dropped the little balls of yarn down from her seat on the rock, and one of Washington's men would eventually pick it up. After the drop was conducted, Moly packed up her knitting and went back to serving drinks to the British soldiers.

According to local legend, Molly, sometimes called Mom Rinkle or Molly Runker, was believed to be a witch who lived on the rock that now bears her name. A passage from a book titled: *The Story of Philadelphia* by Lillian Ione Rhoades sums up the legend well:

"here is a legend that Mom Rinker was a witch; that she rode to the moon on a broomstick; that she drank dew from acorns; that she had an evil eye that soured the neighbor's milk, and that she fell from this cliff and was killed. It is undoubtedly true that she brewed strange decoctions from the herbs, roots, and bark of trees, but the rest of the story is fanciful."

A man known as Mr. Meehan was quoted in a 1901 edition of *The Philadelphia Record* with a little more information about the 'witch's' demise:

"From this rock towering over the dark waters of the Wissahickon, she nightly mounted her broomstick and set off on her weird flights. But, one night, whether owing to excessive indulgences in the witch's revels or some other cause, instead of soaring from the rocks, she fell — the sharp crags dashed the life out of her — and the waters of the creek toyed with her lifeless body."

Molly was a patriot who took extraordinary risks to help her compatriots. That some locals thought she was a witch or that she conducting witchcraft is a travesty; she was a heroine in her own right; that she was possibly drunk from a homemade concoction of corn mash and plummeted from the rock to her death is a much more plausible explanation of her demise.

Marine Corps Tie-In...Enter the "J" Hat.

After two and a half cycles serving as a third or fourth hat, I thought I had a better understanding of what fatigue was and how being completely drained of energy felt. I even believed the previous cycles had conditioned me to cope better with the effects of fatigue. I could not wait to be a J-Hat and take on the responsibility of teaching close order drill and in-house procedures. As the J Hat, I would be the Senior's second, his right-hand man, and there would be no wasting myself with the constant running, screaming, and high-level intensity constantly demanded of a junior Drill Instructor.

I studied my J notes and Drill Manuel to exhaustion to be as mentally agile and prepared as possible prior to the next recruit pick-up. Finally, the day came when the recruits were all sitting on the quarterdeck waiting to meet their Drill Instructors. I knew that once the speeches were made, it was going to be almost exclusively my show for the rest of the weekend and for most of the cycle's drill periods. Not only would I have almost exclusive control of the recruits, but I also had control of but was not responsible for, the junior hats on the team.

After the Senior's speech, he turned to face his team and stoically commanded, "Drill Instructors, take charge of the platoon and train them to become United States Marines." All hell broke loose as the Senior stepped into the duty hut with an entourage of VIP spectators, and I started to run the deck. During the ensuing couple of hours, the squadbay was in total chaos, but by design, to establish command

and control over the platoon quickly. Recruits and Drill Instructors were blurs of human movement as gear was pulled out, inventoried, kicked around, put away, and pulled back out again. Drill Instructors sweated through uniforms, running up and down the squad bay, screaming orders to dazed and confused recruits, while I attempted to control it all by screaming instructions over the bedlam. No close-order drill or in-house procedures were taught during the first few hours by design; the platoon needed a proverbial punch in the face to let them know who threw the punches in the house; as my wife sometimes says, "Give them a forehand for attention and a backhand for respect." After the house was hastily put back together, the platoon was herded to the chow hall for a quick noon meal and then returned to the house for more instruction.

After the noon meal, time was set aside to teach in-house procedures such as making a rack, properly staging gear, maintaining a shoe display, head call procedure, setting up a classroom, and forming a school circle. After each lesson was explained and demonstrated, the recruits were ordered to imitate and practice with the Junior Drill Instructors; the instruction was controlled, but the practice was chaotic.

The in-house instruction continued into evening chow, and the recruits were expected to demonstrate the chow hall procedures they had been taught. Manufactured friction is constant throughout recruit training: it is either generated by the recruits or imposed by the Drill Instructors. The tiniest infraction of a rule committed by a recruit guaranteed unwelcomed, one-on-one attention with a Drill Instructor and sometimes by several Drill Instructors; the attention was not for the faint of heart.

With the recruits back in the house after evening chow, it was time to teach them evening basic daily routine (BDR). Recruits were taught how to prepare for the next day's events by staging PT gear on footlockers or placing empty canteens for the fire watch to refill at night. Recruits were also rudely introduced to how the hygiene ritual would be conducted every night.

When I was a Junior Hat, I did not need to teach the BDR, but I had to make sure I was very intensely reinforcing what was being taught by the J-Hat. That meant I had to go into the middle of the 'rain room' which was equipped with four shower trees, with thirty naked recruits while I was fully uniformed and wearing my campaign cover, to make sure the recruits showered by the numbers. In these moments, I was glad I was a J Hat; although my voice was completely shot by the end of the day, at least I was not inhaling soap suds and ruining a uniform, shoes, and campaign cover in the shower room.

The next day consisted of teaching more in-house procedures and reiteration of lessons taught very concisely and with a lot of repetition. That day would also be the first day that the seal to the Drill Manual was cracked and introduced to the platoon. After the recruits were finally ordered to bed, fire watches stood up, and lights turned out, I went into the duty hut to study my J notes and Drill Manuel for the following day. I was so tired I fell asleep during my studies, and woke up sometime later in a pool of drool that had gathered on the laminated pages of my manual.

When you pick up a platoon of recruits, they have not been taught precision movements, and the platoon resembles a mob of recruits for the first few days of training. By the time the platoon transitions through initial and final drill, they do not look like a platoon of individuals; they move as one entity, a cohesive unit of Marines. The transformation seems just short of miraculous, and the amount of detailed work put into the effort is almost unbelievable.

Every drill movement is taught with precision, and the commands are driven by the rise, inflection, and rhythm of the Drill Instructor's voice. Movements are taught with verbal 'isms' to help the recruits remember the drill movements, counts, and the timing at which they will be executed. An ism used when teaching columns for the first time begins with the Drill Instructor commanding in cadence, "Turn to your right," where the recruits respond by shouting, "By pivoting on the left foot, left foot, left Foot." When the platoon is proficient at pivoting on the proper foot, the ism evolves to the Drill Instructor commanding in cadence, "Column Right, March- left right, left, right!" The recruits respond by shouting: "Hold back, align to the base." Drill instructor: "Left, right, left, right." Recruits: "Pivot in teams of four." Eventually, by third phase, the platoon is proficient enough to come off isms for most drill movements.

I struggled with my voice the first few weeks; I was doing so much teaching and talking that I kept blowing my voice out. I would blow my voice out and it would eventually come back stronger and louder. Dill Instructors are known for talking with a 'frog voice,' some people believe that Drill Instructors intentionally manipulate their voices in this fashion, and perhaps some do, but my frog voice was well earned. It wasn't until I worked the J-Hat cycles that I understood why Senior Drill Instructors wanted their hats to scream at the recruits nonstop every day for three months. I assume most, like myself, thought we were doing all the screaming to sound really intense and intimidating. After pulling a double hernia from screaming without properly engaging my diaphragm as a junior DI, and after constantly blowing out my voice during my first J cycle, it occurred to me that the seasoned Seniors were trying to prepare their junior Drill Instructors for the eventuality of becoming a J-Hat and the rigors that come along with it. I learned too late that it would have been better for me to have blown out my voice as a junior.

During graduation, the J-Hats have the honor and distinction of participating in a very brief but emblematic event called Retiring the Guidons. During this ceremonial interlude, each platoon guide symbolically closes out the platoon's three-month ordeal by returning the flag and symbol that represented it back to their Drill

Instructors. Few events on the depot ever emotionally moved me, but taking the guidon back from the platoon guide was special enough to be considered a hair-raising experience for me. It had that effect on me for each of the three cycles I took custody of the guidon from a platoon guide, tucked it into my shoulder, and marched it off the parade deck. I get the same sensation now as I recall the memory for some odd reason.

Historical places to visit in and near Wissahickon State Park, Pennsylvania.

Wissahickon State Park is another beautifully maintained preserve with several access points to the park. Spend the day hiking on an extensive but well-marked trail system. Some trails are wide, heavily trafficked improved trails that meander along the Wissahickon Creek while others provide a more challenging experience over rugged and elevated terrain. To visit the Tedyuscung Statue or the Toleration Statue of William Penn, you will have to negotiate difficult terrain if you want to get close. These historical points of interest are located on opposite sides of the park so plan your route with care. If you want to visit the Toleration Statue of Penn without roaming through the park, making a short drive to 6588 Park Line Drive, Philadelphia, is an option, but parking at the trailhead is limited, and you will still have some moderate to challenging trails to deal with, but the distance is much shorter. The rocky precipice the statue occupies can be dangerous, so I do not recommend visiting with small children. The rocky promenade is also the likely spot Molly sat whenever she needed to drop valuable intelligence to the trail below the rocks for Continental Soldiers to 'discover'. Bring a picnic lunch to the park and stay for the day or sit up at a table at the historic Valley Green Inn for a meal or refreshments. Just be aware that there are sometimes transients in the park and the poignant smell of marijuana is usually in the air near the bridge leading to the Inn during the summer months.

<u>Wissahickon State Park</u> is located at Valley Green Road, Philadelphia, Pennsylvania.

<u>Tedyuscung the "Lenape Chief" Statue</u> is located in Wissahickon State Park.

<u>Toleration statue of William Penn</u> is located in Wissahickon State Park.

<u>Thomas Mill Covered Bridge</u> is located in Wissahickon State Park.

<u>Cedars House</u> is located in Wissahickon State Park.

<u>Harper's Meadow</u> is located in Wissahickon State Park.

<u>Bells Mill</u> is located in Wissahickon State Park.

<u>Magargee Dam</u> is located in Wissahickon State Park.

<u>Valley Green Inn</u> is located in Wissahickon State Park.

<u>Cave of Kelpius</u> is located in Wissahickon State Park.

<u>The Goldmine Caves</u> is located in Wissahickon State Park.

<u>Rock Climber's Rock</u> is located in Wissahickon State Park.

<u>The Devil's Pool</u> is located in Wissahickon State Park.

Tredyffrin, Pennsylvania

"So long as our Corps fields such Marines, America has nothing to fear from tyrants, be they Fascists, Communists or Tyrants with Medieval Ideology. For we serve in a Corps with no institutional confusion about our purpose: To fight! To fight well"!

~General Jim Mattis, 26th Secretary of Defense.

The countryside surrounding Valley Forge served as the Continental Army's third of eight winter encampments during the War for Independence. In September 1777, Congress fled Philadelphia ahead of the British occupation of the city. Washington led his Army into winter quarters at Valley Forge in December after several attempts to draw Howe into a defensive battle. The American Army that limped into Valley Forge on December 19th was a beaten, beleaguered group of about 12,000 soldiers, craftsmen, women, and children.

The encampment was primarily situated along an easily defendable natural plateau east of Mount Joy and south of the Schuylkill River. Aside from the concentration of soldiers at Valley Forge, Washington also ordered nearly 2,000 soldiers to camp at Wilmington, Delaware after the British left the area. He posted the Army's dragoons at Trenton and established additional pickets and posts at Downingtown, Newtown Square, and Radnor.

Political, strategic, and environmental factors shaped Washington's decision to establish his encampment at Valley Forge. Washington considered advice given by his officers, but he also had to listen to the recommendations of politicians and other influential citizens. They wanted the Continental Army to be in a position where it could protect the countryside around Philadelphia. There were even some near-sighted members of Congress who thought a winter campaign against the British forces in Philadelphia was possible.

Other sites for a winter encampment were also recommended, including Lancaster and Wilmington. However, following the inconclusive Battle of Whitemarsh, an obvious need to defend the Philadelphia countryside from British foraging took precedence. Valley Forge became the Continental Army's first encampment consisting of large-scale construction of living quarters.

Washington tasked Brigadier General Louis Lebegue de Presle Duportail to select grounds for the brigade encampments and plan their defenses. Duportail appointed officers from each regiment to determine the precise location of every officer and all enlisted men's huts. Although the shelters were designed to be standard, they varied in size, materials, and construction techniques. There is no accurate account of the number of log huts built, but historians estimate between 1,300 and 1,600 huts were constructed in the area based on the correspondence of Washington and other soldiers' letters and notebooks that recorded the camp's construction and layout.

The Continental Army faced and overcame several challenges during the Valley Forge winter encampment, including poor organization of the Army and sustainment. Two years of fighting a desperately uphill war, a revolving door of officers, uneven recruitment, and short enlistment terms resulted in inconsistent unit organization and depleted strength. During the winter encampment, Washington reorganized his Army into five divisions, which helped improve unit strength. Terms of service for officers and enlisted became more standardized, which helped retain experience and improved the Army's continuity and efficiency. Throughout the winter, commanders and politicians faced the challenge of supplying and feeding a population the size of Philadelphia. Although the Continental Congress authorized the reorganization of the supply department in the early summer of 1777, those changes never fully took effect because of the rigors of the Philadelphia Campaign.

Consequently, the supply chain was broken before the Continental Army arrived at Valley Forge. Supplies became so scarce through the neglect of Congress that by the end of December, Washington had no way to feed or adequately clothe his soldiers. This changed when the five-man Continental Camp Committee arrived at Valley Forge to "rap a demi-god over the knuckles." The committee witnessed the Army's deplorable condition firsthand. That and Washington's lengthy letter to Congress addressing those conditions contributed to Washington being authorized to choose his quartermaster instead of dealing with an appointment from an incompetent Congressional committee. This eventually resulted in a better supply of food and arms for the Army.

One popular myth about the Valley Forge encampment was that a harsh, snowy winter decimated the Army. Contemporary depictions of the winter of 1778 described the encampment as blanketed in snow, causing exposure and frostbite, claiming the lives of hundreds of soldiers. Although amputations and exposure injuries indeed occurred, there are no corroborating sources that suggest that death occurred from the freezing temperatures alone.

That winter, it seldom snowed, above-freezing temperatures were prevalent, and icy conditions were uncommon. Stories of a harsh winter encampment likely originated from the previous Continental Army winter encampment at Morristown, New Jersey where the Army experienced the coldest winter of the entire war. Records indicate that two-thirds of the deaths that occurred during the encampment at Valley Forge didn't even happen during the winter months. They emerged during the warmer spring months of March, April, and May, a time when soldiers were kept busy outside cramped cabins training and drilling. Food and other supplies were even more abundant and easier for the Army to acquire by this time.

Diseases proved to be the most significant contributor to deaths at Valley Forge. By the end of the six-month encampment, approximately 2,000 men, or roughly one in six, died of the flu, fever, typhus, typhoid fever, and dysentery. Conditions most likely were aggravated by poor hygiene and sanitation at the camp.

The Continental Army was hindered in previous battles because units were trained and drilled by officers with various military backgrounds, making coordinated battle formations between units awkward and difficult to control. There was no concept of formations and tactics common to all who served in the Continental Army. A great example occurred at Brandywine as General Sullivan desperately tried to reorganize battle lines to fight off a British attack on the American flank. That all changed at Valley Forge when Baron Friedrich von Steuben, a Prussian military officer, stepped in with a plan to standardize training and drill for the entire American Army.

Von Steuben arrived at the winter encampment on February 23rd 1778. Washington, who had learned from experience to be wary of foreign officers, was nonetheless impressed by Von Steuben's shrewdness and candor, so he appointed Von Steuben as the temporary Inspector General of the Army. Von Steuben wasted no time setting new standards for the camp layout, sanitation, and conduct, including insisting that latrines be dug, facing downhill, on the opposite side of camp from the kitchens.

Von Steuben also became the Continental Army's chief drillmaster at Valley Forge. Although he spoke rudimentary English, Von Steuben still found ways to run troops through intense Prussian Army drills. The vastly undisciplined soldiers learned to quickly and efficiently load, fire, and reload muskets, conduct coordinated bayonet charges, and march in compact columns of four instead of being strung out in a long single file where it was challenging to keep stragglers in the file. Von Steuben developed a standard drill manual called "Regulations for the Order and Discipline of the Troops of the United States." This manual, also called the "Blue Book," remained the Army's official training manual until the War of 1812.

Another common myth about the winter encampment at Valley Forge is that hundreds of soldiers died and were buried there. This is due to stories and images of men starving, freezing, and dying of sickness. These ideas were especially prevalent during the Victorian age when people were typically obsessed with the macabre. One mass burial site identified during the Victorian Age is near Varnum's Quarters, just below the Washington Chapel along Route 23. A headstone marked with the initials "JW" was rumored to have marked the site. In 1901, the Daughters of the Revolution of 1776 commissioned a monument to be erected near the lone headstone containing the initials JW, identified as John Waterman's initials. Although it is called the Waterman Monument, the obelisk commemorates all soldiers "who sleep in Valley Forge."

The other rumored burial ground at Valley Forge was along Outer Line Drive as it winds around the bend from Wayne's Woods and his monument. An anonymous letter written in 1898 described how the ground had naturally eroded to unearth the skeletons of soldiers buried in a crouched position. This area is marked with a monument erected to commemorate these soldiers.

Although mass burial sites at Valley Forge make the encampment more interesting, the evidence for them is almost entirely circumstantial. Soldiers who became ill in the camp would have been immediately evacuated to outlying hospitals for treatment to contain, isolate and prevent the outbreak of a communicable disease from spreading through the camp. In addition, archaeological investigations conducted in the park failed to reveal any human remains at either of the above mentioned grave sites. The controlled digs did unearth several offal pits, where soldiers would have buried bones and waste from the livestock butchered for their meals. National Park Service historian Joseph Lee Boyle has gone on record to confirm that "no substantiated human graves have ever been found in the park".

John Waterman's supposed burial at the obelisk below Varnum's headquarters also has its problems. John, who was a quartermaster for the 2nd Rhode Island Regiment, died from smallpox, which was a highly contagious disease. He would have exhibited early signs of the infection and likely would have been immediately evacuated to an outlying hospital, where he would have been buried after he died. In addition, the headstone containing Waterman's initials was removed from the field near Varnum's headquarters in 1939, and the original site has been lost to antiquity. The Victorian interest in death and graves naturally led to the fabrication of Valley Forge ghost stories based on vague reports that ghostly campfires and the ghosts of Revolutionary soldiers were visible on the hillsides during stormy nights.

Despite the harsh conditions, disease, and ghosts, Valley Forge is sometimes considered the birthplace of the American Army. When the Army broke camp in June to pursue General Clinton's Army across New Jersey, the ragged, battle-weary, half-starved troops that limped into Valley Forge emerged with a rejuvenated spirit. Better trained, provisioned, and organized, the Army was transformed into a formidable fighting force that could face their British foe with poise and confidence and more than hold their own on future battlefields.

Continental troops established a key outpost at Radnor. Its headquarters was the Friends Meeting House, part of the same fieldstone building that survives today at Conestoga and Newtown Roads. The military and intelligence surveillance of the neighborhood, in fact, of the entire country between Matson's ford on the Schuylkill and the market towns of Darby and Chester to the south, was of great importance to General Washington, who was encamped from December until June of 1777-1778 at nearby Valley Forge. The Radnor' picquet', which worked closely with another smaller post at Newtown Square, was commanded by the cream of the American military. General Stirling, Colonel Morgan, General

Potter, and Colonel Bigelow, a veteran of the Lexington Alarm, were all detailed to Radnor. Colonel Stewart of the Pennsylvania Line also did patrol duty in the neighborhood.

Another picket consisting of an element of Potter's scouts organized to prevent the British from plundering the countryside was established at the Blue Bell Inn along Darby Road. On November 12th Cornwallis, with 3,000 troops, crossed the Middle ford and began a march toward Chester. Along the way, they passed the inn where the column was allegedly fired on. The British rushed into the tavern, bayonetted five scouts, and took the remaining scouts prisoner. The tavern still stands today and is located at 7303 Woodland Avenue.

Marine Corps Tie-In…The Senior Drill Instructor.

In my last full year of Drill Instructor Duty, I worked two platoons as a Senior Drill Instructor, and I gave each platoon the Senior Drill Instructor's Speech:

"Sit up straight and get your eyeballs on me! My name is Staff Sergeant Moyer, and I am your Senior Drill Instructor. I am assisted in my duties by Drill Instructor Staff Sergeant… and Drill Instructor Staff Sergeant… Our mission is to train each one of you to become a United States Marine. A Marine is characterized as one who possesses the highest military virtues. He obeys orders, respects his seniors, and strives constantly to be the best in everything that he does. Discipline and spirit are the hallmarks of a Marine. Each of you can become a Marine if you develop discipline and spirit. We will make every effort to train you, even after some of you have given up on yourselves. Starting right now, you will treat all Marines with the highest level of respect, for we have earned our places as Marines, and we will accept nothing less than that from you. We will treat you as we do our fellow Marines: with firmness, fairness, dignity, and compassion. At no time will you be physically abused or verbally threatened by any

Marine or recruit. If anyone should abuse or mistreat you, I expect you to report such incidents immediately to me or one of my drill instructors. Further, if you believe I have mistreated you, I expect you to report it to your series commander, Captain Thornton. From now on, my drill instructors and I will be with you every day and everywhere you go. I have told you what my drill instructors and I will do. From you we demand the following: You will give percent of yourself at all times. Obey all orders quickly, willingly, and without question. Treat all Marines and recruits with courtesy and respect. You will not physically abuse or verbally threaten any Marine or recruit. Be completely honest in everything you do. A Marine never lies, cheats, or compromises. Respect the rights and property of others. A Marine never steals. You must work hard to strengthen your body. Be proud of yourself and the uniform you wear. Above all else, never quit or give up. We offer you the challenge of Recruit Training and the opportunity to become United States Marines."

The Senior Drill Instructor billet comes with its own unique set of responsibilities, and a Senior, by necessity, needs to transition into a more accommodating role with the recruits. As a Senior, I was responsible for the health, welfare, training, and success of the recruits as well as a team of Drill Instructors. My J-Hat taught most of the Drill Manual, and I would step in only if needed. I never corrected or countermanded the J-Hat while he was teaching. I would no longer be expected to portray the intense and insane Drill Instructor and had to become more approachable for the recruits. Seniors take on more of a mentorship role with the recruits and Drill Instructors, and there were times when I was expected to sit down with them, remove my cover, and teach from a more humanistic approach. Although it was customary for Senior Drill Instructors, staff personnel, and officers to sit during chow, I never did.

One morning during chow, I supervised my third-phase recruits as they ate breakfast. By this point in the cycle, they were on autopilot for most routine events and were generally led by the platoon guide and squad leaders. It was a low-key morning with none of my Drill Instructors sharking tables and kicking stress. Even as a Senior, I stood up instead of partaking in the chow hall mess or merely sitting at a table, and I did this for a couple of good reasons. I remember seeing a Senior from another battalion who always sat in the chow hall while his recruits ate, shoving food in his face as fast as his recruits did. As I wondered how he could buckle the iconic black duty belt around his fat waist; I was determined I would never be that guy. Another chow hall observation makes me shudder even as I recall it, making me glad I never partook of depot cuisine.

While I was a Drill Instructor in San Diego, the Marine Corps was phasing out some occupational specialties and farming them out to private contractors, including food service. A food service company was awarded the contract to provide workers for the depot chow halls, and judging by the aptitude of some of the employees; the company was not too particular about who they hired. We suddenly had problems that we were not used to dealing with. The food service employees began side hustles selling cigarettes and contraband to recruits, and some of the female employees were rumored to have sold themselves to recruits.

One female food service employee, in particular, was well known for her infatuation with the hats, and we would often catch her staring at them with melancholy eyes or clandestinely attempting to snap pictures of them with her flip phone. She was pudgy, had short, ratty hair, and wore heavy makeup that looked like a three-year-old had plastered it on her face. One morning, while observing my platoon in the chow hall, I caught the woman staring at a hat in my training company. She was wiping the same spot at the same table for several minutes without looking down at the table once. The hapless Drill Instructor she was in love with was the incessant brunt of many jokes and course remarks for several cycles.

During my first Senior cycle, I had a young J-hat who was decidedly more hands-on with the recruits than what was probably suitable for the progression and preservation of his career. However, I had warned him several times of the adverse effects an allegation from a recruit could have on a Marine's career.

One afternoon, I worked on admin tasks in my duty hut when a rude and urgent slapping sound outside the hatch disrupted me. When I opened the hatch, I came face to face with a red-faced and visibly distressed recruit who immediately blurted the most disconcerting words heard by a hat on the depot: "I want to make an allegation on my Drill Instructor."

Without hesitation, I ordered the recruit into my office to calm him down and investigate the nature of his allegation. The recruit immediately stated that the J-hat had assaulted him with a footlocker. Finding the recruit's statement a bit far-fetched, I told him to take a breath and think about what really happened. The recruit repeated the allegation and added that he was afraid to return to training. Usually, a good Senior Drill Instructor can persuade a recruit to retract an allegation, and a really good Senior can even convince a recruit that he was in the wrong. I could not do either with this recruit, who soon requested permission to speak with the series commander.

Exasperated, I happened to glance in the direction of the J-hat's desk, and a McDonald's meal he hadn't had an opportunity to indulge in was sitting beside his drill manual. An idea quickly sprung into my brain and I told the recruit to have a seat at the desk in front of the meal. As I began talking with the recruit about the possibility that he may have inadvertently gotten too close to the Drill Instructor, he must have caught a good whiff of the burger or fries as I intended because I saw his eyes shifting toward it.

I asked the recruit if he missed eating a good cheeseburger and fries, to which he hesitantly affirmed with a slight head nod. I told him he could have whatever was in the bag, but he had to wolf it down quickly. By the time the recruit had downed the combo meal and licked his fingers clean, I almost had him convinced that the Drill Instructor had accidentally struck him. Inviting the recruit to wash the meal down with the large Coke was the proverbial straw that broke the camel's back. By the time he began gulping away at the Coke, the recruit was positive he had carelessly gotten too close to the Drill Instructor and got in his way.

The recruit was almost finished with the Coke when the duty hut door swung open, and the J-hat stormed in to see the recruit sitting in his chair, feet propped on the desk, sipping away at his Coke. Red Faced, the Drill Instructor was about to explode on the recruit when I put my hand up and told him to take a walk. The recruit finished his cold, bubbly beverage and returned to training; the J-hat came back to protest the ill-treatment of his dinner.

There was no way I was going to believe that a flying footlocker struck the recruit, but I did believe that the hat likely struck him, as evidenced by the red welts on the recruit's face. Before I allowed the Drill Instructor to get too excited during his explanation of the alleged event, I calmly asked him, "What are you going to value more right now...your career or a Happy Meal"? The Drill Instructor paused for a few seconds before grudgingly acknowledging that the Happy Meal Likely saved him from investigation and possible Relieved for Cause (RFC), a career-ender for any Marine on the receiving end of this instrument of good order and discipline.

During the same cycle, one of my Drill Instructors was a brand-new hat that we picked up at the Weapons and Field Training

Battalion. The DI was a seasoned, very professional Marine who had already completed a successful tour as a Marine Recruiter. The Drill Instructor was an instant menace to the recruits, and he viciously slayed them at every opportunity he had on quarterdecks and in sandpits. One morning, the hat was busily thrashing ten recruits at a time outside the squad bay when I heard him scream Senior Drill Instructor! Thinking a recruit was injured or worse, I ran out onto the catwalk, which overlooked the pit where the hat was conducting IT. When I asked what was going on, the hat exclaimed, "One of the recruits is running toward the front gate"! I said, "Go get him!" As the new Drill Instructor attempted to run down the recruit, I sent the other nine recruits away, then called and alerted the guard shack at the main gate. The new hat became a J-hat after his first full cycle and a Senior the next. After his senior cycle, he was promoted to Gunnery Sergeant and became a Chief Drill Instructor before being assigned as the battalion's Drill Master. The gunny was eventually selected as an instructor at DI School. I told him once that I was confident that he would become Sergeant Major of the Marine Corps one day, and he looked at me and replied, "I know". He was not boasting; he was simply confident that he would one day be appointed SMMC. In May 2023, that Drill Instructor was appointed as the Marine Corps' 20th Sergeant Major of the Marine Corps, replacing the SMMC who was once my Drill Instructor in 1993.

Toward the end of my last Senior cycle, I was preparing a Drill Composition Card for Final Drill the following day, and it had to be scrubbed one final time because changes could not be made to the platoon composition once the card was submitted. I had sent my hats home because the last thing I wanted them to do was kick stress when I needed the platoon to be focused and smooth for the following day. I had planned to pull the platoon together in the evening, work through the Final Drill Cards, and then show them a clip from a comedy movie to get them loose but not too loose. I had a Follow-Follow platoon that cycle, and it was larger than a usual summer platoon due to the OIF surge. Follow-Follow was usually the largest platoon in the training company anyway, and it served as a net for recruits dropped from other platoons. I didn't have lofty expectations of winning Final Drill but did not want to place last, which is called 'taking booger' on the depot.

I went through some administrative tasks with the platoon and then asked if there were any recruits who didn't think they could go out and whip it on when I took the X in the morning for the Final Drill event. I was about to turn on the movie clip when I saw a hand raise among the massed recruits. I said, "Speak freak," and waited impatiently to hear what the recruit had to say so I could quickly dismiss it and move on. The recruit very hesitantly requested permission to go to sick call in the morning, which would have automatically disqualified him from participating in Final Drill. I ordinarily would have had little issue removing a recruit from the Drill Comp but this recruit was one of the best I had in terms of close order drill in the platoon. I said, "Why do you need to go to sick call?" the recruit replied, "It's personal, Sir, I am embarrassed to say out loud." I said, "You will tell me, and you will right now." As I demanded an answer, the recruit became more agitated and disheveled. Finally, he burst out, "Sir! This recruit reports that last night this recruit had a problem with his butthole, so he asked the witchdoctor (the recruit designated to hand out Band-Aids and salves) for some ointment... Sir! My butt is on fire!"

I quickly bit my lip and hid my face in my campaign cover. I was on the verge of completely losing my bearing while the platoon, struggling with theirs, lost the battle and gave in to spontaneous laughter. The recruit went to sick call the next day, and the platoon did not win Final Drill, but the recruits didn't booger either. The moral of the story...there are more soothing ointments to use on an inflamed hemorrhoid than Tiger Balm.

Places to visit in or near Tredyffrin, Pennsylvania.

Start your historical tour of Tredyffrin at Valley Forge National Historical Park, which encompasses over 3,500 acres of rolling hills, historical homes, and monuments. With over twenty miles of trails within the park, it serves as a central hub, with access to miles of connecting trails. The Sullivan's Bridge to Joseph Plumb Martin Trail at County Line Road and Valley Forge Road intersects with the Schuylkill River Trail. This trail runs south to Philadelphia with the Chester Valley Trailhead in Norristown, running west to Exton. The trail north leads to Phoenixville Near Oaks and links up with the Perkiomen Trail, which runs north to Reading.

For the ultra-trail enthusiast, a trailhead to the Horseshoe Trail will take you on an extended journey west to Dolphin, Pennsylvania. There, it connects with the Appalachian Trail, where one can hike south to Georgia or north to Maine...you choose!

If you decide to stick to the trails in the park, they will lead you on an incredible journey through history as you visit Washington's headquarters at The Potts House, the headquarters of Knox, Lafayette, Varnum, and Maxwell, along with the Maurice Stephens House, which served as officer's quarters. Tour examples of the meager log huts the troops would have spent the winter in and visit over 40 monuments and memorials spread throughout the park, including the United States National Memorial Arch. An online calendar will provide visitors with dates of events held at the park throughout the year, highlighted by the mid-December "March In," where reenactors dressed in period uniforms muster. Visitors can take the 'oath of enlistment' with the soldiers and march a short distance to exhibition camp cabins.

Outside the park's boundary, you can travel a short distance to Wayne, Pennsylvania, and visit the historic Old Eagle Graveyard, where Continental soldiers, militiamen, and Loyalists are interred together in peace. Many soldiers buried in this graveyard lay in unmarked graves, but five Revolutionary War graves are marked with a headstone and an American flag. Beside the headstone of another grave, the Union Jack waves, a testament to this person's loyalty to the King during the revolution. A large boulder has also been placed in the graveyard. Four bronze plaques commemorating these brave Americans have been affixed to the boulder.

Finally, swing into Valley Forge Military Academy and Collage, where you will find an 18th-century mortar, buildings named for Revolutionary War generals, and the World War II Battle of the Bulge Monument. Walk into Richard King Mellon Hall and turn left into the office of the curator of the academy's small museum. Tour the museum and the rest of Mellon Hall, check out the historic chapel with its beautiful stained-glass windows depicting American battles and heroes, and ask about the building's cornerstone, which was once part of the White House. Walk down the hill to Wheeler Hall, the barracks where the movie Taps, starring Tom Cruise, was filmed and then onto Eisenhower Hall. Take in this building's beautiful paintings, busts of American presidents, and rich architecture. Finish your academy visit in the Reviewing Area on the parade field where three American Presidents once stood watching the cadets march Pass and Reviews in their honor.

Valley Forge National Historical Park the Visitor Center and parking are located at 1400 North Outer Lane Drive King of Prussia, Pennsylvania.

Old Eagle School Graveyard is located at 1 Private Way Wayne, Pennsylvania.

Blue Bell Inn is located at 7303 Woodland Avenue, Philadelphia, Pennsylvania.

Valley Forge Military Academy and College is located at 1000 Eagle Road Radnor, Pennsylvania.

General Stirling's Headquarters is located at 553 Yellow Springs Road, Malvern, Pennsylvania

General Wayne Headquarters is located at 14 Walker Rd Wayne, Pennsylvania.

Newtown Square, Pennsylvania

"The war does not end when you come home. It lives on in memories of your fellow soldiers, sailors, airmen and Marines who gave their lives. It endures in the wound that is slow to heal, the disability that isn't going away, the dream that wakes you at night, or the stiffening in your spine when a car backfires down the street".

~Barack Obama, 44th President of the United States of America

By late October, Potter had established his headquarters in the house of Mr. Garrett in Newtown, near the Radnor township line. By November 13th he had moved his headquarters to a house belonging to Mr. Lewis on Goshen Road in Newtown. Also quartered in the house was Major John Clark Jr. a Pennsylvanian on General Greene's staff who had been attached to Potter's militia. To prevent British foraging parties from requisitioning valuable supplies outside of Philadelphia, Washington wrote to General John Armstrong to order Potter and 600 Pennsylvania militiamen to interrupt "the enemy's intercourse with vessels on both the Delaware and Schuylkill Rivers and with the inhabitants of Chester County."

In other words, Potter was ordered to intercept convoys, seize British Army dispatches, and conduct long patrols out of Newtown Square, a base of operations specifically recommended by Washington, to prevent country provisions from falling into British hands. Potter was ordered not to get bogged down but to strike swiftly, surely, and then move on. Any locals found provisioning the British were to be punished by death according to a decree enacted by Congress. Finally, citizens of Chester County who had not taken the oaths of allegiance and abjuration to the Crown were subject to seizure of what weapons and extra clothing they might possess. Potter's boldness and diligence in intercepting the forage parties sent out from Philadelphia was appreciated by Washington, who frequently commended him for his actions. As vigilant as Potter and his men were in the performance of their duties, neither the Radnor outpost nor Potter's men at Newtown engaged or detected a lightning raid made on December 11th by troops under Cornwallis' command that cut a devastating swath through Radnor resulting in livestock, provisions, clothing, liquor, small valuables, and 1,000 fence rails seized by the British.

James Fitzpatrick, also known as Sandy Flash, was Newtown's very own Robin Hood or highwayman, depending on which side of the war one was on. He conducted his rogue operations in Chester and Delaware counties during the Revolutionary War. In 1775, Sandy volunteered for the Continental Army and joined one of the Pennsylvania Flying Camps. He served at Long Island with the Pennsylvania militia in the summer of 1776, where he was wounded in battle. Fitzpatrick deserted the Army after he was flogged as punishment for some minor infraction. He swam across the Hudson River under the cover of darkness and made his way to his home in present-day Ridley Creek Park. He wasn't home for very long when he was arrested in Philadelphia. Sandy was released from the Walnut Street jail on the condition that he rejoin the Army, which he did; then he promptly deserted a second time. In September 1777, Patriot militia from Wilmington, Delaware, attempted to arrest him at a farm where he worked, but Sandy threatened them with a rifle and forced them to flee.

When Howe invaded Chester County in September 1777, Sandy joined the British Army, guided troop movements, and fought at the Battle of Brandywine against his former compatriots. After the battle, he roamed Chester and Delaware County (then a part of Chester County), waylaying and robbing Whig militia officers and tax collectors whom he had an apparent distaste for while working as a British scout. Although he was known to call himself a captain, there is no evidence that he ever held a British military commission, much less commanded troops.

After the British withdrew from Philadelphia in June 1778, Sandy stayed near his home and continued to harass the Continental Army and its supporters in the area, waging a personal war against Whigs.

Occasionally, he rode with the Doan Outlaws of Bucks County and partnered with fellow outlaw and boyhood pal Mordecai Dougherty. He and Dougherty established a hideout at Hand's Pass near Coatesville and began his vendetta with the Whigs and the rich in earnest, becoming notorious for his audacity. After robbing two tax collectors, Sandy stripped them, tied them to trees, and flogged them. On another occasion, he captured a militia officer who prided himself on his long hair. After stealing the officer's weapons, Sandy cut off the man's hair as an added insult. He once purportedly walked into a Kennett Square tavern crowded with Whigs, who were busy bragging about what they would do to Fitzpatrick once they caught him. Sandy ordered a drink, but before he was recognized, he drew a pistol and backed out, covering himself before disappearing into the woods. On yet another occasion, Sandy attended a public meeting unarmed and in disguise and captured another boastful militia officer after fooling him into thinking that an iron candlestick was a pistol.

Although Sandy was well-known for harassing and intimidating the Whigs and the rich, he was never accused of murdering or seriously wounding anyone. Like Robin Hood, Sandy cultivated a reputation for gallantry among some locals. He was even reported to have given gifts to the poor and reputedly never stole from the poor or mistreated a woman. According to a local legend, Sandy was chased to his home by American soldiers where he and his mother lived in a log cabin along the Crum Creek, near the present-day Springton Reservoir. He eluded his pursuers and went to Castle Rock, which became another base for his operations. It was rumored that he buried a substantial treasure in the Castle Rock area, a rocky hill in the eastern part of Edgmont near Crum Creek, but no treasure has ever been found. The rock formation is on private property but can easily be viewed from the roadside, but the cave was blasted shut in the 1930s to prevent treasure seekers from injuring themselves.

The house at the corner of Newtown Street Road and Goshen Road was used as a tavern in the 1700s and also served, at times, as a hideout for vagabonds. Although Sandy's usual victims were Whig tax collectors, he did not overlook wealthy landowners and merchants. He also had a propensity for knocking over a tavern when the till was filled with cash. One local legend has it that he held up the Old President Inn at the intersection of West Chester Pike and Providence Road. Particularly mortified, the patrons Sandy had intimidated with drawn pistols were members of a posse who had been out searching for him and dropped in for a quick drink. Sandy came in, ordered a drink, tossed it down, and left before anyone recovered from their astonishment. Although this story adds to Sandy Flash's colorful reputation, there are problems with dates. The small log house Joseph Griffith built, which eventually became the Old President Inn, was built in 1798, twenty years after Sandy was tried and executed for his crimes. Perhaps the most interesting, documented crime that took place in the old Inn didn't happen until 1966 when a regular patron, disgruntled at being thrown out of the tavern too many times, convinced an accomplice to break a side window and throw home-made Molotov cocktails into the building. The old inn miraculously survived the fire-bombing and exists today as an Italian restaurant called La Locanda.

Things took a turn for the worse for the man called Sandy Flash when, on August 23rd 1778, he entered the Edgmont home of Militia Captain Robert McAfee (present-day Edgmont Square Shopping Center) in order to rob him. McAfee and a servant girl, Rachel Walker, subdued the infamous outlaw after a struggle when Sandy put down his weapons to pull on a pair of McAfee's shoes. When he was turned in to local authorities, the Supreme Executive Council of the Commonwealth of Pennsylvania split the 1,000-pound bounty offered for his capture between McAfee and Walker. On September 15th at the original Chester County Courthouse (which still stands on the Avenue of States in Chester), Sandy Flash was convicted of burglary, theft, and highway robbery, crimes to which he confessed, and was sentenced to be hanged. He attempted to escape from prison, filing off his irons and getting out of his cell, but was caught. He was sent to a more secure jail in Philadelphia, where he managed to get out of his wrist irons twice more prior to his date with the county executioner at the gallows.

On September 26th Sandy was hanged from a tree at Gallows Hill at the intersection of Edgmont and Providence Avenue, but the public execution was botched. The rope used to hang him was too long; when he dropped from the gallows, his toes touched the ground, allowing him to take pressure off his airway. The hangman had to climb onto Sandy's shoulders to force him down, strangling him to death. Sandy's confederate, Mordecai Dougherty, was never captured and is thought to have fled to Canada. Shortly after Sandy danced his jig at the end of a rope, Tory sympathizers burned Captain McAfee's haystacks and maimed his horses. McAfee received 200 pounds in compensation from the revolutionary government in 1783.

The Square Inn is one of the most important surviving historic buildings in Newtown Township. The inn still stands at the corner of Goshen and Newtown Street Roads, which was the town's central square in the 18th Century. The evidence that the preserved section was built in 1742 by Francis Elliot may be discovered by examining several 18th-century Chester County Tavern License Petitions. Apparently, by November 24th 1741, Francis Elliot "of the Township of Newtown" Chester County was living in a house built on the corner where the Square Inn now stands. This is evidenced by Elliot's 1741 Petition, where he requests a "license... to keep a publick House of

Entertainment, at the Intersection of Darby (Newtown Street) and Goshen Great Roads." He complains, "Your petitioner is frequently burthened with Travelers on the Sd Roads and the approaching season of the year (is) like to mate it more So to be."

Toward the close of the seventeenth Century, a group of Welsh settlers moved into the area known as Radnor Township. In 1704, the settlers petitioned the Society for the Propagation of the Gospel in England for prayer books and a Bible written in Welsh, especially for a Welsh-speaking missionary. In 1714, some of Radnor's inhabitants began constructing a beautiful stone church named Saint David's Church after the Patron Saint of Wales. The cornerstone was laid on May 9th 1715. During the prelude to the Revolutionary War, a wave of resentment against the Church of England swelled among the patriots of the congregation. One of these patriots was Anthony Wayne, who faithfully served his country throughout the Revolutionary War and eventually became Commander in Chief of the Army after Washington was elected President of the United States. During the war, the church provided shelter for soldiers on both sides of the conflict.

Marine Corps Tie-In...Going on Quota- A Well Earned Respite?

As demanding and physically challenging as Drill Instructor Duty had been, after eight cycles of spending hours on the parade deck, mini-grinding, PT, and eight crucible events, it was time for me to go on quota. Nearly all hats go on quota at some point during their assignment at the depot, and it provided transitioning Drill Instructors a much-needed opportunity to reprogram themselves to be normal Marines before returning to the fleet since no dignified Lance Corporal wants to be on the receiving end of a 'knife hand.' A few Senior DIs roll into Chief Drill Instructor positions while fewer still become Drill Masters or Drill Instructor School Instructors. Most are assigned to the Training and Support Battalion for Platform Instruction, MCMAP, Swim Qualification, and other support roles.

Two hats are assigned to the Weapons and Field Training Battalion as a liaison with platoons training on the rifle range and during the crucible at Edson Range on Camp Pendleton. I was assigned as the platoon sergeant for Weapons and Field Marines while my counterpart coordinated the crucible events.

The Weapons and Field platoon provided basic combat instruction for the training companies. It ran an M-249 Squad light Machine Gun familiarization fire, an unguided, man-portable, disposable, shoulder-fired, recoilless, anti-tank weapon (AT-4) Familiarization fire, the Confidence Chamber, and a non-fire combat infiltration course. In addition, the platoon was responsible for setting up and maintaining the ranges and targets recruits used.

Of the two live fire ranges conducted, the AT-4 range was the most controlled and scrutinized and drew a host of VIP spectators for every live rocket firing. I performed the collateral duty of Range Safety Officer for both live-fire ranges, but since a live rocket was fired during every AT-4 firing event, I was required to draw a sidearm and ammunition from the armory and escort the rocket from the Ammunition Supply Point where they are stored, to the range where it was to be fired because the rocket had to be under constant armed guard until it was fired. Usually, the fam-fire is executed very well and has few issues; only one recruit in the training company fires a live rocket while the rest fire 9 MM tracers through an AT-4 trainer, considerably reducing the risk of a mishap. The recruit chosen for the live rocket shot is usually the recruit who obtained the highest score during rifle qualification the previous week.

When the recruits finished their Tracer Training block, they were seated on bleachers placed in a safe area so they could observe the live rocket shot. Two reliable Marines very carefully controlled the procedure on the firing line. Once the live rocket was unpacked, I transitioned to the tower to clear and control the range for the shot. A call must go out to Range Control and PMO to alert them to the live fire sequence. A stop-move and no-fly order is issued base-wide to adjacent training areas to prevent anyone from entering the impact zone.

The company high shooter shouldered the AT-4 and carefully went through the firing procedures while a line NCO ensured the business end of the AT-4 was always facing down range in a safe direction. The recruit was instructed to aim at a tank hulk at least 700 meters distant. The range was cleared hot and the back-blast area was verified clear for the shot. As the recruit pressed the button of the three-stage trigger system, he inexplicably tilted the launcher forward, just before the rocket cleared the tube, sending the live warhead careening into the ground less than 50 meters from the firing line. As the warhead hit the ground and began to tumble, it broke into small pieces scattered down range in every direction. The issue wasn't that the rocket failed to impact the target or that it malfunctioned. The problem was that the rocket's warhead failed to detonate where it had finally settled and was laying somewhere on the range as unexploded ordinance (UXO).

Range Control was notified, the recruits were taken off the range, and most of the VIPs departed. As everyone hastily left the range, PMO and an Explosives Ordinance Disposal Team were called in to locate and destroy the warhead. It was a long, time-consuming task, but hours later, the warhead was eventually found and destroyed by a C4 charge, finally placing the range into a cold status. We were fortunate that the rocket broke up on impact approximately 50 meters from the Marines and the recruit on the firing line. They were well within the minimum safe distance of the warhead; had it exploded on impact, we would likely have had casualties. This is never good in a training environment, especially when involving recruits.

The Marines assigned to the Weapons and Field Training Battalion were not necessarily what I considered the cream of the crop. Most of the Marines were assigned to the battalion through the Corps Fleet

Assistance Program (FAP). The vast majority of Marines assigned to a FAP from an owning unit fall under a few categories, they are working through a family hardship, are on limited duty, they are transitioning out of the Marine Corps, or the command just wants them re-assigned because they are turds. Suffice to say, I spent a lot of time on brig visits, court hearings, and hospital visits supporting my Marines.

One afternoon, I got a call from the Provost Marshall's Office (PMO) that one of my Marines was going to be arrested and placed in the brig, pending unspecified charges. The Marine lived in base housing with his wife and young children. While the Marine worked on a range, his children played with an ammo can stored in the family's garage. When his spouse discovered that the ammo can was emitting an odd rattling noise, she called PMO. PMO responded with a bomb squad, which immediately isolated the can and conducted a careful investigation. Fortunately for the Marine's wife and young children, they didn't open the ammo can because when the bomb squad got it open, they discovered several very angry rattlesnakes. It turned out that the Marine went out onto the ranges and caught the snakes, which wasn't unusual because we inspected the ranges daily. Any snakes discovered would be caught, stored in ammo cans, taken into a remote field, and released to ensure a recruit wasn't bitten. Instead of releasing the snakes, the Marine illegally sold them to exotic pet stores.

A more gut-wrenching experience I had was when I attended a court hearing for a Marine who struck and killed young children walking along a road while driving under the influence of alcohol. I was no fan of the Marine or his selfish, senseless act and secretly hoped he would spend a lot of time in prison to reflect on the heinous act he had committed. The courtroom set-up was odd; the judge and attorneys were behind desks on the floor while the Marine was led in shackles to a caged area adjacent to the judge. The spectators were seated in an elevated seating area. I felt very awkward and conspicuous as I sat in uniform amongst the victim's family and supporters. It was an event I never want to witness again, and I couldn't help feeling deep sadness for the family while simultaneously feeling ashamed to represent the Marine charged with the senseless act. The victim's father could not contain his anger and anguish and had to be removed from the proceedings as he vehemently raged at the shackled Marine and even directed some of his anger toward me...and I could hardly blame him at all for his anguished outburst.

The last event I will share is one where one of the platoon members gained dubious celebrity status when he was featured on Date Line- to Catch a Predator. Evidently, the Marine had been chatting online with a girl who had disclosed she was 'underage' several times. The Marine continued to pursue the minor online and eventually set up a date at the girls' home...only the Marine wasn't chatting to an underage female; he was chatting with an adult posing as a teenager.

The Marine drove to the girl's home and entered the kitchen, where he was unexpectedly confronted by adults, cameras, and very uncomfortable questions. The Marine wasted no time and fled the scene but was quickly arrested before he cleared the garage by local law enforcement and detained. He was remanded to the custody of the Marine Corps pending trial, and it became my responsibility to drive him to California's Inland Empire for his arraignment.

The Marines who represented the platoon were not all terrible, and there were a few exceptions to the usually unfavorable quality of the FAP Marines. One of the exceptions was a very dependable young sergeant who was assigned to the FAP so he could deal with a family hardship. This young Marine's infant son was diagnosed with an aggressive cancer, and the child was being treated at nearby Balboa Naval Hospital in San Diego. The Marine was a real warrior; he handled daily issues with his section of Marines professionally and with an indomitable spirit, inspiring those who knew what he was battling in his personal life. Treatments were touch and go with the Marine's son, but the family courageously dug their heels in and held fast to the hope they had that the Lord would take the cancer from the child and restore his health and strength. I often visited the family at the hospital and supported them in any way I could. I was invited to attend the child's second or third birthday party, but soon after, I lost touch with the family after transitioning to the East Coast. I follow the sergeant and his family on social media and am happy to report that they are all doing well.

Historical places to visit in and near Newtown Square, Pennsylvania.

Many historical homes along this segment of the Patriot's Path are now private homes but can be easily viewed from the roadside, and several have historical plaques. Old Saint David's Church is a great place to visit the Revolutionary War patriots interred in its historic graveyard. The Square Inn is another beautifully preserved 18th-century building open for tours from spring to autumn. The Inn sits at the head of a trail that runs west into the countryside toward the White Horse Historic District. The 1798-era district consists of 15 contributing buildings, including a blacksmith shop. Castle Rock still exists and is easily accessible along a public road, but the rock formation is now located on private property.

Nearby Ridley Creek State Park is open to the public year-round. With multiple entrances around its boundaries, it is one of the more easily accessible parks in the area. Walk along Sandy Flash Lane or hike miles of improved trails through the park. More challenging routes on rugged trails crisscross the main thoroughfare and lead you on an adventure along Ridley Creek and through the woods. Visit the beautiful Hunting Hill Mansion built in the 18th Century or plan an interactive experience at the Colonial Pennsylvania Plantation. This working farm is open to the public from spring through autumn, and for a small fee, you can watch people dressed in period clothing doing everyday chores during the weekends.

Last but certainly not least, visit the Delaware County Veterans Memorial, located just north of Castle Rock along West Chester Pike. This breathtaking memorial was built as a tribute to all the brave American patriots who faithfully fought for freedom and liberty. It features an eternal fountain, statues, monuments, and 18 granite panels that provide a history of American wars and conflicts from the Revolutionary War to Operation Enduring Freedom.

Old Saint David's Church is located at 763 Valley Forge Road Wayne, Pennsylvania.

The Square Inn is located at North Newtown Street Road and Goshen Road Newtown Square, Pennsylvania.

Pratt Lewis Springhouse is located at 209 North Newtown Street Road Newtown Square, Pennsylvania.

The Samuel Caley House is located at 3523 Caley Road Newtown Square, Pennsylvania.

The Thomas Thomas House is located at 311 North Newtown Street Road Newtown Square, Pennsylvania.

The Nathan Newlin House is located at 103 Tanglewood Lane Newtown Square, Pennsylvania.

Fox Chase Inn is located at 3405 West Chester Pike Newtown Square, Pennsylvania.

Castle Rock is located along Castle Rock Road, Edgemont, Pennsylvania.

Richard Fawkes House is located at 5 Hidden Springs Circle Newtown Square, Pennsylvania.

Settler's House is located at Paper Mill Road Newtown Square, Pennsylvania.

Dunwoody Barn is located at 3500 West Chester Pike Newtown Square, Pennsylvania.

Skunk Hollow Park is located at 600 Darby Paoli Rd, Radnor, Pennsylvania.

Freight Station is located at 4200 West Chester Pike Drexel Lodge Newtown Square, Pennsylvania.

Ridley Creek State Park is located at 351 Gradyville Road Newtown Square, Pennsylvania.

Delaware County Veterans Memorial is located at 4599 West Chester Pike Newtown Square, Pennsylvania.

Eastown Township, Pennsylvania

"The safest place in Korea was right behind a platoon of Marines. Lord, how they could fight"!

~General Frank E. Lowe, Aide to President Truman during the Korean War

During the winter of 1777-78 and throughout the spring, communication with the Valley Forge Encampment by horse was protected via signals relayed by a network of sentinels posted high in trees growing on natural prominences. The signal Oak on the David Thomas Farm along Newtown Road in Newtown Township (the Aronimink Golf Club) was the first link in the chain. It stretched to a tree on a hill along Newtown Road above Scott's farm in Easttown (the outpost of Captain Henry Lee). It continued north to another tree on the east side of what is now Waterloo Road, Berwyn. The line of signals extended to a tree on a hill between the Old Lancaster Road (Conestoga Road) and what later became the Pennsylvania Railroad and onto another on a hill between the present Old State Road and Contention Lane. The line of sentinel trees ended on Mount Joy, the right flank of the American encampment at Valley Forge.

On the morning of January 18th 1778, a small detachment of less than a dozen American soldiers under Captain Henry Lee repelled an assault of around 200 British dragoons, commanded by the notorious Colonel Banastre Tarleton, on a wooded hill known as Signal Hill in Eastown Township. With the outbreak of the Revolutionary War, Colonel Henry 'Lighthorse' Lee, father of General Robert E. Lee, received a commission as a Captain of a Virginia dragoon detachment. This detachment was a unit of 1st Continental Light Dragoons. Lee fought in many Revolutionary battles, including the Battle of Paulus Hook, Edgar's Lane, Brandywine, Germantown, Guilford Court House, Eutaw Springs, and Yorktown.

In 1778, Lee, who had gained a reputation as a capable leader of small units, was promoted to major and placed in command of a corps of cavalry and infantry. This mixed unit became known as Lee's Legion. Lee's Legion served as Washington's bodyguard at the Battle of Germantown and was assigned to one of several outposts suggested by Washington while the Continental Army was encamped for the winter at Valley Forge. Its purpose was not only to provide intelligence for Washington and his staff but to harass British foraging parties during their efforts to obtain food and supplies for the British Army occupying Philadelphia. The detachment consisted of thirteen men from Colonel Theodore Bland's Virginia regiment.

Lee's headquarters at Scott's Farm was along Newtown Road, which happened to be one of the principal routes used by British foraging parties. The outpost was established on high ground overlooking the road, on the northeast corner near its intersection with Sugartown Road. A tall chestnut tree served as a sentry tree in a chain of signal trees for communication with Valley Forge, a stone house was used as a headquarters for the detachment, and a barn large enough to warehouse supplies captured from the British wagons was available. The outposts were so successful in disrupting British foraging, particularly those south of the Schuylkill River, that General Howe was determined to take action to protect his foraging parties. Through Loyalist spies, the location and size of Lee's detachment were known to the British. Howe ordered Colonel Tarleton to surprise and capture the isolated outpost. The British troops left Philadelphia on January 17th and spent the night at a farmhouse near Lee's headquarters.

Advancing to attack the following day, which was described as "a clear, crisp, cold January morning," Tarlton's Dragoons surprised the outpost's quartermaster and three men, who were out on a foraging expedition themselves and captured them before they could give any alarm. It was only when the British rode up on the hillside behind the house that the rest of the detachment became aware of their presence. The Americans only had time to barricade themselves in the house before the British attacked.

With Lee's headquarters quickly surrounded, Tarleton demanded the unconditional surrender of Lee and his entire party, adding that otherwise, he would set fire to the house and its occupants. Lee's reply to the British was comedic, "Who but a fool ever threatened to burn a stone house?" Lee conferred with his men, stating his intention to fight it out, and promised to recommend those who did likewise for promotion. All agreed to make a stand. In the meantime, the patriot owner of the property, who had been working in the barn, was able to get away unnoticed to try to get additional troops from a larger detachment of the Army quartered in the valley only about two miles to the north.

Tarleton's threat to fire the house was yet another fold in Revolutionary War history. On December 13th 1776, Tarleton commanded a reconnaissance patrol to gather intelligence on the movements of General Charles Lee (no relation to Colonel Lee) in New Jersey. Tarleton's patrol surrounded the house and forced Lee, still in a dressing gown, to surrender by threatening to burn down the house.

Captain Lee described his defense of the picket post in his report to General Washington. "We immediately manned the doors and windows," he reported, "the contest was very warm; the British Dragoons, trusting to their vast superiority in number, attempted to force their way into the house. So well directed was the opposition that we [also] drove them away from the stables and saved every horse; we have got the arms of their wounded; the enterprise was certainly daring, though the issue of it very ignominious. I had not a soldier for every window."

At one point in the encounter, Colonel Tarleton was within point-blank range of the carbine of Private O'Neil, only to be saved by a misfire and "flash in the pan." According to tradition, the end of the attack came when Lieutenant Lindsay, wounded in the hand at the beginning of the assault and unable to take part in the fighting, stood at an open window on the second floor, calling and beckoning to relief troops still some distance away, as though they were close at hand, encouraging them to hurry. The ruse was successful. Assuming that American reserves were nearby, the British became distracted and disengaged from the fight. Galloping their horses out of danger, they headed back to Philadelphia, but not before leaving a wake of destruction in their path.

The British losses were officially reported as four killed and four wounded. Major Tarleton came away from the skirmish with a wounded horse, a jacket full of buckshot, and the loss of his helmet. In a letter to Captain Lee's father a month later, General George Weedon wrote that five of the attacking party were killed, with several wounded. Other estimates have placed the British dead as high as twelve, all of them buried in an old Welsh graveyard that is located on the northwest corner of the intersection of Newtown and Sugartown Roads.

Henry Lee wrote to General Washington describing the skirmish:

"They were near two hundred. in number and by a very circuitous route endeavoured to Surprize me, in quarters. About day break, they appeared & we were immediately alarmd & manned the doors and windows. The contest was very warm, the British dragoons trusting to their vast superiority in number, attempted to force their way into the house. In this they were baffled by the bravery of my men. After having left two killed & four wounded they desisted and sheered off. We are trying to intercept them. Col. Stevens has pushed a part of infantry to reach their rear. So well directed was the opposition, that we drove them from the Stables & saved every horse. We have got the arms, some cloaks &c. of their wounded. The only damage at present know of is [a] slight wound received by Lt. Lindsay. I am apprehensive about the patroles The enterprize was certainly daring, tho the issue of it very ignominious. I had not a soldier for each window.

I have the honor to be with most perfect respect Your Excellency's most obt &c Servt

Henry Lee".

Three days after the skirmish, Washington wrote a personal letter to Lee, saying:

"Although I have given you my thanks in the general orders of this day for the late instance of your gallant behavior, I cannot resist the inclination I feel to repeat them again in this manner. I needed no fresh proofs of your merit to bear you in remembrance... Offer my thanks to the whole of your gallant party, and assure them that no one felt more pleasure more sensibly or rejoiced more sincerely for your and their escape, than yours affectionately, etc. George Washington."

Lee and Tarleton continued their revolutionary feud when the war shifted to the south. During one of their cat-and-mouse-like encounters known as The Battle of Haw River, or if you are a British partisan, Pyle's Massacre, on February 24th 1781, Lee pulled off an epic impersonation of his antagonist. Lee's Legion wore green uniforms remarkably similar to those of Tarleton's British Legion, and the British Legion encampment was only a mile away. When Lee's green-coated dragoons rode into their midst, it was natural for the Tories to assume they were Tarleton's men. Lee boldly rode before four hundred North Carolina loyalists, and the militia, eager to join General Cornwallis' army, had lined up for review. With Lee's cavalry by his side, he was enthusiastically greeted by the unit's commander, fifty-eight-year-old Colonel John Pyle, an Alamance County physician loyal to the crown who had actively raised the men to fight for the king. Lee paused to admire Pyle's militia, drawn up in review with their weapons harnessed or slung over their shoulders. As he shook the doctor's hand, he smiled. Pyle eyed the impressive cavalryman in a green uniform and immaculate trim, that of a British dragoon. He returned Lee's compliments in kind, saying, "Colonel Tarleton, it is a pleasure to meet you." Within moments, the killing began. With Pyle's column essentially surrounded, Lee's Legion opened their attack, killing 90 Tories and wounding 150 more.

After the Revolutionary War, President George Washington placed Lee in command of an army of approximately 13,000 militiamen to put down the Whiskey Rebellion in western Pennsylvania. Washington accompanied the army to western Pennsylvania, but a peaceful surrender was accepted, and there was no fighting. In 1798, Henry Lee was appointed a major general in the U.S. Army. He petitioned President James Madison for a commission at the onset of the War of 1812 but without success. Lee settled into public service as the 9th governor of Virginia.

Although able to avoid several attempts of being captured by Lee, Colonel Tarleton fared far worse than his antagonist during the remainder of the war. On January 17th 1781, Tarleton's forces were virtually destroyed by General Daniel Morgan at the Battle of Cowpens, famously depicted in the movie *Patriot*. William Washington, cousin of George Washington, commanded the American cavalry at the Cowpens when Tarleton and two of his dragoons attacked him. Washington countered the attack with his saber, shouting, "Where is now the boasting Tarleton?" Washington survived the encounter and, in the process, wounded Tarleton's right hand with a saber blow. In the exchange, Tarleton managed to crease Washington with a pistol shot that also injured his mount. Tarleton and his men scattered, and Washington pursued them about sixteen miles before giving up the chase.

After the Cornwallis surrendered the British forces at Yorktown, the senior British officers were invited to dinner by their American captors. The only one who did not get an invitation was Tarleton. He returned to Britain on parole and finished the war at the age of 27.

Marine Corps Tie-In...NROTC Villanova University.

After a relatively routine deployment with Second Battalion, Sixth Marines, I returned to the States. I was contemplating my next career move when I stumbled upon a rare opportunity to work on a college campus for three years. My wife and I had been married for several months, and we recently found out that she was pregnant with our first child. The timing for an opportunity to be undeployable for a few years could not have come at a better time if I was selected for the prestigious duty.

To be selected for duty at an NROTC Unit as its Assistant Marine Officer Instructor (AMOI), a Marine has to have successfully completed a tour as a Drill Instructor, be promotable, and be in good standing with their parent unit. Once selected, the monitor assigns you to a university or the Naval Academy. Although, as part of the package, you list the available schools in the order you want to be assigned, it is infrequent that a Marine selected for the duty is assigned to a school inside the top ten of their lists. I submitted my package to the special duty monitor and chose Villanova University, the University of North Carolina, and Cornell as my top three schools.

While I waited for the disposition of my AMOI package, my wife and I found out that her pregnancy was considered high-risk. After deciding the best course of action would be for her to remain close to her family during and after the pregnancy, I called the special duty monitor and asked if he could possibly assign me to Villanova due to the possible hardship. The monitor was understanding but powerless to determine the outcome of the selection board. He told me the best he could do was forward my request to the board, who had the final say.

It was from a call from a Sergeant Major who had deployed to OIF as my platoon sergeant that I learned I was selected for the duty and had been assigned to Villanova University. It wasn't time for celebration because my current Sergeant Major insisted that I needed another deployment with the unit before executing orders. After trying to get my orders for special duty canceled and finding out he had no authority to do so, the disgruntled Sergeant Major attempted to send me to Afghanistan as a member of a Military Transition Team (MiTT). That effort failed when the Division Sergeant Major, for whom I had recently planned and organized the 2nd Marine Division Senior Enlisted Birthday Ball on behalf of my battalion Sergeant Major, who was supposed to plan and organize it, found out what was going on and promptly reassigned me as his Division Assistant Family Readiness Officer until it was time for me to execute my orders to Quantico.

On an evening when our training company at OCS was minutes away from stepping off on a twelve-mile night hike, my wife called to say that our baby was on the way and she was headed to the hospital. I jumped into my SUV and drove to Media, Pennsylvania, battling through four or five hours of D.C. and Route 95 traffic to get there in time. That night, I just made it in time to welcome our first daughter into the world. Since the OCS company was at the end of its first increment, I was authorized to take a couple of weeks of leave to help with the baby, but it wasn't enough time for my wife to recover from birthing our daughter. I called the Sergeant Major at OCS and asked if I could work the second increment the following year. Even though there were instructors slated for the bullpen that the Sergeant Major could have drawn from, he told me that I needed to return to Quantico to work the second increment. My wife decided to spend the second increment on base with me, so we packed up our new addition and headed to OCS, where we lived in a hotel room for six weeks. After the increment graduated, we headed south to Camp Lejeune to pick up my orders for Villanova before heading back home and settling in with our new daughter.

While serving as Villanova University NROTC Unit's AMOI, I had the unique privilege to help shape four years' worth of Villanova Marine Officers with the even more unique opportunity to see a freshman class all the way through the program to their graduation and commissioning. We ran a weekend training evolution for the Philadelphia consortium of Marine option midshipmen at Fort Indiantown Gap or Fort Dix-McGuire twice a year. The training evolution held in the fall was geared toward basic leadership and field skills for underclassmen, and the Spring evolution was planned with the upperclassmen in mind. I conducted training to prepare the seniors for The Basic School (TBS) upon graduation and the junior class for OCS that summer.

The NROTC Unit also attended a Military Excellence Competition (MEC) in Cornell and hosted its own MEC at Villanova every year. In the first three years, I worked at the university, we grew the number of participants in our event to a number much larger than it had been in the previous twenty years. I had my only disagreement with the Marine Officer Instructor I worked for, a Major and one of the finest officers I ever worked with in the Corps. We grew our MEC event to the point where we were inviting vendors and VIPs to participate. For the last MEC we planned, the Major had reached out for Miss Pennsylvania, a beauty pageant queen, to sing the National anthem to kick off the closing ceremony and award presentation. When it was time for the National anthem to begin, Miss Pennsylvania, who had shown up late, informed us she didn't sing; she only performed interpretive dancing. I didn't want her to go out in the middle of the floor and dance in front of everyone while we played the anthem over the P.A. system and asked her to kindly 'do her thing' off to the side. The Major was all for the young woman conducting her dancing routine in front of the massed formation of uniformed midshipmen; a disagreement between myself and the Major quickly escalated. I knew I was wrong to argue with a Major of Marines, especially in public, but I didn't want interpretive dancing included in my closing ceremony. The equally flabbergasted Major finally asked if we needed to take our argument outside, and I wisely let the issue drop, and I embraced the suck.

It was well known around the unit that 'the Gunny' liked his strong, black coffee, and nobody messed with Gunny's coffee pot. One year, I taught a freshman-level Military Science course, and I had one strictly enforced rule... nobody shows up late to Gunny's class. I had been teaching the class for around fifteen minutes when a Navy option freshman sauntered through the doors, disrupted the class, and immediately raised my ire. I stopped teaching and angrily pointed at the door for the freshman to leave. I followed the midshipman out of the classroom, and the student began to spout off about how important his education was and that fifteen minutes was not a big deal. I ordered the midshipman to stand outside my downstairs office until my classroom instruction was completed.

An hour and a half later, I finished the class and went to my office, where I found the belligerent freshman leaning against my wall. After ripping him for 'propping up my wall with his stinking carcass,' I marched off with my coffee pot in hand to fill it with water. On my way back to my office, I inadvertently dropped the pot, which shattered at the feet of the freshman when it hit the floor. I cleaned up my mess, ripped open my office door, and sat behind my desk. After a few minutes, I called him into the office to stand in front of my desk at the position of attention. As soon as the midshipman's heels came together, I addressed the freshman's behavior viciously and very loudly. About midway through my tirade, the kid carelessly shrugged his shoulders, let out an audible sigh, and rolled his eyes.

The Drill Instructor in me let loose in an even more explosive diatribe as the desk mysteriously levitated and then flipped over in front of the suddenly wide-eyed freshman. I stood on the overturned desk screaming at the unfortunate freshman, and uninvited spectators rushed down the hallway to see what was happening. I didn't even notice my commanding officer, a grizzled Marine Colonel, standing in the hallway. He patiently redirected foot traffic and kept people from my office until my verbal assault on the midshipman had ended. Eventually, the colonel came down the hall to my office, took a turkey peak in, and asked with a crooked grin, "You good, gunny"? as he pointed at a puddle the freshman had deposited on the yellow footprint mat he was standing on; I was so amped up I didn't even notice that the midshipman had apparently pissed himself. A few years after I retired and several years after the infamous butt-chewing episode, I chaperoned some Valley Forge Military Academy cadets at a National Day of Prayer luncheon Villanova NROTC students were also attending. A senior midshipman walked up to my table and introduced himself as the very freshman I ripped into four years prior; we had a happier time recalling the incident.

Graduation was always a special occasion because it also entailed commissioning a brand-new crop of Marine and Navy officers. A formal commissioning ceremony was held in the chapel, and the new officers lined up afterward to render their symbolic first salute. The Silver Dollar First Salute traditionally symbolizes transitioning from an officer candidate to a commissioned officer. The newly minted officer chooses an enlisted servicemember who has had the most significant impact on them to give them their "First Salute." As tradition goes, in return, the newly commissioned officer presents a Silver Dollar as a token of gratitude. This military tradition likely originated from British regiments garrisoned in America during the colonial years. However, during that era, the coin would not have been a "dollar" as we know it. Historically, some British traditions and customs were adopted by the newly formed American Army units in the 18th Century. In the British model during colonial times, new officers were assigned an enlisted adviser who 'showed them the ropes.' They taught them the history of the regiment they were assigned to and the ins and outs of customs and the military profession.

Newly commissioned Lieutenants compensated their enlisted adviser with a small amount of money. I have every one of the silver dollars my Marine option Midshipmen presented to me cased in a frame with their names pinned beneath. The monetary value of the silver will never supersede how special the shadowbox is to me or the Marine officers I helped forge. To be asked by a midshipman to render the first salute is a high honor and one I always took seriously. When the newly commissioned officer stepped in front of me, I rendered a smart salute and said congratulations, Sir or Ma'am. Marine and Navy options alike knew I strictly used Sir or Ma'am as a term of respect; I didn't say it because I had to say it; I said it out of respect for the officer facing me. Of all the first salutes I rendered, I only addressed one new officer as 'lieutenant' instead of the usual Sir or Ma'am, and everyone who heard it, including the new lieutenant, knew exactly why.

Historical places to visit in and near Eastown Township, Pennsylvania.

Schedule an appointment to tour historic Waynesborough. The beautifully preserved 18th-century mansion was the ancestral home of General Anthony Wayne. It is a popular venue for weddings, especially on the weekends, so it may be challenging to schedule a tour of the inside of the mansion. The grounds are open year-round if you want to get a closer look at the well-preserved colonial architecture. There are also several historical markers and plaques on the property to check out. The Tarleton School was the location of the skirmish fought between Tarleton's dragoons and Lighthorse Lee's picket post. The best time to visit this historic site is during the summer or on weekends since this is an active school. Another historic home in the area is the Finley House. The house was built in 1789 and was the home of Revolutionary War patriot Captain John Pugh. Today the home serves at the Wayne Historical Society and is open every Tuesday and Saturday for visitors to tour house and its unique exhibit of horsedrawn carriages, wagons, and sleighs.

Scott's Farm is located at 602 Newtown Road Berwyn, Pennsylvania.

The Tarleton School is located at 327 Waterloo Avenue Berwyn, Pennsylvania.

Waynesborough is located at 2049 Waynesborough Road Paoli, Pennsylvania.

The Covered Wagon Inn is located at 629 West Lancaster Avenue Wayne, Pennsylvania.

The Finley House is located at 133 West Beechtree Lane Wayne, Pennsylvania.

Lafayette Hill, Pennsylvania

"Find the enemy that wants to end this experiment (in American democracy) and kill every one of them until they're so sick of the killing that they leave us and our freedoms intact".

~ General James Mattis, 26th Secretary of Defense

In mid-May 1778, Washington ordered Lafayette to establish a Forward Operating Base (FOB) between Valley Forge and Philadelphia to provide security for the American main camp, conduct reconnaissance, and disrupt British supply and communication lines. On May 18th Lafayette led a force of 2,100 troops, five pieces of artillery, and a contingent of Oneida scouts across the Schuylkill River at Matson's ford and marched south on Ridge Road. On Barren Hill, Lafayette established his FOB, placing the guns on the high ground near Saint Peter's Church and orienting them south. A reinforced picket post was established at Ridge Road to the south of the church, and the Pennsylvania militia was sent to guard Germantown Pike to the Northwest. General Howe quickly learned that Lafayette's force was nearby when a spy embedded in Lafayette's command delivered detailed intelligence to him; acting on the information, Howe decided to attack.

Howe, who had been recently recalled to England, decided to take the opportunity to capture such a high-value target as Lafayette before departing Philadelphia and vowed to make him a prisoner of war. On May 19th 1778, around 10:30 PM, Howe ordered 'No Flint' Grant and a 5,000-man British force, including 15 artillery pieces, to march toward Lafayette's FOB on Barren Hill. Howe planned an indirect route to the junction of White Marsh Road and Ridge Road to repel any American reinforcements and cut off the likely line of retreat for Lafayette. Howe planned for 2,000 grenadiers and dragoons to move along Lafayette's left flank while another assault force would move into position on his right flank. Howe devised the plan to encircle Laffayette's FOB from three positions and trap them against the river. Howe ordered his assaulting forces to wait until morning and then attack and destroy or attack and capture all the Americans operating on Barren Hill.

On May 20th the British launched their attack. The undisciplined militia occupying outposts scattered at the sight of the British troops; they didn't offer any resistance and even failed to notify Lafayette of the impending attack. On Ridge Road, Lafayette finally learned of the British attack, but it was too late for him to devise a counter-attack strategy. Shortly after Lafayette learned of the pending attack from Ridge Pike, a militiaman who had been posted on Germantown Pike told him that the British had advanced up the White Marsh Road. The British were suddenly and very unexpectedly in close proximity to Lafayette's forces, and they seemed to be everywhere around him, but the young general kept his head about him and did not give way to panic. In an uncalculated and risky move, Lafayette decided to evacuate his FOB via a low road, dangerously placing the tactical high ground at his back. He knew of a small road that led back to Dickison ford that would hopefully bypass the British force. It ran along low ground, offering the Americans a concealed escape route from the attacking British. The British apparently did not know about the road, and Lafayette had a secure route to the fording area. Lafayette ordered his men to retreat down the road while a rear guard delayed the British at the FOB.

A few men were sent out in small teams spread across the forward edge of the battle space to engage and delay the British. These teams would fire and displace while another would advance and fire on the British, making them think the American force intended to stay and fight. Essential actors in the American delaying force were a contingent of around 50 Oneidas, whose primitive tactical expertise precisely described this type of guerilla warfare. The Oneidas were longstanding members of the Iroquois League.

They and the Tuscarora Nation were the only ones out of the six Nations representing the Iroquois League that were allied to the Americans during the war; the other four Nations remained allied with Britain. The Oneidas specifically engaged the mounted British dragoons, which posed the most danger to the retreating American patrol. Lafayette calmly and successfully led his retreating force to safety and slipped away with relatively few casualties, reporting nine killed or missing after they crossed the Schuylkill River and settled back in camp at Valley Forge.

Facing increased criticism from his countrymen and their politicians, Sir William Howe, rumored to be sympathetic to the American cause, to begin with, had already sent his resignation letter as commander in chief of the British Forces in America to London in October 1777. When Howe arrived in England on July 1st he and his brother faced national criticism for their failures in America. In 1779, Howe and his brother demanded that the parliament begin a formal inquiry into their military actions in colonial America. The inquiry that followed was unable to confirm charges that either of them mismanaged the war effort. Because of the parliament's failure to come to any conclusion in the Howe brother inquiry, the press continued to attack the Howe brothers in British pamphlets.

Marine Corps Tie-In...the Gunny and His Coffee.

I usually had a metal canteen cup full of robust and steaming-hot coffee in hand or within reach whenever I was on the Villanova University campus. During parade practice one cold, overcast October morning, I was working with the entire battalion of midshipmen, well over a hundred cadets who did not want to spend the morning with me in the cold. I was the NROTC unit's drill master. I was responsible for planning and preparing the midshipmen for parades, close-order drill competitions, and other ceremonial events, and we had a parade to rehearse for that morning.

The senior class advisor, a Surface Warfare Officer (SWO), was shadowing me on the parade field that morning for some reason or another. I eventually got frustrated with the Navy option midshipmen, some of whom refused even to take their hands from their pockets. In a grand effort to display my disgust for their poor performance and get their undivided attention, I hurled my mug of coffee across the parade field. The midshipmen knew of my love for coffee and thus took my brash display to heart. However, I was about to give in to a bout of pure insanity following the coffee cup act when some of them started to break out in laughter. Instead of losing my cool with them, I had to check my own bearing when I turned to see the SWO, coffee spatter staining his white uniform, march angrily toward his office. He had thrown his Styrofoam cup of Starbucks into the stiff wind after I had thrown my heavy iron mug across the field, thus dousing himself with his own brew.

I carefully maintained a rigid working relationship with the NROTC Unit's SWOs and I am sure 'Mr. Coffee' knew how I felt about SWOs in general, but he made efforts to try to get on my good side anyway. Sometime after the coffee catastrophe on the parade deck, he brought a bag of coffee to my office that I took as a peace offering. Though his gift didn't change my opinion of SWOs, I enthusiastically accepted the coffee. The coffee was packed in a black bag with a sticker of a red gorilla affixed to it, and a small white tag was inscribed, "Wake the 'F-bomb' Up Coffee." I opened the bag of coffee, and to my amazement, it smelled a little bit like marijuana.

I debated whether to risk brewing a pot or just throwing it in the trash when my boss, the Marine Major, came to my office frantically asking for coffee. I told him I was out of coffee except for the coffee that was recently given to me, and I explained my reluctance to brew it. He told me he was up all night studying for his MBA final and really needed the coffee. So, setting my apprehension aside, I brewed a strong pot of the stuff and took a steaming mug to the Major. About an hour later, the Major came into my office and shut the door, which he seldom did. Wide-eyed, he asked me if I knew what was in the coffee. When I told him I had no idea but harbored certain suspicions, he burst out, "I drank the whole cup of that coffee, but instead of becoming more alert and awake, I am sleepy...and I have the munchies!" I tried to keep a straight face and replied, "I don't know Sir, but I am not going to volunteer a sample for a urinalysis any time soon!" I don't know for sure if the coffee was laced, and I doubt that it was, but the black wrapper it was packaged in was neatly framed and hung up in the Major's office as a memento of the occasion.

Historical places to visit in and near Lafayette Hill, Pennsylvania

Begin your historical tour of this segment of the Patriot's Path at Saint Peter's Lutheran Church founded in 1752 by Henry Muhlenberg. Here, you will discover historical plaques and stone monuments marking Lafayette's FOB. You will find a monument dedicated to the Oneida scouts who fought here, as well as several graves of Revolutionary soldiers. Drive over to the Masonic Villages at Lafayette Hill and look for a memorial commemorating the Oneida Scouts in the rear parking lot. Just across Ridge Road, you will find a historical marker for the Battle of Barren Hill. If you are into statues of the Marque, there are several in the area. You will find one at the Hill at White Marsh and another at the Philadelphia Art Museum. If you don't mind a longer drive, you will find Lafayette statues at Lafayette Collage in Easton, Pennsylvania and Havre De Grace, Maryland. There is another in York and one at the Moland House in Warminster, Pennsylvania. The addresses for these locations are listed in subsequent chapters of the Patriots

Masonic Villages-Lafayette Hill is located at 801 Ridge Pike Lafayette Hill, Pennsylvania.

Lafayette Historical Marker is located at 2327 Barren Hill Road Lafayette Hill, Pennsylvania.

<u>Saint Peter's Lutheran Church</u> is located at 3025 Church Road Lafayette Hill, Pennsylvania.

<u>Statue at Lafayette College</u> is located at 730 High Street Easton, Pennsylvania.

<u>Statue of Lafayette</u> is located at the Philadelphia Museum of Art 2600 Ben Franklin Parkway Philadelphia, Pennsylvania.

<u>Statue of Lafayette</u> is located at the Hill at Whitemarsh 4000 Foxhound Drive Lafayette Hill Pennsylvania.

<u>Statue of Lafayette</u> is located at Legion Square 425 North Union Avenue Havre De Grace, Maryland.

Warminster, Pennsylvania

"In the Marine Corps, I was used to people doing what they said and saying what they mean. There was a higher purpose and calling in the Corps. Everyone works toward accomplishing something together, and there's a common goal. In entertainment, the same isn't always true. You're in it for yourself in Hollywood."

~Rob Riggle Captain of Marines, actor and comedian

While Washington and the Continental Army were in winter quarters at Valley Forge, Brigadier General John Lacey, Washington's second youngest general at the age of 22, was tasked with patrolling the region north of Philadelphia between the Delaware and Schuylkill Rivers to deny British foraging parties from operating in the area. Washington also ordered Lacey and the militia to prevent farmers from taking their goods into Philadelphia to sell to the British, who paid higher prices in gold, and to protect patriots in the region from harassment by British and Loyalist troops.

Washington was as critical of Pennsylvania's militia as he was with Lacey's performance. Despite promising 1,000 militiamen to patrol the Warminster region, Pennsylvania only raised a small fraction of that number, so Washington considered calling in militia from neighboring states to supplement Lacey's force. Washington wrote that "militia stipulated by the state had never been above half kept up and that General Lacey had only 70 men left in the field". In late April, Lacey began a series of maneuvers and patrols across Bucks County that ended with his arrival on April 27th at the Crooked Billet Tavern in present-day Hatboro. Lacey's men responded poorly, if at all, to repeated small-scale raids in their area of responsibility, and his troop movement to Crooked Billet made him vulnerable to a surprise attack.

In Philadelphia, General Howe ordered Colonel Simcoe to "secure the country and facilitate the inhabitants bringing in their produce to market." In April, Simcoe secured permission from Howe to launch a coordinated attack on Lacey and his militia. On the afternoon of April 30th he and Lieutenant Colonel Abercromby led their troops out of Philadelphia and marched towards the Crooked Billet Tavern. By then, Lacey's troop strength had improved to about 400, including fresh arrivals from Cumberland and York Counties. That night, Lacey ordered Lieutenant William Neilsen to begin a patrol between 2 and 3 AM and ordered Thomas Downey's brigade to stand on alert. Neilsen failed to follow his orders, and his patrol only left camp shortly before daybreak on May 1st. They had not gone far from the Crooked Billet when they spotted the advancing British troops.

Simco had planned a pincer-style attack, with his troops attacking from the north and east and Abercromby's troops from the south and west. Lacey's pickets, in place to warn against any type of threat, noticed the British troops but failed to fire off a warning shot for fear of being killed or captured. Neilsen sent a runner back to the camp to raise the alarm, but he never arrived. Lacey was sleeping in a nearby house and was awakened by musket fire when the attackers were only 200 yards away. Surprised and outnumbered, the militia were soon routed and forced to retreat into Warminster, losing their supplies and equipment at their bivouac site. As a result of this engagement, the American forces lost ten wagons full of much-needed supplies, and Lacey had almost 20% of his force killed, wounded, or taken prisoner. Lieutenant Nielson, the officer in charge of the pickets, was court-martialed and drummed out of the militia for disobeying orders. On May 11th General Potter returned from a leave of absence, and Lacey was subsequently relieved of his command.

In the television series Turn: Washington's Spies, Simcoe is depicted as a ruthless sociopath. Perhaps after discovering the following historical accounts, Hollywood got this one right. Almost immediately after the battle, reports surfaced that British and Loyalist troops had committed various atrocities, including brutally murdering defenseless prisoners of war and setting fire to American wounded. On May 7th Washington ordered Brigadier General William Maxwell to conduct an investigation into these allegations so that a formal protest could be sent to General Howe. Washington's orders to Maxwell:

> "As great complaints have been made of the disorderly conduct of the Parties which have been sent toward the enemys lines, it is expected that you will be very attentive in preventing abuses of the like nature, and will enquire how far the complaints already made, are founded in justice. You will make particular enquiry into and obtain the most authentic testimony of the conduct of the British Troops toward the Militia under the comd of Brigr Genl Lacey on the Instt that if the facts alledged be true a proper representation of it may he made to the Comr in chief of the British Troops".

Andrew Long, a justice of the peace in Bucks County, took the depositions of Colonel Watts and four residents who witnessed the battle: Samuel Henry, William Stayner, Thomas Craven and Samuel Erwin. Watts reported, "We found the bodies of the dead usid in a most inhuman & barbarous manner" and that "the most cruel Barbarity that had ever been exercised by any civilised Nation; nay, Savage barbarity in its utmost exertion of cruelty could but equal it."

Lacey's report to Major General John Armstrong further documented the atrocities:

> "Some of the unfortunate, who fell into the merciless hands of the British, were more cruelly and inhumanely butchered. Some were set on fire with buckwheat straw, and others had their clothes burned on their backs. Some of the surviving sufferers say

they saw the enemy set fire to wounded while yet alive, who struggled to put it out but were too weak and expired under the torture. I saw those lying in the buckwheat straw—they made a most melancholy appearance. Others I saw, who, after being wounded with a ball, had received near a dozen wounds with cutlasses and bayonets. I can find as many witnesses to the proof of the cruelties as there were people on the spot, and that was no small number who came as spectators. The Rangers lit the fires and disfigured many, though British regulars tried to stop them. Capt. John Downey of Plumstead made a fight of it until shot through the shoulder. He lay bleeding on the ground when the Rangers set upon him. "They dispatched him in a cruel manner, for his body was found with one of his hands almost cut off, his head slashed in several places, his skull cut through."

One of the statements received by Judge Andrew Long seems to indicate that the wounded were not intentionally burned alive by the British, but the field where they lay wounded was set on fire by the militia's own musket fire. Samuel Erwin testified on May 15th that on the day of the battle he:

"saw a smoke in one of his Fields, and after the Enemy had retreated, went out to see what was the occasion thereof, was much surprised to find one of the Militia men lying dead, his Clothes Burning and nearly consumed, which had burnt the body black, he thinks the man was set on fire before he was dead, from this sircumstance that his Arms were standing nearly erect, he further sayeth that he saw three other Bodies in Thos Cravans Field burnt in an inhuman manner, & further sayeth not".

Thomas Craven swore on May 15th that:

"after the battle he was called on by one of the Brittish Light Horse to carry some Milch to one of their Wounded Officers, when he came into the Field he was asked by a Trooper if he did not see some fires round the Field, to which he said he did, the trooper said they were men, & that their own Amunition set them on fire after the Brittish lef[t] the ground he went again into the Field where he saw four or five men burnt to a Shocking digree".

Unfortunately, there was no recorded account by the British regarding this skirmish to compare to the depositions gathered from the Americans. Regarding the inquiry into British atrocities, the investigation appears to have been passed from Maxwell to Potter, who collected and forwarded the few depositions to Washington. A letter to Howe from Washington regarding the alleged atrocities is not included in the Washington Papers, and there appears to be an absence of a historical conclusion from other sources. Either the atrocities occurred, and Simcoe was indeed a madman who burned helpless wounded soldiers alive, or the field was set ablaze by musket fire from one side or the other, and some men were simply too injured to remove themselves from the inferno...you get to choose how the story ends.

Despite Simcoe's portrayal of a devious sociopath in three seasons of Turn, the historical Captain Simcoe, in contrast, had the reputation of a respected, forward-looking British officer. Simcoe came to Long Island, New York, in the fall of 1776, along with 23,000 other British and Hessian soldiers. His company was one small part of the overwhelming force that pushed General Washington out of Brooklyn. The same British force also pushed Washington's Army off Manhattan Island and pursued them through New Jersey.

Simcoe participated in the Philadelphia Campaign and suffered a wound at the Battle of Brandywine. During that period of the war, Simcoe kept lobbying his superiors to form a light infantry force that could maneuver more quickly and effectively than regular regiments. After the Battle of Brandywine, he got his wish, receiving the rank of major and command of the Queen's Rangers, a corps made up of American Loyalists. Instead of the standard army drill, Simcoe's training emphasized physical fitness, speed, and the deployment of bayonets. His corps also included a company of hussars or light horsemen.

The rangers' bayonets became notorious among Americans after the Battle of Quinton's Bridge in March 1778, when they made a night-time raid on a house full of patriots. Simcoe's men stabbed up to twenty Continental soldiers, as well as the house's owner. Although Americans called the raid a massacre, the incident was within eighteenth-century rules of warfare.

Whether carrying out raids, hunting for spies, or fortifying his regiment's positions, the historical Simcoe performed to the standards of any British Army officer in wartime. The Queen's Rangers were especially effective at fast strikes and reconnaissance. Simcoe survived the Revolutionary War and became the first governor of Upper Canada.

Marine Corps Tie-In... a Marine on Duty Has No Friends.

While waiting on a ship date to one of the recruit depots, a diligent recruit will have the eleven general orders for sentry duty memorized if they want a fraction of the peace it buys them at boot camp. Not committing these orders to memory will result in a lot of hate and discontent for the recruit who cannot confidently recite any of them on demand. A recruit assigned to fire watch was posted behind three stacked footlockers in front of the barracks' main entrance; the recruit's mission was primarily security. Unfortunately for the recruit standing fire watch, he would get blasted by every Drill Instructor walking through the entrance, and the footlocker podium was almost always violently kicked across the squad bay during the process.

Sentry duty in the Marine Corps begins with the first assignment of fire watch for a recruit, and the collateral duty will follow every Marine, enlisted and commissioned, throughout their career. Fire watch literally referred to watching for fires when the militaries of old maintained warming fires near flammable tents or when a fort was attacked with flaming arrows. The term still consists of this essential duty in modern times, but it is no longer the post's primary purpose. The primary responsibility has shifted to the safety of Marines within sight and hearing, and the secondary responsibility of maintaining the security of a building, bivouac, or weapons.

In the fleet, a Marine stood fire watch in the field, and the duty typically rotated through junior Marines in one-hour shifts. One of the more difficult tasks a Marine on fire watch had was to get the next fire watch on the roster to get out of his sleeping bag and stand his post in a timely manner. It is no secret amongst Marines that the best hours to draw fire watch was the first or last hour because it would give one the best opportunity to get a bit more uninterrupted sleep. Conversely, the worst two hours to draw fire watch were the hour after the first watch and the hour before the last watch because you're getting a two-for-one deal.

Fire watch morphs into Duty and Assistant Non-Commissioned Duty Officer of the Day in garrison. Every Marine unit from the company level up always has two Marines on duty. In a regiment, the chain starts with a duty and assistant duty NCO at each company, an Officer of the Day (OOD) and Staff Non-Commissioned Officer of the Day for each battalion, and an Officer of the Day and Staff Non-Commissioned Officer of the Day at the regiment. The duty is continuous at the company level, but at battalion and higher, the duty begins after 1600; on weekends and holidays, all Marines on duty stand a 24-hour post. A good night on duty is when everything can be quickly covered during a morning debrief with a commander or Sergeant Major. A bad night on duty is one where one or both have to be woken with a phone call to give them an immediate briefing of a situation gone wrong.

A duty logbook is meticulously kept on all levels of the duty chain and serves as a legal document whenever required. Suffice it to say that I logged my fair share of strange and unusual events while serving on duty. The first unusual log I recorded was an unauthorized guest in the barracks at 8th and Eye; unfortunately, that guest's host was my squad leader. It was a difficult moral dilemma to be in, especially after said squad leader shoved his half-dressed date out of his room and instructed me to sneak her out of the building, call a cab, and get her in it. Stranger still, some young Marines were in a room watching a video with the door ajar. We walked by the room as I tried to whisk the girl away. As we passed the room, she peered in quickly, looked at me, and said, "Hey, I am in that video!" Fortunately, the squad leader made sure I was absolved of any responsibility for the incident after word quickly spread.

The worst night I ever had while serving on duty was as Officer of the Day (OOD) for the Weapons and Field Training Battalion in Camp Pendleton, California. As I was getting ready to tour my duty area late one night and check on the Duty NCOs, one of them came to the OOD shack, frantic to report a dire situation. He informed me that while touring the barracks, he thought he saw a Marine loading several magazines with live rounds while glancing through a gap in the room's curtains. When I arrived at the room, I immediately verified that a Marine was, in fact, busy loading Magazines with live rounds. While I held the Marine at gunpoint, I instructed the Duty NCO to call the Provost Martial Office (PMO) for support.

Within minutes, PMO arrived on the scene with shotguns and long rifles drawn to secure the room and take the Marine into custody. Once the Marine was removed from the room (and it wasn't gently), we recovered several loaded magazines and an AR-style rifle. Among several whiskey and vodka bottles that littered the room, a hand-written manifesto was found crumbled on the floor. The manifesto made known the mentally unstable Marine's plan to sit on an overpass spanning eight lanes of Highway 5 and take out as many motorists as possible before ultimately taking his own life. The Marine's previously diagnosed mental condition made the situation much more volatile since he was prescribed narcotics that were not supposed to be mixed with alcohol, and it was pretty obvious he had done so.

While the last example is in a league of its own, a typical night of duty was spent dealing with the idiotic stuff drunk Marines come up with, especially on the weekends. This generally ranges from finding women of ill-repute in barracks rooms to drunk Marines tying ponchos to themselves and attempting to glide off third-story catwalks like flying squirrels... every now and then, a stabbing between drunken roommates was thrown in the mix.

Historical places to visit in or near Warminster, Pennsylvania.

The historical gem in this segment of the Patriot's Path is the Moland House, built around 1750 by John Moland. The estate served as an unplanned camp for the American Army after Washington received dispatches from John Hancock that a substantial British armada of 220 ships was sighted fifty miles below Cape Henlopen. Washington used the beautiful stone house as his headquarters while his Army camped nearby and, pulling his generals in, held a Counsel of War. The historical site claims that the Betsy Ross flag was first presented to Washington while he quartered here, but it's another Betsy Ross rabbit hole I will not dive into. What is most significant about the Moland House is that the Marque de Lafayette and Count Casimir Pulaski joined Washington and his Army at this critical juncture in American history. The house now belongs to the Warminster Township Historical Society and is open to visitors from spring to autumn. Take a walk along its hiking trails and visit several monuments and historical plaques on the estate, including a full-sized statue of Lafayette.

Drive over to Crooked Billet Elementary School, where the Crooked Billet Battle Monument stands tall in front of the school. Along the street, you will find a historical marker for the Battle of Crooked Billet. You can drive into the countryside to visit the General Lacey Homestead, but the private residence sits at the end of a long driveway, and it isn't easy to view from the road.

Finish your historical tour at the Wings of Freedom Aviation Museum in Horsham, which currently exhibits 19 military aircraft inside and outside the building. The museum sits on what used to be the Willow Grove Naval Air Station. During the Sounds of Freedom Airshow in 2000, an F-14 Tomcat crashed in the neighborhood after experiencing a catastrophic engine failure while conducting an aircraft carrier demonstration called a wave-off. As the jet banked off the runway and began to climb, the pilot lost control and crashed in a wooded area. Although the pilots managed to eject, they did so while the jet was horizontal to the tree line, tragically killing both of the Naval Aviators. The last airshow at the Naval Air Station was in 2006, and the base was eventually closed in 2011 and turned over to the Air National Guard.

Crooked Billet Elementary School is located at 69 Meadowbrook Avenue Hatboro, Pennsylvania.

The Moland House is located at 1641 Old York Road Hartsville, Pennsylvania.

General John Lacey Homestead is located at Forest Grove Road Buckingham Township Wycombe, Pennsylvania.

Wings of Freedom Aviation Museum is located at 1155 Easton Road Horsham, Pennsylvania.

Coastal Counties of New Jersey

"Not only the Army, Navy, the Air Force, the Marines, everything is going away at a time when certainly we are a top priority for making sure that doesn't happen. We're not respected to the extent we were and if we keep going like this, we won't be respected at all."

~Donald Trump 45th President of the United States

The small coastal community of Chestnut Neck, New Jersey was a thriving international trade center leading up to the Revolutionary War. Chestnut Neck was established along the Little Egg Harbor River about 10 miles north of present-day Atlantic City, New Jersey. Local vessels traveled to Philadelphia, New York, and other eastern seaboard cities, carrying mail, overseas trade goods, and merchandise. When the British occupied Philadelphia and New York City during the winter of 1777–78, General Washington, camped upriver at Valley Forge, was cut off from his source of supplies coming into those major ports. The supplies were re-routed into Little Egg Harbor instead and unloaded at Chestnut Neck. The supplies were floated up the river in flat-bottomed boats and transported across the peninsula to Burlington. The supplies were placed on rivercraft and floated across the Delaware River and overland to Valley Forge.

With the advent of war, American privateers took over the harbor facilities to use as a base of operations. The American privateers would attack and seize vulnerable British ships. Many of the ships seized, held supplies intended for Sir Henry Clinton, who was stationed in New York. The cargo was sent to the American Army along with their usual shipments via Chestnut Neck. The captured British vessels were often modified for use as privateers. In addition, French aid to the Patriots likely made its way through Chestnut Neck, including valuable arms, ammunition, and uniforms.

General Clinton became so exasperated by the constant loss of his ships and cargo that he devised a plan to "clean out that nest of Rebel Pirates." On September 30th 1778, Clinton sent nine warships and troop transports under the command of Captain Henry Collins to Chestnut Neck. An assault force of 300 British regulars and 100 New Jersey Loyalists commanded by Captain Patrick Ferguson sailed on the transports. Governor William Livingston learned of the assault force and sent riders into the countryside to warn the people.

Due to bad weather, the British fleet was also delayed and did not arrive in the vicinity of Little Egg Harbor until late in the afternoon of October 5th 1778. The tide went out during the delay, and the landing craft could not float over an exposed sand bar. Loyalist spies told the landing party that the people had already been warned and that Count Pulaski was on his way with his Legion, so as soon as the tide came back in, Ferguson moved up the river to Chestnut Neck as quickly as possible. The British assault force was put aboard galleys, which departed at daybreak on October 6th. They were delayed when two boats grounded despite the incoming tide, and the assault force did not reach Chestnut Neck until 4 PM, which then was shrouded in heavy fog.

The British assault force engaged with American defenders and retrieved some supplies, destroying any they could not carry away. Around noon on October 7th having received intelligence that Count Pulaski was nearby, the British and Loyalists quickly left Chestnut Neck. On their way back to the coast, they stopped to destroy Eli Mathis's salt works and mills at the mouth of the Bass River. The British burned the houses on his plantation, his home, and his barns before reembarking their ships.

Washington ordered Count Pulaski and his Legion to intercept the British landing force, but they did not arrive until the day after the British attacked. Pulaski's Legion consisted of a corps of dragoons and light infantry and was a unique unit where deserters and prisoners were encouraged to join its ranks. When Pulaski's Legion neared Little Egg Harbor, a German deserter named Gustav Juliet, who held a subordinate command in Pulaski's Legion, also held a grudge against Colonel de Bosen, the commander of the light infantry. Juliet turned traitor and reported the Legion's position to the British, who made a night attack upon De Bosen's camp. Pulaski heard the gunfire and quickly repelled the enemy with his dragoons, but not in time to prevent the Legion from losing forty men.

As soon as Pulaski's Legion arrived at Chestnut Neck, they crossed the river and marched to the town of Tuckerton, arriving there on October 8th. Ferguson and Pulaski watched each other until October 15th when a force of 250 Loyalists under Ferguson's command surprised an outpost of Pulaski's men, bayoneting the sentry and almost all of the other men while still asleep. Locals soon referred to this action as the Little Egg Harbor massacre.

Although Ferguson's raiding party managed to retrieve some supplies and destroy others at Chestnut Neck, they could not capture any of the vessels used by American privateers in the area. As a consequence of the battle, Chestnut Neck lost its status as a trade center.

Two years after the raid at Chestnut Neck, Pulaski and Ferguson were both killed in battle. Ironically, each of these antagonists was killed during the southern campaigns, and they died in separate battles. Pulaski was killed by grapeshot during the Siege of Savannah in October 1779, and Ferguson was killed during the Battle of King's Mountain in October 1780.

Marine Corps Tie-In... Teufel Hunden.

The French government awarded the 5th and 6th Marine Regiments the French Fourragere for actions during World War I. These Marine Regiments are the only Marine Corps units still authorized to wear it on their uniforms while assigned to these units.

The World War I Marine Regiments were also awarded the Croix de Guerre for their brave actions in several battles, including the Battle of Belleau Woods, just 39 miles from Paris. During my twenty-year career, I had the unique honor of serving with the First Battalion, Fifth Marines, Second Battalion, Sixth Marines, and Second Battalion, Fourth Marines (The Magnificent Bastards), which was permanently attached to the Fifth Marine Regiment when the Fourth Marine Regiment was disbanded after World War II.

The Marine Corps has acquired many sobriquets over its illustrious history, one of the more famous is Devil Dog. Devil Dogs, has its roots from German reports on the fighting at Belleau Wood, where they refer to the American Marines as Teufel Hunden (Devil Dog). Legend has it the popular moniker for Marines originated after they attacked a fortified hill occupied by German forces. The Marines wore gas masks as a precaution against German mustard gas attacks. The uphill fighting while wearing the oxygen-depriving gas masks, combined with the heat of the moment, caused the Marines to sweat profusely. The rigorous activity caused them to foam at the mouth, and their eyes became bloodshot. At some points during the assault, the terrain was so steep Marines had to bear climb up the hill. From the Germans' soldier's point of view, they were witnessing a pack of tenacious, growling, dog-like creatures wearing gas masks, with bloodshot eyes and mouth foam seeping from the sides, charging up the hill, sometimes on all fours, killing everything in their path. The German soldiers, upon seeing this horrific sight, began to frantically yell that they were being attacked by "dogs from hell."

I acquired two horses and a Dalmatian, my own Teufel Hunden, from military acquaintances throughout my career; I affectionately called them my 'boys.' I got a hot-headed Arabian Saddlebred from friends who could no longer keep him. He was never saddle broken due to his often-ornery disposition. I got him as a yearling, but he was still a stallion, contributing to his wicked disposition. The horse and I had a love-hate relationship; predominately love on my behalf and hate on his; he kicked a few times, I believe, out of sheer meanness. I eventually realized that he was too much horse for me to handle for someone with my limited equine aptitude when he started to freak out while I was grooming him one afternoon. As he inexplicably began to kick and buck in his stall, I somehow managed an escape before he could connect with a flying hoof. While I was leaning against the stall, waiting for him to calm down, he stretched his head over the bars, bit me in the chest, and ran to the opposite side of the stall. Before I could even collect myself, the horse trotted over and bit me on the other side of my chest.

My second horse was a two or three-year-old American Quarter horse that was rough broken when I acquired him. I knew I would eventually own him because the Marine who had him grew up in Las Vegas and didn't know much about horses at all, and I suspect he was interested in having a horse merely because I had a horse. The Marine asked me to accompany him to a tack shop one afternoon to buy riding gear, and figuring I would eventually end up with the horse and new tack, I 'recommended' a saddle, blanket, and tack at an Inland Empire tack shop. The Marine bought the gear, and within a few months, I ended up with the horse, saddle, and tack for around $2k. I eventually took the quarter horse to a California ranch, where I paid a pretty authentic-looking cowboy to break him in. The horse became my partner when I was a volunteer Riverside Sheriff Posse member. I had him shipped to my new duty station in North Carolina after I left California. Anticipating the lack of time and money I would have raising a new family after proposing to my wife; I sold him to a stable in Maryland a year after I brought him to North Carolina.

My third 'boy' was the aforementioned Dalmatian named Charlie Daniels, whom I acquired from a couple in 29 Palms, California; Charlie came to me because his previous family could not keep him. I noticed right away that something was amiss with the dog. Although happy, playful, and energetic, most of the time, he might have been a bit racist. I don't know if it was preconditioned behavior acquired from his previous South Carolina family or because he suffered from an identity crisis because he was either black with white spots or white with black spots; whatever the reason, he was aggressive toward African Americans.

I babysat my neighbor's five-year-old boy one evening while his parents went out for an anniversary dinner. The boy and the dog were watching cartoons, and I was making dinner when I heard a muffled scream and looked up to see, to my horror, the dog's mouth entirely around the boy's head. I ran over and pulled the dog off the boy; thankfully, the boy did not sustain so much as a scratch from the ordeal. I put the dog in a room and sat with the traumatized little boy; the wait seemed like forever until his parents came home. I met the boy's dad at the door, who was an imposing Navy Chief, blurted out an apology, and explained what had happened. I told the boy's father that I would take the dog to a vet and have him put down, but he adamantly refused to allow me to do that.

I love Penn State football, and one autumn, I was baking a cake while Penn State and Michigan were playing a game being televised in California. It was rare to be able to watch an East Coast game on the West Coast and even rarer that Penn State was favored against Michigan. Going into the fourth quarter, the game was close, and my television was upstairs. While mixing cake batter in the kitchen downstairs, I heard excitement on the TV indicating that Penn State made an interception in the close game. I ran upstairs and watched the ensuing drive, completely forgetting about the cake batter I had carelessly left on the counter. As I celebrated a go-ahead Penn State touchdown, I reached down to pet the dog and put my hand in something wet and sticky. I looked down to see the dog, painted blue for the game, covered in chocolate cake batter. I followed chocolate paw prints downstairs and into the kitchen, where I found cake batter spattered all over the walls and floor.

I got up a little late for work one morning and, jumping out of bed, quickly dressed in the dark. As I walked around the house, the pungent odor of dog poop followed me. Every room I went into in search of the offending turd and came up with nothing but the stench until I realized I had something sticking to my leg. The dog slept under covers in bed every night regardless of temperature. That night, I either rolled on the dog, or he had an accident, but it happened in the bed, where I subsequently rolled in it.

I did a lot with the dog and took him to most of the places I went. One of his favorite activities was catching a floppy frisbee, and he rarely missed it, often launching himself through the air to catch it. I also gave him tombstone power drivers, mimicking the antics of the Undertaker, a professional wrestler I liked to watch. When I performed the wrestling move, I was careful never to let the dog's head hit the ground. I would tuck his head between my legs, pick his butt up in the air and jump up in the air, acting like I was going to drop the dog on his noodle. After I let him loose, he would go nuts, running all over the place, then come back and beg me to do it again. One afternoon, a few Marines from my platoon were helping me move into base housing. I told them about the tombstone pile driver stunt, and they all wanted to see it. Everything was routine as I grabbed the dog, inverted him, and took my jump. What wasn't routine at all was the slick, steaming turd that shot from his butt, landing at the feet of one of the stunned Marines.

Historical places to visit along or near the New Jersey coastline.

My family enjoys a beach vacation in Ocean City, New Jersey, so a natural starting point for us to visit the historical sites along this segment of the Patriot's Path is Somers Mansion, which is not far from the boardwalk. Built in the 1720s, the house that Richard

Somers constructed is the oldest in Atlantic County. Somers and his close friend Decatur were ensigns assigned to the frigate United States commanded by Commodore John Berry at the end of the Revolutionary War. One evening in the ship's wardroom, the two, now senior lieutenants, exchanged friendly insults over clothing. However, to six of the ship's junior officers who witnessed the event, Decatur, slightly junior to Somers, was insubordinate for his insults. Because Somers failed to hold his friend accountable, they believed he acted out of cowardice and was a disgrace to the Navel service. Somers offered the junior officers his wine a couple of days later, which was refused because no one would drink with a coward.

In those days, that was an insurmountable insult that usually led to a duel, and this occasion was no different. Somers challenged all six to duels on the same day, and his challenge was accepted. He missed the first incumbent he faced but received a wound to the arm. This was quickly bandaged, and Somers stood to face his next challenge. Again, he missed his man and received another shot, this time in the thigh. He was patched up again and tried to get to his feet to face the third duelist. Due to the loss of blood, he was unable to stand but resolutely refused to withdraw or allow Decatur to stand in his place. Decatur did help support his friend and steady his aim, and together, they managed to wound the third man. By this time, the six juniors were thoroughly convinced Somers was no coward, and the remainder of the duels were called off. Near the beautiful Somers Mansion is the Somers Point Patriot Park, and near it, a submariner's memorial.

From here, you will begin a marathon distance tour of five historic sites along the Jersey coast: your first stop, Smith's Meetinghouse. Visit the church graveyard, now called the Methodist Union Chapel Graveyard, where you will find the graves of two privateers and two Revolutionary War soldiers. Your next stop on your route is the Battle of Chestnut Neck Monument and Park. For me, this is the most significant place to visit on the Atlantic County list. Check out the indomitable battle memorial, the central attraction in the park, then stroll around and view the British ship anchor, ship's rib, and privateer plaque. Next, head up the road to Tuckerton, where you will find the Pulaski Legion Memorial and Little Egg Harbor Massacre historical plaque, and experience the colonial history of the harbor. The final stop on this leg is Joshua Huddy Park. Joshua Huddy was an American Officer and privateer the British captured toward the war's end. He was 'removed' from the custody of his British captors by a party of angry Loyalists who promptly executed him by hanging. In response, the Continental Army arranged the summary execution of a British Officer. In what had become known as the Asgill Affair, cooler heads prevailed with a little bit of French influence, and the execution was stayed. This would have violated the 1781 Articles of Capitulation and likely caused diplomatic upheaval.

The last few stops will take you southwest along the coast to Cape May. I like to visit these sites on the way home from a weekend beach trip. Visit Sunset Lake Park, where you will find the Battle of Turtle Gut Inlet Memorial and a marble memorial bench commemorating the Americans who died during the terror attacks on 9-11. If you are into the World War II coastal batteries, swing into Sunset Beach and visit Fort Miles Battery 223. The seaside concrete battery is near the Cape May Lighthouse and now defends against the steady erosion of the beach it was built on and continual vandalism. If you visit Cape May Point at low tide, you might even get to see the bow of a World War I era concrete ship. During World War I, some shipbuilders turned to concrete for cheaper, more abundant shipbuilding material. Although concrete is not very durable in salt water, the shipyards built twelve steamer ships of concrete because they estimated the lives of the ships to be rather short anyway because of German U-boat activity in the Atlantic. The SS Atlantus, made several transatlantic voyages where it shipped coal to Europe and brought

American soldiers home at the end of the war. She was retired after two years and tugged from Virginia to Cape May. At Cape May, she was moored to become part of the Lewes-Cape May ferry, but she broke loose from her moorings during a storm and grounded at her present location.

Finally, head north toward Cumberland County, New Jersey, where you will find a beautiful stone monument commemorating the Greenwich Tea Burning of 1774. In the autumn, a British ship called the Greyhound with a cargo of tea from the East India Tea Company. Daniel Bowen, a Loyalist, agreed to hide the tea cargo in his cellar, but unfortunately for him and the tea, this did not go unnoticed by his patriotic neighbors. In December, around forty of these patriots, dressed like Indians, broke into Bowen's cellar, removed the wooden crates of the valuable tea, and stacking it in a nearby field, set it on fire. Greenwich was one of five colonial cities with the distinction of being a tea party town. The four others are Boston, Annapolis, Princeton, and Charleston.

Somers Mansion is located at 1000 Shore Road Somers Point, New Jersey.

Somers Point Patriot Park is located at Bethel Road and Veterans Way Somers Point, New Jersey.

Smith' Meetinghouse is located at 2 Mill Street Port of Republic, New Jersey.

The Battle of Chestnut Neck Monument and Park is located at the intersection of New York Road and Chestnut Neck Road Chestnut Neck, New Jersey.

Privateers Plaque is located at The Battle of Chestnut Neck Monument and Park.

Ship's Rib is located at The Battle of Chestnut Neck Monument and Park.

3rd Battalion Gloucester County Militia is located at The Battle of Chestnut Neck Monument and Park.

The British Anchor is located at The Battle of Chestnut Neck Monument and Park.

Pulaski Legion Memorial is located at 209 Lake Champlain Drive Tuckerton, New Jersey.

Little Egg Harbor Massacre is located at 836 Radio Road Tuckerton New Jersey.

Little Egg Harbor Colonial History is located at 120 West Main Street Tuckerton New Jersey.

Joshua Huddy Park is located at 3M East Water Street Toms River, New Jersey.

Sunset Lake Park is located at New Jersey Avenue and East Miami Avenue Wildwood, New Jersey.

Cape May Point State Park is located at 303 County Highway 629 Cape May, New Jersey.

Greenwich Tea Burning Monument is located at 1031 Ye Greate Street Greenwich, New Jersey.

Marcus Hook, Pennsylvania

"Only those who would be called upon to risk their lives for their country should have the privilege of voting to determine whether the nation should go to war."

General Smedley Darlington Butler, "The Fighting Quaker" and one of only two Marines awarded two Congressional Medals of Honor.

In the early 18th Century, Marcus Hook was a haven for pirates who preyed upon the waters of the Delaware River below Philadelphia. Markets at Marcus Hook provided the pirates a convenient place to sell plundered goods and to resupply away from the attention of authorities and customs officials in Philadelphia. Interestingly, early maps of Marcus Hook indicate that modern Second Street was originally named "Discord Lane" because it was the location where pirates gathered for their drunken revelry whenever they were in town. According to a local oral tradition, Marcus Hook Plank House was once the home of the mistress of the pirate Blackbeard.

By the mid-1700s, Marcus Hook became a major regional center for shipbuilding, turning out wooden sailing ships until around the late 19th Century, when larger ships became more popular than the sloops and schooners built in Marcus Hook. In the beginning stages of the Revolutionary War, two rows of underwater chevaux-de-frise obstacles spanned the Delaware River at Marcus Hook. They were the front line of river defenses to deter British naval forces from attacking Philadelphia. A training center for the Pennsylvania militia was also established at Marcus Hook during the Revolutionary War.

The Continental Army camped at Marcus Hook in the autumn of 1777 during their march to meet Howe's forces in Delaware. The town was subjected to a naval bombardment by British warships, so very few 18th-century or older houses survive in Marcus Hook. In

1812, a defensive post was established in Marcus Hook along the river. It was manned with over 5,000 American troops and placed there to defend the river and Philadelphia's deep-water port.

Marine Corps Tie-In...Ductus Exemplo.

Marine Corps officers and noncommissioned officers are renowned for their troop-leading skills. Sometimes, Marine leaders command Marines with an iron fist, but the best Marine leaders lead by example; juniors will follow their leaders more enthusiastically when inspired. Ductus Exemplo, Latin for Lead by Example, is the motto at Marine Officer Candidate School, and it is one of the more critical leadership traits of Marine leaders at every level.

On my first unit deployment to Okinawa, I was a young sergeant and a squad leader. Regarded as one of the company's top NCOs, I had been sent to several premier' leadership' schools and was selected as the regiment's representative for a division Meritorious Staff Sergeant Board; I thought I was pretty salty and, thus, a pretty good leader. I was in great physical shape, probably in the best shape I had ever been. I strove to train my squad hard and was a very demanding leader. I was a tough-as-nails NCO, and I led my Marines with an iron fist, but I am not sure I always had their respect or even their confidence that I would take care of them when the going got tough. During that deployment, my first team leader was a Marine whom the squad and platoon loved and respected. He was proficient and dependable, a competent young NCO who naturally led from the front. Even though he waged a personal war with unseen demons that he would ultimately and fatally lose, his team members would have resolutely battled the demons with him to the end if he had allowed them to.

Sometimes, the more critical aspects of leadership are not learned in a classroom; great leaders must demonstrate it in cauldrons of conflict and adversity. A better test of leadership is to see how a physically and mentally tired Marine leads. I was soon fed a giant slice of humble pie that radically opened my eyes and transformed my leadership style in the Okinawan jungle. Our company commander was a sturdy, proficient captain and recent recipient of the Marine Corps's annual Leftwich Trophy. This prestigious award is presented for outstanding leadership in the memory of Lieutenant Colonel William Groom Leftwich, United States Marine Corps, who was killed in action during the Vietnam War in November 1970. The captain decided to schedule a field exercise in the jungles of Okinawa to evaluate the leadership skills of his NCO, and his officers and staff were taken out of the planning, preparation, and execution of the exercise to assess the young leaders. I was selected as the company's acting executive officer for the field operation. I immediately immersed myself in the planning and logistics of the operation along with a more senior NCO who was designated the acting company commander. The three-day operation began at Camp Hanson and culminated with an assault on a company-sized enemy objective at a Military Operation in an Urban Terrain (MOUT) town situated deep in the jungle.

Our plan was developed, and we gathered the temporary company leadership around a terrain model and issued our combat order. The foot movement to our attack point on the outskirts of the MOUT Town required patrolling through several miles of undulating triple-canopy jungle; roads and other modern infrastructure were removed from the problem and considered out of play. On the second day of fighting through the thick jungle, we settled the company into a patrol base in a pre-designated location to give the tired and hungry Marines rest. Upon reaching the patrol base site, we discovered a resupply of water and chow. I called the temporary company gunnery sergeant to distribute the food and water. After tasking the platoon commanders to set outposts and security patrols,

I sat down with a Meal Ready to Eat (MRE) and started to work on patrol overlays.

I was in mid-bite when the captain walked up and asked how everything was going. I briefed him on the company's posture and informed him I was working on a company security patrol map overlay. He looked down and asked if I had walked the lines to ensure the Marines all had chow and an opportunity to eat. I was so focused on developing a perfect plan and successful attack that I failed to carry out a basic tenant of Marine leadership, ensuring the troops were taken care of ahead of my own needs. As I tried to swallow the suddenly bad-tasting bite of MRE, I found the captain's words even harder to swallow. I didn't walk the lines to check to make sure the men were fed; I merely assumed they ate when the MREs were distributed. I learned in the moment that winning didn't mean anything if winning was at the expense of the men I led; as the captain's lesson in leadership sank into my mind, it also penetrated my ambitious heart. I was reminded that leadership isn't about being the hardest, fastest, or smartest Marine. In that wet, cold jungle, I learned that a leader is only a leader if he can inspire others to follow his example willingly.

The lesson the captain taught me that evening in the jungle during peacetime training resonated in war a year or so later in the sands of Iraq. RCT-5's movement north to Baghdad was so rapid that supply trains could not keep up, and after a couple of weeks, we were rationing MREs and water. I had my squad, platoon sergeant, attachments, and a few Marines that 'bumped' onto my AAV when theirs broke down, so we had a lot of Marines in a cramped space, sharing dwindling resources. One evening, a couple of days after our MRE rations were depleted, I discovered I had a bunch of hungry Marines on my hands. Stored under a bench in the middle of our AAV were several boxes of humanitarian MREs we were supposed to pass out to Iraqi families whenever possible. I asked the platoon sergeant if I could pass a few out for the Marines to share since we were out of food. The platoon sergeant reminded me that to do so would violate standing orders that the MREs were strictly set aside for Iraqi non-combatants. He wasn't wrong, but my Marines were hungry. I broke down a few of the meals and passed them out to the Marines under the cover of darkness that night. Although I was willfully disobeying a standing order, I did so for the good of my Marines and not in a spirit of insubordination.

During my second full cycle as a Drill Instructor, I was walking the crucible with another Drill Instructor, leading half of our platoon of recruits through various stations comprising the event. The recruits were required to carry a sustainment load in their packs, which weighed 40 or 50 pounds, for the duration of the three-day event. Some of the other Drill Instructors opted to place pillows in their packs instead of the sustainment load the recruits in their charge carried. While I didn't opt to carry what amounted to air in my pack, I only carried what the recruits were carrying when I knew I could hump much more weight. By the end of the second day of the crucible, the Drill Instructor, in his weariness, was developing a tendency to forget his pack when transitioning to another station.

The recruits understood they were never allowed to touch any gear belonging to a Drill Instructor; besides, I was usually quick enough to discover the DI's pack and would retrieve it before a recruit had a chance to. I was completing a task away from the group but made it back just in time to see that the DI had the recruits in a column on a dirt road, ready to move to the next station, but once again, was without his pack. I was about to scan the area for the pack when the platoon's guide reached down for an object, half hidden in the grass. As the recruit braced himself and heaved on the pack to lift it from the ground, he nearly fell over backward, not expecting the pack to be as light as it was. I screamed at the recruit to drop the pack, but the damage was done. The recruits to a man saw what had happened, including an unusually red-faced Drill Instructor. That evening, when the recruits were bedded down for their scant four hours of sleep, I carefully loaded my pack with rocks. The pack was easily as heavy a pack as I had ever carried in the fleet, but I humped it the entire 15 miles of the crucible hike the following day and then some since it was always an implied task that junior Drill Instructors run up and down the long columns making sure each recruit maintained the prescribed interval and cover for the duration of the hike.

Back at the squad bay after the crucible hike, I intentionally left my weighted pack outside our Drill Instructor duty hut, knowing that the recruits would eventually test the pack's weight. The next cycle, word of the pillow trick, made its way among the company's Drill Instructors, prompting the Chief Drill Instructor to randomly check the packs of the hats before the crucible event. To his astonishment, he discovered several loaded with pillows, one filled with an inflated bag, and one loaded with rocks.

Historical to visit in and near Marcus Hook, Pennsylvania.

There are a few historical sites worth exploring in Marcus Hook. The town isn't the safest, but the town's police department is near the three sites listed below, so I recommend staying within the area. Park across the street within sight of the police department and walk over to the Plank House. Built from the planks of an 18th-century ship, the house now serves as a living museum. Plan your visit for mid-September to experience the annual Pirate Festival held at the Plank House. Check out the waterfront from the Municipal Park before walking over to St Martin's Cemetery. Here, you will find the Soldier and Sailor Walk Memorial and the marked graves of 73 American Patriots who served in the Revolutionary War, the War of 1812, the Mexican War, the Civil War, and the Spanish-American War.

Soldier and Sailor Walk Memorial is located in St Martin's Cemetery 225 Church Street Marcus Hook, Pennsylvania.

<u>**The Plank House**</u> is located at 221 Market Street Marcus Hook, Pennsylvania.

<u>**Municipal Park**</u> is located at 11 East Delaware Street Marcus Hook, Pennsylvania.

Book Four: An American Revolution in the Pennsylvania Back-Country

---

York County, Pennsylvania

"A Marine likes a good fight and respects a good fighter. You've got yourself one fine Marine for an escort and the whole Marine Corps is behind you".

~ Bud Rudesill, author

York, Pennsylvania, became the temporary capital of the United States in September of 1777 when the Continental Congress, threatened by the British Army's proximity to Philadelphia, evacuated the city. They settled into the backcountry town of Lancaster but did not feel quite secure on the same side of the Susquehanna River as the British. The Continental Congress moved to York, Pennsylvania, placing a significant water barrier between them and General Howe. York played an influential part in America's early history, hosting the Second Continental Congress for nine months during the winter of 1777-1778, becoming the temporary home of John Adams and John Hancock. During its brief stay in York, The Second Continental Congress accomplished several touchstone events in American history. While hunkered down in York, Congress signed the French Treaty of Alliance, proclaimed the first National Day of Thanksgiving, and adopted the Articles of Confederation.

The Conway Cabal, which was a political conspiracy waged against General Washington, also took place in York, at the Golden Plough Tavern. The Conway Cabal consisted of a small group of senior Continental Army officers and congressmen who conspired to unseat Washington as the Army's commander-in-chief. The conspiracy is named for its main actor, General Thomas Conway, an ambitious and discontent general who wrote several letters criticizing Washington.

General Conway immigrated to France from Ireland with his parents as a child. At the age of 14, he received a commission in the Irish Brigade of the French Army and was promoted rapidly through the ranks to colonel. With the outbreak of the American Revolutionary War, he volunteered for service with the American Army. American diplomat Silas Deane forwarded a letter of introduction to Congress, and he was appointed a brigadier general and sent to Washington.

Washington passed him over for promotion to Major General because he believed that several American-born officers with more time in service deserved the rank ahead of him. This decision caused a fatalistic rift between Washington and Conway. Conway's suggestions in letter form were forwarded to the Second Continental Congress, hoping they would convince Congress to promote him to Major General and sack Washington in favor of his friend Horatio Gates, Hero of Saratoga. The suggestions in Conway's letters were often little more than thinly disguised criticisms and expressions of discontent with either Washington or the general course of the war. When the letters were made public, they had the opposite effect on Congress that Conway had envisioned, inspiring supporters of Washington to take immediate action to assist him politically.

Washington distrusted Conway anyway, as he did the motives of most foreign officers in American service, and he found Conway's character and conduct particularly arrogant and unbearable, although he had proven himself a capable officer. Conway freely admitted that his ulterior motive for promotion was based on the supposition that if he was promoted to major general during the Revolutionary War, he could become a brigadier general in the French Army whenever he returned. Washington supported his own position regarding Conway's promotion by identifying him as an officer "without conspicuous merit" and that his promotion would "give a fatal blow to the existence of the army." Washington continued, "It will be impossible for me to be of any further service if such insuperable difficulties are thrown in my way." Strong words from the Army's commander-in-chief, which was seen as an implicit threat to resign should Congress promote Conway against his wishes. Conway continued his campaign for promotion in a correspondence to Gates. In it, he stated, "Heaven has been determined to save your Country, or a weak General and bad Counsellors would have ruind it."

General Stirling received a letter from Gates' adjutant, James Wilkinson, that contained a quotation of Conway's disparaging remark about Washington. Stirling didn't waste time forwarding the letter to Washington, who received it on November 8th 1777. The quotation caused Washington to wonder if there were more subordinate officers besides Conway making underhanded plans to have him replaced. The idea resonated with Washinton since he was already well aware that the 'Hero of Saratoga,' in particular, was suddenly a more popular figure in political circles.

Lafayette, who treated Washington as his surrogate father, took great offense to Conway's efforts to insult and undermine Washington. One evening, Congress invited Lafayette to York to accept command of a future military campaign in Canada. After Lafayette met with Congress, he was invited to dinner with its members. It was customary in those days to toast one another before dinner. Keenly aware that some of Washington's critics were present at the dinner, Lafayette referred to them as "rascals." When the toasting began, Washington conspicuously was not recognized, so Lafayette stood and toasted his commander-in-chief. The congressmen knew protocol demanded they support Lafayette's toast, or they might lose the Frenchman's support and the vital alliance of his liege with it. Lafayette was America's best hope for a full French military commitment in the war with Britain, and if they lost his support, they would likely lose the support of France as well. This toast was rumored to have helped save Washington's job by forcing the men who opposed him to show support for him publicly.

The toast is sometimes considered to have "saved the nation" because Washington and his future French allies went on to win the Revolutionary War.

Lafayette eventually exposed the duplicity of the Conway Cabal after his failed Canadian invasion. The war board, controlled by the cabal leaders, named Conway to replace Lafayette as commander of the American Northern Army, but Lafayette wasn't having any of that nonsense. Lafayette protested to Congress and even went as far as threatening the vital American and French alliance if Conway was allowed to replace him as commander. Lafayette's efforts had the desired effect, and Congress overruled the war board's appointment.

Despite Washington's veiled threat to resign, Conway received his contested promotion from his war board buddies and was appointed Inspector General of the Army on December 13th 1777. Washington, who wasn't thrilled with Congress' decision, revealed Wilkinson as his source for the letter containing Conway's insubordinate quotation. This uncharacteristic revelation by Washington forced Gates to apologize and then perjure himself regarding his correspondence with Conway. Amid the scandal this created, Conway submitted his resignation to Congress in April 1778, and it was readily accepted.

Still unhappy about the whole affair, Washington's supporters began to challenge Conway and his collaborators to duels. This prompted Wilkinson to turn on Gates and challenge his former boss to a duel. Gates reportedly wept and apologized for any offense caused, and the duel was called off. On July 4th Conway was challenged to a duel by Brigadier General John Cadwalader, another close friend of Washington's. Cadwalader won the duel after he shot Conway straight in his big, belligerent mouth, the bullet exiting through his head, saying, "I have stopped the damned rascal's lying tongue at any rate." Conway somehow survived the encounter and, as he convalesced from his wound, wrote an apology to Washington, which was never answered. After recovering, he returned to France in disgrace.

The failed cabal was the only major political threat to Washington's command during the entire war, and no formal requests were ever submitted asking for Washington's removal as Commander-in-Chief of the Army. Proponents for independence largely rallied behind Washington, who was increasingly seen as a figure of national unity. He would be the overwhelming favorite to serve as the new nation's first president after the war. A statue of the marque making his historic toast is located on the grounds of the General Gates Tavern, which shares a kitchen with the Golden Plough Tavern.

Camp Security was a prison camp with a stockade and living quarters. It was built in 1781 on a confiscated farm in York County. The York County militia was tasked with guarding Camp Security, except for a brief period in 1782, when General Hazen's Continental Army regiment guarded the prisoners. It was first occupied by British General John Burgoyne's troops, who were captured after the Battle of Saratoga. Only enlisted men were confined to the prisoner-of-war camp. Officers were either granted parole, exchanged, or housed in private residences. In 1782, the camp's population increased considerably with the addition of Cornwallis' Army after the British surrender at Yorktown, Virginia. His troops, considered high risk for escape, were incarcerated in the stockade while others were required to remain in the vicinity of the camp. A pass system allowed some prisoners to work for locals, which supplemented the camp's limited supply of food and resources. Some prisoners married locals during their seven years in captivity and became citizens of the new nation.

Camp Security was abandoned after the Revolutionary War. Some former prisoners migrated to Canada, where they were given land in exchange for their service to the British. Some even stayed in the United States, but most eventually returned to Britain. Several prisoners succumbed to a fever outbreak, and others died due to other reasons, and they were buried somewhere near the camp. The site of the graveyard remains unknown.

Major John Clark Jr. of York, County was a noted American spy for Washington and operated Washington's spy network in and around Philadelphia during the British occupation. Clark was commissioned as a first lieutenant in the 1st Continental Infantry (Pennsylvania Rifles) on January 1st 1776, and was made a major of the 2nd Pennsylvania Battalion of the Flying Camp on September 14th 1776. He originally came to Washington's attention during the evacuation of Long Island and Manhattan. Directed to travel across Long Island Sound, Clark scouted troop movements on Long Island.

Clark was the spymaster of one of the most efficient spy rings organized and run by the Continental Army during the war. The clandestine operations of this illustrious ring saved Washington's Army on at least three separate occasions. Clark, who was recovering from a severe shoulder injury, was explicitly tasked by Washington to focus his efforts on General Howe's war efforts while the British occupied Philadelphia. Clark set up a group of informants and couriers, sending at least 30 detailed intelligence reports to Washington, which allowed him to react to British movements. Clark set up a hoax in which he used a false name while pretending to be a Quaker Loyalist who would inform on the Americans to General Howe. The ruse worked, and Howe even offered Clark incentives to support the British cause. When Washington learned of the scheme, he prepared a false report of the Continental Army's strengths and planned movements and ordered it delivered to Howe. A courier also acquired information about British activities while delivering messages on Clark's behalf.

In the television series Turn: Washington's Spies, Washington's Chief of Intelligence was identified as Nathaniel Sackett. In the series, Sackett is murdered by a Simco in Washington's camp, and

Washington chooses Major Talmadge to replace him. Unfortunately, this is historically inaccurate. In early 1777, Washington, indeed, selected Nathaniel Sackett as his first chief of intelligence. Sackett was a leading member of the Committee for Detecting and Defeating Conspiracies, which was organized by John Jay. Major Tallmadge of the 2nd Continental Light Dragoons was appointed Sackett's liaison with the Continental Army soon after Sackett's appointment. Sackett's tenure was brief because Washington was not impressed with his performance, not because Simco brutally murdered him as portrayed in *Turn*. He was replaced by Clark, whom Washington considered a practiced spy experienced in infiltrating enemy lines. Washington also chose Clark to replace Sackett because of the proven success of the espionage networks he already managed in Philadelphia.

In December, with his wound still not fully healed and after having not seen his wife in more than a year, Clark asked Washington to be released from service. Washington agreed and introduced Clark to Henry Laurens, who gave Clark a desk job as auditor of Army expenses. For the remainder of his life, Clark lived quietly and continued to maintain his secrecy regarding the names of the informants and couriers who helped him.

Brigadier General Charles Scott, a veteran of the French and Indian War and several Revolutionary War battles, was chosen as Clark's successor. Major Tallmadge was appointed to assist General Scott as deputy chief. One of Scott's first assignments from Washington was to develop intelligence networks in British-occupied Long Island and New York City. These networks eventually evolved into the renowned Culper Spy Ring depicted in *Turn*. In October 1778, Washington replaced Scott, finally promoting 24-year-old Tallmadge as the Continental Army's new intelligence chief.

Major Clark is buried at St. John's Episcopal Church along with Colonel Hartley, James Smith, and Hessian prisoners of war. Strangely, a little-known historical event also took place in the graveyard. The graveyard was the scene of the dramatic episode associated with the Conway Cabal and the duel that was planned to be fought there between Gates and Wilkinson. All were on hand among the graves, and the pistols were ready for use, but as we now know, the dual was called off.

Marine Corps Tie-In...The Quantico Cabal.

My last training platoon at OCS was also the most challenging one. Some of the new instructors had a difficult time transitioning from working with recruits to working with officer candidates, and to make matters worse, the Marine captain assigned to the platoon seemed distracted and not as engaged as he probably needed to be. The candidates were typical college students from NROTC units across the country who had suddenly discovered they had a lot of personal adjustments to make.

The primary purpose of the enlisted instructors at OCS is to train, screen, and evaluate the candidates for leadership potential and officer ascension. A collateral duty of the job is to provide and create copious amounts of stress throughout the training cycle under the auspice that anyone can lead in a calm, ordered environment, but for potential Marine officers, the antithesis can be expected in a combat environment.

This platoon had issues from the beginning; some instructors were new to OCS and needed to learn to handle candidates differently than recruits. The inside joke between instructors was that officer candidates were Uncle Sam's little Brussels sprouts because they were green, nasty, and easily bruised when handled. The reality was that we were not making basically trained Marines; we were ensuring that the officers commissioned to lead them were worthy of the responsibility.

The platoon's candidates had a difficult time working together to complete simple tasks, and individualism ran rampant among its ranks. The candidates were too concerned about placing first—from completing basic tasks to peer evaluations. The Peer Evaluation process was compromised from the beginning, inundated with personal hacks aimed at one another, and worse, the process was used as a tool to eliminate competition. By just past mid-increment, the platoon was well known for its cannibalistic nature and was generally considered the worst in the company.

The more the negative behavior persisted, the less inclined the frustrated instructors were to mentor the platoon. I was on duty with the platoon one hot afternoon while the candidates waited to move into its Squad Unit Leader Evaluation (SULE) lane. As they were preparing for the SULE evaluation, I spoke with the captain, who was also visibly frustrated with the platoon's performance. I asked him if I could directly address the platoon's behavior, but in a different manner than what was usual or expected from enlisted instructors; after I gave him a quick frag-o, he gave me his consent. I found 14 dry and brittle sticks about two feet in length, and taking the platoon aside, I directly confronted their behavior and performance and gave them the following example from our American Founding Fathers.

I asked if they had a general idea of why our country fought for independence and why it was such a difficult dream for them to achieve. As they nodded their heads in assent, I went on, "You want to achieve a dream that is just as indomitable and just as patriotic as our nation's forefathers, but they couldn't, and they didn't do it alone and neither can you. Before the 13 colonies became one nation, the pieces needed to come together as a whole. The colonies under the Continental Congress wanted one independent nation free from the yoke of England's tyranny, but they each wanted it their way, so they squabbled, and they squabbled a lot. Washington had the same problem with his corps of General officers; instead of working together for a common cause, they constantly undermined each other for promotion. One of his subordinate generals even attempted to unseat Washington as Commander in Chief during the failed cabal".

I asked the smallest candidate in the platoon to stand up and take one of the sticks I had piled before them and continued my narrative. "One afternoon in New York in 1775, Ben Franklin addressed a bickering continental congress, pleading with them to work together for a common cause. Franklin took up a single arrow and said, "Let me borrow a simple euphemism from our Iroquois friends. How much strength does it take to break a single arrow?" Easily snapping the arrow shaft in half, the aged Franklin said, "Almost nothing." I had the smallest candidate snap the stick, which he did with ease. I picked up the bundle of 13 sticks and handed them to the largest candidate in the platoon. I continued, "Franklin then picked up a bundle of 13 arrows and attempted numerous times to break the bundle. After he failed to break the bundle of arrows, he addressed his now captivated audience again. "But bound together, it will be impossible to break these 13 colonies." I told the candidate I wanted him to break the bundle of sticks he held, but he could not, no matter how hard he tried. I told the platoon, "If you bind yourselves into one cohesive team, nothing can break or beat you. There is nothing this platoon cannot achieve if you work together."

I wasn't sure if my message resonated with the platoon that afternoon, but by the end of the increment, it was apparent that something had inspired them to change their approach to Officer Candidate School as their performance increased dramatically. Near the end of every increment, the training company gathers for an afternoon of good food and friendly competition, and each platoon designs a unit tee shirt exemplifying a significant moment during their training. The tee shirt design for the first platoon I trained at OCS featured a raging bulldog immortalizing their notoriously demanding instructor team captioned with the words, "And you want to lead me," a phrase we often used disparagingly with the candidates. The tee shirt design of the final platoon I trained at OCS depicted a fist full of arrows with the words *Thirteen Arrows* embossed beneath the image. I learned during that increment that a Marine can be fierce and demanding and, every now and then, sit down with young people, take off the heavy armor of authority, and mentor them authentically.

Near the end of the increment, a few instructors from another platoon approached me, asking what positively changed my platoon's performance. I told them what helped me was realizing that the young men they were working with were not recruits; they were all officer candidates who all completed their junior year of college and were both intelligent and strong. A few new instructors were infamous for screaming at candidates like banshees; they literally screamed nothing intelligible at candidates. I said to the inquiring instructors that the pointless, wordless screaming might have intimidated recruits on the depot, but for highly educated young college students, it looked ridiculous and was probably a little disheartening for them to see and hear Staff NCOs acting in that way.

One of them said, "I know you get loud and intense with the candidates, but they respond well to you, even without resorting to cussing and cursing." I told them I was careful to demonstrate escalation but cautioned that there must be a discernable purpose. I also reminded them that what goes up will eventually come down. Whenever I spun up the candidates, I brought them back down; I didn't let the winding down process up to the candidates to figure out. I hope my advice resonated with the instructors, but unfortunately, I still witnessed grown men screaming and jumping up and down in front of candidates for no apparent reason as I finished my days in Quantico. In their eyes, they were being intense, or perhaps, that's just what they taught PI-DIs (a friendly dig at my Parris Island Drill Instructor colleagues).

Historical places to visit in and near York County, Pennsylvania.

Begin your tour of York's historical sites at the colonial complex. Liaison with a knowledgeable park ranger who will conduct you on a journey through the 18th Century. You will visit the Golden Plough Tavern, where Lafayette defiantly made his toast in support of Washington. Outside the tavern you will even find a life-sized bronze statue of the marque with a tumbler raised high. The General Gates Tavern is attached to the Golden Plow, and the colonial courthouse and stocks are across the street. Along York's streets, you will find several historical markers on your way to Saint John Episcopal Church. Walk around the church and visit the graves of patriots Major John Clark and Colonel Thomas Hartley. Along one side of the church is a small grassy courtyard, perhaps an ideal spot for a duel. If you visit when the church is open, go inside and ask to see the York Liberty Bell.

York County Courthouse is located at 28 East Market Street York, Pennsylvania.

The Golden Plough Tavern is located at 159 West Market Street York, Pennsylvania.

The General Gates Tavern is located at 159 West Market Street York, Pennsylvania.

The Colonial Courthouse is located at 157 West Market Street, York, Pennsylvania.

Camp Security Park is located at Eastern Boulevard York, Pennsylvania.

Major John Clark Marker is located at 7 South Beaver Street York, Pennsylvania.

General Wayne Marker is located at 107 West Market Street York, Pennsylvania.

Colonel Thomas Hartley Marker is located at 34 West Market Street York, Pennsylvania.

St. John Episcopal Church (Clark and Hartley graves and the York Liberty Bell) is located at 140 North Beaver Street York, Pennsylvania.

Lancaster, Pennsylvania

"Our Country won't go on forever if we stay soft as we are now. There won't be any AMERICA because some foreign soldiery will invade us and take our women and breed a hardier race"!

~ General Lewis 'Chesty' Puller, the Most decorated Marine in the Corps.

Lancaster County was the fourth county created in Pennsylvania and was added to the original three counties of Bucks, Chester, and Philadelphia. The backcountry town of Lancaster began in 1728 after Chester County residents lamented that "thieves, vagabonds, and ill people" had infested the remote areas of its western boundary. Residents on the western border also had to travel great distances over rugged cart paths to reach the Courthouse. They petitioned to create a new county with a local municipality that could quickly deal with crime. Lancaster County was formed on May 10th 1729, to bring a regional seat of government to residents settled in the borderland wilds.

Lancaster was the site of the Great Indian Treaty of 1744, home of the Conestoga wagon, and birthplace of the Pennsylvania long rifle. Famous residents include President James Buchannan, U.S. Representative Thaddeus Stevens, Surveyor Andrew Ellicott, artist Charles Demuth, F. W. Woolworth, and Milton S. Hershey. During the Revolutionary War, Lancaster was the American capital for one day when the Continental Congress was forced to flee Philadelphia and the capital of Pennsylvania from 1799 to 1812.

Timothy Matlack lived on East Orange Street, Lancaster, during much of the Revolutionary War. As the Clerk of the Continental Congress, he penned the Declaration of Independence for members to sign when it approved the Articles of Confederation.

Another great contributor towards American independence was the Pennsylvania Long Rifle, produced in Lancaster. The Pennsylvania Long Rifle was developed because early settlers needed an accurate, reliable rifle that could withstand the rigors of the frontier. Settlers and frontiersmen relied on the rifle to hunt game and for protection from dangerous predators, vagabonds, and hostile Indians. The first long rifles were designed for function, but after 1750, they were often embellished with carvings, engravings, and ornamentation, becoming objects of utility and beauty. A Pennsylvania Rifle was considered a significant investment in the 18th Century; it was the second highest expense next to a home.

During the Revolutionary War, Lancaster became a major supplier of warfighting weapons. Thomas Butler, born in Kilkenny, Ireland, was a gunsmith who immigrated to America from Dublin. Butler set up his first shop in Lancaster and began producing quality long rifles. His five sons all served in the Revolutionary War and the old bull, who would not be left out of the fray, volunteered as an armorer for the Continental Army.

The Pennsylvania Riflemen, mainly from the frontier county of Lancaster, were both feared and respected by the British for their uncanny range and accuracy in battles during the Revolutionary War, providing the Continental Army a slight, psychological advantage over their adversaries. British General George Hager wrote, "I never in my life saw better rifles or men who shot better. A British surgeon wrote, "These men are remarkable for the accuracy of their aim; striking a mark with great certainty at 200 yards distance. . . and their shot have frequently proven fatal to British officers and soldiers who exposed themselves to view, even at more than double the distance of common musket shot"

The reputation of the Pennsylvanians and their long rifles soon made British recruitment difficult and increased the need to procure more Hessian soldiers. Despite the accuracy of these rifles,

Washington and his officers still favored the modes of European warfare and armed most of their troops with faster-reloading smoothbore muskets. Most of these muskets were supplied by France but many others were produced by Lancaster gunmakers.

A Pennsylvania Long Rifle was implicated in an early Lancaster murder in 1846 when John Haggerty, a neighbor of prominent gunsmith Melchior Fordney, rushed into his gun shop one day demanding that the gunsmith shoot his 'demon-possessed' horse. Fordney naturally refused such an outlandish demand. Haggerty then grabbed a rifle from the shop and ran outside to shoot his unfortunate horse. Haggerty leveled the rifle and pulled the trigger, but it failed to fire, so an exasperated (or drunken) Haggerty rushed to his home and returned to the shop with an axe and his own gun. This time the gun fired, but Haggerty merely wounded the horse. It ran down the street into a stable, where it eventually succumbed to the wound. Fordney and his wife watched the spectacle in abject horror.

When Fordney confronted Haggerty demanding he give up the gun, he raised his axe and chased the gunsmith into his shop, where he bludgeoned Fordney to death with the axe and critically injured his wife and six-year-old daughter. Neighbors immediately took Haggerty into custody and locked him in jail. During his ensuing trial, Haggerty claimed, "his horse was the incarnation of the devil and had been climbing trees and talking to goats." He also said, "he had seen chickens turn themselves into images of Martin Van Buren and witnessed balls of fire flying down the street as George Washington was leading bands of saints." The trial was brief and had a predictable outcome. Haggerty was convicted of murder and hanged in the town's jail-yard.

General Edward Hand was born in Clyduff, King's County, Ireland, on December 31st 1744, and earned a medical certificate from Trinity College in Dublin. Hand joined the 18th Royal Irish Brigade as a

Surgeon's Mate. On May 20th 1767, he sailed with the regiment from Cork, Ireland, and arrived at Philadelphia on July 11th 1767. In 1772, he was commissioned an ensign, marched with the regiment to Fort Pitt, and returned to Philadelphia in 1774. Hand resigned his commission and moved to Lancaster, Pennsylvania, where he practiced medicine.

In 1775, Hand was commissioned as a lieutenant colonel in the Continental Army. He was assigned to the 1st Pennsylvania Regiment under Colonel William Thompson. In 1776, Hand was promoted to full colonel and commanded the 1st Continental Line, then designated the 1st Pennsylvania Rifle Regiment. By 1777, Hand was promoted to brigadier general and served as the commander of Fort Pitt, where he fought British loyalists and their Indian allies on the western frontier.

In 1778, Hand's forces attacked a tribe of Lenape during a military campaign to reduce the hostile Indian threat to settlers in the Ohio Valley. Native nations such as the Shawnee, were allied to the British and became the Army campaign's intended target. Hand's soldiers failing to distinguish between native nations in the Ohio Valley, attacked the neutral Lenape instead of the Shawnee. Among the victims of this attack were Captain Pipe's mother, brother, and a few of his children. This naturally turned the Lenape chief against the Americans and border settlers would pay a terrible price for his wrath. After over two years as commander at Fort Pitt, Hand was recalled to serve as a brigade commander in Major General Lafayette's division during the war's southern phase.

In 1782, a plan was being developed for a campaign against the Iroquois, and Hand's frontier experience naturally qualified him as a participant. In the resulting Sullivan Expedition against the Iroquois, Hand was placed in command of the Third Brigade. Units in the Brigade included the Fourth and Eleventh Pennsylvania Regiments, Proctor's Artillery, Captain James Parr's Riflemen, Captain Anthony

Selin's Riflemen, the German Regiment, and included two Wyoming companies. The brigade formed what was considered the "Light Infantry Corps" of Sullivan's Army and was assigned to the expedition's vanguard. Collaborating information from journals kept by the officers who participated in the expedition indicate that Hand's Brigade played an integral role in the campaign's success.

After the campaign, Hand rejoined his family in Lancaster. he was thirty-five years old and the youngest brigadier general in the American Army. Hand was appointed Adjutant General of the Continental Army and served in this capacity during the siege of Yorktown. In recognition of his long and distinguished service, he was promoted by brevet to major general in September 1783.

Marine Corps Tie-In...Primary Marksmanship Instructor Course.

First Battalion Fifth Marines sent me to a premier school to teach the fundamentals of marksmanship and conduct sustainment training for the service rifle and pistol platforms the Corps uses. Over the course of five weeks, the students learned to teach the four supported rifle positions authorized for use on the Marine Corps's static, known distance qualification course and the two authorized pistol positions for qualification. The students were taught to critique and correct each position during snap-in (dry fire practice) while constantly reminding each shooter of the seven fundamentals of a good shooting position. Primary Marksmanship Instructors (PMIs) could not physically adjust a shooter's position during prequalification and qualification day, so each shooter needed to know how to auto-adjust.

Analyzing a shooter's data book was also a skill required by the instructors in training. If a shooter accurately filled out the range data book, it could be read to find trends in shot placement, windage, and elevation adjustments, and weather conditions. A good instructor could then provide good feedback for the shooter to adjust. The students were also taught range procedures, tower commands, and target pit management. The target pit, or 'butts' as it is more commonly known by Marines, is a bunkered area containing fifty target carriages that each hold two large 6-foot by 6-foot framed paper targets. Shooter relays manipulate these frames by receiving commands from the pit NCO. Every shot on paper made a very distinctive, loud snap as it pierced the paper target. Once the target was impacted by a single shot or group of shots, the target was pulled, the shots marked with spotter discs, and ran back up for the shooter to record.

The marksmanship course students were also taught how to set up and run Battle Site Zero (BZO) courses so they could run them whenever their units needed them. Weapon systems only deployed along with units for combat or floats. Every time a Marine was issued a rifle when reporting to a new unit, UDP deployments, or returning from deployments, a BZO course was required to tailor the sights of an unfamiliar rifle to the shooter it was issued to.

While working at Valley Forge Military Academy, I learned discipline can be taught and effectively reinforced through marksmanship. I was asked to run the marksman portion of summer camp. Finding that the military marksmanship program I was skilled in was better than the plate-pinging model that had previously been in place, I recommended implementing a modified two-week instructional and qualification marksman course based on the Marine Corps model. I taught the fundamentals of marksmanship, safety, and firing positions to male and female campers ranging from six to seventeen years of age, emphasizing discipline. The course was broken down into a three-day teaching block, a two-day rifle handling and snap-in (dry fire) block, a three-day prequalification block, a one-day qualification block, and a one-day competition shooting.

The Marine Corps course of fire takes place on an outdoor rifle range, in any weather condition, at distances of 200, 300, and 500 yards with 5.56 caliber, magazine-fed, semi-automatic rifles. The campers fired on an indoor range with a target line distance of 25 yards with 22 caliber, magazine-fed, semi-automatic rifles, so the target sizes were modified to simulate actual standoff distances. The pilot iteration of the summer program went better than I had anticipated, and I quickly realized that the two-week process was actually building and reinforcing disciplinary skills with the young campers.

They were taught the four safety rules: Treat every rifle as if it were loaded, never point a rifle at anything you do not intend to shoot, keep your finger straight and off the trigger until you intend to fire, and keep the rifle on safe until you intend to fire. They were also taught the four rifle conditions: Condition 4- No round in the chamber, rifle on safe, magazine removed, bolt forward on an empty chamber. Condition 3- The bolt is closed in an empty chamber, the rifle is on the safe, the magazine is inserted, and the ejection port is closed. Condition 2- Not applicable. Condition 1- Round in chamber rifle on safe, magazine inserted, bolt locked forward, and ejection port closed. Every day beginning on day one, the class had to recite the safety rules and rifle conditions as a class; before live fire, each camper was chosen randomly to recite a safety rule or rifle condition.

The campers had to execute every iteration of the live-fire courses of fire on command; an example of this is as follows: Campers, this is slow fire portion of your qualification course, firing five well aimed shots on your 200-yard target, standing to sitting, in a time limit of five minutes. With a condition four rifle, muzzles down range. Campers, you're in your prep time. The campers were given three minutes to get into a good shooting position and dry fire on their targets with their ammunition kept out of reach on ready tables. Campers, your prep time has ended. Campers, with a rifle in condition four, STAND! With a magazine of five rounds...LOAD! (Campers insert their magazines). MAKE READY! (Campers, with muzzles elevated rack a round, going from condition four to condition one). Campers, you may begin firing when your targets appear...TARGETS! Campers move into their seated position and fire five controlled, well-aimed shots at their targets. When they have fired their fifth and final round, they are to unload and show a cleared rifle on their own by removing the magazine, visibly and physically inspecting for an empty chamber, and presenting the rifle for a secondary verification that the rifle is cleared. Once cleared, the camper makes a condition four rifle and remains in the shooting position until further instructed.

I was amazed at how fast the campers learned and how well they applied what they had learned. There were no mishaps of any kind on the firing range. I had a high number of expert shooters and relatively few marksmen shooters, and none failed to qualify. Quite a few parents brought their children back to marksmanship camp the following year, and the number of participants doubled. More than a few parents commented about how much better disciplined their children became because of the marksmanship program.

Historical places to visit in or near Lancaster, Pennsylvania.

The next segment of the Patriot's Path will take you to the heart of Pennsylvania's Amish Country. At your first stop, you will learn about Pennsylvania's Dutch heritage at the Landis Valley Museum. The early 20th-century house, though modern compared to other houses listed in this manuscript, is a living museum that can be visited throughout the year, Thursday through Sunday. Explore the house, take a look inside the barn, and check out the horse-drawn farming implements on display.

Head over to the Rock Ford Plantation, which served as General Hand's estate in the 18th Century. Take a guided tour of this beautiful 1794 brick mansion. From furniture to firearms, enjoy exhibits containing rare historical artifacts. During your tour, your guide will tell you about General Hand's medical and military career. Stroll the estate gardens, grounds, and barn. Immerse yourself in another interactive walk through history. On your way out of city limits, make sure you stop at the old courthouse as well as Postlethwaite's Tavern, although the last time I heard that name was in the movie Open Range.

Next, drive over to Ephrata and visit the historic Ephrata Cloister and Mount Zion Cemetery. The cloister was used as a backcountry hospital where hundreds of soldiers were brought in for the treatment of wounds and diseases. A beautiful memorial in the Mount Zion Cemetery commemorates the many soldiers buried in its hallowed grounds after they died from their illnesses or injuries.

Finally, head over to Lititz to visit the Moravian Brethren House, White Swan Hotel, and the Stiegel-Coleman House. Washington used the Brethren House as another field hospital; it is estimated that over one thousand soldiers were brought for treatment and recovery. At least 110 soldiers who died from illness or infection were buried in a graveyard across the street. Unfortunately, the Stiegel-Coleman House is closed to visitors, but you can grab a bite to eat at the 1790 Swan Inn.

Landis Valley Museum is located at 2451 Kissel Road Lancaster, Pennsylvania.

Rock Ford Plantation is located at 881 Rockford Road, Lancaster, Pennsylvania.

Soldier's Monument is located at Mount Zion Cemetery, 803 Oak Blvd Ephrata, Pennsylvania.

Moravian Brethren House Lititz is located at 8 Church Square Lititz, Pennsylvania.

The Ephrata Cloister is located at 632 West Main Street Ephrata, Pennsylvania.

Lancaster County Courthouse is located at 50 North Duke Street Lancaster, Pennsylvania

White Swan Hotel is located at 1264 east Newport Road Lititz, Pennsylvania.

Stiegel-Coleman House is located at 2121 Furnace Hill Pike Lititz, Pennsylvania.

Postlethwaite's tavern is located across the street from the Lancaster Courthouse.

Carlisle, Pennsylvania

"A Marine is a Marine. I set that policy two weeks ago - there's no such thing as a former Marine. You're a Marine, just in a different uniform and you're in a different phase of your life. But you'll always be a Marine because you went to Parris Island, San Diego or the hills of Quantico. There's no such thing as a former Marine".

~General James F. Amos, 35th Commandant of the Marine Corps and first Marine Aviator to be appointed Commandant.

Although far removed from the fighting along the East Coast, Carlisle and Cumberland County still played an integral part in the Revolutionary War. Settlers living in the Cumberland Valley area volunteered to fight in the war, while others produced food, supplies, weapons, and munitions to support the fight for independence. An ordinance center called Washingtonburg was built in December 1776 after the Continental Congress authorized its establishment. Over the years, the barracks were simply called the Carlisle Barracks. It is the second-oldest Army post in the United States and the home of the United States Army War College. Carlisle was also the home to some notable people during the 18th Century. James Wilson for example, was a Cumberland County attorney and one of three from the County to sign the Declaration of Independence in 1776.

Molly Pitcher is another name synonymous with Carlisle, although the story of Molly Pitcher is complex. It is a story that is part fact, myth, and legend. It is a story built up and repeated without documented evidence to support the stories and partly the combination of stories of the exploits of multiple women during the Revolutionary War. Molly was a common nickname for Mary and Margaret; Carlisle's "Molly Pitcher," Mary Hays McCauley, was born around 1754. Like other women, Mary followed her husband from camp to camp during the war. These women were said to "follow the drum." These camp followers worked hard and were very important to the troops they supported. In addition to walking the same great distances as the soldiers, these women cooked, laundered clothing, sewed, cared for the sick, and did many other important domestic jobs.

Mary's husband, William Hays, had enlisted in Thomas Proctor's Artillery in May of 1777 as a gunner. This Artillery Unit was engaged at the Battle of Monmouth, New Jersey, on June 28th 1778. The story goes that during the battle, Molly Pitcher took her husband's place at the cannon after he had received an incapacitating wound. Unfortunately for this Molly Pitcher legend, there is no documented evidence that Mary Hays ever manned a cannon at Monmouth; however, on February 22nd 1822, the government of Pennsylvania did award her a forty dollar a month pension, but it never explicitly stated why it was granted. The pension merely states, "An Act For the relief of Molly M'Kolly, for her services during the Revolutionary War."

Mary McCauley's great-great-granddaughter, Mary E. Wilson, in a deposition she provided, stated, "My grandmother often told me about her grandmother Molly McKolly alias 'Molly Pitcher' telling her about being in the army and about carrying water to the wounded and dying." From Mary Wilson, the Cumberland County Historical Society obtained a pitcher once owned by Molly Pitcher but it is not the same pitcher she used in battle.

After Mary Hays McCauley's death, two Carlisle newspapers ran an obituary for her. On January 26th, 1832, the American Volunteer said, "She lived during the days of the American Revolution, shared its hardships, and witnessed many a scene of 'Blood and carnage.' To the sick and wounded she was an efficient aid, for which; and being the widow of an American hero, she received during the latter years of her life an annuity from the government." Neither obituary made any mention of her firing a cannon in battle.

General John Armstrong was one of Carlisle's first settlers and was responsible for planning the town's layout prior to the Revolutionary War. Armstrong began his military career during the French and Indian War, leading the Pennsylvania militia in the Kittanning and Forbes expeditions as a Colonel. During the Forbes expedition, he befriended Virginia militia commander Colonel George Washington. The two were co-commanders of the successful expedition against France and their Indian allies, and they would continue to serve together throughout the Revolutionary War.

Armstrong commanded Pennsylvania militia at the Battle of Germantown and led the attack that was supposed to skirt around the British left flank and attack from the rear. Unfortunately, because of Stephen's folly and the delay caused at the Chew House, they were not quite in a position to attack, which inspired Armstrong to remark that the battle was "....a glorious victory fought for and eight-tenths won, ...mysteriously lost, for to this moment no one man can ....give any good reason for the flight." Armstrong was sixty years old during the Battle of Germantown and just plain tuckered out from all the fighting he did during his illustrious military career.

He petitioned for and was granted permission to retire, and he returned to his home in Carlisle, but his public service was not over. Armstrong served in the Continental Congress, becoming one of Washington's strongest advocates. After the war, he was appointed to the Congress of the Confederation. After Armstrong's national service, he served on the Carlisle School Board when Benjamin Rush proposed to build a college in Carlise. Armstrong was initially opposed to the idea but later changed his mind and ironically served on the first board of trustees for Dickenson College.

Another influential Carlisle resident was General William Irvine. He was an Irish-American doctor who served as a ship's surgeon in the British Navy during the French and Indian War. Because of his patriotic views, he resigned his commission amid the revolutionary fervor spreading across the colonies in the early 1770s. He was commissioned as a colonel and captured by British forces at the Battle of Three Rivers in 1776. He remained a prisoner of war for nearly two years before being exchanged in 1778.

Irvine was promoted to Brigadier General a year later and placed in command of the 2nd Pennsylvania Regiment in Pittsburgh. In 1781, Washington placed Irvine in command of the Western Department of the Continental Army. While acting in this capacity, Irvine convinced Washington that the British fort in Detroit needed to be neutralized. Irvine then reached out to his friend, Colonel William Crawford. He convinced him to come out of retirement and lead an expedition against the hostile Indians along the Sandusky River to clear the way for an expedition against Fort Detroit.

Crawford was an excellent choice for this assignment, given his service record. He was a highly skilled frontiersman and served in several well-known wars on the American continent, beginning with the French and Indian War and spanning the years to the end of the Revolutionary War, where he served as commander of Maxwell's Light Infantry scouts, acquitting himself with distinction throughout the Philadelphia campaign.

Crawford made out a will and gave it to his son before heading to the frontier. Intuition must have prompted Crawford to write his will because the campaign did not end well for him. A combined force of British soldiers, renegades, and Indians surrounded Crawford's force of 500 men along the Sandusky. Crawford's men were forced into an unorganized retreat, which resulted in the capture of Crawford and dozens of his men, the majority of whom were horrifically tortured to death. Simon Girty, an infamous frontier renegade who served under Crawford before he deserted, and Captain Pipe personally oversaw Craford's violent and gruesome torture before he was burnt at the stake.

After the war, Irvine served in the Continental Congress and later played an active role in ending the Whiskey Rebellion in Pennsylvania. He also served one term in Congress, representing Pennsylvania, and was active in the state's public affairs.

Last but certainly not least are the many important contributions Thomas Butler and his five sons made during the Revolutionary War for liberty and freedom."The Fighting Butlers of Carlise", gunsmiths from Lancaster, set up shop before serving as officers during the American conflict with ferocity and distinction. Washington once made a toast in their honor, and three counties in three states are named for them.

General Richard Butler, the oldest of the three sons, was given the honor, after the British surrender at Yorktown, of receiving Cornwallis' sword. Richard in turn, conferred this honor to his second in command. Before his subordinate commander could receive the instrument of surrender, General Von Steuben demanded the honor. This nearly precipitated a duel between the two General officers. Later while Washington celebrated the victory, he raised his glass and toasted "To the Butlers and their five sons!"

After the war, Richard was placed in charge of Indian affairs in the Ohio Valley and negotiated several treaties, notable among them the Second Treaty of Stanwix, which forced the once mighty Iroquois League to cede most of its lands to the United States.

Richard had four children with his wife Maria and even fathered a son with Cornplanter's sister, Nonhelema, a Shawnee chief. Richard would find himself on opposing sides of a losing battle called St. Clair's Defeat against his half-breed son, Tamanatha, also called Captain Butler. Richard was tomahawked and scalped during the battle...hopefully not by his own son. To this day Richard remains the most senior American officer ever killed in action. The brothers continued to fight for their country and eventually avenged Richard's death when they defeated the Shawnee Chief Tecumseh's Indian Confederacy at the Battle of Fallen Timbers. A few of the brothers even fought alongside their own sons during the War of 1812.

Marine Corps Tie-In…A Commandant Holds a Baby.

During my second OCS increment, a few instructors were invited to attend a Friday Evening Parade at Marine Barracks 8th and Eye by the Commandant of the Marine Corps. I couldn't pass up an opportunity for my wife and her parents to experience a parade in person. My wife and one-month-old daughter were staying with me at Quantico and were with me when I went to pick up our tickets. When the woman handing out the tickets saw us with our daughter, she immediately gave us a difficult time, concerned that our baby would cry during the parade. I explained to the woman that my first duty station was at the barracks and assured her that our baby would not disturb the parade.

Since we were invited guests of the Commandant, we were given a tour of the Commandant's Home prior to the parade. I had been in the historic home on several occasions while I was assigned to the barracks and even had an interesting experience when the 31st Commandant of the Marine Corps invited our platoon to tour the Commandant's House and then meet with him in his office.

After the platoon toured the home, we all crammed into the General's office and waited for his arrival. For his short stature, he was full of piss and vinegar. He affectionately teased his wife as he sat behind his desk, dressed down in a pair of green trousers and a white skivvy shirt. He insisted on us calling him Chuck, which none seemed willing to do except for a bold, usually inebriated, redheaded, Irish sergeant who once had me sneak his date out of the barracks. He walked right up to the general, extended a hand, and said, "What's up, Chuck…I am Brian".

We all expected the sergeant to be immediately reprimanded or worse, but instead, the General's face broke out in a broad smile as he enthusiastically shook the sergeant's hand.

Thankfully the house tour experience for my family was a bit more refined. My family and a small party of other guests were ushered outside into a receiving line on the Commandant's lawn after our tour concluded. When we reached the general and his wife, the General's aide announced Mrs. And Gunnery Sergeant Moyer and party. I shook the General's hand and was about to move on when he asked if he could be introduced to our tiny daughter. I handed her over to the General, who carefully took her up in white-gloved hands. He gave her a lot of attention before his wife finally grabbed her up. My little girl had the rare distention of gently being held by the 35th Commandant of the Marine Corps before the commencement of a traditional Friday Evening Parade. Thankfully the General wasn't dishing out his famous knifehands that evening.

Historical places to visit in and near Carlisle, Pennsylvania.

This segment of the Patriot's Path will take you to three stops in and around Carlisle, Pennsylvania. Begin your historical tour of Carlisle's sites at the Carlise Barracks and look for the 18th-century barracks built by Hessian prisoners while incarcerated during the Revolutionary War. This barracks has been converted into a museum featuring several exhibits that tell a compelling story of the barrack's importance to the Revolutionary War. If you examine an ancient wooden cell door closely, you will find names carved by Hessian prisoners. Take your time and drive around this second oldest post in the Army, where you can discover historical plaques, the site of a period forge, a reproduction of a Revolutionary War redoubt from the 1781 Siege of Yorktown, and a full bronze bust of Fredrick the Great.

Next, Drive into town and stop at the historic courthouse, where you will find several military memorials beautifully arranged in the adjoining Veteran's Memorial Courtyard. Drive on to Hanover Street and find a good parking spot. Along this thoroughfare, you can view the Andre and Despard House. The Historical plaque on this home states that Major Andre and Lieutenant Despard were held prisoner at the house and that both were eventually executed several years after their parole.

Andre and Despard were captured in 1775 near Quebec but were imprisoned in Caleb Cope's home in Lancaster for several months before they were transferred to Carlise. Andre, indeed, was executed as a spy in 1780. However, Lieutenant John Despard would end his career as a General and enjoy a quiet retirement before his death in 1829. It was his brother Edward, a Royal Naval officer, who was implicated in what was called the Despard plot and executed for high treason.

Look for the Blaine House and tour the former Commissary General of the Continental Army's historic brick home. Continue along Hanover Street to an Old Graveyard containing memorials, plaques, graves of American patriots, and a monument dedicated to Molly Pitcher. This beautiful monument is the centerpiece of this historic cemetery and features a life-sized bronze statue of Molly holding a ramrod for a field piece. Finally, head over to High Street, where you will find historical markers for General Armstrong and General Irvine and a massive mural of Molly Picture on the side of a brick building along Pitt Street.

<u>Andre & Despard House</u> is located at 129 PA-34, Carlisle, Pennsylvania.

<u>Blaine House</u> is located at 11 South Hanover Street Carlisle, Pennsylvania.

<u>Brigadier General William Thompson Marker</u> is located at Molly Pitcher Grave & Statue, 223 S Hanover Steet Carlisle, Pennsylvania.

Molly Pitcher Grave & Statue is located at 223 South Hanover Street Carlisle, Pennsylvania.

Carlisle Marker is located at 637-601 PA-34, Carlisle, Pennsylvania.

Carlisle Barracks is located at 860 North Hanover Street Carlisle, Pennsylvania.

Carlisle Fort Marker is located at 31 West High Street 3rd Floor Carlisle, Pennsylvania.

Carlisle Old Graveyard Revolutionary War Soldiers is located at 223 S Hanover Street Carlisle, Pennsylvania.

Dr. Benjamin Rush Statue is located on Dickenson Collage Campus.

General John Armstrong Marker is located at 103 East High Street Carlisle, Pennsylvania.

General William Irvine Marker is located at 103 East High Street Carlisle, Pennsylvania.

Thompson's Rifle Battalion is located at Hauto-Zat Art Gallery 45 East South Street Carlisle, Pennsylvania.

Butler Gun shop is located at 116 Dickenson Avenue Carlisle, Pennsylvania.

Berks County Pennsylvania

"A big grin came over the Marine's face and down came his hand. From then on, I always returned salutes. When George Bush followed me into the White House, I encouraged him to keep up the tradition."

~ Ronald Reagan, 40th President of the United States of America.

Berks County's role in the Revolutionary War is similar to Carlisle and Lancaster County. Reading, the county seat, was used during the war as a storage depot to supply the Army, a prison for Hessians and its courthouse, several churches, and even a shoe shop were used as field hospitals to treat injured and ill soldiers. This chapter will focus on two well-known and influential men who called Berks County their home, Daniel Boone and Conrad Weiser.

Jim Bridger, Kit Carson, Davey Crockett, and Daniel Boone are names synonymous with the term mountainmen and the American frontier. Of these illustrious trailblazers, only Boone once called Berks County home, and he spent much of his life-fighting Britain's Indian allies on the fringe of the American frontier during the Revolutionary War. Boone was born on October 22nd 1734, and was one of eleven children his Quaker parents raised. The family lived in a one-room cabin his father built in the Oley Valley near Reading.

Daniel spent his early years on the Pennsylvania frontier, often interacting with Native Americans. He learned to hunt from local settlers and the natives, and by the age of fifteen, he was renowned as one of the region's best hunters. Many colorful stories about Daniel illustrate his hunting prowess. In one such story, he was hunting in the woods with some local boys when the howl of a panther scattered all of them, but Daniel calmly aimed his rifle and shot the panther through the heart as it leaped. The story is probably folklore, but one of many that contributed to Daniel's iconic frontiersman image.

Daniel preferred to spend his time hunting, apparently with his parents' blessing, at an early age and received little formal education. According to a family tradition, a schoolteacher once expressed concern over Daniel's education, to which his father replied, "Let the girls do the spelling, and Dan will do the shooting." Although on the surface, it appeared education was a low priority for the Boone's, Daniel was tutored by family members, and he acquired a level of literacy that was at least on par with most cultured 18th-century men. Daniel was known to have reading material with him on his hunting expeditions, which usually consisted of the Bible and Gulliver's Travels. Daniel often found he was the only literate person among his hunting companions on hunting expeditions and would sometimes read to them around campfires.

Daniel's family became a source of controversy amongst their Quaker neighbors when his oldest sister married outside of the Quaker faith, and it didn't help that she was visibly pregnant before the wedding. When Daniel's oldest brother Israel married a woman who was not a Quaker a few years later, Squire Boone stood by his son and was subsequently excommunicated from his church and neighbors. In 1750, Boone sold his land and moved the family to North Carolina. Some believe they moved because of Boone's fallout with his Quaker neighbors, but others find it more likely because Berks County was getting too crowded for a frontier family like the Boones.

When the French and Indian War broke out, Daniel joined the North Carolina militia and served as a teamster and blacksmith. In 1755, he returned to Pennsylvania with the militia, which was part of General Braddock's expedition to expel the French and their native allies from the Ohio Valley. Daniel was in the rear with the wagons at the Monongahela River when the battle began. The battle was a very short one. Before Daniel could get to the fighting, Braddock was dying, and his soldiers were in a panicked retreat led by his young subordinate, Colonel George Washington. Daniel had to retreat from the battlefield with the rest of the expedition.

In 1758, conflicts between British colonists and their former Cherokee allies during the French and Indian War escalated to violence. The Cherokee raided the Yadkin Valley, forcing the Boones and many other families to relocate north to Culpeper County, Virginia. Daniel fought the Cherokee as a member of the North Carolina militia in what the colonists considered an uprising.

On August 14th 1756, Daniel wed Rebecca Bryan, one of his neighbors in the Yadkin Valley. They lived in a small cabin on his father's farm and, over the years, had ten children. Daniel and his wife also raised eight children who were related to them.

Daniel supported his large family as a hunter and trapper and was very active in the fur trade industry. Almost every autumn, despite the usually hostile frontier, he would go on long hunts into the wilderness that lasted weeks or even months. Daniel went alone or with a small group of men, accumulated hundreds of deer skins in the autumn, and trapped beaver and otter over the winter. When the long-hunters, as they called themselves, returned after the trapping season in the spring, they would sell their pelts to fur traders.

Along the hunting paths in the wilderness, frontiersmen would leave messages carved on trees or write their names on boulders or cave walls. Daniel's name or initials have been found on several trees or boulders. In Washington County, Tennessee, a tree was found with the inscription "D. Boon Cilled a. Bar on a tree in the year 1760" carved in its trunk. A similar tree carving can be viewed in the Filson Historical Society's museum in Louisville, Kentucky. The preserved tree trunk is inscribed, "D. Boon Kilt a Bar, 1803 but whether the carvings are authentic or not is really up to those who chase the history.

According to another popular story, Boone returned home after one of his more extended hunts only to discover that his wife Rebecca had given birth to a daughter. This came as a bit of a shock to Daniel because Rebecca wasn't pregnant when he left home. She ultimately confessed that, believing Daniel was dead, she slept with one of his brothers, who had fathered the child. Daniel did not blame Rebecca since he had been in a very inhospitable environment for so long. He helped raise the girl as if she were his child.

Daniel marked a trail he named "Boone's Trace," later called the Wilderness Road, which ran through the Cumberland Gap and into central Kentucky. When the group of settlers camped along this trace near present-day Richmond, Kentucky, Indians attacked, killing a slave named Sam and his enslaver. After driving off the attackers, the party buried the two men side by side. Daniel founded a town called Boonesborough along the Kentucky River. In September 1775, despite occasional attacks from Indians, Daniel brought his family and other settlers to Boonesborough.

Some Indians who were unhappy about losing their traditional hunting grounds in Kentucky to treaties saw the American Revolutionary War as a convenient opportunity to drive out the settlers and reclaim their land. Isolated frontier families and hunters soon became the frequent target of attacks and raids, convincing many to abandon Kentucky altogether. By late spring of 1776, Daniel and his family were among the fewer than 200 settlers who remained on the Kentucky frontier. They lived in or very near fortified settlements in Boonesborough, Harrodsburg, and Logan's Station.

On July 14th 1776, Daniel's daughter Jemima and two of her companions were captured outside Boonesborough by a raiding party of Indians. They absconded with the girls, taking them north toward the Shawnee towns in the Ohio Valley. Daniel and a group of frontiersmen from Boonesborough quickly trailed the war party, finally catching up with them two days later. Daniel and his men caught the Indians in an ambush, drove them off, and rescued the girls. The incident became the most memorable event of Daniel's allure. James Fenimore Cooper created a version of this historical event in his classic novel The Last of the Mohicans. Unfortunately, this event did not end the hostilities in the Kentucky region.

In 1777, the British Lieutenant Governor of Quebec, Henry Hamilton, began to recruit Indians to attack the wilderness settlements in Kentucky. That same year, the newly formed Kentucky County, Virginia militia mustered in Boonesborough in March. In 1778, some Shawnee, allied to the British, conducted a siege of Boonesborough. Armed slaves fought alongside their slave masters in defense of the fort. A slave named London ventured beyond the fort walls to engage the war party and was killed. Daniel was shot in the ankle while he fought outside the safety of the fort walls. A recent arrival to the settlement named Simon Kenton came to Boone's rescue, running beyond the walls in withering enemy fire and carrying Boone back inside the fort.

While Boone recovered, the Shawnee, led by Chief Blackfish, kept up their siege of the fort at Boonesborough. While they kept the settlers pinned down inside the fort, the Indians killed the settler's livestock and destroyed crops before they abandoned the attack.

Although the settlers successfully defended the fort, the attack left food supplies dangerously low. Boone was confident they could replenish their supply of meat by hunting, but they had no way to quickly preserve it with the onslaught of winter. Out of salt to preserve venison and other game, Daniel led a party of 30 men to the salt springs along the Licking River. On February 7th while Boone was hunting game for the foraging party, he was captured by Blackfish's warriors. Because Daniel's party was vastly outnumbered, Boone avoided a fight by returning to camp the next day with Blackfish and persuading his men to surrender.

Blackfish had planned to move on to Boonesborough and destroy it, but Daniel argued that the women and children would not survive a winter journey as prisoners back to the Shawnee villages. Instead, Daniel promised that he would surrender to Boonesborough the following spring. The problem with this plan was that Daniel was not able to let his men know that he was merely bluffing to prevent an immediate attack on the settlement. He acted out his strategy so convincingly that some of his men thought he had switched sides. Many of the Shawnees wanted to torture and burn the prisoners to death in revenge for the recent murder of a Shawnee Chief named Cornstalk. Blackfish held a council to seek the consensus of his warriors. Daniel made an impassioned speech that was so convincing the warriors voted not to kill the prisoners. Daniel had saved his men, but, as Blackfish pointed out, Daniel had failed to include himself in the agreement, so he was forced to run the gauntlet through the lines of warriors, which he survived with minor injuries.

When Daniel and his men were taken to Blackfish's town of Chillicothe, some of the people adopted some of the prisoners to replace dead relatives, which was their custom. Some historians believe Daniel was adopted into Blackfish's family and named 'Sheltowee', which means Big Turtle. On June 16th 1778, Daniel found out that Blackfish intended to return to Boonesborough with a large force to destroy the settlements as he had previously planned. Boone promptly escaped from the village, finding a horse, and made his way back to Boonesborough, covering 160 miles in just five days. After his horse gave out, he finished the journey on foot. Biographer Robert Morgan calls Daniel's escape and return "one of the great legends of frontier history."

In 1780, Daniel joined General George Rogers Clark's expedition into the Ohio Valley and fought the Shawnee in the Battle of Piqua.

On the way home from the campaign, while Daniel was hunting with his brother Ned, a Shawnee, mistaking Ned for Dainiel, shot and killed him. The Indian cut off Ned's head and took it back to his people as evidence that Daniel Boone had finally been killed.

In 1781, Daniel traveled to Richmond to take a seat in the legislature, but British dragoons under Colonel Tarleton captured him and several other legislators near Charlottesville. The British released Daniel on parole several days later. During Daniel's term in office, Cornwallis surrendered at Yorktown, but the fighting continued along the Kentucky frontier. In August 1783, Daniel returned to Kentucky and fought in the Battle of Blue Licks. Daniel's son Israel was killed during the fighting, and it ended in a resounding defeat of the Kentuckians. On November 10th 1782, Daniel took part in another Clark-led expedition into the Ohio Valley, the last major campaign of the Revolutionary War, which resulted in the destruction of six Shawnee towns.

Although many of the stories about Daniel are considered folklore, what is indisputable is that Daniel was a warrior and a Patriot. Daniel died on September 26th 1820, at his son Nathan's home along Femme Osage Creek, Missouri. He was buried next to his beloved wife Rebecca, who preceded him in death on March 18th 1813.

Although Conrad Weiser, another resident of Berks County, died fifteen years prior to the beginning of the Revolutionary War, it is still important to recognize his significant contributions toward the settlement of Pennsylvania during the 18th Century. Weizer was born in 1696 in the small village of Herrenberg, in the Duchy of Württemberg, Germany. His father, a member of the Württemberg Blue Dragoons, was stationed in the village. Conrad's father was discharged from the Blue Dragoons when Junior was an infant, and the family moved back to their ancestral home. In 1709, things took a turn for the worse for the family. Conrad's mother, Anna, died of fever when he was a young boy. Then, the family's ancestral lands were ravaged by repeated French invasions and pestilence. After a particularly long and inhospitable winter, the Weiser family and thousands of other refugees left Germany. They traveled to England, which had been willing to support the Protestant refugees.

The Weisers lived in England for about a year when Queen Anne, who encouraged the refugees to migrate to the new world, arranged the transportation of nearly 3,000 refugees in ten ships to the New York colony to help settle the land. However, the passage wasn't free, and most of the refugees had to work off their passage in the form of indentureship in work camps. These camps typically produced ships' stores, such as tar and other materials. After they worked off their passage, they continued their indentureship, trading their labor for land. After Weiser senior worked off the passage for his family, he acquired land in the Schoharie Valley and established a homestead.

When Conrad was 16, a Mohawk chief proposed to Weiser Senior that the boy live with the Mohawk in a village near the homestead to learn the Indian culture and wilderness ways. Weiser Senior agreed to the proposal, and Weiser Junior spent the winter and spring of 1712–1713 with the Mohawk, where he was able to pick up enough of the native language and the customs of the people to communicate effectively. The Mohawk tribe was the easternmost nation of the Haudenosaunee or the Iroquois League. Village life for young Weiser was not easy. He endured long periods of cold, hunger, and bouts of homesickness. He eventually returned to his family toward the end of July 1713, a hardier and more woods-savvy young man.

On November 22nd 1720, at the age of 24, Weiser married Anna Eve Feck. They remained in the Schoharie Valley for about five years before following the Susquehanna River south to Womelsdorf, Pennsylvania, near present-day Reading, where they established a farmstead and started a family. The Weisers had fourteen children, but only seven reached adulthood.

An oral tradition posits that Weiser met an Oneida Chief named Shikellamy while hunting. This is entirely plausible since an old trail called the Tulpehocken Path leads from Womelsdorf to Shamokin village near present-day Sunbury, where Shikellamy lived. Regardless, the two discovered they could communicate using the Mohawk language and became friends. The Oneida chief quickly learned he could trust Weiser and considered him an adopted son of the Mohawk and, by extension, the Iroquois.

When the Iroquois sent Shikellamy to Philadelphia as their emissary for a council with representatives of the province of Pennsylvania in 1731, Weiser accompanied him and entered public service for the first time. Weiser's translator skills during the conference impressed the Pennsylvania governor so much that he enlisted his services as an interpreter, and his skills were leveraged in a follow-up council held in Philadelphia in August 1732.

During the Tulpehocken Treaty of 1736, Shikellamy, Weiser, and the Pennsylvania government negotiated a deed in which the Iroquois agreed to sell lands south of Blue Mountain. This represented a significant change in Pennsylvania's policy toward Indians because the Iroquois had no prior claim to the land.

When Penn's father died in 1670, King Charles II of England owed the knighted Admiral 16,000 pounds, now worth nearly four million dollars. William Penn accepted in payment, forty thousand square miles of land in America from the indebted king. He named his land grant Sylvania, which means woods or forest, but the king prefixed Penn, in honor of Admiral Penn, and it became Pennsylvania or Penn's Woods. Pennsylvania was to become a home in the wilderness for the Quakers, who were persecuted for their religious beliefs in Europe.

Penn firmly believed that the Indians were the original owners of the land and deeds of land purchases bearing the Penn name are on record. Although he was already granted a title to the land he claimed in Pennsylvania, Penn carefully negotiated treaties with its native inhabitants, thus paying for something he already owned. Penn was careful in his negotiations with the Indians and deliberately avoided taking sides in disputes between tribes, which helped keep the peace along the frontier.

Unfortunately, Penn's children had a different viewpoint regarding treaties and negotiations. The formal purchase between Penn's descendants and the Iroquois in the Tulpehocken Treaty suggested that Pennsylvania favored the Iroquois' claim over the claims of the Lenape, who were, in that era, subjected to the Iroquois, for the same land. Along with the Walking Purchase of the following year, the treaties negotiated by Penn's sons strained Pennsylvania-Lenape relations.

On February 27th 1737, Weiser was commissioned by Virginia Governor William Gooch to attempt to negotiate peace between southern tribes living in the Shenandoah Valley and the Iroquois League. The governor feared wars between the Iroquois and local tribes like the Catawba would draw Virginia and Pennsylvania into their conflict. Weiser and Stoffel Stump made the six-week journey to the Iroquois capital at Onondaga, near present-day Syracuse, New York, trekking through deep snow, enduring freezing temperatures, and subsisting on meager rations. Weiser successfully persuaded the Iroquois not to send retaliatory war parties to the South but failed to convince them to send emissaries to negotiate with the Southern tribes. The Iroquois were, however, impressed with Weiser's negotiating skills, so they named him Tarachiawagon, which means Holder of the Heavens.

In 1742, Weiser's interpreter skills were called on for another treaty meeting between the Iroquois and Pennsylvania in

Philadelphia, where the Penns finally paid for the land they purchased six years earlier. During the council, the Onondaga chief Canasatego chastised the Lenape chiefs for engaging in independent land sales and he ordered them to move their settlements northwest beyond what is now Northumberland County. The Lenape were eventually pressured by Iroquois dominance and settlers pushing into Indian territory to migrate further west into the Ohio Valley, which was considered disputed territory between the English and the French. Here, the Lenape were positioned to trade with the French, and having been disillusioned by the English taking sides with the Iroquois over disputed land claims, some became natural allies to the French. During the French and Indian War, they launched raids against English settlements as far east as the Susquehanna River.

Conversely, the Pennsylvania land purchase ensured that the Iroquois League would remain staunch allies with the British during the seven-year conflict with the French. The League helped defeat France and her Indian allies, who were coincidentally, traditional enemies of the Iroquois to begin with.

In 1744, Weiser acted as the interpreter one last time during the Treaty of Lancaster, held between the Iroquois and the colonies of Pennsylvania, Virginia, and Maryland. On the final day of the council, which happened to take place on July 4th Canasatego spoke about how the Iroquois Nation viewed political unity, saying;

"Our wise forefathers established Union and Amity between the Five Nations. This has made us formidable; this has given us great Weight and Authority with our neighboring Nations. We are a powerful Confederacy, and by your observing the same methods our wise forefathers have taken, you will acquire such Strength and power. Therefore, whatever befalls you, never fall out with one another".

Later, amid constant political squabbles between colonial representatives during the First Continental Congress, Benjamin Franklin published Canasatego's speech. Some historians believe the speech delivered by the Iroquoian statesman influenced Franklin's American concepts of political unity and government. Many of these ideas, including his political cartoon *Join or Die*, manifested in Franklin's failed attempt to unite the squabbling 13 colonies during the Albany Plan of Union ten years after Canasatego's speech.

In 1756, the Pennsylvania government appointed Weiser and Ben Franklin to plan for and organize the development of a chain of frontier forts between the Delaware and the Susquehanna Rivers, and in the autumn of 1758, Weiser attended a council at Easton, Pennsylvania, and was instrumental in calming angry Ohio Vally tribes and working out peaceful resolutions. During this treaty counsel, Pennsylvania met with the Iroquois and other Indian tribes. With the Treaty, the tribes in the Ohio Valley agreed to abandon support for their French allies after French soldiers demolished Fort Duquesne and withdrew to Canada.

Weiser died on his farm on July 13th 1760, and was buried near his home. Ironically, Weiser wasn't in the ground very long when relations between Pennsylvania and the Indians began to decline rapidly. Although the Colonial leaders tried to restrict settlement to the east of the Appalachians to preserve sovereign Indian territory, settlers kept pushing west, encroaching on territories and traditional hunting grounds that did not belong to them; in the 19th Century, this concept would become known as Manifest Destiny.

Marine Corps Tie-In...Officer Candidate School- Integrity Violators.

AMOIs are usually required to perform an augmented duty assignment during the summer months. My augmented duties consisted of three Bulldog cycles at OCS Quantico and SNCOIC of

Marine Option Midshipman summer mountain training at Bridgeport, California.

The first two Bulldog training cycles at OCS are non-bargain assignments for new AMOIs and are completed in the summer before checking into an assigned college or university. New AMOIs traveled on Permissive Temporary Assignment Duty orders, which meant I was required to travel back to Camp Lejeune, pick up original orders for my assignment to the Villanova University NROTC Unit, and then drive back to Philadelphia after completing my first two summer increments. I had already checked out of my North Carolina unit before departing for Quantico, so I had nothing else to do but pick up my original orders.

I arrived in Quantico, Virginia, in mid-May, checked in, and settled down in a hotel room that would serve as my Geo-bachelor quarters while working in Quantico. All new and returning AMOIs gathered on Brown Field for a Physical Fitness Test the next day. After the PFT, we all gathered in an auditorium and received a welcome aboard brief from the school's commanding officer and sergeant major. Every summer, all AMOIs and officers participate in a two-week Staff Orientation Course (SOC). During SOC, Officers and staff learn the OCS Standard Operating Procedure, are assigned to a training company, and are broken down into teams.

During SOC, the training companies PT...a lot. During the two-week course, an instructor can expect to run through every PT session the officer candidates will be led through over eight weeks. The prerequisite successful Drill Instructor tour is important because each platoon of officer candidates will conduct close-order drills, MCPAP training, conditioning hikes, and other activities similar to those Drill Instructors conducted with enlisted recruits during boot camp.

Unlike the two recruit depots, where Drill Instructors emphasize making basically trained Marines, the OCS focus is leadership eccentric; each candidate is trained, screened, and evaluated for leadership potential. Although billets are assigned to a few recruits in training platoons, most will not be assigned a leadership billet during boot camp. At OCS, every candidate is assigned several platoon or company-level leadership billets, and their peers and instructors constantly evaluate their performance. Those consistently falling under a particular percentage find themselves the subject of a Performance Board held by the Commanding Officer of OCS. A candidate can usually survive one Performance Board, but a second visit with the Colonel will likely send a candidate back to his or her NROTC Unit with the option to reapply for OCS the following year. A disciplinary board is a different story; depending on the severity of the infraction committed, a candidate can be dropped and told to reapply or dropped and be advised to seek employment elsewhere.

During my second increment at OCS, I worked with a candidate who was having difficulty passing his rifle handling evaluation. The harder he tried, the more frustrated both of us became. He struggled with the basics: muzzle awareness, magazine retention, slinging, and unslinging the rifle. The candidate eventually threw his rifle on the ground (which is a big no, no anywhere in the Marine Corps) and angrily started to walk away from it. I ordered the candidate to pick up the rifle he had thrown to the ground, and he said, "Nope, going to see the colonel." The candidate marched to the Colonel's office to drop on request; he disclosed that he was a conscientious objector but was sure the Marine Corps would give him an assignment where he wouldn't be required to carry a 'gun'. The candidate got what he asked for, and the last time we saw him, he was gathering his personal effects while grumbling about joining the Air Force.

Candidates were typically dropped for any integrity-related incident and depending on the severity of the violation, some were not invited back to OCS. During one increment, we had a cheating scandal during a night land navigation course. Whenever the conspirators involved found a box in the dark, densely wooded training lanes, they would tap on the ammo cans that served as markers so others could find them. Had the candidates known that failure merely meant a second or third attempt to pass the course later in the increment, they likely would not have cheated.

Another integrity-related incident candidates were dropped for was emptying their canteens to lighten their combat load prior to running the Endurance Course. This rugged, hazard-filled obstacle course stretches over several miles. Candidates began the course with the 'Double O' course and ended their ordeal miles later at the top of a hill they were required to assault by fire, using blank ammunition.

I never understood why some officer candidates would have thought that dumping a few ounces of water they could have and should have consumed during the course could give them a significant advantage. I negotiated the course at least a dozen times and didn't feel the need to lighten my combat loadout. Unfortunately, we caught candidates dumping water and required gear all along the trails. We even caught candidates hiding along the looped trails, where they would wait for what they thought was a reasonable amount of time and then jump back onto the trail, cutting out miles and obstacles from the course. During one iteration of the course, instructors had to return to the circuit to find a missing candidate. We eventually found him in some brush along one of the loops. He had fallen asleep while waiting for an opportunity to jump back onto the trail.

I was on duty one night in the squad bay and heard a noise in the laundry room. When I investigated the source of the noise, I discovered a candidate sitting on the floor in the laundry room. The candidate was obviously eating food in the squadbay, which was strictly against the rules. Although he probably would have been assigned a Performance Review, which would have resulted in mild consequences, the candidate decided to lie. The scene would have been comedic if not for the candidate's decision to lie to avoid a performance review. His cheeks were so full of food from a Meal Ready to Eat (MRE) that he looked like a chipmunk with cheeks stuffed with nuts. Whenever he said anything, cracker crumbs would spew from his mouth. Worse still, he was sitting on the rest of the MRE to conceal it; he looked more like a brooding hen sitting on her eggs than a potential Marine officer. The candidate was dropped for integrity but was invited back to OCS the following year.

Medical drops were more unpredictable and could disqualify a person from military service depending on the reason and extent of the injury. One of my Nova midshipmen tripped over an obstacle and broke a bone, which wasn't surprising. Ironically, the midshipman, infamous for his clumsiness, was warned to watch his step before his departure to OCS.

Heat cases were common during the summer months in Quantico, and depending on the severity and frequency, they were another disqualifier from military service. Candidates failing to monitor their fluid intake properly were the most susceptible to heat injuries, which required a core temperature verification via a rectal thermometer. Most Marines have a healthy respect for the rectal thermometer. Dubbed 'the Silver Bullet,' most recruits and candidates were terrified of the prospect of being a recipient of the procedure.

At the depot, DIs would tell their recruits horror stories about the infamous Silver Bullet, akin to stories parents would tell their children featuring the Boogieman. When I was a child, I was terrified that the Boogieman would get me, and if I gave him a place to hide in a messy room or misbehave, I would surely have a run-in with him. Drill Instructors told stories of hapless recruits who, faking injury, would get the Silver Bullet. The instrument was almost always described as a long, thick equine instrument typically used for checking the core temperature of large barnyard animals. Some hats even went as far as suggesting that corpsmen often did not have time to lubricate the instrument before its use.

An instructor could usually discern if a recruit or candidate was faking a heat injury. Most victims of a heat injury were too comatose to resist the procedure, while fakers usually fought the insertion of the Silver Bullet pugnaciously, often amplified with blood-curdling screams. Most heat case injuries at OCS occurred during conditioning hikes, the Endurance Course, and occasionally during PT.

During one increment, an officer candidate completed the Endurance Course but failed to finish in the prescribed minimum time allowance; he indicated to staff it was because he suffered from heat exhaustion. He was immediately sent to a corpsman for medical attention and was administered the Silver Bullet. He was diagnosed with a mild case of heat stress and quickly returned to training. During his second attempt, the candidate's time was much improved, but still not good enough for the minimum requirement to pass, and once again, the candidate requested medical attention for a heat-related illness, and he again received the bullet. The candidate was offered a third and final attempt at the course a few days later. This time the candidate finished the course in time, but incredulously, as his time was being recorded, the candidate fell to his knees with his pants around his ankles and butt bared and looked over his shoulder expectantly for a Corpsman. The candidate packed his bags later that day and was never seen again.

Historic places to visit in Berks County, Pennsylvania.

Begin your journey on this segment of the Patriot's Path with a trip to Reading, Pennsylvania. On the way to the Pagoda, you should pass the historic Hessian Camp marker along Hessian Road. The

Pagoda, built on the summit of Mount Penn in 1908, offers a breathtaking view of the town of Reading and miles of the surrounding countryside.

Head down the mountain towards town, and you will pass by City Park and the bow anchor from the USS Maine. "Remember the Maine to hell with Spain" became America's battle cry after the Maine was sent to the bottom of Havanna, Cuba's harbor, in 1896 from an explosion. Although Cubans were quickly blamed for sabotage, the blast might have been accidentally ignited in the ship's ammunition magazine. Coincidently, the anchor was the only part of the ship that had not sunk since it had already been embedded in the harbor floor before the explosion. Fourteen years after the USS Maine went down, the US Navy raised the ship, recovered the bodies of the American sailors, salvaged what they could, and towed her out of the harbor, where she was properly sunk. Assistant Secretary of the Navy and future president of the United States, F.D. Roosevelt, was on hand in Reading to dedicate the artifact to the city and squash rumors that the anchor was actually not from the Maine.

Drive across town to the regional airport and visit the Mid Atlantic Air Museum and its exhibits of thirty-three military aircraft. This collection includes one of only four P-61 Black Widows known to be in existence and a 1941 Piper Cub trainer from the Philadelphia Navy Yard. Plan your visit for the first weekend in June to experience the annual World War II Weekend. Eighty World War II aircraft are on display, 200 vintage vehicles, and over 1,500 war reenactors.

Next, head to the Daniel Boone Homestead in Birdsboro and swing by The Mordecai Lincoln house. Unfortunately, the Lincoln House is probably a drive-by adventure; it is currently in disrepair, boarded up, and parking is precarious. The history is fascinating, though. Mordecai was President Abraham Lincoln's great-great-grandfather and business partner of Iron Master Samuel Nutt. The Daniel Boone Homestead is nestled in the picturesque Oley Valley on

579 acres and is the home of beautifully preserved homestead buildings and much more. Meet up with a tour guide at the park entrance and get an interactive tour of the house and outbuildings by a knowledgeable guide, often dressed in period garb. Although the Boones took their belongings with them when they migrated south, period-appropriate furniture, tools, and other objects used by 18th-century settlers are meticulously displayed. Visitors can tour the blacksmith shop, the Deturk Barn, the Bertolet Sawmill, and the cabin.

The final destination listed in this chapter of must-see historic places is the Conrad Weiser Homestead in Womelsdorf. Begin your visit of this beautiful 26-acre park at the Scheetz House, which is where you will find the visitor center and another knowledgeable tour guide. You will see exhibits on display on the home's first floor before moving outside to an adjacent house. The house is considered the Weiser home because it is the only dwelling on the property old enough to have served as such. Visitors can walk along a pond on the property, visit the Weiser Family Cemetery, and check out the full-sized bronze statue of Shikellamy, the Weiser Monument, and a statue of a World War II soldier overlooking the road.

Daniel Boone Homestead is located at 400 Daniel Boone Road Birdsboro, Pennsylvania.

Conrad Weiser Homestead is located at 28 Weiser Lane Womelsdorf, Pennsylvania.

Mordecai Lincoln House is located at 930 Lincoln Road Birdsboro, Pennsylvania.

The Reading Pagoda is located at Duryea Drive Reading, Pennsylvania.

The Hessian Camp Historical Marker is located along business route 422 and Hessian Road Reading, Pennsylvania.

<u>Mid Atlantic Air Museum</u> is located at 11 Museum Drive Reading, Pennsylvania.

Luzerne County, Pennsylvania

"We have a saying in the Marine Corps, and that is, 'no better friend, no worse enemy, than a U.S. Marine.' We always hope for the first…friendship, but are certainly more than ready for the second".

~ General John F. Kelly retired Marine general, White House Chief of Staff and Secretary of Homeland Security under the Trump Administration

In 1777, The British in Canada were busy recruiting Loyalists and native allies to take the war to the American frontier along the northern and western borders of Pennsylvania, New York, New Jersey, and Virginia. Their Indian allies included the majority of the formative Iroquois League; only the Oneida, having maintained their friendship with the colonists, supported the American Cause.

British Indian Department officer John Butler, a prominent loyalist and an officer of the British Indian Department, was granted permission to enlist other Loyalists into a regiment known as Butler's Rangers to begin raiding the frontier. The Iroquois soon got into the action after Seneca chiefs Sayenqueraghta and Cornplanter encouraged their warriors to begin raids against frontier settlements. Mohawk war chief Thayendanegea, also known as Joseph Brant, influenced Mohawk participation in a joint effort to harass the frontier and even recruited Loyalist volunteers to fight with him. Unlike the fictional companions in James Fennimore Cooper's Last of the Mohicans novel, Brant actually was educated at the Reverend Wheelock School in Connecticut and had very close ties with the British, which is more accurately portrayed in a movie titled *The Broken Chain*.

By April 1778, Seneca war parties were ravaging settlements along the Allegheny River and up and down the West Branch of the Susquehanna River. In late May, Brant's Mohawks raided Cobleskill in

Tryon County, New York. In June Butler, Sayenqueraghta, and Brant met at Tioga Point in present-day Athens, Pennsylvania, near where the Chemung River and the North Branch of the Susquehanna River meet. Butler and the Seneca planned a major joint attack on the Wyoming Valley settlements while it was agreed that Brant would return to Onaquaga in New York and prepare to raid settlements in that quarter.

The combined Loyalist-Indian force arrived in the Wyoming Valley on June 30th and killed three settlers who were working in an unprotected gristmill. This alerted the rest of the settlers and gave them enough time to move into a local fort. The following day, Butler demanded the surrender of Wintermute's fort. Terms were arranged that required the defenders to surrender the fort, all their weapons, and food stores. The militiamen occupying the fort were released on the condition that they would not actively fight for the duration of the war. On July 3rd however, Butler's Rangers discovered that the militia was gathering at nearby Forty Fort.

With Patriot militiamen located a mile away, Butler set up an ambush. He set his plan into motion with an order to burn Fort Wintermute, which, by design, drew in the militia, who thought the rangers were retreating, into Butler's well-laid trap. Butler directed the Seneca warriors to lie flat on the ground to conceal the ambush element from the militia. The militia advanced to within a hundred yards of Butler's Rangers and engaged them. After an exchange of volleys, the Seneca rose from their concealed positions, fired one time, and then charged the militia with tomahawks and knives to engage the militia in hand-to-hand combat. The battle lasted about 45 minutes. An order to re-form the American line turned into a frantic rout when the inexperienced militiamen panicked and began to run away. The howling Seneca warriors gave chase, and only about 60 Americans escaped. Of the militia not killed in the ambush or during the chase, Loyalists and Seneca warriors tortured and killed all but five men. Butler reported that his rangers and Seneca allies had taken 227 militia scalps. The next morning, Colonel Nathan Denison surrendered what remained of his militia, Forty Fort, and two other smaller posts to Colonel Butler. The militia were paroled on their promise to take no part in further hostilities. The Loyalists molested a few inhabitants after the forts' surrender but spared all the non-combatants.

After the forts fell into enemy hands and news got around about the devastating ambush on the militia, many settlers evacuated the area in a panic, spreading news and rumors about the American defeat along their flight. This caused a general alarm among settlers across the frontiers of New York and Pennsylvania. Some American newspapers picked up these rumors and embellished the accounts, producing unsubstantiated and exaggerated accounts about Butler and the Seneca burning women, children, and wounded militia inside Forty Fort on the day after the battle on July 4th. The American public was duly outraged by the reports of the atrocities. Many settlers saw it as one more reason to support the American cause for independence.

A few months later, Colonel Thomas Hartley arrived with his 'Additional Continental Regiment' to defend the Wyoming Valley and protect settlers while they harvested their crops. Captain Denison joined Hartly's Regiment along with a few other militia companies. In September, Hartley and Denison, with 130 soldiers, moved up the east branch of the Susquehanna, destroyed Indian villages as far as Tioga, and recovered a significant amount of plunder taken by the Seneca and Loyalists during their raid. They skirmished with Seneca War parties but withdrew from the country on intelligence that Joseph Brant was assembling a large force at Unadilla, New York.

Many Seneca were angered by the accusations of atrocities committed during the Battle of Wyoming, which they denied committing. The accusations, along with resentment toward

American militiamen ignoring their paroles, encouraged some warriors under Cornplanter, Joseph Brant, and Colonel Butler to attack settlers in what is known as the Massacre at Cherry Valley in New York in November 1778. The Battle of Wyoming and the massacre at Cherry Valley drew a strong American response to strike back at the Loyalists and Iroquois along the frontier. In the summer of 1779, the Sullivan Expedition, commissioned by General Washington, would become that strong response.

The western state of Wyoming was introduced in a bill to Congress in 1865 to provide a temporary government for the territory. Colonists had used the name earlier for the Wyoming Valley in Pennsylvania, and it is derived from the Lenape-Munsee word meaning "at the big river flat."

Marine Corps Tie-In...An Unlikely Companion.

Early in my youth, I was enthralled with stories about American Indians. According to my maternal grandmother, Cherokee blood runs through my veins. I spent hours upon hours walking corn rows, searching for arrowheads that proliferated my grandfather's farm. An artesian spring existed not far from the farmhouse that feeds a small pond my grandfather had excavated. According to my grandfather, a Delaware camp existed near the valuable water source. No one knows whether a small village existed near the spring or if the area served as a temporary hunting camp, but ample evidence has been discovered over the years to support the claim that some primitive camp once occupied part of the farm. I had found dozens of arrowheads, a well-preserved spear point or knife, and many partial arrowheads, likely products of failed knapping projects. Others found arrowheads in the area, and my father even found a clay trade pipe and an old silver Spanish coin near the spring.

My late uncle inadvertently focused my interest on the Iroquois League at an early age by introducing me to a book series I had read through several times. The White Indian Series chronicles the life and adventures of a fictional white child taken by the Great Sachem of the Iroquois League during a raid and raised the boy as his own. The series spans generations of the original white Indian and is considered a historical fiction since it weaves its way through touchstone wars and battles such as the French and Indian War, Revolutionary War, Seminole War, and the Battle of Fallen Timbers, to name a few. Unfortunately, in his book series, Porter places the Iroquoian capital in Seneca lands, writes that the Seneca nation remained neutral during the Revolutionary War and descendants of the White Indian served directly as Washington's personal scouts, which is not even close to being historically accurate.

A lot of native Indian micro-history exists near my grandfather's farm. From an Indian cemetery on the outskirts of a town a mile away from the farm to a small Indian village and burial site on the Isle of Que, along with little-known battles and massacres along Penn's Creek that happened within a ten-mile radius of the farm, served to intensify my interest in native American history. I eventually learned the art of tomahawk throwing and became proficient in its use. I bought a hand-forged tomahawk from a self-proclaimed modern-day mountain man who lived in a teepee down in the valley (Flint Valley) where I grew up. I practiced throwing the tomahawk until, after many shattered handles, I could regularly hit the targets I aimed at.

The tomahawk eventually became a combat companion to my K-Bar fighting knife, and they served as my backup weapons to my rifle in OIF; I kept both razor sharp and painted the tomahawk in a desert tan pattern. I pulled it from my belt one time during OIF on the outskirts of Saddam City. Our platoon was tasked with controlling a displaced crowd, becoming more agitated the longer we prevented them from re-entering the city. At one point, I found myself surrounded by Iraqis, and because of the language barrier, everyone was agitated. Some cultural tendencies don't translate well, especially in a combat zone. One of these is the Arab custom of close, hands-on communication. In other words, they tend to communicate through physical touch, and I am a no-touchy, touchy kind of guy unless you happen to be my wife or daughters.

Along the outskirts of Sadam City, an Iraqi man grabbed the sleeve of my blouse and frantically pointed across the river toward the town. We clearly could not verbally communicate, but I tried several times, to no avail, to get the man to stop grabbing at my sleeve. Finally exasperated, I pulled the sinister-looking tomahawk from my belt in a quick, sweeping demonstration and returned it swiftly to my belt. I then pointed to the man, held out my hand, and made a chopping motion with the other. The man ran off, and I soon discovered I had a widening bubble of space around me and my squad members...I learned the fine art of communication using sign language with a primitive tomahawk. The tomahawk never left my belt again in Iraq, and like myself, has been retired. I store it in a box with the rest of my military relics.

Historic places to visit in Luzerne County, Pennsylvania.

Most of these historical points of interest are located in Forty Fort, Pennsylvania. Begin your tour of this historic town at Jenkins' Fort Historical Marker, then travel downstream to the other stopping places along the river. Following this path, your next stop is at the Wyoming Battle Monument. This towering stone obelisk stands proudly over the common grave of the patriots who died during the Wyoming Massacre.

After visiting this piece of hallowed ground, continue along the river to the Swetland Homestead. Although the house was built in the early 19th Century, it is still one of the oldest surviving houses in Forty Fort and is well worth visiting. After your Swetland Homestead visit, continue to the Colonel Nathan Denison Homestead. Denison built this house after the Revolutionary War in 1790 and lived there until his death in 1809. The Luzerne County Historical Society now owns the home.

Your last two stops in Forty Fort will take you to the historic Forty Fort Cemetery, where you will find the graves of American patriots and several beautiful monuments raised in their honor. Finally, Drive down to 242 River Street to a beautiful brick building where you will find a small memorial commemorating the fort and a historical marker facing the river. Tioga Point is the last historical point of interest on this segment of the Patriot's Path, but history enthusiasts, be warned, it is at least an hour's drive the New York border and Tioga Point.

Jenkins' Fort Historical Marker is located at 11 Exeter Avenue West Pittston, Pennsylvania.

The Wyoming Monument is located at US 11 Wyoming Avenue and Susquehanna Avenue Wyoming, Pennsylvania.

Swetland Homestead located at 885 Wyoming Avenue Forty Fort, Pennsylvania.

Nathan Denison Homestead is located along Wyoming Avenue Forty Fort, Pennsylvania.

Forty Fort Cemetery is located at 20 River Street Forty Fort, Pennsylvania.

Forty Fort is located at 242 River Street Forty Fort, Pennsylvania.

Tioga Point Museum is located at 724 South Main Street Athens, Pennsylvania.

Lycoming County, Pennsylvania

Marine Corps Credo: To catch us, you have to be fast. To find us, you have to be smart. To beat us, you have to be kidding.

~ Anonymous

When the American Revolutionary War broke out in 1775, most of the settlers in the Lycoming area were patriots who supported independence from Britain. About 75 settlers from Lycoming County volunteered to serve in the Continental Army, and many more were actively defending the borderlands as members of local militias. Although fighting had erupted far from home along the eastern seaboard cities of Boston, New York, and Philadelphia, Lycoming County soon became another battlefront in the war. Frontier communities, devastated by the British and the Seneca along the northern and western branches of the Susquehanna River during the Wyoming Massacre, along with the mania created by fleeing settlers, prompted local militia leaders to order an evacuation of the frontier. The evacuation would become known as the Big Run Away.

Most of the refugees traveled downriver to the fringe of civilization to escape the raiding Loyalists and Seneca war parties and were temporarily relocated in or around Fort Augusta at modern-day Sunbury. While the settlers were taking advantage of the relative safety of the fort that defended the forks of the North and West Branches of the Susquehanna River, their abandoned houses, farms, and mills were being razed and destroyed. Some settlers returned to their land soon after the raids, but the attacks were renewed the following year, leading to a second evacuation known as The Little Runaway.

In 1768, Pennsylvania and the Iroquois Confederacy signed the First Treaty of Fort Stanwix in New York. The treaty expanded the boundary between colonial, and Iroquois lands in exchange for money and guarantees that settlers would be restrained from pushing beyond the limits set by the treaty. It did not take very long for settlers to move into the newly annexed territory known as the 'New Purchase.'

The treaty between Pennsylvania and the Iroquois League recognized Lycoming Creek as the western boundary of the New Purchase, so any settlements established west of the creek were encroaching on Indian land and violated the treaty. Despite this, settlers built farmsteads and mills west of the treaty boundary, near modern-day Lock Haven. The settlements that fell outside the treaty boundary received no protection or government from Pennsylvania because they willfully violated the treaty agreement, so they formed their own system of self-rule, known as the Fair Play System.

The Fair Play Men recognized that some form of municipality was needed to govern the settlements. They wrote their own Declaration of Independence from Britain and delivered it to the settlers in Lycoming County at the mouth of Pine Creek on July 4th 1776. Tradition suggests that when the Fair Play Men did this, they were unaware of the Continental Congress' Declaration, a coincidence that is hard for me to believe.

There had always been tensions between the settlers and natives along the frontier, notwithstanding the influence British agents and Loyalists had on Indians near the territories the Fair Play System governed. Atrocities were committed by Indians and settlers alike, which became more severe during the winter of 1777–78 when war parties killed two settlers in separate incidents. After this, two Indians in a war party were killed by Colonel John Henry Antes' men in a skirmish. Later, a war party plundering homesteads along Buffalo Creek near modern-day Lewisburg, Pennsylvania, was stopped near present-day Jersey Shore by militia, and their plunder was confiscated.

June 10th 1778, war parties attacked three parties of settlers in what has been considered the bloodiest day in the annuals of the county. Near Muncy, a party of twelve, including a friendly Indian, left the fortified walls of the Wallis house to search for horses that had been stolen or had runoff. Robert Covenhoven, a soldier, woodsman, and Fair Play Man, was sent out to find the party and guide them back to safety. When Covenhoven located the party commander, Captain Berry refused to return without the horses, so Covenhoven agreed to scout for the party. The party failed to find the horses and followed the same route they had taken earlier back to the settlement.

Covenhoven advised the party to take a different route, but they refused. The party was ambushed by a war party that lay waiting for the men to return along the trail. Several settlers were killed in the ambush; six were captured, including a black man who was a member of the party. The Indians burned the black man at the stake; only Covenhoven and a few others escaped. Three men left the Wallis house on the same day to retrieve cattle from an outlying farm. They were ambushed at the farm by another war party, which included a Tory. Two of the settlers were killed in the ambush, and the third was wounded and taken prisoner.

Later that same day, in what is known as the Plum Creek Massacre, a party of sixteen settlers was attacked by a war party on its way to Lycoming Creek in Williamsport, Pennsylvania. Four men, two women, and six children were killed and scalped; the war party carried off two girls. Two other children managed to escape but were unable to tell settlers where the attack occurred. An armed search party was sent out to investigate, and all three ambush sites were found. It was generally believed that war parties were from a large contingent of Seneca and Tories that had descended the Sheshequin Path into the region for the very purpose.

A woman was one of at least two riders who braved death or capture to sound the alarm to the settlements. Departing from the relative safety of Fort Muncy, she went out into the hostile woods after the men apparently refused to go. She rode into the wilderness along Muncy Creek and the Wyalusing Path, warning several settlers to evacuate to the fort. Colonel Hunter sent word to Colonel Hepburn, who then commanded Fort Muncy, to order all the troops above him on the river to return to Fort Augusta. However, Colonel Hepburn had difficulty finding a messenger willing to carry the order up to Colonel Antes because of recent Indian attacks. Covenhoven volunteered to relay Hunter's order and started on his risky venture. He crossed the Susquehanna and ascended Bald Eagle Mountain, keeping along its summit until he reached a gap opposite Antes' Fort. After cautiously observing the fort, he slowly descended through the gap and proceeded to the stockaded walls. It was later in the evening, and it was beginning to grow dark when Covenhoven heard the distinctive bark of a rifle. Covington soon discovered that a girl had gone outside the fort to milk a cow, and an Indian lying near the walls ambushed her. Fortunately, the Indian missed his intended target, the rifle ball passing through her skirts, and she escaped uninjured.

The wilderness forts, homes, and fields were abandoned, and settlers headed east to Muncy. Women and children rode the river on rafts with a few meager possessions while the men walked the shoreline, driving livestock and providing security for the rafts. Muncy was just a temporary stopping point along their journey as the settlers moved south to Fort Augusta. Their abandoned forts and homesteads were burnt by the war parties as evidenced by some settlers reporting that the glow of their burning settlements lit the sky behind them as they fled the wilderness.

Of all the forts and settlements in the New Purchase and beyond, only Fort Antes, built of hard-to-burn peeled oak logs, and the stone Wallis House survived the destruction.

Fort Antes was built by militia Colonel John Henry Antes in 1777. He built the fort on a plateau above his house and his mill on the east side of a creek that bears his name. Colonel Antes was a prominent man on the frontier in civil and martial life. He was a justice of the peace and twice elected sheriff. When hostilities broke out in Lycoming County in 1775, he was appointed captain of a militia company in a battalion commanded by Colonel James Potter. The battalion was raised for the defense of the frontier. Two years later, Antes was commissioned a lieutenant colonel of the Fourth Battalion of Militia. A militia company was stationed at Antes' Fort. The garrison kept a vigilant lookout for raiding Indians, and scouting parties were frequently sent out to keep lines of communication open with Fort Muncy.

Some settlers eventually returned to what was left of their homesteads, a few soon enough to find their homes still smoldering. Many of those who fled were recent immigrants from New Jersey who fled the war on that front. Some of those settlers were poorly provisioned to begin with and ill-equipped to withstand Indian attacks. These wayfaring strangers returned to New Jersey. Colonel Samuel Hunter, who was in command at Fort Augusta, received a lot of criticism for ordering the evacuation. Many people thought that military intervention would have allowed the settlers to withstand the attackers, but it was a big frontier, and Hunter simply did not have the men to form such a protective umbrella.

Pennsylvania eventually did send military aid, and Colonel Thomas Hartley, one of Wayne's subordinate commanders during the Paoli Massacre, rebuilt Fort Muncy to protect settlers returning to their devastated homes. On September 24th 1778, Hartley led a strong force of about 200 men up the Sheshequin Path to the North Branch of the Susquehanna to strike back against the Seneca, believed to be principally responsible for raids on the Fair Play settlements. Hartley's expedition covered about 300 miles in just two weeks, engaged with and killed several bands of Seneca, and burned a few of their villages. This demonstrated the feasibility of a larger force operating in the Iroquois territory and set the wheels in motion for the punitive Sullivan Expedition the following year.

In the spring of 1779, all Continental troops were ordered from Fort Muncy to join General John Sullivan and his expedition assembled at Wyoming, for the largest frontier expedition of the entire war. Only a few militiamen were left at Fort Muncy, and they offered little defense against a combined raiding force of Iroquois and Butler's rangers. Sometime before or shortly after the July 28th 1779 raid on Fort Freeland, the second Fort Muncy was burnt during the Second Runaway.

Beginning in 1780 and continuing through 1783, Pennsylvania rangers were the first line of frontier defense for north-central Pennsylvania. Captain Thomas Robinson and his men, under the leadership of Lieutenant Moses Van Campen, rebuilt Fort Muncy for the third time. After an eventual declaration of peace ended hostilities in the region, the fort's garrison was removed. The fort was abandoned, its grounds consecrated with the memories of three forts, their triumphs and trials. Unfortunately, a farmer eventually acquired the land and cleared it, removing any noticeable trace of this historical landmark. Muncy Historical Society hosted the rededication ceremony of the official state historical marker commemorating the site of Fort Muncy on Memorial Day, May 29th 2017, at the marker's permanent location along Lycoming Mall Drive.

American patriot Captain John Brady was one of the earliest settlers in Lycoming County. He had been a captain in the Scotch-Irish and German forces during the French and Indian War under Colonel Henry Bouquet. As payment for his service, Brady along with other officers, received a land grant. Brady built a house on the fringe of the frontier. The house was large for its day and location but was protected by a stockade of 12-foot-high logs. The stockaded home became known as Fort Brady.

Brady was appointed a captain in the 12th Pennsylvania Regiment during the Revolutionary War and was wounded at the battle of the Brandywine. His 15-year-old son John was also wounded in that battle. His eldest son Sam was in another division and was not injured at Brandywine. During this time, most of the men along the Pennsylvania frontier were fighting Revolutionary battles far from home, which left the settlements prone to attacks by Tories and Indians. When word of the perilous situation on the frontier got to General Washington, he sent out several officers to organize a defense of the area. Captain John Brady was one of those officers mustered out for that purpose and soon after the Battle of Brandywine, he went home to organize its defense.

Fort Brady quickly became a place to offer protection for nearby settlers. On April 11th 1779, Brady took a wagon and a guard up the river to Fort Wallis to procure much-needed supplies. On the trail back to Fort Brady, he and his guard were attacked by a Seneca war party and Brady was killed. His body was retrieved, brought to his home, and interred in the Muncy burying ground four miles away. By May, the area was overrun by war parties, and most of the people evacuated.

Although there were forts and an occasional presence of soldiers, the principal defense fell upon the settlers of the regions they protected. The Indians seldom attacked these places with any persistence unless Loyalists accompanied them. Fort Reid was essential to the garrison since it covered the river on both sides and the lower Bald Eagle Valley. Along with Forts Horn, Antes, and Muncy, Fort Reid protected the whole region between the Bald Eagle and the Susquehanna down to White Deer Creek.

Reid's Fort was the home of Mr. William Reid and was stockaded in the spring of 1777. It was built along Water or River Street, east of the mouth of the Bald Eagle Canal. A large Indian mound existed on the riverbank, described as a mound as high as a two-story house, surrounded by a circle of small ones. When the Bald Eagle Canal was dug, workers cut away the western half of this mound, exhuming numerous human bones and stone implements. Immediately to the east of the mounds stood Reid's fort, traces of which could still be seen after 1820. Reid's Fort was the left flanking defense of the series of forts built on the frontier, but it was vacated by order of Colonel Hunter, who had overall command of the forts.

Moses Van Campen, then an orderly sergeant of Captain Gaskins' company of Colonel John Kelly's regiment of Northumberland County militia, said the regiment was stationed at Fort Reid during its six months' service in the summer of 1777. He thought Fort Reid must have been fortified at that time, as the position was on the extreme outer limits of the settlements and much exposed. This is, without doubt, correct. Scouting duty was performed by the regiment, and guarding the inhabitants was performed vigilantly. In the West Branch of the Susquehanna River near the mouth of the Bald Eagle Creek, the "Big Island," comprising a few hundred acres of very fertile soil, basked in the shadow of Fort Reid. The island was a popular attraction for early settlers. Van Campen had a wrestling match with the champion of the Indian landmen or "those settlers on the north side of the river". Unfortunately for Van Campen, "Northumberland's activity and muscle prevailed".

Marine Corps Tie-In... Letters from the Presidents.

Over the course of twenty years that I served our great nation as an active-duty United States Marine, I was fortunate enough to have received a Letter of Appreciation from two sitting American Presidents. In February 1997, I received the first letter while stationed at Marine Barracks 8th and Eye, and it was delivered in a box wrapped in security tape. The letter, from President Clinton was presented to me for supporting his Inauguration ceremony. The letter reads:

Dear Lance Corporal Moyer,

Thank you for serving as a stand-in during the Inauguration rehearsal. I appreciate your help in making this exciting day run smoothly. I'm grateful for your participation in this special role and for your daily service to your country.

Hillary joins me in sending you best wishes.

Sincerely,

Bill Clinton

The irony in receiving the letter is how quickly the President's patriotism toward Marines faded in just a few months. One evening during the summer of 1997, I was assigned to the White House to support a State dinner. My job was simple enough: look immaculate in uniform, open and close a glass door for each of the President's dinner guests, and salute officers and dignitaries. For that State dinner, the President hosted his Chinese counterpart. When I opened the door for the President and his guest, the Chinese dignitary returned my salute, but the President of the United States walked through the doors without even glancing at me. I can only assume that the President somehow failed to recognize me as a United States Marine in my Dress Blues.

On the day of my retirement from the Marine Corps, I received my second Letter of Appreciation from President Obama in recognition of twenty years of service.

"I extend to you my personal thanks and the sincere appreciation of a grateful nation for your contribution of honorable service to our country. You have helped maintain the security of the nation during a critical time in its history with a devotion to duty and spirit of sacrifice in keeping with the proud traditions of military service.

Your commitment and dedication have been an inspiration for those who will follow your footsteps, and for all Americans who join me today in saluting you for a job extremely 'well done'.

My best wishes to you for happiness and success in the future."

Barak Obama

Commander in Chief

Historical places to visit in Lycoming County, Pennsylvania.

This segment of the Patriot's Path takes you out of the suburbs to the mountains and farms of central Pennsylvania. Most of these historical sites consist of signs or roadside monuments, but there are a few places along the route that offer a place to get out of the car, stretch your legs, and look around. Muncy Historical Society, established in the former 1700s Wallis House, offers a tour of their small museum, complete with a miniature version of what Fort Muncy would have looked like in the 18th Century. Walk the grounds and check out the monument located on the property.

Captain John Brady Historic Marker is located at John Brady Drive by Muncy Creek, Pennsylvania.

Fort Muncy Marker is located along Lycoming Mall Drive/State Route 2014 Muncy, Pennsylvania.

Muncy Historical Society and Museum of History is located at 40 North Main Street Muncy, Pennsylvania. (by appointment only)

Fort Antes is located at 1454 South State Route 44 Highway Jersey Shore, Pennsylvania.

Fort Reed Marker is located at the intersection of West Water Street and 6th Street Lockhaven, Pennsylvania.

Fort Reed Stockade Monument is located along East Water Street near the Veterans Bridge in Lockhaven, Pennsylvania.

Danville, Pennsylvania

"I selected an enormous Marine Corps emblem to be tattooed across my chest. It required several sittings and hurt me like the devil, but the finished product was worth the pain. I blazed triumphantly forth, a Marine from throat to waist. The emblem is still with me. Nothing on earth but skinning will remove it."

~General Smedley Butler, a son of Newtown Square, Pennsylvania and one of only two Marines to be awarded two Congressional Medals of Honor

Major General William Montgomery was born in Mill Creek Hundred on August 3rd 1736, the third of six children; he spent his childhood working on the family plantation and gristmill. In 1743, his father, Alexander, and his business partner William Nevin, purchased 650 acres adjacent to Faggs Manor in Londonderry Township, Chester County, Pennsylvania. In 1747, at age 11, William and his siblings were orphaned when their parents died. In 1756, William married Nelvin's daughter, Margaret, and settled on the 822 acres he inherited in Londonderry Township. Over the next 14 years, they had six children, including Daniel Montgomery, and they made it the most prosperous farm in Chester County.

The Pennsylvania Militia Act of 1755 compelled "all males between 17 and 45 years of age, having a freehold worth 150 pounds a year, to arm himself and appear for training on the first Monday of March, June, August, and November" to protect the country during the French and Indian War. William joined the Associators in 1757 and continued to serve for the next 17 years. Montgomery's battalion was re-designated the 1st Pennsylvania Regiment and mobilized for the fortification of New Jersey in 1776. They arrived at Perth Amboy in mid-July, established a command post at the Proprietary House, and conducted rotating patrols along the 35-mile strait to Fort Lee. They must have been shocked to witness the sudden arrival of the British Navy off the coast of Staten Island: 160 transport ships carrying 33,000 infantrymen, 35 frigates, and 25 ships of the line bearing 64 cannons each. Five of the ships of the line alone had more collective firepower than the entire Continental Army.

While countering British reconnaissance efforts in New Jersey, the 1st Regiment learned of the defeat of the Continental Army at Long Island. After peace talks failed, Montgomery ordered four companies to Fort Lee and four companies to Fort Washington to buffer General Howe's landing at Kip's Bay Manhattan. When the American defenders of Fort Lee and Fort Washington were routed, most of Montgomery's men were taken prisoner and sent to prison hulks, Montgomery and his remaining men, along with General Washington and what was left of the Continental Army, retreated to Pennsylvania, closely pursued by General Cornwallis.

By December, Montgomery's Regiment was sent to Philadelphia to put down a Loyalist uprising. He was joined by his son William Jr. who enlisted on his 14th birthday and served as a drummer in Captain James McDowell's company.

Following Washington's victory at the first Battle of Trenton, Montgomery received General Cadwalader's dispatch for militia reinforcements. Along with 1,800 militia, the 1st Regiment arrived at Crosswicks, New Jersey on January 1st then marched to Trenton, where General Washington's army engaged with General Cornwallis at the Battle of Assunpink Creek (Second Battle of Trenton). Montgomery's Regiment, among others, provided a vital diversion that deceived Cornwallis into believing that Washington's forces were still encamped and simultaneously removed their supplies to Burlington, New Jersey.

William's oldest brother, Captain John Montgomery, was also a revolutionary Patriot deeply involved in the grassroots effort for independence in the Province of North Carolina, culminating in the War of the Regulation. He commanded a company in the Battle of

Alamance and was wounded by a cannon ball. He also commanded a company at the Battle of Guilford Court House and was wounded again, then imprisoned. He was sentenced to execution but escaped.

In November 1773, William Montgomery began buying land in Northumberland County from J. Cummings. On November 26th 1774, he purchased 180 acres along Mahoning Creek and Susquehanna River. Following his service in the New York and New Jersey Campaigns, William moved his family from Chester County to Northumberland. Originally referred to as Montgomery's Landing, it became known as Danville, named after his son Daniel.

After establishing his farm, William built a gristmill, sawmill, and trading post. In 1778, his family fled downriver to Fort Agusta with the rest of the settlers during the Big Runaway and returned to their homes following the Battle of Wyoming. In 1792, William built the General William Montgomery House. General Montgomery's exploits during the Revolutionary War were portrayed in the television series Turn: Washington's Spies, season 1, episode 5, "Epiphany," which features Montgomery's division after the Battle of Princeton. Montgomery died May 1st 1816, in Danville, Pennsylvania, and is buried at Old Presbyterian Church Cemetery in Danville.

Marine Corps Tie-In...Band of Brothers.

A typical Marine will come away from their military experience with friends forged through service and sacrifice, bonding like blood brothers, whether served together in war or peace. I grew up in rural central Pennsylvania and was not a popular kid; I was decidedly introverted and had few friends. In boot camp, you develop some loose friendships with other recruits, but they usually develop due to mutually experienced misery; you will rarely serve in the fleet with boot camp brothers, and rarer still that you remain in contact with them. It wasn't until after I arrived at my duty station at Marine Barracks Eighth and Eye that I met the first Marine I consider a friend and a brother. This young Marine was a West Coast Cat from Bakersfield, California, who was chosen by an 8th and Eye screening team to serve in Washington, DC. He was assigned to Alpha Company, 2nd platoon 'Earth Pigs' after he graduated from the Marine Corps School of Infantry West (SOI). I attended SOI on the East Coast when the screening team from Washington selected me to serve at Marine Barracks 8th and Eye.

The screening team began the selection process by elimination. They only needed to select a few of us, and there were hundreds of hopefuls. If a Marine had a history of drug use, they were asked to leave the auditorium. If a Marine had a criminal history, they were asked to leave. If a Marine wasn't at least six feet tall in socks, they were asked to leave. The elimination process continued until there were about thirty Marines left in the auditorium. These were interviewed by a company First Sergeant on the screening team.

Somehow, I had made the cut and was among the few who received orders to Washington. I was incredulous when I learned a particular Marine had also been successfully screened because his mouth was bigger than he was tall. I remember a cold night on an SOI range in the Verona Loop Training area where his big mouth got him in a lot of trouble. One of our troop handlers at SOI was a tobacco-spitting corporal who spoke with a thick southern drawl. The NCO was one to fear a little and avoid a lot; for some reason, he really didn't like the height-challenged young Marine. We had just completed a night shoot and were in a large formation waiting to be cleared out before hiking back to the huts we would spend the night in. After what felt like hours, we were ready to step off on the hike when the NCO with the southern draw tersely reminded us to check and make sure we all had our gear.

The short one standing next to me said, "crap, I don't have my helmet." I suggested he tell the corporal, a proposition he adamantly refused until the corporal held the helmet in the air like a sinister beast holding up a severed head. We all knew that whoever's name he found stamped on a piece of medical tape in the helmet band was in a lot of trouble. He screamed out the name, but the short one remained unusually silent. The corporal screamed again, and the Marine sheepishly moved out of formation to retrieve his gear. When he made it to the angry NCO, the corporal threw the helmet to the ground and demanded the Marine to get on his face. The Marine reluctantly assumed a push-up position but couldn't keep his big mouth shut and started to talk back. As soon as the grumbling Marine assumed the position, the corporal gave him a vicious kick in the ribs that fairly levitated the Marine in the air and left him in a cloud of dust.

When we arrived at the barracks in Washington, we were placed in one of the two marching companies, assigned rooms, and fitted for ceremonial uniforms. The next few weeks were spent learning the ins and outs of barracks life and ceremonial marching. Uniform and grooming standards were so high that some of us would struggle to maintain them. The rooms we lived in had to be kept in an immaculate condition. Everything in our wall lockers had to remain inspection-ready, rooms needed to be set up in a particular way, and the floors had to be polished to a mirror finish. We set up a wall locker display and never touched it again; we never walked on the floors in shoes or bare feet, and beds were carefully made and held tight with straps but never slept on. We were taught how to spit shine boots to a professional level, using a technique that involved baking boot polish into the leather using a conventional oven. Although most of our dress uniforms were professionally cleaned and pressed, everyday work uniforms such as cammies or Service Charlies were up to each Marine to clean and press. In Ceremonial Drill School, we had to clean, starch, and press the uniforms ourselves, and the camouflage utilities were starched stiff as a board.

One afternoon, I was in my room in my skivvies, pressing out my Cammie trousers, when someone shouted, "Attention on deck!" There I stood in my skivvies at the position of attention with a hot iron in my hand when two short-statured but very important Marines stepped into my room. I gave the appropriate greeting of the day, and the Sergeant Major of the Marine Corps (SMMC) looked up at me and asked whether I knew who stood beside him. I was a slick-sleeved private with less than three weeks at the barracks; I knew the man beside the SMMC was a four-star general, but I did not recognize him. Confused, I replied, "Yes, Sir, he is a four-star general!" The SMMC gave me an exasperated look and said, "That's correct, but do you know who he is?" When I failed to answer, the SMMC asked, "They didn't teach you who the 31st Commandant of the Marine Corps is in boot camp?" Of course, the chain of command was drilled into my head during boot camp, and when the SMMC said that I knew who the general was, it was the first time I had ever seen either of the senior Marines in person, but it would not be my last.

My Bakersfield brother and I had a great time as we served together at Marine Barracks 8th and Eye, along with the other Earth Pigs of 2nd platoon Alpha company. There was a Marine from New Jersey, twins from the Chicago area, the short Marine from SOI, and a hillbilly from West Virginia among the notables in the platoon. The hillbilly was a unique individual, to say the least. He drove a beat-up Geo Tracker around town and was a roommate out in town with my Bakersfield buddy.

One hot summer day, I walked over to their apartment along Pennsylvania Avenue and caught the smell of death as I walked by their garage. When I went into the apartment, I mentioned the foul smell to my buddies. We hesitantly investigated, fearing we would find someone's corpse stashed there. Finding nothing, we stopped searching for the source of the overwhelming smell. A few days later, I asked the hillbilly for a ride to the train station. The smell was almost unbearable as we started our short drive. When I made it back to Washington after a long weekend, I was told that the source of the stench had been discovered... under the seat of the Tracker were shoved several packages of rotting deer steak.

Community spit bottles were popular at the barracks. During an afternoon of long, tedious classes, the Marines had almost filled a large Gatorade bottle of a fine concoction of dip spit when someone made a lucrative offer to the hillbilly. We agreed to give him five bucks if he chugged the spit bottle. He readily accepted the challenge and, tilting the bottle to his lips, chugged it down! It was indeed a difficult sight to witness. I fought waves of nausea as the hilly Billy struggled unsuccessfully to keep the dip spit down. With a heave, the hillbilly spewed dip spit everywhere, clearing the room and making a vile mess of the place. The crazy part of the whole story is that only two Marines paid for the show.

We all eventually moved out of the barracks to apartments in the town and were given a wall locker in a large space we called the Brown Bagger's room. One Friday evening, we were getting ready to dress for an Evening Parade, and I was sitting in a folding chair by my locker, edge-dressing my shoes. I felt someone tapping my head while engrossed in a deep conversation with another Marine. Irritated at the interruption, I continued talking with the Marine, trying to ignore the tapping on my head. Finally having enough, I tilted my head back and immediately saw the hillbilly and his vile method of getting my attention.

My usually short fuse lit, I jumped up in blinding fury, grabbed the offending redneck, and executed a textbook DDT that Hulk Hogan would have been proud of. As I tried to calm myself down, a group of Marines gathered around the comatose hillbilly who lay sprawled at my feet. When he eventually gained consciousness, his eyes were crossed, and he had a large, angry welt growing on his forehead. As his eyes came back into line and focused, he looked up at me and said, "I guess we both got smacked on the head."

The hillbilly was excited one afternoon to receive an 8 by 10-inch box sealed in security tape. Most of us had received one of these boxes during our service in Washington. The boxes came from the White House and usually contained a Letter of Appreciation from the President of the United States. As the hillbilly tore open the box in anticipation, his excitement turned into astonished dismay. Instead of the usual letter, the box contained an 8x10 photo of the Marine, which was signed by the 42nd President of the United States. The photo was of the hillbilly standing at attention outside the White House during a combined service full honors arrival. The photo was typical until we all got a closer look, discovering that the hillbilly's eyes were plainly straining to the left to look at a beautiful young lady in a short skirt as she walked with the foreign dignitaries, instead of keeping his eyes fixed to the front. Scrawled on the photo above the President's signature was a suggestion from the Commander in Chief to keep his eyeballs forward and off the dignitary's daughter.

Another interesting Marine within our peer group at the barracks was one we very affectionately dubbed Dominican Dan. This Marine was notorious for falling asleep in formation during ceremonies. During evening parades, Dominican Dan's head would start to slowly fall to his chest and then spring back up as if the movement startled him into consciousness. Eventually, he would settle into a nap as the long ceremony continued, and it was usual to hear Marines desperately try to wake Dominican Dan up from his ill-timed naps before the platoon received a command to bring it out of ceremonial parade rest.

During a retirement ceremony for the Secretary of Defense, Dominican Dan, once again, fell asleep on his feet during the lengthy joint ceremony. After many long-winded remarks and just before the pass and review, I could hear Marines try to wake him from his vertical slumber again, but to no avail. The effort didn't fail because Dominican Dan was sleeping so soundly, but because we all had to maintain our ceremonial pose and minimize excessive movement, including lips. When our captain faced the platoon and gave the command, we all snapped to attention except Dominican Dan, who slept on. The captain ordered right face, which somehow startled Dominican Dan into the position of attention, but he faced left instead of right, which put him nose to nose with me. The abashed Marine executed an about-face when the captain commanded right shoulder arms. After the captain gave the command forward march, Dominican Dummy somehow managed to get his rifle onto his right shoulder and march without so much as missing a step.

In 1997 Marine Barracks 8th and Eye received an invitation to Central Park, New York, from a wealthy philanthropist and businessman who was instrumental in saving the USS Intrepid from the scrap yard. Alpha and Bravo Company were bused to Andrews Airforce Base and flown to New York City on a C-130. When we arrived in the city, a steady downpour of rain greeted us, and the forecast didn't indicate it would end in time for the Silent Drill Team to parade in the park. Canceling the parade was not an option for our host, who quickly made accommodations on the USS Intrepid for the 8th and Eye Marines while he looked for an indoor venue for the Drill Team. We finally got word that he had arranged for the Armory to accommodate the Drill Team and his quests, but it would be far too small for the two companies to parade.

It was quickly decided that the three supporting platoons would line the inside perimeter of the building while the Silent Drill Team and the Band performed their routines. We all dressed in our blue/whites and were bused through the city to the Armory. After the Drill Team and band performed, we boarded buses; our host wanted to treat the Marines to dinner and treat us he did after the buses pulled up to the World Trade Center Towers. We all took turns cramming into high-speed elevators that quickly whisked us up to the top of tower two for the most exquisite meal I ever had. Two open bars served the Marines whatever they wanted with no limits imposed. I didn't drink so my memory of the night is probably a bit sharper than most of the Marines who had depleted one of the bars before the meal was even served. I remember seeing a senior officer, completely wasted, in a bathroom, trying in vain to zip up his trousers before finally giving up and returning to his table with his barn door open. Marines threw up all over themselves during the bus ride to the airport and a much more unpleasant plane ride back to Andrews Airforce Base was in store for the few of us not too drunk to care.

As we grew into our roles as Marines in Washington DC, I began to take my Bakersfield brother home on weekend trips so he could get away from the city grind and experience slower urban life. One weekend on the farm, my dad asked us to dispose of a bunch of rogue roosters running the roost and gave us carte blanche as soon as my mother and sister were away to dispose of them as we saw fit. My friend and I decided to dispose of them by firing squad. I loaded up my late grandfather's 30 ought six hunting rifle, chased the offending roosters in a killing field where we could safely fire the rifle, and handed it off to my friend for some fun and entertainment.

As the Marine placed his eye on the old, steel-rimmed scope and carefully lined up his shot, I tried to warn him about proper eye relief. Years earlier, I had learned the same brutal lesson with the same old scope and still bear the scar to prove it. He told me he knew what he was doing and yanked back the trigger: Rooster 1 Marine 0. The rooster was doing a little chicken dance in the field as the Marine was trying to pick himself up from the ground, a small trickle of blood running down from a cut over his brow. I asked the Marine if he wanted me to knock down one of the roosters, but he angrily pumped another round in the chamber and let her go bang. The rooster got the message and hurried to the safety of the barn while the Marine, a little slower to get back on his feet, had a tiny cut on his brow just over the one he received a minute earlier. The final score was Rooster 2 Marines 0, and the roosters lived to see another day.

My brother left the Marines after completing his initial enlistment, but not before he had his revenge for the rooster incident. After leaving Marine Barracks 8th and Eye, most of us received orders to 29 Palms, California. In California, I quickly discovered the proverbial shoe was firmly on the other foot, as I spent some weekends taking in the urban scene of his home in Bakersfield. One morning, after waking to a beautiful California morning, we went out into the yard to help his father with some landscaping before going to a vast orange grove to hunt coyotes. Seeing a bush bearing small, purplish berries, I asked my friend what they were. To my chagrin, I missed the twinkle in his eye as he told me they were California berries and tasted like a cross between a strawberry and a raspberry.

Helping myself to a small handful, I popped them in my mouth, immediately discovering they tasted nothing like any sweet berry I had ever eaten but were easily the hottest 'berry' I had ever bitten into. Nothing but time quelled the fiery torrent I was experiencing in my mouth and throat. Worse even than CS gas, I learned, to my dismay, that milk or copious amounts of chocolate would not take away the sting. Ironically, that friend married a woman near my hometown, bought a house near Danville, raised two children, and is near the completion of a long, distinguished career at a local state prison. While he was doing this, I served in the Marines for another sixteen years before finally settling down to raise my daughters in the sunny Philadelphia suburbs.

Historical places to visit near Danville, Pennsylvania.

<u>General William Montgomery House</u> is located at 1 and 3 Bloom Street Danville, Pennsylvania.

American Revolution Marker is located at Memorial Park Danville, Pennsylvania.

Northumberland County, Pennsylvania

"Remember that America keeps an insurance policy, a hedge against uncertainty. It's called the United States Marine Corps!"

~Sergeant Major Mike Barrett, 17th Sergeant Major of the Marine Corps

By 1779, Northumberland County was still considered on the edge of the American frontier. As Major General John Sullivan's expedition was busy savaging the Iroquoian homeland in Northern Pennsylvania and New York, Loyalists and the Seneca attacked settlers in the remote wilderness, hoping to draw a portion of Sullivan's force out of the northern tier and thus weaken it. At Warrior Run in Northumberland County, another harrowing tragedy Called the Battle of Fort Freeland occurred, claiming the lives of at least 108 Americans, toward the end of the Revolutionary War.

Garrett Vreeland's farm was one of the best-developed properties in the upper portion of Northumberland County. Local settlers attempted to fortify the site following the Great Runaway of 1778; at least 12 families spent the winter of 1778-79 inside the fortification. On February 10th 1779, Mary Vincent, whose brother Isaac died five months later, was one of three children born inside the fort. She lived a long life and was buried in the Warrior Run Church Cemetery upon her death. Issacs's son was born and raised without ever knowing his father.

The following spring, the fields had been planted under watchful guards, and the colonists seemed to settle into a life of constant danger. In April, seven members of the militia were killed or captured at the fort, and a few miles north near Muncy, twelve settlers were killed or captured by Indians when they went searching for stray horses. On July 20th, five boys and young men were sent from the fort to cultivate a nearby cornfield when a war party attacked them. Isaac Vincent, Elias Vreeland, and Jacob Vreeland, Jr. were killed, and

Michael Vreeland, aged 17, and Benjamin Vincent, aged 12, were captured and spent more than a year as British prisoners.

On July 28th a large Indian war party attacked the fort. Mary Jamison, a loyalist wife living in the area, recalled that the war party consisted of 300 Seneca led by her Seneca husband Hiokatoo and as many as 100 British regulars led by Captain John McDonald. The outnumbered settlers defended the fort until they ran out of ammunition and were forced to surrender. Non-combatants were allowed to leave the fort unmolested, but men of fighting age were taken prisoner. Hiokatoo, who was known for his bloodlust, killed wounded who were unable to evacuate the fort or travel with the war party. Fort Freeland was plundered of its valuables, and the victorious party paused along the creek to enjoy a meal.

During the raiding party was distracted by their picnic, 30 militiamen led by Daniel Boone's cousin, Hawkins Boone, arrived on the scene. Boone had found that the combined war party was in the vicinity of Fort Freeland, intending to attack it, so he set off to stop them, but he arrived too late. Boone, after realizing that the party had killed several of the settlers, organized a hasty ambush, ordering the militia to fire directly into the Loyalists and Seneca resting along the stream, killing several dozen. The Indians and British quickly assumed the defensive and fired back, killing half of Boone's men and scattering the rest.

Among the women and children set free to make their way to Fort Augusta was 16-year-old William Kirk, dressed as a girl so he could escape with the women and children. Much later in life, he built the brick farmhouse, which still stands across Interstate 180 from the Warrior Run Church on what is today known as Kirkland Estates. A few weeks after the battle, Benjamin Franklin reported the event in the Pennsylvania Gazette, where he talked about the "brave defenders of the Warrior Run." The 'Defenders' later became the mascot of the Warrior Run High School, which today stands on the former Vreeland farm. The Seneca and Loyalists continued to raze the area after their attack on Fort Freeland, driving most of the remaining settlers out of the region. Most of these settlers did not return to their homesteads until the end of the war.

Fort Agusta, named for Augusta of Saxe-Gotha, the mother of King George III, was constructed by Colonel William Clapham in 1756 on the site of the Lenape village of Shamokin, which was abandoned a few weeks before construction of the fort began. The fort was the main stronghold of the British at the junction of the East and West branches of the Susquehanna River during the French and Indian War. The fort was the largest of the Pennsylvania forts, and it was initially built to defend against the raids of the French and their Algonquin allies from the upper Allegheny region and Canada.

During the French and Indian War, a raid force was gathered from the French forts at Duquesne, Kittanning, Venango, and Le Boeuf for a campaign to attack and seize Fort Augusta. The French and Indians consolidated at the mouth of Anderson Creek, in Clearfield County, Pennsylvania. The party hastily built Crude boats, rafts, and bateaux to travel down the Susquehanna River to Fort Augusta. They managed to transport two small brass cannon to support their raid force. When they reached their proposed attack point on high ground, now called Shikellamy's Lookout, across the river from the fort, they found the guns did not have the range to reach it. The French commanders determined the defenses at Fort Augusta were too strong for a direct assault or a successful siege, so they decided to abort the attack and return upriver. Had the French and Indians been able to seize and control this strategically placed fort, it could have altered the outcome of the war in favor of the French.

During the Revolutionary War, Fort Augusta became the military headquarters of the colonial forces operating along the frontier of the upper Susquehanna Valley. Colonel Samuel Hunter was placed in command of the fort and directed all the activities related to the defense of the region and provided protection to the frontier settlements. The ultimate plan of the British and its Iroquoian allies was to destroy Fort Augusta in Sunbury. The fort was lightly garrisoned and contained a large store of supplies and food for the upcoming Sullivan Expedition. The combined Loyalist and Seneca war party did not go much further south than Fort Freeland and inexplicitly called off the planned attack on Colonel Hunter's fort in Sunbury. The war party's losses at Fort Freeland may have been the reason, but failing to take Fort Agusta preserved the valuable supplies for the Sullivan Expedition. It was Sullivan's well-provisioned expeditionary force that permanently ended Iroquois supremacy in America.

I attended Maclay Elementary School in Sunbury, Pennsylvania, as a kindergartener and first grader. I didn't know the school's namesake's historical background until recently. William Maclay was born in the small village of New Garden in Chester County, Pennsylvania; his parents were Presbyterian immigrants from Portadown, Ireland.

Maclay pursued classical studies before serving as a militia lieutenant during the French and Indian War. He served in several expeditions of that war, including the Battle of Fort Duquesne, where he served under Forbes and Bouquet in 1758. After the war, he studied law and was admitted to the bar in 1760. MaClay practiced law until he became a surveyor in the employ of the Penn family. In 1769, Maclay married Maty McClure Harris, the eldest daughter of John Harris, Jr. and they raised nine children together. In 1772, the family moved to the newly established Northumberland County, where he helped survey and lay out the town of Sunbury. He eventually became a prothonotary and clerk of the courts of Northumberland County in the 1770s. During the American Revolution, he marched with the Northumberland County Associators and participated in the battles of Trenton and Princeton.

After serving in those touchstone battles, Maclay continued to serve in the Continental Army as a commissary.

After the Constitution was ratified, Maclay was elected to the United States Senate and served in the 1st United States Congress from March 4th 1789, to March 4th 1791. He served a two-year term instead of the usual six-year term for senators after he lost a lottery with the other Pennsylvania senator, Robert Morris. In the Senate, Maclay was one of the most radical members of the Anti-Administration faction.

He constantly feuded with Vice President John Adams in the Senate after Adams rejected Maclay's political deal to support his vice-presidential candidacy during the 1789 presidential election. In July 1789, Maclay issued a motion requiring the President to request the Senate's permission to dismiss Cabinet members, but it was defeated when Vice President Adams voted against it. During Senate debates over the Residence Act, which was to establish the site of the permanent national capital and seat of government, Vice President Adams worked with Morris, who preferred Philadelphia as the capital, to defeat Maclay's motion to place it in Harrisburg near his landholdings on the Susquehanna River.

In his journal, which is the only diary and one of the most important records of the First United States Congress, he criticizes Vice President Adams and President George Washington. He also criticized many of their supporters who ran the Senate and named particular senators, believing that their ways of running the Senate were inefficient. He was unsuccessful in his attempt to be re-elected by the state legislature of Pennsylvania and subsequently retired from national politics.

Maclay became a Pennsylvania State House of Representatives member from 1795 to 1797. He was also a presidential elector in the 1796 presidential election and voted for Jefferson. He was a county judge from 1801 to 1803, and he was a member once again of the state House of Representatives in 1803. Maclay sold ten acres of land to the Commonwealth of Pennsylvania prior to his death in 1804. In 1811, architect Stephen Hill began constructing the Capitol building and state office buildings on that land purchase after Governor Simon Snyder agreed to relocate centrally within Pennsylvania. He was buried in Old Paxton Church Cemetery in Harrisburg.

Marine Corps Tie-In…The Boys of CATT 1- A Twilight Tour.

My assignment to Second Battalion 4th Marines, "aka the Magnificent Bastards," ended up being my twilight tour in the Corps; I was destined to not raise my hand again and swear an oath to serve my nation. When I checked in with the battalion sergeant major before the unit's deployment, he asked if I planned to retire or reenlist. When I told him I was on the fence but leaning toward retirement, he offered me any of his open gunny billets in the battalion. I chose the platoon Sergeant billet for Combined Anti-Armor Team 1 since I had never had the opportunity to lead a mechanized platoon, and I felt it was a good potential exit for an old grunt.

The team consisted of eight up-armored gun trucks: two mounted a 50. Cal machine gun, two mounted MK-19 automatic grenade launchers, and two trucks mounted SABER-guided TOW missile systems. CAAT 1 was led by a fresh-faced, rock-star wannabe 2nd lieutenant who has an entertaining TBS video titled *The Most Interesting Man on Camp Barrett* posted on YouTube. The platoon's backbone consisted of a core of some of the best NCOs I had ever served with, led by two sergeants, section leaders who were expert machine gunners,   and outstanding young Marines.

Although I arrived at the unit toward the end of the unit's workup, I had the opportunity to participate in the battalion's MCCRE. The platoon started the MCCRE on a pair of Navy Landing Craft Air

Cushioned (LCAC) that took us over the horizon and then back on shore, simulating a ship-to-shore landing. Once back on shore, we operated in training areas across Camp Pendleton, screening, setting in overwatch positions, conducting reconnaissance patrols, and an occasional attack.

I had a great deployment in Okinawa with CAAT 1 and could not think of a better note to retire on. During the six-month deployment, the platoon honed its skills in gun drills, land navigation, and other combat skills. We spent Christmas and Easter together. Two of my former Villanova Marine option midshipmen were passing through Okinawa and visited me in Kinville for dinner one evening. I also spent a lot of weekends golfing at two local courses with the Company First Sergeant and Operations Gunny.

Although we spent most of the deployment on Okinawa, we did get an opportunity to drive our gun trucks to the dock and embark on the USS Ashland for a Dog and Pony show in South Korea. Our gun trucks and high-back HMMWV were driven from the beach onto a Landing Craft Utility (LCU) and remained chained to its deck. The LCU was drydocked in the ship's lower V, a large, internal bay at the stern of the ship that opens to the waterline via a massive stern gate. After a couple of weeks at sea working on gun drills and cross-training with a track company who were deployed with us on LSD 48 Ashland, we began our approach to the South Korean shoreline. The *Ashland* stopped on the horizon, CAAT 1 strapped into our vehicles, the ramp was dropped, and the lower V flooded to allow the AAVs and the LCU, loaded with our vehicles, to float off the ship. We remained in our vehicles as the LCU and AAVs transited toward the beach. At a position about 100 meters from the shore, a Navy beachmaster signaled for CAAT-1 to begin launching trucks from the LCU.

The first two unarmored trucks swam to shore with no issues. Unfortunately, the third and fourth gun trucks did not launch as successfully as the first and second. As soon as the third truck accelerated off the LCU's ramp, it sank over its engine snorkel, flooding the engine compartment with seawater and dead-lining the vehicle. The platoon commander, who had gone ashore with the first vehicle, radioed for the fourth to launch. I radioed my advisement against that order, but he insisted, and Truck Four sank alongside Truck Three. I told the LCU commander we were done sinking trucks in the drink, and he concurred, raised the ramp, and disembarked the rest of our trucks directly onto the beach.

The Koreans got to see a Dog and Pony contingency plan in action. The Navy had to deploy a duck boat to retrieve our dead-lined vehicles, and the lieutenant was steadily losing his cool, already worrying about the possible repercussions the sunken gun trucks might bring. I tried to reason with him by shifting the blame to the beachmaster and LCU commander. I also offered my opinion that the beachmaster's survey was inaccurate, the LCU commander failed to keep his craft on the sand bar, the sand bar could not sustain the weight of the trucks, or a combination of the factors was to blame.

The young lieutenant was not interested in my synopsis as we tried to figure out how and what to do with the two flooded trucks on the beach. The lieutenant was quickly acquitted of any responsibility or wrongdoing and he decided to split the platoon; since the water-logged trucks could not move on their own or be towed back onto the LCU, I would dead-tow the broken trucks, all weapon systems, personnel, and serialized equipment of one CAAT section from the beach several miles through a town, to a small South Korean Navy Base while the other continued to live-fire ranges inland according to the plan.

Dead-towing the vehicles may have been a violation of the Status of Forces Agreement (SOFA) we had with South Korea, but the battalion either obtained special permission or went with the 'get the trucks back on the LCU and beg for forgiveness later' route. Either way, we got the vehicles safely to the base and, after linking up with the docked LCU, had them craned onto the craft. I remained with the stranded section, marooned on the small base with the LCU's crew until the training was complete. We cleaned weapon systems for a few days until the other CAAT section linked up with the LCU, and we returned to the *Ashland*. The dead-lined trucks were unceremoniously craned and secured to the LPD's flight deck, where they remained until we made it back to Okinawa. The trucks were then dead-towed back to Camp Hanson, where Marine mechanics soon had them dried out and back in good operating condition.

Historical places to visit in Northumberland County, Pennsylvania.

Plan a September tour on the first weekend of the month at the Hower-Slote House to get a unique experience of what life was like on a Pennsylvania frontier homestead during Fort Freeland's Heritage Days. Spend a couple of hours with period reenactors and historians as they take you back to the July 28th 1779 Battle of Fort Freeland. Spend the rest of the day learning how to butcher or boil apple butter, take part in an apprenticeship parade, and listen to 18th-century music. Over the course of the weekend, you can experience well over 50 different 18th-century homesteading demonstrations. Walk the property and check out the memorials commemorating the pioneering men, women, and children who lived on the frontier in those tumultuous days.

Head down the river to Sunbury next and stop in at the Hunter House Museum on this segment of the Patriot's Path. Fort Augusta was dismantled in 1796 but the Northumberland County Historical Society has its headquarters established at the Hunter House Museum on the site of the old Fort. A well and one of the fort's magazines still exists. The museum contains exhibits featuring historical and archaeological artifacts related to Fort Augusta. A model of the fort is displayed in the front of the museum. The model of the fort was reconstructed in 2013 and rededicated on July 5th 2014. The majority of the markers and memorials are within walking distance or a short drive. You can drive to Shikellamy lookout where the combined French and Indian assault force looked down on the fort in 1756 before changing their plan to attack it. Go down to the marina for the best view of Shikellamy's profile.

Hower-Slote House is located at 246 Warrior Run Boulevard Turbotville, Pennsylvania.

Wyoming Path Marker is located at 1150 North Front Street Sunbury. Pennsylvania.

Fort Augusta Marker is located at 1150 North Front Street, Sunbury, Pennsylvania.

Hunter House Museum is located at 1218 Fort Augusta Avenue Sunbury, Pennsylvania.

Thompson's Rifle Battalion Marker Hunter House Museum

The Bloody Spring is located at 338 Memorial Drive Sunbury, Pennsylvania.

The Sullivan Expedition is located at Hunter House Museum, Sunbury, Pennsylvania.

Shikellamy Marker is located on North Front Street on the right when traveling south, Sunbury, Pennsylvania.

Shikellamy Marker II is located at North Front Street near Augusta Street Sunbury on the right when traveling north, Sunbury, Pennsylvania.

Shikellamy's Profile Marker is located at the intersection of North Front Street and Julia Street Sunbury, Pennsylvania.

<u>William McClay Marker</u> is located at the intersection of Front Street and Arch Street Sunbury, Pennsylvania.

<u>Historic Fort Halifax Park and Preserve</u> is located at 570 North River Road Halifax, Pennsylvania.

Bedford, Pennsylvania

"Why we fight and why we win is unchanged. Its our ethos, our character and our unapologetic resolve to be the most capable and most lethal fighting force in the world."

~Sergeant Major Troy E. Black , 5th Senior Enlisted Advisor to the Chairman and 19th Sergent Major of the Marine Corps.

William Phillips was an American patriot appointed a Captain in the Bedford Militia in 1780 to raise a company of rangers and defend Morrison's Cove against raiding Seneca and Tories. By July 14th 1780, Captain Phillips had formed a company of ten men, plus his son Elijah, as members of his Rangers. On July 15th 1780, a war party of Seneca and Tories arrived in the wilderness of Bedford and forced settlers to evacuate to Shoup's Fort, located near the modern town of Saxton. After the settlers in Shoup's Fort found out the war party consisted of at least fifty Loyalists and Seneca, they decided the safest course of action was to abandon the small fort and evacuate further east, where it was more civilized.

Captain Phillips and his rangers tried to locate the war party but found no sign of the raiders as they trekked across Tussey Mountain and into the Woodcock Valley; they also did not find many settlers to warn because most had already fled from their homesteads. The rangers arrived at the Heater homestead, which they found recently abandoned. Discovering the Heater house to be fortified with stout walls, and loopholes through which guns could be fired, Phillips decided to hunker his men down for the night. It had rained that night, so the small company of rangers slept well and woke early the following morning to prepare their breakfast. During the breakfast preparations, one of the rangers opened the door to find that a group of Seneca and Tories had surrounded the house during the early morning hours.

Since Phillips and his rangers were secure behind the thick walls of Heater's house, he decided to wait and see what the war party was going to do. It didn't take very long to find out what the war party was going to do, and it was calculable that the war party would have at least tried an attack on the house. The attack began suddenly with a hail of bullets and arrows; no one knows who fired the shot that initiated the battle or whether surrender was demanded first.

The war party fired on the house all morning and continued into the afternoon. The defenders were fairing better than their antagonists, and they managed to kill at least two attackers and wounded two others. At some point in the afternoon, the war party attempted to fire the house with flaming arrows. The roof turned out to be the house's soft underbelly; although it had rained throughout the night, the flaming arrows managed to ignite the roof. The rangers were able to extinguish the fire, but it didn't stay out, and the roof was set ablaze again. A few rangers went up to the attic and kicked out portions of the flaming shingles. Unfortunately, the burning shingles slid down the roof and landed next to the walls, eventually setting the whole house on fire.

Realizing his rangers could not escape the burning building, Captain Phillips called out to the war party, asking for a ceasefire. He surrendered his men under the agreement that he and his men would be taken prisoner and not harmed. The men laid down their weapons, and their arms were bound tightly. Captain Phillips and his son were detached from the group and marched away from the burning inferno. Father and son were eventually separated somewhere along the trail and taken to Canada along different paths.

Unfortunately, the rest of Phillip's Rangers faired far worse. Securely bounded, they marched to a small clearing roughly half a mile from the Heater House and tied to trees. The rangers, completely helpless, could not have even imagined the horrors that awaited them. The Iroquois were notorious for torturing their enemies, especially when they limited their cruel devices to strong men. They shot arrow after arrow into their helpless victims, careful to avoid vital areas so they could draw out their cruel game as long as possible. As the rangers became weak and started to lean against their bindings for support, the Seneca would introduce even more devious methods to the fray before disemboweling and scalping the men alive. The savaged and lifeless bodies of the rangers were discovered later by another group of militia led by Colonel Piper, ravaged bodies still bound to the trees. The rangers were cut down and lowered to the ground; they were buried in a common grave.

Captain Phillips remained a prisoner in Canada for two years before effecting his escape and making his way back to the Woodcock Valley. His son also eventually returned to the valley as well, but the exact time of his return is unclear. Captain Phillips left Bedford County around 1787 and moved southwest to Kentucky. Some local traditions posit he was buried near the burned homestead in Saxon beside his men, a short distance from a monument erected in his honor. This is unlikely, however, since he died in Kentucky, and some of his descendants have verified that he is buried there.

On July 16th 1926, on the one hundred and forty-sixth anniversary of the massacre of Phillips' Rangers, a monument that was constructed in the general location where the massacre was thought to have happened was dedicated to the eight brave patriots. Some locals living during the 18th Century thought they knew the general area of the burial site, but the exact location was lost until January 25th 1933, when the mass grave was finally located by accident, not design. A Work crew was clearing an area to build a stone wall when a skull was uncovered a couple of feet from the monument. The lost grave had finally been found. The remains were carefully removed and re-buried in a crypt under the monument during the memorial services that year.

Marine Corps Tie-In...Retirement Day.

After my last deployment, I flew home to my wife and daughter as fast as I could get on a jet. We wouldn't be in Philadelphia long because we decided to take our daughter on a road trip across America where they would spend the summer in California to give them an opportunity to experience family life in the fleet Marine Corps; it served as a good test bed for us to determine whether to re-enlist or retire.

After my nephew's high school graduation, we jumped in the SUV and headed west; I drove through to Chicago, and then my wife and I switched in the morning. We stopped at a monument called the Freedom Rock in Iowa before arriving at our first stop in Platte, Nebraska; we visited the Buffalo Bill Center of the West, had a good dinner, and then took it easy for the rest of the evening. The next morning greeted us with a hail storm shortly after we got back onto the road. Fortunately, the storm abated just as we crossed into Wyoming for our visit to Cheyanne. We drove through the big sky country and into the Grand Tetons, where we had a room waiting for us at the Snake River Lodge and Spa. It was a great place to stay, and very difficult to get my daughter out of the pool, which was half indoor and half outdoor. The next morning, we drove into Yellowstone National Park and visited the geysers. We finished our day in Montana at the Grizzley and Wolf Sanctuary before driving down through Idaho to the Snake River and our room at the lodge.

The third leg of our adventure was probably the most forgettable. We drove most of the day through Utah, finally reaching the Great Salt Lake, which wasn't as great as I had envisioned. There was not much to see, not much to do and it smelled bad. After an abbreviated visit, we got back on the road and headed to our next hotel. When we got to the poorly maintained room, which was already paid for, my wife took one look at it and, refusing to stay, went back to the SUV. After a lot of persuasion, we finally went to look for something to eat, finding a brick oven pizza joint that was much better than the hotel room.

The next morning we jumped back into the car and headed south to the Valley of Fire in Northern Nevada. Our next stop was to the Hoover Dam and the Grand Canyon. The Grand Canyon Skybridge was an incredible experience. As we walked out into seemingly bottomless oblivion, grown people, overcome with fear, were maintaining death grips on anything they could hold onto. My daughter, on the other hand, decided to lay on her little belly and make snow angels on the glass floor. As she was doing this, she looked at us, pointed down at a hawk, and said, "Look, Mom, a baby bird".

After an evening at Kingman, we got on the road for the final leg of our trip to Oceanside, California. We drove through the Mojave Desert to 29 Palms and MAGCC before heading to a diner in Yucca Valley, where we met one of our favorite midshipmen from Villanova. Just getting out of the SUV was enough to convince my girls that the desert wasn't for them. After a great meal and some catching up, we headed south, passing the windmills at Palm Springs before finally arriving at our Vista, California, rental.

The summer was filled with Disney hoppers, trips to Sea World and Lego Land. We found a great church off the Carlsbad coast, and my wife had some of her friends fly out from Pennsylvania for a visit. We filled out the rest of our time together with fire pits on the beach, Pedro's Tacos, trips to Camp Pendleton, and MCRD San Diego. But good things must, indeed, come to an end. My daughter needed to return to school in the fall, and my wife needed to return to work. We still had not made a final decision about my career, and we even visited a potential Christian School in Vista for my daughter to attend.

The day came when I drove them to the San Diego Airport for their flight home. I knew it would probably only be for a few months, but it was still tough to do. As my wife and five-year-old daughter made their way down a long jetway toward their departure gate, my little "Bug," dragging her small, wheeled suitcase in tow, periodically turned to blow kisses to her daddy. My daughter had helped push me off the fence as I stood there sweeping away shameless tears...she needed a full-time daddy under her little foot, and I was determined to retire and give her just that.

A few weeks before my retirement ceremony, invitations were sent out. When the day had finally come for my retirement ceremony to take place on the hallowed ground of the Fighting Fifth's Memorial Garden, it was absolutely beautiful: sunny and mild, with an autumn breeze kicking up off the nearby ocean. On reserved seating sat my beloved wife and daughter, who were there to share such a significant milestone in my life.

The well-rehearsed ceremony ended with a column of enlisted Marines ranked from Private First Class to Gunnery Sergeant, Marines whom I just spent my last overseas deployment with. As the flag... my flag, was ceremoniously passed from one enlisted rank to another, representing my twenty-year journey through those ranks in the Corps, each Marine reverently saluted it. Finally, the flag, which had been flown over Valley Forge National Historical Park to honor the occasion, made its way to the front of the line and was handed to me. As each Marine held the flag, a paragraph in the Poem, I am the flag of the United States, written by Howard Schnauber was read.

"I am the flag of the United States of America. My name is Old Glory. I fly atop the world's tallest buildings. I stand watch in America's halls of justice. I fly majestically over great institutions of learning. I stand guard with the greatest military power in the world. Look up and see me.

I stand for peace ... honor ... truth ... and justice. I stand for freedom. I am confident. I am arrogant.

I am proud.

When I am flown with my fellow banners, my head is a little higher, my colors a little truer. I bow to no one. I am recognized all over the world. I am worshipped, I am saluted, I am loved, I am revered, I am respected, and I am feared.

For more than 200 years, I have fought in every battle of every war: Brandywine, Gettysburg, Shiloh, Appomattox, San Juan Hill, the trenches of France, the Argonne Forest, Anzio, Rome, the beaches of Normandy, the jungles of Guam, Okinawa, Japan, Korea, Vietnam, Beirut, Iraq, Afghanistan, and a score of places long forgotten by all but those who were with me.

I was there.

I led my Marines and Sailors ... followed them ...I watched over them. They love me. I was on a small hill in Iwo Jima. I was dirty and battle-worn, and I was at ground zero in New York City on September 11th as cowardly fanatics attacked America. I was raised from the ashes of once-proud buildings by brave firefighters, heroes who risked their lives to save others, showing all that America, though bloodied, will never be beaten. Those who would destroy me cannot win, for I am the symbol of freedom, of one nation under God, indivisible with liberty and justice for all.

I have been burned, torn, and trampled on the streets of countries I have helped set free.

It does not hurt, for I am invincible. I have been soiled upon, burned, torn, and trampled on the streets of my own country, and when it is by those whom I have served in battle, it hurts.

But I shall overcome.

I am strong.

I have even slipped the bonds of Earth and stood watch over the uncharted frontiers of space from my vantage point on the moon. I have borne silent witness to all of America's finest hours. But my finest hours are yet to come. When I am torn into strips and used as bandages for my wounded comrades on the battlefield, when I am flown at half-mast to honor my sailors, Marines, soldiers, and airmen, or when I lie in the trembling arms of a grieving parent at the grave site of their fallen son or daughter.

I am proud.

My name is Old Glory. Long may I wave. Dear God, long may I wave".

How fitting that family, friends, comrades, and brothers in arms were there for the moment. How appropriate that the moment took place where my brother Billy is memorialized along with many other Fighting Fifth Marines who made the ultimate sacrifice in Iraq or Afghanistan. How grateful I am that I survived my career to witness my service flag handed to my wife.

Historic places to visit in Bedford County.

Driving through Pennsylvania's mountains near Raystown Lake, it is difficult to imagine that the wilderness has changed much since settlers first built their homesteads there. Drive into Bedford to the site of Fort Bedford. This replica of the old French and Indian fort that once stood overlooking the stream is a museum. Next, drive over to the Bedford Cemetery where you can pay your respects to 43 Revolutionary War soldiers buried there. About an hour or so from Bedford sits Fort Robereau, which holds its annual Revolutionary War Days event during the second weekend in August and a Tribute to Veterans on the last Saturday in October. Fort Robereau was built in 1778 to protect nearby mining operations from Tories and Indians. The fort walls protected an officer's quarters, barracks powder magazine, and a lead smelter. The fort and the buildings it protected have been reconstructed and can be visited year around. Take a guided tour if you want or walk the grounds yourself and take advantage of miles of hiking trails and picnic areas the park provides. Finally, head over toward Raystown Lake, visit the Phillips Ranger Memorial, and pay your respects to those brave patriots of a mostly forgotten battle.

Phillips Rangers Memorial is located at Captain Phillips Monument Road Saxton, Pennsylvania.

Lieut. Col. Levin Powell Marker is located at 309 South Richard Street Bedford, Pennsylvania.

Revolutionary War Burial is located at 3390 Business U.S. 220 Bedford Pennsylvania.

Site of Fort Bedford is located at 110 East Pitt Street Bedford, Pennsylvania.

Fort Roberdeau Park is located at 383 Fort Roberdeau Road Altoona, Pennsylvania.

Selinsgrove, Pennsylvania

"If you are in these reviewing stands today, it is because there were moments in our careers where we bonded...it's those moments that entwine our lives for the rest of our lives".

~Sergeant Major Carlos Ruiz, 20th Sergeant Major of the Marine Corps.

I grew up on the outskirts of the small rural town of Selinsgrove in Snyder County, Pennsylvania, which happened to be founded by and named for an American Revolutionary War officer and scout who fought heroically for the independence of his adopted country. This immigrant-American patriot didn't fight a few battles in the Revolutionary War and go home like many others; he valiantly fought through to the very end of the conflict. He was present during most of the battles and skirmishes detailed throughout this book and interacted with many of the heroes and anti-heroes these pages record.

Most local historians who have written articles about Captain Anthony Selin over the years merely gloss over his military service, some making blanket statements that he fought with Washington or fought beside him; some have even suggested an actual friendship existed between the Commander-in-Chief and Selin, but I have found through careful research, that these claims are a bit exaggerated. Few existing letters were written between Selin and Washington, but they were strictly written regarding military interests during the war. Washington mentioned Selin in a few of his letters and orders to his subordinate generals, but nothing in any of the letters or documents suggests anything more than a professional relationship between the two compatriots. It is more accurate to say they knew of each other, and perhaps Selin even saw Washington in passing, on battlefields, along roads, or in camps, but I scarcely believe there was more interaction than that based on a lack of personal correspondence or mention in diaries or memoirs.

Regardless, my interest and certainly my excitement is generated from where Selin served and fought on battlefields I am very familiar with, most of which I visit frequently and usually with my daughters at my side in Chester, Delaware, and Montgomery Counties. My retirement flag was even flown over the Valley Forge encampment, where historical documentation indicates Selin camped with the Continental Army in 1777-78. His story is much bigger than a mere sentence or two in a local historical pamphlet and it is well worth reading.

Antony Selin was a Swiss Catholic who came to the Susquehanna Valley after the Revolutionary War. Period sources had described Selin as dark-eyed, dark-skinned, and tall. He came to the colonies on December 5th 1777, and was commissioned a Captain in Major Nicholas Dietrich, Baron de Ottendorff's Corps, which is described as a partisan or free unit. Partisan units were typically used as light infantry by European armies and worked independently from the main body. They were usually assigned reconnaissance, screening, scouting, and assault missions on enemy combatants, outposts, and convoys. Selin commanded the Second Partisan Company, which consisted of two lieutenants and 47 men. Von Ottendorf and Selin were probably friends or, at the very least, acquainted before the Corps was formed since both men had petitioned Congress for money to raise Ottendorf's Corps. It is also likely that Selin was the first officer commissioned in Ottendorf's Corps for the same reason. The unit was formed in Great Plains, New York, and placed under General Washington's immediate command.

Several historical records, orderly books, and letters indicate that Captain Selin served in the Continental Army for the duration of the conflict, which for him, began in April 1777, when he arrived in Bound Brook, New Jersey, with his company and fought in that battle.

April 4th 1777 From George Washington's General Orders:

"The detachments, commanded by Capts. O'Hara, Bicker, Talbot, and Selin, to hold themselves in readiness (with two days' provision) to march tomorrow morning. They will receive their orders from Major General. St. Clair".

In February 1777, the American outpost at Bound Brook, New Jersey, commanded by Major General Benjamin Lincoln, consisted of 1,000 soldiers. These men represented the 8th Pennsylvania Regiment, the 4th Continental Artillery, and provisional companies from the Wyoming Valley. Of this force, half of that number would muster out of the Army due to expiring enlistments in March. Selin commanded one of the provisional companies mentioned above.

Late on the evening of April 12th 1777, four thousand British and Hessian troops commanded by General Cornwallis marched from the British garrison at Brunswick, New Jersey, towards Washington's Army, which had wintered in Morristown. The combined assault force reached positions surrounding the Bound Brook outpost of 500 Americans before the battle began near daybreak the next morning. During the lop-sided battle, most of the American garrison narrowly escaped through an unblocked route. Reinforcements from Morristown arrived in the afternoon, but not before the British plundered the outpost and began the return march to Brunswick. During this minor skirmish, Selin fought against several of this book's anti-heroes, including British Generals Cornwallis and No Flint Grant, Hessian Colonel Donop, and Jager Captain Johann Ewald, who wrote detailed account of the battle of Bound Brook in his memoir, *Diary of the American War.*

"On the 20th, several hours before daybreak, I put an amusette behind a false hedge which I had fashioned from bushes, placing it so that the barn could be pierced easily. I sent Lieutenant Trautvetter with twelve jagers to a small hollow on this side of the river across from the parsonage, with orders to keep hidden until the Americans were dislodged from the barn by the fire of the amusette. Then, they were to rise and accompany the piece with sharp rifle fire. All went well. As soon as day broke, the riflemen began their harassing with their long rifles. After the third cannon shot, the barn became silent and the enemy left it, whereupon he fell into the jagers' fire. Since the road ran up along the river, which was not over a hundred paces wide, the jagers had the best possible range, and every jager killed or wounded his man.

After several hours, an officer with a trumpeter appeared and requested permission to take away the dead and severely wounded on a wagon. I permitted this and asked the officer if he would not visit us again soon. He shook his head, and they took away their dead and wounded on two wagons. There were five dead and two badly wounded".

Colonel von Donop reported that the American commander, General Lincoln, "must have retired en Profond Négligé," meaning profoundly undressed or naked, since his military papers and various personal effects were discovered when he left them behind in his haste to escape.

The British plan to surround and decisively engage the American post was negated when Ewald prematurely skirmished with the Americans, and British companies sent to block the road to Morristown arrived too late. This was the very route the Americans used to escape relatively unscathed. Several weeks later, Howe tried to spring a trap on another of Washington's detachments. This effort would have effectively cut off an American retreat into the New Jersey hills if it were successful. This effort was repulsed by the American detachment, including Selin's company, but not without a lot of bloodshed for Ottendorff's Corps during the engagement.

Historical sources indicate that Von Ottendorff never fought with his Corps; during the Battle of Bound Brook, he was away recruiting and, at some point, due to his relatively poor organizational skills, lost

General Washington's confidence, which was evident when Washington recalled the truant commander. On June 11th 1777, just prior to the Battle of Short Hills, a French officer, Colonel Charles Armand, Marquis de la Rouerie, was given the command of Ottendorf's Corps.

In a letter, Washington writes to Armand:

"Sir: You are forthwith to take upon you the command of the Corps heretofore under Major Ottendorf and to do all the duties thereof as commanding Officer, according to the rules and regulations established for the government of the Continental Army and according to the usages of War."

It seems that Ottendorff failed to report to Washington and, instead, absconded back to Europe. On July 15th 1778, Ottendorff reappeared based on a letter from General Heath to George Washington from Heath's headquarters in Boston, which reads:

"Dear General, this moment Col Armand & a Major Ottendorff called at my quarters and being about to set out for the Army, the major desires I would write your excellency that he is exceedinly sorry for leaving the service the last year, and wishes overlook it, that he desires to again serve in the Army. He has made several applications to the navy board to serve in the navy, he is now requesting Col Armand to let him serve in his Corps if agreeable to you and Col Armand informs me he would like him as a major if your excellency should approve of it, and has desired me to mention it. I know nothing of the Major's abilities or the reasons his leaving the Army, both of which (illegible) are known to your excellency".

Apparently, Washington was not having any of the baron's nonsense, which is plain from the following reply to Heath on August 14th 1778:

"Dear Sir:

Within a few days past I have been favoured with your several letters of the 15, 17 and 25 Ulto. and of the 6th. Inst. Mr. Attendorff shall never act as a Major or in any capacity as an officer in the Army with my consent, and I am much surprised that he should entertain the most distant idea that he would be received. His conduct deserves a very different notice."

Ottendorff reappeared a year or two later as an officer in the Revolutionary War, but this time, on British payrolls. A letter Ottendorff wrote on August 15th 1781, contains a deposition he took from a female spy who had infiltrated the French armies fighting on the American side, indicating Ottendorff was either spying for the British cause or he was at least handling spies for General Sir Henry Clinton, the British commander that replaced Howe in the American Campaign. Interestingly, a Cipher code in which the Cipher key is part of a book or other piece of text is called an Ottendorf cipher and was presumably named after Ottendorf, providing more tangible evidence that Ottendorff had probably spied for the British. The letter and pay receipt from a British paymaster can be sourced upon request from the University of Michigan, which maintains the Clinton Papers.

Around mid-June, General Howe marched most of his Army into central New Jersey to try to lure George Washington's Army into the open plains, and into a decisive engagement that would favor the British Army. During the ensuing skirmish, called the Battle of Short Hills, elements of Howe's Army engaged with elements of Washington's Army but failed to dislodge the Americans from their defensive position in the Watchung Mountains. Washington's forward divisions, including Lord Stirling's, shadowed Howe's movement, playing a dangerous game of cat and mouse with Howe's professional Army. Howe seized upon this opportunity and, on June 26th marched two columns of troops out on the plains to cut

Washington off from his defensive high ground. The British Army engaged in a running skirmish with Lord Stirling's troops, including Selin's company, which retreated to a more easily defendable position in a swamp.

Colonel Armand had a direct role in the Battle of Short Hills and reported he had a certificate of commendation:

"from Lord Sterling for my conduct at the battle of Short Hills in the jersey--where out of 80 men, 32 were killed & taken in the action & after the corps was ordered to defend a piece of cannon which happily, though making the rear guard in the retreat, I saved from the enemy--thus as I may remember were the expressions of Lord Sterling--the loss of men and the deffence of the peace of canon are the fact".

William Grant, a Virginia rifleman, provided eyewitness testimony as to the fate of the majority of Ottendorff's Corps of Volunteers:

"They drew up immediately in order to defend their field pieces and cover our retreat, and in less than an hour and a half were entirely cut off; scarce sixty of them returned safe out of the field; those who did escape were so scattered over the country that a great number of them could not rejoin the Army for five or six days."

Stirling's courageous resistance, including Selin's Corps, likely gave Washington enough time to withdraw his Army safely to high ground. Historically, the battle is considered a strategic victory for the American Army. After spending the night at Westfield, New Jersey, Howe returned to the British post at Perth Amboy and completely evacuated New Jersey by June 30th. During the battle, John Paul Schott, commander of the third company of Ottendorf's Corps, who joined the Corps with his independent company in time to fight in the Battle of Short Hills, was taken Prisoner.

After the battle, Colonel Armand began recruiting for his newly inherited Partisan Corps, with the base consisting of what was left of the Late Ottendorff's Corps. Selin, along with some of the other original officers of the Corps, led the unit during Armand's absences. Captain Bauer retired, Captain Dreisback was Court Martialed and removed from command, Captain Schott was a prisoner, and Bedkin left the Corps for another command. This left Selin to command the Old Corps and some newly recruited officers during the Philadelphia campaign.

The Corps was recognized as Armand's Corps, but Armand's early recruiting and his focus were directed more toward building a cavalry element and probably included the recruitment of replacement officers. However, Selin's Corps continued to serve as a light infantry unit under Armand during the Battles of Brandywine and Germantown before eventually wintering at Valley Forge.

Before those touchstone battles of the Philadelphia Campaign, we pick up Selin's trail at the Head of the Elk, Maryland, where Howe disembarked his Army to engage Washington's Army, end an American bid for independence, take Philadelphia or at least deprive Washington of their vital supplies stored in the Pennsylvania backcountry. Before Howe even landed, Washington received complaints that members of the Continental Army had allegedly participated in criminal activity against the people living in the area. Washington ordered Selin's Partisan Corps to investigate the allegations and retain any soldier suspected of potential criminal activity.

Elkton, MD

September 2, 1777

George Washington to William Maxwell, Head Qurs., Wilmington, September 2, 1777.

"Sir: I have your two favours of this date.

In consequence of the remonstrance from the Inhabitants near Elk, I have commanded Armand's Corps to repair immediately to this place. If any of the people who have been injured can point out the particular Persons, either Officers or Soldiers, they shall be made Examples of."

On September 2nd Washington sent Colonel Charles Armand's four-company Partisan Corps to join the newly formed Light Infantry, commanded by General Maxwell. Maxwell's newly minted American Light Infantry fought in the skirmish at Cooches' Bridge, then moving north towards Chads' ford, it engaged Knyphausen's Hessians at the Kennett Meetinghouse before finally falling back to defend the western bank of the Brandywine at Chads' ford. The unit eventually crossed the ford and occupied defensive positions on the eastern bank with the rest of the American Army. Selin's Corps was among the American patriots who covered the retreat of the main body of Washington's Army at Dillworthtown, collecting stragglers and the wounded as the American Army retreated toward Chester.

On September 16th Selin's Partisan Corps was in present-day East Goshen Township during the Battle of the Clouds. General Wayne's division led the left flank along the North Chester Road (Route 352), and Maxwell's Light Infantry led the right. Sixteen-year-old eyewitness Jacob Nagle watched as Maxwell's men engaged Colonel Abercromby's forces in the vicinity of Hershey Mills: "Our artilery was ranged along the ridge on the hill on the road side between the bridge and the enemy. Morgan's riflemen were in a wood on the opposite side of the road next to Sculkill. The rifelmen begun the action with their advance guard and Hessians. But the enemy not being nearanuff, the artilery had not fired a shot, when it begin to rain, that we could not engage".

The torrential rain forced the British to shelter in and around Goshen and Washington's Army to retreat across the Great Valley to Yellow Springs. Selin's Partisans, still attached to Maxwell's Light Infantry, were ordered to remain in the Great Valley to harass the British and confiscate their baggage trains. This American force, commanded by Generals Wayne and Maxwell, were the same Americans who were surprised by the British in Paoli.

Maxwell's Light Infantry was disbanded on September 25th and Maxwell resumed command of his New Jersey Brigade. The Light Infantry was reconstituted on September 28th although only at about half its original strength. It was held in reserve with Stirling's division during the battle of Germantown on October 4th 1777, and was permanently disbanded shortly after that. I believe Selin's Partisan Corps likely remained with General Wayne's Division after Maxwell's Light Infantry was disbanded based on the absence of historical data placing them elsewhere and because there is reliable documentation that places his Corps at the encampment at Valley Forge, Pennsylvania, during the winter of 1777-78 as evidenced by the following order issued to Selin in Washington's Orderly Book of May 26, 1778:

"It is ordered that an independent corps commanded by Captain Selin are immediately to bury the offal and carrion near the black bull. The commanding General of the staff will in future apply to the commanding officer of that Corps for a party to bury any offal which may be near his stall".

On June 17th 1778, Selin continued to command Armand's Light Infantry Corps whenever he was absent. He was likely still attached to Wayne's division when the American Army left their winter camp at Valley Forge. Selin's Corps would likely have served in the Army's forward screening effort to intercept and engage with General Clinton's newly acquired British Army near Monmouth Courthouse after it had evacuated Philadelphia for fear of becoming trapped between Washington and a French fleet possibly transiting the unprotected Delaware River.

On June 25th Washington ordered Wayne to follow General Scott with another 1,000 hand-picked men to reinforce the Army's vanguard. Washington offered General Lee command of the vanguard, to which he declined, stating the force was too insignificant for a man of his high rank and position to command. Washington appointed Lafayette instead and gave the eager young general orders to attack "with the whole force of your command" if the opportunity presented itself.

Lee, having realized Lafayette's assignment was more significant than he first thought, had a sudden change of heart and requested command of it. Washington ordered Lee to take Scott's former brigade and the brigade of General Varnum, link up with Lafayette, and take command of all advanced forces. Lee went forward with Wayne to reconnoiter Monmouth Court House, where they discovered the British rearguard. Estimating the British strength at around 2000 men, Lee decided to envelop the rearguard. He left Wayne with orders to fix the rearguard in place and returned to the remaining vanguard to lead it on a left flanking maneuver. Lee's confidence crept into reports sent back to Washington that implied "the certainty of success." Unfortunately for Lee, he quickly lost control of the vanguard and, with it, his tactical advantage.

Washington led to believe by Lee's reports that the American situation was well at hand, was astonished when he encountered an American straggler on the road bearing the first news of Lee's retreat just before witnessing whole units in retreat with his own eyes. None of the officers Washington met could tell him where they were supposed to be going or what they should be doing. As Washington rode on ahead towards the front line, he saw the vanguard in full retreat but saw no sign of the British.

On the trail, Washington met Lee, who, expecting praise for a retreat he believed had been generally conducted in good order, was chagrined when Washington asked sternly, "I desire to know, sir, what is the reason – whence arises this disorder and confusion?" When Lee regained his composure, he attempted to explain his actions, blaming faulty intelligence and his officers for pulling back without orders. Lee complained he had no choice but to retreat in the face of a superior force, which reminded Washington that Lee had opposed the attack in the first place. This untimely reminder did little to elevate his case with Washington, who said, "All this may be very true, sir," he replied, "but you ought not to have undertaken it unless you intended to go through with it." making it abundantly clear he was disappointed with Lee, to say the least as he rode off to re-organize his Army and personally lead the fight he expected Lee to be capable of doing.

Washington was able to turn his Army toward the sound of the gun and engaged the British, who occupied defensive positions around the Monmouth Courthouse. The British soon found themselves facing Wayne's detachment, which reformed about 350 yards away. As the British Grenadiers advanced to engage Wayne, they came under heavy fire from Stirling's artillery, which was unlimbered another 350 yards behind Wayne. Colonel Monckton became the highest-ranking British casualty of the day. In the face of an unexpectedly strong and determined enemy, the Grenadiers retreated across the bridge and back to a hedgerow from which they had chased Lee earlier. After realizing he had lost the initiative and had little to gain by continuing the fight, Clinton withdrew, and Washington decided not to pursue the battle, ending in another stalemate.

Lee continued in his post as second-in-command after the battle, and the issue at Monmouth would likely have gone away if he had let it go. His pride wouldn't allow him to let it go though. On June 30th after protesting his innocence to anyone who would listen, Lee finally wrote a scathing letter to Washington, blaming "dirty earwigs" for turning Washington against him. Lee asserted that his decision to retreat had saved the day and added that Washington was "guilty of an act of cruel injustice" towards him. Instead of the apology Lee was tactlessly seeking, Washington replied that the tone of Lee's letter was "highly improper" and that he would initiate an official inquiry into Lee's conduct. Lee's response was to demand a court-martial, which was once again regarded as insolent in tone; Washington ordered his arrest and set about obliging him with the court-martial he was seeking.

The court convened on July 4th. Lee was charged with disobeying orders in not attacking on the morning of the battle, contrary to "repeated instructions," conducting an "unnecessary, disorderly, and shameful retreat," and disrespect towards the commander-in-chief. Lee was found guilty on all four charges and was suspended from the Army for a year. The movie series Turn: Washington's Spies, Season Two- Gunpowder, Treason, and Plot, portrayed Lee's retreat from Monmouth Courthouse and his encounter with Washington and was inspiring, if not a bit too theatrical. The Battle of Monmouth marked the last major Revolutionary War battle fought in the Northern theatre.

A little talked about historical event rarely associated with the American Revolutionary War took place on the Pennsylvania, New York, and New Jersey frontier between 1777 and 1778 yet it holds its own among the more famous battles of the war. Although the Iroquois League had initially taken a stance of neutrality in what they regarded a "quarrel between a father and son," they were soon drawn into the bitter war between the 'Long Knives'. British commanders at Forts Niagara and Detroit began making concentrated efforts to encourage members of the League or any native they could convince, to attack settlements along the frontiers.

The British garrisons provided the warriors with firearms, ammunition, and other valuable accouterments, which enticed the warriors to take up the hatchet against the settlers. In addition, the British commanders paid a high bounty for any scalp taken by the warriors. Colonel Henry Hamilton, commander of the British fort in Detroit, bought so many scalps that he became infamously known as the Hair Buyer.

By the winter of 1778, Selin and his Corps were ordered to New York to defend its frontier against raiding Iroquois warriors and their Tory allies. Selin commanded one of the outposts on the New York frontier of the "Minisinks," which is evidenced by a letter from Washington to Edward Hand, Head Quarters, Fredericksburg, November 20, 1778:

"... I have thought it would be more agreeable to you to remove down to the Minisink settlement and take the command of a Body of troops which we are under the necessity of assembling there to protect that Frontier against the incursions of the Indians. The Corps at the Minisink will consist of Count Pulaski's Legion, Colo. Armands Corps, and Colo. Spencers Regt. making about 500 Horse and Foot. Colo. Cortlands Regt. is at Rochester in the neighborhood of Minisink".

On December 25th 1778, Selin sent a letter to General Hand from the Minisinks. He reported that:

"he had received his orders but had fallen from his horse and was injured." I cannot leave Minisink for three or four days but will send Lt. Lawrence Myers... with the Core tomorrow morning to the Place you Direct..." 7. Selin signed this letter as "Antoni Selin, Capt., Commander at Present."

Colonel Armand, who continued to focus on his mounted units, had little time for Selin's partisan corps. Eventually, Selin and Schott's company broke from Armand's division when Armand attempted to promote two of his newly recruited French countrymen over his senior company commanders. On February 7th 1779, George Washington wrote to Hand, proof that Captain Selin and Schott had separated from Armand's command. In part, Washington writes:

"...There is a small corp under the immediate command of Capt. Schott, which formerly belonged to Colo. Armands old and now attached to his new Corps. As they are unhappy in their situation on account of a disagreement in point of Rank..I have thought it best that they shall also march to the Southward with Pulaski's Legion. You will therefore give Capt. Schott orders to march to Lancaster, where he will also find orders on how to proceed."

Washington soon changed his mind when, on February 8th he wrote, "...I have determined that Captn Schott's Corps shall remain where they are, as I find they occupy a small detached post...as they are unhappy in their situation on account of a disagreement in point of Rank," This was written in reference to Armand's continual attempts to have officers that he recruited promoted into the ranks with no regard for Selin and Schott's earlier commission dates and seniority.

Washington reassigned Selin and Schott's companies to General Hand's Brigade, and Colonel Armand was ordered to a court martial and subsequently arrested for an unrelated incident. Armand was eventually acquitted of all the charges brought against him, was eventually promoted to Brigadier General, and, being one of only a few foreign officers who impressed Washington, corresponded with him well after the American Revolution.

George Washington to Charles Armand-Tuffin, Marquis de la Rouerie:

"...without delay, march your Corps towards Bedford to join the troops at or near that place under the command of Colonel Moylan. You are not for the present to go with the Corps yourself...as there is a complaint of a serious nature against you made by Mr. Vandeburgh..."

On June 28th, 1779, Washington again wrote to Armand, instructing him:

"Sir: The complaints of your Corps daily increased. You will immediately on receipt of this send it off under the Officer next in command, to join Col. Moylan, at or near Bedford. Yourself will remain with the Witness you have to attend a Court Martial which will sit tomorrow morning at 10 oClock at New Windsor.

Head Quarters, West-point, August 14, 1779:

On August 23rd, 1779, Capt. Schott and Selin were transferred to Gen. Hand's 3rd Brigade, as noted in Rev. William Rogers' journal: "...By this day's orders the 4th Pennsylvania regiment and Rifle Corps are annexed to General Hand's brigade."

Selin and Schott spent the winter of 1778-79 in the Minisink region, commanding small frontier forts. They remained there until they were ordered to the Wyoming Valley in the Spring of 1779 to prepare for the Sullivan-Clinton Campaign. General Washington sent Captain Schott to Philadelphia for supplies for the Corps while Captain Selin marched the two companies into Wyoming.

On March 24th 1779, Washington wrote to General Hand:

"... As soon as the Weather will admit I intend the German Battalion, Armand's and Schott's Corps shall move over to Wyoming to take post there..."

The Wyoming Valley is in present-day Luzerne County, Pennsylvania, but in the 1700s, it was disputed territory claimed by Pennsylvania, Connecticut, and the Lenni-Lenape. The controversy started when 1662 King Charles II granted the land north of the 41st parallel to Connecticut and included the land along the north and west branches of the Susquehanna River. The same king, nineteen years later, granted William Penn lands west of the Delaware River and north to the 42nd parallel, so each colony claimed the land between the two parallels.

Penn bought the disputed territory from representatives of the Lenni-Lenape for around four hundred pounds, which was considered a bargain even in those times for Penn. Years later, however, the Lenni-Lenape disputed the purchase. To settle the dispute, the Penn family devised what was called the Walking Purchase in 1737. The treaty between the Penn family and the Lenn-Lenape would cede lands from the Lehigh Valley north as far as a man could walk in a day and a half. The Lenni-Lenape, reasoning that the furthest a man could walk in a day and a half was but 40 miles or so, thought they were making a pretty good deal. The Penn brothers, however, hired a runner who covered nearly 70 miles in the allotted time. The Penns drew a line on a map from the Lehigh Valley north to what is now known as Jim Thorpe and considering that line the western boundary of the purchase, claimed all the lands east of the two points to the Delaware River, forcing the Lenni-Lenape to move west, settle along the Susquehanna River.

At the Albany Conference in June 1754, the Iroquois League agreed to sell seven million acres in western Pennsylvania to the Penns. At this juncture of history, the Lenape were subservient to the league, had no representative power in the land sale, and were forced to be displaced again within a year after the land was ceded. This precipitated retaliatory attacks on German and Swiss settlers who had already begun to settle the land along the Penn's Creek region. One of these attacks known historically as the Penn's Creek Massacre, utterly wiped out several families. At the same time, those who survived the attacks, primarily women and children, were taken into captivity, sold, or adopted in the place of a deceased relative.

John Harris Jr, a woodsman who laid out the present city of Harrisburg on his father's land grant, led an expedition of around 50 men up the Susquehanna River to the town of Shamokin to quell the attacks through negotiations. When the expedition arrived at Shamokin, they found a large gathering of Lenni-Lenape warriors painted for war. Andrew Montour, a half-breed Oneida, warned Harris to return home immediately and to travel east of the river. Harris took the advice and immediately left the town but traveled south on the west side of the river. Near the mouth of Penn's Creek, on the northern end of Selinsgrove, a Lenape war party ambushed Harris' expedition, resulting in three killed by the warriors and five more of Harris' party drowning in the river as they attempted to swim to the eastern bank. A doctor riding behind Harris was shot in the back and killed just before the horse was shot from under Harris. Harris was fortunate to have survived the ambush and the swim across the river.

As if the land disputes between the natives and European settlers were not enough, armed disputes often occurred between Pennsylvania and Connecticut settlers over the original land granted to the two colonies by King Charles II. Although the armed conflicts generally ceased during the war, tensions remained high. Colonel Hunter, who commanded the garrison at Fort Augusta, confiscated boats loaded with military supplies being sent upriver to the Wyoming garrison. When militiamen from the Wyoming garrison complained, Hunter explained to Governor Reed that the supplies were drawn from Pennsylvania stores in Carlisle and Lancaster and should be provided to Pennsylvanians and that Connecticut should provision the garrison at Wyoming. Hunter also cited a rumor that the Wyoming garrison was giving the supplies to settlers who were posing as soldiers drawing rations. Washington settled the dispute in 1780 by ordering a detachment of the Jersey line of the Continental Army to occupy the post, and the supplies resumed without seizure.

Selin, tasked with commanding a detachment to move supplies up the Susquehanna to the Wyoming post in June 1779, was likely subjected to one of Hunter's seizures of the military supplies near Fort Augusta in present-day Sunbury. Given Hunter and Selin's historical headbutting during the Revolutionary War, it is kind of ironic that one of the most significant Susquehanna Valley rivalries in high school football today is the cross-river rivalry between the Selinsgrove and Shikellamy (Sunbury) high schools. Although Congress unanimously ruled in 1782 that the disputed territory belonged to Pennsylvania and Connecticut had no legitimate claim to the land, the Seals and the Braves continue to fight annually for supremacy over the gridiron.

During the summer of 1779, General Sullivan was tasked with leading an expedition intended to knock the British-allied Iroquois out of the war permanently and remove them as a threat to the Pennsylvania and New York frontiers. To achieve this, Sullivan resorted to a scorched earth tactic and destroyed multiple villages and crops throughout Pennsylvania and New York. Toward the end of the Revolutionary War, the Iroquois received very little support from the British or Loyalists, so they avoided large-scale engagements as much as possible. Because of this, most of the combat during the Sullivan Expedition consisted of minor skirmishes or ambushes, with one exception occurring in Newtown, New York.

Captain Schott left the Sullivan campaign sometime in early March, and Captain Selin assumed command of "Schott's Corps" along with his own Corps. Historical references to "Captain Selin's Independent Rifle Company" replaced The Armand Corps designator at this juncture. Selin's Independent Rifle Company, together with a Corps of Pioneers, cleared the path for Sullivan's march during the campaign. In August 1779, after nearly two months of burning Iroquoian crops and villages, Sullivan and his men reached Newtown, New York. Newtown was situated near the border of New York and

Pennsylvania near present-day Elmira. A force of 1,000 Iroquois, roughly half the warriors they could even field, and 200 Loyalists waited in a fortified position on a large hill, hoping to ambush and destroy the Continental expedition.

Selin commanded the group of scouts during the expedition, who were instrumental in discovering the ambush being set up in Newtown, New York. They discovered the hidden breastworks and reported to General Hand, who ordered his light infantry troops to concentrate their fires on the earthworks. The defenders tried repeatedly to lure Sullivan's forces into their ambush zone, but failing to do so, a lull in the fire gradually fell over the field.

Sullivan devised a complex plan to encircle the defenders. Although skillfully executed by Sullivan's well-trained troops, not enough consideration was given to the swampy terrain, which slowed Sullivan's troops. This delay allowed the Iroquois and Loyalists just enough time to escape encirclement and destruction. A brief counterattack led by the Mohawk chief Joseph Brant did little to change the outcome of the battle, which resulted in a crushing defeat for the Iroquois that left the once proud warriors completely demoralized. Sullivan operated virtually unopposed in the region for the following month, allowing him to end the Iroquois threat on the American frontier. With a significant number of Iroquois villages destroyed, the Iroquois, dispersed and homeless, suffered from famine after the destruction of their crops and homes. At the end of it all, their British allies were nowhere to be found.

After the end of the Sullivan Campaign, Selin was again joined by Schott, and they returned to and took up posts in Wyoming to help protect the frontier settlements. In the Spring of 1780, another dispute in rank erupted again, this time between Captain Selin and Schott, resulting in the Corps splitting up and working separately. In January of 1781, Selin requested and was given command of a company in General Hazen's 2nd Canadian Regiment. He held this position until the end of the Revolutionary War and retired with the rank of Major.

On January 1st 1783, Selin resigned his commission and moved to the Susquehanna Valley. In 1785, he purchased land north of the Conrad Weiser tract (The Isle of Que), surveyed it, and laid it out in lots, eager to sell them and start a town. He eventually went into the milling and store business with Simon Snyder, married the future Pennsylvania Governor's sister, Catherine, and settled on a farm just north of the town to raise their son and daughter. Anthony Selin died on February 3rd 1792, and is buried at the Trinity Lutheran Church in Selinsgrove.

His son, Anthony Charles, was commissioned a major and served in the War of 1812. A great-great grandson, Captain Charles Selin Davis, organized a company of volunteers in 1862 to fight for the Union cause during the American Civil War. Captain Davis was mortally wounded while leading a charge during the Battle of Taylor's Ridge in Georgia. Son and great-great-grandson are buried beside their patriot patriarch.

Marine Corps Tie-In...a full circle.

In late July 2023, having learned that my friend and brother Marine, a fellow Lima Company Drill Instructor I briefly worked beside in the hot, chaotic trenches of Marine Corps Recruit Depot San Diego, had been appointed the 20th Sergeant Major of the Marine Corps, which is kind of a big deal. I immediately sent him a message congratulating him on his prestigious appointment. I reminded him of a brief conversation we had one day on the depot when I told him I thought he would be the Sergeant Major of the Marine Corps one day. I was so impressed by the Marines' professionalism, tact, and humility. He looked at me, smiled, and said, "I know," not in a boastful or arrogant tone but with unwavering confidence and certainty. In my message to the Sergeant Major, I told him it would be an honor to make the trip to Washington, DC to support him and happily stand in the back of the bleachers if he had no room on his guest list to accommodate me. I really did not expect a reply to my message because I assumed the Sergeant Major would be extremely busy and his usage somewhat limited on social media platforms. I received a reply from him a few days later that read, "Send me an address, brother!"

In a few more weeks, I received an envelope addressed to myself and a guest. Inside was an invitation from the 39th Commandant of the Marine Corps on embossed cardstock inviting my wife and me to Marine Barracks 8th and Eye for the Relief and Appointment Ceremony of the 19th and 20th Sergeants Major of the Marine Corps. My wife and I made plans to attend, and on the morning of August 10th we were in our car and headed south to Washington, D.C.

We arrived at the Washington Navy Yard in good time, parked in a garage, and made the 10-minute walk to Marine Barracks 8th and Eye. So much had changed in the city, yet the old bones I remembered were still there. As we walked to the barracks, waves of nostalgia started pelting me like well-aimed bricks. Marine Barracks 8th and Eye was the first duty station in my Marine Corps career, and those memories returned to me in an overwhelming deluge. When we arrived at the barracks, Marines in full dress or Service Delta's were fairly swarming the place.

We walked through security, and a young Marine greeted us and inquired whether we were the VIP guests of one of the sergeants major. I told the young motivator that we were invited by the 20th Sergeant Major of the Marine Corps but that I didn't think we were VIP guests as I showed him my invitation. He ushered us to Center Walk, and as we made the short walk, I asked the Marine if he was assigned to one of the marching companies. I really wanted to ask him whether he was even old enough to play Marine, but I figured I would have been aging myself. He replied that he was assigned to

Alpha Company, and I shared that I was once a member of Second Platoon Alpha Company, the venerated Earth Pigs, in 1996. He looked at me wide-eyed and grunted 'rah,' but I was not sure if it was out of shared comradery or astonishment. When we arrived at Center Walk, the Marine inquired with a gunny who verified that we were, in fact, VIP guests and had us seated directly behind the Sergeant Major's family.

My wife and I were seated for no more than five minutes when I heard a booming voice, all too familiar, even though it had been seventeen years since I heard it. The voice belonged to none other than a Senior Drill Instructor who had once given me a tongue-in-cheek order to "IT a recruit to death," a Marine who took the time to teach me how to be a Drill Instructor and who is a Marine I respect tremendously. As we struggled with our mutual shock at the unexpected reunion, more happy reunifications were in store for us.

The parade sequence for the Relief and Appointment Ceremony for the Sergeant Major of the Marine Corps differs from a usual parade in that it is an enlisted parade, absent of officers, except the Commandant of the Marine Corps. The Sergeant Major of Marine Barracks 8th and Eye presided over the parade as the Commander of Troops. When the barracks Sergeant Major took his position on center walk to commence the parade, we were in for another shock. My former Senior Drill Instructor exclaimed, "No way," as he stared in disbelief. The barracks Sergeant Major was another Lima Company Drill instructor from our training company whom we affectionately dubbed Jesse James, the Green-Eyed Terror.

The Marines of 8th and Eye performed to their usual high level of precision, and the speeches of the Sergeants Major were well presented. When the Relief and Appointment Ceremony was concluded, the 20th Sergeant Major of the Marine Corps walked toward his family when I believe he noticed us for the first time. He could scarcely contain his excitement as his face broke out in a huge, boyish grin, and he began to double-fist pump our hands. He then turned to his wife and said what sounded like, "These two guys are reasons I am standing here today." I have rarely received such high praise if that is indeed what the Sergeant Major said. In the moment, it left me wondering if I even did enough to earn such a reverent accolade from an obviously much more accomplished Marine than myself.

We were eventually ushered to a reception for the guests of the Sergeants Major. As we made our way across the well-manicured grass parade deck, I startled myself when it suddenly dawned on me that I was breaking a very sacred Marine Barracks law...only VIPs walked on the parade deck grass. The only reason a barracks Marine ever broke this unwritten law was to practice for or march in a parade. In the reception hall, a receiving line for each Sergeant Major was established for guests who wanted a rare and very brief opportunity to offer well wishes or take a photo. I was about to make my move to a receiving line when a giant of a man yelled and grabbed the Senior Drill Instructor up in a huge hug. Yet another Lima Company Drill Instructor, though one I only knew in passing.

I finally made my way to the 19th Sergeant Major of the Marine Corps, and recently appointed 5th Senior Enlisted Advisor to the Chairman (SEAC) who, believe it or not, was the same Platoon 3050 Drill Instructor I had inadvertently called a Drill Sergeant on a rifle range in Parris Island, South Carolina, on a sunny afternoon in 1995. I introduced myself and said, "I heard you mention you were a recruit in platoon 3050 in your speech, and I was wondering if you remember platoon 3050 in 1995," as I showed him my old recruit photo with our Drill Instructors lined up in front of the platoon. He grimaced and said, "I remember the platoon, but I didn't want it because when I was a recruit in 3050, the entire Drill Instructor team was relieved." I asked him if he remembered an occasion when one of his recruits inadvertently called him a Drill Sergeant" on a rifle range. The SEAC smiled and said, "One would never forget something like that." He then asked if I remembered the consequences of the occasion. I smiled at him and said, "A recruit would never forget something like that!"

I reminded him that on the same evening, he made me a squad leader in the platoon, a coveted billet I held until just before final drill when I was fired because I couldn't get column of files down. He shrugged and said, "Easy come, easy go." I told him that the irony was that I was assigned to a ceremonial marching platoon at Marine Barracks 8th and Eye a scant couple of months after boot camp. Later in my career, I became a Drill Instructor and even went on to become a Drill Instructor at Officer Candidate School." He seemed impressed, but I don't think for my accomplishments as much as it was for the irony of the moment.

The SEAC asked if I could stick around for a photo. He told me that the Marine who was his 3050 Drill Instructor when he was a recruit was also in the room. He insisted on a group photo to commemorate such a rare opportunity to have such a combination of Marine Drill Instructors together...A third battalion Lima Company Senior Drill Instructor of platoon 3050 with his former recruit, who eventually became a Lima Company Drill Instructor of his own platoon 3050. That DI, 19th SMMC and recently appointed 5th SEAC, in turn, with his 3050 recruit who eventually became a Senior Drill Instructor for Lima Company in San Diego...I just missed picking up my own platoon 3050. With a grin, the SEAC said, "Occasions like the one the three of us are experiencing in this space and time never happen...we have a better chance of being struck by lightning".

I eventually had my opportunity to meet the 20th Sergeant Major of the Marine Corps in his receiving line and I brought my fellow Lima Company Drill Instructor with me. I was so overwhelmed in the moment that I could only tell him how proud I was of his prestigious accomplishment. After several photos, the Sergeant Major insisted on a group photo of the old Lima Company hats, reunited again on such a monumental occasion.

The next morning, when I had sufficiently regained control of my emotions, I sent a message to the Sergeant Major to tell him what I wanted to convey the previous day. The message was:

"Carlos, thank you so much for the invite to a very special day...in all the hoopla, I didn't get a chance to tell you that my family and I are praying for you and yours as you embark on this special service to our Corps...my father-in-law, who was recently diagnosed with stage four cancer, is also very patriotic and wanted me to tell you he is going to pray for you every day as you lead our Corps forward! He wanted a signed picture of you to place on his desk but told me a photo I took of you during your speech would do just fine! I am also committed to praying for you and our Corps every day, and if there is anything I can do to support you, please don't hesitate to ask...we had some great times in those hot San Diego trenches, didn't we?"

Again, I never expected the Sergeant Major to have the time or inclination to reply, but again, true to his nature, he did: "Shane, thank you for making the journey, brother. It was wonderful to see you!"

The un-relinquished, boundless brotherhood of Marines is what I will always cherish and sorely miss as I live out the rest of my days in retirement. A Marine Corps where you can unconditionally trust the man to the left and right of you with your very life among a community of warriors where color, demographics, or socioeconomic differences are meaningless. A Marine Corps where you can begin at the very bottom of a highly competitive organization, work hard, and become worthy and deserving of such high mantles of leadership and responsibility as the Sergeant Major of the Marine Corps and SEAC.

Time has a fleeting way of slipping by us all...not long after I finally finished this last chapter of the book, my father-in-law (Pop-Pop) finished his long, illustrious journey through life. He succumbed to complications from his illness at the very impressive age of 84 after a brief but intense fight with stage four cancer. He was a great man in his own right- a servant, shepherd, and steward; a promise keeper, mentor, and dutiful man of God. He diligently prayed for Carlos, the Marine Corps, and its leadership, just as he prayed for all his family and friends, even when cancer made it almost unbearable for him to do so in the end.

On one of the last evenings that he was able to walk on his own and have coherent conversations, he pulled my wife and me aside and told us he believed the Lord was going to use the two of us and our girls in great and mighty ways for His kingdom. He also looked me in the eye and paid me the ultimate honor, one I am sure will never be surpassed. It echoed to a time over fourteen years ago when I very nervously asked him for his daughter's hand in marriage. He told me that on that day, he gave me his blessing, a father's blessing, and he accepted me as his son-in-law. He went on to say that he no longer looked at me as a son-in-law but that he considered me one of his own sons. I gave him the first of only two printed copies of my rough draft just before he was diagnosed with cancer. An ardent patriot, he was so enthusiastic to read it through to the end... but the manuscript is long, and this last chapter wasn't even included in the original rough draft I gave him. We all simply ran out of time, a stark and terrible reminder that "tomorrow may be one day too late."

Historical places to visit in or near Selinsgrove, Pennsylvania.

Our journey ends with this final segment of the Patriot's Path. Travel to Selinsgrove in beautiful Central Pennsylvania. This small town is nestled along Penns Creek and the Susquehanna River in a valley surrounded by great blue mountains. This segment will have you driving from marker to marker and include a visit to a couple of cemeteries where the heroes of this chapter rest in eternity. While visiting all the historical sites, be sure to stop by the many small shops along Market Street and make a reservation at BJ's Ribs for a wonderful dining experience.

The Isle of Que is located along front Street Selinsgrove, Pennsylvania.

The Governor Snyder House is located at 121 North Market Street Selinsgrove, Pennsylvania.

Simon Snyder Historical Marker is located along 12o South Market Street Selinsgrove, Pennsylvania.

Simon Snyder Monument is located along Union Alley, 0.1 miles south of University Avenue Selinsgrove, Pennsylvania.

Selin's Monument at Trinity Lutheran Cemetery is located at West Spruce Street and David Street Selinsgrove, Pennsylvania.

The Penn's Creek Massacre Monument is located at 319 South Old Trail Selinsgrove, Pennsylvania.

The Penn's Creek Massacre Sign is located along 357 North Market Street Selinsgrove, Pennsylvania.

The Albany Purchase Historical Marker is located along 980 North Susquehanna Trail Selinsgrove, Pennsylvania.

Albany Purchase Line Stone is located at 367 South Old Trail Selinsgrove, Pennsylvania.

Revolutionary War Memorial is located at the intersection of Pine Street and University Avenue Selinsgrove, Pennsylvania.

John Harris, Founder of Harrisburg Monument is located at 319 South Old Trail Selinsgrove, Pennsylvania.

About The Author

Coming home from my final deployment

I was born and raised in central Pennsylvania. Growing up on stories told by my grandfathers and metal detecting with my father, I developed a passion for local history, especially the colonial and pre-colonial eras. Although a career spent learning and researching local historical events was alluring, it wasn't powerful enough to keep me from achieving my deep-rooted desire to serve our nation as a United States Marine.

On October 10th 1995, I started my 20-year career as a United States Marine at Parris Island, South Carolina. During my career, I served at Marine Barracks Eighth and Eye, Third Battalion, Seventh Marines, First Battalion, Fifth Marines, Marine Corps Recruit Depot San Diego, Second Battalion, Sixth Marines, Villanova University NROTC, and Second Battalion, Fourth Marines.

In 2003 I deployed to Iraq as a member of Regimental Combat Team 5 in direct support of Operations Iraqi and Enduring Freedom. During this deployment, I was awarded a Navy Achievement Award with a combat 'V' for valor, a Combat Action Ribbon, and a Presidential Unit Citation.

I received an undergraduate degree in Religion from Liberty University and a Master of Divinity from Liberty Baptist Theological Seminary, and I was ordained in 2013. My interests include volunteerism, long-distance running, traditional hunting, and spending time with my wife Diane, thirteen-year-old daughter Sadie Grace, and five-year-old daughter Savannah Irene.

I retired from the Marine Corps and settled down with my family in the Greater Philadelphia area, where I am a Campus Safety Officer at a local school district. Three long summers running on trails through rich historical areas, pushing my youngest daughter in a beefed-up stroller, revitalized my passion and appreciation for history. At four years old, my daughter was too big for a stroller and had little interest in riding in one, so we started exploring the Patriot Paths of Pennsylvania together. As we began to research each town, county, and battle site, I gained a deeper understanding of the part Pennsylvania played in securing a free and independent America during the Revolutionary War. It is a fantastic, vibrant story and history that is worth sharing.

Bibliography

Architecture & Archaeology. "National Register of Historic Places Inventory Nomination Form:

Ashmead, Henry Graham (1884). History of Delaware County, Pennsylvania. Philadelphia: L.H. Everts & Co. p. 290.

Bedford County Genealogy Project "The Massacre of Captain William Phillips' Rangers" https://www.pa-roots.com/bedford/history/massacrecaptphillips.html Bedford County Genealogy Project.

Bennett, M. Busenkell, M. Edmunds, F.L. Morris, E, Murphy, K. and Stoudt, V. (1976) "Warwick Furnace Farm History". Nomination Form for Warwick Furnace Farm.

Blairsville, PA (August 4, 2014) "Sketches of the Life and Indian Adventures of Captain Samuel Brady, a Native of Cumberland County, Born 1758, a Few Miles Above Northumberland, Pa" Hardpress Publishing.

Blount, Jim (1989). "The Butler We're Named For, Gen. Richard Butler". Hamilton Journal-News.

Brigadier General John Lacey, Jr., to General Armstrong, dated May 11, 1778.Moore Hall" (PDF).

Brigadier General John Lacey, Jr., to Thomas Wharton, President, Supreme Executive Council of Pennsylvania, dated May 4, 1778.

The Brinton House (2021) "The Brinton House: Our Story" https://www.brintonfamily.org/copy-of-our-mission The Brinton Association of America, Inc.

Brower, D.H.B. (1881) "Danville, A Collection of Historical and Biographical Sketches" Lane S. Hart.

Brubaker, Jack (April 16, 2010) "Remembering Lancaster County: Stories from Pennsylvania Dutch Country" The History Press.

Buckalew, John M. (1896) "Report of the Commission to Locate the Site of the Frontier Forts in Pennsylvania: The Frontier Forts Within The North And West Branches of the Susquehanna River. Vol. 1" Clarence M. Bush, State Printer of Pennsylvania.

Caerter, W.C. (June 1, 2009) "History of York County, Pennsylvania, 1729-1834" Genealogical Publishing Company.

Carlisle, Pennsylvania (2023) https://www.carlislepa.org/about_us/about_carlisle_borough/history.php Carlisle, Pennsylvania.

Cash, Kerry H. (February 2, 2005) "A Table in the Presence: The Dramatic Account of How a U.S. Marine Battalion Experienced God's Presence Amidst the Chaos of the War in Iraq" Thomas Nelson.

Chase, Philander D. and Lengel, Edward, eds. (2001) "Clement Biddle to George Washington, September 16, 1777, in, The Papers of George Washington August-October 1777, Revolutionary War Series": University Press of Virginia.

"Continental Powder Works". Iron & Steel Heritage. Archived from the original on 2022-12-07.

Davidson, Jane L.S. National Historic Landmarks & National Register of Historic Places in Pennsylvania (Searchable database). "Cultural Resources Geographic Information System". "National Register of Historic Places Inventory Nomination Form: Roger Hunt Mill" (PDF).

Deposition of Col. Frederick Watts & Sam'l Henry by Andrew Long, dated May 14, 1778.

Detterline, Elinor J. (1970) "A Brief Glimpse of East Whiteland" Tredyffrin Easttown Historical Society.

Dillman, David, Dillman, Caroline, Cohn, L. and Powell, Doris M. National Historic Landmarks & National Register of Historic Places in Pennsylvania (Searchable database). "Cultural Resources Geographic Information System"). "National Register of Historic Places Inventory Inventory-Nomination: White Horse Tavern" (PDF).

Dixon, Mark E. (2010) "The Hidden History of Delaware County: Untold Tales from Cobb's Creek to the Brandywine" (pp. 25-29) The History Press.

Dorchester, Jane E. (2009) National Historic Landmarks & National Register of Historic Places in Pennsylvania" (Searchable database). "Pennsylvania's Historic Architecture & Archaeology".

Dunkerly, Robert (November 24, 2007) "Women of the Revolution: Bravery and Sacrifice on the Southern Battlefields" The History Press.

Durschmied, Erik (April 2, 2001) "The Weather Factor: How Nature has Changed History", (pp. 41–44): Bargain Price.

"Ellis Woods Revolutionary War Cemetery" https://eastcoventry-pa.gov/index.asp?SEC=DEC91E78-207F-49D4-9D33-4E28F458C22F&Type=B_BASIC

Ewald, Johann and Tustin, Joseph P. (1979). "Diary of the American War: A Hessian Journal" Yale University Press.

Faragher, John M. (November 15, 1993) "Daniel Boone: The Life and Legend of an American Pioneer" Holt Paperbacks.

Farrell, Joe, Knorr, Lawrence and Farley, Joe ("Pennsylvania's Patriots: Their Lives, Contributions and Burial Sites" Sunbury Press.

Federer, William J. (November 1, 2019) "Miracles in American History: Amazing Faith That Shaped the Nation", (pp. 17–19): Amerisearch, Inc.

Ferling, John (1977) "The Loyalist Mind: Joseph Galloway and the American Revolution" Pennsylvania State Univ Press.

Federer, Susie and Federer, William J. (December 12, 2012) "Miracles in American History: 32 Amazing Stories of Answered Prayer" Amerisearch, Inc.

Figueroa, Joe A. (2001). "Old Breed of Martial Artists Still Kicking". United States Marine Corps.

Fischer, David H. (2004) "Washington's Crossing" Oxford University Press.

J. Smith Futhey and Gilbert Cope (1995) "History of Chester County, Pennsylvania: With Genealogical and Biographical Sketches, Vol. 1".

Futhey, J. Smith and Cope, Gilbert (August 19, 2020) "History of Chester County, Pennsylvania with Genealogical and Biographical Sketches" Southern Historical Press, Inc.

"Gen Persifor Frazer (1736-1792) - Find a Grave..." www.findagrave.com.

George Washington to John Armstrong, dated March 27, 1778

General George Washington to Brigadier General William Maxwell, dated May 7, 1778.George Washington to John Lacey, dated January 23, 1778.

Hamilton, John C. (1840) "Alexander Hamilton to John Hancock, September 18, 1777" The Life of Alexander Hamilton, 2 vols. (pp.85) D. Appleton & Company.

Harris, Michael C. (2014) "Brandywine: A Military History of the Battle of that Lost Philadelphia but Saved America, September 11, 1777" Savas Beatie LLC.

Harris, Michael C. (2020) "Germantown: A Military History of the Battle for Philadelphia, October 4, 1777" Savas Beatie LLC.

Hastedt, Glenn P. (2003) "Espionage: A Reference Handbook. ABC-CLIO, Inc.

Heite, Edward F. Norton, Joan M, Troy, Rosemary, Benenson, Carol A. and Bower, Mark. "Cooch's Bridge Historic District, NRHP Nomination, amendments". NRHP Focus. U.S. Park Service.

"Historic Chichester Meetinghouse" http://www.chichestermeetinghouse.org/histroy

Historical sketches: a collection of papers prepared for the Historical Society of Montgomery County, Pennsylvania (contains extracted reprints of primary accounts)

Horn, Joshua (November 9, 2015) "Peter Muhlenberg: The Pastor Turned Soldier" Journal of the American Revolution.

Hunter, William (January 1, 1999) "Forts on The Pennsylvania Frontier: 1753-58" Wennawoods

Hugins, Walter (1983) "Hopewell Furnace: The Story of a 19th-Century Ironmaking Community, in Hopewell Furnace, Hopewell Village National Historic Site, Pennsylvania, National Park Handbook 124. Washington, D.C.: National Park Service. pp. 28–33. ISBN 0912627182.

Jackson, John W. (1992) "Valley Forge: Pinnacle of Courage" Thomas Publications.

James A. Northington (2010) "Forging a Revolution: John Taylor at Sarum" https://pabook.libraries.psu.edu/literary-cultural-heritage-map-pa/feature-articles/forging-revolution-john-taylor-sarum Penn State University Library.

John Conrad Weiser Family (1960). "The Weiser family: a genealogy of the family of John Conrad Weiser, the elder (d. 1746) prepared on the two hundred fiftieth anniversary of his arrival in America, 1710-1760" (pp. 168) John Conrad Weiser Family Associates.

"John Peter Gabriel Muhlenberg". aoc.gov. Architect of the Capitol.

Jordan, John Woolf (2004). "Colonial and Revolutionary Families of Pennsylvania" (pp. 524) Genealogical Publishing Company.

Joseph G. Bilby and Katherine Bilby Jenkins (2010) "Monmouth Courthouse" Westholme Publishing.

Kaat, Linda (2023) "Friends of Martin's Tavern" https://www.martinstavern.org/martins-tavern

Kennett Township (1971) "History of Kennett Township" Kennett Township.

Kent, Bill (December 28, 1997), "JERSEYANA; One Soldier's Battle to Preserve the Memory of Others", The New York Times

Lee, Henry (1869) "Memoirs of the War in the Southern Department of the United States" (pp. 90-91) University Publishing Company.

Lin, John B. and Egle, William H., eds., (1879) "Pennsylvania Archives-Second Series": Lane C. Hart.

United States Marine Corps. (2010) "MCO 1500.59: Marine Corps Martial Arts Program (MCMAP)".

Mark Edward Lender and Garry Wheeler Stone (2016) "Fatal Sunday: George Washington, the Monmouth Campaign, and the Politics of Battle" University of Oklahoma Press.

Marris W. Mullen Parkesburg: Our Town History 1681 to 1972 https://www.parkesburg.org/DocumentCenter/View/142/Mullen-History-PDF?bidId=

Martin, John Hill (1877). Chester (and Its Vicinity,) Delaware County, in Pennsylvania. Philadelphia: Wm. H. Pile & Sons.

McCullagh, David (January1, 2006) "1776" Simon and Sehuster Paperbacks.

McGready, Blake (November 28, 2016) "Abigail Hartman Rice, Revolutionary War Nurse" https://allthingsliberty.com/2016/11/abigail-hartman-rice-revolutionary-war-nurse/ Journal of the American Revolution.

McGuire, Thomas J. (2007) The Philadelphia Campaign: "Germantown and the Roads to Valley Forge" Stacklpole Books.

McGuire, Thomas J. (2000) "Battle of Paoli" Stackpole Books.

Moore, John L. (January 23, 2018) "Scorched Earth: General Sullivan and the Senecas" Sunbury Press.

Moore, John L. (June, 2019) "1780: Year of Revenge" Sunbury Press.

Mowday, Bruce E. (2021) "Lafayette at Brandywine" The Making of an American Hero" Barricade Books Inc.

Myers, Jack (2019) "The Delco Files: 101 Stories of the Most Amazing and Unusual People, Places and Events in Delaware County, PA" Jack O'Lantern Press Publication.

National Historic Landmarks & National Register of Historic Places in Pennsylvania "Cultural Resources Geographic Information System". Archived from the original (Searchable database) on September 14, 2005.

"National Historic Landmarks & National Register of Historic Places in Pennsylvania" (Searchable database). CRGIS: Cultural Resources Geographic Information System. Note: This includes Pennsylvania Register of Historic Sites and Landmarks (August 1971). "National Register of Historic Places Registration Form: Dilworthtown Historic District" (PDF).

"National Register of Historic Places Registration Form: Continental Powder Works at French Creek". National Park Service. 2015-11-24. Archived from the original on 2022-12-07.

Newtown Square Historical Society (2021) https://nshistory.org/ Newtown Square Historical Society.

Nordheimer, Jon (May 6, 1993). https://www.nytimes.com/1993/05/06/nyregion/port-republic-journal-where-the-biggest-news-is-something-from-1778.html New York Times.

Online Etymology Dictionary (December 31, 1999) "Frazer" https://www.etymonline.com/columns/post/frazer Douglas Harper.

Patterson Emma C. (May 2, 1952) "Blue Ball Inn layout, Owners: Bernhard Vauleer, Prissy Robinson, Croasdale, Wagner families, skeletons unearthed, ghosts" https://radnorhistory.org/archive/articles/ytmt/?p=190 Radnor Historical Society.

Patterson, Emma C. (May 2, 1952) "Blue Ball Inn layout, Owners: Bernhard Vauleer, Prissy Robinson, Croasdale, Wagner families, skeletons unearthed, ghosts" https://radnorhistory.org/archive/articles/ytmt/?p=190 Radnor Historical Society.

The Pennsylvania Magazine of History and Biography. Historical Society of Pennsylvania. 1902. (pp. 341) Google Books.

The Pennsylvania Rambler (June 24, 2020) "The massacre of Captain Phillip's Rangers" World Press.

"The Plank House". www.marcushookps.org. Retrieved 17 December 2017.

Puls, Mark (2008) "Henry Knox: Visionary General of the American Revolution, Biddle to Washington September 16, 1777" (pp106): Palgrave MacMillan.

Quarles, Benjamin (1961) "The Negro in the American Revolution". (pp. 72) Chapel Hill: The University of North Carolina Press.

Reed, John F (1965) "Campaign to Valley Forge: July 1, 1777 – December 19, 1777. Philadelphia" University of Pennsylvania Press.

Richards, Tom (2022) "Seven Stars Inn" https://www.sevenstarsinn.com/history/ Seven Stars Inn.

Roberts, Robert B. (1988) "Encyclopedia of Historic Forts: The Military, Pioneer, and Trading Posts of the United States" (pp. 505–506) Macmillan.

Salav, David L. (1975). "The Production of Gunpowder in Pennsylvania during the American Revolution". The Pennsylvania Magazine of History and Biography. (pp. 422–442.

Selig, Robert Selig and McGuire, Thomas (October 25, 2013) "Battle of the Clouds Technical Report" https://www.chesco.org/DocumentCenter/View/17453/CloudsTech Report?bidId=

Sheridan, Kevin P. (2015) "The Timepiece Chronicles: The Battle of Brandywine Creek" Dancing Do"Short History" (PDF). West Chester Public Library. Archived from the original (PDF) on October 5, 2014. Iphin Productions.

"Short History" (PDF). West Chester Public Library. Archived from the original (PDF) on October 5, 2014.

Showman, Robert K. (1980) "Proceedings of a Council of General Officer, 23 September 1777 The Papers of Nathaniel Greene, 1 January 1777-16 October 1778" Chapel Hill: University of North Carolina.

Sipe, Hale (April 25, 2022) "The Indian Chiefs of Pennsylvania" Sunbury Press Inc.

Sipe, Hale (December 2, 2008) "The Indian Wars of Pennsylvania" Heritage Book

"The Skirmish at Barren Hill | Oneida Indian Nation | History". www.oneidaindiannation.com. Archived from the original on 6 January 2009. Retrieved 22 May 2022.

Smith, Charles Harper. "General Lacey's Campaign in 1778", Bulletin of the Historical Society of Montgomery County, Pennsylvania, Volume II (1941), No. 4, pp. 261–296.

Smith, George (2017) "The History of Delaware County, Pennsylvania" HardPress.

Smith, Paul H. (1981) "Hancock to Philemon Dickinson or Alexander McDougall, September 19, 1777," Letters of the Delegates 1774-1789 26 vols: Washington: Library of Congress.

Stacks, David (1973) National Historic Landmarks & National Register of Historic Places in Pennsylvania (Searchable database). CRGIS: Cultural Resources Geographic Information System. "National Register of Historic Places Inventory Nomination Form: Uwchlan Meetinghouse" (PDF).

Spivey, Larkin (2010) "Miracles of the American Revolution Divine Intervention and the Birth of a Republic", God and Country Press.

Sterwart, Chris and Stewart, Ted (October 14, 2009) "Seven Miracles That Saved America: Why They Matter and Why We Should Have Hope", Shadow Mountain.

Stryker, William Scudder (1894). The affair at Egg Harbor, New Jersey, October 15, 1778. Trenton, NJ: Naar, Day & Naar.

Syrett, Harold C. and Cooke, Jacob E, eds, (1961) "Hamilton to Hancock, September 18, 1777, in The Papers of Alexander Hamilton, 1768-1778, 28 vols" (pp. 326-327) Columbia University Press.

This Haunted Place "Prissy Robinson's Blue Ball Inn" http://thishauntedplace.com/content/prissy-robinsons-blue-ball-inn Amazon Services LLC.

Tomlinson, Everett T. (2017) "In the Wyoming Valley" HardPress.

Tucker-Jones, Anthony (2014) "The Iraqi War" Operation Iraqi Freedom 2003-2011" Pen and Sword Military.

Twaddle, Meg Daily (1984)"This Haunted Place Prissy Robinson's Blue Ball Inn" http://thishauntedplace.com/content/prissy-robinsons-blue-ball-inn Country Publications.

Vanacore, Roderick (November 29, 2021) "Battle of Wyoming Casualties: The Battle for Wyoming for Liberty and Life" Kindle Unlimited.

"Vincent Baptist Church and Graveyard: Who Slumbers Here?" https://www.westvincenttwp.org/_files/ugd/16c450_8c0083ec893c4ca4a73758a36c1cc2e1.pdf?index=true

Walker, Wendy (September 12, 1991) "Dowlin Forge: Saving the Remnants of an Iron Forge" https://uwchlanconservationtrust.org/dowlin-forge/ Uwchlan Conservation Trust Inc.

Warrior Run - Fort Freeland Heritage Society "Battle of Fort Freeland" https://freelandfarm.org/battle-of-fort-freeland/ Peggy Inc.

Washington, George (October 3, 1789) "George Washington's Thanksgiving Proclamation" https://www.si.edu/spotlight/thanksgiving/proclamation The Smithsonian Institute.

Weir, William (2005) "50 Battles that Changed the World" (pp. 55–59): Barnes and Noble Books

Weiser, Clement Z. (February 9, 2021) "The Life of Conrad Weiser: The German Pioneer, Patriot, and Patron of Two Races" Distelfink Press; 3rd edition.

Wentz-Eisenstadt, Cathy (February 18, 2009) "Charleston Township Presbyterian Cemetery" https://sites.rootsweb.com/~pacheste/chester_twplist_charltwn_cem_cha.htm American History Local Network.

Winsor, Eleanor and Freedenberg. (August 1972) "National Historic Landmarks & National Register of Historic Places in Pennsylvania (Searchable database)". "Pennsylvania's Historic

"Who served here? Physicians, Surgeons and Mates with Washington at Valley Forge". ushistory.org. Archived from the original on 22 October 2010.

Wrobleski, Joseph (April 14, 2010). "Pulaski Legion Memorial Little Egg Harbor Massacre". Historical Marker Database.

Woodman, Henry (1922) "The History of Valley Forge" (pp,37) John U. Francis.

Zanine, Louis (April 1981). "Brigadier General John Lacey and the Pennsylvania Militia in 1778". Pennsylvania History. 48 (2): 129–142.

Zarrelli, Natalie (March 16, 2022) "The Wartime Spies Who Used Knitting as an Espionage Tool Grandma was just making a sweater. Or was she?" https://www.atlasobscura.com/articles/knitting-spies-wwi-wwii Atlas Obscura.

Zellers-Frederick, Andrew (May 27, 2010) "Hallowed Ground: Valley Forge, Pennsylvania Military History Vol. 27": Historynet.